ft®

# Microsoft® Office SharePoint® Server 2007 Best Practices

*Ben Curry and Bill English,*
*with the Microsoft SharePoint Teams*

PUBLISHED BY
Microsoft Press
A Division of Microsoft Corporation
One Microsoft Way
Redmond, Washington 98052-6399



Library of Congress Control Number: 2008927271

Printed and bound in the United States of America.

3 4 5 6 7 8 9 WCT 3 2 1 0 9

Distributed in Canada by H.B. Fenn and Company Ltd.

A CIP catalogue record for this book is available from the British Library.

Microsoft Press books are available through booksellers and distributors worldwide. For further infor-mation about international editions, contact your local Microsoft Corporation office or contact Microsoft Press International directly at fax (425) 936-7329. Visit our Web site at www.microsoft.com/mspress. Send comments to mspinput@microsoft.com.



**Acquisitions Editor:** Martin DelRe
**Developmental Editor:** Karen Szall
**Project Editor:** Melissa von Tschudi-Sutton
**Editorial Production:** Custom Editorial Productions, Inc.
**Technical Reviewer:** Daniel Webster; Technical Review services provided by Content Master, a member of CM Group, Ltd.
**Cover:** Tom Draper Design

Body Part No. X14-80907

I want to thank my parents, Jerry and Betty Curry, for always believing in me and standing behind me. Your love and support mean more to me than you will ever know. This book is dedicated to you.

*–Ben Curry*

To Kathy, David, and Anna.
I dedicate this book to you three,
who are the most important people in my life.

*–Bill English*

# Contents at a Glance

# Table of Contents

# Part IV Operating

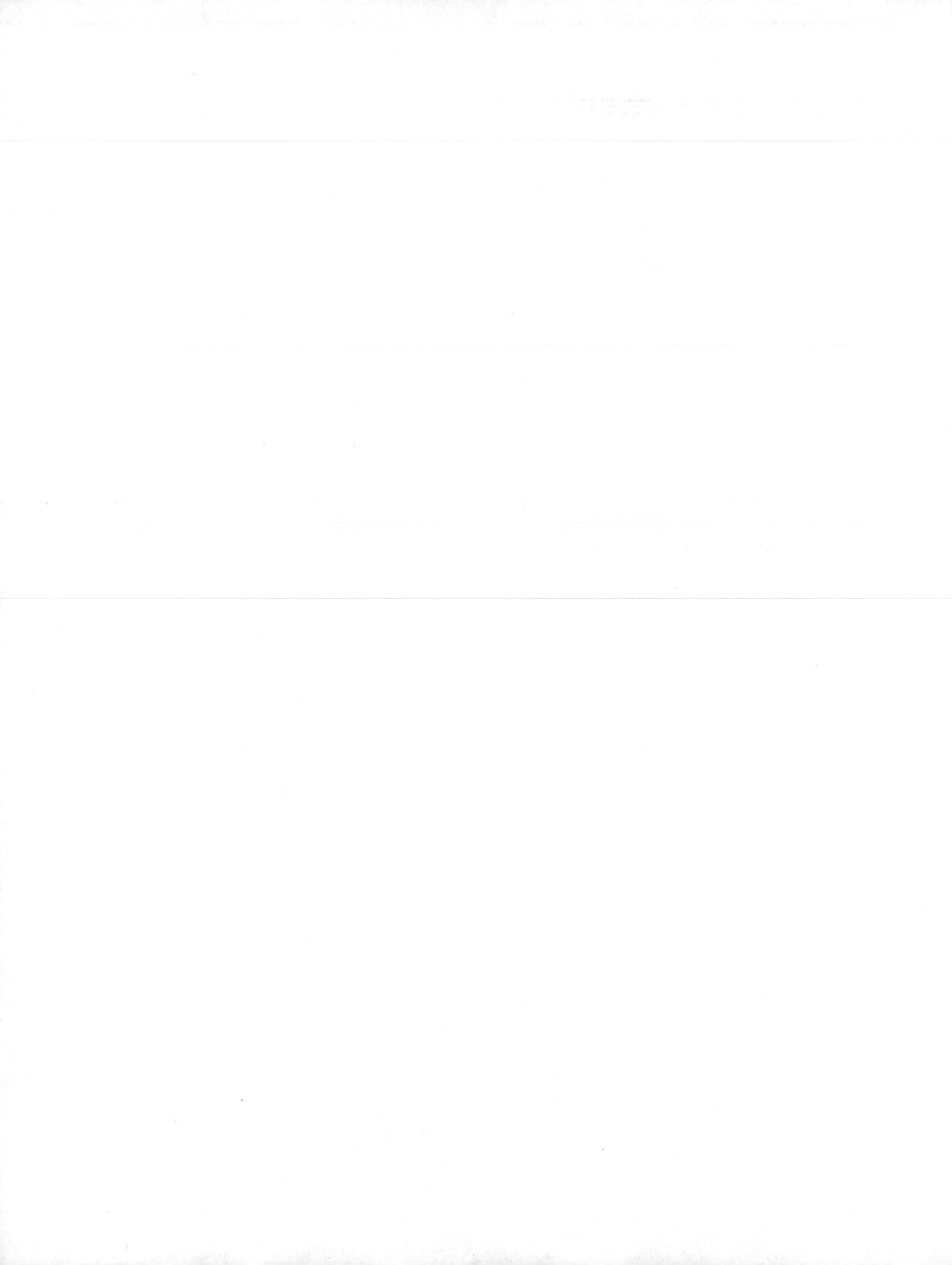

# Acknowledgments

In some wisdom literature, Solomon wrote that "iron sharpens iron," meaning that two people could push each other to be sharper and better than they thought they could be and that together they would both grow more than had they not relied on each other. When it comes to Microsoft Office SharePoint Server 2007, Ben Curry and Daniel Webster have been my "iron" in ways that I'm sure I can't fully articulate.

I want to thank Ben, who initially envisioned this book, acted as the lead project manager for the project, and worked with Microsoft Press to make it a reality. I also want to thank him for bringing me onto this project and allowing me write the chapters in which I was most interested. He brought me in only after he was sure that Microsoft Press wanted to do the book and he was ready to get started on it. Ben Curry is an outstanding technologist who has a very bright future. He's a gifted writer and speaker, and he is fast becoming one of the thought leaders in the SharePoint space. Thanks, Ben, not only for letting me work with you on this project, but also for being a great friend!

I also want to thank Daniel Webster for being a great technical editor on this book. Daniel is much more of a detail-oriented guy than I am, and he found numerous places in my chapters and others that needed to be re-worked or "beefed up." Daniel is one of the best technologists on the planet when it comes to Microsoft Office SharePoint Server 2007. The SharePoint Server 2007 community is better off for having his contribution on this book.

I'd like to thank Martin DelRe at Microsoft Press for helping us envision the book and make positive adjustments to the book's content roughly halfway through the project. Since this is the first book in the new Best Practices series, we were all a little confused at times as to how the series elements should be incorporated into the text and what the focus the chapters should be. Martin helped with this part quite a bit and also got this book project approved by the editorial team at Microsoft Press. Thanks, Martin, for being a great guy with whom to work. I look forward to working with you on other upcoming projects.

I can't say enough good things about Melissa von Tschudi-Sutton and Karen Szall, our two Microsoft Press editors for this book. You two are fabulous to work with. You know when to push, when to help, when to let go, and when to correct. I really hope we can work together on some of the other upcoming projects. You two are the best!

I'd like to express my gratitude to my wife Kathy, my daughter Anna, and my son David for being in my life. Anna even took an interest in writing one day and asked me if she could help write my book, so I agreed. She typed out two words in Chapter 8, so I suppose I should credit her with co-authoring that chapter. Anyway, I love you three more than life itself, and I'm highly blessed that we're together in life. And for those who care to know, yes, my *trainsbydave.com* domain name is named after my son, David. I'll tell you the story sometime if you ask me.

Finally, I'd like to express my love and gratitude to the Lord Jesus Christ, who gave me the opportunity and talent to write my part of this book and without whom I would be lost forever.

*Bill English*

Well, Bill made my part here very easy! I want to thank Bill and all of the authors who wrote on this project. I share his sentiments completely and can't thank the supporting authors of this book enough. SharePoint Server 2007 is a dynamic, fluid monster that is only tamed with proper planning and governance. I hope you find this book useful, and if you didn't like something written, it was Bill's fault. (Just kidding, Bill).

I also want to thank Kim Lund, who kindly let me sap her internal authors at Mindsharp on a continual basis.

I, like Bill, am always amazed at the spiritual gifts bestowed upon all of us. I hope you find this book as fruitful to read as it was to write. Without God, I would not be alive to write this book. Thank You.

I also want to thank my wife Kimberly, and my children, Madison and Bryce, for 'letting' daddy write another book. I know it takes countless hours away from you. Hopefully, this book is worth the effort and will instill hope and confidence for the readers when deploying SharePoint Server 2007. My daughter wanted to draw a picture for the book, but I'm not sure Karen and Melissa would let me get away with that!

*Ben Curry*

# Introduction

One of the perks of our job is that we get to speak at SharePoint user groups around the country. We genuinely enjoy getting out and meeting those who work in the trenches with SharePoint every day. You're the men and women who use this product, day in and day out. We admire every one of you who makes this product work for your environment on a daily basis. You're working in the midst of a sea of change in regard to how information is created and managed, which means you're at the epicenter of significant changes on how we are learning to do business moving forward. It's an exciting time to be in technology.

Bill was recently asked to speak at the San Francisco SharePoint users group. The opening presenter covered planning and governance topics. The speaker's presentation was filled with solid information and great recommendations. The presentation could have lasted for days because there were so many questions: How does this bullet point apply to *my* situation? How would I accomplish that in *my* environment? The questions were great, and his answers were on target. But the sheer number, complexity, breadth, and depth of the member's questions surprised us. At other user groups, we received similar questions privately from administrators struggling with how to map the features and functionalities in Microsoft Office SharePoint Server 2007 to their environments. Many of the answers to their questions and more are included in this book.

## Why We Wrote This Book

We wrote this book to provide a starting point for design and best practices discussions and to present what we consider to be best practices for an Office SharePoint Server 2007 deployment. Even though many of us who are considered leaders in the SharePoint Server 2007 community have been trying to communicate ideas about design and deployment best practices, it remains painfully obvious that many, many administrators and architects working in the SharePoint Server 2007 vertical have penetrating questions that seem to go unanswered. In blog postings, conference presentations, white papers, and other mediums, product team members, SharePoint MVPs, and others have been writing, speaking, and posting about governance and best practices for SharePoint Server 2007 deployments. Yet in spite of a sky-rocketing increase of governance and best practice information that is available today, it seems that our discussions are not really coalescing into any coherent whole.

Because everyone has an opinion on these topics, the noise level has become rather high, and it is difficult to know to whom you should listen. Administrators and architects are finding it hard to differentiate between fact and fiction because some of the advice being given is just plain wrong. For example, one of the authors on this book attended a training class in which the instructor advised the class members that they could (and should) perform all of their collaboration in one site collection. This instructor went on to say that she couldn't see why multiple site collections would be needed in most collaborative environments. That information was just plain wrong, and yet the students who knew little about SharePoint were making notes: "Got it. All collaboration–one site collection."

To guard themselves against doing something wrong, many of our customers want to know what others are doing *right*. We can't tell you how many times we've been asked a variation on this theme. Unfortunately, the scenarios are so varied and atypical that it becomes difficult to identify common patterns for SharePoint Server 2007 deployments. We've yet to see any two scenarios for a SharePoint Server 2007 deployment to be similar in terms of their business requirements, culture, and the resulting design decisions. Yet this doesn't mean that we can't find common threads of best practices across our deployment scenarios. It is the aim of this book to set forth many of the best practices that can be utilized across a number of different deployment scenarios.

This book will probably answer some questions for you, but it also may lead to more questions specific to your environment, culture, requirements and deployment. Frustrating as this might be, you need to view this as progress. In talking with one product team member at the SharePoint 2008 Conference in Seattle about information architecture, governance, and deployment best practices, he commented that sometimes, the best we can do is to help customers understand what are the *right* questions to ask and answer." While I agree with this statement, we also know that administrators and architects are looking for something more. They'd like to know, generally speaking, what the best practices are. Their final design might not follow all of the best practices, but they'd still like to know what the best practices are.

Now, we know well that this book is full of opinions. Hopefully, you'll see the logic in our thinking. Some best practices are based on hard-coded limits in the product. But most are based on how we view this product–how we connect the dots of the various parts of the product to arrive at a best practice. We haven't just dreamed these up, mind you. These practices have been vetted and discussed with many, many students and customers over the past two to three years. In our public and private classes, as well as our private design and architecture engagements, we have discussed, analyzed, bisected, dissected, chopped, shredded, sliced, and diced these ideas in numerous different ways.

# Best Practices versus Design

As you'll see when you read this book, there is a fine line between best practices and design decisions. Best practices tend to be built on the proper use of the technology, taking into account what the technology does, what it does not do, and what it was intended to do. Design decisions tend to account for how that technology can fit into the current culture and how it will map to meeting the business and technology requirements. At some point, design concepts and best practices are intermingled. At other times, best practices are presented with a notation that other design choices might be possible and might be the best choice given a different scenario. Consider this e-mail we recently received from an administrator:

*Sure, we've recently got the Extranet Collaboration Toolkit for SharePoint, but my takeaway is that it's based on a virtually useless premise: that everything we'd like to access via SharePoint is in a perimeter network. It addresses some self-service functionality far more than my security concerns. My security concerns:*

- *Given a dual-homed perimeter network, how best to authenticate and ****authorize***** external users (suppliers or customers) accessing data located in our ****intranet*****?*
- *Assuming Windows Credentials are used by the intranet databases (Analysis Services basically demands this), Microsoft suggests "the perimeter network must trust the corporate network."*
- *OK, but...*

  *a) my intranet system administrators would never want to manage extranet accounts, so...*

  *b) where do we store the extranet accounts? It can't be in the intranet Active Directory.*

  *c) How should/can clients maintain their accounts if their LDAP is in our intranet?*

*Thanks for any thoughts!*

Now, regardless of what you think might be the answer to our friend's design question, what we want you to focus on is how *different* the answers or choices would be if the system administrators were willing to manage extranet accounts or if the SharePoint Server 2007 farm was placed in the perimeter network. We think that it would be a best practice for the system administrators to manage the external accounts. But in this case, asserting that position as a design choice for his scenario would likely lead to the design being rejected. Take the same scenario; change a couple of details, and suddenly what is a best practice in one scenario is a non-factor or perhaps a poor design choice in another. So often, the art of the design is found in applying the combination of the requirements and the culture of the organization to the features of SharePoint Server 2007.

It is impossible for us to discuss every possible scenario that might exist in the market today. You'll likely need to adapt our thinking to your scenario in order to arrive at a good design for your environment. This book will provide a starting point for discussions about SharePoint Server 2007 deployments world-wide. But the results of your discussions may be shaped by responses that disagree with our recommended best practices as much as those that do align with our recommendations. As long as your design and deployment is improved, either through agreement or disagreement with the ideas we offer in this book, we will consider our efforts as having borne fruit.

It would be good to let you know that our ideas have been vetted with several different groups within Microsoft, including some who support this product directly with Microsoft customers, the internal group that is responsible for implementing and managing SharePoint within Microsoft, and team members whose full-time responsibility is developing and communicating best practices for SharePoint Server 2007. This is not to say that every word is somehow endorsed by the product team, but we have incorporated the input of different groups who work with this product all day, everyday. Their input has both improved this book and sharpened our thinking on the product. Any mistakes in the book, of course, belong to us.

## Who This Book Is For?

Regardless of your title, if you're responsible for designing, configuring, implementing, and/or managing a SharePoint Server 2007 deployment, then this book is for you. If you're a member of the team in your organization that is responsible for SharePoint Server 2007 in your environment, then this book will help you understand what your team is up against when it comes to your SharePoint Server 2007 deployment. If you're responsible for managing a consulting firm that is implementing SharePoint Server 2007 on your behalf in your environment, then you need to read this book. And if you just want to learn more about SharePoint Server 2007 from a design perspective, then this book will help inform your own thinking about SharePoint Server 2007. This book rarely issues prescriptive guidance–you should use the online Microsoft resources for that.

## How This Book Is Organized

This book is organized into the following four main sections:

- Part I: Planning and Design
- Part II: Building
- Part III: Deploying
- Part IV: Operating

Because of our strong belief that well-defined business requirements and governance standards must be in place for a robust, successful deployment of SharePoint Server 2007, we have dedicated entire chapters to these two topics in Part I. When you read these chapters, you might be tempted to think that they don't really cover SharePoint Server 2007 here or that they don't include many best practices for SharePoint Server 2007. Please understand that the development of well-defined business requirements and technical requirements *is* a best practice, so the entire chapter represents our discussion about a single best practice. The same is true for the governance and project planning chapters.

In Chapter 1 we provide a brief overview of SharePoint Server 2007. In Chapter 2 we've written about topics that are seldom discussed with customers regarding a SharePoint Server 2007 implementation. This chapter discusses the cultural impact, power shifts, and conflict points that a SharePoint Server 2007 deployment can introduce into an organization. Ignore these potential effects at your own peril. In Chapter 3 we discuss the design life of a SharePoint Server 2007server and offer best practices related to this topic. In Chapter 4 we shift gears and discuss how to define business requirements for your SharePoint Server 2007 deployment. In Chapter 5 we follow up our discussion about business requirements definition with a discussion on the development of governance standards. This chapter will show you how to create an environment in which those standards can be created. In Chapter 6 we highlight

SharePoint Server 2007 deployment best practices as they relate to the sample SharePoint Server 2007 deployment project plan that the product team has published and that you can find on this book's companion media. We end Part I with Chapter 7, where we discuss how to develop an information architecture for your organization.

Part II focuses on building out your SharePoint Server 2007 deployment. We start with Chapter 8 on document management best practices. Chapter 9 explores Enterprise Content Management best practices, and Chapter 10 outlines the best practices for business processes and workflows. For our readers who are also developers, we have two chapters in which you'll be interested. First, in Chapter 11, we discuss the branding and customization best practices for developers who are want to create a consistent look and feel for their SharePoint Server 2007 deployments. In Chapter 12 we discuss the best practices as it relates to Web parts, features, and solution management. In Chapter 13 we cover the best practices for creating and managing publishing sites. We round out Part II with a brief introduction to Microsoft Search Server 2008 and some best practices as they relate to this new platform.

In Part III we focus on best practices for deployment topics. Specifically, we discuss how to create an optimal search topology in Chapter 15. Then, in Chapter 16, we outline the best practices for your Shared Service Provider implementation. In Chapter 17 we discuss the best practices for information security management in SharePoint Server 2007 and use the CISSP model for securing SharePoint Server 2007 objects. In Chapters 18 and 19 we include an extensive review of business intelligence and the best practices for basic and advanced business intelligence implementations. We finish our discussion of deployment best practices in Chapter 20 with a strong chapter on deployment design for intranet, extranet and internet scenarios.

Part IV deals with enterprise operations and we begin with disaster recovery best practices in Chapter 21. Then Chapter 22 wades into the thorny area of upgrade best practices. Finally, we conclude the book in Chapter 23 with an interesting look at capacity planning and monitoring best practices.

## What This Book is Not

This book assumes that you have a working knowledge of SharePoint Server 2007 administration or that you have access to that information. We will assume that you understand most SharePoint Server 2007 concepts and the how-to of those concepts. This is not a how-to book. Instead, this is a book about deployment best practices and design concepts. If you need to learn how to install, configure, and administrate SharePoint Server 2007, then we would advise you to read the following two books:

- *Microsoft SharePoint Products and Technologies Administrator's Pocket Consultant* by Ben Curry (Microsoft Press, 2007)
- *Microsoft Office SharePoint Server 2007 Administrator's Companion* by Bill English with the Microsoft SharePoint Community Experts (Microsoft Press, 2007)

## System Requirements

This book is designed to be used with the following software:

- Windows 2000 or later
- 128 MB of RAM
- P4 processor or higher
- 100 MB of available disk space
- Internet Explorer 6.0 or later

The following are the minimum system requirements to run the companion provided with this book:

- Microsoft Windows XP, with the latest service pack installed and the latest updates installed from Microsoft Update Service
- CD-ROM drive
- Display monitor capable of 1024 x 768 resolution
- Microsoft Mouse or compatible pointing device
- Adobe Reader for viewing the eBook (Adobe Reader is available as a download at *http://www.adobe.com.*)

**Digital Content for Digital Book Readers:** If you bought a digital-only edition of this book, you can enjoy select content from the print edition's companion CD.
Visit *http://go.microsoft.com/fwlink/?LinkId=120121* to get your downloadable content. This content is always up-to-date and available to all readers.

## How You Can Contact Us

We like to stay in touch with our readers. To help accomplish this, we will have a Best Practices Web site at *http://sharepointbestpractices.mindsharp.com*. You can also contact Bill English at *bill@mindsharp.com* and Ben Curry at *bcurry@mindsharp.com*. Because of the volume of e-mail that we receive, all we ask is that when you e-mail us, you give us a week to respond before e-mailing us again.

## Support for This Book

Every effort has been made to ensure the accuracy of this book and companion content.

Microsoft Press provides corrections for books through the Web at the following address:

*http://www.microsoft.com/mspress/support/search.aspx*

To connect directly to Microsoft Help and Support to enter a query regarding a question or issue you may have, go to the following address:

*http://support.microsoft.com*

If you have comments, questions, or ideas regarding the book or companion content or if you have questions that are not answered by querying the Knowledge Base, please send them to Microsoft Press using either of the following methods:

E-mail: *mspinput@microsoft.com*

Postal mail:
Microsoft Press
Attn: Microsoft Office SharePoint Server 2007 Best Practices editor
One Microsoft Way
Redmond, WA 98052-6399

Please note that product support is not offered through the preceding mail addresses. For support information, please visit the Microsoft Product Support Web site at

*http://support.microsoft.com.*

## Part I
# Planning and Designing

**In this part:**

Chapter 1

# Introducing Microsoft Office SharePoint Server 2007

**In this chapter:**



Microsoft Office SharePoint Server 2007 is often confused with the earlier versions of SharePoint Products and Technologies, and much earlier versions of software in general. As a result, many organizations view the implementation of Office SharePoint Server 2007 as an "I agree, Next, Next, Finish" installation. With the exception of very small organizations, this couldn't be farther from the truth. What the market is learning is that a well-running SharePoint Server 2007 implementation takes significant planning and designing first. In fact, the farm topology is relatively easy once the proper planning has taken place for the features in SharePoint Server 2007 that you want to use.

The purpose of this book is to record some of the best practices to provide you with an overview of the planning process, with solid, real-world examples of implementations. In addition, when it makes sense from a learning perspective, you will be presented with the "wrong way" of implementing some SharePoint Server 2007 functionality as well as ideas on what a better way might be.

### SharePoint Editions

With the new versions of SharePoint Products and Technologies, the product names have changed a bit. The new versions are Windows SharePoint Services 3.0 and SharePoint Server 2007. These can be roughly equated to Windows SharePoint Services 2.0 and SharePoint Portal Server 2003, respectively. Most of the previous functionality continues in these versions of the products, but with significant changes and additions.

# Windows SharePoint Services 3.0

Windows SharePoint Services 3.0 provides the foundation for SharePoint Products and Technologies. It provides essential capabilities that are leveraged by SharePoint Server 2007. The following sections give an overview of the functionality of Windows SharePoint Services 3.0, but they are by no means exhaustive.

## Delegation of Administration

Windows SharePoint Services 3.0 provides a distributed management model that allows for delegation of administration. Central Administration access can now be limited to SharePoint Products and Technologies farm administrators, but not to machine administrators. This allows for separation of duties between the staff who manage servers and those who manage SharePoint Products and Technologies.

In addition, farm administrators do not, by default, have access to site collections. If a farm administrator escalates his or her privilege to access an unauthorized site collection, that action is now audited. A site collection administrator can further delegate authority to site owners and list managers. A well-thought-out Windows SharePoint Services 3.0 implementation will leverage these capabilities and move much of the administrative overhead from IT to power and end users. A best practice is to trust your server farm administrators and database administrators. Either group has total access to all SharePoint Server 2007 content, and can most likely find a way to access any data in your system.

## Provisioning of Web Applications

The provisioning of Web applications, including Internet Information Server sites and content databases, is also included with Windows SharePoint Services 3.0. Web applications are foundational to any SharePoint Products and Technologies implementation. A Web application provides the ability for users to interact with your content via a Uniform Resource Locator (URL). Web applications are associated with one or more content databases that hold the majority of user and administrative content. While one Web application, Central Administration, is provided for you to manage your farm, you should exclusively use the Central Administration Web application for farm administration, not for user collaboration.

> **More Info** Web applications are explained in great detail in both the *Microsoft Office SharePoint Server 2007 Administrator's Companion* (Microsoft Press, 2007) and the *Microsoft SharePoint Products and Technologies Administrator's Pocket Consultant* (Microsoft Press, 2007).

Logging, reporting, and usage analysis are provided by Windows SharePoint Services 3.0. Diagnostic logging allows you both to set specific events and select the level at which you want to capture them for later analysis. It is much more extensive than the last versions of SharePoint Products and Technologies—so much more that your farm can suffer significant performance degradation if not carefully planned and configured.

**On the Companion Media** On the companion CD, you will find a Logging and Reporting command line script and associated spreadsheet that can be modified to suit your needs. The Central Administration logging and reporting interface provides an effective but time-consuming method to set all logging levels. In addition, many logging levels can only be set using the command line.

Used in conjunction with Internet Information Services (IIS) logging, you can get close to real-time logging of your server farm. A good monitoring plan is covered in Chapter 23, "Capacity Planning and Performance Monitoring," and includes using performance counters installed with SharePoint Products and Technologies. In addition to the logging provided, usage analysis is provided by Windows SharePoint Services 3.0 and creates log files for reporting on how your site is being used. This information can be accessed in many ways, including site collection administration, site administration, and SharePoint Designer 2007.

## Backup and Restore

The backup and restore functionality of Windows SharePoint Services 3.0 is greatly improved over the previous versions. First, you no longer need the SQL Client Tools loaded on your SharePoint Products and Technologies farm servers to back up and restore content. Second, you can create farm level backups and restores from the command line. The ability to create farm level backups from the command line allows you to create batch files that are scheduled within Windows Server. Many third-party tools offer SharePoint Server 2007 backup and restore capabilities, but it is a best practice to learn the native tools first. What we have learned is that the native tools always work!

In addition, a Recycle Bin is provided natively. The Recycle Bin is a much-anticipated addition to Windows SharePoint Services because most of the restore scenarios were for individual documents and list items. This should greatly reduce the number of support incidents that previously required database restores. Like much of the product, the Recycle Bin is managed at three different levels–Web Application (farm administrators), 2$^{nd}$ stage (site collection administrators), and 1$^{st}$ stage (end users). Properly configured, the Recycle Bin should reduce the total cost of ownership for SharePoint Products and Technologies over Windows SharePoint Services 2.0 and SharePoint Portal Server 2003.

### Behind the Microsoft Firewall **Recycle Bin Usage**

Are you curious about storage requirements for the Recycle Bin? Here are Microsoft IT's numbers as of September 26, 2007: We have 9850 site collections using the Recycle Bin with 845 GB of storage used by the Recycle Bin. This translates into 5 to 10 percent storage overhead for something that previously was resulting in daily support calls.

*Joel Oleson, Senior Technical Product Manager, Microsoft*

## Security

Windows SharePoint Services 3.0 also provides the foundation for security. Almost identical to the last versions of SharePoint Products and Technologies, it provides granular permissions that can be grouped together in permission levels. These permission levels can be restricted or enabled at the Web application level and site collection level. The ability to restrict at the farm level allows SharePoint Products and Technologies administrators to restrict available permissions in all site collections in a given Web application, possibly assisting you in your governance plan.

User rights and roles are also included with Windows SharePoint Services 3.0 and leverage native or custom permission levels. User permissions are then natively used to "trim" objects in the user interface (UI). Unlike the last versions, Windows SharePoint Services 3.0 will display items only when users have the proper authorization. Figure 1-1 shows some of the available permission levels in SharePoint Server 2007.

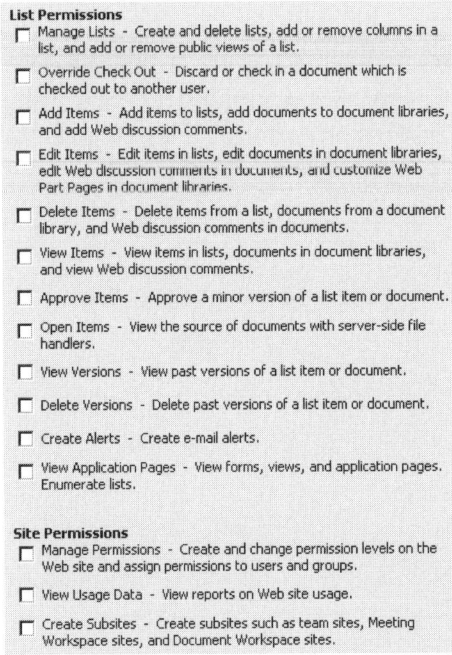


**Figure 1-1** You can assign permission at a granular level.

Web application policies have been added to Windows SharePoint Services 3.0 and are a welcome addition. Web application policies can restrict or escalate privileges based on the URL being browsed. Web application policies explicitly grant or deny, effectively overriding the permission levels anywhere in site collection. For example, you can have two URLs associated with the same content database, rendering the same content via both URLs. Then, via Web application policies, you can restrict access on a very granular level based on the user and a

URL. A common implementation is exposing your intranet to the Internet via a different URL and restricting the ability to manage sites and lists. Another common scenario is developing and testing all custom code on an internal URL, such as *http://www-test.contoso.msft*, and exposing the same content on *http://www.consoto.msft* using a combination of Extending and Web application policies. You can restrict all write access on *http://www.consoto.msft* to reduce the surface area available to hackers, as shown in Figure 1-2.

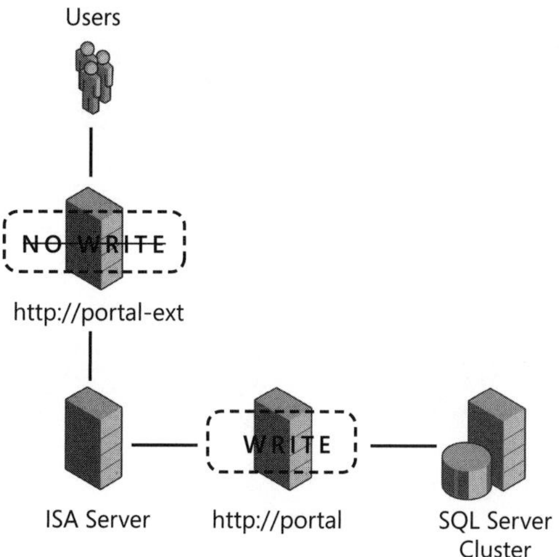


**Figure 1-2** Custom Web application policies allow users to access the same content via two unique URLs.

Authentication is provided by ASP.NET and consumed by Windows SharePoint Services 3.0. This version of Windows SharePoint Services 3.0 allows for authentication to almost any source, including third-party Line-of-Business (LOB) systems, databases, or LDAP directories. Active Directory is the preferred authentication mechanism and provides the most functionality. However, developers can create custom authentication providers to authenticate users through Forms Based Authentication and Single Sign On (SSO). This is often leveraged for extranet and Internet Web application deployments.

# Storage

Content databases are the back-end storage for Windows SharePoint Services 3.0. Having your content stored in SQL Server databases allows for easy, multiple server scaling, in addition to increased functionality over file system storage. While not necessarily recommended, every database used by Windows SharePoint Services 3.0 could be hosted on a separate SQL Server instance, providing extreme scalability if needed.

## Site Columns

Through Site Columns, metadata collection is also provided by Windows SharePoint Services 3.0. Site Columns give you the ability to collect many forms of metadata that can be used as the foundation for building your enterprise-wide taxonomy. If your users have Microsoft Office 2007, you may also collect this metadata through the Document Information Panel (DIP). Both of these metadata collection methods are natively supported by Windows SharePoint Services 3.0. The DIP is a Microsoft Office InfoPath 2007 form and can be customized to suit your needs. Figure 1-3 shows an example of a native Office 2007 Document Information Panel.

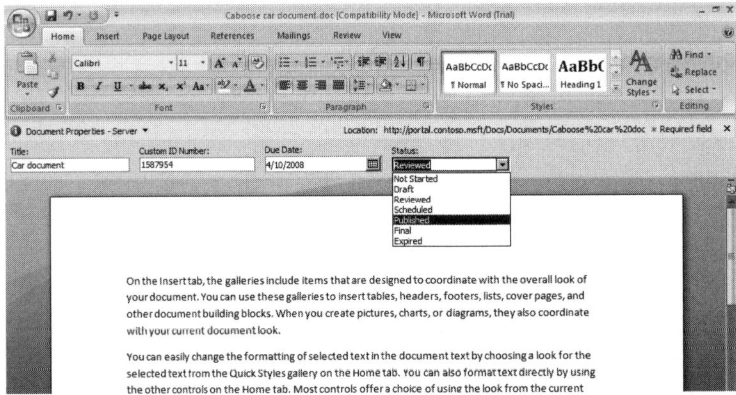


**Figure 1-3** Document Information Panels can be used to seamlessly collect metadata from users.

## Item Versioning

Item Versioning is much improved over Windows SharePoint Services 2.0. The Item Versioning functionality that was available in SharePoint Portal Server 2001 was brought back in the current version of Windows SharePoint Services. You now have the ability to control the number of major versions that exist for any given document pedigree in addition to the added functionality of minor (draft) version support. The granular control over versioning was needed for true, enterprise-scale deployments of Windows SharePoint Services 3.0. Figure 1-4 shows the granular ability to manage document versions.

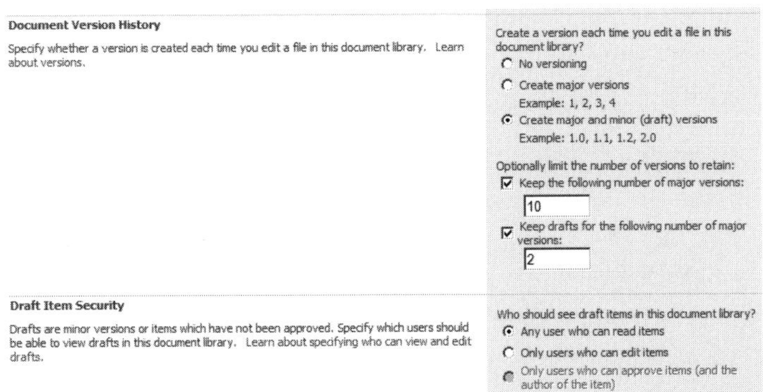


**Figure 1-4** You can control Major and Minor versioning, as well permissions based on the version level.

## Server Farm Topology

The basics of server farm topology are provided by Windows SharePoint Services 3.0. The heart and soul of any SharePoint Products and Technologies server farm is the configuration database. The configuration database contains the majority of your farm configuration and is much more important than in previous versions. Web applications are contained, almost in their entirety, within the configuration database and associated content databases. In addition to Web applications, farm configuration such as logging and reporting, farm topology, services on servers, antivirus, content database, authentication, and much more is hosted in the configuration database.

While SharePoint Server 2007 offers much more functionality than what is provided in Windows SharePoint Services 3.0, Windows SharePoint Services 3.0 provides the foundation upon which a SharePoint Server 2007 farm is built. For example, you can extend your farm well beyond a single server to provide extended search and Web capabilities. Figure 1-5 shows an example of a medium-scale Windows SharePoint Services 3.0 server farm.

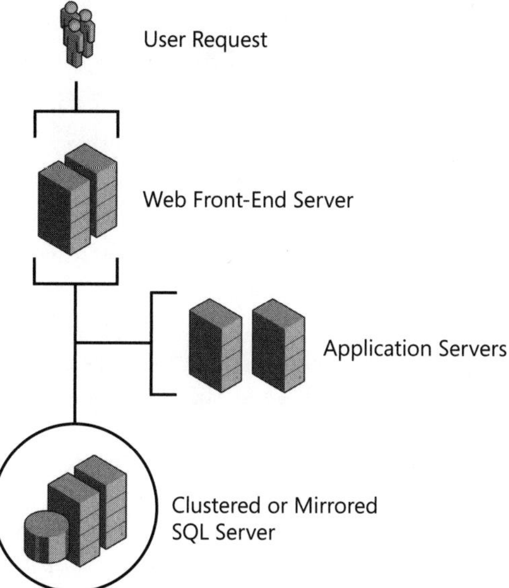


**Figure 1-5** Windows SharePoint Services 3.0 provides the basic functionality of server farm scaling.

## Site Model

Similar to Windows SharePoint Services 2.0, this version of Windows SharePoint Services provides the site model. This model begins with a *site collection*, which is a collection of one or more sites. These sites are not randomly organized, however. There is always a top level site within the site collection, also referred to as a *root web* or *top level site (TLS)*, with sub-sites possible underneath. The hierarchical structure of the site collection beneath the TLS can be deep or wide, or both. For the most part, site collections will not bump up against the 2,000 sites at a level performance limit, but it's good to know that you can scale that large if needed. Figure 1-6 shows an example of the site hierarchy.

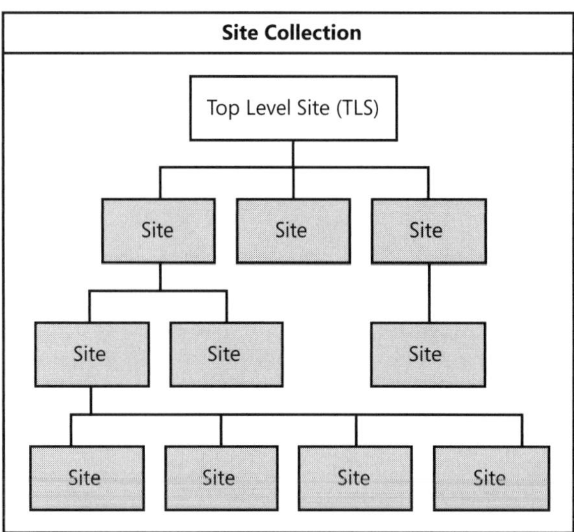


**Figure 1-6** Site collections are a structured collection of sites.

Content rendering of user content is provided by Windows SharePoint Services 3.0, in addition to customization, branding, and extension. Most SharePoint Server 2007 custom development work actually occurs within Windows SharePoint Services 3.0, not SharePoint Server 2007. One of the most commonly customized components of Windows SharePoint Services 3.0 is Site Templates. While the native templates are technically Site Definitions when stored on the file system, they appear as templates to the end users. The ability to use the native Site Definitions and add new ones is a function of Windows SharePoint Services 3.0. If you want custom Site Definitions, you must employ a developer to create these in Visual Studio 2005 or 2008.

Your site collection administrators can create their own templates from any site, including colors, navigation, lists, and even content. When they save and use one of their templates, it is basically applying a "macro" to the original Site Definition upon which the template was based.

## Application Programming Interfaces

There are two ways to access SharePoint content programmatically: the Object Model and XML Web Services. SharePoint Products and Technologies provides an extensive collection of Namespaces that can be used to write applications that run on the SharePoint server. XML

Web Services are more limited but can be used to access data from anywhere. If you will run code directly on a local farm server, the SharePoint Object Model provides a leaner and more robust approach. The Object Model makes SharePoint extensible. By leveraging the Object Model, SharePoint can be used as a development platform to meet unique business requirements not covered by the product natively. The Object Model is extensively featured and very friendly for developers because it behaves in a manner familiar to any.NET developer. But, the Object Model is available only to applications that run on the SharePoint server. XML Web Services is used to access the data from a client.

### Web Services

Web Services allow for interaction with much of the SharePoint Object Model using standard Web service calls. Web Services interaction with SharePoint 2007 is possible from a Windows Client, Console Applications, and non-windows development platforms. Essentially, Web Services surface a portion of the Object Model in a manner that allows a developer to interact with it from outside the browser. With this flexibility, you can consume SharePoint Products and Technologies services via any third-party application, like Apache server or a JAVA application.

### Fields and Forms

Fields are the fundamental underlying data types of SharePoint lists and Site Columns. Custom field types can be created to represent custom data types and provide custom data validation. Field controls can be created for field types to provide for custom presentation. Forms capability is extended by the SharePoint Server 2007 Enterprise Edition and allows users to input data that may not have the Office InfoPath 2007 client loaded.

## Collaboration

Windows SharePoint Services 3.0 provides good collaboration functionality that can be extended programmatically or extended by installing SharePoint Server 2007. Lists form the center of collaboration in Windows SharePoint Services 3.0. There are many types of lists, such as document libraries, calendars, task lists, and many others. Basically, the different types of lists have specialized features and different views.

Document libraries are one of the most common list types and are easily recognizable to any current SharePoint Products and Technologies end user. Document libraries give you the ability to store, version, link to, manage, automate processes, and enforce information policies on documents. While most of this functionality is provided in any list type, document libraries are where the bulk of end user content lives. Figure 1-7 is an example of a native document library.

Documents

Share a document with the team by adding it to this document library.

New ▾ Upload ▾ Actions ▾ Settings ▾ View: All Documents ▾

| Type | Name | Modified | Modified By |
|---|---|---|---|
| | Caboose car document ! NEW | 10/30/2007 11:03 PM | TRAINSBYDAVE\Administrator |
| | Caboose customers ! NEW | 10/30/2007 11:03 PM | TRAINSBYDAVE\Administrator |
| | Cattle car customers ! NEW | 10/30/2007 11:03 PM | TRAINSBYDAVE\Administrator |
| | Cattle car document ! NEW | 10/30/2007 11:03 PM | TRAINSBYDAVE\Administrator |
| | Christmas train set ! NEW | 10/30/2007 11:03 PM | TRAINSBYDAVE\Administrator |
| | ctrlogo_header_off ! NEW | 10/30/2007 11:03 PM | TRAINSBYDAVE\Administrator |
| | Engine Customers ! NEW | 10/30/2007 11:03 PM | TRAINSBYDAVE\Administrator |
| | Engine document ! NEW | 10/30/2007 11:03 PM | TRAINSBYDAVE\Administrator |
| | Eurodollars futures ! NEW | 10/30/2007 11:03 PM | TRAINSBYDAVE\Administrator |
| | Futures ! NEW | 10/30/2007 11:03 PM | TRAINSBYDAVE\Administrator |
| | more trains ! NEW | 10/30/2007 11:03 PM | TRAINSBYDAVE\Administrator |
| | Refrigerated car document ! NEW | 10/30/2007 11:03 PM | TRAINSBYDAVE\Administrator |
| | Refrigeration Customers ! NEW | 10/30/2007 11:03 PM | TRAINSBYDAVE\Administrator |
| | SALES ! NEW | 10/30/2007 11:03 PM | TRAINSBYDAVE\Administrator |
| | train image ! NEW | 10/30/2007 11:03 PM | TRAINSBYDAVE\Administrator |
| | trlogo_header_off ! NEW | 10/30/2007 11:03 PM | TRAINSBYDAVE\Administrator |

**Figure 1-7** Document libraries can store many types of files and have controls, such as Information Management Policies, in place.

Blogs are new in this version and can be very useful for sharing information within an organization, or exposing information to the outside world. In conjunction with the new ability to enable any list with RSS (Really Simple Syndication), blogs give your users the ability to quickly and easily share information with any number of people. This information can be indexed by SharePoint Server 2007 and be available for search consumption. The aggregation of blog content can assist you in limiting the loss of institutional knowledge due to employee turnover.

In addition to RSS, there is also improved e-mail integration with lists. Lists can be enabled to accept incoming e-mail and sort attachments for use in workflows or custom processes. In addition, there is functionality provided for managing the contacts associated with these lists in Active Directory via the Directory Management Service (DMS). DMS can manage the creation of distribution lists that contain SharePoint group members. This allows your users to e-mail members of a SharePoint group without typing addresses individually, or even knowing the members of that SharePoint group.

## Wikis

Windows SharePoint Services 3.0 also provides Wikis in addition to blog functionality. Wikis provide an easy to use method for capturing knowledge from your users. In SharePoint Products and Technologies, *Wikis* are lists containing user-created Web pages. Because they are simply another list, they have the full functionality of versioning and content approval. So no matter what your governance stance, Wikis can be very useful in getting tacit knowledge into your search index. While blogs provide a means for individual publishing of content, Wikis are a good way to tie a complex site collection hierarchy together, quickly capture creativity between team members, and allow inexperienced users an easy way to contribute to the collective knowledge of the organization.

> **Note** A very nice addition to this version of Windows SharePoint Services 3.0 is two-way synchronization with Microsoft Office Outlook 2007. While not perfect, it does provide a useful interface for keeping tasks and calendars synchronized with a corresponding Windows SharePoint Services 3.0 Web part. Office Outlook 2007 can synchronize tasks, calendars, and document libraries.

# SharePoint Server 2007 Standard

SharePoint Sever 2007 Standard Edition adds much functionality to Windows SharePoint Services 3.0. Windows SharePoint Services 3.0 is installed automatically when you install SharePoint Server 2007, but you can also easily upgrade an existing Windows SharePoint Services 3.0 implementation. The following sections provide an overview of what SharePoint Server 2007 adds to the Windows SharePoint Services 3.0 functionality stack.

## Search and Indexing

The first noticeable difference between the two products is the use of a common search engine along with dramatically extended search and indexing functionalities in SharePoint Server 2007. SharePoint Server 2007 search capabilities allow content aggregation for almost any content source and the ability to create almost unlimited search scopes. Windows SharePoint Services 3.0 is limited to searching "this site and below," while SharePoint Server 2007 gives you the ability to search for anything in the index.

In addition, SharePoint Server 2007 search provides you with the capability of scaling out multiple servers to service a single index, something Windows SharePoint Services 3.0 cannot do. SharePoint Server 2007 search also allows you to manage crawled properties, allowing you to create a robust scope and advanced search solution. For example, all documents written in a company division can be queried using common metadata assigned to them, along with scopes that focus your query that are built on a combination of Site Columns and Managed Properties. This helps provide a more relevant result set for your users.

## Shared Services Providers

Shared Services Providers supply the services that all Web applications need to run properly. For example, it is assumed in SharePoint Server 2007 that all sites need search capabilities. For sites built on the SharePoint Server 2007 code base, search is provided via a Shared Services Provider, which means that one index can be exposed to multiple sites in multiple Web applications to provide a common search experience.

By analogy, a Shared Services Provider can be compared to a public utility provider for high cost services, whether that cost is human, financial, or technology capital. A good example would be your local water company. While you might be able to dig a well for your own water supply, it is usually easier simply to purchase clean water from a central utility company. Table 1-1 describes the shared services provided.

**Table 1-1 Standard Version Shared Services Provider**

| Service | Description |
|---|---|
| User Profiles | User profiles and properties provide a method for synchronizing properties from Active Directory, or from a third-party profile source. These properties can then be used to target content, expose properties, create search scopes, and collect information directly from end users. |
| My Sites | My Sites, in their simplest form, provide a one-to-many collaboration space in a single server farm. For small to medium SharePoint Server 2007 implementations, you will have a single My Site provider. In larger or specialized instances, you can have multiple My Site providers across multiple server farms to localize geographically dispersed installations, role-based My Sites, and different service levels. |
| Published Links to Office Applications | With SharePoint Server 2007, you can specify 'Save As' locations to Office 2007 applications. These locations can be targeted to Audiences or Active Directory groups. This targeting ability assists governance by suggesting relevant file locations to your users. |
| Personalization | There are many personalization features in SharePoint Server 2007, such as My Links, regional settings, alerts, and personalization sites. |
| Audiences | Global audiences are a very powerful enhancement in SharePoint Server 2007. Audiences can be used to target content to users in Web parts, list items, global navigation links, and more. Global audiences are pre-compiled and thus faster than directly targeting via Active Directory groups. |
| Excel Calculation Services (Enterprise Edition) | Excel Calculation Services include an Excel Web Service, custom Web parts, and Office Excel 2007 publishing capabilities. |
| Business Data Catalog (Enterprise Edition) | The Business Data Catalog provides an interface to back-end systems, such as third-party databases and Line-of-Business systems. Content from these sources can then be used for dashboards, search, and custom applications. |

# Portals

Portals are exposed via the publishing features in SharePoint Server 2007. The publishing features, in conjunction with specialized site templates, offer a rich foundation on which to build your intranet, extranet, or WWW site. Because portals are much like snowflakes in that no two are identical, Microsoft has provided a customizable and extensible platform upon which you can build any portal structure required.

SharePoint Server 2007 provides two native portal templates: Collaboration Portal and Publishing Portal. The *Collaboration Portal* was envisioned for small to medium intranets and provides a starting point to connect people, content, and third-party systems. The Collaboration

Portal functionality includes the Site Directory, customizable Search Center, Document Center, Report Center, and all Publishing features. The *Publishing Portal* has fewer active features turned on than the Collaboration Portal, and was envisioned for large intranets and public-facing Web sites.

## Site Collection Auditing

SharePoint Server 2007 Standard Edition also provides an often-overlooked added capability of site collection auditing. While this can be added to Windows SharePoint Services 3.0 using custom code, the functionality is provided natively in SharePoint Server 2007. Auditing capabilities include the item type, userID, event date, and action taken on the item. For example, you can audit every time any item is deleted or restored. Site collection auditing must be turned on manually at the root of each site collection, as shown in Figure 1-8, or programmatically.

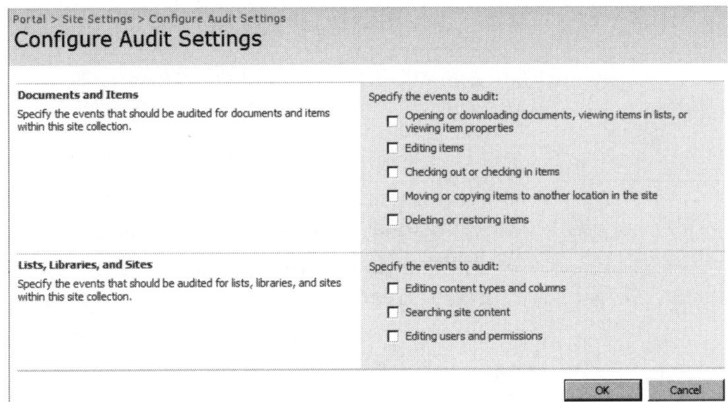


**Figure 1-8** Site collection auditing is a function of SharePoint Server 2007.

With many aspects of SharePoint management the design is decentralized control with more focus on site collection administration. Auditing follows this design with the scope of both management and reporting being the site collection. There is no centralized tool that you can use to manage auditing across all the site collections hosted within a Web application or at the farm level. Also, reporting is not amalgamated across site collections to offer you a composite report. While this can be done manually, it is not commonly done because of the human expense involved in bringing together different reports into one common report.

## Enterprise Content Management

Enterprise Content Management is a welcome addition to SharePoint Products and Technologies. SharePoint Server 2007 provides many tools to manage content, including the following:

- **Content types** Now an essential part to any SharePoint Products and Technologies deployment. Content types provide a way to manage documents on an enterprise scale, including custom metadata, default templates, policies, workflows, and auditing.

- **Auditing policies** Created at the site collection or content type level. While the best practice to scoping policies will be detailed in Chapter 9, "Enterprise Content Management," policies are usually created at the site collection level and used by individual content types. Auditing policies are sometimes confused with site collection auditing, but they are very different in application. Auditing policies are scoped to an individual content type, while site collection auditing applies to the entire site collection. An example of site collection policies is auditing a sensitive content type when a user opens or downloads documents, views items in lists, or views item properties.
- **Retention policies** Aid in meeting regulatory compliance and reducing the amount of outdated content. A solid file retention plan can narrow the gap between the cost of SharePoint Server 2007 versus legacy file system storage.
- **Custom document information panels (DIP)** Allow you to leverage InfoPath forms to collect many types of metadata as part of the Office 2007 experience.
- **Records Repository** Provides a specialized site collection where official files are accepted and managed including the creation of holds for legal events. It is a necessity for organizations that must comply with regulations such as HIPPA and SOX. Additionally, the Records Repository can accept incoming content from third-party systems, reducing the need for multiple solutions.
- **Document Center** Provides a centralized place for approved organizational documents. Using permissions in conjunction with content approval and versioning, organizational documents can be authored in place, with only the last approved version available for user consumption. Alternatively, these documents can be authored and revised in collaborative sites or workspaces with only the approved version being sent to the Document Center.
- **Page layouts** Provided by the publishing infrastructure and provide a method for organizations to define the look and feel of their sites. This allows the content creators to focus on the content and not the design. These page layouts can also contain Web parts, making them very flexible.

# SharePoint Server 2007 Enterprise

SharePoint Server 2007 Enterprise Edition includes all of the functionality of Windows SharePoint Services 3.0 and SharePoint Server 2007 Standard Edition, with the addition of Forms Server 2007, Excel Calculation Services, and the Business Data Catalog.

## Forms Server 2007

The addition of Microsoft Forms Server 2007 gives you the ability to create forms in Office InfoPath 2007 and allow Web-based and mobile access to forms for process automation. These forms can then be stored in SharePoint Products and Technologies lists, Line-of-Business systems, or any third-party system. Allowing a power user to create and manage forms reduces the overall costs associated with custom programming, with essentially the same end results. This allows your programming resources to be used where they are better needed. Forms also provide a method for validation at the time of entry, reducing the total cost of collecting and streamlining information.

### Excel Calculation Services

Excel Calculation Services is a Shared Service and offers many benefits, including Web viewing of spreadsheets, secure spreadsheet sharing, performance caching on the server, and centralized management of business data. While many IT professionals might argue that SQL Server is the best place for business data, that isn't reasonable for many organizations that have decentralized IT, or are short-staffed in the Database Administration area.

### Business Data Catalog

The Business Data Catalog (BDC) provides a straightforward way to connect to back-end server application storage systems such as SQL, Oracle, Siebel, SAP, and PeopleSoft. While many developers will simply connect directly to the content source, the BDC provides administrators a way to communicate with these back-end systems. Additionally, the BDC allows for the indexing of third-party systems for searching.

## SharePoint Server 2007 for Internet Sites

SharePoint Server 2007 for Internet Sites is simply SharePoint Server 2007 Enterprise Edition with special licensing. The license allows you to use SharePoint Server 2007 for external users, not including employees. SharePoint Server 2007 for Internet Sites is a per-server license, and does not need Client Access Licenses. It is primarily targeted to WWW applications or extranet applications.

## How Can SharePoint Server Help My Organization?

If you asked ten IT professionals how SharePoint Server 2007 could help your organization, you would probably get ten different answers. The truth is that SharePoint Server 2007 can solve countless business problems, while at the same time increasing overall productivity. But be careful when deciding to implement SharePoint Server 2007, because you probably don't need the entire spectrum of functionality. A good plan will include an implementation performed in stages, allowing your organization to grow with the product as you become more familiar with it through training and experience. For example, if you needed to implement an intranet, an extranet, and a public-facing Web site, you would want to deploy only one at a time. This approach allows you to become familiar with the pitfalls associated with implementing in your environment.

This section discusses five core functions that SharePoint Server 2007 brings to your organization. You may find that you'll implement all of them or only one of them, but it's nice to know the breadth and depth that SharePoint Server 2007 brings to you out of the box.

## Collaboration

Collaboration is the first of the five core functions provided by SharePoint Products and Technologies. The foundation of collaboration is provided by Windows SharePoint Services 3.0, with SharePoint Server 2007 offering extended features. Windows SharePoint Services 3.0 provides the site model that is the foundation for a successful collaborative workspace. These workspaces are then used to encourage and foster collaboration for a team or process, but without proper training they often fail.

The key to a successful collaborative workspace is educating your users in the proper setup and management. The workspace should be tailored to your organization's goals. For example, large site collections can be tied together with the SharePoint Server 2007 provided functionality of Wikis. Wikis help users share ideas quickly, while linking to content throughout the site collection and elsewhere. But without the training to know how and where information should go, it could become a disorganized mess. Simply moving content from tens or hundreds of legacy file shares to SharePoint Products and Technologies workspaces will solve nothing. If you do not properly plan the migration of this content, you will move from disorganized content on file shares to disorganized content in SharePoint Products and Technologies.

SharePoint Products and Technologies provide a much better framework for collaboration than legacy file shares and most third-party systems. To begin with, SharePoint Products and Technologies provide Information Management Policies to assist with automated pruning of outdated documents. This ability can greatly reduce content sprawl in your organization. Additionally, workflows, versions, and content types help to manage your content while collecting valuable information about the content. Lastly, SharePoint Products and Technologies provide a Web-based solution that can be accessed from anywhere, according to your needs. Windows SharePoint Services 3.0, and thus SharePoint Server 2007, allows for self-creation and management of site collections. This functionality allows users the ability to collaborate quickly and easily, without the need for the IT staff to become involved. But once again, your users need training to know how and when to create these site collections.

Another benefit of using Windows SharePoint Services 3.0 for your collaboration is the seamless interaction with Microsoft Office 2007. New in this version is the ability to populate metadata for documents using the Document Information Panel (DIP), start and stop workflows, check-in/check-out, and publish content from within the desktop application. This makes it easy for your users to abide by your governance policy, without the need to know a bunch of complicated rules.

SharePoint Products and Technologies collaborative workspaces can be extended to include your extranet partners, or provide collaboration to your employees remotely, both via *zones*.

These zones allow you to define who has access to your content remotely, and what that access might be. For example, you could allow the sales team full access to content while visiting the site from within your firewall boundaries or during a VPN session via *http://portal*, but extend the same site to *http://portal-ext* for external access. You can then limit the permissions, such as delete and restore, on the external URL.

SharePoint Server 2007 also provides a robust search and indexing capability. This search capability is often overlooked when discussing collaboration. In Windows SharePoint Services 3.0, users can only search in the current site and below–possibly missing previously created content in another site collection, or in a higher site in the hierarchy. A well-running search and indexing implementation can greatly increase your users' efficiency. SharePoint Server 2007 also extends collaboration by providing profiles and personalization. *Profiles* are the basis for People Search and allow users to quickly find others with relevant information, such as a skill set.

## Content Aggregation

The second main functionality that SharePoint Server 2007 brings to your organization is content aggregation. One of the most frustrating aspects for many who are working with information on a daily basis is that much of the information they work with is in disparate locations. Being able to aggregate that content through a common interface can help ensure that you work with the most relevant, important, and up-to-date content.

In most SharePoint Server 2007 designs, content aggregation can reduce the amount of time your users spend looking for what they need to do their job. SharePoint Server 2007 provides several methods of aggregation, including Really Simple Syndication (RSS) of almost any SharePoint Products and Technologies list, News Web parts, Document Centers, Report Centers, and most importantly, Portals and Search.

### Portals

As you have noticed by now, "Portal" has been removed from the product name because it offers so much more. SharePoint Server 2003 wasn't the best document management system, nor the best search engine, but it offered a very nice portal experience when correctly implemented. The new version of SharePoint Server is greatly enhanced and offers much more than a portal experience, hence the name change. That should not overshadow the fact that the portal experience has also been enhanced, and is a very flexible framework on which to build your portal solution. To begin with, the SharePoint Server 2007 portal templates include the publishing framework for enhanced navigation, Web content management, in-browser editing, reusable content, and more. Less-specialized deployments will find the native templates to work quite well. But for specialized implementations, you can easily customize via custom Web parts, master pages, and page layouts, in addition to the native sites such as the Site Directory.

### Search

Do your users frequently create the same content over and over again? Do your users spend much of the time looking for the information they need? The answer to both questions is a resounding yes. Microsoft invested much into Share Point Server 2007 search services because legacy "click and find" portals are becoming a relic of the past. Modern portals are much smaller and leaner because your users have already been trained to search for what they need on their home computer! Because Search is such a huge part of a successful SharePoint Server 2007 implementation, two chapters have been dedicated to the subject in this book. You must first understand what your users need and how to give it to them before you can decide on details like Index and Query server placement.

### Knowledge Transfer

There are essentially two types of knowledge: tacit and explicit. *Tacit knowledge*, or tacit knowing, is "know-how" or "institutional knowledge"–basically, the information in your users' heads. By contrast, *explicit knowledge* can be defined as "know-what." Both are vital to the success of your organization, but tacit knowledge is usually lost when an employee resigns or retires. Many features of SharePoint Products and Technologies can help you capture this tacit knowledge so it isn't lost. Examples are Wikis, e-mail–enabled lists as part of a discussion group, My Sites, and blogs.

A boon to your organization would be planning for the transfer of different types of knowledge throughout your design. A common practice is using Wikis to get information out of people's heads quickly and easily, and then using that information as part of another organizational process. The latter transfers that information to explicit knowledge that can be internalized. You should plan for tacit-to-tacit knowledge transfer; this is best accomplished via blogs and Wikis. In addition, you should design your end-user training so that site collections are built to encourage tacit-to-explicit knowledge transfer. Most of this depends on your Information Technology governance plan and information architecture, both of which are discussed in this book.

## Content Organization

If you're going to aggregate content, then you'll need to organize it. There is little sense in pulling together much of your information into a common location (either via hosting it in SharePoint, linking to it, or indexing it) if you're not also going to organize it.

The main reason that you organize information is so that you can find it later. When we talk with IT professionals and knowledge management directors around the country, what we find is that the sole reason for organizing content is to make it findable.

You can use several tools to organize your content. For example, you can organize your SharePoint sites using the Global Sites Directory in the collaboration portal. By default, this feature organizes only the root sites of each new site collection plus all the sites within the collaboration portal, but you can always add links to this directory to help organize any URL-addressable location.

Another tool you can use to organize your information is the Summary Links Web part. This Web part allows you to build a set of links that can be grouped and displayed in columns within the Web part. Since all of the work in this Web part is manual, you may not see this Web part as being highly helpful in building a complex taxonomy simply because it would take too much time and effort. But for those teams that need to build a simple taxonomy of their links and locations, the Summary Links Web part provides good, basic functionality for them to use.

A third tool that might help with the organization of information is not a Web part but a feature: content types. A *content type* is nothing more than a core data element with at least one metadata field associated with that element. Because the metadata are exposed via Site Columns and whose population can be enforced via the DIP in Office 2007, a content type is a great way to ensure that individual content items are properly described (or *tagged*) with the correct metadata values.

What makes this even more helpful is that custom Web parts can be built that pivot on certain metadata fields to provide a browsable view of the content items that have common metadata attached to them. Moreover, the advanced search Web part can be modified to allow users to query just on that metadata field, enabling them to commit a surgical query into your index to find only those content items that are described in a common way. Multiple metadata fields can be combined in the Advanced Search Web part to provide even more refined results to the user.

There are several more methods of organizing information in SharePoint Server 2007, and we don't have space in this book to do them all justice, but as you look to deploy SharePoint Server 2007, be aware that additional methods of organizing information are readily available.

## Content Presentation

In this context, presentation is much more about making the right content available at the right location than the more common ideas of branding or "look and feel" of a site. When we talk about content presentation tools in SharePoint Products and Technologies, we're talking about features like the Data Form Web Part, which can connect to a number of different data sources and present that data with sorting, grouping, and filtering functionalities available to the data consumer. We could also consider the RSS (Really Simple Syndication) Web part as a method of presenting content. The RSS Web part can connect to any anonymous or Kerberos authenticated RSS feed and re-present that data within SharePoint.

Nearly every list type within SharePoint Products and Technologies can be considered a content presentation tool, whether we have Announcements in view, documents, contacts, or nearly any other type of data–it can all be presented within the SharePoint interface.

The BDC is another way that content from Line-of-Business (LOB) databases can be re-presented within SharePoint. What is especially interesting is the LOB information from different databases can be aggregated within the same view to make data available to those who need it within the same web part or InfoPath form.

Finally, there is an entire set of metric and reporting Web parts that ship with SharePoint Server 2007 to allow you to connect to SQL databases and other data sources so that you can present Key Performance Indicator (KPI) bits of information in a reporting dashboard. The ability to gather key metric and performance data and present it in meaningful ways to managers and knowledge workers is one of the key content presentation features in SharePoint Server 2007.

## Content Publishing

The term *publishing* is used in a variety of ways within the information management industry. For our purposes in this section, we mean the ability of the user to make content available to a wider audience using controlled, predictable methods inherent within SharePoint Server 2007. For example, the ability to publish a document means that we're making a finished document available to a wider audience, such as all users in a division or company or even on the Internet.

Making published content available on a public-facing Web site is usually referred to as *Web Content Management*. Controlling, managing, and releasing content internally is usually referred to as *Records Management* and/or *Document Management*. All of them falling loosely under the Content Publishing umbrella, each one of these major features in SharePoint Products and Technologies provides your users with the ability to control when and where content is deployed and by whom it is consumed.

# Summary

This chapter introduced you to all editions of SharePoint Server 2007and provided a general overview of how the five areas SharePoint Server 2007 can help your organization. These concepts are summarized here:

- Windows SharePoint Services 3.0
- SharePoint Server 2007 Standard Edition
- SharePoint Server 2007 Enterprise Edition
- SharePoint Server 2007 for Internet Sites
- How can SharePoint Server 2007 help my organization?
    - Collaboration
    - Content aggregation
    - Content organization
    - Content presentation
    - Content publishing

Chapter 2

# Change, Power, and Conflict

**In this chapter:**



It is not unusual for those implementing Microsoft Office SharePoint Server 2007 to experience a fair amount of change and conflict as part of their deployment process. Other than e-mail, no other product that you will implement will have as wide or personal "touch and feel" as Office SharePoint Server 2007 if you intend to implement this product in a wide, deep, and pervasive way. When SharePoint Server 2007 is implemented in your environment, you're not just implementing a simple document management or Web-based collaboration solution. You're implementing change. Culture change. Business process change. Information management change. And usually, when change happens within an organization, power balances get shifted and conflicts can ensue.

In this chapter, we're going to explore the less-talked-about side of SharePoint that many encounter during deployment—the change that SharePoint introduces to an organization with the predictable effects that such a change imports. You should note that the problems we'll discuss in this chapter are not about your SharePoint implementation *per se*. Yet changes that can cause conflict that result in power wars, if not anticipated, discussed, and managed properly, can kill your deployment. We're not kidding.

Since this book's focus is on deployment best practices, we'll be offering some best practices regarding change, power, and conflict. Like several other chapters in this book, this chapter can be read as a single best practice about a SharePoint Server 2007 deployment. But in another sense, we'll discuss several best practices about how to manage change, power, and conflict as part of your overall SharePoint Products and Technologies deployment. Before we discuss the changes that this technology introduces that are specific to SharePoint, let's consider the more general concept of change within a corporate environment.

## Understanding Change in a Corporate Environment

It was once thought that a manager could simply tell everyone that they were going to do things a certain way and everyone would salute and follow. In today's corporate environment, that is a misconception. In fact, there are several misconceptions about change that need to be recognized.

The first misconception is that a great idea, like SharePoint, will be accepted just because it is a great idea. When it comes to SharePoint, it might be a great software product with lots of helpful features that solve many existing information management and collaboration problems, but that doesn't mean it will be readily accepted. The fact is that even some of the best ideas are not readily accepted. Remember the old Sony Beta technology for videocassettes? Sony had a clearly superior technology to the VHS videocassettes, but due to poor marketing and other factors, the VHS became the adopted standard. If we borrow from family theory for just a moment, family therapists will tell you that the family system will put pressure on the individual who is changing to remain the same—even if the change is for the better. Human beings are wired to resist change. Just because it's a good (or even a great) idea doesn't mean the idea will be automatically accepted.

### Notes from the Field **When You "Get It" and Your Users and/or Managers Don't**

In our work with customers, we meet a number of highly talented administrators and developers who are sold on SharePoint as a key solution in their organization's environment. Often, they are baffled at how the rest of the company doesn't appreciate SharePoint. They've explained SharePoint to their managers and co-workers and are perplexed as to why everyone hasn't signed on to the idea. And that's the point: a great idea, by itself, isn't enough.

A somewhat extreme example comes from one client with whom I worked who had a rather talented team of technical people—both administrators and developers. But they had made some unwise decisions in the previous 12 to 18 months and their managers were skeptical of their abilities to really fix their current problems. As a result, their managers froze the IT budgets and told the team members that until they could fix their existing problems using current technologies and budget monies, no approval for more money or new technologies would be forthcoming. This team knew that SharePoint Server 2007 could resolve a number of their existing problems, but because of their past activities, coupled with their current restraints, they were unable to implement SharePoint Server 2007. Their managers simply wouldn't hear about this new, great idea from a team of people in whom they had little confidence.

In addition to a great idea, there must be a methodical and consistent approach to implementing change. Some of that approach will involve persuasion. And the change must be viewed as a step forward, not a lateral move that only increases costs and chaos.

*Bill English, Microsoft MVP, Mindsharp*

Another misconception is that all you have to do is explain the new idea and the explanation, by itself, will remove the resistance to change. Explain it. Do some training. Get people excited and you're done. No follow-up is needed. No care and feeding is warranted. If you're thinking this way, please be prepared for a long, sustained effort. The reality is that introducing change in an organization requires persistence. You need to be in this for the long haul if you're going to be successful.

### Lessons Learned **Passive Acceptance Doesn't Equal User Investment**

While mandating change from the top-down is a quicker way to apparent success, this method rarely resolves the natural resistance to change that you will likely encounter. The passive-aggressive resistance to change that exists in many organizations isn't resolved or overcome by a top-down change management approach. Carly Fiorina's experience when she became president of Hewlett-Packard is a prime example. She tried to implement major changes and because the changes were implemented quickly, many in the workforce were not involved or consulted, so they were skeptical and resistant. They didn't openly attack her new ideas, they simply appeared to meet her goals while continuing to do things as they always had in the past. The resistance was so subtle and so pervasive that it was difficult to accomplish anything.

New software roll-outs always represent change at the desktop. (You need to consider SharePoint to encompass a similar effect as updating the Office suite at the desktop because of its pervasive and persistent touch and feel.) Have you ever rolled out a new software product only to find that, over time, the product is not persistently used and the old methods are still the primary methods of accomplishing work? In many organizations, change can be an illusion while the old reality persists.

### Notes from the Field **Solidifying Change at the Desktop**

I recently worked with a customer who has 12,000 employees. This customer's IT team was thoughtful and experienced at bringing about change at the desktop level. Their current desktop environment (at the time of this writing) includes Windows 2000 and Windows XP as their desktop operating systems as well as Microsoft Office 2000. They are planning to implement SharePoint Server 2007 in the next six months.

One of the business requirements for their SharePoint Server 2007 implementation is the adoption of a software package that will both enable and, at times, require end-user population of metadata on documents before the document can be saved to the document management system. They know that Office 2007's Document Information Panel feature will accomplish this for them. But they are also smart enough to know that rolling out Office 2007 to the desktop while also rolling out SharePoint Server 2007 to their users would represent too much change at the desktop for their users. They have not used a prior version of SharePoint, so most of their user base is inexperienced with SharePoint products and technologies.

As I discussed their situation with them, it became clear that they needed to do an Office 2007 rollout before the SharePoint Server 2007 rollout. Because this created a delay in their SharePoint Server 2007 rollout timeline, they decided to use that time to test some Phase 3 and Phase 4 ideas before their Phase 1 rollout. They also decided to roll out Office 2007 first to those groups who most wanted SharePoint Server 2007, concluding that their motivation would be high to learn Office 2007 because that would clear the way for that team to get SharePoint Server 2007 sites faster.

*Bill English, Microsoft MVP, Mindsharp*

A third misconception is that implementing change slowly while building grassroots support will result in nothing getting done. In fact, the opposite is true. What research has shown is that while bottom up change is more gradual, it addresses resistance more effectively. The emphasis in bottom-up change is on participation and on keeping people informed about what is going on, so uncertainty and resistance are minimized. Furthermore, research has revealed that people are not resistant to change, they are resistant to being changed. People are better at coping with change if they have participation in bringing the change to reality. This is why—with or without grassroots support—the best way to introduce SharePoint into your environment is through a gradual, collaborative process where your users, managers, and executives all have input into the overall deployment objectives and direction.

## Common Types of Change in a Corporate Environment

Experts in change management tell us that organizations can experience several common types of change:

- **Structural change** This type of change looks at the organization as a set of functional parts that need to be restructured. The parts are re-configured (re-organized) to achieve greater overall performance. Mergers and acquisitions are two examples of structural change.
- **Cost cutting** This type of change focuses on the elimination of nonessential activities or on other methods of squeezing costs out of operations.
- **Process change** This type of change focuses on altering how tasks and activities are accomplished. Examples include re-engineering processes or implementing a new decision-making framework. The introduction of new software products onto the desktop clearly falls into this type of change.

- **Cultural change** This type of change focuses on the human side of the organization, such as a company's general approach to doing business or the relationship between its management and employees. Cultural change nearly always involves relational change. Since relationships are built on personal interaction, how people communicate and interact helps build the culture. Introducing SharePoint Products and Technologies into your environment introduces culture changes because SharePoint Products and Technologies introduce new communication paths and new ways of relating to co-workers, partners, vendors, and customers.

We believe that SharePoint represents change in three out of the four areas: structural, process, and cultural. It is structural in that the major parts of the business (however this is defined) will need to adjust their work habits to incorporate SharePoint's features into their daily work routines. For example, end-users will be managing Web sites while power users will be managing a range of Web site administrative tasks including the security of the information that resides in SharePoint. Another example is managing documents in a library versus a file server. This is a significant change that will be felt by everyone in the organization.

SharePoint represents huge process change because we're now going to ask everyone in the organization to (more or less) get on the same page when it comes to information management and information process management. And since SharePoint has a huge touch and feel at the desktop level, the process changes will be experienced by nearly everyone in your organization who uses a desktop computer.

Finally, SharePoint represents significant cultural changes because of the way it handles information and the new communication paths that are created by its introduction. Collaboration moves from e-mail threads to team sites. Discussions are handled online while offline synchronization involves Microsoft Office Outlook or Groove. Workflows introduce an electronic way of gaining document approvals, and communication about approvals involves both e-mail and the browser. Hence, implementing SharePoint Products and Technologies in your environment represents significant, pervasive change. If this aspect of your deployment is not managed correctly, the chances are increased that your deployment will either fail or not be as successful as initially envisioned.

## How Different Individuals Accept Change

Not everyone in your organization will accept change in the same way or at the same pace. This thinking has been around since the early 1900s, but was refined in 1953 by E.M. Rogers in his book, *Diffusion of Innovations*. Rogers defined *diffusion* as the process by which innovation is communicated through channels to the members over time. In this thinking, diffusion included four main elements:

- **Innovation** The new idea is incubated and defined.
- **Communication channel** The methods or paths that messages flow over between individuals.

- **Time** Three factors were mentioned here, but for our purposes, the innovation's rate of adoption is the one factor that is most important. How fast the new idea is accepted and utilized is part of the diffusion process.
- **Social system** The set of interrelated groups that are working toward a common goal.

The overall thrust was that a new idea or an innovation needed to be defined, communicated, and, over time, adopted within the social system of the organization. From a diffusion viewpoint, SharePoint represents the new idea or the innovation. The communication channels that currently exist in your organization will need to be utilized to introduce SharePoint Products and Technologies to your environment. The rate of adoption will likely depend on how adept you are at working with the five groups described below and meeting each of their needs. And a solid understanding of your social system, the stakeholder's needs, and your overall culture will enable you to manage the potential pitfalls along the way. As you look to implement SharePoint in your organization, you'll need to be aware that these four factors cannot be avoided: You must define, communicate, be patient, and work within the social structure of your organization if you're going to be successful.

The theory of diffusion holds that a new idea will be adopted faster when the following is present:

- The new idea is perceived to have more value than the current system.
- The new idea is compatible with existing values, past experiences, and current needs.
- The new idea is not overly complex.
- The new idea is testable before its production implementation.
- The new idea results in visible, measurable positive outcomes.

Critical mass is achieved once enough individuals in the organization have adopted the new idea so that the idea is commonplace and self-sustaining. In short, critical mass means the new idea will survive. The problem with achieving critical mass is that there is a time lag in how fast new ideas are adopted. This is why it is important to understand the different groups that naturally exist in your environment as you try to introduce SharePoint Server 2007 into your environment:

- **Innovators** This group makes up about 2.5 percent of the overall population. They accept new ideas quickly and need little persuasion. They often like new ideas simply because they are *new*. They tend to be venturesome, daring, and risk-takers. They also tend to have the financial resources to absorb a loss if the new idea proves to be unprofitable. Finally, this group has the ability to cope with a high degree of uncertainty about the innovation along with the time to understand and apply the technical knowledge the innovation represents.
- **Early Adopters** This group represents about 13.5 percent of the overall population. They are open to new ideas, but will accept them only after serious consideration. This group usually holds the greatest degree of opinion and thought leadership within an

organization. They tend to look for the strategic opportunity an innovation can provide. They serve as role models for others in the organization and they tend to be highly respected.

- **Early Majority** This group represents about 33 percent of the overall population. These folks frequently interact with one another and tend to be followers, not leaders. They want to see that others have been successful with the innovation before they adopt it themselves. Critical mass is usually achieved once this group has adopted the new idea.
- **Late Majority** This group is also about 33 percent of the overall population. These folks tend to be skeptical and cautious and will usually adopt new ideas only when pressured to do so.
- **Laggards** This is the last group to adopt a new idea, which by the time they adopt it, is a current or fading idea. This group possesses no opinion leadership at all. They tend to be isolated and suspicious of new ideas and will filter these ideas through referential points in the past. Their acceptance of a new idea results from other's pressure coupled with the certainty that the innovation cannot fail.

## Managing Environmental Change

Once we understand the basic ideas in Rogers' (and others') work, there is an opportunity to apply how change should be managed when it comes to doing a SharePoint implementation.

First, in some environments, SharePoint will be perceived as a huge step forward by the decision-makers because of the features and benefits inherent in the program, such as collaboration, information aggregation, or publishing. Many customers with whom we work don't have a problem seeing the obvious advantages that SharePoint brings to the organization. Yet sometimes, there is little grassroots, managerial, or information technology support; when this support is absent, the task of working within existing communication channels and the social culture will be foundational to success.

Second, SharePoint is rarely seen as a system that is incompatible with the organization's values and goals. Because the system is so flexible, it can be used by nearly any organization. We have yet to encounter a customer who found that SharePoint was inherently in conflict with his organization's goals and values.

Third, SharePoint is sometimes thought to be a system that is highly intuitive for non-technical people who work with it on a day-to-day basis. This assumption needs to be challenged. While SharePoint's interface is rather easy to use and is somewhat self-explanatory, we still find that users need a solid base of education on how to use the product and the scenarios in which certain features would be used. Some customers have balked at purchasing SharePoint until they knew their user-base would be adequately educated to use the software appropriately. In short, everyone in your organization will need education if you are planning on obtaining a robust Return on Investment (ROI) for the money your organization has spent on SharePoint licenses.

### Why End-Users Need Education

The design of SharePoint Products and Technologies is that non-technical end-users will manage their Web sites while securing their information. To place this much administration on the shoulders of your end-users represents *significant* change, both for them and for you.

It is change for them because they must now learn and execute an entirely new skill set—Web site management and information security management. Prior to the development of SharePoint Products and Technologies, these activities were reserved for IT personnel. But now they have been shifted to the non-technical end-user. It is a change for you, the IT administrator, because you are accustomed to being in control. You're also probably a bit scared that your end-users will do something foolish and cause you more work than you would have had if you had administered the Web site yourself. This is significant change for you, potentially, if you have a low level of trust in your end-users.

Implementing a robust training program that is cost affordable but that also delivers the right training at the right time to your users is important. End-users will not know how to manage their sites without education, regardless of how often others might tell you that running a SharePoint site is intuitive and easy.

The most important part of end-users' education cannot be purchased from a third-party vendor. Communicating the governance rules and the SharePoint policies and procedures that your organization has created will be the most important part of their education. Developing your own educational materials or purchasing third-party materials will also be a decision-point for your organization. But in our opinion, one important best practice is to include a robust SharePoint training program that is embedded in your SharePoint deployment plan.

Fourth, SharePoint can be (and should be) tested in a proof-of-concept (POC) before it is deployed into production. POCs can be great tools to learn about a new software product and simulate a production environment. In our experience, however, the danger is that the POC often morphs into a production environment because the test team members tend to *really* test SharePoint, find that they like it, and then dump all sorts of mission-critical information into the POC. After that, they have little interest in pulling out the information and re-doing their work in a production environment. So while a POC or some type of pre-production test is a good idea, you should also have clear agreements about when the POC will start and stop and the expectations that users will have regarding the information they have placed into their POC sites.

Finally, the ability to measure SharePoint's ROI is probably the highest pain point in this entire discussion. How "success" is defined is elusive and this results in measurements that tend to be more emotional or anecdotal in nature as opposed to being more structured and objective. But there are some ideas you can work with to help understand if your implementation is successful or not. First, count the number of site collections in your farm. Just add up the number of "sites" on your content databases and this will be a rough equal to the actual number of site collections in your farm. Second, you can measure database growth patterns and determine if the growth rate is what you had hoped it would be. Third, you can count the number of people who have attended SharePoint training as another metric of success. Or you could use one or more of these metrics plus others that you develop yourself and then use those numbers to determine if your implementation is successful or not. While still a subjective measure, it will add some statistical support to your conclusions.

Most organizations don't roll out SharePoint to everyone on the same day. Most IT personnel would strongly advise against this. Given that there are five types of people in your organization (from an adoption-of-innovation standpoint), best practice is to find one or two groups that like to work with new technology and roll out SharePoint just to those groups. Not only will they enjoy having a new technology with which to work, but you will have the opportunity to refine and mature your rollout processes so that by the time you're rolling out to the Early Majority, you've fixed the bugs in the rollout process and have better defined how to use SharePoint in your environment and how to present its usage to your users.

So find out who your Innovators are in your environment. Go to them with SharePoint. Let them use it and get excited about it. They tend to be opinionated, so get their feedback on how to use SharePoint better in your environment and then use them as your first "win." Others will see what is happening, the Early Adopters will likely want to get going with SharePoint, and your adoption will spread. In our experience working with customers, most have a hard time throttling their deployment because the demand for this product is so strong. Don't give in to the large demand. Stay methodical about your deployment and ensure that you move along at the rate you had hoped. Don't let demand push you into going too fast. If you do, you might find that the demand was more vocal than serious. Going more slowly will help you resolve nagging problems early in the deployment so that those in the Early and Late Majority groups will have better experiences once they start using SharePoint.

### Notes from the Field Energy Company's Innovators

We recall the Innovators in one company in the energy industry with whom we worked. This company of roughly 1300 employees had a strong, talented IT staff and a CIO and CEO who fully supported SharePoint implementation. This company had two groups that were clamoring for SharePoint collaboration. Apparently, a key individual within one of the groups had seen it at a friend's company and wanted to get it for his team as quickly as possible. He had been asking about it for several months and had been influential in developing grassroots support for SharePoint adoption within the second team.

The IT staff had decided to roll out SharePoint using a phased approach where these two groups would receive the functionality first. In addition, not all of the SharePoint Server

2007 functionalities would be given to them. The plan was to engage these two groups first and give them basic collaboration functionalities, with a view to introducing other functionalities into these groups as they matured using SharePoint's basic functionalities. These groups were happy to get the technology first and were willing to "learn" about how SharePoint would be used optimally within their company. They were also willing to use their experiences to help improve the SharePoint deployment to the rest of the company.

The IT staff rightly identified these two groups as their Innovators. Innovators will often be the individuals or groups who are pushing IT for SharePoint's adoption. They'll be excited to get the technology first and they'll enjoy learning how to use it. At times, they might irritate you regarding the pace at which SharePoint is or is not being adopted. Don't regard these folks as difficult or demanding. Quite the opposite is true. In some respects, they can't help it. They're Innovators.

*Bill English, Microsoft MVP, Mindsharp*

Having said all this, it is highly probable that you'll roll out SharePoint Products and Technologies to a departmental team composed of people from all five groups. If possible, try to avoid this scenario. But if you must roll out to a group that is mixed in their attitudes about adopting SharePoint Products and Technologies, then please take the time to communicate with them about the "hows and whys" of SharePoint Products and Technologies and ask for their input and help in adopting SharePoint Server 2007. While bottom-up changes take longer, the resistance will be less and, in the end, you'll have a more successful deployment of SharePoint in your environment.

## Understanding Power Dynamics and Change

If you're like most information technology professionals, it is likely that you don't spend much time thinking about the power dynamics in your organization. Yet, there is nothing more demoralizing than feeling you have a creative idea or a unique skill to help solve a significant problem and then encountering resistance to your ideas from individuals within your organization. You might even be someone who has become disillusioned and cynical about the realities of how managers and peers improperly use their power in ways that negatively affect you.

What is power? Power is the *potential* of an individual (or group) to influence another individual or group. Influence, in turn, is the exercise of power to change the behavior, attitudes, and/or values of that individual or group. It is easier to change behavior than attitudes, and in turn, it is easier to change attitudes than values. Power and influence are always at work within organizations. For example, most organizations experience conflict over resources, schedules, or personnel. These conflicts are inevitable and their resolutions often require the intervention of someone with influence and power. Organizations consist of individuals and groups with divergent interests who must figure out how to reconcile these interests.

Power comes from several sources within an organization, and those sources are as follows:

- **Formal authority** Formal authority refers to a person's position in the organization hierarchy. The higher in the corporate hierarchy or the greater the scope and scale of responsibilities, the more power that person will have. Most workers today don't respond well to the raw use of formal authority.
- **Relevance** Relevance refers to a person's ability to align work activities with corporate priorities. The more relevant a person is in his or her job, the more powerful that person will be. For example, in a company that focuses on innovation, the vice president of research and development will likely yield power and influence that is beyond her stated job description.
- **Centrality** Those occupying central positions in important networks in organizations tend to have power because others in the organization must depend on them for access to resources or for help in getting critical tasks accomplished. Hence, a person's position in the *workflow* can yield power or influence beyond a stated job description or place in the organizational chart.
- **Autonomy** The greater one's ability to exercise discretion or freedom in his position, the more power and influence that person will have within the organization. These people generally do not need to seek out approval from a superior. Tasks that tend to be novel or highly technical tend to have considerable autonomy, since it is difficult to develop guidelines or rules on how the work should be done.
- **Visibility** Those whose job activities tend to be highly visible to other powerful people within the organization will tend to have more power than those whose job performance is less obvious.
- **Expertise** Those who possess technical expertise or hard-to-find skills typically are people who are in a position to influence the opinions and behavior of others. This is because others need to rely on their expertise or skills to accomplish their own goals and objectives.

What are the implications of all this for a SharePoint Server 2007 deployment? First, you need to understand who your "champions" are for your SharePoint Server 2007 implementation. The more influence your champions have at the enterprise level of your corporation, the more likely it is that your deployment will be successful. As part of your pre-deployment planning, be sure to assess your current situation and ensure you have champions outside of your IT department who also hold positions of influence and power in your organization. Second, as part of your cultural assessment, be sure to understand the power dynamics in your organization by asking and answering these questions:

- Who are the relevant stakeholders in this SharePoint Server 2007 deployment?
- Who is dependent on whom and for what?
- In which areas do we need our stakeholders to cooperate?

- What is the source of power or influence in our stakeholders?
- What are the common goals or values among our stakeholders?
- What are the divergent goals or values among our stakeholders?
- As a result of these divergent goals or values, what tradeoffs can we expect to make to realize a successful SharePoint Server 2007 deployment?
- If conflict arises during the deployment, how are the key stakeholders likely to react?
- What can we do now to help ensure these conflicts have as little impact as possible?
- What power do we on the SharePoint Server 2007 deployment team have within our organization?
- How can we use our power effectively to influence the broader culture of this organization to accept and use SharePoint Server 2007 on a daily basis?

There are two main activities where you can exercise influence within your organization while also furthering your SharePoint Server 2007 deployment to a successful outcome. First, you need to be willing to *empower* those on whom you are dependent. For example, if you're dependent on a particular manager's approval of your deployment because that manager is an opinion leader within your organization, then you should proactively work with that manager to help her understand the benefits and advantages of using SharePoint Server 2007. If she is particularly opposed to a SharePoint Server 2007 implementation, then working with those who have influence on her job, as well as maintaining a connection with her, will provide the best opportunity to change her opinion.

Second, you need to cultivate relationships within your organization's networks. As you align your tasks with the organization's goals and develop solid relationships with other influencers in your organization, those relationships can help you achieve a successful SharePoint Server 2007 deployment as well as success in other IT initiatives. If those in the network see your efforts as a one-time appearance for a SharePoint Server 2007 deployment, you won't get very far. They need to see that you're working with them to help achieve the organization's goals and objectives.

## Managing Your Boss

Many IT administrators and developers find that they are in the cross-fire between end-user demands and manager demands. Sometimes, they feel powerless to affect any real change that will positively impact the organization. While serving the needs of your end-users is essential to a successful SharePoint Server 2007 deployment, a compatible relationship with your manager is *essential* to being effective in your job and in achieving a successful SharePoint Server 2007 deployment. If you're an IT administrator or developer, here are some principles that you can use to effectively manage your boss.

First, recognize the *mutual dependence* between you and your manager. While it is true that you depend on your manager to provide decisions and resources that help you become effective in your job, it is also important to realize that your manager is dependent on you to perform your job well so that she can receive good reviews and achieve her own goals and objectives. Some IT staff behave as if their bosses were not very dependent on them. They fail to see how much their boss needs their help and cooperation to do her job effectively.

Second, recognize that you are two *fallible* human beings. You will make mistakes. So will your boss. Failure to recognize and accept this fact may lead to unrealistic expectations.

Third, be sure that you understand your work style, needs, strengths, and weaknesses. You also need to understand these same elements in your manager. Misunderstandings can arise from your lack of understanding about what your boss really needs and how she really works. For example, instead of waiting for your manager to request information from you that you know she will need in the future, you could provide it in advance so she has more time to understand it and offer feedback about what she really needs. At a minimum, you need to appreciate your manager's goals and pressures, her strengths and weaknesses if you are to understand the environment in which you work.

# Understanding Specific Changes that SharePoint Introduces

Now that we have discussed change from a general perspective, let's discuss some of the more common changes that users experience when SharePoint is introduced. This discussion will be from the viewpoint of the user, not the administrator or architect. There are several key changes that users will experience pretty quickly. We'll cover them under the general umbrellas of how information is accessed, how information is managed, and how collaboration occurs. Note that we cannot cover all of the changes that SharePoint will introduce into your environment, so we'll need to focus on the more common changes that organizations often experience.

## Information Access Changes

For those who are new to SharePoint, an immediate change will be how documents are accessed and consumed. At present, many companies have shared network drives that host large data sets with hundreds or even thousands of folders with tens of thousands of documents. It is not uncommon to hear of shared network drives that host a terabyte or more of data, much of it redundant, old, outdated, and unusable. So, two problems immediately present themselves in this scenario.

First, as SharePoint is increasingly used, users will not access the shared network drive to work with a document. Instead, they will access the document using a URL namespace via their browser or their Office client. The catch is that it's difficult to use the Office client to access a document library until the user has manually created a Web folder client connection to the document library, or the user has created a mapped drive to the document library, or the user has visited the library and worked with documents in such a manner as to have the Web folder client connection automatically created in their My Network Places on their desktop. This need to "visit-first" in order to obtain a shortcut route to the document library can be frustrating for your users.

Logically, the shared drive's contents will likely not be hosted in the same document library. In nearly all scenarios, this shared drive's content will be re-hosted in SharePoint spanning many, many document libraries. So, what once was a single drive mapping for the end-user that resulted in wading through countless folders to find their documents now becomes accessing information through a plethora of Web folder client connections while learning to manage documents across many different document libraries and sites.

Our recommendation is that users be taught how to use Favorites, My Links, and shortcuts to help them organize the document libraries for quick access to these locations. In addition, we recommend that users be taught how to create mapped drives for certain document libraries in which they will be working most often.

### Lessons Learned **International Non-Profit Adopts SharePoint**

We recall a non-profit organization with whom we work that has members located literally all over the world. This organization's members go into other countries and live there for several years at a time. In many respects, these individuals are considered entrepreneurs—even though they are not in a for-profit business—because their work demands similar skills and characteristics of entrepreneurs.

These individuals usually form small teams in their respective cities to carry out their work. Yet these teams often need to collaborate with one another and, to date, they have been using e-mail as their only form of collaboration. Because all of their e-mail must be routed through a single set of servers for security purposes, these individuals find that sending larger documents or pictures is both time consuming and difficult, especially when sending from locations that don't have high-speed and/or reliable bandwidth. In addition, their documents are stored in multiple locations around the world, mostly in peer-to-peer, small networks where each team hosts its documents on a local desktop that other local team members can access.

These teams needed a new way to share their documents so that work that was accomplished in one city could be made available to other teams in other cities. In addition, there were times when multiple teams needed to work on a single project with shared documents and calendars. SharePoint provided the platform in which these teams could collaborate more effectively. With SharePoint, their ability to share documents and calendars was streamlined and made more simple. Uploading documents to a centralized Web server is still slow, but at least users are now working with a single pedigree for each document and can collaborate on a single version of the document.

A second problem with moving documents from a shared network drive to SharePoint is that you'll need to communicate with your users *where* the documents will be placed or instruct them on how to move the documents themselves. Knowing where the documents will land in SharePoint means that you've already finished your Information Architecture work and that you've fleshed out your taxonomies in SharePoint (if you're planning on implementing a robust taxonomy). In addition, when documents are added to the document library, if they need to be described with new types of metadata, then your users will need training on this as well.

We strongly recommend that you implement a user-oriented information taxonomy training if your documents will need to be tagged or described with metadata that users heretofore have not been asked to manage. A new tagging effort can be a real sore point for many users, so be sure to spend time explaining and working through the issues involved with this effort.

### Notes from the Field **Energy Company Implements Taxonomy**

Remember the energy company with the strong Innovators group? We introduced them earlier in the Energy Company's Innovators sidebar. Well, not only did they have a strong Innovators group to which they could initially roll out SharePoint, but they had just completed a two-year analysis of all of their information corporate-wide.

What they found was that they had 56 core data elements and an additional 258 supporting data elements. They had already gone through the effort to identify, describe, and organize all of their data elements and how they rolled up into forms, reports, and metrics for their organization.

So when it came time for them to implement SharePoint, they were ready to take their data element models and transform them into content types, and then apply those to their site collection structure. We worked with the company to develop a logical plan on how to build their taxonomy and data hosting topology. They started with their data elements, then they rolled up those elements into forms and reports, then rolled up the metrics from the reports into a set of dashboards that were initially exposed in a set of elementary Web parts. In a future phase, the company will use the Report Center in SharePoint to extend and mature their reporting as they learn about using the Business Intelligence and SQL Analytics capabilities to deliver the metrics management and team leaders need.

*Bill English, Microsoft MVP, Mindsharp*

## Breaking Down Information "Kingdoms"

A second scenario that we commonly encounter is department-level file servers. Similar to a shared network drive, users work on documents that are hosted on a local file server. From a user's perspective, this scenario is similar to the shared network drive scenario. But from a manager's perspective, this scenario might result in change, power, and conflict issues. Consider a manager who believes her department's information is *her information*. In other words, she believes that what she and her department users produce belongs to her department first. This manager is likely to resist having that information placed in some remote, Web-based collaboration system on servers that she can't control. Sound familiar? Many of you are undoubtedly nodding your head "yes."

This type of scenario, whether it be a manager or single end-user or a project team, represents a power issue. If these folks believe that SharePoint will infringe on their ownership and manageability of the information, they will see it as a direct threat to their power over the information. You'll need to work with them to help them see that they still maintain power and control over the information if it is hosted in SharePoint through site collection and Web management.

> **Important** If this scenario isn't managed correctly, you'll likely end up with significant resistance, conflict, and perhaps an elongated implementation for this team or department. Use the Group Adoption and Identification Job Aid to assist you with identifying to whom you should pay special attention and why.

## Document Development and Collaboration

Nearly everyone who is reading this chapter has had the experience of collaborating on the development of a new document. For many years, we have e-mailed documents back and forth, putting version numbers inside the document and/or in the name of the document while implementing a manual workflow to gain approval for the finished version of the document.

SharePoint represents a new collaboration path for documents that are in development. Having written several books using SharePoint as our back-end system, we can attest that even those whom you would not suspect will have a difficult time *remembering* to use the check out/check in features for simple document collaboration. The culture change of *not* e-mailing documents to team members for their consideration is huge. The idea of putting a document in a team site and then inviting others to the site so they can check out, read, modify, and check in a document is vastly different from the immediate gratification of sending an e-mail with instructions about the attached document.

Don't assume that simple document collaboration will be understood or will be intuitive for even your advanced users. Best practice is to ensure your users have received collaboration and governance training on how to work with documents in SharePoint. Since document collaboration is one of the key selling points for SharePoint, making document collaboration training a core part of their training experience is smart.

## End-Users as Web Site Administrators and Creators

SharePoint is designed to have both a centralized administrative architecture that parallels a distributed administrative architecture. Some functions, such as Web application creation, alternate access mappings, or configuring policies for Web applications, are reserved for those who manage the SharePoint farm from a central location. These functions are grouped under the Central Administration site.

All other administrative functions—at the site collection level as well as the site level—are distributed to those who create and manage sites and site collections. In the vast majority of implementations, these two levels of management are performed by non-technical, non-IT users who happen to have some technical acuities and interests.

Having said this, it is important to note that once you open up My Sites to the masses in your organization, each person who is able to create a My Site also becomes both a site collection administrator as well as a site administrator. This is because each My Site is a separate site collection. So, in the long run, everyone who has a My Site will need education on how to manage and utilize the features in their My Site as well as more generic site collection and site administration. Failure to do this will result in both a lower ROI (Return on Investment) as well as increased help desk calls asking about how to use this or that feature or administrative link.

We often have customers whose SharePoint farm administrators want to "lock down" their SharePoint implementation. They want to retain centralized administrative and security controls over all of the site collections and sites within SharePoint. Often, they use global groups from Active Directory to centralize their security control and force users to request new sites each time a new collaboration space is needed. They have very little trust in their end-users and usually are rather cynical about their users' abilities to manage a Web site. They conclude that by retaining centralized control, they will avoid a number of support incidents that would otherwise be created by users who might commit unwise actions with the site.

While we believe that much of the "lock down" mentality is more emotionally driven based on poor end-user support experiences, we have found there are some scenarios where this type of implementation makes sense. Usually, these scenarios have some or all of the following characteristics:

- The centrally managed sites are part of a larger process where *ad hoc* or team collaboration isn't performed within the site.
- The site is templated as a publishing portal and the security management for portals in the overall SharePoint implementation design calls for IT to secure all portals and their pages and subsites.

- The ability of the business to create income is greater than the cost of having a centrally managed SharePoint implementation. The legal vertical is one that we commonly find in this scenario because, given their bill rate, it is more profitable for the business to have their legal employees working on client matters while the IT staff manages the entire implementation.
- The centrally managed site hosts old reference documents and is not involved in collaboration activities.
- The centrally managed site is an extranet site where tight security is required to ensure those users authenticated into the site do not have access to any other part of the SharePoint implementation.
- The centrally managed site hosts highly sensitive information whose security must be closely monitored by IT professionals.
- The centrally managed site is a records repository where IT personnel are expected to secure the records in the organization's official records repository.
- The Phase I deployment, as part of a multi-phased deployment, calls for centralized IT security management. As users become educated and experienced with SharePoint, IT control is released to the user population in subsequent phases of the rollout.

What is helpful to understand is that all of these characteristics are either function specific or time specific. And in nearly all of these scenarios, we find that while there is justification for locking down these sites, there is also justification for having other parts of the deployment more open to end-user control. Rarely do our designs for customers fall 100 percent in either the "open" or "locked down" camps. Commonly, a combination of both aspects is included in a complete design.

So, don't be afraid to lock down those sites that should be locked down by having your IT staff centrally control the security and functionality in the site. But also, don't shy away from having some areas where the collaboration sites can be self-created and self-organized by the end-users without looping through your IT staff. One of the hallmarks of a highly collaborative system is that the collaboration spaces are self-organizing with a low transaction cost. SharePoint has the flexibility to provide both centrally secured sites alongside user-created and secured sites.

Also, from a sheer workload perspective, it is often unwise to have IT manage all of the sites. For example, let's assume that your implementation calls for seven Web applications and that, over a period of one year, each Web application has an average of 40 site collections with an average of four sites within each site collection.

If we do the math correctly, that will mean a total of 1,120 different Webs within your farm. With an average of 11 Web parts and lists per Web, that's a total of 12,320 lists. If each site has an average of four different SharePoint groups and each group is secured by a corresponding global group in Active Directory, this would mean creating 4,480 global groups in Active

Directory. So, for IT to granularly manage the security for each site, your IT staff would have to pay attention to 1,120 different Web sites and potentially secure thousands of lists while creating, populating, and managing nearly 5,000 global groups. By any standard, this would represent enough of an additional workload on your IT staff that you would need to hire additional employees to keep up with the SharePoint management tasks. And the coordination of efforts across all the sites and Active Directory groups would be substantial too.

Now, we realize that some will find this illustration a bit absurd, but in our customer work, we encounter those who seriously think about doing this. But when we illustrate what this really means in terms of objects managed, the number becomes overwhelming and, usually, customers end up deciding to allow their users to manage a significant portion of their implementation.

Like it or not, SharePoint Products and Technologies is an administrative-heavy platform that doesn't appear to be so mainly because the administrative workload is distributed across many end-users at the desktop. Centralization of the administrative workload will require additional full-time employees that will need to increase in number as your SharePoint deployment increases in scope.

So, best practice is to train a sub-set of your end-users to be SharePoint Power Users (or whatever title you wish to give them) who can effectively administrate and secure major portions of your SharePoint deployment, including site collection administration. We feel it is simply impractical to centrally administrate a SharePoint farm in all but the smallest of deployments.

### Tradeoff **Centralizing SharePoint Administration versus Increased IT Support Costs**

This illustration goes against our best practice recommendation, but we offer it to help illustrate what a fully centralized administrative environment means to the IT staff and the users. We have worked with several law firms. Each one had over 600 lawyers, plus administrative and support staff. One firm that we worked with stands out in their effort to totally centralize all SharePoint administrative activities. Because this firm routinely bills at rather high rates, they don't want their lawyers and paralegals taking the time to administrate SharePoint. They have concluded that even simple administrative tasks, such as adding users to a team site, is too costly for their billable people to perform and that it is more cost effective to hire additional IT staff to perform these functions or to generate scripts to perform many mundane administrative functions.

Consequently, the firm's IT department has grown considerably. Beginning with an IT staff of roughly ten individuals, the firm has hired two additional full-time employees to whom the initial implementation was offloaded. Two to four more individuals (mostly developers) will be hired to help with SharePoint implementation over the first two years of deployment. The reason the additional staff is needed is because each matter (which is a new pleading with facts that may or may not be opposed) requires a new team site.

Larger clients receive their own site collection, which may or may not be exposed via an extranet scenario.

The creation and maintenance of each team site requires direct involvement of the IT staff. When a new site is needed, the requesting assistant to the lawyer fills out a short online form in the company intranet that informs IT of the following information:

- Name of the site
- URL name
- Site members and their role assignments
- Selection of Web parts that should appear on the site with all others assumed to not be exposed on the page
- Name(s) of any custom created Web parts, including new document libraries
- Explanation of any custom permission levels that are needed and who should be assigned to those custom levels
- Explanation of any lists or list items that should be explicitly permissionized
- Explanation of any customizations that might be needed
- Other notes of interest that might help explain what is needed in the site

After IT receives the request, they create an organizational unit (OU) in Active Directory that corresponds to the site. Every site collection's hierarchy structure is mirrored in Active Directory's OU structure. For example, if they create a site collection called *http://contoso* with three sub-sites, *contoso/matter1*, *contoso/matter2,* and *contoso/matter3*, then they will have an OU called *contoso* with three child OUs called *matter1*, *matter2*, and *matter3*, respectively. Inside each OU, IT will create a global group for each role in the site. Their group naming convention is descriptive, so they can specifically identify the global group by its name alone. For example, the members SharePoint group in the *contoso/matter2* site would have a corresponding global group called Contoso Matter2 Members. They use global groups only for permission assignments to end-users within SharePoint, and the IT staff is mandated as the only site collection owners across the entire deployment.

On average, IT will create 15 to 20 new matters each week, so you can see that the effort to create these objects and sites is substantial. They are scripting the creation and population of the global groups in Active Directory and, at the time of this writing, are looking into ways to script site and Web part creation as well. What they find incredibly time consuming are the ongoing day-to-day administrative on a site-by-site basis, such as the following tasks:

- Managing user account changes as employees enter and leave the firm
- Documenting breaks of permission inheritance within site collections and sites

- Re-configuring user accounts for commonly used workflows
- Passing user account information to non-employees, such as customers or co-counsel in other law firms
- Implementing customizations on a site-by-site basis, based on the unique requests of each partner in the firm

This law firm illustrates that a centralized administrative approach to a SharePoint deployment is both possible and doable. But it also illustrates the additional workflows, processes, and human resources that will be required to be successful. And the fulfillment of those requirements could be costly and time consuming. This firm has dedicated additional IT staff and have accepted the increased IT overhead expenses in exchange for a fully centralized deployment. Your organization may or may not desire to fully centralize your deployment, but if you do, bear in mind that your IT overhead costs, as illustrated here, will increase substantially.

## End-Users as Security Agents

What sends some Type-A administrators into a panic is when they realize, for the first time, that their users will become the masters of their documents, not only in terms of the documents' management, but more so in terms of securing those documents. More than once, we have engaged in extended discussions about the potential exposure to legal liability should a document containing sensitive information be made available to the wrong person(s).

It's interesting how users react to this newfound responsibility. Some become much more ferocious about securing their information than their system administrators ever were. It's as if they (finally) have ownership of their documents and are making the most of their ability to secure their information. Some take the responsibility in stride and correctly secure their documents without any need to feel as if they "owned" their content. Still others appear to secure their documents but sometimes let the wrong people in for a few minutes, which results in the information being exposed to the wrong people.

But there will always be a few individuals in your organization who will quietly break the security rules now and then. It may be only.01 percent of your user base, but some of them will do it. Most will unwittingly expose information to the wrong individuals, but others will purposefully engage in this activity.

For this reason, best practice is to have a serious discussion with your legal team about the potential problems of having the different types of information exposed to the wrong people and how that information should be managed. Don't allow highly sensitive information to be secured by anyone who hasn't been properly trained and who meets other criteria that you might need to implement for your environment.

Another best practice will be for your information security policies to explicitly call out how documents are secured within your SharePoint environment and who is responsible for securing them. Content owners should be named for content that is hosted within SharePoint, and those owners should be the site collection owners and/or site administrators who are responsible for securing that content. Penalties should also be called out in the policy and then enforced when broken.

Finally, there needs to be a culture shift in how your organization thinks about information security. Your organization needs to understand that they should not look to IT to secure information that is hosted by SharePoint (except in highly centralized deployments) and should not hold the IT staff responsible for information that is wrongly secured and exposed.

# Strong Governance and Potential Conflicts

In Chapter 5, "SharePoint Server 2007 and Governance," you'll learn how to implement proper governance for a SharePoint Products and Technologies deployment. In this section, we'll discuss the effects that a lack of governance will create from a conflict and power perspective. We can't stress strongly enough how important proper governance is for your SharePoint Products and Technologies deployment. Hopefully, if you're on the fence about developing strong governance for your SharePoint deployment, this section will help you understand the problems that inherently exist in a deployment without strong governance.

Without strong governance, you'll likely encounter at least three major conflicts in your SharePoint deployment:

- Confusion about where information should reside
- Confusion about how information is to be handled
- Confusion about who makes which decisions in SharePoint

Let's discuss each point individually in the following sections.

## Knowing Where to Put Information

You cannot assume that users will know where their information should be hosted in your SharePoint environment. Without communicating a corporate-wide set of expectations about where information goes in SharePoint, users will be left to make the decision on their own and you'll find that each one will have a different idea as to where their own information should reside. For example, should customer project collaboration information go under the Customers site or the Projects site? Should new product information go under the Research or the Products site? Should extranet information be shared with internal users or not? These examples illustrate that users will not have clear choices about where their information should reside. Placing this burden on them to make such decisions, especially in the absence of any deployment-wide information architecture, is a bit unfair to the average user.

If your organization can't bring itself to make core governance decisions like this, then conflict is bound to erupt based on the lack of direction for your SharePoint deployment. Because users will decide where their information goes, they will necessarily end up negotiating where they will collaborate within SharePoint. Turf wars will likely happen with organic coalitions that form out of conflict and compromise. Users will spend cycles and energy resolving differences when their focus should be on collaboration and decisions.

Someone in your organization needs to make some high-level decisions about where information will go and who will manage it. These decisions need to be communicated and then enforced if you plan on avoiding conflict surrounding where information goes in SharePoint.

## Knowing How Information Is to Be Handled

In most organizations, there are different kinds of information with different security levels. For example, payroll information is often highly secured, whereas public Web site information is generally less secured.

When users are developing information within SharePoint, they cannot be assumed to know how their information should be managed. For many, the prospect of managing and securing their information is a new task; in the absence of direction, they're bound to violate some unwritten rule or expectation. Best practice is to have an organization-wide information architecture from which document-type definitions can be described and then implemented in SharePoint.

For example, how should the site administrator that hosts the organization's payroll file manage that file? To whom should the administrator give permissions to that file? How should the research and development team manage new research information? What security level should be given to this information? How should it be described? When does information in your organization become legally compliant and publicly available?

These types of questions relate to how information is managed. In the absence of clear governance for how information should be handled, conflict will likely occur and some information security policies might be violated. Best practice is to map out your information types and then communicate how these types should be managed within SharePoint.

### Tradeoff **Mitigating Conflict Through Governance Planning and SharePoint Design**

We routinely work with customers who have been charged with replacing their file servers with their SharePoint Server 2007 implementation. There are a number of problems with this approach, not the least of which is that such a mandate inherently places several groups in the company in a position where conflict is likely to erupt.

For example, consider the tasks that will need to be performed in order to undergo a bulk migration of documents from a file server to a SharePoint Server 2007 platform, illustrated in Figure 2-1.

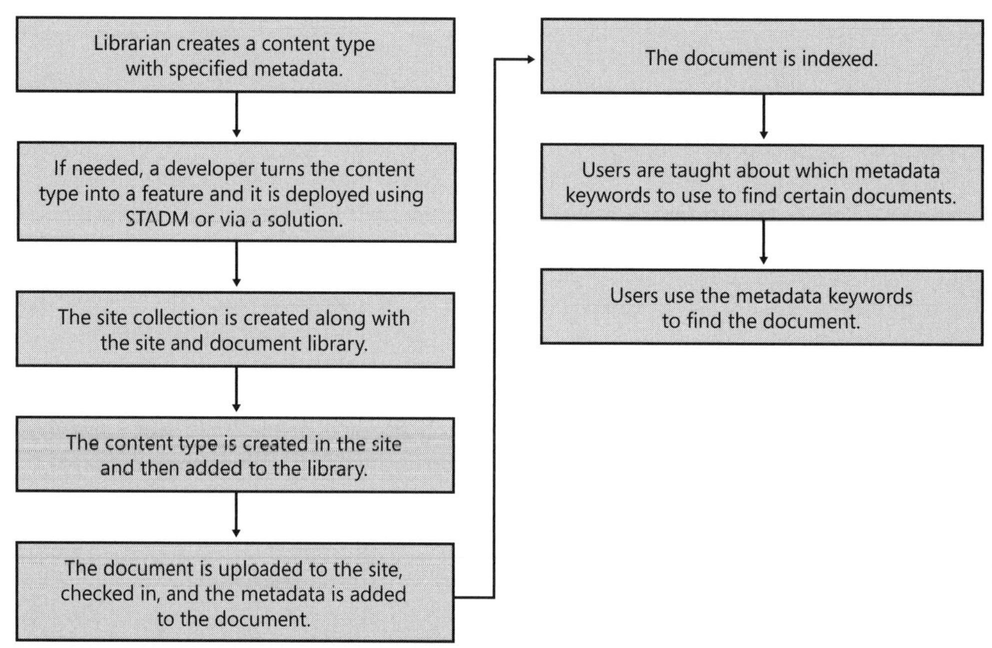


**Figure 2-1** Process flow of the tasks necessary to import documents into SharePoint Server 2007

In order for the documents to be findable, they need to be accurately described with global keywords that are pre-defined for the organization. These keywords need to be highly discriminating and communicated to the users so that the users can use them to quickly and easily find the documents. Simply uploading hordes of documents into SharePoint will not make those documents more findable, especially if hundreds of thousands or millions of documents are uploaded into many different libraries.

This process also involves several groups of people and requires them to work together in ways that they never have before. The opportunities for conflict are obvious. The groups are as follows:

- Librarians need to create global keywords and metadata fields, mapping them to content types and then mapping those content types to sites and libraries.
- Developers may need to create the content types into features and have them deployed either through STSADM or through solution deployments so that end-users need not be tasked with manually creating content types that are shared across many site collections.

- Farm administrators and power users will need to create a plethora of site collections, sites, and libraries with a predetermined set of site and library names that will be both intuitive to the end-users and compliant for the SharePoint farm deployment.
- Site owners will add the content types to the libraries.
- IT team members and/or power users will need to populate the libraries with the documents. Using third-party tools, metadata can be applied at the time the documents are checked in to the library.
- Farm administrators ensure the documents are indexed.
- Trainers will need to train end-users on the keyword meanings and how to use them to find the documents they need to find.
- Users need to be informed about the unique metadata field names that should not be used as site column headings or in new metadata field names for new content types.
- Users use the keywords to query and find the documents.

As you increase the number of documents in SharePoint, you'll find that the same words will be used for very different meanings, rendering a syntactically correct result set increasingly irrelevant. Keyword searches on content cannot help a user express meaning in a keyword search. And getting all of these groups on the same page regarding the meaning of keywords and metadata fields that are attached to documents can be the source of conflict. The conflict can be avoided by regularly communicating project goals and keyword meanings and by ensuring that key stakeholders are informed of the process and are in agreement with ongoing decisions as the project moves forward.

The tradeoff decision is to invest resources into laying out the information architecture groundwork upfront versus just moving the documents into SharePoint Server 2007 and hoping that by indexing their content, the documents will be findable enough and that you will have avoided conflict altogether between these groups.

## Knowing Who Makes Which Decisions

At the core of your governance plan is the need to decide who can make decisions within your SharePoint implementation. A myriad of configuration settings are available for manipulation at four basic levels: farm, Web application, site collection, and site. Generally speaking, SharePoint farm administrators will manage the options at the farm and Web application levels, whereas power users with advanced training will manage the options at the site collection level. Nearly everyone in your organization who is involved with content creation or management will manage configuration values at the site level.

Your governance plan needs to specify which people and positions will be able to make decisions and commit changes at each of these four levels. Planning this out before you deploy SharePoint Server 2007 is the optimal method of ensuring success for your SharePoint deployment.

By default, site administrators and site collection administrators have broad powers to make decisions and affect configuration changes within their scope of influence. The breadth and depth of influence is often not fully understood, but a quick look at the administrative options in Site Settings tells the story better than nearly any other method we can think of. Consider Figure 2-2, which illustrates the options that are available to a site administrator for a team site template with the publishing features activated. Take a moment and look at all of the configuration, security, and customization options that are under the purview and authority of the site administrator.

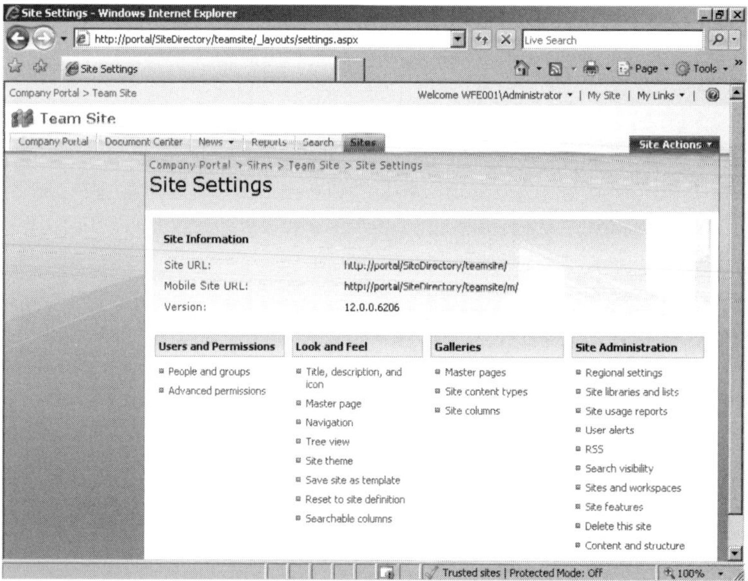


**Figure 2-2** Site Settings page for a default team site

Site owners can do things like create content types, enable and disable features, set permission levels for users and groups, and create e-mail–enabled lists and distribution groups (assuming this feature is enabled at the farm level) without ever having to loop in a System Administrator. Site administrators can break permission inheritance from parent sites and can customize the navigation for their site. Site administrators have significant authority and ability to pervasively manage their sites. Unless their configuration abilities are explicitly allowed or denied by a governance plan, it is highly likely that some might engage in administrative activities that you might not want them performing. This will cause conflict that is difficult to resolve because the conflict occurs within a scenario that lacks overall direction.

Figure 2-3 illustrates the additional responsibilities of the site collection administrator in a site collection with the publishing features turned on. What is important to note here is that once My Sites are opened to the end-users, when they create their My Site, they become both a site administrator and a site collection administrator. The My Site site collection administration matrix is somewhat different than that which is illustrated in Figure 2-3.

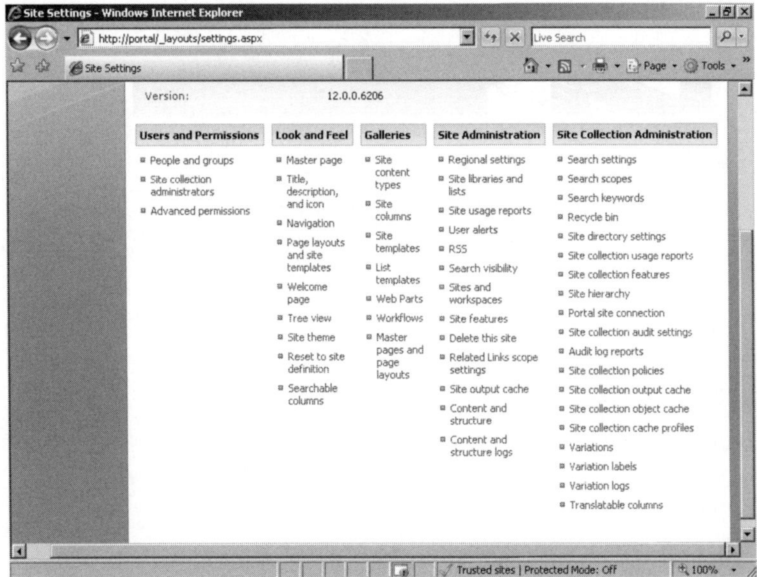


**Figure 2-3** Site Collection Administration Settings

By default, site collection administrators can create and configure the search scopes that appear in the search Web parts, keywords and best bets, and language variations as well as turning on and off features that have been applied at the site collection level. Site collection administrators have access to all content stored within their site collection and can manage permissions throughout the collection. In addition, site collection administrators can implement collection-wide auditing, work with the Recycle Bin, rearrange the hierarchy of sites (when the publishing features are turned on), and configure the cache properties.

Both Figures 2-2 and 2-3 point to the strong need to thoroughly train your users on the proper administration and maintenance of a site and/or site collection in your environment. Best practice is to not allow your users to use the SharePoint technology without first receiving training on the proper methods of use and administration of a SharePoint site.

In addition, because site collection administrators have both pervasive and robust administrative capabilities, it is imperative that the organization either explicitly support their role or state where they want the site collection administrative activities reserved for the IT staff or the SharePoint farm administrators.

# Summary

In this chapter, we have discussed at a high level how different groups respond to change and some common, specific changes that your organization will encounter with an implementation of SharePoint Server 2007. We've also offered some best practices regarding these changes, and they are summarized for you here:

- Find one or two groups that like to work with new technology and roll out SharePoint just to those groups.
- Ensure that your users have received collaboration training on how to work with documents in SharePoint.
- Train a sub-set of your end-users to be SharePoint Power Users (or whatever title you want to give them) who can effectively administrate and secure major portions of your SharePoint deployment, including site collection administration.
- Have a serious discussion with your legal team about the potential problems of having the different types of information exposed to the wrong people and how that information should be managed.
- Information security policies should explicitly call out how documents are secured within your SharePoint environment and who is responsible for securing them. Penalties should also be called out in the policy and then enforced when broken.
- Have an organization-wide information architecture from which document-type definitions can be described and then implemented in SharePoint.
- Map out your information types and then communicate how these types should be managed within SharePoint.
- Do not allow your users to use the SharePoint technology without first receiving training on the proper methods of use and administration of a SharePoint site.

Chapter 3

# SharePoint Server 2007 Design Life Cycle

**In this chapter:**



Imagine you are a movie director who is responsible for a major motion picture. You are responsible for everything that must happen, such as set construction, location for film shooting, actors, and scripts. Your job is to produce a quality movie by managing all of the details and ensuring that everyone works together in a common purpose to produce a great movie.

When designing for Microsoft Office SharePoint Server 2007, you are the director! Much like an Office SharePoint Server 2007 installation, many of these activities are happening simultaneously and you must plan for tasks to complete on time and in sync. Your set construction is analogous to your farm and Web applications, actors are your end-users, and the scripts are the policies and training.

SharePoint Server 2007 does require some planning and design, but it doesn't always need to be rigidly designed and implemented. If you are interested only in getting it installed, you should still review the basics of design processes and the commonly asked SharePoint Server 2007 design questions sections. If your goal is a well-running SharePoint Server 2007 implementation that will grow with your organization and adapt to future challenges, then you should consider using a framework for your design. This chapter isn't about any one industry framework, but rather an overview of the SharePoint Server 2007 design points and associated processes. You can take this information and incorporate the details into your organization's design process. If you do not have a framework in place, this chapter will serve to provide a SharePoint Server 2007 design life cycle for your organization. Additionally, it is important to understand this entire chapter is a single best practice and doesn't necessarily contain granular best practices. This chapter will cover the following topics:

- Foundations for a SharePoint Server 2007 design life cycle
- Process models
- Defining stakeholders
- Providing training
- Gathering requirements
- Designing
- Building
- Operating

However you choose to proceed with your SharePoint Server 2007 implementation, consistency is crucial. It is usually possible to fix a consistently incorrect installation, but very difficult to fix an inconsistently installed SharePoint Server 2007 server farm. You should consider using a framework to ensure consistency, even if it is very simple.

# Overview of Frameworks that Can Be Used with SharePoint Server 2007

Design life cycles have been around for quite some time and are based in many verticals such as retail manufacturing, computer software, systems engineering, and academia. Design life cycles are becoming more commonplace in the IT industry and will continue to do so because they lower the overall cost of a service while simultaneously improving its delivery. The following section provides a brief overview of the frameworks and processes that serve as the foundation for this chapter.

## Information Technology Infrastructure Library

The Information Technology Infrastructure Library (ITIL) is a library of over 30 books that provide a foundation for designing, implementing, and management of IT services. The following ITIL books are the most commonly used depending on the size of your implementation.

- **Service Support** Provides the basics for the daily processes required to maintain IT services.
- **Service Desk** Can be roughly correlated to the Help Desk function in many organizations, but encompasses much more than answering a phone call.
- **Incident Management** Outlines the fundamentals of service restoration in the event of a service outage.
- **Problem Management** Will assist you in detailing a plan to minimize the disruption to valuable IT Services.
- **Configuration Management** Is a mechanism in which you identify, manage, and maintain versions of configuration items.

- **Change Management** Helps you to methodically manage configuration changes in your environment.
- **Release Management** Provides the foundation for releasing new software, whether done manually or automatically, ensuring appropriate control and communication.
- **Service Delivery** Is widely used in large organizations to manage processes such as Service Level Agreements (SLAs), Service Level Requirements (SLRs), availability management, capacity management, financial management, and service continuity.

> **More Info** For more information on ITIL, see Chapter 7, "Developing an Information Architecture," or browse to *http://itil-officialsite.com*.

## Microsoft Solutions Framework

This section is a brief overview of the Microsoft Solutions Framework as it applies to SharePoint Server 2007. There are entire books on the topic, so the inclusion of more than a brief overview as it applies to SharePoint Server 2007 design isn't possible. The Microsoft Solutions Framework (MSF) originated to address Microsoft's need for software design life cycle management. The MSF process model is the basis for developing solutions, while the Microsoft Operations Framework is the framework for managing the solution. Figure 3-1 shows the MSF process model.

**Figure 3-1** The MSF process model encompasses the life cycle of a solution.

As seen in Figure 3-1, the MSF life cycle consists of five phases:

- The Envisioning Phase identifies the stakeholders in the project, such as the financier, users, departments, and Information Technology. It is the time where the stakeholders and IT agree on the functional requirements for the project. Be sure to stay with functional requirements such as the need to automate document workflows, and away from technical requirements like implementing SharePoint Server 2007 in conjunction with Microsoft BizTalk Server to enable workflows. The MSF process model addresses technical requirements in a later phase.

- The Planning Phase is where you decide what the best technical solutions are to meet the functional requirements. You should do some high-level testing and present your findings to the stakeholders in a project planning review.
- The Developing Phase is when you prototype and test the solution, including testing the system dependencies. Example dependencies for SharePoint Server 2007 are SQL Server 2005, Active Directory, firewalls, routers, storage, and Windows Server operating systems. Present the solution in a stakeholder and peer review, and attempt to freeze the project and not allow any new requirements.
- The Stabilizing Phase would begin with pilot testing of the solution. A general rule is testing the solution with 5 to 10 percent of your user population. Rarely does everything work as planned, so this phase gives you the opportunity to fix those issues and stabilize the implementation for mass deployment.
- The Deploying Phase is where the solution is deployed to the users. Verify that you have provided the proper training to your users, administrators, developers, and Help Desk staff before deployment. You should identify and tweak any required training during the stabilizing phase.

## Microsoft Operations Framework

The Microsoft Operations Framework (MOF) compliments the MSF process by providing "operational guidance that enables organizations to achieve mission-critical system reliability, availability, supportability, and manageability of Microsoft products and technologies," as stated in MOF documentation. The Microsoft Operations Framework is divided into four unique quadrants, as shown in Figure 3-2.

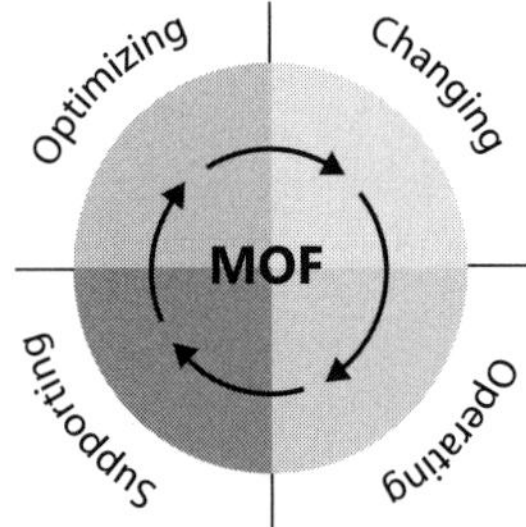


**Figure 3-2** MOF was divided into four unique quadrants to compartmentalize solution operations.

While MOF has been developed for Microsoft technologies, much of the framework aligns with ITIL. The four quadrants of MOF are as follows:

- The Operating quadrant is more Microsoft-specific and addresses directory services administration, job scheduling, network administration, security administration, service monitoring, storage management, and systems administration.

- The Supporting quadrant aligns with ITIL and includes incident management, problem management, and the Service Desk.
- The Optimizing quadrant describes eight key service management functions–availability, capacity, financial, infrastructure, service continuity, security, service levels, and workforce management.
- The Changing quadrant addresses three key areas as described by ITIL: Change Management, Configuration Management, and Release Management.

> **More Info** For more information on the Microsoft Solutions Framework, browse to *http://www.microsoft.com/msf*. For more information on the Microsoft Operations Framework, browse to *http://www.microsoft.com/mof*.

## Structure versus Freedom

Before you begin your design, consider your IT governance plan, if it exists. While an IT governance plan obviously isn't required to implement SharePoint Server 2007, you do need to consider how much freedom you will give your users within the product.

> **More Info** See Chapter 5, "SharePoint Server 2007 and Governance," for more Information Technology governance information.

Many times the IT department will exert too much control over the functionality of an application, thus limiting the true capability. SharePoint Server 2007 is definitely one of the products designed for end-users, and built for the end-users to manage their own workspaces. SharePoint Server 2007 was designed to delegate much of the administration to power users and end-users. The more restriction placed on these users, the less functional the product will become. In essence, control and usability are inversely proportional with SharePoint Server 2007.

> **Note** If you require a rigid structure in place, then you will need to perform a significantly more detailed design. Your requirements planning process must identify most, if not all, possible uses of SharePoint Server 2007. A real-world example of this detailed planning is content type planning. If you will allow your users to leverage only pre-determined content types, then you must completely plan your content types before production deployment. A complete content type planning process is impossible for the majority of organizations because you cannot predict how SharePoint Server 2007 will be used in the future. If you educate and train your users on the proper way to create and use content types, they can create their own content types according to your Information Technology governance plan.

Another common design mistake is attempting to control the site structure within site collections. This is an almost impossible task for all but the smallest SharePoint Server 2007 installations. If you try to control the site structure, you will require a much larger Information Technology staff. A better way is to educate your users and allow them to decide on the best structure for their processes. When using the latter method for site management, you will not need to know all of the processes within your organization because the users can implement the structure themselves. If you exert too much control over the application, users will just find ways around your controls inside or outside SharePoint. Experience has shown that hard-working employees will get their jobs done, whether you provide the technology or not. This non-compliance with your policies results in multiple systems. Because multiple systems providing the same service is difficult and expensive to manage, your goal should be providing a solution employees will use, thus allowing you to effectively control content and automate policies and processes.

## Process Models

While many process models exist for designing solutions, the two basic process models in the Information Technology field are the waterfall process model and spiral process model. It is not important to completely understand the details of each, but you should at least be familiar with them as concepts. You will most likely use a combination of both to effectively design and implement SharePoint Server 2007 in your environment.

The waterfall process model waits for one activity to complete before the next consecutive activity can begin. For example, your requirements analysis must be completed before you start a design. According to the MSF 3.1 overview:

> *This model uses milestones as transition and assessment points. In the waterfall model, each set of tasks must be completed before the next phase can begin. The waterfall works best for projects where it is feasible to clearly delineate a fixed set of unchanging project requirements at the start. Fixed transition points between phases facilitate schedule tracking and assignment of responsibilities and accountability.*

In other words, it works in organizations that have a rigid design process in place and have time to wait for the solution. Many readers of this book will not have those processes in place, and many others needed SharePoint Server 2007 installed yesterday. But one of the primary benefits of a waterfall process model is that there are milestones–both intermediate and major. First, the intermediate milestones help to segment efforts in large SharePoint Server 2007 implementations. Second, major milestones signal time for peer and stakeholder reviews, and for comparing progress against the overall project timeline. Figure 3-3 gives an overview of the waterfall process model.

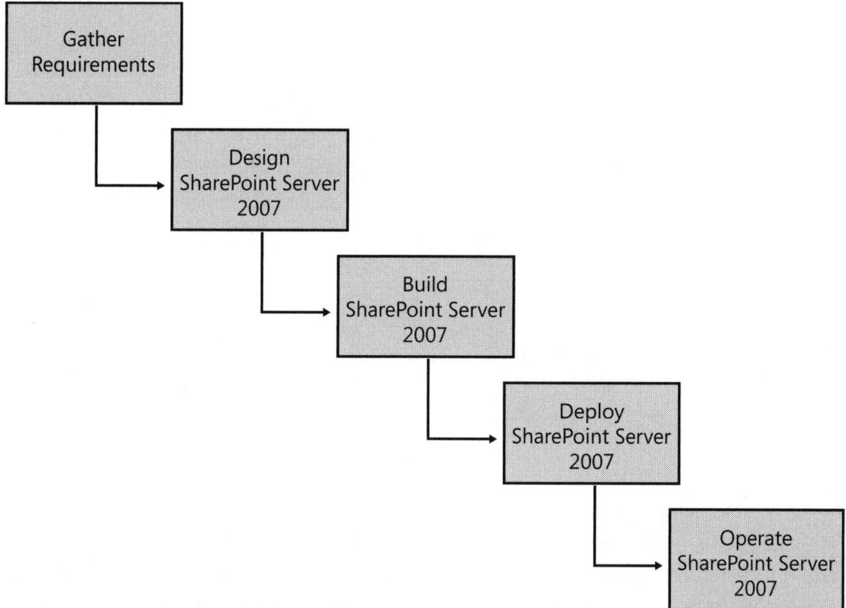


**Figure 3-3** The waterfall process model requires each task to be completed before the next can begin.

In the MSF 3.1 overview, the spiral process model is described as follows:

> *This model focuses on the continual need to refine the requirements and estimates for a project. The spiral model can be very effective when used for rapid application development on a very small project. This approach stimulates great synergy between the development team and the customer because the customer provides feedback and approval for all stages of the project. However, since the model does not incorporate clear checkpoints, the development process may become chaotic.*

Spiral process models are very effective for rapid deployment because you essentially build it quickly, then continually improve and add to your solution, in addition to requirements redefinition. The spiral process model is also useful for small- to medium-sized projects that do not require the great deal of overheard that the waterfall process model dictates. The downside to a spiral process model is the lack of milestones and the difficulty in providing a clear vision of success. An example of a spiral process model is shown in Figure 3-4.

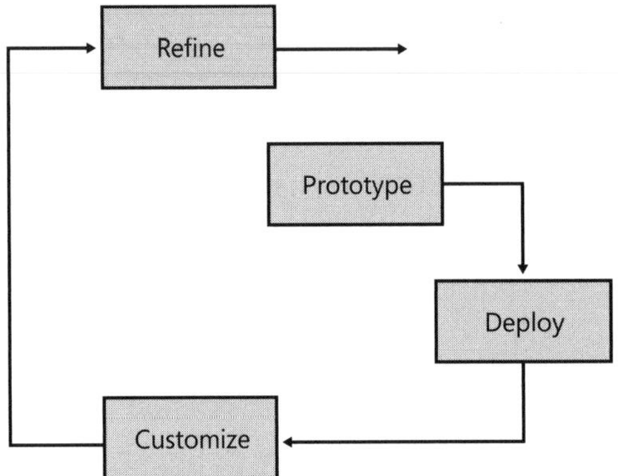


**Figure 3-4** A spiral process model is iterative in nature.

## Best of Both Worlds

So which process model do you use? An approach taken by many large organizations, including the development of SharePoint Server 2007 itself, is to combine the two process models and take the best traits from each. Deploy the most critical parts immediately, and add secondary and tertiary requirements in a versioned fashion. Figure 3-5 shows how these two models can be combined for a positive outcome.

> **More Info** If you would like more information regarding process models in solution development, try reading *MCSD Self-Paced Training Kit: Analyzing Requirements and Defining Microsoft .NET Solution Architectures, Exam 70-300* (Microsoft Press, 2003) (*http://www.microsoft.com/mspress/books/index/6460.aspx*).

A good starting place is a milestone-based approach, borrowed from the waterfall process model, which will allow you to define the points in your implementation where peer and stakeholder reviews should occur. At a minimum, the following reviews should take place:

- Requirements review
- Design review
- Build readiness review
- Operational readiness review

While these reviews may be quite complex, they don't have to be. A small or simple SharePoint Server 2007 implementation might require only a few Office PowerPoint slides and Office Visio diagrams. Your reviews are meant to "get everyone on the same page," so to speak. You should have the stakeholders, Help Desk, Information Technology staff, and any individuals who would like to see your project fail. Why would you want your opposition at the design reviews? It is much like in martial arts, where you use your opponents' strengths against them. They may not realize that you have a phased implementation and may point out every mistake and weakness in your design and the product itself. Great! They will eventually help you to create a solid solution because they have pointed out the design flaws. It is also important to educate the stakeholders about the design process model you will use.

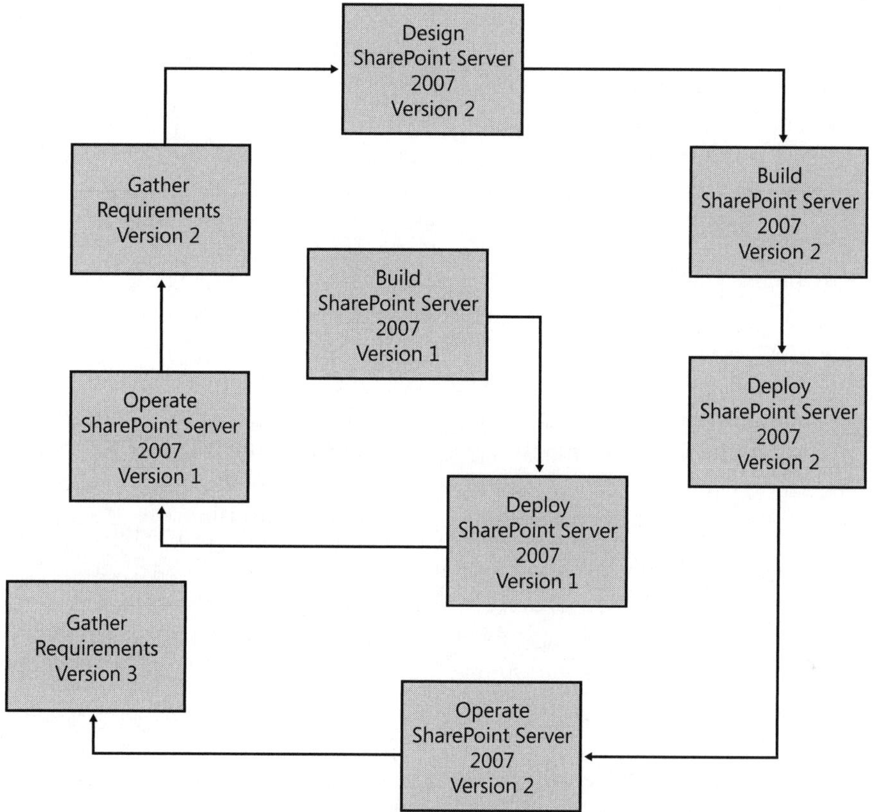


**Figure 3-5** A combination of both models provides the benefits of each.

Major milestones are often used as synchronization points in a project. If you are using Project Server 2007, it is quite easy to publish Office Project 2007 schedules so they are viewable via a Web browser. These major milestones are where your multiple solutions teams synchronize on your project. As an example, your developers might be creating custom Web parts and site definitions. At the same time, your search team has been building test server farms to validate requirements. Your system administrators may also have been building intranet and extranet solutions to test a different set of requirements. The major milestone reviews are a great place to bring all of these teams together and see where there are common solutions, or conflicts in the different teams' designs.

Minor milestones may prompt for reviews within a team, but rarely will the entire project team meet for a review. Minor milestones in a SharePoint Server 2007 deployment might include the completion of a custom Web part, successful validation of a search topology, or the creation of a server farm. Minor milestones can also be used within teams when a large task is split up into smaller tasks, documenting and tracking the segmentation of efforts.

## Define Stakeholders

The very first thing you must document is the stakeholders. The term *stakeholder* has come to mean something very different than its original meaning. Merriam-Webster defines a stakeholder as "1: a person entrusted with the stakes of bettors; 2: one that has a stake in an enterprise." Until recently, the only definition was the first. In the modern era of engineering, the term stakeholder has come to mean those who have an interest in a project–essentially those who will gain or lose from the project. If you are following a framework such as ITIL in your environment, the term stakeholder may have already been defined for you. The following are stakeholders you will commonly need to deal with as you implement SharePoint Server 2007:

- **Customers** Often, the person or group responsible for paying the bill becomes the most important stakeholder. We refer to this person or group as the *customer*. Unfortunately, customers are not always the users, and they do not always agree with those who will actually use the product. While the customers' opinions are certainly important, try to help them understand that if the needs of the users are not met, the project success rate is greatly decreased. If the customers are unwilling to listen to the users, you are in for a long, uphill battle.
- **Users** SharePoint Server 2007 is an end-user product. It was developed for end-users to empower them to quickly and efficiently collaborate. Unfortunately, users are often not asked their opinion about SharePoint Server 2007 until after it is installed. End-users are arguably the most important stakeholders in your design. As was discussed previously, people are resistant to change unless they are included in the change. Including your end-users early in your SharePoint Server 2007 project increases your chances for success. You could have a free lunch and learn, hang posters about SharePoint Server 2007 and why it is good for them, provide end-user training, or even show them their favorite Web sites that were implemented using SharePoint Server 2007.
- **Departments** Another important stakeholder is the departments or divisions themselves. Examples are Sales, Engineering, Manufacturing, Marketing, Information Technology, Human Resources, and Security. Many times departmental input can make or break a design. Try to find the people who make these departments run smoothly, and ask what the software can do for them. If you have a prototype system currently running, department managers can often provide valuable input into the future design and use of the system. Be sure to show examples of SharePoint Server 2007 functionality and ask what their current pain points are with their current system.
- **Executives** Executive input is almost a necessity when implementing a product like SharePoint Server 2007 because it is likely to have a wide-reaching impact in your organization. We say almost, because if given enough time and money, you can be successful without their support. In a perfect world, your SharePoint Server 2007 implementation is being driven by the executives. You should explain and demonstrate that, before it is installed, SharePoint Server 2007 needs to be properly planned and designed. This will be much more difficult if you have simply been ordered to install SharePoint Server 2007.

If you were told to "install SharePoint Server 2007" with no executive support, then you must document how a hastily implemented SharePoint Server 2007 project will negatively impact your workplace and present this information to your executives.

- **Supervisors** One stakeholder not to forget is usually the person you work for. If you an administrator, it may be the CIO or Information Technology Manager. If you are the CIO or Information Technology Manager, it may be the CEO or another executive. Whoever it might be, it is very important for this person to be involved in the process as much as possible because SharePoint Server 2007 almost always changes the culture in an organization. At a minimum, be sure to invite the person you work for to every design review.

After you have defined stakeholders and gained some support and momentum, you must train the project staff. You cannot skip training and go directly from defining stakeholders to gathering requirements because you will not know the questions to ask.

# Training

Training is one of the most critical components to a successful SharePoint Server 2007 deployment. It is essential that your architects and administrators be trained before starting the design process. More importantly, your end-users and Service Desk must be trained before deployment. Because SharePoint Server 2007 is an end-user product, the long-term success of deployment greatly depends on the level of training provided them. You should create customized training when customizing SharePoint Server 2007; otherwise, your end-users will not be able to apply the training they receive. What follows in the next few sections are some groups that we believe you should strongly consider training as part of your SharePoint Server 2007 deployment.

## Administrators

Administrators should probably be trained first, if you must decide an order. Your administrators will learn how to install the farm, design for success, and learn the overall technical functionality of SharePoint Server 2007. It is almost an impossible task to properly design SharePoint Server 2007 without training. At a minimum, your SharePoint Server 2007 administrator training should include the following:

- Logical architecture and supporting dependencies
- Installation best practices
- Farm operations and application management
- Shared Services Providers installation and configuration
- Content aggregation
- Search and indexing configuration and administration
- Enterprise content management including document management and content types
- Disaster recovery

## Developers

If your SharePoint Server 2007 installation will include custom Web parts, branding, or customization of the look and feel, then your developers should receive training as well. Their training should take place very early in the design process because items such as custom site definitions, list definitions, workflows, and master pages are more easily applied *before* you begin deployment. At a minimum, your developer training should include the following:

- SharePoint Server 2007 authentication and authorization
- Building features and solutions
- Custom site definitions
- Learning the Windows SharePoint Services 3.0 and SharePoint Server 2007 Object Model
- Building custom Web parts
- Working with SharePoint Server 2007 events and workflows

## End-Users

End-user training doesn't need to be as rigid as administrator and developer training, but it is just as important. If possible, classroom training of end-users has proven to be the best learning technique, when the classroom includes a competent instructor and hands-on labs. You could provide a short classroom experience and extend end-user training through computer-based training (CBT) sessions. Many times, organizations will encourage their end-users to take these training modules by offering incentives. Additionally, organizations require users who will become site collection administrators to complete training before they are allowed to create and manage site collections. Here are some foundational components to look for in an end-user training product:

- How to navigate and search SharePoint sites
- How to work with document libraries and lists
- How to add and modify content
- How to use the document management features
- How to use the new Outlook integration features
- How to use the Recycle Bin
- How to set and manage alerts
- How to manage lists
- How to use workflows
- How views are used in SharePoint

- How to create and use document and meeting workspaces
- How to contribute to Wiki and blog sites
- How to create and manage lists, libraries, and views
- How to manage users and groups
- How to create and delete sites, workspaces, and Web pages
- How to customize a site
- How to administer a site

One special set of SharePoint Server 2007 end-users are those who will customize sites using SharePoint Designer 2007. It is a very powerful product and extremely useful for branding and building customized workflows, but if used improperly it can cause negative effects. For example, you should never open master pages in the _Layouts folder, or it can cause site outages. Because of issues such as this, always train users before giving them SharePoint Designer 2007 access. It should be considered a power tool and users trained as such.

### Help Desk

Your Help Desk, or Service Desk, will probably receive a combination of the previous training. Depending on the level and depth of your Help Desk, you should provide training that aligns with their responsibility. For example, if your Help Desk only forwards requests by end-user calls, then they should at least have end-user training. In addition, you can compile a frequently asked questions list to assist end-users and the Help Desk with common problems. You could even create and manage this knowledge base via SharePoint Server 2007!

## Gathering Requirements

Once you have defined your stakeholders and received SharePoint Server 2007 education, you can move on to gathering requirements. One of the most common mistakes made with SharePoint Server 2007 implementations is the lack of clear requirements. We have seen many instances where nobody asked the end-users what they wanted! Gathering your requirements doesn't have to be difficult; it just needs to be done. There are entire engineering sciences around requirements engineering (RE), but it isn't necessary for most SharePoint Server 2007 installations. Many of the RE processes were designed for building spacecraft, airplanes, skyscrapers, and other very complex systems. Therefore, the following processes are derived from RE but show only the steps required for SharePoint Server 2007.

### "I Need" versus "I Want"

It can be very difficult to differentiate between a user's *need* and a user's *want*. You should attempt to draw a line and allow only legitimate requirements into your design. What is legitimate? If a user's wants don't incur exorbitant expense or slippage to the schedule, including those wants that will help your users adopt the product. However, human emotions often enter the picture and those with political influence often get their *wants,* even when they are expensive or cause delays. One of the keys to success when implementing SharePoint Server 2007 is your understanding of the political and cultural change it brings. Introduction of SharePoint Server 2007 affects the very way your users do their jobs, changes the power structure and communication paths in your organization, and may even change the original requirements your system was built for. Try to give stakeholders examples when using the following techniques for gathering requirements.

## Elicitation Techniques

Merriam Webster defines elicitation as "1: to draw forth or bring out; 2: to call forth or draw out." Because not every stakeholder will communicate requirements the same way, several different methods of gathering requirements are covered in this section. Many of the following techniques were derived from the International Council of Systems Engineering document "Requirements Engineering: A Roadmap." They have been changed to meet the needs of SharePoint Server 2007, but the basic best practices are followed. Rarely will one technique be sufficient. A best practice is to use a combination of the following techniques:

- Traditional elicitation techniques are the most common when building SharePoint Server 2007 solutions. The strengths of traditional techniques are the familiarity in the format, the ability to gather specific information about a problem, and a general forum to collect information. Traditional elicitation techniques include questionnaires, surveys, and discussion groups. Of course, you can use SharePoint Server 2007 to collect the surveys and information in discussion groups! Interviews can also be very useful when defining requirements for SharePoint Server 2007, but they are time consuming. Try to keep interviews to a minimum, and only with stakeholders such as managers, power users, and executives.
- Existing systems should always be the starting point for a new system. While these are often overlooked, existing systems usually provide the basic functionality required in a new system. Additionally, the pain points of the legacy system should be addressed in the design of your SharePoint Server 2007 installation, if possible.
- Pain points are essentially requirements unfulfilled by a current system, or problems within the business itself. Many of your stakeholders are uncomfortable discussing business and technical requirements but are willing to discuss pain points. They are essentially one in the same and allow you to fill in the gaps of your design. A design that isn't accepted by the stakeholders is doomed to failure.
- Group elicitation techniques include brainstorming sessions, focus groups, and consensus building workshops. Group elicitation is an effective requirements gathering technique because it allows stakeholders to bounce ideas off of one another. Many times, conversation about requirements prompts others to think of additional requirements that might otherwise have been overlooked.

- Prototyping should almost always be used when defining SharePoint Server 2007 requirements. Prototyping helps clarify requirements when there is doubt about functionality, such as incoming e-mail, records management, or search services. While this prototype can be very elaborate, it doesn't have to be. You could use the same system for gathering requirements as you would for prototyping. This simplifies and integrates both processes. Additionally, prototyping allows users to find new ways SharePoint Server 2007 can address their pain points and allow real-world testing during group requirements sessions. Be sure to get feedback from the stakeholders during these early prototype sessions.
- Contextual requirements gathering includes the observation of the stakeholders and customers on the current system, or in their daily non-computerized business processes. Remember that you are not only addressing the weaknesses in the previous computerized system, you are also addressing their needs to automate processes that are currently manually performed. Contextual requirements gathering can be as simple as following and documenting a stakeholder's job duties or as extreme as hiring psychologists to analyze and recommend better ways of doing business. The depth of your requirements analysis depends on the scope and complexity of your SharePoint Server 2007 installation, so don't overcomplicate it.

> **Note** When leveraging the strengths of both the spiral and waterfall process models, you can build a prototype SharePoint Server 2007 installation in the very beginning. Using this system for your requirements gathering and other project activities gives the stakeholders an opportunity to see the system in action, and allows for "real-time" elicitation of requirements. You should use much of the native functionality in this prototype system, including Wikis, blogs, document libraries, tasks lists, contact lists, and search. If you plan on integrating Project Server 2007 with SharePoint Server 2007, this is also a perfect time to showcase the capabilities of that product.

## Modeling Requirements

As you gather requirements, model them in your prototype system. This allows you to see conflicts in requirements and provide real-time validation of requirements. Your model should include much of the advertised functionality of SharePoint Server 2007, allowing your stakeholders to select capabilities for their processes. A good example of a modeled requirement is search and indexing. You could crawl several file shares and Web servers to demonstrate the functionality of SharePoint Server 2007 Search. This demonstration could include search scopes, stemming, managed properties, and federated search results. Whatever the functionality you model, be sure it addresses the legacy system's basic requirements, if applicable, and add new requirements as they are defined. The model should clearly address business requirements and map those to functional requirements. You could even identify the functional requirements that are met as the label for objects such as sites, document libraries, Wikis, blogs, portals, and searches.

> **Note** When defining your functional requirements, you can simply number them as 1, 2, 3, and so on. For example, if you had the requirement for a portal, you could assign the number 1 to the requirement. If you had the requirement for a Wiki, you could assign the number 2. You can then simply reference these requirements by a simple numbering scheme. If you have a complex SharePoint Server 2007 implementation, you can also provide minor requirements, as is usually the case with a Portal Site Directory. Using this example, if the portal's requirement identification was 1, then the Portal Site Directory's identification number might be 1.1.

Using requirements labels in your prototype clarifies where requirements are met. Figure 3-6 shows an example of functional requirements labeling for a portal site that contains minor requirements of a site directory, Wiki library, and blog site.

**Figure 3-6** You can label your requirements within the prototyped objects themselves.

## Agreeing on Requirements

If you have many stakeholders, or stakeholders from multiple organizations, consensus on SharePoint Server 2007 requirements may be the hardest part of your design. First, you should create a communication plan so all stakeholders are updated with the design process. This can be as simple as an e-mail list, but SharePoint Server 2007 functionality such as discussion lists and blogs usually work much better than e-mail alone.

One idea that has served us well in the past is getting the stakeholders to agree on the *problem* before getting them to agree on the requirements. If your stakeholders cannot agree on why the solution is being installed, it is very unlikely they will agree on how it is to be installed. More fundamentally, your stakeholders must agree there is a problem. You must realize by now that stakeholders have many goals for your project, and some may conflict. A prime example of this is authentication mechanisms for your Web applications. One group might ask you for Kerberos authentication, while another wants two-factor smart card authentication. While you can accomplish this via multiple URLs, generally you cannot accomplish this on a single URL. In this example, you must work with both parties and identify some common ground, and maybe even a compromise. Many of your requirements must be proved to be technically feasible through requirements modeling, while others are more social in nature and can be validated only through actual use.

## Dealing with Requirements Creep

Requirements creep, also known as scope creep, occurs when the requirements never stop coming in. If you had an initial design, but stakeholders continued to add requirements to the design, that is requirements creep. If you use the spiral process model, it is easy to deal with continuing requirements because they are included in the next version of the project. This next version doesn't have to coincide with the product version of SharePoint Server 2007: You could have two versions of your specific implementation while still being in SharePoint Server 2007! Requirements creep is usually thought of as a bad thing, but continuing requirements usually mean you have a project that has meaning and value in your organization. There are two groups that align with the scope creep—those who want your project to succeed and those who do not. The first are your allies, and the last thing you want to do is alienate them from your project. So the best way to deal with this type of requirements creep is to define functional requirements and don't deviate throughout the project. When new requirements are added, simply refer those to the next version in your product life cycle, i.e., version two. Those who are against your project will also continue to add requirements, hoping to doom your project to failure. While you welcome those comments to help the stability and functionality of your SharePoint Server 2007 implementation, you should provide the functional requirements for the project and use the executive stakeholder support you have already gained to address your opponents' issues in the next version.

Another way to deal with requirements creep is to develop a vision statement that defines the functional requirements for your project. In a perfect world, you should get all stakeholders to sign this vision statement with the understanding that additional requirements must be added in the next version of the project. Be careful, however, because some of your peers may try to make original requirements look like new ones, to reduce their risk or gain extra budget to meet their political goals. Likewise, additional requirements sometimes must be added to the current version for success. As your project progresses, always reference your functional requirements in design documents. If a design point is not backed by a functional requirement, you might be experiencing requirements creep.

# Major Milestone 1: Design Phase

Once you have gathered your base requirements, communicated them among the stakeholders, and defined the process for your design, you enter the design phase. The design phase should be very flexible so you can adapt to additional requirements that you must include, as well as changing requirements based on the iterative learning process. As you begin your design and modeling, things don't always work the way you thought. So be ready to change your design to meet these challenges. As you proceed with your design, remember that SharePoint Server 2007 isn't a stand-alone system; rather it is part of a "system of systems" (SoS). As such, you should include the people responsible for those dependencies such as SQL Server administrators, network administrators, security teams, the Active Directory team, and the Help Desk. In many circumstances, these roles are shared throughout the Information Technology department and will make this process easier.

## Mapping Functional Requirements to Design Features

While creating functional requirements may sound very technical at first glance, real work cannot begin until you map those requirements to SharePoint Server 2007 design features. We also call the mapping of functional requirements to design features *technical requirements*. Technical requirements should map directly to SharePoint Server 2007 features, and the system dependencies such as Active Directory and SQL Server. For example, a functional requirement for SharePoint Server 2007 could be to automatically collect and archive e-mail for your current discussion lists. The technical requirement in SharePoint Server 2007 would be enabling incoming e-mail, and the supporting requirements such as Windows Server 2003 SMTP service and Active Directory.

> **Note** When creating your first design, include the functional requirement label, such as F3.1, on the SharePoint Server 2007 object itself. An example would be creating a portal named Portal_F3.1, if creating a portal was a functional requirement labeled F3.1 in your design document.

In order to understand what functional requirements you'll have for your SharePoint deployment, you may need to ask some specific questions of the right people to fill out that information.

## Common Functional Design Questions

When communicating with the stakeholders, try to keep the communication streams high-level. The following functional design questions are examples to assist you in communicating with the stakeholders. From these functional design questions, you can extrapolate technical requirements. Here are some example questions you might ask the stakeholders:

- Will you move file share content to SharePoint Server 2007?
  - What content is being migrated from file shares to SharePoint Server 2007?
  - Do you understand that large files should probably remain on file shares?
  - How will this content be organized?
  - Who is responsible for the data?

- Will you create an enterprise portal?
    - What do you consider to be a portal?
    - Who will manage it?
    - What type of aggregation do you want?
    - What should be in the portal?
- How will you implement a search solution?
    - What is your expectation?
    - Who is on the search team?
    - What do you want searched?
    - What are the desired search scopes?
- Will you allow secure access to intranet content from the Internet?
    - Is SSL sufficient for external access?
    - Can we have two URLs for the same content?
- How will you reduce content sprawl?
    - What are the current information management policies?
    - If there are no current policies, how will we determine the length of time to keep files?
    - How many versions should we keep?
- Must you adhere to corporate Information Management Policies?
    - Must we abide by regulations (HIPPA, SOX)?
    - Do we need a records center?
- What would a desirable outcome be?
    - Without defining a successful outcome, it is very difficult to measure the growth and success of your SharePoint Server 2007 installation. Some examples of metrics for success might include turning off legacy collaborative file shares, using SharePoint Server 2007 as your Web platform in addition to collaborative platform, turning off legacy Web servers, automating a business process, or integrating with a Line-of-Business (LOB) system.
- Is the project being driven by Information Technology or the business principals?
    - You need to quickly know if the project is IT driven or business driven. An IT-driven project rarely gains as much traction as a business-driven project, and is usually less supported. If you are not implementing for business stakeholders, it is even more important to educate the executives and departments about the advantages of implementing SharePoint Server 2007.

- Is your Information Technology management centralized or decentralized?
    - Early in your design, you should map out administrative delegation. If you have a centralized IT department, you can manage your SharePoint Server 2007 implementation with a single team. But if you are geographically dispersed or very large, you may have many SharePoint Server 2007 administrators. If this is the case, you should create a systems management plan so you have a consistent architecture in place.
- Will you integrate SharePoint Server 2007 with third-party systems?
    - If you need to connect to LOB systems, it is best to do so after the initial version. But, you may need to integrate with these systems in the very beginning to meet fundamental project requirements or to gain stakeholder buy-in. Try to clearly define what systems you are connecting to, and what level of integration is expected. For example, simply crawling an LOB system is of no use unless the end-user can connect to the content source returned in a search result.
- How important is SharePoint Server 2007 compared to other Information Technology projects?
    - Let's be honest: If SharePoint Server 2007 isn't high on the priority list in your organization, it will be difficult to get support from management. SharePoint Server 2007 isn't the type of product that does well when low on the implementation priority list. Either try to move SharePoint Server 2007 towards the top of the list using methods within this book, or consider implementing only in small increments.
- Who will be on your search team?
    - If search is important to your organization, and it usually is, you need to involve many people in your search design. Ask your stakeholders who is responsible for making decisions such as gaining access to content sources for search authentication, security audits of content sources before crawling, permission to crawl corporate Web servers and file servers, and how federated indexing will be performed in your environment. You also need end-user feedback to create search scopes and customize the end-user experience in the Search Center and site collections.
- Will you brand/customize team sites?
    - You must also make the decision if you will brand team sites. It should be obvious that not branding SharePoint Server 2007 will make your life easier as an administrator. But if you must customize and brand, you need to plan for this and apply branding and customization best practices as outlined in Chapter 11, "Branding and Customization."
- What content will you crawl?
    - Early on, you must decide what content to initially crawl. Because a stable search service is very important, consider crawling only SharePoint Server 2007 content

in the beginning. As your understanding of search and the impact on other services increases, add content sources gradually. This will help your users trust your search implementation and give you time to grow with the product.

Once you have defined the functional requirements, you must map them to technical requirements. Carefully plan what technical requirements you actually need, and don't hurry your implementation without planning.

## Understanding How to Implement Technical Requirements

When installing SharePoint Server 2007, be aware that there are many interwoven dependencies. Many times, tweaking one portion of SharePoint Server 2007 can affect a seemingly unrelated function. An example is the content database change logs. A customer struggled to understand why search always full-crawled his SharePoint Server 2007 content, even though incremental crawls were scheduled. What was the reason? He had set the change log database settings to 3 Days in Central Administration Web application general settings. Because it was taking longer than three days to crawl their environment, and search uses the content database change logs for incremental crawling of SharePoint Products and Technologies content, an incremental crawl couldn't be performed. This is an example of many of the intricacies covered through the book and how changing one part of SharePoint Server 2007 can affect one or many other parts. Because of these interdependencies within SharePoint Server 2007 and other systems integrated with SharePoint Server 2007, you must continually refine your design through an iterative process. Figure 3-7 shows a possible design process that will change with your design.

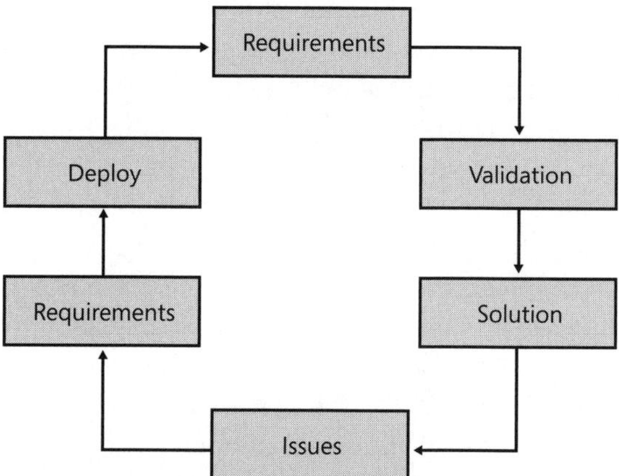


**Figure 3-7** A tried-and-true design process

Microsoft provides planning, architecture, deployment, design, security, and operational guides at *http://technet2.microsoft.com/Office/en-us/library/3e3b8737-c6a3-4e2c-a35f-f0095d952b781033.mspx*. Real-world experience in conjunction with the thousands of pages in the preceding TechNet location were used to derive the following common technical questions that you can use to begin your design.

## The 25 Most Common Design Questions

The following section is not meant to be all-inclusive. It simply provides an overview of design questions that are commonly asked and points you in the right direction for finding the answers specific for your environment. Because it is impossible to list every design variable for every SharePoint Server 2007 installation, we will explain *how* to answer the question. You will be provided with a foundation to research each of these design questions for your environment.

- **Should you migrate all content to SharePoint Server 2007?** A common mistake is moving lots of file share content, from tens or hundreds of file shares and systems, to tens or hundreds of SharePoint Server 2007 sites, without a plan. If you move disorganized content to SharePoint Server 2007 without a plan, you will simply have disorganized content in SharePoint Server 2007! Part of your content migration plan should be an information architecture design. More importantly, you must educate your users on the correct way to store and retrieve content, or your well-laid plans can quickly erode.

### Tradeoff **Where Does Content Reside?**

One of the most common design questions we get from students and clients is "what do I put in SharePoint Server 2007?" It is a question that isn't even agreed upon by the authors of this book! Many believe that only collaborative documents and documents involved in a SharePoint Server 2007 activity, such as a workflow, should be stored in SharePoint Server 2007. This does lower the overall *bit* cost of storing documents, and takes the load off of the server farm. You can then simply crawl this content on a file share and expose it, or make it *findable*, via the search interface. The tradeoff is that users must go to more than one place to find content and, more importantly, they need to know *where* they should put *what*. Many users simply want one place to store everything. Putting everything in one place allows for a single location experience, making it easier for the user to find information and collaborate. While it does initially increase the per-bit cost of storage, leveraging information management policies for expiration can decrease the long-term cost of storage. The tradeoff on the latter solution is that all files simply cannot be stored in SharePoint Server 2007. Files over 2GB cannot be stored in SharePoint Server 2007, and files such as Microsoft Office Outlook 2007 personal folders cannot be accessed over HTTP. There is an external storage API that can be leveraged to store large files such as CD images on a file share, but be accessed through the SharePoint Server 2007 interface.

- **How large can your content databases be?** That is a very common question that is directly related to your service level agreements (SLAs). An SLA defines, among other things, the maximum time to return your application to service. If you do not have an SLA, you should ask the stakeholders how long your system can be down in the event of failure. You must take the maximum amount of time you can be down and calculate how long it will take you to restore a database in the event of a problem. For example, if your SLA defined four hours as the maximum down time, you would need content databases no larger than about 150-GB with the average tape system on the market today. You should test your backup and restore speeds to a SQL Server instance to benchmark performance for your system. Once you have calculated the maximum size your content databases can grow to, divide that size by the site quotas used in the Web application associated with those content databases. Table 3-1 shows an example of calculating content database sizes using two different site quotas and 2nd stage Recycle Bin settings. You must estimate your backup throughput, populate content databases with information, and test in your environment. Nobody can tell you exactly what your numbers should be.

**Table 3-1 Content Database Size Planning**

| Site Quota | Number of Sites per Database | Total Database Size | Add % of Recycle Bin 2nd Stage | Actual Database Size |
|---|---|---|---|---|
| 30 GB | 4 | 120 GB | 50% | 180 GB |
| 50 GB | 4 | 200 GB | 20% | 240 GB |

As you can see in Figure 3-8, the default settings of 9,000 sites before a warning and 15,000 sites maximum are unlikely to be accurate in your environment. If you thoughtfully set these, you will assuredly have multiple content databases per Web application. Details on content database size and planning are covered in Chapter 23, "Capacity Planning and Performance Monitoring."

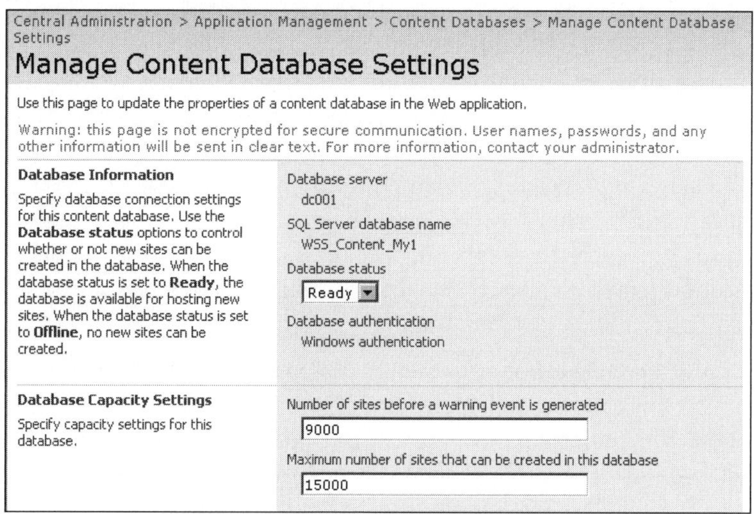


**Figure 3-8** Change the default limits for warning and maximum.

- **How many Web applications do you need?** This will be very different for every installation, but there are some general guidelines to follow. A good rule of thumb is that fewer are better. Keep it simple and create new Web applications only when necessary. Chapter 20, "Intranet, Extranet, and Internet Scenarios," will help you understand when to create multiple Web applications. In the beginning, most organizations will have at least the following:
    - **Portal** A Web application is usually created for your intranet, regardless if it is actually called a portal. It is a centralized, governed Web application where content is aggregated. Unless you have specific requirements to do otherwise, this is also a good place for your collaborative site collections.
    - **Shared Services Provider Administration Web Application** While it is not required that you have another Shared Services Web application to host Shared Services Administration, it is useful for the purposes of backup and restore, inter-farm shared services, and application isolation.
    - **My Sites Web Application** It is also not required that you create a dedicated Web application to host My Sites. But doing so eases administration of My Sites in that you can leverage Web application permission levels, policies, and authentication for the hosting Web application. If you choose to host My Sites in another Web application, be sure to install the My Site Host template in the same Web application. This specialized site collection is used for default settings and for the crawler to index profile settings for people search functionality.
    - **Central Administration** The best practice is to always have Central Administration in its own Web application. This is the default setting. You should not use Central Administration to host any other services.

    Unfortunately, additional Web applications are often created due to politics within an organization. While a managed path is usually sufficient to meet a requirement, customers and executives sometimes drive designs that are needlessly complex. For example, you might have a Human Resources executive who demands a Web application named *http://HR*, when a sub-site or embedded managed path site collection in the corporate portal named *http://portal/HR* would work just as well. Another Web application usually means more resources, additional content databases, and additional IIS Server configuration. But even after explaining the benefits of not creating another Web application, you may still be forced to create the *http://HR* Web application. That's okay; just try to keep them to a minimum.

- **How do you enable intranet/extranet access to content?** A major question from many is, "How can I securely access my content from either the intranet or Internet?" This is such an important topic that it is included in Chapter 20, "Intranet, Extranet, and Internet Scenarios," but the general concepts are discussed here. You can extend an existing Web application, *http://portal.contoso.msft*, for example, to use another IIS Web application and additional URL *http://portal-ext.contoso.msft*. Using Web application policies and zones, you can restrict access based on the URL. There are other options as well, such as legacy virtual private network (VPN) access and, more recently, SSL VPN access.

> **Important** We often work with customers who want to leverage the native functionality of extended zones and Web application policies to extend collaborative information to the Internet. But when you get to the meat of the problem, many times this cannot be done securely. For example, if you were to serve up *http://portal.contoso.msft* externally as *https://portal.contoso.msft* you are only slightly minimizing the risk of being hacked. In fact, organizations that must comply with NIST guidelines or HIPAA regulations probably cannot implement zones and Web application policies to enable Internet access to their content. The most likely solution is either classic IPSEC virtual private network (VPN) connections or SSL VPN connections. Another option is creating a second farm in its entirety, including SQL Server. Why? Because if any Internet-facing Web application in the farm is compromised, the risk of compromising all other applications in the farm is very high. If a hacker has gained access to your SharePoint Server 2007 server farm, you must assume the SQL Server has also been compromised. Therefore, carefully plan your intranet/extranet access.

- **What level of content type planning must you do?** Content types are a very important part of SharePoint Server 2007. In fact, every Web page, document, task item, and meeting request–virtually everything stored in the database–is a content type. You can use the default content types in the beginning and methodically expand your usage, but depending on your organization's policies, judicial use of content types from the beginning may be needed. An example of this would be requiring metadata collection as part of a content type. You may need to know if an item is confidential, secure, belongs to a division, or has a project identification code. You can always go back and tag items later with metadata values, but defining them in the beginning can make your content management easier down the road. Experience has shown that you are better to use the defaults than to set them up incorrectly. Details of content types are in Chapter 8, "Document Management," and Chapter 9, "Enterprise Content Management."
- **Do you need an information architecture plan?** The short answer is YES. Without some planning of the Web application, managed paths, and site collection structure, you could easily end up with a mess that cannot easily be fixed. Information architecture is a lengthy topic, and is covered later in this book in Chapter 7, "Developing an Information Architecture." For the sake of designing in this chapter, you simply need to gather input from the stakeholders on how your Web application, managed path, and top-level site structure will be. Try to help your stakeholders understand the importance of getting it right from the very beginning. A mistake with your information architecture in the beginning can make corrections later very difficult.
- **Do you need records management?** If your stakeholders require records management for legal or regulatory compliance, then you should consider implementing a records center. Otherwise, you should attempt to manage your document life cycle in-place.

Most organizations will be fine using information management (IM) policies via content types and lists. IM policies include auditing, labeling, expiration, programmatic workflows, time-based approvals, and barcodes. Creating a records center usually complicates your administration more than it resolves issues. If you do require a records center for compliance, plan for the additional Web application and Shared Services Provider needed for proper isolation.

- **Do you need search?** You needn't have a robust search topology and plan before implementing SharePoint Server 2007. Search will benefit you greatly, but don't let the fear of planning search stymie your plans for SharePoint Server 2007. In the beginning, just use the native search functionality, and expand as your knowledge and requirements increase. One word of caution–because your users have been trained by Internet search engines to find what they need via search, you do need a reliable search center in the very beginning. You want your users to trust SharePoint Server 2007 search early because otherwise it is very hard to gain back their trust.
- **Will you configure version pruning policies?** You should decide what the official policy is on version pruning. If you leave it completely up to your users, they could turn on versioning with no limits. This action leaves you in the same state as SharePoint Portal Server 2003 and means there is no limit to the number of versions in document libraries. This is generally bad practice because it can dramatically increase your disk space usage. You should decide how many major versions to maintain, how many major versions you will keep minor versions for, and what the security will be on each. These decisions will vary greatly depending on your requirements, but at least one major version is recommended for content recovery due to user error and data corruption.
- **Will you allow users to modify sites with SharePoint Designer?** With proper training, your users can modify sites with SharePoint Designer 2007 and produce very elegant, customized SharePoint Server 2007 sites. Without proper training, your users can break sites and pages, customize pages that should not be customized, and affect overall server performance. A best practice is to provide the SharePoint Designer tool only after users have received the proper training.
- **Will you leverage the publishing infrastructure?** Chapter 13, "Creating and Managing Publishing Sites," details why and how to use publishing sites. But, you need to decide *when* to use publishing sites. Because of the increased overhead associated with the publishing infrastructure, you don't want to turn it on unless there is a requirement to do so.
- **What content will you crawl?** From a technical perspective, you should define what content sources you will crawl. You should always crawl your local SharePoint Server 2007 content including My Sites. But you may need to crawl additional sites from the very beginning, such as file shares and Web servers. Be sure to apply search best practices when doing so and plan for crawler authentication. Also, be careful when crawling file shares because you may expose information that was previously secured through obscurity.

- **How many Shared Services Providers will you have?** You should plan for the number of Shared Services Providers you will have. Most installations should have only one. Leveraging Shared Services Providers is discussed in Chapter 16, "Leveraging Shared Services Providers". You can safely assume the best practice is a single Shared Services Provider. If you are not sure or don't know why to create more than one, don't.
- **Who will create new site collections?** SharePoint Server 2007 was really designed to allow users to manage their own destiny in regard to workspaces. Your goal should be to train users and allow them to create their own site collections. If you choose to do otherwise, you should seriously consider training a set of site collection administrators to perform the creation and management. Otherwise, the IT department usually does a poor job of managing site collections, including the creation thereof.

> **Note** Thousands of laws govern how highway systems are built, the chemistry of the concrete, how signage is used, how automobiles are built, how motors are maintained, how emissions are controlled, and when to stop for oncoming traffic. If you had to know and understand every single rule of highway systems before you could drive, nobody would! Instead, you only need to know the basic rules of the road, take a test, and you are issued a license to drive. SharePoint Server 2007 is much the same way. If you levy complex governance rules on your site collection administrators, they will feel overwhelmed and find another way to do their jobs. Instead, analogize site collection administrator training with a driver's license. Train them on the basics of site collection management within your implementation and encourage them to adhere to your governance policy through education.

- **Will you enable incoming e-mail for lists?** Enabling incoming e-mail for lists and libraries isn't as simple as selecting the option in Central Administration and the target list. You must install an SMTP server, configure DNS, and allow the proper security in your network and e-mail server. You should work with the respective teams and explain the functionality and requirements of incoming e-mail.
- **Will you mail-enable SharePoint groups?** Mail-enabling SharePoint Server 2007 groups has the same requirements as incoming e-mail for lists, but also provides a method for approval. Unfortunately, this approval can be done only in Central Administration, so you must plan for approval rights, if necessary. You don't have to approve groups, but you lose control over the naming convention otherwise. Once again, training your end-users is very important.
- **Do you have workflows that should be created organization-wide?** If you have workflows that are needed in all or many sites, consider creating the workflows in Visual Studio and deploying them as features. A best practice is to create workflows as needed, and only deploy globally after verifying their need and functionality in a prototyped site.
- **Who will manage your code access security?** Code access security (CAS) is widely regarded as a developer responsibility and not an administrator responsibility. But the best practice has been proven to be the opposite. Developers often create code in a "full

control" environment to ease application development. But writing code with no security boundaries can be a vulnerability when deployed. You need to decide who will manage code access security and how it will be audited.

- **What logging and auditing policies do you need?** As outlined in the *Microsoft SharePoint Products and Technologies Administrator's Pocket Consultant* (Microsoft Press, 2007), defining and setting logging and auditing policies is an important exercise when implementing SharePoint Server 2007. If you don't set your policies, the defaults are rarely enough to help when a problem arises, yet impact server performance. Don't simply set your logging levels to Verbose; you should make informed decisions about logging and auditing settings. Many SharePoint Server 2007 administrators set logging levels only to report errors, and increase the level of auditing when troubleshooting an error. This has proven to be a good starting point.
- **How will you monitor your solution?** You should decide what to monitor, and to what level you will monitor services in your SharePoint Server 2007 server farm. Too much system monitoring, and you could miss important facts because of too much information. Too little monitoring or using wrong performance counters will have the same result. Chapter 23, "Capacity Planning and Performance Monitoring," will assist you with monitoring best practices.
- **How will you back up and restore your content?** Disaster Recovery, to include backup and restore, should be paramount in your SharePoint Server 2007 design. Chapter 21, "Data Protection, Recovery, and Availability," will assist you in disaster recovery best practices.
- **Should we migrate My Documents to My Sites?** Many of you want to replace My Documents with SharePoint Server 2007 personal portals, also called My Sites. This isn't altogether a bad idea, but you need to carefully plan what content will be migrated. Remember that SharePoint Server 2007 has limitations on file upload size and file types, and drastically changing these can have negative repercussions. But My Sites are often a good starting place for an enterprise SharePoint Server 2007 deployment because of the immediate value stakeholders can see in work efficiency and collaboration. Large organizations have seen the value in Exchange Server installations, and My Sites are a natural extension to that in the minds of many executives. If your users currently store music, video, ISO, and other large file types, you should consider some type of file storage other than My Sites.
- **What should my farm topology be?** Many administrators are concerned with the farm topology in the very beginning of their design. The truth is, your farm topology is almost always the last design consideration. You should start with the end-user's experience with the product (it is, after all, an end-user product) and design toward the farm topology. Figure 3-9 shows the logical architecture of SharePoint Server 2007 containment.

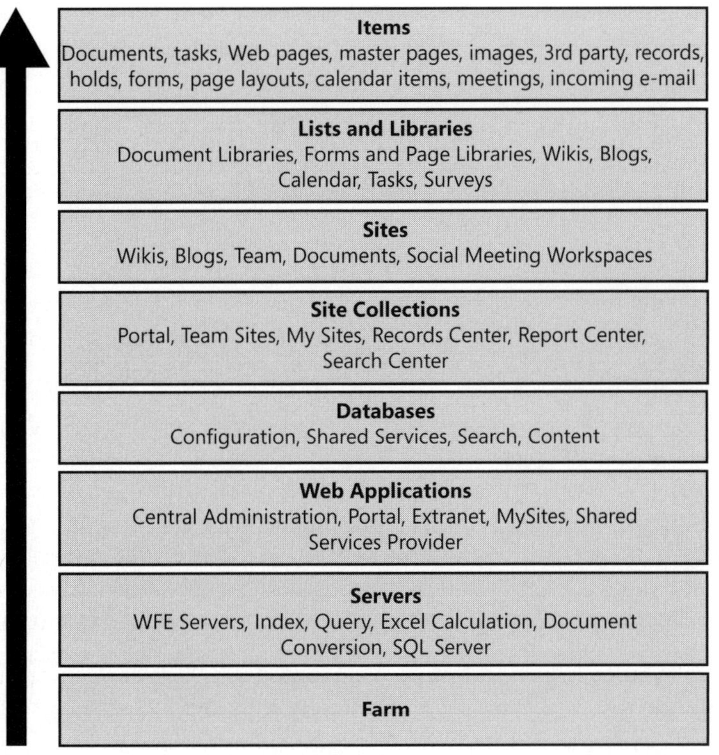


**Figure 3-9** Start your design with items such as documents, Web pages, and images.

You should first decide your information architecture, Web application design, search requirements, security, governance stance, and user requirements. If you must buy hardware immediately, plan for a medium server farm topology. A medium farm topology consists of two Web front-end servers, one application server, and one SQL Server. Alternatively, you can continue developing on your prototype system and scale outwards as needed. Either way, your farm topology is changed with relative ease later.

- **Will you enable integration with third-party systems?** If you need to integrate SharePoint Server 2007 with third-party systems, such as a Line-of-Business system, be sure to include the administrators from that system, and know what information your stakeholders expect you to surface from that system. You may need to connect to many third-party systems, but experience has shown that you should build out the native functionality first, then connect to these systems in a systematic fashion.
- **What are your security controls?** Early in your design, you should decide what security authentication and authorization you will use. You essentially have two choices for authentication—Windows Authentication and Forms Based Authentication (FBA)—although other pluggable choices exist. Windows Authentication has the deepest functionality in SharePoint Server 2007, but support for FBA is rapidly gaining. If you can use Windows Authentication with SharePoint Server 2007, it is easier to install and easier to

maintain. There are two types of Windows Authentication–NTLM and Kerberos. One isn't necessarily better than the other from a design perspective, but Kerberos is generally a better choice from a performance point of view, while NTLM is easier to configure and install. There are instances, however, where FBA is preferable. An example is a partner extranet where you want to authenticate users against a Line-of-Business system. Carefully test your SharePoint Server 2007 functionality when using FBA.

## Dependencies

As you progress through your SharePoint Server 2007 design, it is imperative that you include the system dependencies. System dependencies are any software and hardware services that are required for your SharePoint Server 2007 installation to run properly. You require a building to host your servers, utilities such as A/C to power them, battery backups, lights, monitors, network switches, hubs, cables, routers, firewalls, and software to manage these. The following list should be considered the *minimum* dependencies you should plan for. If you are not the administrator for the following dependencies, be sure to include the respective system administrator.

- **Active Directory** Not required for SharePoint Server 2007, but most installations will be built using Active Directory as the identity manager. The service accounts and Web application pool identities should be domain accounts, when possible, but should not be domain administrators or local administrators. You can enable the farm account as a local administrator during the installation process and the permissions will be set automatically. Then move the farm/installer account into the local users group afterwards.

> **Note** If possible, you should use Active Directory for all SharePoint Server 2007 farm services and application pool identities. Using Active Directory simplifies the setup and administration of SharePoint Server 2007.

- **SQL Server** A common bottleneck in SharePoint Server 2007 installations. Because your valuable user content is stored in SQL Server along with your farm configuration database, it is critical that your SQL Server configuration be capable of the load, and stable enough to meet your SLA requirements. You should research methods of fault tolerance for your SQL Server instances including clustering, mirroring, log shipping, and third-party solutions. SQL Server transaction log shipping and database mirroring for SharePoint Server 2007 is covered in Chapter 21, "Data Protection, Recovery, and Availability."

- **Storage** For the most part managed by your SQL Server instance. But don't forget to plan for file system storage of items such as event logging, trace logging, indexes, temporary storage for content deployment jobs, and usage analysis processing files. Remember to include planning for your Shared Services Provider database, search database, content databases, and configuration databases. If leveraging SQL Reporting Services, you may also need to plan for related databases.

- **Network** Configuration would include switches, routers, firewalls, hardware load balancers, storage area network (SAN), and proxy servers. It is critically important that you include each of these administrators if you do not manage these systems. You should ask questions like: What is my required network speed? What firewall rules do I need? Do I need hardware or software load balancing for my WFE Servers? Do I need source-based routing? How will I manage remote access? Do we need to use inbound and outbound proxy servers? What capacity and speed do I need in my SAN solution? Will SharePoint Server 2007 change the capacity requirements for these hardware and software dependencies? Are all tiers of dependencies sufficiently engineered to support fault tolerance to meet SharePoint Server 2007 SLAs? For example, if you require four-hour return to service for SharePoint Server 2007, then all supporting tiers must support a four-hour return to service or less. Remember, SQL Server must be restored before you can begin your SharePoint Server 2007 database restoration.

## Define Performance and Capacity Requirements

You should plan for performance and capacity from the very beginning. Usually, the medium server farm requirement for fault tolerance is sufficient for several thousand users. Performance and capacity come into play with extreme customizations or very large implementations. As was discussed in process models, you should plan for an iterative deployment when servicing large user populations. Another advantage to an iterative design and implementation process is the ability to monitor your server farm for performance as you add users and custom code.

## Contingency Factors

As you progress with your design, you need to plan for contingency factors. Contingency factors are anything that may affect your implementation for the worse, but are not certain to occur. You must balance the risks with the costs of mitigation. Since we live in the real world, your design may not always progress or function like you planned. There could be technical limitations, political obstructions, and many unforeseen risks and issues encountered along your design path. You should understand the differences between risks and issues, and design accordingly.

Risks are a part of life, and your SharePoint Server 2007 implementation is no different. Risks aren't necessarily a problem, as long as you notice them and plan for them. Risks usually have a negative outcome if allowed to fruition, but sometimes have a positive outcome. Some examples of SharePoint Server 2007 design risks might be Active Directory migrations, SQL Server versions and upgrades, hardware instability, lack of training by technical staff, lack of executive support, and no IT governance plan. All known risks should be documented and a mitigation plan presented at your design reviews. Even if you know it will not be mitigated, at least you have performed due diligence by documenting the risk and bringing it to the team's attention. Risks should be stated in simple terms such as *If X happens, then issue Z will exist.*

For example, a non-clustered SQL Server instance would provide a risk as follows: *If the SQL instance hosting SharePoint Server 2007 fails, user content and search will be unavailable until the content is restored. All user content could be lost since the last backup occurred.* Mitigation for this risk might be: *By using SQL Mirroring and SQL Clustering, we can decrease the downtime and user content loss in the event of a SQL Server outage.*

When the risk becomes fact, then it is an *issue*. It is quite possible that a design dependency, such as your network, may already be an issue. An issue should not be overlooked because they often happen again. Yes, a current *issue* might become a future *risk*. If you have an issue, you should thoroughly document the issue and redesign or involve someone to fix the problem. Examples of issues are slow throughput on WAN links, service provider instability, contractor non-performance, slow storage speeds, and lack of load balancing capability. Issues should be documented in simple terms like: *X happened and can be prevented by Y*. For example, an issue might be documented as follows: *A network outage occurred because of insufficient network bandwidth. You should plan for increasing the bandwidth, or you risk the reoccurrence of the issue.*

## Test Initial Design

Once you have designed your prototype environment and installed according to your technical requirements, you should test it against the *functional* requirements. In other words, will it do what your stakeholders want it to do? Look at the functional requirements you started with in the beginning and see if all are met in your design. Conversely, look at implemented technical features that *don't* align with functional requirements, and consider removing them. Extraneous functionality often causes unneeded problems in the future. Don't forget to ask the stakeholder's opinion, and realize you may need to tweak requirements and re-prototype before moving to the build readiness phase. Problems are much easier to fix now, rather than after you have implemented in full-scale.

## Approval

Last, but definitely not least, is the approval process. Depending on the complexity of your design, the approval could range from an e-mail containing some design PowerPoint and Visio diagrams, to a multiple-day design review with the stakeholders. The best practice is to get written approval from the stakeholders. While this isn't always possible, you should have correspondence from the stakeholders approving your design before moving into the build readiness phase. Be clear about the design in your reviews, and point out any risks or issues more than once.

> **On the Companion Media** On the companion CD, you will find examples of design review PowerPoint and Visio files (Design and Planning.ppt, Acme Phase 1.vsd, Acme Phase 2.vsd, and Acme Phase 3.vsd). If you do not currently have a design process in place, you can use these as starting points for your design reviews.

# Major Milestone 2: Build Readiness

The next major phase of your SharePoint Server 2007 implementation is build readiness. This phase begins with preparing to implement SharePoint Server 2007 for production use. Because of space constraints in this book, you should reference the MSF documentation for a complete overview of the build readiness phase. Only critical points are referenced in the following section.

## Prototype Approved by Stakeholders

While it is possible to simply proceed with your prototype system, you should leave it in place when possible to support question-and-answer sessions with the stakeholders. By this point, your prototype should have been approved by the stakeholders via e-mail, or preferably a formal design review. This is the point in your project where you will need real funding and support to move forward. You will need to build out at least one SharePoint Server 2007 server farm and supporting infrastructure services such as SQL Server, Exchange Server, Active Directory, Windows Server systems, and the supporting hardware to proceed. If these do not already exist, you need to procure these dependencies along with the software licensing required for SharePoint Server 2007.

## Design Constraints

Design constraints may be based on your risks and issues, change in technology, or unforeseen usability limitations in SharePoint Server 2007 itself. Examples of SharePoint Server 2007 design constraints might be:

- Incompatibility of customizations with legacy Office applications
- Inability to upgrade clients from Office 2003 to Office 2007 for reasons not associated with your SharePoint Server 2007 deployment
- Inability to upgrade your clients to the latest version of Internet Explorer due to legacy custom Web application requirements
- Regulatory limitations on upgrading the Windows Server operating systems or Exchange Servers
- Delayed training of administrators, developers, designers, and end-users

You should document your design constraints and communicate these constraints to the stakeholders. Be sure to clearly explain the impact these constraints have on the functionality and deployment schedule of SharePoint Server 2007. It is possible that some constraints can be resolved when the impact of not fixing the constraints is greater than the impact to your SharePoint Server 2007 implementation.

## Build Out Production System

When your team and the stakeholders have agreed with the requirements, approved the prototype, and have funded your project, you are ready to proceed with building the production system. When building your system, be sure to refer to the many articles on TechNet and MSDN, along with the materials from your training sessions, to properly build-out for production use. This section is not a technical reference for building SharePoint Server 2007; that is covered in many other books and on *http://www.microsoft.com/sharepoint*. Instead, this section is a brief overview of the activities that should take place as you build for production.

### Prepare Dependencies

You must first prepare the SharePoint Server 2007 dependencies such as SQL Server, Active Directory, and Windows Server. If you have defined your requirements at a granular level, this should simply be a process of following your design documents. If you have not granularly defined the requirements, you may have some trial and error while configuring these dependencies.

### Document SharePoint Server 2007 Installation

You should document absolutely everything you do when installing SharePoint Server 2007, but especially if you didn't granularly define your technical requirements. If you have only a few servers and do not have a complex design, you can create a Microsoft Office Word document with the installation requirements and installation walk-through. When you begin installation, you are also beginning your disaster recovery plan. In a worst-case scenario, you must rely on your documentation to bring your system back to the state it was in previously. Without a carefully documented installation, this is almost impossible.

## Test Production Build

Once you have your SharePoint Server 2007 server farm ready for production, you should always complete comprehensive testing, no matter the size or complexity of your implementation. At a minimum, the following items should be tested before moving to the pilot phase of your deployment:

- **Functional Requirements** You should always test your production system for the functional requirements defined by your stakeholders. This should be fairly straight-forward. For example, if your stakeholders asked for mail-enabled lists and libraries, then you should test this functionality with all of the possible list and library settings for e-mails and attachments. Don't forget to test fault tolerance of functional requirements, such as the example with incoming e-mail.

- **Performance** Performance can be a difficult metric to define and measure. Chapter 23, "Capacity Planning and Performance Monitoring," discusses many techniques for measuring performance, but *perceived* performance is what your SharePoint Server 2007 installation is measured by. This can vary greatly if you have customized code because the developer must understand how to build code that paints the screen, even if a background process must run. Ask a few of your stakeholders to test the functionality of the new system and gauge their perception of system performance. This is often more important than the actual system performance.
- **Capacity** You should start with 5 to 10 percent of your expected user population and incrementally increase the user base. Using performance counters defined in Chapter 23, continually measure the system's capacity as you add users.
- **Integration Testing** If you added integration to third-party systems, test for the functional requirements defined by your stakeholders.
- **Custom Development Testing** Always completely test third-party code for any variance you can imagine. Custom code, especially poorly written Web parts, can crash an entire Web application. When deploying custom code, it is a best practice to mimic your entire user base accessing the custom code using Visual Studio Team System 2008.

## Refinement of System

As you deploy your project and continue to refine the system's functionality and performance, you need to communicate with the stakeholders and verify that your refinements are not impacting the original functional requirements. An initial system deployment should always begin with a set of pilot users. These pilot users can help refine the system and identify where these refinements may impact functional requirements. An example of a SharePoint Server 2007 refinement might be integration with client authentication. Many times, client computers do not have your SharePoint Server 2007 Web applications included in the appropriate Internet Explorer security zone, like Trusted Sites, and therefore do not automatically authenticate. This is easily missed in an initial design but probably cannot wait until version *n* of your SharePoint Server 2007 implementation. But this could possibly impact other areas of your design that require clients to be in a different zone, perhaps Local Intranet. This is merely an example and your refinements could be much different.

### Pilot Users

We have talked about pilot users occasionally, but here we will more clearly define how to choose and classify pilot users. Many use *personas* to identify and validate a design during pilot testing. *Personas* correlate to a type of user in your environment, like an executive, Help Desk employee, average user, developer, or power user. If you are in a complex environment and your organization is very large, you should consider using several personas in your pilot.

Try to identity the four or five largest groups of users by function, and map the most commonly used SharePoint Server 2007 features. Evenly spread 5 to 10 percent of your target production user base across these defined personas. As you progress with your operational pilot, survey these users against the persona requirements to see if your design works as expected. Remember, you will also be gathering requirements for the next version of your SharePoint Server 2007 deployment.

### Fix Bugs

If you deployed more than a basic SharePoint Server 2007 installation, you will no doubt find bugs in the deployed software, dependent systems, or custom code. You need a method to document these bugs and get them fixed. Always verify that bug fixes do not affect the functionality and performance of your deployment. SharePoint Server 2007 lists and library functionality can be leveraged to collect bugs and bug fixes. Don't forget to deploy your bug fixes to all affected areas of your design.

# Major Milestone 3: Operational Readiness

Once you have built your system, verified functionality against your requirements, completed pilot testing, fixed bugs, and completed system refinements, you are ready for an Operational Readiness Review (ORR). Be prepared to show the final design, how that design maps to functional requirements, refinements, bug fixes, risks, issues, and lesson learned during your pilot user testing. The ORR is when you get the final approval to proceed with an operational deployment. Do not proceed if the stakeholders do not agree it is ready, or if you have risks, issues, or bugs that will significantly impact your deployment.

## Disaster Recovery Testing

You should always perform a disaster recovery test before production deployment. We have never seen a disaster recovery plan work as initially designed. They always require refinements that you cannot foresee and design for. Your disaster recovery test should be real-world, using identical hardware and software being used in your production environment. If possible, include the dependencies such as Active Directory and SQL Server in your disaster recovery test. Additionally, involve your stakeholders and pilot users in the disaster recovery testing scenario.

# Operating and Supporting

Operating and supporting your newly installed SharePoint Server 2007 installation is discussed throughout this book, on TechNet, and MSDN. The following sections should be considered the minimum required processes for supporting SharePoint Server 2007.

- **Systems and Network Administration** Proper systems and network administration is essential to the well-being of your SharePoint Server 2007 installation. Without the supporting operating system and network infrastructure, your hard work designing and implementing SharePoint Server 2007 is for naught. Your operating plan should include contacts for each of the dependent systems, to include contact numbers, backup administrators, and a disaster recovery plan.

- **Database and Storage Management** SQL Server forms the foundation for SharePoint Server 2007 content. All of your important user content is stored in content databases on the SQL Server instance. You should plan for a fault-tolerant solution and monitor for performance and capacity. If you are not familiar with SQL Server, but must administer your own database, seriously consider obtaining outside assistance with installing and configuring your SQL Server instance. A properly installed SQL Server instance can make management of that system much easier.

- **Systems Monitoring** Monitoring is vital to the long-term success of your new SharePoint Server 2007 installation. This chapter has discussed the benefits of incrementally scaling to meet changing requirements and growing user consumption. Without systems monitoring, you will be unable to adapt to these changes and tweak future system requirements. Additionally, you should monitor your systems for problems. The last chapter on performance monitoring will detail methods to monitor your SharePoint Server 2007 installation for performance and security.

- **Knowledge Base** A knowledge base is fairly simple to create and will save time and energy in the future. It doesn't have to be elaborate–you could use native SharePoint Server 2007 functionality using a Wiki. While there are many online and written resources for SharePoint Products and Technologies, having a knowledge base with information tailored for your specific installation is invaluable.

- **Documentation Repository** You can easily build a document library in SharePoint Server 2007 and store all of your project documentation in it. Be careful that you have another copy because if you need to rebuild your SharePoint Server 2007 installation, and the documentation is on the same SharePoint Server 2007 that failed, you won't have it. Regularly update and keep this documentation in more than one location.

- **Configuration and Change Management** You need to create a configuration management and change management plan. If you have a native SharePoint Server 2007 installation, creating a document library in Central Administration can assist with documenting all changes in your farm. You should encourage your site collection administrators to also document changes in their respective site collections. But change management is more than tracking changes, it is also about testing changes before they are implemented. Refer to the MOF documentation when creating a change management plan.

- **Incident and Problem Management** Last, you should plan for incident and problem resolution. Break down the hierarchical structure of your SharePoint Server 2007 installation and obtain agreement from the stakeholders on who will support each of the tiers. For example, SharePoint Products and Technologies administrators may support SharePoint Server 2007, while SQL Server administrators will support SQL. But who will support site collection administrators? Who will fix problems in custom Web parts? How will users report these errors? Will the Help Desk know to whom to route problems? Inform your Help Desk who to contact for each of these problems.

# Summary

This chapter discussed best practices when designing and implementing SharePoint Server 2007. Don't make your design more difficult than it has to be. But if you are implementing an enterprise SharePoint Server 2007 solution, you need to carefully and methodically design and implement. Remember the following points during your design:

- Implement in an iterative fashion
- Incrementally grow your solution
- Gather requirements
- Involve your users
- Train your people
- Test your theories
- Have design reviews
- Document, document, document

# Additional Resources

- Microsoft Operations Framework: *http://www.microsoft.com/technet/solutionaccelerators/cits/mo/mof/default.mspx*
- Microsoft Solutions Framework: *http://msdn2.microsoft.com/en-us/teamsystem/aa718795.aspx*
- International Council on Systems Engineering: *http://www.incose.org*
- On the CD: PowerPoint and Visio design review templates

Chapter 4

# Defining Business Requirements

**In this chapter:**



Business requirements are essentially a list of targeted accomplishments that are articulated in a way that can be understood by all of the stakeholders. To really enhance the project's chances of success, it is nice to articulate these targeted accomplishments in a way that can be measured. The targeted accomplishments that make up the goals of the project are known as *requirements*, and it is a best practice to write down requirements, agree upon them, and then get them done.

When you consider the development of business requirements for any software product, the process is essentially the same. That process is outlined in this chapter. Therefore, you might be tempted to think that this chapter is not about Microsoft Office SharePoint Server 2007 at all and should not have appeared in this book. Nothing could be farther from the truth. While this chapter will not mention Office SharePoint Server 2007 very often, it is important to note that *we believe this is one of the most important chapters in the book because, in the absence of well-articulated business requirements, your SharePoint Server 2007 implementation will lack purpose and direction.* Stated another way, the development of business requirements is *essential* to your SharePoint Server 2007 implementation. Those requirements define the business environment into which SharePoint Server 2007 is deployed. Hence, the development of business requirements is a best practice.

> **Note** Few SharePoint Server 2007 best practices will be presented in this chapter because we feel that the entire chapter represents a single best practice for your SharePoint Server 2007 deployment—to develop well-articulated business requirements that are technology agnostic.

In this chapter, you will learn how to do the following:

- Understand the relationship between business and technical requirements
- Recognize the characteristics of good requirements
- Use requirements to solve problems
- Define requirements for your implementation

We will discuss what good requirements look like and how SharePoint Server 2007 can make the requirements management process more effective and efficient. We will also discuss mapping relevant requirements to SharePoint Server 2007 product functionality.

# Requirements

A requirement is a concise written description of a function or capability that a software solution must have in order to solve a specific business problem. The requirement is considered valid if it can be clearly and objectively measured, if it describes a single function or aspect of the desired solution, and if it is understandable by the project's stakeholders.

## Business Requirements

The software development process must always start with one or more business requirements. If the software project does not address a clear business need, then it should be rejected. A business requirement is a simple description of how the organization is to be improved or enhanced by the new technology solution. Sample business requirements include:

- Lower order-entry costs
- Speed up product time-to-market
- Improve communications with regional offices
- Improve order-to-ship times
- Expand into overseas markets

## Functional Requirements

The project team must work with the business stakeholder to break the larger business requirements down into a set of simple and measurable functional requirements. Functional requirements are measurable descriptions of the new features or functions that must be developed in order to meet the needs of the business requirements. For instance, the business requirement to lower order-entry costs could yield the following requirements:

- Reduce the number of order-entry screens from five to two
- Pre-populate key information, such as customer identification and address, automatically
- Change a form from fill-in-the-blank to pick-list data entry
- Provide better training to order-entry personnel to reduce the learning curve

## Constraints or Nonfunctional Requirements

Projects are also bound by constraints or nonfunctional requirements. These are requirements that do not add functional value to the software being developed, but must be included in order to meet regulatory, cost, or quality requirements imposed on the organization as a whole. Examples of these constraints can include:

- Adherence to corporate document management policies
- Corporate security policies
- Requirements to integrate with other technologies
- Conformity with corporate enterprise architecture standards

## Testing Requirements

Remember that, by definition, requirements must be objectively testable. Therefore, the testing requirements are written before the solution is designed or developed! This occurs to ensure that the requirements being handed to the technology stakeholders are valid before the development team begins working on a solution. Therefore, a test requirement must be written for each of the business, functional, and nonfunctional requirements that the technical team is being asked to develop. This provides a "meeting of the minds" between the various stakeholders even though they speak different professional languages. The agreement is that the technology stakeholders will provide a solution to the business requirements that will objectively meet the testing requirements articulated in the requirements document.

## Technical Specifications or Requirements

After the project stakeholders have all agreed on the validity of the requirements outlined previously, the technical team must determine how it will provide a solution that meets the test requirements. This leads to the creation of technical requirements or specifications. These requirements spell out precisely what technologies will be used and how they will adhere to best practices. The technical specifications are validated by whether they fulfill the test requirements and whether a development team is able to take them and begin work on a solution.

## Notes from the Field **Moving from Business Requirements to Technical Requirements to SharePoint Server 2007 Features**

One customer we worked with had a business requirement need similar to that of many others who work with SharePoint Server 2007. Table 4-1 shows how the customer envisioned each of the three parts of this equation.

**Table 4-1 Business and Technical Requirement Translation**

| Business requirement | Technical requirement | SharePoint feature |
|---|---|---|
| Increase collaboration efficiency. | Collaboration must have asynchronous and Web-based abilities. | SharePoint team site can provide asynchronous communication plus Web-based tools to collaborate on documents and ideas, such as a document library, a Web-based discussions list, or a links list to link to other information resources. |
| Provide document management capabilities to all users who create content. | The software must have check-out, check-in, versioning, and item-level security on all objects in its scope. | SharePoint document libraries have check-out, check-in, versioning, and item-level security. |

As you can see, a business requirement can be translated into a technical requirement that supports the business requirement but still remains technology agnostic. After articulating the first business requirement, you'll develop at least one (and often more) technical requirements that support the business requirement. For example, referring back to Table 4-1, each of the document management technical requirements could have been (and perhaps should have been) a separate line item.

Developing business requirements is time consuming. Turning those requirements into technical requirements that are technology agnostic but support the business requirement is essential to understanding the role that SharePoint Server 2007 will play in your environment. If you can "connect the dots" on how SharePoint Server 2007 meets both business and technical requirements, then you'll have an implementation with direction, clarity of purpose, and stakeholder support.

*Mark Schneider, PMP, sharepointplan.com*

Concise and measurable written requirements are the foundation of a successful project. Requirements keep the project team together and focused on the business needs that are driving the project. They also provide the key to the project team's ability to validate and test the solutions it develops and are the organizing principle for user manuals, installation instructions, and technical support plans. Even though they understand how important requirements are, project teams often record inadequate requirements or skip the process entirely. The reason requirements are often skipped is simple: They are very difficult to develop without a dependable and robust document management and collaboration tool. SharePoint Server 2007 is just such a tool.

## How SharePoint Server 2007 Helps the Requirements Process

All project documents, including requirements, are just that–documents. SharePoint Server 2007 is an excellent tool for organizing and managing documents in the context of a collaborative team. So, a SharePoint Server 2007 Team Site is an excellent tool for coordinating the collaborative efforts of a project's stakeholders. Project documents can be stored in a common library, and the stakeholders can be kept informed of changes by using alerts within SharePoint. Also, the requirements can be placed in a SharePoint Server 2007 list to make it easier to review, filter, and manage each individual requirement. Filtering can also be used to isolate the genealogy of a given requirement without having to visually search through a large and confusing table of information.

Figure 4-1 illustrates what a basic team site looks like with a few calendar entries. Figure 4-2 illustrates the Gantt view of a calendar, which allows a project manager to better manage tasks over a given timeline. Project documents, tasks, and workflows can be utilized to help manage a project within SharePoint Server 2007. Obviously, for more robust project management functionality, you'll want to use Microsoft Office Project Server 2007.

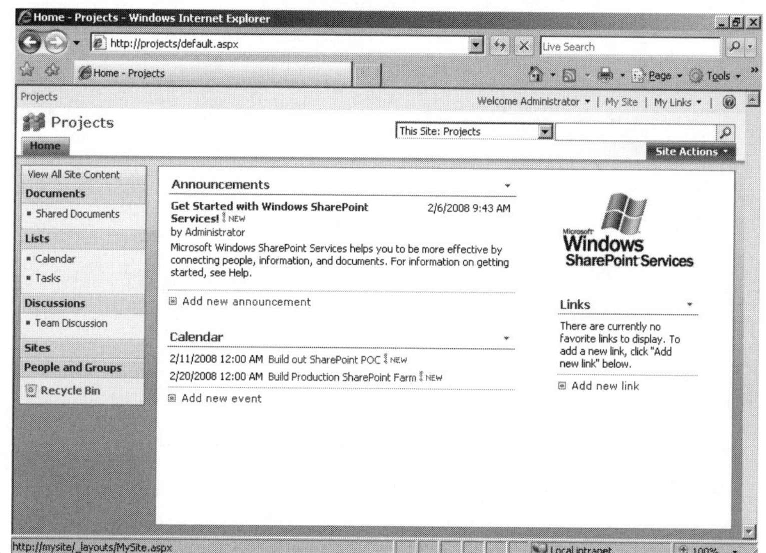


**Figure 4-1** Default team site with a few calendar entries

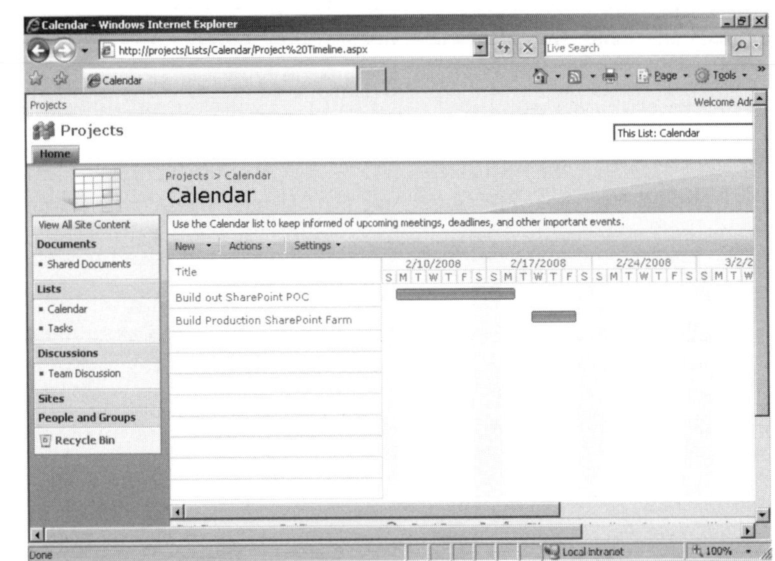


**Figure 4-2** Calendar using the Gantt view with the same entries shown on a timeline

SharePoint also takes document management and collaboration functions that were formerly contained within individual applications and delegates them down to the level of an operating system service. Thus, each application in an environment doesn't need to provide its own document version control, workflow capabilities, e-mail integration, Web presentation, and other document management capabilities. These are now shared services provided across applications by SharePoint. This means that these features and functions do not need to be re-defined with each software application the organization purchases or develops. SharePoint provides these services as a given. The requirements process can focus on the actual business need that the project seeks to address rather than getting bogged down in the "nuts-and-bolts" services in the operating system.

# Bridging the Gap Between Business Need and Technology Solution

In grammar school, most of us learned how to solve mathematical story problems. The hardest part in solving a story problem is learning to isolate the key information needed to create a mathematical expression and ignore the extraneous information. A similar process holds true for defining business requirements. In grammar school, you understood the story problem properly if your answer matched the teacher's answer. Unfortunately, when dealing with business requirements' story problems, most technical teams forget to validate their understanding of the problem before they begin creating a solution. Appropriately enough, the process used to make sure the technical stakeholder's translation of the business stakeholder's story problem is known as *requirements validation*.

Business stakeholders generally deal with complex issues involving people, market drivers, regulatory agencies, financial tradeoffs, and other realities of daily business. Although these problems can be modeled and tracked using mathematical methods, the business stakeholders generally describe problems using analogies. This isn't a failing; it is as necessary to the language of business as procedural logic is to technical design.

The technology stakeholders talk a different language—that of specific tools, syntax, languages, system design, methodologies, and other minutiae of software and hardware. To the business stakeholder's bewilderment, a technical discussion can quickly spiral into a vigorous argument over seemingly irrelevant fine points that each party defends with fanatic ferocity. Although the technology stakeholders generally view their discussion as being one of fact, at the end of the day, it is just as subjective as the business analogies they dislike and misunderstand.

The *requirements definition process* helps the business stakeholders and technology stakeholders understand each other, validate that understanding, and use the resulting requirements information to build and test a solution that satisfies both parties.

When the business and technology stakeholders agree on a high-level requirements document, it becomes the foundation of the *project charter*, which serves as a contract governing the project and its participants (Figure 4-3). Any change to the requirements or the charter represents a change to this contractual agreement and must be validated with cost and schedule impacts. In other words, once the charter has been written and approved by the business and technology stakeholders, it becomes the governing authority for the project.

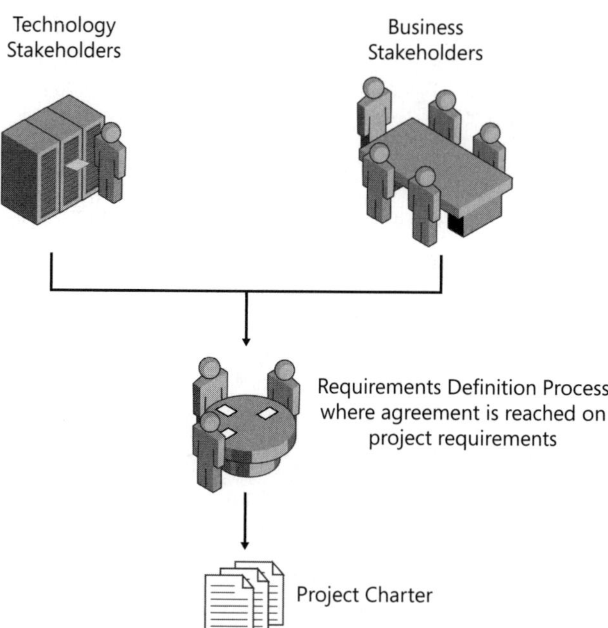


**Figure 4-3** Illustration of the project charter development process

Although it is critical, a requirements definition doesn't need to be complicated or lengthy. Simply stated, it is a dialogue in which the business stakeholders articulate a measurable need and the technology stakeholders negotiate a reasonable strategy for meeting that need. At the beginning of the process, the technology stakeholders usually find the business requirements to be very imprecise because businesspeople integrate their understanding of new technologies through analogy, as was mentioned earlier. This is one of the great challenges in establishing business requirements. It is the task of both the business stakeholders and technology stakeholders, working together as a project team, to resolve the business analogy into measurable and executable technical requirements.

## Characteristics of Good Requirements

While the greatest risk to project success is a lack of requirements, it can be argued that the next-greatest risk to project success is the development of overly specific or restrictive requirements. The author of the requirements must be prevented from mandating the technology solution to meet the requirements. Most requirements authors are tempted to "play engineer" and dictate not only the business problem to be solved but also the technical solution to be chosen. The requirements process is intended to provide checks and balances between the business requestor and the technical developer. This creative tension and the ensuing negotiations keep the design balanced between business objectives and technical expedience.

So, how can you distinguish a good requirement from a bad requirement? A good requirement should have the following characteristics:

- **Transferable** Requirements must be written down in a way that the other stakeholders and team members are able to understand. Anything not written down is an urban legend, a rumor, an idea, a prejudice–but not a requirement.
- **Business focused** Aligns with business strategies, priorities, and drivers.
- **Concise** Contains just enough information to deliver the service, no more and no less.
- **Unique** Does not duplicate the information provided by other requirements, by the technology strategy, or by the business strategy. Requirements that recur in multiple projects may be candidates for inclusion in the business strategy or technology strategy document.
- **Technology agnostic** Does not mention, dictate, or assume the technologies to be used in meeting the requirement. The requirements articulate a desired goal-state to be brought about by a change in business processes or services.
- **Verifiable** Describes a goal-state that is both measurable and verifiable.
- **Specific** Focuses on a single business process or service to be improved.

- **Identifiable** A method must be applied to record and track each requirement individually. This need not be complex and may be as simple as a numbering system or naming convention, but the requirements must be differentiated from all other requirements.
- **Traceable** To avoid having requirements overlooked during a project and having new and changing requirements added ad hoc to the project, it is important to be able to trace the requirement. This means that it must be possible to show which detailed requirements arose from the stated business requirements, what testing requirements were developed as a result, and the resulting design.

### Lessons Learned "I've Already Purchased a Software Solution and Now You Need to Make It Happen."

The software sales process has evolved to make use of the communication differences between business stakeholders and technology stakeholders. Software sales representatives are generally trained to "sell up," which means that they engage the senior business stakeholders in an organization, listen to their business story problem, and then promise that their software product meets those needs. Because the business stakeholders generally deal in story problems, the technology salespeople often use testimonials and application sheets to show that other businesspeople with similar story problems met their needs using the offered software package. Unfortunately, the current business problem might bear only a superficial resemblance to the problem solved in the testimonial and might not meet the needs of the current business stakeholders. Even when purchasing turn-key products and solutions, you need to work through a detailed and measurable requirements process. Well-defined requirements are the only defense against purchasing an inappropriate or ineffective turn-key software solution.

For example, I often have students in my classes who have been charged with replacing their file servers with SharePoint Server 2007. The reasoning given is that a Microsoft salesperson convinced their CIO that the search engine and collaboration features in SharePoint Server 2007 would both help the company grow and help employees find their documents quickly and easily, so it stands to reason that if all their documents were hosted in SharePoint Server 2007, then all of their documents would be quick and easy to find.

This solution meets a strongly felt need—to allow employees to find information quickly and easily and to allow companies to relieve themselves of the growing number of documents on their file servers. Unfortunately, most CIOs don't take the time to define, precisely, what it means to have a system that is able to more easily and quickly find documents. As a result, SharePoint Server 2007 is purchased with a promise that it can act like a file server and relieve fundability problems, even though SharePoint Server 2007 is not a file server and never purports to be one.

> Because most organizations don't take the time to understand their need from a granular level, they also don't learn about the problems associated with using a collaborative platform as a document repository. If a detailed and measurable system was put in place, many would realize that, while a large number of documents are appropriate candidates for SharePoint Server 2007, others are not and should not be moved into SharePoint Server 2007. In the absence of well-defined requirements, SharePoint Server 2007 can be construed to solve nearly any problem, which would obviously be untrue.

# Implementing Requirements Traceability and a Requirements Matrix

When a solution has been created, how do you know that the developers have created one specific to the original business requirements, no more and no less? A requirements traceability matrix is a simple documentation tool that can be used to help align the various kinds of requirements throughout the course of a project. A *traceability matrix* is a table of information that lists the business requirements in the left-most column, the functional requirements that make up the business requirement in the next column, and the testing requirements in the right-most column. This helps the project team visually determine the genealogy of a specific requirement. If a functional requirement can't be traced to a specific business requirement, then it should be removed from the project. The traceability matrix can be extended to include nonfunctional requirements and technical specifications as well. Note: *Scope creep* is the uncontrolled growth of a project's scope and objectives. Scope creep occurs when requirements drift in meaning, new requirements are added to the project in an uncontrolled fashion, or the technology stakeholders add features to the solution that are not defined by the requirements. One of the most useful tools in keeping track of the project scope is the requirements matrix. While the requirements matrix outlines the project's scope and objectives, the requirements traceability matrix outlines the origin or the genealogy of the technical requirements that are part of the project's scope.

The requirements traceability matrix, as shown in Table 4-2, is a simple table with four columns. The first column on the left lists the high-level requirements; the next column adds refined and detailed requirements; the third column records the method for testing and validating the requirement; and the fourth column points to the technical documentation describing the solution for each requirement. This matrix gives the project team a tool that helps to ensure that all of the business requirements have been addressed by the technical specification. It also helps make sure that the technical team has not inadvertently added a new feature or capability that the business did not in fact request. This method for recording requirements therefore helps to prevent scope creep.

Table 4-2 Requirements Traceability Matrix

| Business Drivers *(Justification)* | Business Requirement *(Interpretation)* | Test Requirement *(Validation)* | Technical Interpretation *(Specification)* |
|---|---|---|---|
| Reduce operating costs. | Reduce IT service delivery costs by 10 percent. | Pro forma cost projections validated by finance department and showing a 10-percent cost reduction over three years. | Consolidate applications into fewer servers and reduce data storage costs.<br>Retire older systems with highest maintenance costs. |

# How Many Requirements per Project?

There is a tension between the need to keep project requirements simple and concise and the need for complete and thorough definition. For smaller projects, it is best to limit the number of business requirements to five or ten if possible. This has a number of advantages. People are able to clearly remember and act upon only about ten tasks or goals from memory. More complex lists require constant reference to a written document, which makes deviation more likely.

How can larger projects, which often necessitate hundreds or even thousands of distinct and concise business requirements, be simplified without losing important information? Several approaches are available to structure projects so that the requirements remain simple, fresh, and immediate without losing vital information needed for project success.

## Establishing Subprojects in Parallel

It might be advantageous to organize a project with thirty requirements into a portfolio of three subprojects with ten requirements each. This is especially useful if the project requirements can be neatly grouped by common subtopics. Under these circumstances, all three projects may be managed by a common project manager, with separate technical team leads for each of the three subprojects.

## Establishing Subprojects in Sequence

Many organizations make use of *phased* project management. This strategy breaks the project into subprojects with separate requirements and measurable deliverables and then executes the projects sequentially. Ideally, the phases are organized so that the most important requirements are met in the first phase. Succeeding phases address groups of requirements in descending order of importance until the project is finished.

The advantage of phased project management is that the project team can focus on a limited number of requirements, and the stakeholders are able to evaluate preliminary results to determine whether the project is on track and the requirements are still valid. In addition, if the project must be terminated early, the most useful solutions were delivered up front, ensuring the best return for the amount of time and effort put into the project. This makes it easier for the organization to change its spending patterns quickly by canceling or delaying less vital project phases.

## Implementing Iterative Project Management

*Iterative* project approaches develop the solution while the requirements are being developed and refined. This class of methodologies includes variations known as *spiral*, *rapid*, and *radical* project management.

> **More Info** See Chapter 3, "SharePoint Server 2007 Design Life Cycle," for more information on process models.

The less information gathered prior to development and the more hectic the development process, the cooler the methodology's name. Presumably, a project methodology performed completely in ignorance, in a darkened room, without food or water, would have the coolest name of all.

Iterative project methodologies continue to gain popularity with development teams for a number of reasons. Most importantly, technology development tools increasingly use object-oriented technologies. At a very high level, object-oriented technologies allow development teams to use self-contained programs known as *objects* to develop solutions. Objects can be quickly assembled into unique configurations and combinations. They can also be quickly recombined and rearranged into other configurations in response to shifting requirements.

Similarly, the ability to develop user interface screens by recombining graphic elements and then linking them to underlying software objects has made it possible to quickly develop a prototype solution from even scant requirements. In an iterative context, the technical team might first create user interface screens based on the information gathered from the business stakeholders. After reviewing and refining these screens with the business stakeholders, software objects and other modular tools may be added to gradually create a solution to fulfill the business stakeholders' requirements. In an iterative methodology, changes in scope and requirements are not treated as enemies of the project–rather, they are seen as an integral and organic part of the process.

The business stakeholders and technical team gather just enough requirements to develop the first prototype screen or function, and then more requirements are generated from discussions about this first deliverable. If this process is guided by the standards and best practices defined in a technical strategy, then the solution will integrate into the larger computing environment when it is declared complete.

Iterative methodologies also recognize that a solution is never truly finished, and the project ends when the evolving solution is declared "good enough" by both the technology and business stakeholders.

## Using Hybrid Methodologies

It is also possible to develop some aspects of the solution using an iterative approach, some in parallel and some in sequence. This places a much larger burden on the project manager, but it often has the best results. When fulfilling a complex system of requirements, it is often true that some groups of requirements can be met using an iterative approach, while others require a systematic and laborious effort accomplished in concert.

The ability to employ a hybrid methodology in meeting complex systems of requirements hinges on the use of a mature technology strategy. The technology strategy is necessary both in determining which methodology best fits the solution set and in making sure that the component solutions can be successfully integrated with each other and the larger computing environment.

# Using Requirements to Solve Problems

To understand how technology stakeholders use requirements to solve problems, it is important to understand how project management methodologies are organized. Countless project management methodologies have been developed over the years. Some work well with smaller projects, some work with larger projects, and some are effective with hybrid methodologies. Some methodologies are very thorough and powerful, while others are simple and easy to learn. Although each methodology has its own nomenclature and structure, they all essentially tell the same story. Table 4-3 is a project management meta-methodology diagram that shows the logic that underlies most, if not all, project management methodologies.

**Table 4-3 Project Management Phases and Activities**

| | **Decide**<br>Deliverable: Project Charter<br>Result: Go/No Go Decision | **Plan**<br>Deliverable: Project Plan<br>Result: Approval to Build and Deploy | **Do**<br>Deliverable: SDLC Documents<br>Solution | **Finish**<br>Archive<br>Lessons Learned<br>Life-Cycle Plan |
|---|---|---|---|---|
| What | ■ Scope<br>■ Requirements | ■ Requirements document | ■ Develop solution | ■ Contract and financial closure |
| Why | ■ Business justification | ■ Communication plan | ■ Organizational change | ■ Lessons learned |
| How | ■ New architectures<br>■ New best practices | ■ Design document | ■ Production plan | ■ Process improvement plan |

**Table 4-3 Project Management Phases and Activities**

| | **Decide**<br>Deliverable: Project Charter<br>Result: Go/No Go Decision | **Plan**<br>Deliverable: Project Plan<br>Result: Approval to Build and Deploy | **Do**<br>Deliverable: SDLC Documents<br>Solution | **Finish**<br>Archive<br>Lessons Learned<br>Life-Cycle Plan |
|---|---|---|---|---|
| Who | ■ Core technical team<br>■ Key business stakeholders | ■ Full project plan<br>■ Staffing plan<br>■ Training plan | ■ Support team identified and trained<br>■ End-user training | ■ Product owner |
| When | ■ Key project milestones | ■ Project Schedule<br>■ Team management plan | ■ Technology roadmap updates | ■ Life-Cycle plan |
| Where | ■ Production model | ■ Deployment model<br>■ Maintenance model | ■ Recovery plan | ■ Archive plan |

What follows is a discussion of the project model described in Table 4-3.

## Deciding Whether to Pursue the Solution

The first phase of any project is focused on gathering enough information to determine whether the project should continue. The first phase is called a number of different names depending on which methodology is used, but its purpose is to decide whether to continue the project effort.

## Developing the Project Charter

The first phase produces a written document known as a *project charter* or *contract*. The project charter is usually written by a project manager at the request of the project sponsor, who is the project's "owner." Once it is written and approved, the project manager is responsible for managing the charter document. If changes are required after approval, the project manager must obtain approval from the project sponsor to make alterations. This document describes the estimated benefits, costs, and deadlines in sufficient detail to justify further analysis. The project charter is structured as follows:

- Project information
- Scope
- High-level requirements
- Business justification

- Success criteria
- Key deliverables
- Technology strategy
- Roles including sponsor and core team members
- Milestones
- Operations strategy and deployment plan

## Project Information

The front of the project charter document identifies the project, establishes its official name, and identifies the timing, sponsor, and project manager. It may seem obvious to provide an official name for the project, but it is amazing how many organizations generate competing unofficial names for a single project, causing confusion and opportunities for error. The project name on the front of the project charter is the authoritative name for the project. All other names should be discouraged or eliminated.

## Project Scope

Listen to the business stakeholders' story problem. Get the business stakeholders to tell their stories. Don't criticize them for being vague, don't argue with them, don't get defensive. Just listen and ask questions that help the business stakeholders refine and articulate their problems and needs.

## High-Level Project Requirements

The purpose of the high-level requirements is to identify the key features and services that represent the focus of the project's efforts. Later in the planning phase of the project, after it has been approved and the project charter has been approved and funded, the requirements can be further defined if needed.

To develop the high-level requirements, the project manager works with the project sponsor to articulate which business drivers are being addressed by the project scope. For each of the identified business drivers, the project manager works with the project sponsor to identify five to ten measurable business features and services that will be developed to address the project scope and business drivers.

For each of the high-level requirements, the project sponsor creates a limited number of test or measurement criteria to be used to prove that the requirements are met. It is important to base the test requirements on the business requirements and not the technical design, as is often done, because the proof of the solution will be the degree to which it meets the business needs and not how well it conforms to the technical design. The design is useful only if it helps the team efficiently and effectively meet the requirements.

## Business Justification: Making Sure Your Project Meets a Business Need

The business justification is often the most dreaded aspect of project initiation. However, it is necessary to clearly state why the project is being proposed and what the business will gain from its successful completion. To arrive at a meaningful and compelling business justification, the project's goals must be well understood in light of the business goals and drivers prioritized by the organization. The total cost of ownership must also be taken into consideration so that the project sponsor and steering committee are able to judge the technology investment in terms of opportunities lost, money invested, and resources that are not available for other tasks.

The bottom line in the project initiation process is that the effort should be quickly cancelled if there isn't sufficient business interest to obtain approval. If the business stakeholders don't support the project, it will most likely fail. Even if the project team manages to muscle the project to completion, there will be little or no interest in the project and possible resentment over money being spent on technology for its own sake. Technology projects should proceed only if there is a solid business reason to do so. Technology should never be pursued for its own sake.

Having said this, it is also important for the business stakeholders to understand that technology requires continual improvement and uplift if it is to be an effective and agile platform for delivering ongoing business solutions. The business must recognize and support the concept of technology life cycle management where technologies progress through an ordered life cycle and are retired just before obsolescence. This means that the business must support routine maintenance and uplift projects even though they do not necessarily represent a direct improvement in performance or services. Without continual refresh and uplift, the technology environment will be unable to extend to provide new business services and features.

## Success Criteria

In project management, every decision requires a trade-off between cost, resources, and schedule. If new features are added, cost goes up and the schedule goes out. If the schedule must remain the same while scope increases, cost increases dramatically. It is a best practice to rank the project's success criteria in order of emphasis. Project management decisions involve making intentional tradeoffs between the three success criteria: resources, schedule, and scope. These three are ranked in order and provide a common understanding that the success criterion listed first is the most important and should be the last to change. The third success criterion is the least important to the project's success and therefore the first to change if the project must be adjusted. This is also true in business agreements in which the contract may stipulate that cost, or time, or performance is the essence of the agreement. The essence can't really be all three because a change in one significantly impacts the other two.

## Key Deliverables

As the project progresses, is it more important to guard the cost, timing, or features being developed? Keep in mind that a change in the project goals, schedule, or budget will require approval by the project sponsor and the steering committee, so this ranking doesn't remove accountability from the project team. It does, however, help the project team keep the primary goals of the project in mind at all times.

## Technology Strategy

The technology strategy identifies whether an existing or new technology is needed to meet the project goals and how the technology will be implemented. Although the purpose of technology is to meet a high-priority organizational need, the development of new technical solutions often presents an opportunity for new technologies or an uplift to existing technologies. Often, the business needs a new technology or service because it is trying to diffuse business pressures that result when rivals gain a competitive advantage by leveraging improved or even disruptive technologies.

So, although the best practice is to drive technology projects from a business perspective, it is also important to invest in new or disruptive technologies to gain an ongoing technology advantage over the organization's competitors. If the solution is expected to require or facilitate the assimilation and deployment of a new technology base, this should be described in the project charter. This may work against project approval if the new technology is beyond the core skills of the organization. New technology can present a serious risk to project success because it usually requires the development of new skills and integration into legacy technologies. By definition, new technologies are being deployed to bring about a significant change in the technology base of the organization. Significant change increases the chances of unintended consequences and impacts with existing technologies. The results are very difficult to predict in advance. If the project presents an opportunity to extend the technology base of the organization without incorporating significant risk, it may work for the approval of the project.

## Roles

A project is nothing more than an organized effort by people working as a team. Critical to a project's success are the individuals who will be engaged in supporting and staffing the project team. The most important member of the project team is the project sponsor, who provides and controls the budget for the project, as well as the project scope and schedule considerations. The project sponsor is, in short, the project's customer. The steering committee is a team of advisors chosen to support the project sponsor's decision making. The steering committee is often made up of representatives from various business groups within the organization who have a vested interest in the project's successful completion. Ideally, they represent a wide variety of viewpoints and backgrounds so that the project sponsor receives feedback and advice from many different perspectives.

### Project Milestones and Deadlines

The project charter also must provide the stakeholders with a rough idea of the major phases of the project and their timing. From the perspective of the project charter, the major milestones include the timing of the project phases themselves as well as any major deliverables or activities that embody the major focus of the project.

### Operations Strategy and Deployment Plan

Technical solutions must be hosted in a physical location, the operations support must reside in a physical location, and the user community is located in one or more physical locations. The project charter presents a concise overview of these physical locations and their impact to project success so that the business stakeholders can evaluate the validity of the project. Is the target user community in a closed country or a country not currently supported by the organization?

Does the solution require hosting in a location or circumstance that is outside the organization's existing best practices? If so, these must be concisely documented and included in the project charter.

## Managing Change Control

It would be unwise to build a house without first spelling out the layout, plan, location, schedule, details, and contract terms of the project. Generally, once the plan is agreed to by the homeowner and the builder, the builder is held to the estimates. However, if the homeowner makes a change to the initial requirements, the builder provides an incremental estimate of the cost and schedule impacts of the changes being proposed. This impact estimate is then submitted to the homeowner for approval. If both parties agree, the contracts and plans are formally amended. This is a legal change process that is binding on both parties. No sane individual would tell a builder to build a four-bedroom home at a certain cost per square foot and leave it to the builder to fill in the gaps in the plan!

Quality and consistency in the housing industry is maintained by an integrated system of standard materials, tools, construction codes, best practices, ordinances, and inspection processes. This common body of knowledge has enabled the housing industry to follow a common strategy to efficiently and economically build homes in a wide range of markets. In general, a power outlet can be taken from one house and installed seamlessly in another house, even if the two are separated by long distances and decades of time. Why are the parts interchangeable? Because the construction teams and suppliers followed common standards and rules.

In a similar fashion, technical standards and best practices give individual project teams the ability to develop solutions independently and quickly while maintaining interoperability.

Requirements are time dependent. Requirements describe a need to adapt the business to the demands of its internal and external environments. The delay between the need for this adaptation and its fulfillment leaves the organization vulnerable to competition, litigation, regulatory punishment, elevated operating costs, and other threats. Good requirements must, therefore, be timely as well as measurable, concise, commonly understood, and change controlled. The systematic use of business and technology strategy documents also makes requirements development faster by focusing the description on what is being added to the overall framework rather than describing the solution requirements from the beginning.

## Governance Defined

Technology standards and policies require a great deal of maintenance and administrative support. There is an exception to every rule, and the consistent use of technology standards requires that exception or variance requests be consistently evaluated and managed on merit. Even where they provide adequate guidance, the organization's technology standards rapidly become obsolete and must be constantly refreshed.

### Standards and Best Practices

- *Standards* are the chosen technologies that the organization will consistently use to solve technical problems.
- *Best practices* describe how standard technologies are to be used in different circumstances.
- *Business processes* define how the business will use the technology solution in daily operations once it has been deployed.

As an example, technology standards define which server technology is to be used under specific circumstances, while best practices describe how the server is to be built, configured, deployed, backed up, and maintained. Business processes describe how the end-user will use the server technology to improve business operations and services.

The process of creating, reviewing, updating, and applying technology standards is known as *technical governance*. Governance also includes evaluating and handling exception requests and providing a roadmap showing how the technology standards will evolve over time. This roadmap includes the preferred technologies and standards, acceptable technologies, technologies that have been retired, technologies that are being retired, and future technologies that are being evaluated and are planned to replace the current preferred technologies.

Business process engineering should always be tightly coupled with the technology roadmap because technologies must be used by people in the context of performing their work within the organization. Technology always impacts the business model, and the business model always impacts technology. If the technology doesn't impact the business model in a favorable way, you should question why the technology is being deployed in the first place.

Best practices are those recommended policies, operations, and methods used to integrate, use, maintain, and update the technologies described by the enterprise architecture and its roadmap. Best practices generally define how systems are built, deployed, and maintained, while the architecture describes which technologies and components are to be used. Taken together, enterprise architecture, business process engineering, and best practices form a very powerful tool for effectively creating repeatable and maintainable solutions to address the needs of the business.

As a result, the technology governance team should include solid representation from the community of business stakeholders. Although the details of the technology strategy are "behind the curtain" as far as the business stakeholders are concerned, the inclusion of business stakeholders in the governance process provides the opportunity to provide an ongoing reality check for the technology stakeholders when choosing solutions and strategies. It also forces the technology stakeholders to think through the standards, best practices, and technologies chosen because they must be explained to the business stakeholders during the governance process. Also, business stakeholders have a remarkable ability to detect bias, meaningless arguments, and other tangents that often distract technology-focused teams. The final major reason to include business stakeholders in the technology governance process is that it raises the business stakeholders' trust in the technology stakeholders' thinking and decision-making processes. In organizations where there is no joint governance process, the business stakeholders usually hold the technology stakeholders in suspicion or outright hostility. A collaborative effort involving both the business and technology stakeholders can quickly alleviate this situation.

## Business Drivers: The Building Blocks of a Business Strategy

Just as the technology stakeholders must provide an over-arching technology strategy to keep all of the development projects aligned and to minimize the burden on the requirements process, so must the business stakeholders identify the overall goals of the business.

The organization's business goals are generally developed in response to external business drivers that have been identified and prioritized by the business stakeholders. *Business drivers* are the high-level business needs that the business requirements seek to address. Business drivers can include, but are not limited to:

- **Changes in the regulatory environment** Are there new laws or guidelines being imposed by the government or some set of professional organizations? Are these constraints mandated or just recommended? What is the timetable for adherence?

- **Changes in the competitive environment** What is the organization's position relative to its competition? Is its position improving or getting worse? Are there new competitors or new product offerings that have changed the stability of the organization's competitive standing?
- **Changes in the market** How has the market changed? Has it grown or gotten smaller? What are the key business drivers impacting the organization's customers, and can new product or service offerings help the customer meet those objectives?
- **Changes in technology** Has a new disruptive technology come into play that will destabilize the competitive environment? Does this new technology provide an opportunity for the organization to leapfrog its competition or enter new markets? What is the risk in adopting the new technology? What is the risk in not adopting the new technology?
- **Changes in personnel** Have key individuals or skills left the organization? Has a competitor gained a recruiting and retention advantage? Has the organization lost its ability to differentiate high-performing and low-performing individuals? Has the organization lost the ability to hold employees and departments accountable?
- **Changes in distribution** Has the organization's ability to deliver goods and services changed for the better? If so, how can the organization further capitalize on this improvement and exploit it to advantage? Has the organization's ability to deliver goods and services changed for the worse? What is the long-term risk to the organization? How can the organization correct this downward trend?
- **Geopolitical changes** Have disruptions in government, the environment, and other large-scale population impacts affected the organization's ability to continue doing business? What business continuity plan or activity can be implemented to bring operations back in line with the organization's normal best practices?

# Negotiating Service Level Agreements

In the context of technology development and management, the business drivers give rise to Service Level Agreements (SLAs) that are negotiated between the business and technology stakeholders. An *SLA* is an agreement between two organizations that formalizes an agreement for service and support and identifies the roles of all participants. The SLAs are then compiled into a service catalog that includes cost differentials for various levels of service. It is common for service delivery to be organized in the three distinct levels for each of the standard requirements that arise from the business drivers. The three levels go by different names, but refer to low, medium, and high levels of service and support. Increasing levels of support obviously give rise to increased operating costs.

Although there is a near-infinite number of individual services that may be used to define the standard requirements between the business and the technology stakeholders, the following are a few examples:

- **Availability** What is the maximum amount of time a particular technology or service can be unavailable to the business or the customer? This is usually applied on an application-by-application basis or a service-by-service basis. Is a 24-hour worst-case outage acceptable, or does the system require instantaneous fail-over in the case of failure?
- **Response time** If a business stakeholder or customer navigates to a Web screen, how long should it take to load? How long should it take a search to execute? How long should it take a data to entry screen to return with confirmation that the information has been posted into an application or database?
- **Security** How secure does the information need to be? Is casual due diligence enough, or is there some mil-spec security standard to which the solution must adhere?
- **Disaster recovery** If a technology or service is interrupted by a large-scale disaster, what is the maximum length of time it should take to re-establish service?
- **Stability** How consistent does the technology or service need to be? Is it acceptable if it is slow one day and fast the next?
- **Accuracy** How accurate does the information need to be?
- **Retention** How long does information created or used by the technology or service need to be retained?
- **Refresh** How often does the technology or service need to be uplifted, replaced, or improved? Some organizations may need to keep their members equipped with the latest technologies. In other organizations, it may be possible to lengthen the time between technology refresh cycles and save time and money.
- **Support response time** How much time may be allowed between a service request and its fulfillment?
- **Extensibility** How often and how quickly will new requirements be added to the service or technology?
- **User experience** Is the end-user able to find, access, and use the information and services provided with a minimum of training and Help Desk support? Is there a high degree of frustration with the service or technology, or are the users comfortable with its operation? Is the technology or service able to incorporate multiple sources and genres of information in order to enhance the user's experience and the practical effectiveness of the service or technology?

Table 4-4 contains a sample service catalog. You can use this catalog to help you define the overall service levels that your technology solutions must meet.

**Table 4-4 Sample Service Catalog**

| Service | Silver Service | Gold Service | Platinum Service |
|---|---|---|---|
| Availability | 24 hours maximum outage. / Cost = $$ | 4 hours maximum outage. / Cost = $$$$ | Less than 1 minute maximum outage. / Cost = $$$$$$$$ |
| ResponseTime | 2 seconds max per user input. / Cost = $$ | 1 second max per user input. / Cost = $$$ | Less than 0.5 second max per user input. / Cost = $$$$$$ |
| Security | No more than 1 unauthorized data penetration per 1,000 session hours. / Cost = $ | No more than 1 unauthorized data penetration per 10,000 session hours. / Cost = $$$ | Absolutely no unauthorized data penetration. / Cost = $ |
| Disaster Recovery | Recovery time no more than 100 hours. / Cost = $ | Recovery time no more than 24 hours. / Cost = $ | Recovery time no more than 1 hour. / Cost = $ |
| Stability | Variance in performance no more than x% over any 2 consecutive hours. / Cost = $ | Variance in performance no more than x% over any 20 consecutive hours. / Cost = $ | Variance in performance no more than x% over any 100 consecutive hours. / Cost = $ |
| Accuracy | Data accurate to .000. / Cost = $ | Data accurate to .000. / Cost = $ | Data accurate to .000. / Cost = $ |
| Data Retention | Data retained 1 year online and 6 years off-line, with automated record destruction after the 7th year of retention. / Cost = $ | Data retained 3 years online and 4 years off-line, with automated record destruction after the 7th year of retention. / Cost = $ | Data retained 6 years online and 1 year off-line, with automated record destruction after the 7th year of retention. / Cost = $ |
| Refresh | Workstations replaced and uplifted to current base configuration every 3 years. / Cost = $ | Workstations replaced and uplifted to current base configuration every 2 years. / Cost = $ | Workstations replaced and uplifted to current base configuration every year. / Cost = $ |
| Support Response Time | 8 hours by telephone or e-mail after initial request, with 70% closure on first contact. 72 hours on-site if issue is not resolved using telephone/e-mail escalation. / Cost = $ | 1 hour by telephone or e-mail after initial request, with 70% closure on first contact. 24 hours on-site if issue is not resolved using telephone/e-mail escalation. / Cost = $ | Immediate response by telephone or e-mail after initial request, with 70% closure on first contact. 4 hours on-site if issue is not resolved using telephone/e-mail escalation. / Cost = $ |

Table 4-4 Sample Service Catalog

| Service | Silver Service | Gold Service | Platinum Service |
|---|---|---|---|
| Extensibility | Extension of service and capacity requires IT design and development participation. | Ability to meet 50% of requirements for extension through administration use of configuration parameters. | Ability of end-user to meet 80% of requirements for extension without IT involvement. |
| User Experience | User is able to successfully learn and use the technology with 40 hours training and no more than 1 Help Desk call per month. | User is able to successfully learn and use the technology with fewer than 8 hours of training and the use of peer support. | User is able to extend the technology to novel and unique situations without IT involvement after 40 hours of training. |

**On the Companion Media** You can use the Sample Project Charter Document from the companion CD if you need a place to get started building the project charter for your SharePoint Server 2007 deployment.

# Summary

In this chapter, we have discussed and outlined the need to have clearly articulated business requirements for your SharePoint Server 2007 deployment project. You have learned about defining business requirements that are turned into technology requirements that can be mapped to the features of SharePoint Server 2007. The performance of the concepts and tasks in this chapter combine to form a best practice for your SharePoint Server 2007 deployment. Without these requirements, your deployment will falter and might even fail. In the next chapter, we'll discuss governance topics that are built on business and technical requirements. So, let's turn our attention to the governance topics.

# Additional Resources

- On the CD: Sample Project Charter Document

Chapter 5

# SharePoint Server 2007 and Governance

**In this chapter:**



Information technology provides the knowledge worker with the tools necessary to independently create, share, and manage information without the intervention of a system administrator or a software developer. Good governance balances this freedom with just enough organization to guide individual decisions toward the organization's goals. The balance point between structure and chaos is unique to each organization and often changes over time. Obviously, then, good governance is difficult to achieve, but it is critical to a successful deployment of Microsoft Office SharePoint Server 2007.

The creation of governance and high-level taxonomies for your Office SharePoint Server 2007 deployment is, in and of itself, a best practice. So if after reading this chapter you think that you've not found many references to SharePoint Server 2007 or its deployment best practices, it is because the entire chapter represents an overall best practice that requires significant explanation.

Many organizations don't even try to find the right governance balance because the task seems quite intimidating. Those organizations usually move to one extreme or the other in the governance continuum; either they "lock down" everything and remove freedom from the knowledge workers, or they move toward chaos by removing all restraints. Either extreme is damaging. A locked-down computing environment becomes a constraint that knowledge workers must avoid entirely or surrender their minds. At the other extreme, organizations often choose to unleash a tool on the organization and wait to see what happens, hoping that intelligence and understanding will arise from a chaotic mass of undifferentiated information and random activity. In the end, neither approach will deliver a desirable outcome (see Figure 5-1).

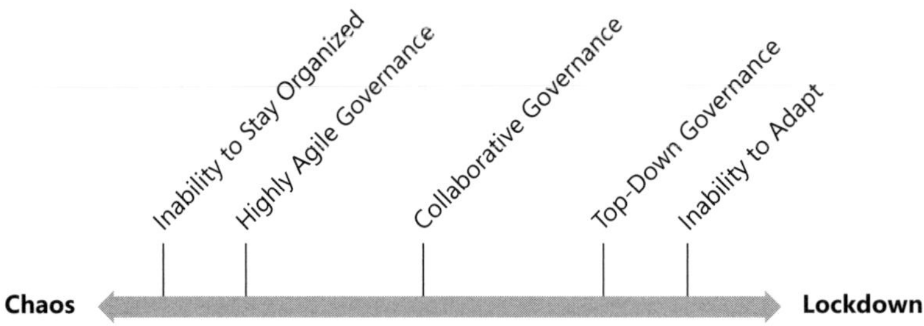


**Figure 5-1** Governance continuum between chaos and lockdown

The difficulty behind effective and balanced governance lies in real-world execution. Although it goes by many names, *governance* ultimately involves a small committee of professionals who set policies and standards that limit the flexibility and use of a computing environment. Historically, the governance committee existed in order to say no to requests for new technologies or new uses of existing technologies. Governance has typically been driven by a desire to reduce technology costs, improve system stability, ensure security, and meet regulatory compliance requirements. Up until recently, information management technologies have been narrowly targeted on specific functions and capabilities. These technologies were then grouped into a technology portfolio that was zealously controlled. In fact, the role of most corporate governance committees has been to detect and prevent change to the information technology portfolio. The introduction of a new technology generally meant the retirement of an existing class of technology from the portfolio. Therefore, governance had more to do with life cycle management than with identifying and encouraging adaptive behavior among knowledge workers.

Governance has received a bad name in many organizations because it has often been driven by emotional loyalty to existing vendors and outdated products that no longer met organizational needs. The tendency of the governance committee to avoid change at all costs often necessitated underground efforts to circumvent its policies and decisions in order to keep the business running. So, the more the governance committee attempted to set and enforce policies and standards, the more diverse and uncontrolled the information technology became. In defense of the historical efforts of governance committees, the available technologies did not provide a meaningful alternative to technology lockdown.

The key information management systems that made up the organization's technology portfolio were either best-of-breed collections that were ultimately incompatible or integrated enterprise solutions that usually provided strong applications in some key areas and extremely weak offerings in others. Because open anarchy was not a viable option, what were the governance committees supposed to do to bring order to the computing environment?

Innovation is driven by impossible demands. The growing management tension between technology control and the need for organizational agility has given rise to a new genre of technology embodied by SharePoint Server 2007. SharePoint Server 2007 is a new layer in the information technology architecture that makes it possible to have both agility and standardization. It is agility and creativity without chaos. Before SharePoint, each application in an organization's information management portfolio had to provide for its own user interface, security, database management, communications and networking, and other needs. Each application in the portfolio duplicated many of the functions provided by other applications, and usually these duplicates were not compatible across applications.

This ad hoc use of technology resulted in a very fragile information management environment. Unintended consequences from even the simplest change could render the entire environment inoperable. Governance had good reason to seek out and block all change–any change could be a disaster in the making. With no way to analytically prevent failure, governance decisions were based on exhaustive and expensive empirical testing. Older and less useful technologies were dogmatically supported and preserved simply because the organization had learned how to use them without experiencing disaster. New technologies, no matter how appealing, were simply too risky to use.

SharePoint Server 2007 provides basic information management services to all users and applications within the computing environment. Upon request, SharePoint provides an interface to operating services that provides for storage, information life cycle management, version control, security, messaging, scheduling, workflow management, Web session management, and other services that are common across information management tasks. With these services standardized by SharePoint, the applications within the organization's technology portfolio are free to focus on the specific business processes they seek to support and automate.

No longer does the accounting application need to manage its own database operations, storage locations, security, search, indexing, and integration with other applications. These services are provided and managed automatically through SharePoint Server 2007. Applications designed to cooperate within a SharePoint Server 2007 environment are automatically able to share information, provide security, integrate with enterprise workflow management, support information auditing, send and receive e-mail, and automate messages simply by issuing requests to operating systems services through SharePoint.

Now application software providers are free to focus on their areas of expertise. They can provide maximum value to the knowledge worker without having to focus valuable resources on managing low-level services that should be (and now are) provided by the operating system and hosting environment. Governance teams are free to choose the best information technology solutions without having to obsess over stability, compatibility, and interoperability issues. In short, governance teams are now able to focus their energies on actual business needs and requirements rather than endless technology discussions and compatibility testing. The ability of SharePoint Server 2007 to provide both stability and agility with minimal governance intervention has placed a great deal of stress on traditional governance committees. Now that governance teams are able to focus on organizational effectiveness, efficiency, and competitiveness from a business perspective, how do they operate? What are the new best practices for a SharePoint Server 2007 environment?

When SharePoint Server 2007 is effectively deployed and used, the governance team must achieve balanced thinking. To govern effectively, the governance team must give up direct control of information in favor of influencing the daily decisions made by the knowledge workers. For governance teams that have heroically struggled to protect fragile systems by preventing change, this is going to be an uncomfortable transition in thinking. It is important to recognize that they weren't wrong to avoid change in the past, but with the advent of SharePoint Server 2007, the rules have changed for the better.

# Governance Best Practices

So what is an intelligent and measured approach to governance in light of the agility and stability provided by SharePoint Server 2007? How can technology governance transform information technology into a strategic organizational asset rather than a tactical constraint? As mentioned previously, no two organizations will decide upon exactly the same governance model and processes, nor should they try to do so. Each organization has unique goals, constraints, and technology histories that must be taken into account in evolving an effective technology governance model. However, there are common characteristics that describe effective governance, whatever form it takes. The following are a few best practices to help your organization achieve an effective, sustainable, and well-balanced technology governance strategy.

## Fit the Organization's Existing Workflow and Culture

Technology is a tool used to meet the organization's business objectives and not an end in itself. In the end, there are no technology issues, only technology solutions to business issues. So when establishing technology governance, look for a successful governance process from elsewhere in the organization and emulate it. If none exists, then you'll be starting from the beginning. Give yourself time to grow into a working governance model, and allow yourself and your team to make mistakes.

## Keep Technology Aligned with Business Objectives

Although technology is a supporting activity that enables the business to pursue its goals, it is probably the most pervasive and strategic asset of the organization. The major purpose of technology governance, then, is to keep technology investments and activities focused on the goals that will provide the greatest benefit to the organization.

## Define and Manage the Organization's High-Level Information Taxonomy

Taxonomy has become one of the hot buzzwords surrounding SharePoint Server 2007, and unfortunately, very few people understand what the word means. With guidance from a technology governance team, SharePoint Server 2007 is able to automatically categorize and manage information as it is created in a collaboration setting. In order for SharePoint to do this, it needs a basic set of definitions it can use to place the information in broad and meaningful categories. These broad categories are defined by the organization's high-level taxonomy, which is much simpler than it sounds.

A *taxonomy* is a system of definitions that are used to describe, categorize, recognize, organize, and manage information. Because a taxonomy represents an organization's world view, it can be very painful and difficult to change a taxonomy. It is especially important in SharePoint Server 2007 to make sure that the high-level taxonomy does not change. High-level taxonomy definitions are not agile.

### Notes from the Field **A Successful Information Taxonomy: The Dewey Decimal System**

The Dewey Decimal System was created by a single individual to provide a high-level taxonomy for classifying information in libraries. It is simple enough that a young child can learn and apply it. It is also robust and extensible enough that it is still in use today even though many topics contained in libraries were not known when the system was originally created. It is able to classify all library-based information into only ten categories:

- 000 – Computer science, information, and general works
- 100 – Philosophy and psychology
- 200 – Religion
- 300 – Social sciences
- 400 – Language
- 500 – Science
- 600 – Technology
- 700 – Arts and recreation
- 800 – Literature
- 900 – History and geography

The following are some observations about the Dewey Decimal System's success as a prototype for information management taxonomies:

- It is well over 100 years old and still works without disruption or discontinuity.
- It is not dependent on a physical deployment: It works in libraries that span multiple buildings as well as single-room libraries.
- It works in virtually all languages and has been adopted around the world.
- It has a governance model that enables it to extend to new ideas and concepts without disrupting the legacy information in the library.

- It is very simple.
- It is organized to facilitate the creation of a search index (the card catalog) that is based on metadata about the books and records in the library. The metadata model provides enough information about the books to permit the reader to find and choose books without having to refer to the book itself.
- It is technology independent and works equally well with books, tapes, disks, magazines, and other information formats.

*Mark Schneider, PMP, sharepointplan.com*

## Simple Is Beautiful in the World of Taxonomies

Big, broad categories bolstered by a simple method of extension are the way to a sustainable taxonomy. The following are a few ideas to help you develop your taxonomy plan:

- **Keep the top-level categories of the taxonomy as simple as possible.** Hold to no more than ten topics.
- **Use broad, horizontal categories that are *not* tied to the organizational chart.** Good examples are Documents, People, Projects, Knowledge Areas, Marketing/Sales, Reports, and Finance. Although Marketing and Sales are often supported by a single organization or department, no company can last long if it doesn't sell something to somebody sometime.
- **Consider the organization's "noise words."** For example, law firms, when searching internally, will ignore their most important keywords, such as Lawyers, Litigation, and Clients, as "noise." And teachers' unions will ignore words such as Teachers, Curricula, and Certifications. These words are candidates for top-level categories. They are certainly candidates for seeding search engines outside the company. One person's noise is another person's keyword.
- **A simple taxonomy governance group must be created to govern and maintain the taxonomy definitions.** From a strategic viewpoint, the chief purpose of governance is the creation and maintenance of taxonomy definitions.

Organizations of all kinds have taxonomies, whether they've written them down or not. Organizations outgrow their taxonomies as well. This usually happens because of mergers, reorganizations, an increase or decrease in sales volumes, the introduction of disruptive technologies, and changes in markets or regulatory constraints. When two organizations merge, the winner is often the one whose taxonomy dominates the new organization. Never underestimate the power of words on daily life. Sometimes, when organizations merge and the taxonomies are not reconciled, it is possible to have vice presidents reporting to managers who report to directors who report to vice presidents, and so on. What happened? There was a collision of taxonomies. People from the "old school" cling to their obsolete taxonomies in an effort to retain their position, influence, and effectiveness.

So the high-level taxonomy is a simple roadmap of an organization's information culture and world view. By implementing and managing the taxonomy in SharePoint, you can fit the information to the organization automatically. You can also easily capture intellectual property that arises from collaboration within the organization's operations because the information that is developed and owned by the organization is more easily findable. In the end, the most important benefit of governance is in its ability to define, manage, and protect the organization's taxonomy, and therefore its intellectual property and culture.

### Notes from the Field **How One Company Implemented a High-Level Taxonomy**

We are working with one customer who has documents dating back to 1928 that need to be entered into a single taxonomy in SharePoint Server 2007. The company is modifying all of its content types to start with six basic metadata assignments that are unique to its industry. Every record—whether document, e-mail, tiff, or any other type of electronic record—will be tagged with at least these six metadata fields. Most will include other metadata fields as well.

Deciding on these six metadata assignments required several months of planning and negotiating among the business stakeholders and the company's information control department. Eventually, they created a matrix that would serve as the basis for more intricate taxonomies within the different verticals of the organization.

*Ben Curry,* Microsoft MVP, *Mindsharp*

## Keep the Organization Aware of the Financial and Performance Impacts of Its Technology Decisions

Technology governance provides a means for an organization's leadership to understand and evaluate the technical impacts of their decisions. This is especially useful in that the leadership may be unaware that nearly all business decisions will, at one level or another, impact the organization's technology base for better or worse.

## Balance Long-Term and Short-Term Views When Making Technology Decisions

Staffing the governance team with a representative mixture of business and technology stakeholders provides an opportunity for the business to understand how short-term and long-term technology decisions are intertwined. A short-term decision to reduce the investment in technology may hinder the organization's ability to meet its objectives in the future. The organization's leadership must decide whether this tradeoff is wise, and technology governance should be designed to support their decisions with integrated business and technology information, impact assessments, and expert opinions.

## Encourage Excellence and Innovation

It is a tragedy when the community of knowledge workers in an organization views technology governance as the end of innovation, creativity, and job satisfaction. To prevent this, it is imperative that the technology governance team emphasize its goal of finding and promoting excellence whenever and wherever it is found. Excellence is created through the experience, dedication, and wisdom of the worker. Technology governance's role is to identify this excellence and, where possible, fit it into the tapestry of technologies and best practices that it promotes and supports. If the governance team is able to establish itself as the champion and rewarder of individual excellence, then it should enjoy enthusiastic "grassroots" support.

## Guide Through Merit and Service

Knowledge workers are best led through influence rather than dictatorship. When given the option, knowledge workers will use the simplest, easiest, and most effective methods to accomplish their daily tasks. Very few will pound a nail with a rock when a hammer is within reach. If the technology governance team is able to make the preferred method of accomplishing information tasks simple, easy, and effective, then the knowledge workers will voluntarily use the standard methods. No coercion is necessary if the standards and best practices are based on merit and governed by a representative group of knowledge workers.

## Handle Questions and Issues Quickly, Concisely, and Effectively

Knowledge workers are judged on their ability to manage information quickly, concisely, and effectively. They will rightly judge technology governance as a failure if it does not meet their needs in a similar fashion. This doesn't mean that the technology governance team must say yes to every, or even most, requests. It means that the community of knowledge workers must know that the technology governance team will hear, evaluate, and respond to their requests for help quickly and decisively.

In order to remain responsive, the technology governance committee must have an effective means of triage to screen out requests that have a low chance of adoption. It also means that the technology governance committee must have a well-known charter that delineates its scope of responsibility. Knowledge workers need to understand when the technology governance team should be involved–and when they should not be involved–in making technology-related decisions.

## Maintain a Technology-Agnostic Viewpoint

The technology governance team should remain technology agnostic in its viewpoint. In other words, governance defines the business objectives and needs to be met by the knowledge worker community, but it does not dictate the technologies used in meeting those needs. The technology selection process must be owned and driven by the technology professionals and stakeholders responsible for delivering technologies and services to the organization. The governance team is the reviewer and validator of the technology choices made by the technology stakeholders, but the technology governance team does not dictate technologies.

## Start Small and Grow Over Time, Intentionally

Technology governance teams must avoid the temptation to build the entire framework of standards and best practices immediately. The first decision the technology governance team must address is the alpha process. The *alpha process* refers to the process that describes how the team will create and implement new processes. The team must have a consistent method for considering, approving, and implementing its policies and decisions, even when those decisions focus on the team's self-governance.

After the alpha process is established, the next task is to identify key processes, standards, and best practices that are working well and to consider them for addition to the technology governance team's body of standards and best practices. All organizations have best practices and standards whether they realize it or not. They may be unwritten, poorly organized, and even conflicting, but any time an organization accomplishes something, a de facto standard is being used. After it organizes itself, the technology governance team must focus on identifying, documenting, refining, and socializing the best of these de facto standards.

## Standardize Enterprise-Wide Information with Minimal Intrusion

The technology governance team focuses on standards and best practices that impact the entire organization while giving departments and teams freedom to innovate and discover ways to collaborate on information-related tasks. However, when a team is ready to publish its information to a larger audience, some level of formal or informal governance must be employed to make sure that the published information meets information quality standards and best practices.

# Getting a Technology Governance Team Started

Figure 5-2 offers a typical technology governance team structure. You can use this sample team structure as a reference for our discussions in this section.

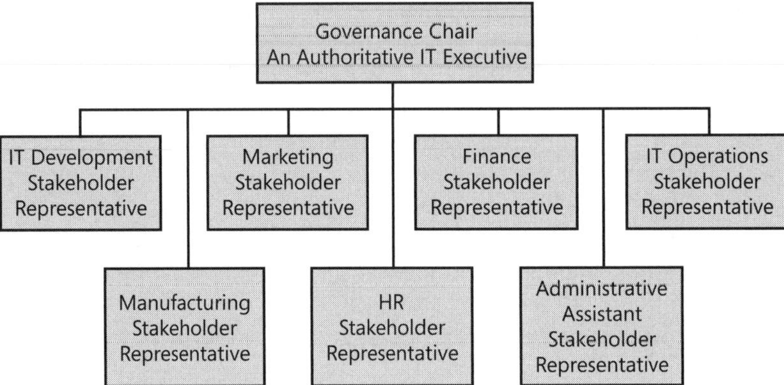


**Figure 5-2** Typical technology governance team structure

## Assign the Governance Team

The technology governance team is a microcosm of the people in the organization who most rely on the technologies being governed and should be composed of no more than 12 members, including the CIO (or the CIO's delegate), who serves as chair. If the CIO elects to delegate the chair to a staff member, then the CIO serves as the sponsor of the technology governance team and is responsible for supporting the team and making sure that its decisions are validated and enforced.

For the team members, membership rotation seems to work best on an annual or biannual basis. Shorter terms of office do not provide enough time to learn the role. The rotation should be staggered so that the team is a mixture of experienced members and new members with a fresh perspective. At first, the team should meet at least once a week as it drives to create its initial set of processes, standards, and documentation. Because startup efforts can drag on indefinitely, it is important to plan the startup effort to last between three and six months. Any issues still outstanding may be dealt with during ongoing meetings.

To be effective and avoid group-think, the members should be representatives of the major functions or departments in the organization. At minimum, the technology stakeholders should be selected from IT Operations or Service Delivery, Development, and, if needed, Desktop Support or the Help Desk.

The governance team should use a team site in SharePoint to develop and maintain its governance standards.

## Evaluate Organizational Goals and Business Drivers

In order to fulfill its strategic role in focusing technology investment and activities on mission-critical projects, the technology governance committee must thoroughly understand its role in the organization and the business imperatives the organization seeks to address in its business plan. A well-managed organization evaluates the key business drivers that shape its market position relative to competing organizations. The organization that develops the best mix of capabilities, products, and services in response to the business imperatives that form its marketplace wins.

Technology governance must keep its technology base agile enough to adapt to shifting business drivers while maintaining enough focus and standardization to target specific accomplishments that will help address those drivers. Each organization either implicitly or explicitly develops a business strategy that identifies and prioritizes market drivers in an effort to provide a competitive advantage over other organizations. With the trend toward ever-increasing organizational dependence on timely and accurate information, the ability to capture, organize, and use information is usually the critical factor in determining an organization's strategic success.

## Evaluate Current and Planned Business Initiatives

After an organization identifies and prioritizes its business imperatives, the business will construct a portfolio of business initiatives to focus its resources on the biggest threats and opportunities it has identified. The portfolio will be critically dependent upon the organization's technology base, but the business planners might not realize this until it is too late to effectively adapt the technology investments and activities to support their initiatives.

It is important that the technology governance team be made an integral part of identifying, prioritizing, and planning the initiatives. The team will be able to provide important insight into the impacts of the planned initiatives on technology investment, projects, and costs. Early information about long-term initiatives will also provide the team with information necessary to shape long-term technology investment to meet upcoming challenges. The result will be faster and more effective application of technology solutions in helping the organization meet its business imperatives.

Figure 5-3 outlines a sample governance approval process. You can use this process to help your governance team establish a method of accepting or rejecting new ideas for governance in your organization. Note that you'll need to work with your site collection owners to help them identify new ideas that are working at the site and/or site collection level that should be considered for inclusion in the enterprise standards. This will require good training of your site collection administrators as well as an ongoing relationship development and maintenance effort that is initiated by the governance team.

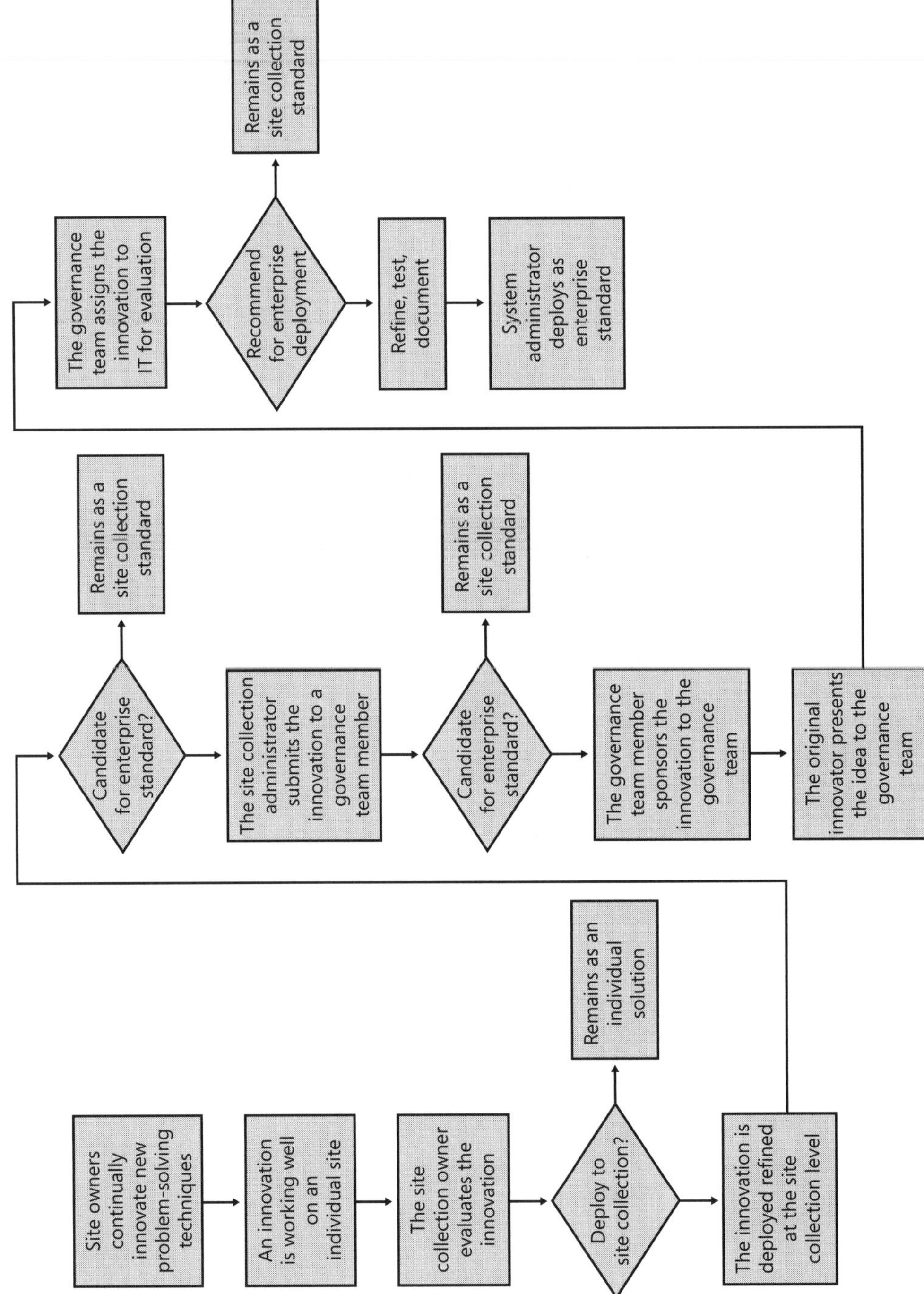


**Figure 5-3** Sample governance approval process

## Define the Business Requirements

Once the governance team has a solid understanding of the organization's business imperatives and planned initiatives, it can develop a technology strategy that will align its investments with the business's long-term needs. This end-state description of the capabilities and services to be developed by the technology stakeholders in response to the organization's business imperatives is expressed as a series of business requirements as described in Chapter 4, "Defining Business Requirements."

### Evaluate the Technology Base

After the business requirements for supporting the business initiatives are written and approved, the technology team performs a gap analysis by comparing the current state of the organization's technology base with its planned future-state technology base as described in the business requirements. A *gap analysis* defines the difference between what exists today and what needs to exist in the future in order to fulfill the project requirements.

### Develop, Publish, and Maintain a Technology Roadmap

A technology roadmap provides an ordered list of projects and investments that will need to be undertaken to evolve the organization from its current state in order to meet the business requirements established. This roadmap may span several years and encompass both minor and drastic changes to technology and practice in the organization. Because market imperatives are fickle and technology is in constant flux, this roadmap must be refreshed and revisited on a quarterly or at least annual basis.

The roadmap is the primary tool for selecting, prioritizing, defining, and funding technology projects each fiscal year. Enough buffer must be built into both the schedule and budget to address ad hoc and unforeseen projects and activities, but the major thrust of technology development will be governed by the roadmap. This, then, is the tool for keeping the business and technology strategies aligned.

## Evaluate Existing Governance and Oversight Processes, Documents, and Activities

Although they might not be documented, the organization undoubtedly has existing governance processes, standards, and decisions that must be identified, at least superficially documented, and discussed. It is always important to find out what has been done in the past, what worked, and what did not. If there are existing processes and standards that have worked well, make an effort to incorporate them into the new governance model.

**Notes from the Field Using Existing Standards as Templates for Governance**

It can be useful to refer to existing industry-standard frameworks to guide the creation of governance taxonomies and processes. However, the governance team should not follow any process slavishly as each organization is to some degree unique. On the other hand, no organization is truly unique in its processes or it would no longer be in business! So, standard governance taxonomies can be very useful if applied carefully. Even when using a framework, it is still important for the technology governance team to apply the framework gradually rather than all at once. Below is a partial list of potential frameworks to review in establishing a framework of governance terms and processes:

- ITIL
- Existing Process
- Theory of Constraints
- MSF/MOF
- COBIT
- CMM and CMMI
- COSO and COSO-ERM
- IT Governance
- ITIL/IT Service Management (ITSM)
- IT Portfolio Management
- PMBOK
- PRINCE2
- Six Sigma

*Mark Schneider, PMP, Sharepointplan.com*

# Create an Effective Governance Team Site

SharePoint Server 2007 not only provides a technical organizing principle for information management, but it can also serve as the practical vehicle for governance activities in daily practice. SharePoint's team sites provide a means for governance team members to accumulate and organize source information, publish policies and standards, debate and discuss options, and vote on decisions without having to align schedules for meetings or conference calls. The simple inability to get busy decision-makers together for a meeting often defeats an organization's efforts at governance. The burdens of organizing and maintaining documentation, as well as the difficulties involved in communicating decisions to the community of knowledge workers, often render the governance team ineffective.

To offer maximum service to the organization, the governance team must center its activities on its own SharePoint team site. In the next sections, you'll learn how practical, day-to-day governance activities can be supported by a SharePoint team site.

## Membership Management

Technology governance requires that stakeholders from different areas in the organization participate in different roles within the governance team's activities. This means that the team must be able to support a rotating membership and be able to systematically leverage the skills of a constantly changing group of subject-matter experts and resources. The team must also be able to capture, evaluate, prioritize, and act upon a broad range of supporting and source documents in the course of creating its policies and standards. This requires source and draft document management for use internally by the governance team as well as the ability to author, validate, and publish official policy documents to the larger organization. Governance teams, in other words, need the support of a SharePoint team site.

## Governance Team Roles in SharePoint

Governance teams are typically composed of six to twelve members. These members usually serve a term of office and are then rotated out and replaced at staggered intervals, which provides continuity. Because all members are not rotated at once, team veterans are complemented with a supply of fresh viewpoints and opinions.

The SharePoint governance team site must provide a role for team members who are able to do the following:

- Read and alter the team's source and draft documents
- Submit documents for consideration by the team
- Review, comment, and approve documents prior to publication
- Participate in online forums and discussions
- Electronically vote on decisions considered by the team

Normally, this role would be the Members role within the site.

### Governance Team Ex-Officio Members

Governance teams also typically include non-voting individuals who participate in discussions but do not have the right to vote or issue policies. These individuals may be subject-matter experts in a particular discipline that is vital to the company, an external vendor or consultant, or an expert in a mission-critical technology.

The SharePoint governance team site must provide subject-matter experts outside the team who are able to do the following:

- Read but not alter selected source and draft documents
- Submit documents for consideration by the governance team
- Participate in subsites while working on subcommittees

In most instances, either the Reader or the Visitor role will suffice for ex-officio members.

## Governance Team Approvers and Sponsors

Governance teams also must fit within the larger management structure of the organization. When a governance team must address an issue that will impact the larger organization, it must escalate the decision to a higher-ranking leadership or executive body. In some cases, technology governance decisions are so strategic to the operation of the organization that the governance team must submit its recommended policies to a broader leadership or executive body for ratification and approval before putting the policy in force.

The SharePoint governance team site must provide a role for senior executives outside the team who are able to do the following:

- Read but not alter the team's source and draft documents
- Submit documents for consideration by the governance team
- Review, comment, and approve documents prior to publication
- Review, recommend, and approve the addition of new members and removal of others

In most cases, this will be a customized role created by the site administrator.

## Governance Team Readers

Governance policies and standards are useful only if they are effective in guiding the thoughts and behaviors of the knowledge workers they serve. The organization's community of knowledge workers must have permission to:

- Read published documents
- Submit new ideas and suggestions for consideration
- Seek clarification
- Pursue variance requests
- Point out problems in the existing policies
- Find and use relevant policy and standard information in a timely fashion

In most cases, the Reader or Visitor role will suffice, with special rights being given to a list where new ideas and suggestions can be uploaded for the team's consideration.

## SharePoint Lists Included in the Governance Team Site

At a minimum, a number of informational lists should be included in the governance team site in order to accumulate, manage, and communicate key information needed by the site's members and readers.

### Governance Team Calendar

In order to provide effective leadership for the organization's knowledge workers, the governance team must be predictable. The most important step in governance predictability is to provide the governance team's members, sponsors, subject-matter experts, and readers with a published calendar of its important events, deadlines, and meetings. Some of the major items to include and track in the governance team calendar are the following:

- Deadlines for submitting requests
- Deadlines for the issuance of new policies
- Meeting dates
- Term of office end dates
- Orientation meetings to explain new policies and standards to the community of knowledge workers
- Informational meetings, broadcasts, vendor presentations, brown-bag lunches, and training opportunities

### Governance Team Task List

Governance teams must proactively identify, document, assign, and complete tasks. This may seem obvious, but every information worker has participated in meetings that assigned no specific tasks and had no measurable results–nothing was accomplished! In order to keep the governance team moving measurably toward its objectives and in order to communicate that progress to the larger community, the governance team must establish and use a SharePoint task list as part of its team site. This allows a central location for documenting, assigning, and tracking governance tasks. Some of the tasks to be supported are the following:

- Evaluation of documents
- Drafting of policies
- Research and analysis activities
- Assignment of resources
- Triage and evaluation of requests
- Scheduling of meetings, presentations, and educational opportunities

## Governance Team Issues List

In contrast to the proactive nature of a SharePoint task list, a SharePoint issues list provides a method for reactively dealing with a broad mixture of unplanned events and problems. Typically, these events represent problems caused by a malfunction of or gap in a policy or technology. Issues lists keep track of the individual who brought the issue to the team's attention, who is responsible for resolving the issue, what the progress is, and what other issues are related to the listed item. This provides a method for identifying trends in the issue log that may indicate the issue is merely a symptom of a larger problem that can only be seen as a trend. The following are some of the potential issues that may come to the attention of the governance team:

- Security breach due to inadequate policies
- Conflicting policy requirements
- Policy gaps
- Inconsistent policy wording or structure
- Inadequate policy communication and enforcement
- Duplicate policies
- Regulatory issues that must be addressed by policy
- Negative impact of policies on operations or costs

## Governance Team Contacts List

The governance team may need to keep track of outside resources, vendors, regulatory contacts, competitors, partners, and resources that are not listed in the company directory. The SharePoint contact list provides an excellent method for the team to manage and use important lists of external and internal contacts.

## Governance Team Documents Library

Governance teams are primarily focused on the creation, elimination, management, and publication of policy documents. The SharePoint document library provides version control, archiving, publication, collaboration, review, and editing support that makes this process simple to manage. Some of the functions that can be automated or supported are the following:

- Group document editing
- Group document review
- Draft document obfuscation
- Approved document publication
- E-mail–enabled reception of document drafts and requests

- Historical retention and management of past versions
- Notification of changes to draft and published documents

### Governance Team Forums

SharePoint forums provide an effective means for governance team members to discuss policies, suggestions, and other details of the team's operations. The use of a forum means that all members of the team will remain informed because all have access to the same information. No one will accidentally be left off a copy list or miss a hallway conversation if the information is entered into a SharePoint forum. Also, a permanent record of the discussions leading up to an important decision can be recorded for historical reference and to provide context when evaluating the decisions of the team.

Over time, the governance team may wish to expand its site to take advantage of additional lists and libraries as well as custom workflows and other SharePoint features. But, as always, it is wise to start small and grow the scope of the site over time.

## Summary

In this chapter, we have discussed the high-level concepts of technology governance and how SharePoint Server 2007 can help keep it on track in your organization. We've also discussed some of the key concepts involved in establishing a technology governance team capable of balancing strategic structure with tactical agility to provide an effective balance between chaos and rigidity.

## Additional Resources

- A blog dedicated to the governance and planning for SharePoint Server 2007: *http://www.sharepointplan.com*.
- Microsoft Governance site, which contains tools and resources to help business decision makers and IT professionals govern their SharePoint Products and Technologies environment. By using the governance techniques and best practices available from this page, an enterprise can align its policies for using SharePoint Products and Technologies with its culture and goals while still enabling teams and individuals to effectively collaborate and share information: *http://technet.microsoft.com/en-us/office/sharepointserver/bb507202.aspx*.
- Codplex Governance Site, which is designed for governance and manageability samples and tools designed to help IT Professionals: *http://www.codeplex.com/governance*.
- SharePoint Governance Checklist Guide: *http://office.microsoft.com/download/afile.aspx?AssetID=AM102306291033*.

- Governance and Planning Job Aid Poster, a checklist for ensuring you've covered all of your governance decision points; includes a 2' X 3' poster that outlines the planning, governance and decision points for a SharePoint Server 2007 deployment: *https://www.mindsharp.com/Default.aspx?page=Login&destPage=Default.*

Chapter 6

# Project Plans for a SharePoint Server 2007 Deployment

**In this chapter:**



Project planning for a Microsoft Office SharePoint Server 2007 implementation is a critical part of the process. The lack of a project plan will most likely result in an unstructured and ill-conceived installation. The best practices of information architecture, governance, design life cycles, and business requirements analyses are usually poorly done, if at all, without a proper project plan. When you begin your project plan, be sure to state how Office SharePoint Server 2007 is addressing your business problems.

Most SharePoint Server 2007 deployments do not have any type of project plan. Because the deployment of SharePoint Server 2007 can be one of the most complex projects you might have undertaken to date, it's important to understand that the existence of a project plan, in and of itself, is a best practice when it comes to the deployment of SharePoint Server 2007 in your environment.

Using a bad project plan can be just as detrimental as not having one at all. Because opinions vary on what constitutes a great project plan, the way we'll approach this topic in this chapter is to use Microsoft's sample SharePoint Server 2007 deployment project plan and then discuss parts of it in order to draw out insights and ideas on best practices for a SharePoint Server 2007 deployment.

**On the Companion Media** On the companion CD that ships with this book, you will find the sample project plan from Microsoft that we're referencing in this chapter. See the Project Sample Plan.mpp file on the CD. Note that you will need Microsoft Office Project 2007 in order to open and use this file.

## Understanding Microsoft's SharePoint Server 2007 Deployment Plan

Microsoft's sample deployment plan consists of 381 tasks that are mostly divided into four main sections:

- Envisioning
- Planning
- Deployment, Implementation, and Configuration Management
- Post-Implementation Operations, Optimization, and Business Review

It will not be possible to discuss each step in the project plan, but there are certain steps in the plan that we wish to highlight as they relate to some best practices in SharePoint Server 2007.

## The Envisioning Stage

In the envisioning stage, there are several steps that highlight some best practices. The first step we want to comment on is to evaluate corporate objectives for SharePoint Server 2007 (corporate knowledge sharing). We believe that this step cannot be fulfilled until you have technology-agnostic business requirements and technical requirements that have been discussed and agreed upon by both the technology team and the business stakeholders. Once you have the project charter (discussed in Chapter 4, "Defining Business Requirements") finalized, then you can start to map the corporate objectives to the features found in SharePoint Server 2007. A best practice is to *always* define what a successful outcome will be in your project charter, as well as the metrics that define it. Without the inclusion of your vision for success, you simply cannot measure your progress throughout your implementation life cycle.

### Lessons Learned "Why Are We Implementing SharePoint?"

We know of one company that was in a position of implementing SharePoint Server 2007 without clear articulation of the business and technology requirements that had been mapped to the features of SharePoint Server 2007. In other words, there was no project charter and no written agreement between the technology and business stakeholders on the problems that a SharePoint Server 2007 implementation was supposed to resolve. In fact, most of the business stakeholders were unaware that SharePoint Server 2007 was even being implemented. It wasn't that there was disagreement concerning the implementation of SharePoint Server 2007. It was more that they had not taken the time to establish a well-articulated agreement about how and why SharePoint Server 2007 was being implemented. Because of this, they experienced several negative, unforeseen effects due to not having clearly articulated requirements that had been agreed upon at the highest levels of the organization.

One of the negative results was reflected in the use of the developer's time. As users began to use SharePoint Server 2007, they started requesting customizations. Like a good soldier, the developer accommodated these requests. But the CIO didn't have a clear vision for the use of SharePoint Server 2007 in the company's overall service structure, so she didn't voice her disapproval of the developer's work in providing these customizations. She did, however, admit that she should not have allowed these customizations because they represented a growth of the product in a direction that she had not envisioned.

Second, because the SharePoint team didn't have a clear project charter from which to work, it was unable to articulate why the users should use SharePoint Server 2007 and the business goals for which SharePoint Server 2007 would *not* be used. In other words, because the team couldn't define the specific business goals their SharePoint Server 2007 implementation was supposed to support, it was unable to refuse user requests for divergent, sometimes conflicting, uses of SharePoint Server 2007. In addition, the team took on management tasks within collaboration spaces that should have been rightly left to the site collection owners and site administrators. Because team members didn't understand the distributed administrative architecture (including the distributed security administrative architecture), they found themselves spending precious time performing user permission assignment requests and creating lists and sites that could have easily been accomplished by the users themselves.

Third, SharePoint team members had not performed any governance work in conjunction with their SharePoint Server 2007 implementation, so when they tried to decide the answers to thorny questions–such as who the data owners would be, who would manage sites and site collections, or who had the power to make these decisions–the discussions usually deteriorated into circular, no-win conversations. Team members weren't fighting with one another, but were fighting with a vacuum: They were trying to determine governance issues with little direction on the goals and purposes of their SharePoint Server 2007 implementation and even less direct authority to make these decisions. Their governance effort was stuck before they even started.

Finally, this team's emerging vision was increasingly different than the CIO's vision for SharePoint Server 2007. The CIO wanted a platform in which to implement several core business processes and had been assured by Microsoft sales that SharePoint Server 2007 could perform what she needed. In fact, SharePoint Server 2007 fell short on one key requirement: the ability to group documents into a single set and treat that set as a single unit for approval and workflow purposes. In addition, the CIO had not been informed about the planning and governance tasks that would be required to complete a successful implementation, so the CIO moved forward with the deployment in good faith.

When the team began to learn more about SharePoint Server 2007, how it works, its architecture, and its possibilities, the team's vision increasingly expanded beyond the CIO's vision. Because of the good rapport that existed between the team members and the CIO, the members found themselves "managing up" by helping the CIO to understand the additional benefits that SharePoint Server 2007 brought to their organization. However, because the CIO had not been able to garner enough of a coalition of other C-level individuals (including the CEO) and in the absence of additional funds for an expanded implementation, the CIO was forced to deny the team's requests. While the team members accepted her decision, they felt that they had been placed in a no-win situation in which their ideas were not accepted, they were not empowered to move forward with a successful implementation, and they were not given the direction they needed to know which actions and decisions might be considered going too far by the CIO. At the time of this writing, the team still feels positive about the SharePoint Server 2007 implementation, and the relationships between team members and the CIO are solid, but there is a residual tension and frustration that, if not managed properly, could grow to be a political and emotional mess for everyone involved.

*Bill English, Microsoft MVP, Mindsharp*

In addition to evaluating corporate objectives, a second task—determining project scope—should be clearly communicated and agreed to by all parties involved. Several times, we have seen a proof of concept (POC) environment morph into a production environment. The problem with this morphing is that, in nearly all cases, the POC is not running on the hardware that is supposed to host the final production farm, and it often has third-party software that is going through a governance and/or quality assessment process that may or may not be accepted into the production environment. We recommend that all POCs (sometimes called *pilots*) have a firm end-date with a firm commitment to rebuild the SharePoint Server 2007 environment in production.

A third task—securing executive sponsorship and funding—is another key part of the envisioning stage. Our firm belief is that this sponsorship and funding should be secured during the development of the project charter. The specific funding cannot be known until the particular technology is selected, but the commitment to funding within a given range can be discussed and committed to during the development of the project charter. The actual funding of the project will come in stages anyway, so the funding of the project deployment phases should be included in the tasks that roll up to the successful completion of a milestone.

# The Planning Stage

In the Microsoft sample project plan, the planning stage is broken into 19 subplans, with each subplan containing multiple steps. These 19 subplans include the following:

- Assemble project teams and define roles
- Review technical requirements
- Review preliminary end-user and business requirements

- Determine preliminary design objectives
- Identify coexistence strategies
- Establish test lab environment
- Perform risk analysis
- Define communication strategy
- Define education strategy
- Review client hardware and software
- Create governance plan with mission, vision, and strategy
- Plan server configuration
- Plan security
- Plan for performance
- Plan failover and disaster recovery
- Plan for localization
- Plan integration
- Plan maintenance
- Plan content and navigation structure

In the following sections, we'll discuss individual tasks within some of these areas and comment on the best practices for a SharePoint Server 2007 deployment.

## Assemble Project Teams and Define Roles

This section highlights the assembly of the various roles that will be needed on the deployment team. This team should consist of 6 to 12 members. Be careful not to place too many roles on a single individual unless there is no other choice. Larger implementations may have more than 12 team members, but in such cases, roles need to be clearly detailed with expectations for how each person will contribute to the overall SharePoint Server 2007 deployment. These roles include the following:

- Development/customization members who can help inform the project team about the costs and opportunities that exist in customizing SharePoint Server 2007
- Communications members who are focused on ensuring that the right messages are communicated to the right groups at the right time using the right communication methods
- Project management members who are charged with ensuring that the overall project and its subprojects' tasks are being accomplished on time and within budget

- SharePoint farm administrator(s) who can help inform the team about the management of a SharePoint Server 2007 farm and the effects that decisions can have on the farm's deployment and overall operations
- A deployment administrator who is experienced in deploying new technologies to the desktop and who can help the team understand the effects of decisions at the desktop
- An extranet/Internet administrator who can inform the team about security risks and other decisions that might need to be made in order to expose SharePoint Server 2007 in an extranet or Internet environment
- Database administrator(s) who can work with the team to help ensure that the SQL back-end is configured and managed in accordance with the deployment plan objectives
- A testing/QA lead who can test new ideas and configurations as they arise during the course of the deployment
- A training lead who can write technical information and train the various groups on how to use SharePoint Server 2007 in your environment

If possible, we recommend including representatives from your business stakeholders who can be kept informed of the deployment process. Now, to be fair to Microsoft's project plan, they may have intended stakeholders to be members of the communications team. But if not, we would strongly suggest that the stakeholders be involved at some level in the SharePoint deployment process.

We believe that the project manager should be the public face of the project team; thus, the communications role can filter through this position. We also believe that a technical writer or someone who can document the technical aspects of the deployment is a role that needs to be fulfilled on the overall deployment team.

## Review Technical Requirements

The review of the technical requirements should be fairly straightforward. By the time the deployment plan is drawn up, the project charter should have been completed and the process for testing SharePoint Server 2007 against its competitors finished. The business requirements that translate into technical requirements should be well known to all now. The final agreement on the deployment between the technical staff and the business folks should have been firmed up. Reviewing the technical requirements should be done with a view to understanding and implementing–not with a view to changing or modifying–unless unforeseen context variables force the discussion and decision of change or modification.

Governance rules should have already been drawn up by this stage. You'll use the governance rules to understand who in the organization can change the technical requirements and the methods that must be employed to have them changed.

## Review Preliminary End-User and Business Requirements

There are a few specific tasks that need attention. The first task is determining the user experience requirement. What you should consider regarding this task is the determination of the types of customizations that are needed for various users who will be using SharePoint Server 2007. Accountants will need something different than salespeople. Executives will need a dashboard. Customizations will likely be a part of your deployment. Understanding and reviewing the customizations that will be needed is a part of this process. But you shouldn't expect that all of your customization needs will be known in advance. As users use SharePoint Server 2007 and become more familiar with it, they will ask for more functionalities down the road, so you should be prepared to have development help available to you by hiring a consulting company or a full-time developer.

### Notes from the Field **Skills Needed in SharePoint Server 2007 Developers**

We are often asked what skills a good SharePoint developer needs. Our response is that a good SharePoint Server 2007 developer will need to understand the .NET 3.0 framework (note that .NET 3.5 is supported for SharePoint Server 2007, so this level of understanding is good, too), C# coding abilities, and an understanding of how to code in Microsoft Windows SharePoint Services. This individual will need to either know or learn the various object models in Windows SharePoint Services.

A top-notch SharePoint developer will need VS.NET and a full SharePoint Server 2007 environment in which to code solutions (assuming the solutions are SharePoint Server 2007 based), as well as access to some type of assembly file storage, such as Microsoft Visual Studio Team Services or the older Microsoft Visual Source Safe.

*Keith Richie, Microsoft MVP, Barracuda*

The second task that quietly appears in this list is to determine content migration requirements. Those who are migrating content to SharePoint Server 2007 well know that this is an entire project plan and effort in itself, and it often defines the entire deployment effort. If you have information from other sources that needs to be migrated, take your time to determine how this information should be imported into SharePoint Server 2007. For example, if you're moving large sets of files from one location to SharePoint Server 2007, you'll want to ensure that you have SharePoint Server 2007 set up correctly to receive those files.

Third, coupled with this migration strategy is the task to review the taxonomy and content type requirements. When moving information into SharePoint Server 2007, it is *essential* that the correct content types exist so that the documents can be described correctly via metadata assignments. Contrary to popular belief, moving documents into SharePoint Server 2007 does not make those documents more findable. The larger the document set that is migrated into SharePoint Server 2007, the more true that statement becomes.

Why? Because as the size of the document set grows, the meaning of individual words within the document set will become more randomized. Our natural use of language is to use the same words to mean different things. For example, if we were to look at a set of documents about music, the word "horn" would likely have a singular or very narrow meaning. But if we were to download all of the words from the United States Patent and Trademark Office (where the foci of documents is highly randomized), then the word "horn" would take on multiple meanings across the entire document set.

In most organizations, you'll have documents that have widely divergent foci, and thus the same words within those documents will mean different things. If you index just their contents and then execute a query, you might receive a syntactically correct result set, but the meaning of those keywords will be widely divergent. It is a horn, a horn, or a horn?

### Lessons Learned **Moving 1.5 Terabytes of Files into SharePoint Server 2007**

One organization that we recently worked with was charged with moving 1.5 terabytes of data into SharePoint Server 2007 from several workspaces in Microsoft SharePoint Portal Server 2001.

> **Important** The principles that we'll discuss in this sidebar are directly applicable to those who need to move file sets from file servers, so don't bypass this sidebar just because you're not moving files from SharePoint Portal Server 2001.

This customer had already determined that its method of migrating documents would require users to drag-and-drop their documents from the Web folder client of their SharePoint Portal Server 2001 workspaces to predetermined document libraries in SharePoint Server 2007. The customer's design was to host those documents for their useful life in SharePoint Server 2007, but then move them to their SAP implementation for long-term document storage. Whether or not you think this is a smart idea is really beside the point: The customer has teams deeply committed to both platforms, and this was the compromise struck between the stakeholders and the technology teams when the project charter was developed.

Most of these documents are Standard Operating Procedure documents that outline how the company's products are to be produced. This company produces thousands of products and then ships them worldwide. Because the documents have a similar format and outline, with different content based on the product in question, the company decided to use categories in SharePoint Portal Server 2001 to, well, categorize its documents based on its product matrix. This strategy worked pretty well. Documents are quickly and easily findable via their intuitive navigation structure.

However, because SharePoint Server 2007 has no concept of assigning categories to documents and then exposing the metadata hierarchy via a set of nested pages, the customer was really in a quandary about how to assign metadata to documents and how to make those documents quickly findable in SharePoint Server 2007. Moreover, whatever taxonomy and navigation structure the customer develops in SharePoint Server 2007 will need to be repeated in SAP so that users can find current and older documents in either system using a consistent findability pattern.

One thing is certain: This company will need to create hundreds of content types and assign them across hundreds of document libraries before the documents are moved in SharePoint Server 2007 if users are going to have any chance at finding their documents quickly in to SharePoint Server 2007.

As part of its migration strategy, this company has been forced to add some time to its project deployment plan to ensure that the content types are created and assigned to the right libraries before users drag-and-drop their documents in SharePoint Server 2007.

*Bill English, Microsoft MVP, Mindsharp*

## Determine Preliminary Design Objectives

The two tasks in this stage deal with communication and branding. First, the task of disseminating project information (presumably at the right time and to the right people) is essential to keeping everyone on the same page and reducing surprises as the rollout moves forward.

The second task is determining branding requirements. When you see this, think "master page customizations" because this is precisely why master pages were created in the first place. Farm-wide branding and navigation structures can be backed into the master page set so that certain elements appear across all or most sites in SharePoint Server 2007.

## Identify Coexistence Strategies

Several coexistence strategies need to be considered, but the most prominent one for our discussion is third-party software for SharePoint implementations.

More than a few third-party vendors make software that increases the value that SharePoint Server 2007 brings to your organization. These products vary in terms of quality and effectiveness, so you'll need to test products you're considering before you purchase them. When it comes to third-party software purchases, we find that it is a best practice to purchase third-party software that does not need to be restored as part of your overall farm restoration plan. In the event that you need to restore your farm, it would be better to simply restore your SharePoint Server 2007 farm and then have the option to restore the third-party software at a later time—perhaps a few days or even a few weeks later. We recommend this because not all third-party software platforms restore with the same quality and reliability as SharePoint Server 2007.

Products that install themselves in such a deeply nested way as to require a restore scenario where you must restore SharePoint Server 2007 should be thoroughly tested and approved before moving ahead with their purchase. In addition, look at the history of the third-party software company and ensure (as best you can in this cottage industry) that it has the stability and reliability to "be there" for the next release of SharePoint Products and Technologies.

## Establish Test Lab Environment

We encounter customers who regularly tell us that, for various reasons, their management won't pay for a lab environment in which they can test their SharePoint Server 2007 implementations. It is a best practice to have a lab environment where SharePoint Server 2007 can be tested and new ideas tried out before they are encountered in production. Not to have such a lab is analogous to a sports team not having a place to practice before it plays its games. Reasons to stand up and maintain a test environment include the following:

- Test new Web parts before placing them in production
- Test third-party software before purchasing and using in production
- Test home-grown code
- Test master page changes
- Test connectivity to other LDAP databases
- Test backup and restore scenarios
- Stress test certain aspects of SharePoint Server 2007
- Test service pack and hotfix updates
- Test farm topology changes

The reason that you do all of this in a lab environment is because you want to closely manage your changes in production. Effecting changes directly in production can have unforeseen side effects and can sometimes cause your production environment to be offline for a period of time. Proper change-control management dictates a testing environment of changes with evaluation and review before committing those changes to production. Don't underestimate the value of having a test lab available to test changes to your production environment.

### Notes from the Field **Standing Up a Test Environment**

One of the questions we frequently receive is whether the test environment needs to mirror the production environment and, if so, how this is achieved. Generally, we find that our opinion matters less than the amount of available funds and time that administrators have to invest in a lab environment. In larger corporations, there are usually strict change management controls in place that require changes to a production environment to be tested and documented before they can be implemented in production.

But in many (perhaps most) of the environments that we encounter, we find that administrators are fortunate if they can get a single SQL Server and a single SharePoint Server 2007 Server for testing purposes. Although virtualization is changing this situation somewhat, it still seems to be a common scenario.

Our recommendation is to have a test environment in which the roles are replicated across servers, but the number of servers in each role need not be replicated. For example, your production environment might have three Web servers, but your test environment will need only one–unless some of your testing has to do with network load balancing of the Web applications. If you have the index role quarantined on an individual server in production, then your testing environment should mirror this fact. In our experience of working with customers, the need to exactly mirror your production in your test environment has not proven to be essential. However, having the roles separated out on different hardware servers as it is in production has proven to be very helpful in different testing scenarios, especially third-party software.

*Bob Fox, Microsoft MVP, B&R Business Solutions*

## Perform Risk Analysis

Every so often, our customers will ask us if SharePoint Server 2007 is really secure. Since this is a relative term, our answers tend to be given against a more defined context. What is meant by "secure?" Can the servers or farm be placed in a perimeter network? Where should extranet accounts reside? What is the level of risk that is assumed when SharePoint Server 2007 is opened to externally initiated connections?

What the administrator is really asking is this: Is SharePoint Server 2007 security implemented in such a way that it is difficult to hack from the outside? Our answer is yes, but like all products, it needs to undergo a security test or audit to ensure that it meets your security requirements. Every software product you purchase carries a certain level of risk. We do not believe that SharePoint Server 2007 is any more risky than any other Web-based software product. Properly implementing Internet Information Services (IIS) and your firewall has as much to do with securing your SharePoint Server 2007 content as properly securing SharePoint Server 2007 itself.

Traditional risk analysis involves the identification of three basic elements:

1. Assets that are exposed to the risk
2. Risk vectors
3. Countermeasures that are used to lessen the risk threat

Like it or not, your users will likely upload highly sensitive information into their sites and use SharePoint Server 2007 as the collaboration platform in which this information is further developed and/or refined. Because of this, part of your governance and content planning should specify if there are any types of information that should not be hosted in SharePoint Server 2007. This isn't a tacit admission that SharePoint Server 2007 is insecure. Instead, it is a recognition that some levels of information, based on their security clearance or method of authentication, are not appropriate for a Web-based information management system. Presumably, the same decision would be made regardless of which Web-based collaboration program was under consideration.

One risk factor for your deployment will be the level of education and expertise your farm administrators and developers have to support your deployment. Unwise administrators who make unwise decisions can cause significant difficulties for your deployment. Developers who write insecure code or write Web parts that cause significant rendering time and processor cycles can injure your deployment.

A potentially fatal risk factor is the absence of clear business and technical requirements for your SharePoint Server 2007 implementation. Closely associated with this risk factor is the absence of clear governance for your SharePoint Server 2007 implementation. Organizations that lack these three elements—clearly articulated business requirements, clearly articulated technical requirements, and clear governance standards—face a very high probability that their deployment will be, at best, minimally successful and, more likely, a failure.

### Notes from the Field **Managing Resistance to Change**

Every SharePoint Server 2007 implementation that we have seen represents significant change for everyone involved with the organization. When implementing change, one of the main aspects that you'll need to understand is how to assess resistance to that change. You can consider both overt and covert resistance to the SharePoint Server 2007 deployment as a potentially fatal risk factor that must be managed. (Other risk factors that can originate within your organization are a lack of grassroots demand for a SharePoint Server 2007 deployment; lack of an approved, funded budget; lack of high-level support in your company [think vice president levels and higher]; and a lack of control over your project, its goals, its objectives, its measurements, and the hiring and firing of team members.)

Resistance can be assessed and managed by proactively mapping the influence landscape. This means that you identify who needs to be persuaded and how they can be influenced. This will involve mapping the key groups and subgroups that will need to be influenced, along with any groups that are already positive toward a SharePoint Server 2007 implementation. Be sure to work with opinion leaders in your organization because they often exert a disproportionate amount of influence on others' opinions and decisions. Chapter 2, "Change, Power, and Conflict," discusses how early adopters also serve as opinion leaders within an organization.

The source of resistance varies:

- Loss of comfortable status quo: The users see no reason to change in ways that might force them work harder or differently.
- Loss of a sense of competence: The users will feel less competent working with new technology and will be unable to perform as required in the post-change environment. This may cause them mistakenly to assume that the new technology is too difficult to learn (think about all the tasks and responsibilities of a site administrator and/or site collection administrator).
- Loss of security due to uncertainty about their future: If the proposed change is implemented and users are unable to adapt, will their jobs be at stake?
- Negative consequences for key allies: They fear the consequences for others they care about within the organization who they feel may not be able to adapt to the new technology.

The key to dealing with resistance is to understand driving and restraining forces. *Driving forces* push users in the direction of adopting new technology. *Restraining forces* push users to resist new technology. The key is to identify both the driving and restraining forces and then find ways to strengthen the driving forces, weaken the restraining forces, or both.

Your users may face a "force-field" something like the following:

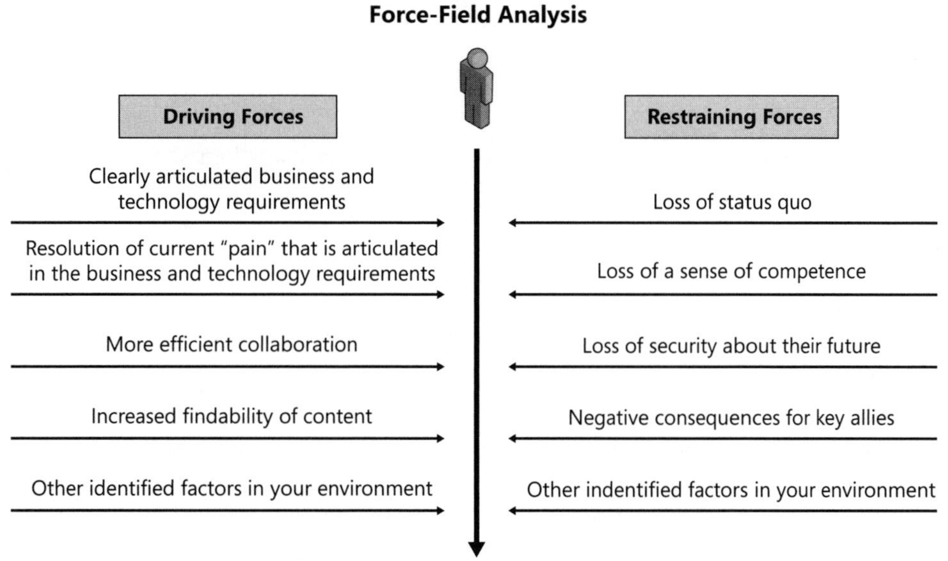


Assessing the driving and restraining forces to a SharePoint Server 2007 deployment will help you understand how to address users' covert and overt resistance. In many cases, training, education, and an insidious (as opposed to acute) onset of the technology's use will help lower resistance. Users may not see the driving forces as adequate tradeoffs for the restraining forces. They won't think of it in these terms, but they'll still do the cost/benefit analysis. Your job (or someone on your team) is to help them see that the perceived tradeoffs can be turned into a win/win for them personally as well as for the organization. No small task, we understand, but an important one that must be accomplished nevertheless.

One other note: Accentuating the positive outcomes that SharePoint Server 2007 brings to your organization in fulfilling business and technology requirements will go a long way toward answering users' "why" questions.

*Mark Schneider, PMP, sharepointplan.com*

## Define Communication Strategy

Writing an effective communications plan is an essential part of a successful SharePoint Server 2007 deployment. This plan needs to be understood and agreed upon as part of the project plan, and it needs to be faithfully followed. The guidelines of a solid communications plan include the following elements:

- Every message should be audience specific.
- Specify the appropriate communication mediums for each message type.
- Provide regular, unbiased reporting of project progress.
- Communicate what other people need to know *before* they need to know it. Provide time for people to move past an emotional reaction and on to effective involvement.
- Offer opportunities for private communication as appropriate.
- Offer opportunities for public feedback as appropriate.

Table 6-1 offers an example of a communications matrix.

**Table 6-1 Communications Matrix**

| Audience | Message type | Method/Medium | Timing/Frequency | Responsible party |
|---|---|---|---|---|
| Business stakeholders | Task updates; project updates | E-mail; in-person meetings | E-mail weekly; bi-monthly in-person meetings | Project manager |
| Project charter board | Policy issues; project deliverable updates | E-mail; in-person meetings | E-mail weekly; monthly in-person meetings | Project manager |

As you can see, this communications plan can become somewhat complex, but if followed, it will help everyone affected by the deployment to be informed as events that affect them occur. Possible groups that will need to be informed of deployment options include the following:

- Stakeholder representatives
- Upper management
- Accounting personnel
- IT personnel
- Site collection owners
- Site collection members
- Project charter members
- Third-party vendors

The types of messages that need to be communicated include the following:

- Project status updates
- Project status milestone completion
- Policy issues
- Policy updates
- Task-related messages
- Project overview
- Project deliverables
- Contact information
- How-to information

This list is not exhaustive, but it is a starting point for your effort to build out a good communications plan. Be sure not to bypass this step of creating a good communications plan in your overall project deployment plan.

## Define Education Strategy

One of the aspects of Windows SharePoint Services and SharePoint Server 2007 that caught many off guard was the pervasive need for education across all groups at all levels within an organization that was adopting SharePoint Server 2007. It is not uncommon for us to hear about how intuitive the interface is to use, and it is true that the interface, in and of itself, is intuitive to use. But understanding the *how* of completing a task is vastly different and less important than understanding the *why* of engaging in the task in the first place.

While some education needs to focus on how-to topics, much of it needs to focus on the integration of how the product works with your governance and use policies. For example, you might turn on Self Service Site Management, which allows everyone with permissions to create new site collections within one or more managed paths. Yet, in order to control the growth of the site collections in your farm, you may need to propagate business case criteria for when a new site collection is created. So not only does your education need to inform users about *how* to create a site collection, it should also inform them about your organization's policies on *when* to create new site collections.

We find that the following groups need education:

- Executives
- Developers
- Administrators
- Web masters
- Web developers
- Help Desk personnel
- Desktop support personnel
- Power users
- Knowledge workers
- Site collection owners
- Site administrators
- Workspace administrators
- Customers
- Partners
- Vendors

Now, you might wonder who in your organization will need which levels of education. Best practice is to err on the side of offering too much education as opposed to too little. For example, once you open up My Sites, you'll find that every person who creates their own My Site will automatically become a site collection administrator because each My Site is a separate site collection. Site collection administrators will be able to manage individual sites, so they will need site administration training, too. In many organizations, we find that the vast majority of users will be both site collection administrators and site administrators within the first two years of SharePoint Server 2007 implementation. Of course, this isn't true for all organizations, but it is certainly true of those who are content-centric where information is created, managed, modified, and used by the wide majority of users within the company.

We strongly recommend a robust training program for everyone in your company. In fact, in many situations, if a company can train its workforce appropriately, we find that the company's need for consulting services diminishes significantly. Training that teaches you to know more so that you can do more is the type of training that you should pursue.

> **On the Companion Media** In the Additional Resources section at the end of this chapter and on the companion CD, you'll find links to various free training modules from Microsoft.

## Review Client Hardware and Software

In this section, the most often-asked question that we receive is whether a company should upgrade to Microsoft Office 2007 at the desktop. Our response is that those companies that are running Office 2007 at the desktop will experience a higher return on investment (ROI) for their SharePoint Server 2007 implementations than those who remain at Microsoft Office 2003 or earlier.

One of the main reasons for upgrading to Office 2007 is the existence of the Document Information Panel (DIP), which interacts with the content types in SharePoint Server 2007 to ensure that required document metadata information is input before the document can be uploaded or utilized by others within SharePoint Server 2007. Note that the DIP doesn't ensure that site columns in the library are populated when the document is uploaded. The DIP is intended to populate document metadata that is attached directly to the document through its content type or through customized metadata fields embedded in the document.

There are other points of integration between SharePoint Server 2007 and Office 2007, but this is an obvious feature that might drive an upgrade to Office 2007 as part of a larger, overall SharePoint Server 2007 deployment. One other obvious integration point between Microsoft Office 2007 and SharePoint Server 2007 is the list synchronization between Office Outlook 2007 and SharePoint Server 2007.

It is a worst practice to upgrade to Office 2007 at the same time that SharePoint Server 2007 is being deployed. This is too much change for your end-users to assimilate at one time. Instead, conduct the Office 2007 upgrade either before or after the SharePoint Server 2007 deployment so that the change the users encounter can be spread across a longer timeline.

## Create Governance Plan with Mission, Vision, and Strategy

Even though most of Microsoft's sample plan has a planning task at this stage of the deployment process, the creation of a governance plan should be in place before starting your SharePoint Server 2007 deployment. The governance plan need not be complete, but the high-level standards need to be in place. More importantly, the process for gathering and evaluating new standards from your users needs to be settled.

## Plan Server Configuration

There is a range of decisions to be made in this area—not just about hardware and server roles, but about other configurations for your deployment. In fact, any configuration that can be effected in Central Administration or a Shared Services Provider could be included in this section. These decision points include elements such as the following:

- Type and number of content sources
- Which Web applications will have Self Service Site Management turned on
- Which Web applications will have which type of authentication provider

- Will there be any anonymous access to any content
- What Business Data Catalog connections need to be built
- What site quotas need to be created

Many of these decisions are discussed in other parts of this book. But suffice it to say that each decision should be measured in light of whether it supports, either indirectly or directly, the business and technology requirements as well as whether it is in line with the governance standards that have been established.

## Plan Security

Probably the largest consideration when planning for security is the interaction of how you'll configure authentication providers for Web applications, the zones to which each Web application and its extended Web application are assigned, and the security policies for users and groups that you'll assign to the zones and Web applications. With the appropriate use of policies that are applied to zones, you can tightly define who has access to which content and the level of access they have.

Best practice is to identify certain users who must have or must not have access to certain content and then use policies and zones to achieve the configured security that you need.

In addition, how users will secure their sites is an important discussion. By default, site administrators have the ability to secure objects within their sites using either Active Directory directory services group or user accounts. IT administrators who like to "lock down" their SharePoint Server 2007 deployments prefer to use group accounts instead of user accounts because the group accounts can be assigned once and user access can be controlled through group membership assigned in Active Directory. Users like to user accounts because they often don't understand the group account naming convention in Active Directory and can't enumerate that group's memberships. Therefore, it's easier to use user accounts to assign permissions, even if this means assigning more than a few users to an object.

On the face of it, assigning permissions using group accounts seems to be the fastest, easiest, and best way to manage permissions. The groups are already familiar to IT personnel. They know how to assign permissions in SharePoint Server 2007 (presumably), so it seems a natural, logical extension of their functions.

But upon closer examination, using groups to secure objects in SharePoint Server 2007 is fraught with opportunities for mistakes. Because site administrators cannot enumerate group memberships in Active Directory, there is an inherent opportunity for miscommunication to occur between the Active Directory administrator and the site administrator. Let's assume that the site administrator needs 70 people to have various levels of access to her site. First, she needs five people to be site administrators, so she and the Active Directory administrator will need to communicate and set up an Active Directory group with herself and the five other members. Then, she needs 30 of those 70 people to be members in the site with collaboration permissions, so she needs to communicate to the Active Directory administrator a second

Active Directory group that needs to be created for the members in the site. Third, the other 40 members need to be placed in the visitors group, so she communicates the membership to the Active Directory administrator and has a third Active Directory group created.

Now let's assume that four of the visitors need to be upgraded with member permissions in the site. The site administrator communicates this to the Active Directory administrator, who then removes them from the visitor's Active Directory group and adds them to the members group for the site. A few days later, three people leave the company and four more are hired, so the three who were members of the visitors group need to be removed in Active Directory and the four who were hired need to be added to one of the groups in the site. So the Active Directory administrator must communicate with the site administrator about which Active Directory groups in which to add these four new people, and the site administrator communicates this back to the Active Directory administrator.

Now let's assume that 15 of the 30 users in the members group need to be given permissions to create subsites. The site administrator creates a new SharePoint group for this group of 15 users and communicates this to the Active Directory administrator, who in turn removes them from the members Active Directory group and adds them into the newly created Active Directory group for members who can also create subsites.

Five of the users go off and create new subsites, which would be expected behavior. However, they decide to break permissions inheritance and thus become the sole administrators of their subsites. They need to add users into their sites, so they send an e-mail to the Active Directory administrator requesting new Active Directory groups with a list of users for each group. Now the Active Directory administrator is working with at least six different site administrators to keep permissions consistent between the group memberships in Active Directory and the needed permission assignments at the site level.

In this scenario, the administrators of all of these sites have no method of remembering who is in which Active Directory group, so the Active Directory administrator will be responsible to help the site administrators understand who has been added to which Active Directory group so that the site administrator can responsibly administrate security within her site. Unless the site administrator manually tracks who is in which Active Directory group, she will sometimes forget the Active Directory group's membership and will need to have those members re-enumerated. This will add administrative effort for security management for both your site administrators as well as your Active Directory administrator(s).

Multiply this by 1,000, 5,000, or even 10,000 sites, and you soon realize that, unless you're prepared to hire additional full-time staff for your Active Directory team, implement a robust permissions workflow between your Active Directory administrators and your site administrators, and implement some type of Active Directory group membership enumeration that can be accessed by the site administrators without involving the Active Directory administrator, this scenario will grow out of control pretty quickly. While the use of groups to manage sites seems best in most cases, the workload on the Active Directory staff becomes overly burdensome, and the workflow to get new groups created that match the needs of the site administrator becomes too cumbersome.

It is best practice to allow site administrators to assign permissions directly, offering them some global groups that have wide memberships in case they want to expose portions of their sites to the rest of the organization. It is a best practice to place all of your Active Directory groups that will be used exclusively in your SharePoint Server 2007 implementation inside their own organizational unit (OU). Through the use of third-party permissions control software, site collection administrators and site administrators can effectively control all of the permissions for those sites that they administrate.

> **Note** To control permissions at the farm and site level using third-party software, please take a look at the DeliverPoint 2007 software and documentation at *www.deliverpoint.com*.

## Managing Permissions Using Active Directory Groups versus Active Directory User Accounts

Even though we have argued that it is a best practice to use individual user accounts to manage permissions at the site and object layer, this method is not without its problems and drawbacks. Without the use of third-party software, user permission management is randomized and highly dependent on each site administrator being proactive to keep permission assignments up to date. What follows in Table 6-2 is an overview of the advantages and disadvantages of permissions management in SharePoint Server 2007.

**Table 6-2 Permissions Management Tradeoffs**

| Scenario | Active Directory Groups | Active Directory User Accounts | Tradeoff |
|---|---|---|---|
| A new site collection needs to be created. | The root site's template will have various permission levels as part of the template. New Active Directory groups will need to be created for the root site and any sites that will inherit permissions from this site. When permission inheritance is broken within the site collection, a new set of Active Directory groups will be need be created for the new subsite that has broken inheritance. | Users are added directly to the default SharePoint groups. | If you are using Active Directory groups, the creation of a new site collection is throttled by the need to loop through the Active Directory administrator to create the new Active Directory groups that will correspond to the permission levels in the site. For example, if you'll have administrators, members, and visitors, then three Active Directory groups will need to be created to accommodate those three permission levels. |

Table 6-2 Permissions Management Tradeoffs

| Scenario | Active Directory Groups | Active Directory User Accounts | Tradeoff |
|---|---|---|---|
| A new subsite within a site collection needs to be created, or inheritance needs to be broken between a parent site and a subsite. | The Active Directory administration will need to be notified, and a new set of Active Directory groups will need to be created for this site if permissions are not inherited. | The new subsite can be quickly and easily created by the users themselves without looping through the Active Directory administrator. | The use of Active Directory groups to secure sites will hamper the self-organization features of SharePoint Server 2007 and likely will create bottlenecks in the security assignments for each site. |
| A user needs to be added to a site at a certain permission level. | The Active Directory administrator needs to be notified to add this user to the appropriate group in Active Directory. | The site administrator adds the user to the SharePoint group directly without looping through IT personnel. | The user account method is faster with a much lower transaction cost. The Active Directory group method keeps IT in the loop and makes them responsible for the security on the site. |
| A user needs to be added to the site collection as a site collection administrator. | Groups cannot be added as site collection administrators. | User accounts must be used for site collection administrators. | |
| A user needs to be given unique permissions within the site. | A new Active Directory group must be created and the user's account added to the group. Then the site administrator must add the Active Directory group to the newly created SharePoint group. | The user account can be assigned unique permissions directly by the site administrator. | The user account method is faster with a much lower transaction cost. The Active Directory group method keeps IT in the loop and makes them responsible for the security on the site. |
| A user leaves the company or is transferred outside the "scope" of the SharePoint Server 2007 farm. | The Active Directory administrator disables the user account and eventually removes the account from Active Directory completely. There are no "left-over" accounts in SharePoint to clean up. | Each administrator must be notified or otherwise learn that the user has left the company and then must go through each site with explicit permissions and remove the user's account manually. | Most site administrators will not take the time to methodically remove user accounts. In most cases, the user account will persist in SharePoint Server 2007. This does not represent a security problem because SharePoint Server 2007 only performs authorization based on authenticated accounts, but it may place your SharePoint Server 2007 implementation outside of compliance with current laws and regulations. |

**Table 6-2 Permissions Management Tradeoffs**

| Scenario | Active Directory Groups | Active Directory User Accounts | Tradeoff |
|---|---|---|---|
| Need to discover permissions on an individual user farm-wide. | Active Directory administrators can manually report in which Active Directory groups the user is a member. Complete reporting would depend on up-to-date documentation that reports which Active Directory group has been assigned to which SharePoint group. Also, documentation would be needed to disclose which Active Directory groups are nested within which Active Directory groups and then which nested Active Directory groups have been assigned to which SharePoint groups. | There is no method to discover user permissions within SharePoint Server 2007 outside the view of the permissions for the current object in focus. | Third-party software will need to be utilized to provide a thorough reporting capability. |
| Need to discover who has permissions to an individual object, such as a document or library. | The Active Directory administrator cannot provide this information because his responsibility stops at creating Active Directory groups and populating them as requested by the site administrator. | The site administrator can see who has permissions to a document or library, but cannot know if any Active Directory groups are nested within the Active Directory groups that have been assigned permission to the object. | This functionality is best served through the use of third-party software. |
| There are 50 subsites within a site collection. The site collection administrator needs to know where permissions inheritance has been broken. | The Active Directory administrator will not be able to provide assistance in this scenario. | There is no method native in SharePoint Server 2007 to provide this functionality. | Third-party software must be utilized to display where permissions inheritance has been broken within a site collection. |

Table 6-2 Permissions Management Tradeoffs

| Scenario | Active Directory Groups | Active Directory User Accounts | Tradeoff |
|---|---|---|---|
| The site administrator has lost track of which users are members of which Active Directory groups. | The Active Directory administrator will need to provide this information to the site administrator, and/or the site administrator must manually keep track of who is a member of each Active Directory group and regularly "sync up" her list with the Active Directory group membership assignments in Active Directory. | The site interface will inform the site administrator about which Active Directory groups have been assigned permissions but will not enumerate the group's membership in the display. The use of individual user accounts can immediately inform the site administrator of permission assignments. | This is probably the most thorny aspect of using Active Directory groups to secure sites in SharePoint. The lack of local security control by the site administrator places her in a position of being responsible for the site's security but not directly having the power and control to secure the site properly. |
| The site collection administrators need to swiftly secure a site in an urgent or emergency situation by removing all permissions and assigning themselves only to the site's permission structure. | For each unique set of site collection administrators, an Active Directory group will need to have been created in anticipation of this scenario. If Self Service Site Management is turned on, a manual workflow will need to be created to ensure that each new site collection's ownership assignments are reflected in an Active Directory group. As site collection owners are added later, the workflow will need to ensure that additional users are added to the Active Directory group. Note that Active Directory groups cannot be added as site collection owners. | The site collection owners simply go into the site, give themselves full permissions, and then remove everyone else from the site. | It is highly unlikely that most users will pay attention to this type of workflow and participate in it, in part because this scenario will seldom be a reality. In addition, enumerating, tracking, and "syncing up" the site collection ownership assignments to their Active Directory groups would be difficult to achieve outside a manual process. It would almost certainly require custom code of some type. |

**Table 6-2 Permissions Management Tradeoffs**

| Scenario | Active Directory Groups | Active Directory User Accounts | Tradeoff |
|---|---|---|---|
| By default, each My Site is considered a site collection and is secured with the NT_Authenticated Users group having full read permissions and the individual user having full ownership permissions. | When a user creates her My Site, the user's account is placed into an Active Directory group for that site collection and then is assigned the proper permissions in the My Site by the Active Directory administrator or the user herself. | Users can directly assign permissions to individual users without having to loop through the Active Directory administrator. | The use of Active Directory groups to secure objects in My Sites is cumbersome and will require custom code. |
| A user creates a subsite in his My Site and needs to add three co-workers to the site. | A manual workflow process will need to be created that allows the individual user to either request or create a new Active Directory group with himself and his three co-workers added to the group. | The user is able to add these three co-workers directly without looping through the Active Directory administrator, thereby making the new collaboration space truly self-organizing with a low transaction cost. | The potential for backlog requests to pile up for the Active Directory administrator is high. If you have 2,500 users, each of whom have a My Site, plus another 5,000 site collections in your implementation, the sheer number of requests for new Active Directory groups and modifications to current group membership will likely be very, very high. As your implementation grows, the number of requests will grow because nearly every user in the company will, at one time or another, make a security request to the Active Directory administrator. |

As you can see, permissions management in SharePoint Server 2007 is difficult at best because the normal tools that you would use are not available in SharePoint Server 2007, and the substitution of Active Directory groups for user accounts does little to solve the overall permissions problem. The federated, decentralized design for administration in SharePoint Server 2007 also means that the security management of information in SharePoint Server 2007 is also federated and decentralized. No matter how much you try to centralize it, you'll probably fail without extremely tight controls and additional IT personnel to manage it all.

Another area of security to consider is the use of Secure Sockets Layer (SSL) certificates for your SharePoint Server 2007 Web applications. SSL certificates have to be assigned to the Web applications after they have been created. There is no place in the interface to specify an SSL certificate as part of the Web application creation process. Likewise, for those who need to use IP-bound Web applications, you'll find yourself unable to assign an IP address to the Web application during its creation process.

When a Web application is created, the information that you enter on the extendvs.aspx (Figure 6-1) page is downloaded into the configuration database. After being written to the configuration database, it is then pulled back into memory on the Web servers and used to create the Web site in IIS and then extend it with Windows SharePoint Services to create what we know as a Web application.

**Figure 6-1** Extendvs.aspx page

If the Windows SharePoint Services Web application service (Figure 6-2) is stopped, all of the Web sites and their configurations will be deleted from the SharePoint Server 2007 server. This happens by design because only those servers fulfilling the Web role need to have Web sites installed on them. If the service is then restarted, the Web sites will be rebuilt using only the information they can find in the configuration database. This means that any customizations or modifications you made to each Web application after it was created will need to be reapplied to the Web application, including IP address assignments, SSL certificate assignments, customizations for the web.config files, and any other file customizations or additions to the Web application's files.

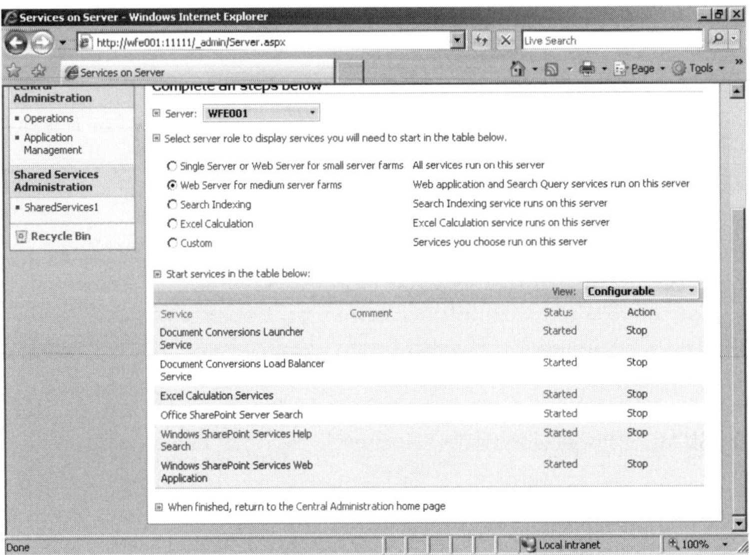


**Figure 6-2** Server service page in Central Administration

> **Note** The Web applications are not removed and rebuilt during a reboot of the server or during the running of the IISRESET command.

Given all this, best practice is to completely document any changes you make to your Web applications in IIS after the Web applications have been created.

## Plan for Performance

We think that most readers will stipulate the argument that planning for performance is a good idea. What most will want to know are the performance benchmarks that should be considered in regard to SharePoint Server 2007 servers.

Unfortunately, that type of benchmark data is difficult to find and even more difficult to generalize because networks are as unique as they are numerous. What would be considered a bottleneck number for an individual counter in one network wouldn't be considered as such in another. This is due to differences in hardware, network equipment, user demand, and services running on each server.

Best practice is to use the information found in Chapter 23, "Capacity Planning and Performance Monitoring," to help you develop your own baseline of counters that you consistently log for the same period of time each month. After a few months, you'll have baseline counters from which to predict future usage given different sets of variables. While we can't say what numbers will represent a best practice for your organization, we can say that monitoring your farm to build out a baseline set of numbers is a best practice, both for performance and for capacity planning.

## Plan Failover and Disaster Recovery

Obviously, backup and restore are an essential part of any software deployment model. SharePoint Server 2007 is no exception. The most thorny problems that we encounter are those with geographically dispersed environments trying to figure out how to failover SharePoint Server 2007 from one datacenter to another. The problem with planning a failover for SharePoint Server 2007 is that SharePoint Server 2007 itself isn't written to work in a clustered environment. Microsoft SQL Server 2005 is, but SharePoint Server 2007 is not. So, it's wrong to say that SharePoint Server 2007 can failover in a clustered environment because it can't. It's not written to do this.

Any way you look at it, the failover capabilities apply only to SQL Server 2005 and its databases. While this will work for the content, you still need to contend with a failover plan for everything else in SharePoint Server 2007, including the Web application and its files, the metabase (or configuration files if running IIS 7.0 or later), the SharePoint Server 2007 binaries, the 12 hive where most of the farm's files are placed, the index and any customized Web part assemblies, or application-specific files and information. Failing over all of this, which in our minds represents the *entire farm,* is not easy. To our knowledge, there is no built-in or third-party tool that will handle all of this for you easily, seamlessly, and quickly.

So, you will need to ensure that the various parts of SharePoint Server 2007 are synchronized on a regular basis between your data centers. To be specific, the parts that need synchronization are as follows:

- SharePoint Server 2007 binaries
- 12 hive
- Web application files
- Web application metabase (if running IIS 6.0) or the configuration files (if running IIS 7.0)
- SQL databases

## Plan for Localization

Variations can be used to publish site templates in different languages if you need to expose different sites in your farm or a different farm using different languages. However, you need to know that the publishing of content in different languages will need to be routed through a human workflow for translation of the content. You can also check for third-party products that might translate the content for you before it appears on the target site in a different language.

Because variations depend on different language packs being in existence, best practice is to install the language packs early in your deployment.

> **More Info** For more information on language packs and variations, please see Chapter 4, "Multilingual Planning, Deployment, and Maintenance," of the book *Microsoft Office SharePoint Server 2007 Administrator's Companion* (Microsoft Press, 2007).

## Plan Integration

The sample project plan lists the following integration points with SharePoint Server 2007:

- Business Data Catalog
- Excel Services
- Microsoft Office Forms Server 2007
- Microsoft Search Server 2008
- Microsoft ForeFront Security for SharePoint
- Microsoft Office Groove Server 2007
- Incoming e-mail

Interestingly enough, the project plan doesn't include the following:

- Microsoft Office Project Server 2007
- Microsoft Office Project Portfolio Server
- Microsoft Office Communications Server 2007
- Microsoft Office PerformancePoint Server 2007

Regardless of which product we include in the interoperability matrix, it is essential to understand what SharePoint Server 2007 doesn't do. After your business requirements and technical requirements have been established, it may be that in order to meet all of the requirements, you might need to plan a deployment of several products, not just SharePoint Server 2007. Having said that, however, much of the functionality you'll want will be found in SharePoint Server 2007, which means that the more specialized functions of project management or business intelligence will be found in add-on server products such as Office Project Server 2007 and Office PerformancePoint Server 2007.

Best practices are obvious here: Test, test, and test some more when integrating these different server products into a common solution. First install the base solution, SharePoint Server 2007, then install the other products and add them over time. Give your project plan room to rest between finishing the installation and deployment of one product and beginning the next product's installation and deployment. Give yourself time to stabilize, evaluate, and assess before moving along to the next software implementation.

## Plan Maintenance

Just because you initially configure and deploy SharePoint Server 2007 correctly doesn't mean that it won't need care and feeding in order to remain in top performance condition. This part of the plan should detail the regular maintenance activities for your SharePoint Server 2007 farm.

Many of these activities are already built in to your timer jobs in Central Administration. Most run at the site collection level, but others run at the Web services level. All of the jobs should be allowed to run based on their schedule, and of all the jobs are necessary to run—even if you don't understand them all. Don't delete them. They are there for a reason and need to run.

Other maintenance activities are built off of your deployment configuration choices. For example, if your deployment doesn't allow databases to grow beyond 50 GB, then a routine check of database sizes would seem to make sense. Creating new databases to accept the new site collections and their information would also be in order when the current content databases reach a certain level, such as 80 percent capacity.

As you grow in your experience and knowledge of SharePoint Server 2007, you'll find that this ongoing maintenance plan will be refined and tailored to meet your organization's individual needs. The best practice for this section is to ensure that you have a regular maintenance plan and that you're methodically and routinely working it.

## Plan Content and Navigation Structure

Regarding plan content and navigation structure, we believe that Microsoft has repeated itself in its project plan. The planning of URLs, custom master pages, and the overall taxonomy of your SharePoint Server 2007 deployment has been covered in other sections of the project plan. We suggest that your plan either move these previously discussed topics to this part of the plan or move the tasks within this part of the plan to an earlier part of the overall deployment, such as that discussed in the "Determine Preliminary Design Objectives" section.

# Deployment, Implementation, and Configuration Management

This major section deals with the creation of a POC or pilot and outlines the tasks and subtasks associated with a real deployment. Much of the planning has already been accomplished earlier in the overall deployment plan under the sections "Identify Coexistence Strategies," "Establish Test Lab Environment," and "Plan Server Configuration."

The pilot is a real implementation of all of the planning that you and your team have accomplished. The pilot is a chance to find the bugs, problems, and roadblocks that are unforeseen to a successful deployment. You'll troubleshoot these problems as needed, and then you'll move on to refine your deployment configuration choices in your project plan.

Microsoft mentions a production go/no-go decision as part of the pilot in its sample project plan. If there is a no-go decision at the end of the pilot, the chances are good that whatever is stopping the deployment has been a known element since the beginning of the project. However, there are times when difficult-to-find technical details will get in the way of a successful deployment. In such cases, every attempt to find a third-party product that will resolve the issue should be considered before the no-go decision is made. Also, don't ignore hiring a development vendor to assess the viability of modifying SharePoint Server 2007 so that the main obstacle is either resolved or worked around.

### Lessons Learned **A Customer Makes a No-Go Decision**

One of our customers had completed its project charter and initial deployment plan. Early in the life cycle of the pilot, the customer noticed that SharePoint Server 2007 didn't support (what seemed to be at the time) a minor detail in the file plan.

Specifically, this customer was accustomed to batching multiple documents into a single set and then routing the entire set through a workflow for approval. It just never occurred to the customer that SharePoint Server 2007 doesn't support this scenario out of the box. Because the development budget was extremely tight, the customer didn't have available funds to hire a development vendor who could, perhaps, have fixed this problem. Therefore, the customer was stuck with either using SharePoint Server 2007 as is and routing each document through an individual approval workflow process or using another system.

In the end, this customer selected a different system to work with because the ability to approve a set of documents in one workflow was perceived as a high value feature that the document management system needed to have. Naturally, the customer wishes it had caught this detail earlier in the evaluation process because a high number of cycles were wasted on evaluating SharePoint Server 2007. But the positive side of the pilot was that it worked: The customer was able to test SharePoint Server 2007 and concluded that it wasn't the right system for its needs.

*Bill English, Microsoft MVP, Mindsharp*

## Post-Implementation Operations, Optimization, and Business Review

After SharePoint Server 2007 has been successfully deployed, you'll find that the ongoing maintenance is essential to a successful, ongoing operation. Based on what we find in the plan, we have two best practice recommendations.

First, perform a regular restore of your farm to offline servers. You need to do this at least twice each year for several reasons. For one thing, it affirms that your backup hardware and software

are working as expected. If, for some reason, the backup solution is reporting successful backups but is not actually backing up as expected, a trial restore will reveal this problem. In addition, performing regular restores of your farm to offline servers keeps your restore skills up to date. It is not an understatement to say that learning how to do a restore for your SharePoint Server 2007 farm at the time when you need to do it in production is not a good idea. Just like an athlete practices his skills to be able to play in the championship game, so administrators need to practice restores in order to know what to do when a real disaster strikes.

Second, as mentioned previously, you need to monitor your servers on a regular basis for the same counters to build a baseline of performance numbers on how your servers are operating.

## Summary

In this chapter, we have discussed some of the best practices that relate to specific tasks found in Microsoft's sample project deployment plan. This plan can be used as a starting point for you to develop your own project plan and ensure that the best practices are both recognized and implemented in your deployment.

## Additional Resources

- DeliverPoint 2007 software and documentation: *www.deliverpoint.com*
- Microsoft Office SharePoint Server 2007 Training Standalone Edition: *http://www.microsoft.com/downloads/details.aspx?FamilyID=7bb3a2a3-6a9f-49f4-84e8-ff3fb71046df&DisplayLang=en*
- Microsoft Office SharePoint Server 2007 Training, built on the Microsoft SharePoint Learning Kit: *http://www.microsoft.com/downloads/details.aspx?FamilyID=673dc932-626a-4e59-9dca-16d685600a51&DisplayLang=en*
- Microsoft Office SharePoint Designer 2007 Training Standalone Edition: *http://www.microsoft.com/downloads/details.aspx?FamilyID=5b10f061-41d4-48ce-85cb-01d46772240d&DisplayLang=en*
- Microsoft Office SharePoint Designer 2007 Training Portal Edition: *http://www.microsoft.com/downloads/details.aspx?FamilyID=6a429664-a911-4ad3-9856-f1b0ae7a136e&DisplayLang=en*
- On the CD: Project Sample Plan.mpp file

Chapter 7

# Developing an Information Architecture

**In this chapter:**



One of the most fundamental design elements in a successful Microsoft Office SharePoint Server 2007 implementation is the underlying information architecture. Information architecture provides a common, well-understood framework for the arrangement of data. A well-considered information architecture includes how data will be structured and divided as well as how it will be presented to and navigated by users. In this chapter, you will review some key implementation motivators, architectural concepts, and lessons learned from some of the larger, more complex implementations performed.

## Common Goals

Customers often have many goals for an Office SharePoint Server 2007 implementation. Depending on the scope and scale of the project and the current or planned capabilities of the underlying network and server architecture, these goals range from delivering basic functionality to a more specific, targeted delivery of rich functionality, or anything in between.

The most common goal is having a centralized place for storing and locating data quickly, yet in conjunction with a consistent, flexible user experience that is in alignment with organizational goals. Another common goal is to provide rich capabilities for working with and providing additional metadata for both internal and external content. By providing a common set of tools and capabilities that empower content owners, reduce information technology support costs, and allow for secure access to information both inside and outside the firewall, SharePoint Server 2007 delivers built-in functionality that is capable of meeting many of these challenges. A well-considered information architecture is essential for implementation success as well as for the overall supportability and longevity of the system over time.

## Architecture Forethought

Information architecture provides necessary alignment between the organization, the users, and the arrangement of data in a way that is rigid enough to provide consistency of user experience, yet flexible enough to endure reasonable change over time. A sound foundation-based approach to information architecture includes defining how the building blocks, data, and end-user activities come together to provide a meaningful experience. Additionally, the details of your information architecture provide the manageable back-end administrative and supportable delivery of the technologies used.

Time spent up front defining a comprehensive information architecture provides a basis for controlled, gradual change over time and limits evolution-oriented "learn-as-you-go" change, which can lead to an inconsistent and unpleasant user experience.

When starting down the path toward an initial pass at your information architecture, consider the following basic questions:

- Who will be visiting a given site?
- What will they be doing within the site?
- What level of information security is necessary within the site?

These questions create a paradigm of sorts that can be used as a basis for framing the initial architecture. This paradigm can be viewed as having both horizontal capabilities and vertical segments. Each horizontal capability symbolizes a primary activity that is performed in sites of a given type. Often, each of the identified capabilities are performed by most, if not all, site participants. Vertical segments subdivide or span across capabilities to form groupings of specific capabilities that are related through application. To apply this theory in practice, imagine the common capability of collaboration and its practical vertical application among salespeople who need information about new products or calling scripts, for example. The next section, "Information Architecture Foundations," describes these categories in more detail.

### Inside Track **Who Owns Information Architecture in a SharePoint Deployment?**

The information architect can be a single person or a group of people, possibly the same group that designed your Active Directory directory services organizational unit (OU) structure. Has that taxonomy worked out? Maybe the group that designed the public folder hierarchy should own information architecture. Is that a touchy subject? Even Distributed File System (DFS) has a namespace with DFS roots and targets, which have limitations and choices with usability considerations. Did you go with product lines, functional, organizational, regional, or simple buckets?

SharePoint consultants stay very busy helping customers figure out this space. Hopefully, you won't just throw it over the fence and hope someone gets it right. They probably won't, and a year or two down the road, someone in IT will be researching how to split databases and move site collections to sites or vice versa. They may even need to tell departments that they no longer have their own Web application–it has been consolidated into a single portal through which they have their own site collection, or they have a site on the portal (a tab in the navigation with the powerful inheritance model).

In a world where SharePoint was growing in leaps and bounds and was even exponential in growth the first year, having site creation go through IT added little value. Many chose to allow employees to create sites for projects and teams and, later on for document and meeting workspaces. These types of sites were ad hoc in nature. However, portals, knowledge management, and document management structured sites required an approval process. The business needed to show it was committed by allocating budget and resources for business development, design, and business processes. Once a business commitment has been made, you can begin to talk about how IT can help meet business goals and where you'll put a portal in the development queue.

At Microsoft, a software development company with nearly 100 percent information workers, it made sense to enable self-service creation (SSC) on a namespace with a defined quota, where ownership, secondary ownership, site descriptions, and other metadata were captured during site creation. Search would later be driven by this list of sites and URLs.

*Joel Oleson, Senior Technical Product Manager, Microsoft*

# Information Architecture Foundations

As is often the case in today's business environment, there are countless advantages to considering the specific capabilities that provide value for a customer, whether internal or external, and packaging or combining those capabilities into product/service offerings that meet specific business needs. An implementation of SharePoint Products and Technologies can also benefit from this sort of model in that specific groupings of functionality can be assembled to meet specific, predetermined business needs and usage scenarios. This provides simplicity in the way the business both views and selects the widget needed to solve a specific problem. Most often, these groupings are expressed as Site Definitions and/or Site Templates within Microsoft Windows SharePoint Services 3.0 or SharePoint Server 2007.

Figure 7-1 illustrates how the out-of-the-box categories (feature sets) in SharePoint Server 2007 come together to create a functioning model that automates simple, single-step operations for users, while allowing smaller teams with more limited needs to work effectively without becoming overwhelmed by the architecture.

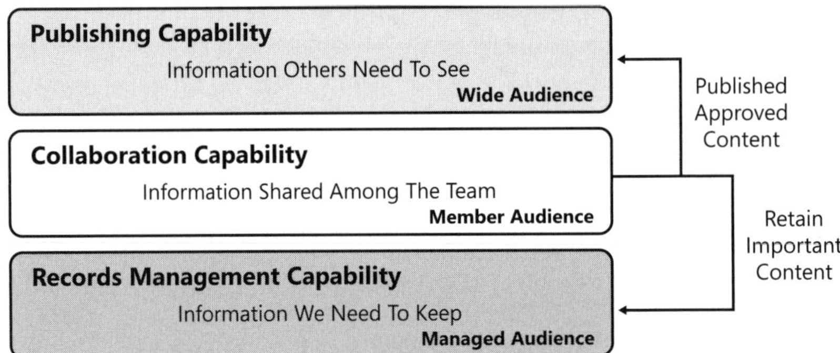


**Figure 7-1** SharePoint Server 2007 capability areas

Let's explore each of these features in more detail. We want to better understand how each feature offers a unique set of capabilities and how those capabilities integrate with other features to create a seamless user experience while providing effective movement of content between features. We will cover the following features:

- Publishing
- Collaboration
- Records Management
- Content Movement
- Opportunity Defined
- Going Vertical
- Shared Services

## Publishing

The Publishing capability consists largely of the features and functionality built into SharePoint Server 2007 from prior versions of Content Management Server. Largely, this is the capability specifically used for the dissemination of information to a targeted, wider audience. Content is often published to these areas through content deployment technologies, such as those built into the SharePoint Server 2007 API or those available from third-party vendor product offerings. See Chapter 13, "Creating and Managing Publishing Sites," for more information.

For example, suppose a large project is underway, and many teams are contributing within one or many collaboration spaces. As these various teams author communications materials that provide project updates and information, they can optionally publish the documents which, pending approval, would be deployed to the associated publishing space for consumption by a wider audience. This capability and its associated site types are typified by their higher viewer-to-author ratio and less restrictive information security, although security might be controlled more closely in highly specific or specialty applications.

What do we mean by "audience?" In this case, we are referring to the group of users who visit the site and, even more importantly, have access to the site and its associated content. This should not to be confused with the audience feature of SharePoint Server 2007 used to target content. So, a wide audience would be markedly less discriminating than a member audience or a managed audience, both of which will be reviewed in more detail as we dive deeper into the remaining capabilities.

## Collaboration

The Collaboration capability of SharePoint Server 2007 is by far the most popular among users, and it is where most of the real action happens in the majority of information management implementations. This is where users are actively engaged with the creation and update of both document and list item content. Figure 7-1 notes that the audience for collaboration spaces is a member audience, meaning that most, if not all, users who have access to this type of site are actively participating in the contribution or management of content. Returning to the project example used earlier, these sites are where the project subteam members spend most of their time creating, editing, and reviewing document and list item content, such as calendar events, tasks, and so on.

Collaboration sites are often viewed as team spaces, with an average membership between 5 and 50 users. The more emphasis placed on this area from a design perspective, the greater the return for the overall implementation effort as well as the long-term viability of the architecture. In larger organizations where process architectures exist for common activities, such as the management of projects, assets, and checklists, it is often easiest to base the initial content layout and functionality on the available information. If an organization has a well-known process for managing projects, sites created by users for the purpose of performing project work using this process should, by default, provide many of the familiar tools, terms, and elements of the process architecture. This makes both the design and the end-user experience easier to create and accept. It also allows improvements in the process architecture to be easily translated into updates of the associated site types.

## Records Management

The Records Management capability in SharePoint Server 2007 provides a unique set of features that, when viewed together, allow for the identification, retention, and ultimate disposition of high-value document content. This is an often-overlooked aspect of an information architecture because, historically, both the people and the technology used to perform the tasks associated with this capability have not been involved in the selection and implementation of organization-wide collaboration/publishing tools. In an age of unparalleled information risk and with many organizations placing an emphasis on information protection, it is more important than ever to look at this foundation-level function carefully. It is a common mistake for those implementing technology to overlook, or even avoid, records management. The information stored and created by users via the two aforementioned capabilities is at risk of both unintentional deletion and being located in sites that themselves need to be life-cycled over time. Records Management sites have a managed audience in that a controlled group of users, who perform specific roles related to the information life cycle, have tailored access to the site in order to perform the various tasks associated with their role.

A best practice to combat these risks is to place high-value information in a separate, secure storage location, thereby allowing that site and the high- and low-value information it contains to be removed when no longer needed or used. The Records Center site provides these services to other sites by way of the Official File Web Service. This Web service allows a Records Center site to receive content from other publishing and collaboration sites as well as from any Web service–enabled application. Once the file is received, it passes through a filter-like routing table, which contains a set of business rules by which the incoming file is classified and filed, in accordance to a pre-defined Enterprise FilePlan. The Document Center is another storage location for completed documents that do not qualify as official records but still need to be accessible to a wider audience.

> **Note** An *Enterprise FilePlan* is a document that lists all of the types of information your organization creates or captures during the course of operations. Some, but not all, of this content will be considered a record, while other types of information might be considered a record once having met specific criteria, such as having been published, reaching a major version, or reaching a specific point in the information life cycle. Often, a good starting point for an Enterprise FilePlan is your organization's retention schedule.

Because the file and its associated metadata are stored separately but remain related, it is possible to reclassify the file as needed without disturbing its disposition schedule. The Records Center site also provides additional interfaces and workflows for managing preservation holds on specific information as well as a set of workflows specific to maintaining and disposing information. An additional add-on pack for Records Center is available, which greatly increases this capability and brings the Records Management feature of SharePoint Server 2007 into compliance with the DOD 5015.2 standards (Department of Defense industry standards for records management systems).

> **More Info** You can find more information on the Records Center add-on pack at *http://office.microsoft.com/en-us/sharepointserver/HA102314141033.aspx.*
>
> For more information on the Microsoft Solutions Framework, go to *http://www.microsoft.com/msf.* For more information on the Microsoft Operations Framework, go to *http://www.microsoft.com/mof.*

## Content Movement

For Publishing, Collaboration, and records manager to work together as a seamless system, you must make the movement of content from one site type in a vertical segment to another as transparent as possible. Returning to the project example, when users participating in the Collaboration sites decide they need an item published so that it becomes available within a Publishing site, they will send the document to a location in the appropriate companion site.

There are a number of ways this can happen. The easiest, but most user-intensive, option is to train users to utilize the Auto-Copy feature of SharePoint Server 2007, which is exposed via the Edit Control Block of a document library as Send To > Other Location. This allows a user to specify the URL of the destination library, after which a linked copy of the document will be sent to that library. The user will have an option to have future updates to the source document automatically update the destination document. It is also possible to set up a default Custom Send To location setting for each document library, which might specify a predefined companion library. Additional options also exist, such as content deployment paths, third-party content replication and deployment tools, and document library event handlers.

You can move content to secure Records Management sites by using many of the methods described earlier. However, it is a generally accepted best practice to use the Official File Web Service, which is the Records Center's cross-application in-basket. This Web service accepts the document itself, along with any metadata, audit details, and actions performed on the document. Specific, pre-configured content types that have been identified as high-value information are configured and made available to end-users through the settings of individual document libraries. There are two primary methods of automating this one-way push of content to the records repository that don't require user interaction.

The first option is to configure high-value record content types with a custom workflow, which includes a final step that calls the *SendToOfficialFile* method. This workflow could be triggered by a document event, such as when a document reaches a major version. The second method involves event handlers on the document library list that detects specific conditions, such as a major version, check-in action, or publishing action, after which the workflow fires to process the document. The URL of the records repository can be set at the farm level through Central Administration. However, it is often preferable to store this URL at the Web application, site collection, or site level using a Property Bag property or list item so that the management of the preferred records repository is more specific to the areas served. The SharePoint Server 2007 Software Development Kit (SDK) and ECM Starter Kit include samples and code to get you on the way to creating these solutions for your implementation. You can find more information on the SharePoint Server 2007 SDK samples at *http://go.microsoft.com/?linkid=6162309*.

## Opportunity Defined

SharePoint Server 2007 ships with ready-made templates for Publishing, Collaboration, and Records Management. These templates provide a feel for the functional expression of the underlying system capability that is available without modifications or heavy configuration. To identify the opportunities that will produce the greatest return for the business, you will need to engage the business stakeholders with the goal of collecting quality feedback, which can then be used to align the technology capabilities with well-identified business needs. It is important that these business stakeholders be individuals with a high level of operational understanding and experience.

One of the most critical aspects of collecting quality feedback from these individuals is the creation and distribution of clear, concise, and effective communications. If financially feasible, it is a best practice to have a dedicated individual or team that is specifically tasked with the collection of this feedback to ensure that proper care is given to both the communications and the collection methods.

The most frequently used methods for collecting business stakeholder feedback include surveys, interviews, and joint sessions. Best practice is to employ a mixture of these methods. For example, you could start with a series of brief interviews with pre-identified stakeholders, followed by a medium-length survey that summarizes the findings common among interview responses, after which a series of joint sessions would be scheduled to explore each of the well-identified opportunities. Expect these sessions to be highly interactive, as each representative of the business holds a somewhat different view of what is important and what kind of system benefits would be most useful to them and their constituents. The final result of these exercises should yield a short list of immediate targets or *vertical segments*. These vertical segments intersect with the horizontal capability layers described earlier in the chapter.

## Going Vertical

While most general implementation opportunities identified will span all three capabilities of the platform, niche or process-specific implementation opportunities might intersect only one or two platform capabilities. For example, a common vertical segment is projects. The project site vertical segment crosses all three of the categories, so a specific business customer might elect to use one, two, or all of the available feature/functionality mixtures provided by each category. A given project may require only the ability to collaborate on project tasks and documents. A different project might require Collaboration capabilities, but also need Publishing and Records Management capability.

By providing a consistent and measurable set of capabilities for a specific vertical segment, both initial adoption as well as return service usage will benefit. Assuming that you implement these products using Site Definitions as opposed to Site Templates, users might even share their own versions or enhancements to the provided base product with other users, which in turn will help improve the product over time. Figure 7-2 illustrates how a few example segments might overlay the categories shown in Figure 7-1.

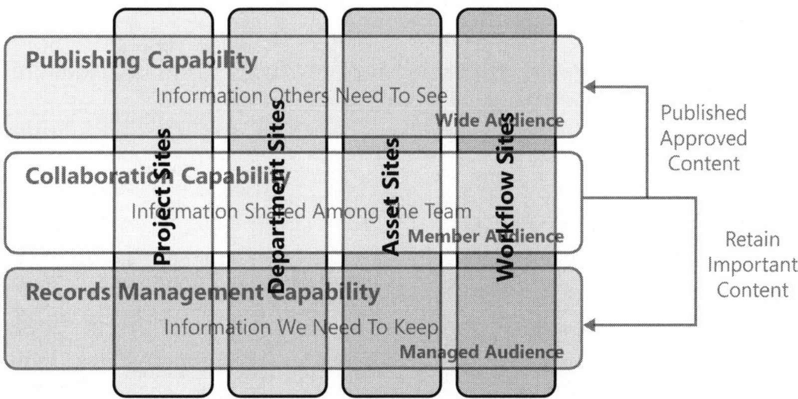


**Figure 7-2** Base architecture categories with example segments shown

## Shared Services

Core services, such as Regional Shared Services Providers, My Sites, Search, and Application Servers, might also be offered in a product/services model to create ubiquity in organizations that are spread out managerially or geographically. When doing so, pay special attention to the limitations of using Shared Services Providers in distributed environments, and avoid consumption of Shared Services across WAN links. Some implementations even include the provisioning of My Site for every user in the organization as part of their user setup routine. While this certainly is not required, it may prove helpful in fostering adoption of the technology within your environment, as many users see their personal site as a place where they can safely learn to use the technology prior to contributing content to shared collaboration sites.

> **More Info** For more information on Supporting Information Architecture with Windows SharePoint Services Manageability Controls, go to *http://go.microsoft.com/fwlink/?LinkId=92896&clcid=0x409*.

> ### Inside Track **Why Is Information Architecture Such a Challenge?**
>
> One of the most common planning topics that can cause a SharePoint deployment to stall is the lack of planning around information architecture. Worse, either an over-ambitious or under-specified information architecture and management plan that is not thoroughly piloted with little thought to change management can easily cause deployments to fail. So why is information architecture such a challenging topic?
>
> Complexity exponentially increases as the scope of the solution increases. If you are planning a small deployment of SharePoint—maybe for a single team, small department, or small business—planning can be relatively straightforward. If you are deploying SharePoint as an enterprise-wide knowledge management solution, especially for companies

that operate globally with complex operating models, the planning process will most likely take weeks and will involve a large number of participants to help identify the requirements of the solution.

There is no right answer. One question we are frequently asked when helping our customers plan their SharePoint deployments is, "How does Microsoft do it?" Although looking toward how other companies have implemented SharePoint can help start the information architecture planning process, it does not alleviate a project team from doing the appropriate diligence and executing the process themselves. There is no one- size-fits-all architecture; what works well for one company may not work for another. Differing cultures, operating models, information worker technical expertise, solution objectives, and functional requirements can drive architecture in completely different directions.

The architecture will mature over time whether you like it or not. It is a rare event to find a Microsoft customer who has used technologies such as SharePoint for more than a few years who has not been through one or more portal re-architecture projects. The reason for this is simple: The information architecture (and how it's implemented in SharePoint) will follow a maturity model just like any other architecture or technology in any enterprise. There is a tendency to try to avoid these maturity growth spurts by trying to come up with an architecture that is perfect on day one. The danger in this approach is never shipping a solution due to never-ending design churn.

So what should you do when it comes to planning your information architecture? The following are a few tips.

### Plan the Process of Designing Information Architecture

An organization may have many different information architectures depending on the scope of the solution, but the process of designing those architectures will be fairly consistent. For example, an intranet portal's information architecture may be different than the information architecture of a large project portal, but the process one goes through to design the architecture will generally be the same. Proactively developing a planning process and adding refinements over time will significantly reduce the amount of time to deploy an information management solution.

It is critical to identify key solution stakeholders and ensure their involvement throughout the planning process. The planning process starts with the identification and alignment of stakeholders by creating a well-articulated information management vision. Stakeholders not only represent the business interests but also IT leadership.

Representation of various business constituencies and the size of the team will be determined by the scope of the solution. It is important for project teams to understand that information architecture directly impacts the way in which people interact with and manage information, and this can be a highly sensitive subject. Without a shared and established vision, an organization runs the risk that the developed solution does not meet the business needs and may result in a loss of productivity.

**Set the Solution Scope Early**

It is absolutely necessary to ensure that the stakeholders understand and agree to the scope of the solution, as this will guide the design. A well-defined scope and the processes to manage scope should be used as a rationale to modify the design and to eliminate features that are introducing too much risk into the project. One scenario where this happens is when a project constituency lobbies for a sophisticated, event-driven business rules engine to auto-populate the attributes defined in a document ontology. A feature like this can take a considerable amount of time to plan, design, and develop and may introduce significant risk to the project. Having a well-defined scope can help avoid introducing inappropriate risks.

**Apply Appropriate Levels of Planning and Governance**

A SharePoint site that is deployed for an organization's intranet requires much more planning and governance than a collaborative team site for a small team. Site attributes such as size, intended purpose, audience, and business criticality will determine appropriate levels of planning and governance.

**Understand the Challenges in Implementing the Architectural Vision**

Avoid designing an architecture that cannot be implemented given the constraints of the technology, time, and resources. If an organization does not have the experience or capability in implementing the vision, it is important to get some outside assistance. A little consulting will go a long way.

**Test Designs Early and Often When Planning a Large or Complex Information Architecture**

Focus groups, including end-users and business leaders, should be utilized to help validate the design. Ensure that the architecture is intuitive and easy to understand.

**Plan for Change**

SharePoint is best implemented in a model that empowers the owners of information to manage and maintain the information architecture. A recommended practice is to start with a simple design and then provide site owners with policies, procedures, and best practices that allow them to evolve their information architecture over time.

*Tom Wisnowski, Senior Consultant, Microsoft Consulting Services*

# Information Arrangement

Once a basis for the site types has been determined in conjunction with the specific functionalities to be provided, it is important to determine how different types of information or entities will be represented in each permutation of a given site type. For example, should a site exist for each project, only specific types of projects, or is this left to the user's discretion? Perhaps projects within the organization are classified into larger flagship projects that are of significant strategic value and smaller, shorter, single-team projects aimed at accomplishing only a few key objectives. It might be determined that the larger flagship projects require their own site collection with one subsite per subteam, whereas the smaller, single-team projects can be expressed in a single subsite within an existing site collection. These conventions provide the basis for organization-specific information management fundamentals and usage guidance. See Chapter 5, "SharePoint Server 2007 and Governance," for more information technology governance information.

Once the entities have been defined for the various permutations of a given site type, you can begin to determine what information types might exist within each. An *information type* is a well-defined classification of information that you expect to be stored or created within a site. In most cases, these information types are specific kinds of document content you expect to accommodate within a site, but they could also be list items, pages, and so on. Later in the chapter, you will take a closer look at how these information types can be arranged to create various permutations of document libraries, content types, and Site Columns.

# Information Context

Context provides a representation of the information that aligns with the way people view the work they do and the information created as a result of that work. Therefore, the three elements of the context equation are people, work, and information. When we consider that all organizations derive value from the information created during the course of operations, we begin to view the information as a type of asset–an *information asset*. Information assets are not unlike other assets from a life cycle perspective in that they enter into existence, are maintained, and are eventually removed.

Because an information asset can enter the architecture only by way of a system, service, or application for which a specific person or group is responsible, the *people* portion of the context equation is easily determinable in most cases. The *work* portion of the context equation is where the most difficulty tends to be encountered when a sound information architecture is created. The concept of work often means different things to different people, groups, and organizations. By leveraging the building blocks described earlier in this chapter, SharePoint Server 2007 provides tremendous flexibility when expressing the context of a given information asset in the system. For example, content types, Site Columns, and lists can be combined in many different ways to express the context of information assigned to, or contained within, them. Example scenarios that illustrate these concepts are provided later in this chapter.

Best practice for creating a meaningful information context within your information architecture is to use a pluggable, building blocks–based design approach that does the following:

- Allows for the significant diversity that can exist in highly distributed organizations or across business functions.
- Provides any single group the ability to get started quickly and with minimal training.

- Provides overall design consistency, while promoting the unique capabilities and work styles of any given workgroup.
- Provides a contextually clear user experience, making it easy for users to understand the significance of a piece of information as well as the context necessary to find or store information quickly, clearly, and easily.

## User Interface and Branding

Although branding may be governed by a set of standards separate from those usually considered core to information management, how users interact with the application interface should be a major focus of the design and development life cycle. In some cases, this may require amending these standards or possibly even creating a new set of standards for pages rendered by Windows SharePoint Services 3.0. For example, it may be decided that all pages rendered within collaboration sites should present the corporate logo in the top right corner of each end-user facing page, as well as some additional adjustments to the style sheets that control the display of the navigational menus. Another example might be the addition of footer information for each page rendered that includes information about the author, department, or site in which the page is located. It is also important to understand how specific functionality will be rendered to the user by making or restricting access to specific list types, Site Templates, and so forth. See Chapter 11, "Branding and Customization," for more information on branding best practices.

## Usability and Acceptance

As with any design element, it is important to review your information architecture design periodically throughout the entire design life cycle, especially during prototyping, with a group of predetermined stakeholders. Even more importantly, you should review the proposed design with sample groupings of the user population that is representative of the business.

After the design is complete and well vetted, it's time to test-drive the design. A great way to do this is to provide a preselected group of users with an initial pilot experience. Use this time to confirm that their movement through the experience is as they expected. Once this initial pilot is complete, consider providing the pilot to an expanded audience that includes additional, randomly selected users from the business. This is where you can expect to get some of the most valuable feedback because these additional users will be exposed to the system for the first time. Create usage, scenario-based scripts to guide the user and capture valuable feedback.

Once a successful pilot has been completed, it's time to perform a post-pilot review of the feedback to determine if the design is ready for deployment. If the resulting feedback is overwhelmingly negative, it might be time to consider a design reset. It is far less painful, both economically and psychologically, to go back and re-evaluate the design prior to deployment. If implementation defects are uncovered during the pilot exercise, be sure these issues are addressed before attempting to deploy to end-users. If the resolution of these defects involves any changes in the user experience or if the presence of the defect created a situation where the user was unable to experience the design in its entirety, the pilot should be performed again upon the resolution of these defects.

## Emergent Capability

Information architecture provides the basis for which future organizational innovation, change, and adaptation can occur, so long as there is a structural cohesiveness to the approach for storing and arranging information. By providing a platform-level convention for performing the tasks associated with the addition of sites, workspaces, namespaces, and even the information itself, you are creating immediate added value while laying the groundwork for emergent capability. So what is the difference between added value creation and the creation of emergent capability?

An *emergent capability* is a new capability that is created as the result of a functioning system that was not present by simply adding together the value created by each individual component of that system. By combining the added value of multiple functionalities, new capabilities manifest, often unexpectedly. For example, by simply possessing or creating all of the individual components that make up an automobile, one goes nowhere. Only after all of those components are assembled in a highly specific manner does the additional capability of transportation emerge. Adding air conditioning or a radio to the automobile might add additional value, but these components are not required for transportation. Remove the rear tires, though, and you have problems. The extensible value delivery mechanism described in this section illustrates the power of information architecture. Information architecture provides highly specific, predefined arrangements for how each of the primary elements (components) in a system fit together to create intended added value. The resulting flexibility and availability of solution options, when properly reinforced, lends to the long-term creation of additional secondary and tertiary system capabilities that were neither planned nor expected but are nevertheless of significant value.

## Information Architecture Building Blocks

This section provides a brief overview of the basic building blocks available for use when designing and building an information architecture. This is not an exhaustive review of each, but rather a simplified review of how each type of object fits into the overall architecture. This prerequisite knowledge is necessary in order to understand how these types of objects can be used to build an information architecture that is usable and sustainable over time. After you have reviewed these basic building blocks, you will review a few permutations of how a simple information architecture might be assembled at both the micro and macro levels. With these examples as a backdrop, you will examine how you might add new sites to an implementation employing this architecture. The following list presents these building blocks and describes each block at a high level by listing a few defining properties and/or constraints.

- Web Application
  - Defined within a farm
  - Topmost object within the hierarchy and the native container of the topmost site collection
  - Representative of a specific Microsoft Internet Information Services (IIS) Web site and defines a specific IIS application scope
  - Has no visual presentation within the user interface and is in no way visually apparent to the end-user
  - Can be extended into multiple zones
- Zone
  - Defined within a Web application
  - Allows users to access the same Web site through separate and independent URLs
  - Has its own load-balanced URL (protocol, host header, and port)
  - Allows for many configurations (multiple authentication stores, caching scenarios, content databases, or custom HTTP modules)
- Managed Path
  - Defined within a Web application
  - Used to incorporate a second tier of top-level site collections
  - Implements either an explicit inclusion (allows you to assign an explicit URL that is appended to the path, e.g., *http://fabrikam.com/dept*) or a wildcard inclusion (automatically assigns a path name, e.g., *http:// fabrikam.com /depts/*)
- Site Collections
  - Defined within a managed path
  - Are the native containers of Office SharePoint Server 2007 sites
  - Contain a single top-level site that in turn may contain any number of child sites
  - Enforce specific feature and security boundaries that cannot be inherited or discovered by a parent or child site collection
  - The top-level site collection in a Web application may contain site collections through the use of managed paths
  - Features that are bound within a site collection and cannot be shared include global navigation, branding, security groups, content types, content sharing Web parts, site aggregation Web parts, usage reports, alert management, and workflows
- Subsites
  - Defined within a site collection

- May share navigation between sites
- May inherit permissions from parent sites
- Allow for the sharing of lists between sites
- Allow for the sharing of design elements (such as themes or styles) between sites

## Lower-Level Data Objects

In addition to the higher-level objects that are used to create the macro architecture, a small, yet equally important set of lower-level objects are used to create and construct the list, libraries, and classification mechanisms within individual sites. A portion of these lower-level elements will be configured by the end-user on an as-needed basis. The goal of the architecture should be to provide end-user workgroups with as many of the feedback-derived elements as possible without creating unnecessary elements.

The item-level storage of individual documents and list entries in SharePoint Server 2007 is made possible through the configuration arrangement of the following four building blocks:

- Content Types (defined within a site collection or subsite)
  - Represent a unique data type
  - May be extended as needed over time
  - May be inherited so as to create new derived data types, allowing for both specificity and simplified management
- Site Columns or Fields (defined within a site collection, subsite, or list configuration)
  - Represent a property of a unique data type
  - May be added/altered over time
  - Provide granular selection and optional required entry of metadata
- Lists (defined within a site)
  - Represent a collection of individual items (data) that are stored by users of the system
  - Provide further requirement-specific configuration capabilities
  - May contain heterogeneous data–items of different content types, with their associated Site Column specifications
  - Can provide additional enhanced functionalities such as information management policy, access control, and workflow, if available and configured
- List Items (defined within a list)
  - The basic data content building blocks; used for storing individual pieces of information

- ❑ Represent a unique instance of defined content type
- ❑ Provide for storage of the unique instance's metadata, security, versions, and workflow executions

## Macro Example

The following example brings many of the design elements discussed in this chapter together in a cohesive manner. The conceptual architecture is shown in Figure 7-3. Figure 7-4 illustrates how you might use the provided building blocks to implement portal and project collaboration services. Specifically, this example:

- Combines the following:
  - ❑ SharePoint building blocks
  - ❑ Well-defined requirements based on comprehensive customer feedback
  - ❑ Generated or feedback-derived taxonomies and metadata elements
- To create the following:
  - ❑ Site collection hierarchy
  - ❑ Common content type hierarchy
  - ❑ Common Site Column definitions
- Expresses content as the following:
  - ❑ Sites: Provide the frame in which people come together to work toward a common objective (shown in Figure 7-3)

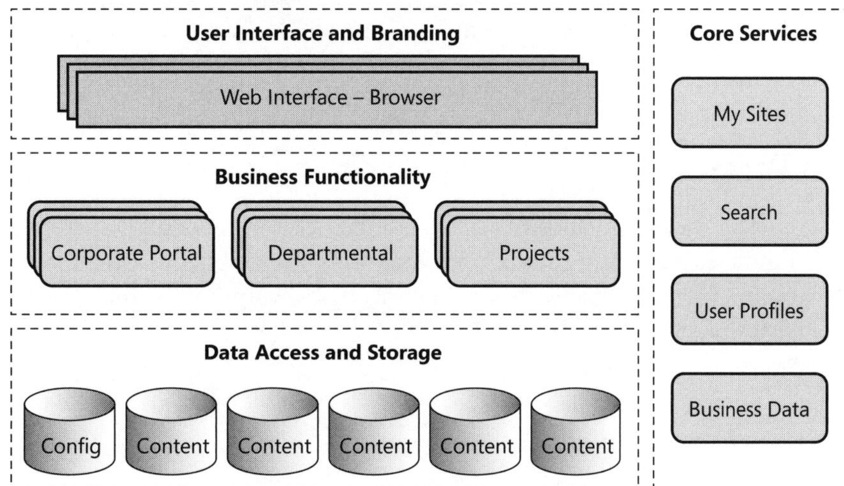


**Figure 7-3** Macro view of example architecture

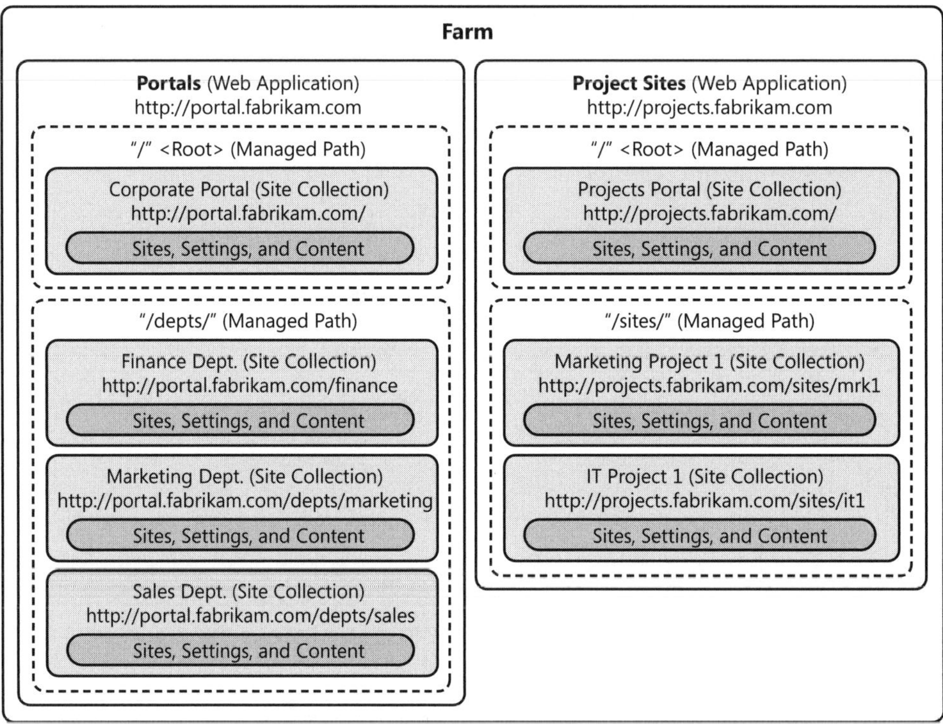


**Figure 7-4** Example of how to use the provided building blocks to implement the portal and project collaboration services

- Content Types: Represent functions performed by people as information outputs generated during the course of their work together (shown in Figures 7-5, 7-6, and 7-7)
- Site Columns (metadata): Provide the granular ability to define those outputs as being related to other entities, items, or designations of significance in a meaningful way (shown in Figures 7-5, 7-6, and 7-7)

## Micro Permutations

Each of the permutations illustrates different possibilities for combining the building blocks described with gathered feedback-derived information types. Each permutation represents an option for how information could be arranged within the architecture to create context and significance.

- **Entities** Something that exists as, or is perceived as, a single separate object, such as the following:
  - Department
  - Project
  - Community
  - Initiative
  - Team
  - Asset
- **Attributes** A quality, property, or characteristic of an entity, such as the following:
  - Name
  - Status
  - Identifier
  - Team
  - Asset

Note that both team and asset can exist as either an entity or an attribute. Based on the provided information architecture, an individual data item could be represented in many ways. For example, Figure 7-5, Figure 7-6, and Figure 7-7 illustrate a few of the options available for creating these representations using different building blocks.

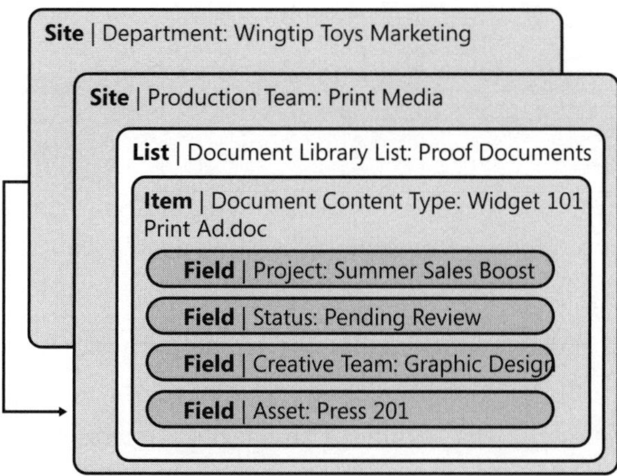


**Figure 7-5** Micro permutation 1

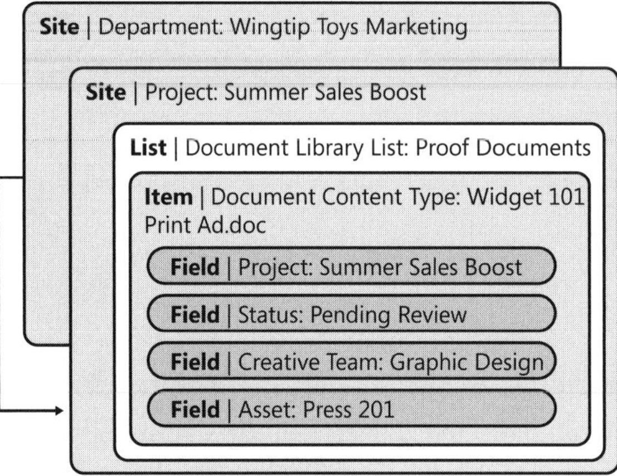


**Figure 7-6** Micro permutation 2

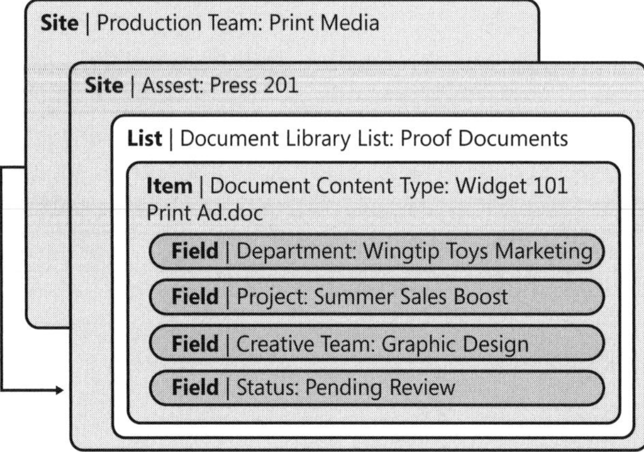


**Figure 7-7** Micro permutation 3

Of course, there are many more permutations possible for arranging this information. Information architecture provides the framework for finding and storing data by defining the following:

- Relative significance of each entity (what should be represented as a site, list, item, or field)
- Arrangement of each entity based on that significance (e.g., departments, then projects, then teams)
- Attributes for each entity, which create the contextual significance between a given item instance and other related entities or designations

## Notes from the Field **When To Use Site Collections, Managed Paths, and Web Applications**

As they consider the multitude of options available while designing an implementation of SharePoint Server 2007, customers often ask us, "When do I use a site collection...or a managed path...or a Web application?" Initially, it might seem that all of these choices are equally viable. It's a common mistake to make these choices based on what is perceived as overall design simplicity, default settings options, or even personal preferences. This is because of the assumption that the use of one object type over another is of little consequence but for the configuration effort required. Let's review some of the best practices relating to each of these object types, which will help guide us though an example.

- **Web applications** Generally, it is a best practice to limit the number of Web applications per farm as much as possible because of the individual memory requirements of each Web application. There are specific scenarios in which an additional Web application is recommended, such as where extranet access or specific Web application-wide security policy requirements differ.
- **Managed paths** More often than not, managed paths tend to be the forgotten option which, when properly used, provide the best balance between the two most common implementation mistakes: overloaded individual site collections and unnecessary Web applications.
- **Site collections** Ideally, site collections should be sized appropriate to their expected use over time. For example, if your restore capabilities and SLAs allow for only 50-GB content databases and the expected size needed for a site collection is 50 GB, this site collection should be provisioned in a dedicated content database. Where the expected use is far less, it could be placed alongside other site collections in a shared content database. The most common mistake made in choosing a new site collection as the best option is disregarding the optimum content storage capacity for a site collection in your environment.

To explain how these tips might be applied to a real-life scenario, consider the following example, which illustrates a commonplace occurrence in many environments.

Fabrikam is performing a new implementation of SharePoint Server 2007. The requirements call for a corporate-wide portal where users can go for company news, events, and announcements. In addition, Fabrikam would like for each department to have its own site where information specific to that department can be made available. Finally, there is a common need for ad hoc team sites in which term project work will be performed. Let's look at a few implementation options that meet these requirements.

**One Web Application, One Site Collection**

This is the most common trap, largely because it's the easiest to configure for both administrators as well as end-users. The problem with this approach is that, despite the ease of setting up a single site collection for the entire site hierarchy, it eventually becomes apparent that this setup is not supportable long term from a capacity perspective and provides little or no data segmentation for protecting against loss or corruption. This configuration often results in a need to split up the site collection, which can prove painful as well as difficult to coordinate effectively.

**Multiple Web Applications, Each with a Single Root Site Collection**

While this approach can provide each department with its own top-level URL (e.g., *sales.fabrikam.com*), the result is unnecessary Web applications, each with its own application pool and each consuming up to a few hundred MB of memory. It is easy to see how this configuration can quickly start to cause performance problems, especially in single-farm environments. However, because this option is complex to configure, it is rarely used.

**One Web Application, One Explicit Managed Path Site Collection per Department, One Wildcard Managed Path for Ad Hoc Sites**

In this configuration, we keep the number of Web applications to a minimum. We locate the corporate portal at the root of the Web application (e.g., *http://corp.fabrikam.com/*). We place each of the departments in its own site collection, which we locate on an explicit managed path (e.g., *http://corp.fabrikam.com/sales*). Finally, we create an additional wildcard managed path for ad hoc project sites (e.g., *http://corp.fabrikam.com/projects/*), under which we can create multiple term-use site collections, one for each project or request. This is clearly the preferred configuration for meeting the requirements.

By taking the time to align the specific requirements with the best practices provided, you can see how, with only marginal additional configurations, you can easily provide an implementation of those requirements that provides the best combination performance and long-term scalability.

*Mark Ferraz, Information Architect, SolutionsMark*

## Provisioning

The provisioning of additional objects within the architecture is a function of the request process as defined by the governance model, as well as the framework and conventions provided by the architecture. Based on the provided example architecture and the nature of the request for additional services, a short list of alternatives for provisioning the request can usually be generated via a quick review of Figure 7-3.

In cases where a clearly preferred alternative is not apparent, the usual culprit is a lack of detail in the request, but there will be occasions when you have multiple options for satisfying a request. In keeping with the example architecture, you can see that requests for additional departmental portal sites will be satisfied by simply adding a new site collection in the Web application for Portals under the /depts/ managed path. Portal sites in your architecture, as in most, will likely be controlled by a request to reduce site sprawl. If you need multiple site collections for each department, you could achieve this by creating a managed path for each department under which all of that department's site collections would exist.

## Self-Service

Requests for new project collaboration sites might be handled by way of self-service site creation, which can be enabled at the Web application level. Self-service site creation allows for the provisioning of new site collections by end-users on an as-needed basis. In our example, this is ideal for project collaboration sites, because new projects, both big and small, are started frequently and need new sites right away. It is important to set up the appropriate quotas and locks, as well as deletion notifications, to prevent a storage overload.

The underlying Site Templates and definitions could include business rules that seamlessly pump content to your Records Center sites to ensure that official record content is always safe from deletion. Enable self-service site creation from Central Administration via the Self-Service Site Management settings link under Application Administration, as shown in Figure 7-8. The option to require a secondary contact can be useful, as both contacts will receive notifications regarding the site.

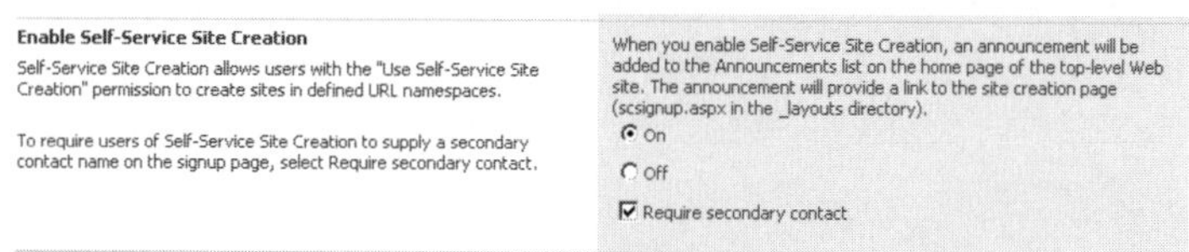


**Figure 7-8** Enabling self-service site creation

# Summary

In this chapter, we highlighted the importance of having a well thought-out information architecture. We reviewed and discussed the building blocks available for creating an information architecture. We also reviewed the primary capabilities provided within SharePoint Server 2007 and discussed common usage scenarios and how they might be approached when defining an information architecture. Lastly, we reviewed some specific features and processes you can use to make it easier for users to leverage your information architecture in a meaningful way.

# Additional Resources

- Determine the information architecture for your site: *http://technet.microsoft.com/en-us/library/cc262873.aspx*

- Design global information architecture and governance: *http://technet.microsoft.com/en-us/library/cc262196.aspx*
- Logical information architecture model: *http://technet.microsoft.com/en-us/library/cc261995.aspx*

# Part II
# Building

**In this part:**

Chapter 8

# Document Management

**In this chapter:**



One of the core functions that Microsoft Office SharePoint Server 2007 is purchased to implement is document and records management. Office SharePoint Products and Technologies has grown from being merely a document collaboration system to one that supports a solid document management implementation.

Because of the increase in complexity of the platform from Microsoft Office SharePoint Portal Server 2003 to SharePoint Server 2007, design and planning issues are also more complex. And with the return of major/minor versioning in SharePoint Server 2007 that we had in Microsoft SharePoint Server 2001, along with the advent of a Records Center that appends each record's name with a unique string of characters plus the added list features and functionalities that are available with a document library, the need to plan and design how documents and records will be managed in your environment has never been more important.

Document collaboration differs from document management in that it allows individuals to asynchronously develop a single document from a single location into a finished product without much concern about what happens to that document within a defined document life cycle. Document management, on the other hand, is concerned about applying governance rules to documents, defining the life cycle of that document, and differentiating between unofficial and official communications. It is concerned about such life-cycle issues as where a document is incubated and developed, where a document is hosted once it is considered official, compliant communication, and how a document will be expired. It is concerned with tracking the "who did what" to the document during certain stages of that document's life cycle. And it is concerned about ensuring that there is only one version of the truth for that document's contents at any given time.

In this chapter, along with document management concepts and their implementation in SharePoint Server 2007, we will discuss some topics that are more collaborative in nature. We will cover these topics only because they support our larger mission in this chapter—namely, to understand document and records management best practices in SharePoint Server 2007. We'll discuss the concept of a document life cycle and will then use that life cycle as a template for how documents are managed within the SharePoint Server 2007 platform. The chapter's flow will follow the life cycle of a document.

But first, we need to understand what a document is and what document management is. Let's start by defining document.

## What Is a Document?

If you were to do much reading in the document management field, you would soon realize that this is a persistent and pesky question. The accepted definition of document is constantly evolving, and our traditional views of documents are difficult to apply in the electronic age. For example, is a .wmv (Windows Media) file a document? Is an .msg file (e-mail message) a document? Some limit the definition of document to communication that is legally compliant or otherwise official. Others broaden the definition to encompass *any* communication—written or electronic—that has been recorded in any format. So using this latter definition, a Post-it note with some scribble on it would be considered a document. Now, don't laugh. One author of this book knows of a municipality in Minnesota that requires every written communication to be indexed and warehoused for seven years, including Post-it notes.

For our purposes in this chapter, we'll consider the term *documents* as mainly referring to Microsoft Office Word, Microsoft Office Excel, or Microsoft Office PowerPoint files, both electronic and hard copy. While Web pages, e-mails, voice mails, and other electronic forms of communication are also considered documents, it would muddy the waters too much to try to discuss these various document types in this chapter. For illustrative purposes, we'll stick with the Microsoft Office suite as our platform in which we'll work with documents. How documents are defined in your organization is up to you, but it is a conversation that should not be avoided. Why? Because if it is not a document, then it may not need to be managed.

## What Is Document Management?

*Document management* is the process of applying policies and rules to how documents are created, persisted, and expired within an organization. *Document collaboration* is merely the process of checking out, checking in, and versioning a document before it is published. Windows SharePoint Services gives you document collaboration, whereas SharePoint Server 2007 gives you document management. *Records management* encompasses all of the functions of document management, but applies those functions to a broader set of content elements—not just documents. Any electronic record, such as a list item or log entry, can be managed as a record in SharePoint Server 2007 if there is a need to do so.

Normally, a document management system (DMS) is used to manage documents. SharePoint Server 2007 forms the basis of an intermediate-level DMS. It is not an advanced system for DMS because it lacks several features that more robust DMSs include, such as:

- Pruning a document's lineage to create a new line of documents
- Grafting dissimilar document pedigrees into a document set that is treated as a single unit
- Managing a set of documents as a single record set
- Working with linked documents that are hosted in other repositories
- Attaching a unique document number to the document that doesn't change its name

### Notes from the Field **When Another DMS Is the Best Choice**

I was working with a customer who had 1,300 users in the oil and gas industry. This customer had already implemented another DMS and was also in the process of implementing SharePoint Server 2007. During our two-day design and architecture engagement, we spent roughly an hour outlining the customer's document management needs that formed the basis of a matrix of customer needs relative to the document management features in SharePoint Server 2007.

At one point, this customer said something to the effect that the documents created by the company's field engineers (as part of the process of pumping oil out of the ground) needed to be grouped together into a document set, and then the set needed to be treated as a single unit in the DMS while the documents remained as individual items.

My suggestion was that the customer place these documents into a single document library or into a single folder within a document library (even though I don't like the use of folders) and then treat those documents as a single unit that way. The customer's response was that the *set of documents* needed to be routed through the company's internal processes and approval workflows, which is something that SharePoint Server 2007 simply doesn't do without custom coding. Since the customer was not going to implement custom coding for documents in Phases I or II of deployment, the company decided to stick with its current DMS and take a wait-and-see attitude about performing this function after seeing the document management functionality in the next release.

*Bill English, Microsoft MVP, Mindsharp*

Generally speaking, the main aspects of managing documents through a life cycle include the following:

- **Creation** These are the methods for envisioning, initiating, and collaborating on a new document's development.

- **Location** There must be a physical location where documents will be stored and accessed. Usually, most DMSs require *single instance storage* (SIS) of a document so that there is only one version of the truth.
- **Authentication/Approval** These are the stated methods of ensuring that a document is fully vetted and approved before it is considered to be official, compliant communication from the company.
- **Workflow** This describes the series of steps needed to pass documents from one person to another for various purposes, such as to gain approval to publish the document or to collect signatures on a document.
- **Filing** In a traditional sense, we'd discuss into which filing cabinet the hard copy was placed. For electronic systems, we file a document by placing it in the physical location and then attaching metadata to the document. The metadata files the document logically by allowing the document to be found based on the metadata values assigned to the document.
- **Distribution** This describes the methods of getting the document into the hands of the intended readers.
- **Retrieval** This refers to the methods used to find the documents, such as querying the index for keywords or using search alerts to find new content that meets the query keywords.
- **Security** This refers to the methods used to ensure the document's integrity and security during the document life cycle.
- **Retention** These are the organization's policies and practices that inform everyone how long different document types are retained by the company.
- **Archiving** Similar in concept to retention, the differing characteristic is that archiving is a subset of retention policies. Archiving focuses on the long-term retention of documents in a readable format after the document's active life has ended. Subsumed in this category is the expiration of documents after they no longer need to be retained.

When we consider the features that SharePoint Server 2007 gives us, what we find is that all the document management characteristics can be implemented using this platform. Table 8-1 outlines the document management characteristics and how they are implemented in SharePoint Server 2007.

**On the Companion Media** This book's CD contains a .pdf file named SharePoint Server 2007 Document Management Poster.pdf, which will print out a 2' × 3' electronic poster on a large format printer. This poster is a graphical representation of Table 8-1. If you would like a free hard copy of this poster, you can sign up to receive one as part of the larger poster set in the premium content site at *www.mindsharp.com*.

**Table 8-1 Document Management Elements and SharePoint Server 2007 Features**

| Document Management Element | SharePoint Server 2007 Feature Support |
|---|---|
| Creation | ■ New Document button in a document library<br>■ Import a document into a document library |
| Location | ■ Documents are held in document libraries<br>■ Libraries are grouped into one or more sites<br>■ Sites are grouped into one or more site collections |
| Filing | ■ Assign metadata to the content type<br>■ Create columns in the document library |
| Retrieval | ■ Internet Explorer<br>■ Windows Explorer<br>■ Native client application<br>■ RSS<br>■ Click a link in a result set |
| Security | ■ Inherited from the document library<br>■ Directly configured on the document<br>■ Audit settings in Information Management Policies |
| Workflow and Approval | ■ Approval workflows<br>■ Collect signature workflows<br>■ Three-state workflows<br>■ Custom workflows<br>■ Require content approval library setting |
| Distribution | ■ Records Center<br>■ Document Center<br>■ Publishing<br>■ Sent to remote location<br>■ Official Records Repository (Central Administration) |
| Retention | ■ Records Center<br>■ Document Center<br>■ Team site<br>■ Expiration settings in Information Management Policies |
| Archiving | ■ Records Center<br>■ Expiration settings in Information Management Policies |

## The Document Life Cycle

In a pragmatic sense, we've outlined a generic document life cycle that can be adapted to most types of documents (refer back to Table 8-1). Spending time on the development of a document life cycle–complete with a document plan and document DDoc about key document types–will help you reduce costs and content duplications while increasing the findability of key documents. Consider these statistics:

- Over 30 *billion* original documents are used each year in the United States.
- The cost of documents to corporations is estimated to be as much as 15 percent of annual revenue.
- 85 percent of documents are never retrieved.
- 50 percent of documents are duplicates.
- 60 percent of documents are obsolete.
- For every dollar that a company spends to create a final document, 10 dollars are spent to manage the document creation process.

> **Tradeoff Short-term Costs versus Long-term Cost Savings**
>
> RFC 1925 outlines *The Twelve Networking Truths*. One of those truths is this: "Good, fast, cheap. Pick any two. You can't have all three." When it comes to implementing a robust document management solution, you'll be faced with competing and mutually exclusive forces in your organization who will want all three. It can't be done. Creating content types and DDoc (discussed later in this chapter) is both time consuming and costly. The short-term costs will need to be accepted if the long-term cost savings are to be realized. Because this is hard to quantify, you might be up against a difficult battle following the recommendations in this chapter. One way to frame your recommendations is to help the decision-makers understand that if they want a great DMS, it will not happen quickly, nor will it happen without up front costs.
>
> *Steve Smith, Microsoft MVP, Combined Knowledge, Lutterworth, UK*

Implementing a document life cycle for your documents will take time and effort, especially if no such plans have existed in your organization before. Developing *Description Documents* (DDoc)–which are documents that describe the envisioned document's focus, content, keyword descriptions, content owner and security, and other important aspects–is even more time consuming and (seemingly) not necessary if you've never done it before.

However, developing a consistent method of creating, managing, and expiring key documents in your environment will go a long way toward ensuring that documents are more easily findable as well as more compliant with current laws and regulations. Disk space usage should also be reduced because you'll minimize duplications on your network. Engaging in document management practices that contain consistent keyword metadata whose fields are assigned at the content type level will ensure that, over time, your documents are findable. Most documents are not findable because they are not adequately described or categorized. If the document isn't findable, then it might as well not exist. Information that can't be found can't be used.

In the following sections, we'll cover some of the features in SharePoint and how they support the document life cycle and document management (refer back to Table 8-1). We'll offer best practice ideas for the implementation of document management within the SharePoint Server 2007 environment and will assist you in understanding the planning and design tasks that you'll face.

## Creation

Every document must be created before it can be used. This understatement deserves some discussion because, when it comes to document management, the creation of a document is much more than going into Office Word or Office Excel and creating a new, empty document.

Indeed, many documents in your environment will not need to undergo the rigors that we'll describe in this section. However, documents that will represent official, compliant, trusted communication from your company will need to be well-designed and envisioned before they are ever created. Moreover, to the extent that you wish all documents to be easily and quickly findable, you will need to adopt the strategies discussed in this section.

The main strategy for document creation that can be employed in a DMS is the development of a DDoc, which we briefly alluded to earlier in this chapter. A DDoc lays out the focus, ownership, security, and metadata of the document that will be created. In the absence of direction, workers will make their own decisions–which could be either correct or incorrect–about document titles, metadata assignments, creation location, and content ownership. The same applies to the creation of a document. Without direction on the keywords that will describe the document, an explicit statement of who owns the content and secures the document, and an understanding of other aspects of the document's life cycle, workers will be left on their own to make these decisions in the absence of support and direction from their managers.

To be sure, some general policies regarding the DMS can be established to help inform workers' decisions when they create documents; not all policies need to be specified on a document-by-document basis. But other decisions are document specific and cannot be formed by broad policy. For example, the keyword descriptors for a document are specific to that document and should be defined in the DDoc. Possible elements of the DDoc are as follows:

- Name of the DDoc
- Date of creation of the DDoc
- Name and title of the target document it will be describing

- Name of position and/or group who will own the document
- Name of the individual responsible for the creation and development of the document
- Name of the SharePoint content type used to create the document
- Specification if this is a stand-alone document or a document that is a member of a larger set of documents; if the latter, specification of the other documents in the set and their current status in the document life cycle
- Keywords that will be used to describe the document
- Other metadata values that must be entered when the document is first saved
- Suggested retrieval methods, especially if there are any native client applications that must be installed on the desktop to retrieve the document
- Workflow information for the document, including named approvers and signatures, if needed
- Location to which the document will be published
- Statement of auditing metrics that will need to be recorded
- Statement of the useful life of the document
- Expiration information, including when and how the document will be expired
- Location to which the document will be sent for long-term archival

> **On the Companion Media** On the CD, you will find a Word 2007 document named Sample Description Document.doc. You can use this sample form as a starting point to help you develop your own DDocs for various types of documents in your environment. This form is not copyrighted, and you are free to use it as needed within your organization.

Once the DDoc has been completed, you now have a roadmap to build the document. The next step, if you talk with most authors, is to prepare the outline that describes the major parts of the document that needs to be written. After the outline is completed, it's time to create and develop the document's contents.

Essentially, you can create the document either inside or outside the document library. In both cases, you will either assign the correct content type to the document when it is uploaded into the library, or you'll use the correct content type to create the document. We prefer that it is created within the SharePoint interface so that the correct content type is used at inception. If you create a document outside of SharePoint, it is conceivable, however unlikely, that some customized metadata will have been assigned to the document before its upload into the document library and that wrong metadata would persist after the document is uploaded. Spurious metadata can result in the document appearing in the wrong result set and, at a minimum, appear out of place. This scenario can occur if a user copies an existing document outside of SharePoint, deletes all of the contents, and then starts writing the new document. In this scenario, all of the metadata will persist and will wrongly describe the new document.

For this reason, if you have gone to the lengths to describe a new document, we think that it is a best practice to create a separate content type for that document and then create the new document from that content type within SharePoint.

> **Note** Content types are discussed in more detail in Chapter 9, "Enterprise Content Management."

## Should SharePoint Replace File Servers?

Many in the SharePoint market claim that SharePoint can and should replace your file servers. Is this a best practice? Should you plan to move all of your files that currently exist into SharePoint? There are pros and cons to this debate, each of which we'll outline below. However, if you don't want to read this entire section, then you should know that our simple answer is no.

The reasons offered for replacing your file servers with SharePoint can be summarized in one thought: Collaborative file shares are on their way out because shared drives that are used for document collaboration are being replaced with SharePoint document libraries. SharePoint Server 2007 provides a better collaborative environment because of the built-in collaboration features, such as check out, check in, versioning, publishing, and single instance storage.

While SharePoint Server 2007 does provide many compelling collaboration features, there are also solid reasons to retain your file servers. First, document storage in SharePoint is generally more expensive than an NTFS file system. This cost can be mitigated to a point with the use of expiration information policies, but not completely equalized. Second, file storage is not the same thing as file collaboration. SharePoint is not a good file storage solution for all scenarios. Hence, file servers are a better storage solution in the following scenarios:

- File servers are preferred for large document storage. SharePoint best handles documents in the 50- to 300-MB range and can handle documents up to 2 GB with configuration modifications, but documents over 2 GB must be stored on a file server.
- Systems Management Service (SMS) distribution points for hotfixes, updates, and application distribution is handled much better from a file server.
- File servers are better suited for My Documents redirection and backups. Many companies use group policies to redirect the location of users' My Documents so that they can back up their content each night. Creating mapped drives to document libraries and then using policies to redirect users' My Documents to those libraries is an untested and unsupported scenario in SharePoint. File servers should be used for this purpose and are supported.

- Storing databases in a SharePoint list is the same as storing a database within a database and is not recommended. If your data need triggers or stored procedures, you may look at the workflows and events as mechanisms for this process, but creating triggers or stored procedures inside the SharePoint databases is not supported. Database type files such as .mdb, .pst, and .ost are best stored on a file server.
- Developer source control of emerging assemblies and new code files are better managed in Visual Studio Team Services, which requires a file server.
- Archive files that will not change and will not be included in future collaboration are best stored on file servers.

The final reason for retaining file servers in your server topology for the foreseeable future is that, for those documents that require long-term storage, file servers are usually a cheaper solution than SharePoint.

So when should you place files in SharePoint? In our opinion, these scenarios point to SharePoint as a great file storage solution:

- When the files need to be accessed over HTTP or HTTPS
- When the files need to be managed in a DMS
- When the files need to be engaged in a collaboration process
- When your document life cycle and governance plans are completed and reflected in technical requirements for SharePoint

After reading these lists, we hope you agree that not all file servers should be replaced with SharePoint and that you should plan to retain certain files on file servers for the foreseeable future. So what do you say to the folks who want you to migrate all of your existing content from your file servers into SharePoint?

The short answer is that unless there is a positive reason to migrate those documents into SharePoint, there is no need to spend the money, effort, and time to do so. Moving documents from one storage location to another simply because someone says you should is not a reason to move those documents. You should be able to demonstrate a value-add that moving the documents into SharePoint brings to your organization that will outweigh the costs of such a move. Admittedly, SharePoint is the popular technology, but that is precisely why cost justifications need to accompany the migration recommendations. It's easy to get on the hot technology bandwagon and find that unforeseen effects burn you down the road. We prefer a more thoughtful, steady pace toward a migration that allows time for hard questions to be answered and cost justifications to be developed.

### Notes from the Field **Replacing Your Current DMS with SharePoint Server 2007**

Many customers with whom I work ask me if they should replace their current DMS with SharePoint Server 2007. My answer always comes back to a clear description of the business requirements that formed the foundation for the decision to purchase their current document management solution. Many of these DMSs are expensive, and the decision to jettison them in favor of SharePoint Server 2007 should not be a rash decision.

I tend to ask my customers questions along the following lines:

- Does your current DMS meet all of your needs?
- Does your current DMS do some things that SharePoint Server 2007 doesn't do?
- Does SharePoint Server 2007 do something that your current DMS doesn't do?
- Is your current DMS paid for?
- Are users familiar with your current DMS's interface and functionality?
- Is there grassroots demand to move from your current DMS to SharePoint Server 2007?
- Is there any loss of functionality by moving to SharePoint Server 2007?

In my opinion, if the functionality offered by your current DMS is not surpassed by the functionality of SharePoint Server 2007, it is paid for, and it meets all of your business requirements, then I see little reason to change DMSs.

*Bill English, Microsoft MVP, Mindsharp*

Having said all this, we must point out that the usability of a SharePoint interface often requires more work (more clicks) than does a mapped drive to a file share on a file server. At the foundation of this discussion is the effect on the daily life of a non-technical knowledge worker who works with documents on an hourly basis. Frankly, in many cases, it is just plain easier to work with files in a file share than it is to work with them in a SharePoint site. This is especially true if the individual is working in the document alone and is not collaborating on the document with others. In addition, in most usability scenarios, fewer clicks are required to work with a document on a file share than in a SharePoint document library, and the interface is familiar to the end-user.

### Notes from the Field **Using SharePoint Server 2007 and File Servers Together**

Before SharePoint was released, I was one of the system administrators, or a jack-of-all-trades type of worker. Because many of you have a large selection of technologies that you need to administrate, some technologies tend to get overlooked. One such technology is file shares, including the directory structure and the setting of permissions on the shares. For most of you who are reading this sidebar, it was and probably is a mess. File shares are notorious as being dumping grounds for everything from Microsoft Office documents to applications, movie files, music files, code—the list goes on and on. Often, these file shares started out as a good idea and had a governance plan that quickly faded due to lack of enforcement. The end result is an environment with a lot of duplicate files and highly sensitive documents that are not secured properly—generally, what I like to call "space wasters."

Now that I'm on the other side of the fence specializing in SharePoint, I have found that many companies I work with look at SharePoint Server 2007 and think a migration would be a good alternative to file shares. So they spin up large, expensive projects to accomplish a file migration from file shares to Windows SharePoint Services or SharePoint Server 2007.

When I work with clients who bring up this subject, I try to help them understand that they first need to properly analyze their file share environments and spend time fixing the security problems in these shares. File shares are not a dead concept, but like any technology, they need to be given some tender loving care and regular management. Numerous third-party utilities can be purchased to help maintain these shares. Once the information is in a useful state, then I ask, "What do you see now as fitting into your SharePoint environment?" It's a tough question, but generally the answer I'm pushing for is one that encompasses a thorough understanding of the points I've made above. For example, this is not where you want to hold your music files for sharing or as a code source repository for your developers.

Both technologies (SharePoint Server 2007 and file shares) can easily coexist, in part by adding your file shares to your search scopes. The only effect this will have in your SharePoint environment is in the size of your index. Assuming that documents are properly tagged with metadata, they will be just as findable on a file server as they are in SharePoint.

*Bob Fox, Microsoft MVP, B&R Business Solutions*

## Location

The location where the document is developed should be in a document library within a SharePoint site. SharePoint Server 2007 is an ideal environment in which to develop documents when multiple people are working together to develop the document. Either a document library or a file share is acceptable for a document location if the document is being developed by a single user. However, as soon as people need to collaborate on the document, it should be uploaded into SharePoint. The document library has several features to configure that we believe reach the level of a best practice.

The first feature is the Require Check Out feature in a document library (Figure 8-1). When selected, a document cannot be modified without first being checked out. The second is the document versioning feature (refer to Figure 8-1). When used together, there is a full history of who checked out the document, when the document was checked out, and what modifications were made to the document before it was checked back in. Now, this history can be truncated with the Version Pruning options, but in the absence of these options, you can keep track of the document's pedigree and pinpoint the user who made each change to the document.

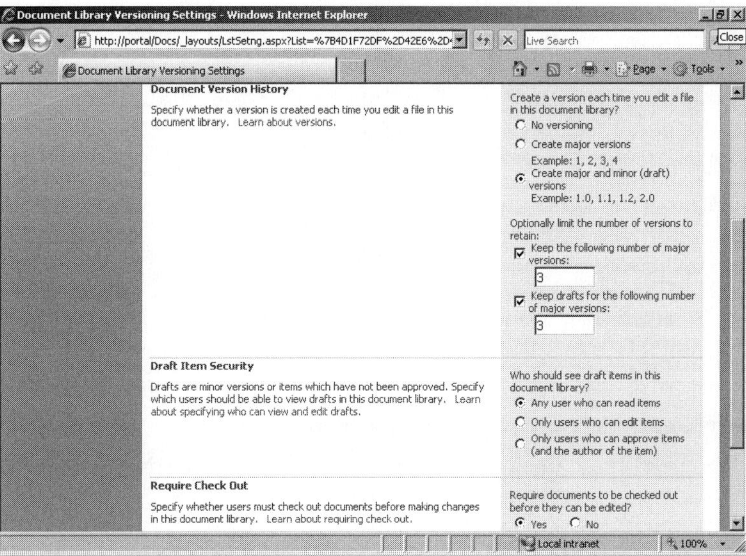


**Figure 8-1** Document library settings for requiring content approval and version settings

> **Note** The check out, check in, and versioning features are applied globally to the document. These features do not replace the Track Changes and Comments features that are so useful in tracking the micro changes that are made to a document. We strongly suggest that your users learn to use the Track Changes and Comments features in each document being developed while using the SharePoint check out, check in, and versioning features that will apply to the documents overall. In the absence of the Track Changes and other in-document Reviewer features, you'll know that the document has changed based on a new version number, but you won't know the *exact* change that occurred in the document. That granular level of tracking changes is a Word activity, not a SharePoint activity.

Third, we recommend that content approval be turned on at the document library when necessary to fulfill the purposes of the library (Figure 8-2). When this is enabled, approval workflows can be triggered when a document is configured to be published as the next major version. Because most of these documents will need to be approved, requiring content approval is the most logical way to allow the workflow trigger to work effectively.

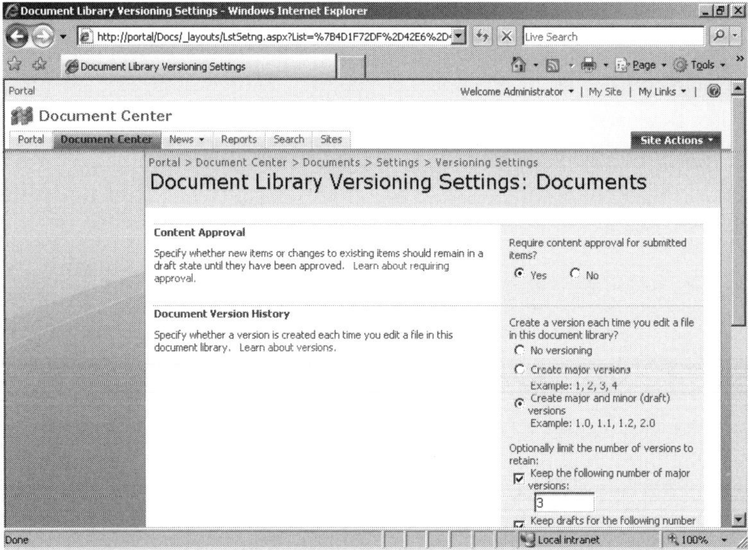


**Figure 8-2** Require Content Approval feature in the document library settings

## Notes from the Field **Naming Document Libraries Can Create Confusion or Findability: Two Best Practices You Should Implement**

When a site is first created, if a document library is created with the site template, the document library will be named "Shared Documents." This default naming of the document library lends to ease of use, but it also creates considerable confusion if it is not managed properly.

When a user first uses the document library, a Web folder client will be created automatically in her My Network Places on her desktop. That Web folder client will use the default naming convention of <name of document library> on <name of root site>. If there is a Web folder client naming conflict, the code will iterate the names by appending a number at the end of the name, as illustrated in Figure 8-3. If the user isn't careful (and in the absence of solid governance and best practice recommendations), she will find that her Web folder client names will be useless because a long list of Web folder client names with the same name across different sites will be created.

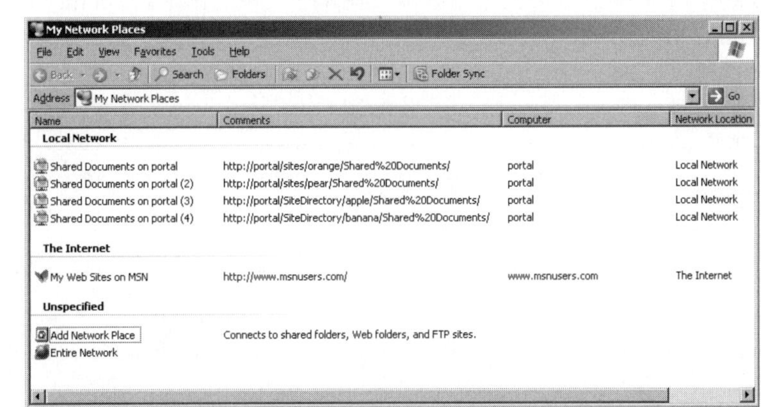


**Figure 8-3** My Network Places with multiple Web folder client connections. Note the numeric suffix iteration when there are naming conflicts.

While it is possible that users could use the URLs listed in the Comments column, it is highly unlikely that the majority will be willing to use this differentiator or that many would understand how to read the URLs in a discriminatory fashion. While elementary to us technologists, many more users will wonder why they have to go to such lengths just to find the right document library when they need to find their documents. And I think they are correct on this point.

This is why I recommend that all of your site definitions and site templates do not include the creation of a Shared Documents document library when the site is created. Instead, instruct your users to create their own document libraries with a naming convention that you propagate. This means that you'll need to go through and modify all of your site definitions and site templates to reflect this best practice.

*Bill English, Microsoft MVP, Mindsharp*

## Filing

Traditional, paper-based documents are filed in filing cabinets. Drawers are labeled–usually with some type of category name–and then documents are placed in the filing cabinets in folders that represented some type of subcategorization of the drawer's category. The name of the folder and drawer really become metadata that is used to help sort, describe, and retrieve the documents.

In SharePoint, the "filing" of the document is accomplished through the creation of a content type, where the metadata fields are created for that type of content. When the document is created using that content type, the metadata fields are inherited (for lack of a better term) from the content type and applied to the document. The first time the document is checked into a document library, the metadata fields are populated with values that will persist for the life of the document unless they are manually modified or removed.

> **More Info** To gain an in-depth understanding of content types, please see Chapter 10, "Configuring Office SharePoint Server Enterprise Content Management," in *Microsoft SharePoint Products and Technologies Administrator's Pocket Consultant* (Microsoft Press, 2007) and Chapter 15, "Managing Content Types," in *Microsoft Office SharePoint Server 2007 Administrator's Companion* (Microsoft Press, 2007).

In a sense, the filing of a document in SharePoint Products and Technologies occurs both before and after the document is created, but for sure, the filing of a document is mostly completed once the first check-in of the first draft of the document is performed in SharePoint.

A number of best practices present themselves as part of this discussion. First, the content types need to be created with forethought and planning. The metadata field names should be unique not only within each content type but also across all other content types. The more robust your content type deployment, the more necessary it will be to have a naming convention for metadata fields as well as (perhaps) a full-time person dedicated to managing and creating content types.

### Notes from the Field **Understanding Data Elements in Your Organization**

I recently worked with a customer who was probably the best prepared customer I've ever worked with in terms of understanding and developing data elements for the organization. This customer had 1,300 users, most of whom worked at the company's main office in Southern California. Because this customer's business is highly process driven, the CEO had mandated an information review that identified 56 primary data elements with 258 supporting data elements. Each element had its own set of metadata, and each metadata field was unique across all 314 data elements. The customer had already done this work when I arrived to do a two-day design and architecture session.

During the session, we discussed how content types would be used to help the company formulate its document management implementation. Their response was one that I've never heard before or since: "We're ready for that." All the customer had to do was turn the 314 data elements into content types.

Not to scare you, but it took the customer two years to develop these 314 data elements. The company had 1.5 FTE (full-time equivalent) positions dedicated to this effort, plus the support of management, starting with the CEO. The company was doing this to support an industry-specific application that tracked its raw materials and manufacturing processes. The fact that the company could easily use this information in SharePoint was a major, unexpected benefit and increased the return on investment on the dollars that had been invested in that project.

> You should not believe that developing content types is just for SharePoint. The identification of the different data types and their metadata elements should be generic, because the information that is developed will likely translate into content types without too much trouble.
>
> One unexpected decision the company made was to not use SharePoint for the conceptual development of its content types. The company found SharePoint itself to be an inadequate system for hosting the ongoing development of its data elements and the mapping of these elements to content types. That work was performed outside of SharePoint using a different management information system with relational databases and relational lists. Essentially, the company developed a metadata warehouse with a data element and content type mapping scheme such that it was able to quickly pivot on metadata elements, major/minor data elements, or content types to look at its data elements from any of the three angles and know that it was viewing accurate information. The ability to move metadata between elements in a relational way as the content types were developed was essential to the company's success.
>
> *Bill English, Microsoft MVP, Mindsharp*

Second, you need to know that every time a new content type is created, a new GUID is attached to that content type. Because these are managed at the site collection level, it is possible to create exactly the same content type in two different site collections with the same name and metadata fields, yet each one will have a different GUID. If you need to programmatically work with the same content types across site collections via their GUIDs, then you'll need to deploy the content types as features wrapped up in one or more solution deployments. Deploying content types in this manner will allow your developers to write code against the content types' GUID across the enterprise. Third, if you create a DDoc for a new document, be sure that the metadata in the DDoc matches the metadata that you'll create for the new content type.

Fourth, the values assigned to the metadata fields need to be communicated to your users so that they will know which keywords and other values to use to help them quickly and easily find their documents using the search and indexing feature in SharePoint Server 2007. Connecting the metadata from content type through value assignment to end-user education is one of the key workflows that deserves attention. It is a best practice to ensure there is consistency in the use of content types, metadata assignments, and end-user education about the metadata and the values assigned to the documents.

The last best practice for this topic is that the development of the metadata fields and their value assignments should be carried out with the aid and input of those who will use those fields and values to retrieve the documents. IT people are the last people on earth who should be deciding the names of metadata fields and the values that will be used to populate them. A robust content type deployment will involve constant chatter with those who will develop, use, and retrieve the documents.

## Retrieval

The preferred methods of document retrieval will vary from user to user. If users know exactly where a document is, they will probably use one or more of the following methods to retrieve the document (this is not an exhaustive list):

- A favorites shortcut to the document (or the document library) in Internet Explorer
- A desktop shortcut to the document (or the document library)
- Shared links in My Sites
- Links that are created in the Summary Links Web part
- If accessed recently, their list of recently accessed documents in Windows XP or Vista
- Physically typing in the URL to the site or document library
- Customized navigation in a SharePoint Server 2007 portal or site
- RSS feeds

As you can see, the methods of retrieval for a document when users know its location are varied and numerous. SharePoint Server 2007 provides a plethora of findability tools in this scenario to ensure that users can find the information for which they are looking. Because there are a plethora of findability tools in SharePoint Server 2007, it is a best practice to cover the various findability methods in SharePoint Server 2007 training.

But what if users don't know where a document is and they need to find it quickly and easily? Well, the most common answer to that question is to use search and indexing–to execute a query against the index that will allow users to find the document. Normally, an advanced search is required if one is to combine multiple metadata queries into a single query. In other words, users will need to be trained on how to enter the metadata values they are looking for in the Advanced Search Web part (Figure 8-4) in order to pinpoint the document they need to retrieve from their query of the index.

Most often, users will need to know how to use the following features in concert with one another in order to execute a highly discriminatory query:

- Keywords and Boolean operators
- Metadata queries
- Scopes

The more skilled users are at using these three features together, plus the more robust the metadata assignments on documents and the scopes topology, the more likely it is that users will be able to pinpoint a document from your index and find the information they are seeking.

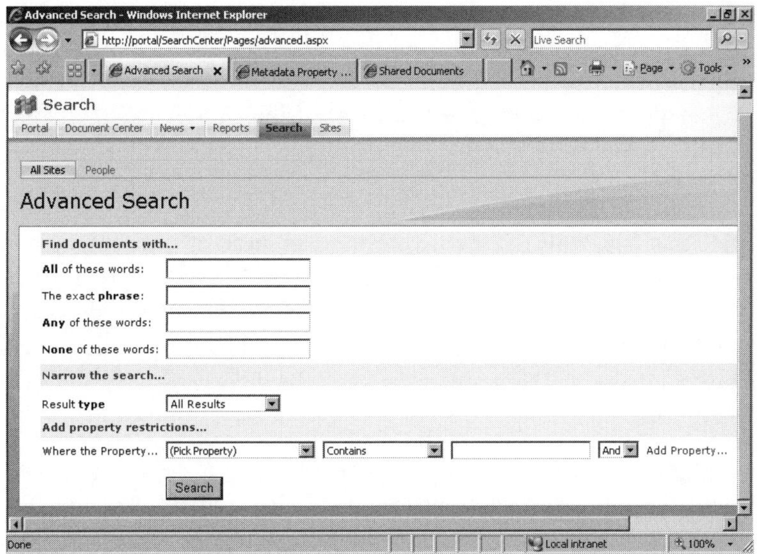


Figure 8-4 Default Advanced Search Web part without the language selection boxes

But the quality of their results depends directly on you, the administrator, tightly defining your content sources such that extraneous information does not appear in the index. Crawler rules that exclude unneeded information, such as ensuring that a Web site's privacy policy is not crawled, is important as you build your content source topology.

Moreover, you need to work with your taxonomist or librarian (whoever is responsible for implementing information architecture in your organization) to ensure that certain metadata reserved for enterprise use is exposed properly in the advanced search Web part.

## Mapping the Features of SharePoint Server 2007 to Your Information Architecture

Most companies that we work with do not have an enterprise-wide taxonomy into which the various types of content are described and codified. While SharePoint Server 2007 gives you the ability to meticulously create metadata for each type of content, it is a time-consuming task, to say the least, and most companies simply don't allocate the budget to get this job done.

The findability of individual content items depends directly on the level of discrimination that the metadata assignments provide your end users. This is why it is so important to set forth a set of primary data elements that represent the core of your business documents and to reserve those documents' metadata fields for enterprise use. Let's consider a somewhat absurd illustration to make this point.

Let's assume that we're in the business of developing tracts of land for new housing projects. As part of our business processes, we go out and find new land to develop. As we consider larger tracts of land, we decide to call those tracts "fields." Inside the fields, we'll have "neighborhoods." Inside neighborhoods, we'll have "lots" upon which individual homes are built. So we develop a land document that describes potential "fields" to buy, and it has a metadata assignment called "field name."

Let's further assume that our company is growing and is in need of some fun company-sponsored events that help our employees get to know each other better. So we assign one of our staff to develop some intramural sports programs. That staff member develops a soccer league for our growing company, and, on the game assignment document, he creates a metadata assignment called "field name" to differentiate between the different soccer fields that our company will use for our games.

Do you see the problem? The metadata assignment "field name" has two entirely different meanings because there was no metadata control at the enterprise level. A "field name" for one department means something entirely different than its meaning for the other department.

This is why it is a best practice to ensure that certain metadata assignments are *not* available for general use within your company. These assignments need to be reserved company-wide and can't be used to create new metadata assignments in content types or be the names of new site columns in a site collection. To the extent that you allow users to create content types and site columns that allow for duplicate metadata names, you injure the findability of those content items in the enterprise and you hurt the discriminatory power of those metadata assignments.

This is not inconsequential. Retrieval of information is one of the key reasons that customers implement SharePoint Server 2007 in the first place. Contrary to popular opinion, placing content into the SharePoint Server 2007 environment does not automatically make that content more findable. You must also be ready to assign metadata to those content items and to ensure that the metadata assignments are unique across the enterprise and that the values they hold are highly discriminatory.

However, when it comes to document retrieval, we humans are as likely to ask other humans where a document is as we are to query the index. So being able to find the right people is as important as finding the right document. Sometimes, it's just plain faster (and perhaps more fun) to ask a person where a document is than to query for it.

In terms of retrieval best practices, we believe that it is a best practice to take the more important and popular metadata keyword terms and make those metadata fields that host the terms available for querying in the Advanced Search Web part. Moreover, be sure to teach your end-users that they can query metadata directly in standard search boxes without having to find those fields exposed in the Advanced Search Web part by simply entering a customized query using the following syntax:

<managed_property_name>: <keyword_query_term_or_terms>

Hence, if we wanted to find all of the documents written by Bill English and the Author field wasn't exposed in the Advanced Search Web part, the user could use any standard search box and enter the query string

author: "Bill English"

Any managed property can be used in this fashion, so another best practice would be to list your managed properties and the included crawled properties if you're going to train your end-users on how to enter metadata queries. This list would need to exist in the Search Center and either be listed below the search box or contain a link to a Web page that would include this information. Using a managed property to filter search results only works in Web parts that use SQL syntax, the managed property must be exposed in the Web part and not entered manually.

## Metadata Results Depend on How You Create Them

What we have learned about metadata creation after working in the field for many years can be encapsulated in the following bullet points. Be sure to understand that how you create metadata will impact how the result set displays it. Obviously, a more concise result set results in a happier end-user. And we administrators live for their happiness, right?

- The ability to execute a query on a managed property really does work, but you need a space between the colon ":" and the start of the query keyword. "DocNum:12345" is interpreted as a single keyword. "DocNum: 12345" is interpreted as a macro+keyword combination by the search Web part. You cannot directly query crawled properties in the search Web part. They must be made part of a managed property first.
- If the metadata is held in a site column that is created from within the document library interface, then the library name will also appear in the result set along with the document when the property query is executed.
- If the metadata is held in a site column that is created from within the content type, then only the document will appear in the result set.
- If the metadata is held in a custom property in the document itself, then only the document will appear in the result set.
- The creation of new managed and crawled properties requires only an incremental crawl to expose them.
- Site columns are added to the SharePoint category of crawled properties whether they are created within the document library or within the content type.
- Document custom properties are added to the Office category of crawled properties.

## Security

When it comes to securing the document, your two main choices are to explicitly assign permissions to the document or inherit permissions from the document library in which the document resides. Item-level permissions can be set on each document if you need to explicitly assign permissions, but in most cases it will be sufficient for documents to inherit permissions from the document library if not the site itself. Setting item-level permissions greatly increases the administrative effort on the part of your end-users, and it increases the chances that some items will be incorrectly secured.

When it comes to securing information in SharePoint Server 2007, most of the security assignments will be executed by your site administrators who are (presumably) non-technical, non-IT end-users. To be sure, some site collections will be wholly managed by IT, but to have IT manage *all* site collections, site collections and sites in the entire farm will require a significant personnel investment to which most organizations are unwilling to commit. So, while the-end-user-is-now-the-security-administrator reality can scare most IT administrators into psychotherapy, it must be managed and addressed. The following best practices will help you in this regard.

First, the content owners of the document should be given site-level management of the site in which the document will reside. To be more precise, the content owners should be site administrators of the site in which the document will reside. This will ensure that the document's security is managed by the content owner or the owner's designee. Use the DDoc's content owner specification to ensure that the content owner is the site administrator. Now, this brings up two related points:

1. Because content owners will be site administrators, they will need training on how to manage and secure a site.
2. The content owners, in some instances, will need direction on who can access the site and document and who cannot. The DDoc should specify any unique security needs.

A second best practice is to ensure that the site owners are not managing documents to which they should not have permissions. Remember that site administrators can grant themselves permissions to any content within their site, so if a document to which administrators should not have access is placed in that site, then security has been compromised. So for each unique set of exclusionary permissions to documents that exist in your deployment, you'll need, at a minimum, different sites in which to develop those documents.

Third, we can't forget about site collection administrators in this discussion. Recall that site collection administrators can grant themselves permissions to any content item hosted within the site collection. So part of your DDoc should specify the potential user accounts that can be listed as site collection administrators and should also specify any user accounts that should not be site collection administrators for sites in which the document will be hosted. For each unique set of exclusive permissions that are developed, you'll need another site collection.

> **Note** Active Directory directory services groups cannot be site collection administrators. Only Active Directory user accounts can be site collection owners.

Remember that site collection administrators do not appear in the groups interface because they are not a group, but an assignment to individual accounts. Figure 8-5 illustrates how the site collection administrators do not appear as a group in the list of SharePoint groups. Figure 8-6 illustrates the people interface with the Is Site Admin check box selected in the default view. Selecting this check box will inform you who is a site collection administrator. Note that while the account bcurry is an owner in the portal, his account is marked as "no," indicating that he is not a site collection administrator.

Fourth, it is a reality that people change roles within organizations and sometimes change jobs between organizations. You will need third-party software to help you efficiently track content ownership changes, site owner changes, and site collection administrator changes in SharePoint Server 2007. If you don't track these human resource changes efficiently in SharePoint, user accounts will be left with access to content that perhaps violates security rules and policies.

> **Note** There is a third-party software package, DeliverPoint 2007, published by Barracuda, available for download from *http://www.deliverpoint.com*. DeliverPoint 2007 will help your organization work with user accounts in a number of ways, including permissions discovery as well as cloning, deleting, and transferring permissions and alerts between accounts at the farm, Web application, managed path, site collection, and site levels.

In addition, you'll need to perform Permissions Discovery reporting for certain documents that you host in SharePoint to ensure that your implementation can meet compliance requirements. Because SharePoint does not offer this functionality, consider using one of the third-party tools on the CD to help you ensure that your security assignments are in compliance with industry standards and regulatory requirements.

Our last security best practice is to ensure that, if major/minor versioning is implemented, only those who can edit the document will be able to see the minor versions. This is a document library setting and is *not* turned on by default.

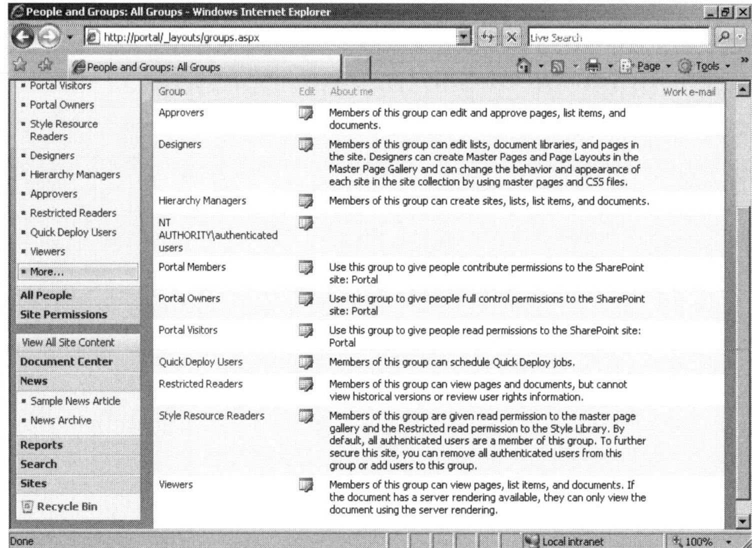


**Figure 8-5** A listing of default groups in the collaboration portal in SharePoint Server 2007

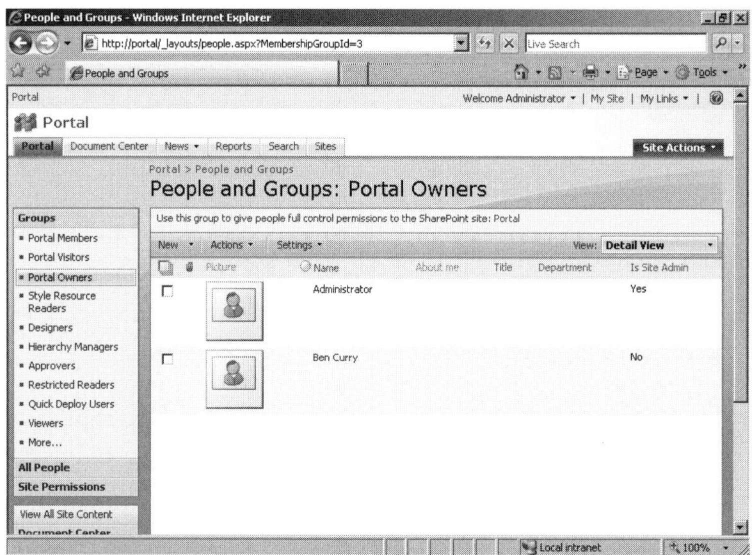


**Figure 8-6** Is Site Admin column showing that the Administrator is a site collection administrator, but that the bcurry account, which is in the portal owners group, is not a site collection administrator

## Lessons Learned **Be Sure You Know Who Has Been Assigned Permissions Throughout Your SharePoint Deployment**

One customer learned the hard way about not understanding the effects of the various permission assignments throughout a farm. We'll explain in just a moment. To understand the background, you need to understand that the following groups and/or accounts have pervasive permissions in a SharePoint Server 2007 deployment that are not revealed or exposed in the user and group interfaces for sites and site collections.

First, the Application Pool account has uber-read permissions to every object within the Web applications that are using that application pool. Be sure to understand that if anyone logs on as the Application Pool account, he can read all of the SharePoint content in all of the sites and site collections in all of the Web applications that are associated with that application pool. Second, the farm administrators have the ability to grant to themselves access to any information in your SharePoint Server 2007 deployment. Be sure that those who are added to the farm administrators group can be trusted not to use their access improperly. If they do add themselves to any part of the farm, that is an audited event. Third, the Default Content Access account has default read permissions throughout the farm. Fourth, any accounts given permissions via a policy will have access to those areas granted, but will not appear in the users and groups interfaces at either the site or site collection levels. Last, site collection administrators can grant themselves access to any information within the site collection, but the granting action is audited by SharePoint.

One client learned that much of his information had been exposed to the wrong group of people because a consultant who didn't understand how to implement SharePoint added the Domain Administrators and Enterprise Administrators accounts to the Farm Administrators group. This individual was under the mistaken assumption that by adding these groups, certain permission problems he was experiencing would go away. When he learned this wasn't the case, the groups were not removed and, for an extended period of time, members of these two groups could have given themselves access to any sensitive information in the farm they desired. Because they also managed Exchange and other platforms, it turned out that they didn't try to take advantage of their position because they were already trustworthy, but the end result could have been very different.

Bear in mind that there are two things that no developer can write code to guard against: an unwise administrator and an untrustworthy administrator. When hiring network administrators, understand that they will have pervasive access to nearly all, if not all, of your most sensitive information. Best practice is to perform thorough background security and personnel checks to be sure the person(s) being hiring have the highest ethical integrity possible.

## Workflow and Approval

Some documents go through an iterative creation-approval-improvement-approval cycle several times before they are ready to be consumed by the larger intended audience. Documents are not written in a vacuum. Every document written, including this chapter, has an intended audience. The main reason that documents are sent through an approval process before being distributed to the intended audience is because the creators need to ensure that the document has the right messaging and focus. It is important to note that workflows are simply electronic restatements of processes that are already occurring in the organization without the use of workflow technology.

The first best practice to creating workflows is to have a clear understanding of the current processes that are being used to publish a document. Following closely behind is a clear understanding of how to improve that process so that the workflow can be written to follow the most efficient path available. If there is not a clear set of policies and procedures in place that users can reference when they create their workflows, the chances are high that the workflows they do create will end up routing documents through the wrong people or leaving out individuals who should have been included. The order might be wrong, too. For workflows to be effective, they must match the written policies and procedures.

A second best practice concerns the way that SharePoint implements workflows. SharePoint Server 2007 causes some consternation among IT administrators because the approvers in the workflow are account based, not position based. To be more precise, the approvers are individual users identified by their Active Directory account instead of users who occupy a particular position in the organization. Usually, a document's approval needs to be performed by a position. The inability to specify a position in a workflow means that every time a user changes positions, the workflows that are related both to the outgoing and incoming user need to be modified.

Hence, a best practice for working around this is to place those users who need to be in a particular workflow into global security groups in Active Directory. The groups should correspond to an organizational position and then the group can be used as an approver in the workflow. Implemented this way, a user can be changed in the group to represent user changes in the organizational positions and the workflow will continue to operate without any changes.

If you choose to not use Active Directory groups to create position-based workflows, then you'll need to notify site owners whenever a user leaves or is added to their site because of positional changes. Site owners may need to modify existing workflows to ensure the correct people are included in the workflow.

Another best practice is to make sure that the workflow names meet a particular naming convention. The reason for this is because the workflow names appear in the e-mail as pronouns for the workflow itself. For example, if the workflow is named "Final Approval," then the e-mail verbiage will say "Final Approval Tasks have started <name of document>." In Figure 8-7, the workflow name is "Final Approval" and the name of the document is "This is the apple document." You can see how this text, put together, is rather confusing. Figure 8-8 shows that when the e-mail is opened, the arrangement of the verbiage in the e-mail makes more sense, but it is still not clear.

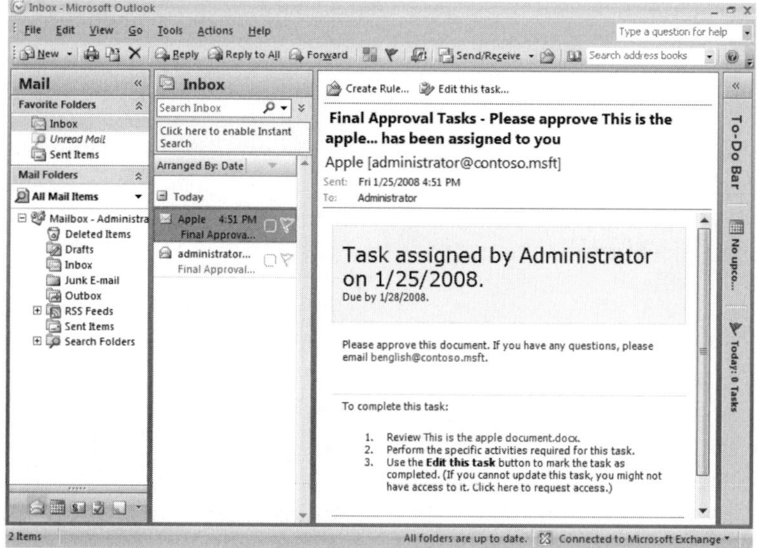


**Figure 8-7** Appearance of the workflow e-mail that indicates there is a workflow task waiting for the Administrator account to perform

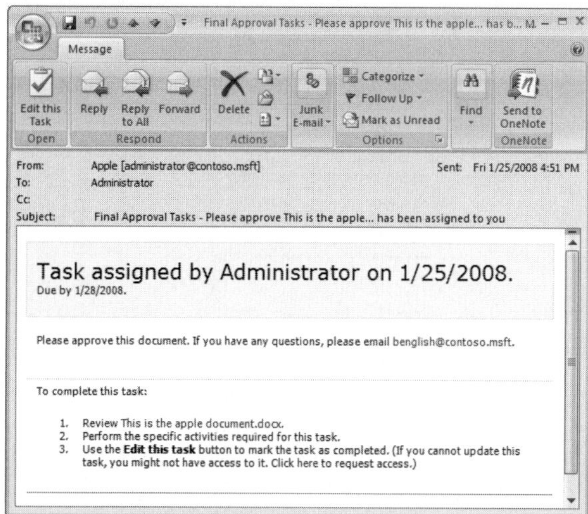


**Figure 8-8** Workflow task e-mail opened in Microsoft Office Outlook 2007

This can be confusing to those at the receiving end of the workflow e-mail. So be sure to set up a workflow naming convention that your users are expected to follow, such as <workflow_name for document_name>. Create a naming convention that will make sense in the e-mail interface so that the users don't confuse workflow task e-mails with alerts and other system-generated e-mails.

# Distribution

The distribution of documents in SharePoint is very different than distributing hard copy documents or routing the documents through a workflow. Distributing a document in SharePoint really means two essential things:

1. Ensuring that the finished document is placed in the correct location
2. Ensuring that those who need to consume the document have permissions to the document in its location

## Location of the Finished Document

Wherever you want the finished document to reside, if that location is within SharePoint, it will be in a document library. Because team sites, Document Centers, and record repositories can host document libraries, the question becomes this: Where should the finished document reside for its active life while it is being consumed by the appropriate audience? There are an infinite number of specific answers to this question, but we can safely group most of those answers into the SharePoint objects illustrated in Figure 8-9.

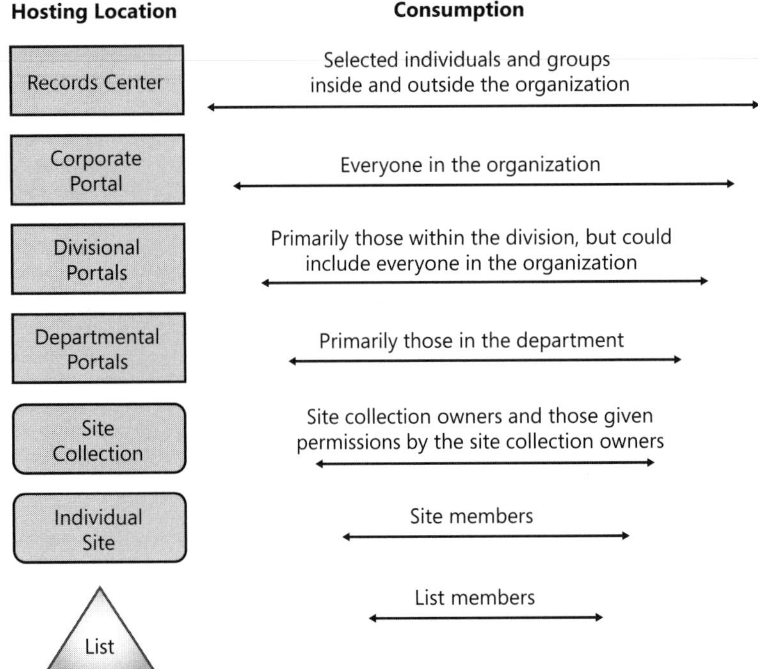


**Figure 8-9** Possible document hosting locations and breadth of consumption illustration

As a general rule of thumb, the wider the audience (those who will consume the document) for the document, the wider or broader the scope of the site should be in which the document is hosted. Stated another way, the breadth of consumption of the document should match the breadth of consumption of the site in which it is hosted. For example, the human resource policy manual is a document that is consumed by nearly everyone in an organization at one time or another. So it would only make sense that the finished (or currently published) version would be hosted in a site that has broad access by everyone in the company, such as a company portal or the HR portal.

From this perspective, SharePoint can be conceptualized as having a series of tools that have intended scopes of consumption. For example, referring back to Figure 8-10, when documents are hosted in a Records Center, they are intended to be official, compliant, (potentially) public, truthful records of communication. Interested parties from inside and outside the company will (potentially) consume this information. By the same token, when documents are hosted in a corporate portal (most often in the Document Center), then it is assumed that those who have access to the corporate portal should also be able to consume (read) the documents in the Document Center. While the breadth of consumption can vary from organization to organization, usually the most widely consumed documents will be placed in the Document Center of a portal. Official records will land in the Records Center. These documents may be consumed by a wide audience, but the more common scenario is that these documents are consumed primarily by the record librarian and selected, interested parties. As you go down the scale, the breadth of consumption narrows to the point where only a few members will consume data in lists.

> **Note** Figure 8-9 is somewhat arbitrary because each of the SharePoint objects can be configured with very wide or very narrow permission sets. This discussion is meant to give you a roadmap on the tools SharePoint offers to host information that is intended for a given breadth of consumption.

In our estimation, we believe that it is a best practice to host data once and link to it from multiple locations if those in other locations than the hosting location need quick access to the information. When multiple copies of a finished document are hosted in multiple locations, there is a very real opportunity to have different "versions of the truth," which is deterrent to clear communication. Most individuals, teams, and organizations constantly struggle with message discipline, message clarity, and message consistency. We believe there is no sense in adding to that struggle by suggesting it is a best practice to host multiple copies of a finished document in multiple locations. Single instance hosting (SIH) should be the goal for your documents.

## Permissions to the Document

Now, there is a line of thinking that says, "We can host a document in a team document library, give everyone read permissions, and place a link to the document in the portal so that we don't *move* the document from its creation location to another location." This is really a carry-over from the design of SharePoint Portal Server 2003. And with proper planning, this is a viable design. But if you intend to do this, then you need to understand the security implications and risks.

First, those who secure the document library will need to understand how to configure the library's permissions so that only those who edit documents in the library can see the minor versions of the document. This setting is configured in the document library settings and is referred to as Draft Item Security (see Figure 8-10).

Second, your overall document plans will need to specify a plethora of team site locations for hosting finished documents. As the number and type of documents are added to your overall DMS planning matrix, you'll find the number of finished hosting locations will grow and will likely become more difficult to manage.

Third, as you randomize a team site's breadth of consumption, you introduce a randomized consumption pattern that will likely irritate most users. Most users would rather find sets of finished documents in one place as opposed to clicking on multiple links that tunnel through to multiple document libraries in which smaller sets of finished documents are exposed. This scenario detracts from an optimal findability solution and should be used only in exceptional circumstances. Best practice is to minimize the number of locations that host finished documents.

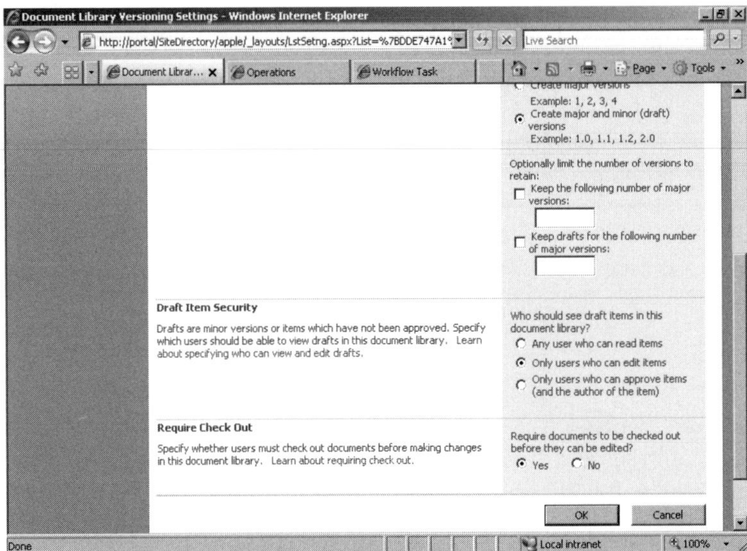


**Figure 8-10** Draft Item Security configuration options in the document library settings

> **Note** For a full discussion of findability, please see Chapter 15, "Implementing an Optimal Search and Findability Topology."

When finished documents are moved to the locations specified in the DDoc, those locations need to be correctly secured so that the intended audience is the *only* audience that can consume that document. You should use a third-party tool that can inform you about the permissions that are assigned to an individual document or library when the security of that document or library is a high priority to the mission or existence of the organization.

## Using the Send To Feature in SharePoint

For each document in a document library, you can have three levels of Send To functions:

1. Other Location Send To field that is filled in by the user for an individual document
2. Document Library custom Send To field that is configured by the document library administrator and appears in all document drop-down lists in the document library
3. Official Records Repository that is configured by the farm administrator in Central Administration and appears in all document drop-down lists farm-wide

The Other Location method is illustrated in Figure 8-11. This method allows a user to set up a connection between the document in the local library and a copy of the document in the remote location. Then, when there is an update in the local copy, a prompt can be configured to remind the document's author to send an updated copy to the remote location. This remote location can be any location within the SharePoint farm. The Other Location method is most often used to send a document from one team site to another or from a child site to a parent site within a site collection. It can be used to keep spreadsheets, reports, and other often-updated information current in two different locations. While this method can be used to publish an individual document from a team site to a portal, it cannot be used to publish a document from a team site to a Records Repository. This feature is implemented on a per-document basis and is best used when there is a one-off need to publish a document from its creation site to its consumption site.

**Figure 8-11** Send To Location feature in a document's shortcut menu

> **Note** Note that the connection in the Other Location method can be set up only in a 1:1 relationship. You can't set up a connection in a Many:1 relationship, which would be helpful if you're editing individual documents in the source location that are then aggregated into a single document at the destination, or what is commonly called a *compound document*. Some will know this as a *thicket*.

The Document Library custom Send To field is illustrated in Figure 8-12. This method allows a single remote location to be made available for copying all the documents hosted in the document library to the remote location. This method is best utilized when a document library becomes the source location for an entire set of documents that are related to one another in some manner and the entire set needs to be copied to a remote location for wider consumption. Because most documents in a set will not be created and finished at the same time, this method allows each individual document to be sent to the same remote location without having to send the entire set at one time or to repeatedly send the entire set to the remote location when there are changes in only one or two of the documents. This method also allows the same Send To field to appear for different authors in the same library, so each author is not forced to set up the same connection individually for each document.

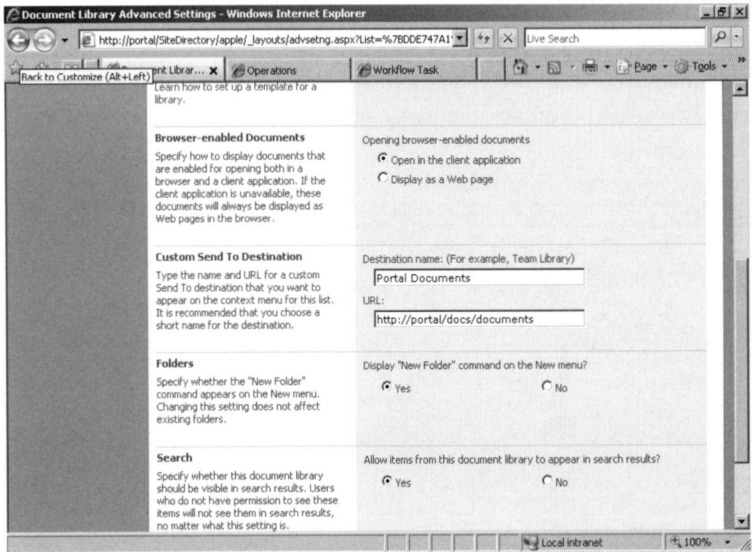


**Figure 8-12** Custom Send To method in the properties of a document library

> **Note** Because each document is sent to the remote location individually, a connection will be created between the source and destination document as if the Send To location has been entered manually for each document.

The Official Records Repository method is illustrated in Figure 8-13. This method allows any finished document that is intended to be a matter of record to be sent to the Official Records

Repository hosted at the farm level. Presumably, the repository will have a matching content type and document library into which the incoming document will be placed as an official record. In the absence of this matching content type, the document will be placed in the Unclassified records library, as illustrated in Figure 8-14. Note that, unlike the Send To method, in the Official Records Repository method, no link is maintained between the source document and the target document in the Records Center. Note also that the name of the document in the Records Center is appended with a unique string of characters and this cannot be modified.

You can create more than one Official Records Repository in your SharePoint Server 2007 implementation. (But only one–and the same one–can be configured at the farm level and appear in the document's shortcut list. Refer to Figure 8-13.) If you do this, use the Document Library custom Send To method to create a Send To connection between documents in a designated source library and the Records Repository so that there is a clear understanding that the source document library is used to create and develop what will be official, compliant, truthful communication and that the same content type is used in both the source document library and the destination document library in the repository site.

When developing an Official Records Repository, it is a best practice to clearly define the source document libraries and locations from which the official records will arrive. The content types and their names must match in the Record Repository's routing table, and documents must be sent to the repository *after* all copy edits, technical edits, and approval workflows have been completed. If there is an update to the source document after it is sent to the repository, another record is created when it is resent to the repository. The first record is neither updated nor overwritten. This is because each record is a permanent record with a unique six-alphanumeric character string attached to it. Any updates to the record constitute a new record, not an update to the current record.

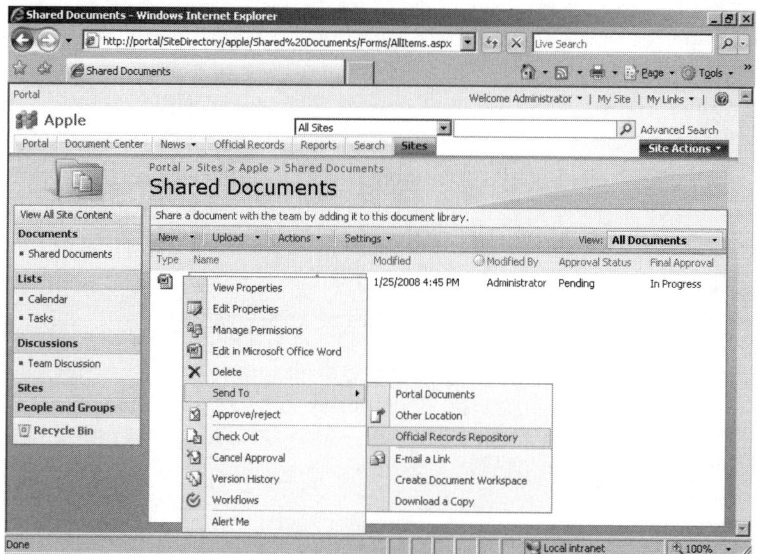


**Figure 8-13** Send To menu shortcut for the Official Records Repository

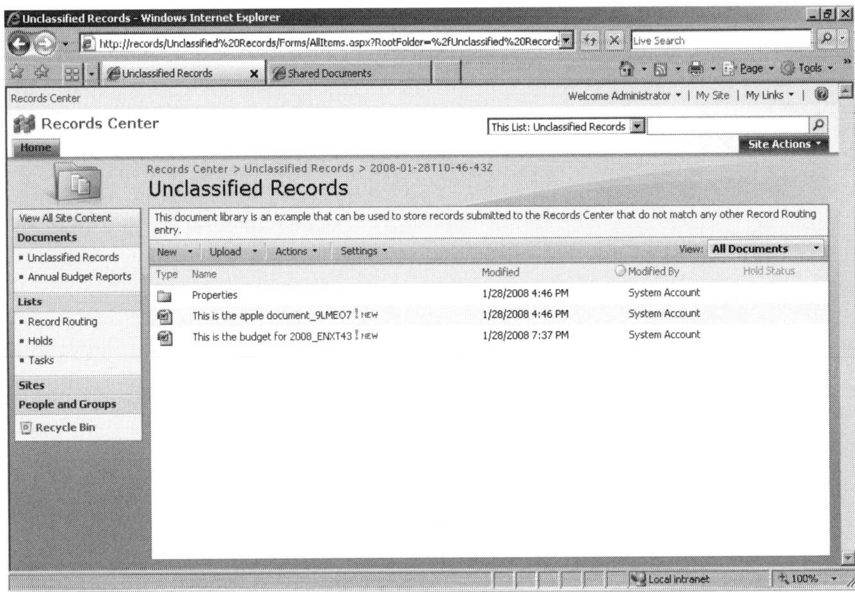


**Figure 8-14** Unclassified documents with their names appended with a random string of characters

## Retention

Retention is the act of retaining a document in a specified location. The decision to retain a document and the length of time it is retained should be made by those who have developed the DDoc well before the document is created. The retention time is set using the expiration policy on the content type or at the site collection policy level.

When the expiration time is set at the site collection policy level, it is just an available setting that needs to be applied to the content type. Interestingly enough, when it is applied through the document library interface, it applies only to the instances of that content type in that library. If the setting is applied at the content type level, then the setting applies to all instances of the content type across the entire site collection. In the absence of site collection policy settings, when you use either the document library interface or the content type interface to set the expiration policy, you're applying that policy at the content type level (there is no document library-level expiration policy) and it will apply to all instances of the content type within the site collection.

If you need to use the same content type across multiple document libraries and have different retention policies within those libraries, then assign the expiration policy to the content type at the document library level using the site collection expiration policy. However, if you need to assign the same retention policy to all instances of that content type within the site collection, then use the information policy setting on the content type.

Note that part of your retention policy is to decide what to do with the document after it has served its useful life. In some instances, you'll decide to delete the document. In other instances, you'll route it through a workflow that may require other individuals to decide what to do with the document—continue to retain it, delete it, or send it to long-term storage (a process commonly referred to as *archiving*). The customized workflow can be created in Visual Studio.NET and then applied to the content type. Whatever decision is made, the disposition process needs to be clearly outlined in the DDoc. It is to the topic of archiving documents that we now turn our attention.

## Archiving

Archiving a document or record means to place that item in a long-term storage solution so that, if needed, it can be retrieved at some point in the future. Usually, records in an archive are useful only for reference and never for ongoing collaboration.

The main enemy of archiving is technological change. As our word processors, security methods, and storage technologies evolve, older information can become inaccessible, defeating the original purpose of hosting the record in an archive. For example, if a document is secured through an Information Rights Management (IRM) program, the certificate and its chain of authority certificates may become outdated or obsolete, rendering the document both inaccessible and unusable. Moreover, a document secured by a password may not be accessible if the correct password cannot be found to open the document. Another example would be if a user tries to open a very old document, such as a WordStar 2000 document or an Ashton-Tate DB III database. While current technologies might still be able to open very old documents like this, the day may come when such documents will no longer be accessible in their original form.

Another enemy of archiving in SharePoint is the enumeration of large lists. SQL is certainly able to handle the storage of millions of records in a single database, but the enumeration of that database can be very difficult once the number of items in the list grows very large, such as a list of over 10,000 records. In many instances, a list this large is simply not renderable in the browser. Over time, your organization can have hundreds of thousands or millions of records in a long-term archive. Enumerating large lists will quickly become a factor in your archive architecture decisions.

Several best practices present themselves and should be seriously followed if you're going to use SharePoint as a long-term archiving solution. First, plan where records will land in the long-term storage and the technologies that will be used to display them to the user.

One of the drawbacks to SharePoint is its inability to enumerate large lists in the browser. Recommendations for best practices vary based on who you ask, but we suggest that your lists in a single view not exceed 1,000 items. When a list is viewed via the browser, the entire list is loaded into memory on Web front-end, then presented in chunks to the end-user via the browser. For smaller lists, this is acceptable, but for larger lists (usually over 2,000 items), the list enumeration may time out because the server can't load the entire list fast enough or lacks sufficient memory to perform the function.

If you need to exceed 1,000 items in a list, then a fall-back best practice is to use the Data Form Web Part (DFWP) to view the list rather than the browser or a filtered view in the browser. The reason for this best practice recommendation is two-fold: First, the DFWP can be configured to have sorting, grouping, and filtering available for end-users to employ when they initially view the list. This allows for a faster, better findability solution across a large set of records. Second, the DFWP does not retrieve the entire list in one call. Instead, it retrieves only the number of records it is configured to retrieve for any given display. For example, the DFWP can be used to view a list of 10,000 records but be configured to present only 100 records at a time. Unlike the browser that will first attempt to retrieve all 10,000 records, when the DFWP displays the first 100 records, it retrieves only the first 100 records. It will not retrieve any more records until asked to do so, and then it will retrieve only the next 100 records. This results in a faster, more performant viewing of the records in a large list.

A second best practice that relates to long-term archiving of records is to implement a process that updates the base records to new technologies on a regular basis. For example, if the original document was created in Microsoft Office Word 97, when the latest edition of Office Word is released, make it a point to upgrade the document to the latest version so that the content stays current with technology changes. We realize this practice is costly and somewhat cumbersome, but we assume that if your organization values the information enough to retain it in long-term storage, then the cost of upgrading the format of the data elements will be approved.

**Note** In some instances, the organization will want to retain the information but will not want the burden and cost of upgrading the base formatting of the information every seven to ten years. If this is the case, the records can be printed, scanned into .tiff files, and then placed back into SharePoint where the Optical Character Recognition (OCR) technologies can be used to index the content for fast retrieval. The need to upgrade .tiff files and OCR technologies will not be nearly as important as upgrading other platforms, such as Word, Excel, PowerPoint, and other word processing and spreadsheet programs.

A third best practice concerns records that are secured using certificates. If the records in the archive are secured through a certificate-based technology, then you'll need to ensure that those certificates are updated on a timely basis or the records will become unusable because they will become inaccessible. If there are passwords on the record, then the passwords will need to be recorded and securely stored. If your organization does not want to bear the costs associated with retaining the security on the records in the archive, then the security can be removed and the record retained in the archive using SharePoint security. Alternately, the record could be printed out to hard copy and retained in a secure location.

## Other Best Practices Concerning Documents and Document Libraries

Regardless of where the document is hosted, several document library best practices are worth mentioning. First, we do not find that a pervasive use of folders in a document library is either helpful or desirable. While an occasional use of folders might help categorize documents, folders are really just a way to apply metadata to a document without having to create a column in the library. Their usability is generally not thought to be helpful in the document library interface. Having said this, for performance reasons, we favor the use of folders over filtered views because folders are twice as fast at bringing up a list of documents as opposed to filtered views of a larger list.

Second, all other things being equal, we would recommend that larger lists be broken down into multiple document libraries. In many instances, large lists of documents can be divided into logical groupings that can be placed in individual document libraries.

### Lessons Learned **Enumerating Large Lists Can Cause Difficult Problems Without Proper Planning**

One author of this book worked with a company that had 9,000 users and was growing rapidly. This company received an average of 100 resumes for every open position that it advertised. To help its recruiters manage the heavy resume load, the company contracted with a consultant to customize a document library that would be the landing location for resumes that were submitted through the company Web site. The library had code that immediately notified the correct recruiter for each open position when a new resume was submitted.

The company did not stress test the code that came from the contractor. It simply implemented the customized document library in production and found that it worked exactly as desired. However, the company soon realized that the list of resumes was becoming increasingly difficult to enumerate. After about 1,800 resumes had been received, the list of documents in the library was no longer enumerable. No matter how the company tried to enumerate the documents, the list couldn't be enumerated. Because the code didn't take the recruiter directly to the individual document, the recruiters were no longer able to open new resumes, which was obviously cause for concern.

To avoid losing the documents, the company called the consultant back and asked him to pull all of the documents directly from the SQL database. Then the consultant had to re-code the library to move the documents to other multiple locations based on new design specifications he built into the revised Web part.

This customer not only learned about the difficulties of enumerating large lists of documents, but also about the value of testing custom code and stressing that code beyond expected limits.

# Working with the SharePoint Server 2007 DoD 5015.2 Add-On Pack

The default Records Center that ships with SharePoint Server 2007 has some basic functionality within it. If you need more advanced functionality in your Records Center, you should seriously consider downloading and using the SharePoint Server 2007 DoD 5015.2 Add-On Pack (DOD5012). Some of the additional features that you'll receive for free from Microsoft include the following:

- Global periods and events
- Records declaration and versioning
- Disposition and cutoff instructions
- Improved search center
- Constrained columns that use supplemental markings and/or access control column values
- Record relationship, move, and copy
- File plan builder
- Improved workflow process

What the add-on pack does not provide is the ability to batch documents into a set and to treat that set as a single entity for workflows, approvals, and dispositions. It would seem to us that the use of this add-on pack would add significant value to your overall document and records management system. Best practice would be to consider the use of this add-on pack, especially if your business requirements call for more advanced record management methods than that which ships with the base SharePoint Server 2007 system.

# Summary

In this chapter, we have discussed the best practices for document management and document libraries. We have also discussed how to ensure that official documents are placed in the right location when they become matters of official records. Lessons learned and notes from the field have been offered on these topics as well.

# Additional Resources


- *Document Management for the Enterprise.* Michael J. D. Sutton (Wiley, 1996).
- *Information First.* Roger Evernden and Elaine Evernden (Elsevier, 2003).
- The SharePoint Server 2007 team blog: *http://blogs.msdn.com/sharepoint/default.aspx.*

Chapter 9

# Enterprise Content Management

**In this chapter:**



The use of personal computers has led to an explosion of information in most companies, and managing that information effectively has become a critical component of being competitive in today's global economy. But that very wealth of information causes its own problems. Many companies are drowning in a sea of digital information. They are asking, "How can I foster creativity, innovation, and collaboration among my employees and still manage the massive amount of content that they produce?" Additionally, companies must comply with increasingly stringent legislation that dictates how access to this information must be audited and controlled. Enterprise content management (ECM) is no longer just a luxury, affordable by only the largest corporations. It has become a tactical and strategic necessity for companies of every size and every market sector.

In this chapter, we'll explore how Microsoft Office SharePoint Products and Technologies can facilitate the management of information in your company. Much of this technology is multipurposed and covered elsewhere in this book, such as in the chapter on content types. But in this chapter, we'll consider how you can empower your employees with a collaborative environment that distributes control effectively by allowing both local ownership and centralized standards. By the end of this chapter, we will have completed the following objectives:

- Explore the reasons why managing content across the enterprise is critical.
- Discuss specific Office SharePoint Server 2007 capabilities that can be used to implement ECM.
- Enumerate a number of best practices for deploying ECM using SharePoint Products and Technologies.

## What Is Enterprise Content Management?

The first thing we should do is clearly define what we mean by enterprise content management. From a high-level perspective, ECM actually refers to managing all of the content in your enterprise. But for the purpose of this book, ECM refers to technologies used to capture, manage, store, archive, and deliver content used in the business processes of a company. Clearly, both SharePoint Server 2007 and Microsoft Windows SharePoint Services 3.0 fit within this broad definition. But most of our discussion will focus on SharePoint Server 2007 because a number of the more sophisticated capabilities related to ECM, such as the Publishing feature, Records Center, and Microsoft Office InfoPath Forms Services, are available only in SharePoint Server 2007.

## Structured versus Unstructured Content

Because ECM is about technologies used to manage content, it's important that you understand what content is. Content in organizations can be divided into two categories: structured and unstructured. Structured content separates the storage of the content from its display. It can be searched, added to, modified, and deleted without affecting other content stored in the same repository. Some examples of structured content are listed below:

- Records in a relational database can be selected using a query and viewed in a list or report separate from the database.
- Items in a SharePoint list can be filtered or sorted using a ListView Web part.

Unstructured content, however, is content that cannot be viewed or modified separately from the format in which it is stored. Some examples of unstructured content are listed below:

- The contents of Microsoft Office Word documents can be viewed only if the document itself is opened.
- Cells in a Microsoft Office Excel spreadsheet can be accessed programmatically only by loading the document into memory.

Unstructured content can be more retrievable by storing additional metadata. Metadata provides information about a certain item's content. For example, a text document's metadata may contain information about the length of the document, who authored it, when it was last modified, and an abstract of its contents. But this only represents the unstructured content—it doesn't make the content itself directly accessible. SharePoint stores structured content in lists and stores unstructured content in libraries.

> **Note** While much of this chapter focuses on storing information in SharePoint Server 2007 and not in file shares, it is important to plan for content that cannot be stored in SharePoint Server 2007, such as ISO images and databases. Any items not stored in SharePoint Server 2007 should have the detail of metadata required so they can be found via search. You should plan on crawling much of your file share content so these items can be found from SharePoint Server 2007, Internet Explorer, and desktop search.

Most organizations have several times the amount of storage dedicated to unstructured content than to structured content. Making use of unstructured content is a challenge for most organizations because there is no easy way to directly access, catalog, or prevent duplication of information stored in documents. An ECM system provides tools for storing metadata that can be used to categorize both unstructured and structured content to make it easily retrievable. This also makes it easier to both detect and prevent storage of duplicate copies of the same unstructured content. By gaining control of your unstructured content, you can leverage it to create a competitive advantage. This is one of the reasons why companies are increasingly interested in ECM in today's marketplace.

### Migrating Content

Starting primarily with Microsoft Office SharePoint Portal Server 2003, many organizations began mass content migrations to SharePoint Products and Technologies, hoping to solve the problem of unorganized and disconnected content. The problem of hundreds and thousands of files in various file shares that couldn't be managed was simply transferred to hundreds or thousands of SharePoint Products and Technologies sites that couldn't be managed. You should have a migration plan as to what you will move into SharePoint Server 2007, where it will live, and who will manage it. This chapter talks at length about managing this content via policies, but these policies take time and effort to be effective. A good plan is moving immediately valuable collaborative content to SharePoint Server 2007 first and then deciding on a migration plan for legacy content later. This adheres to the iterative design life cycle described in Chapter 3, "SharePoint Server 2007 Design Life Cycle." In other words, move the content to SharePoint Server 2007 for which you need SharePoint Server 2007 functionality, such as workflows, auditing, expiration, Site Columns, Document Information Panel (DIP), sharing, and streamlined templates. If you only need to archive the content or if there is infrequent use of the content, consider letting it "die on the vine" on its current storage platform.

## New Legal Requirements

Another factor driving companies to implement ECM systems is new legal requirements. Regulations such as the Sarbanes-Oxley Act of 2002, the Health Insurance Portability and Accountability Act (HIPAA), and the Family Educational Rights and Privacy Act (FERPA) have made it mandatory for organizations to have control of their content. These laws require companies to enforce retention policies on specific types of documents and be able to prove that the documents were handled appropriately before disposal. Equally important is protecting your own valuable intellectual property. Most folks think only about defending litigation. But a proper ECM plan can protect your interests, such as inventions. Because you have implemented an ECM system that will withstand scrutiny in a court of law, you can prove when the invention occurred. This makes the availability of features such as item-level security, auditing, and automated expiration of unstructured content critical for all but the smallest of companies in today's marketplace.

## Other Driving Forces

As previously mentioned, legal requirements are one reason that companies are implementing ECM solutions. In this section, we'll explore other reasons for implementing ECM. First, it is imperative that companies gain control of the mountain of unstructured material being produced to maintain efficiency. Failure to control this information will result in, at best, a duplication of effort. What are the odds that someone in your business creates a document unlike one ever created before? Very bad odds indeed. ECM is as much about the reuse of content as it is about managing the sprawl.

Second, not knowing what content you have can result in missed business opportunities. The management of unstructured content becomes a critical component as companies strive to automate business processes to achieve greater efficiency. The breakdown of information transfer between inside sales, outside sales, and marketing is very common and definitely hurts businesses. Using workflows and Site Columns that exist in the SharePoint Server 2007 ECM feature set, you can control these processes and ensure that correct information isn't lost. Imagine a scenario in which a form was created by inside sales on a cold call, a basic set of questions was asked, and the customer's answers were recorded in the form. The form could then be automatically routed to outside sales, who could then follow up on the information collected in the form. Marketing could get a report on the answers that were generally positive and could develop a marketing strategy for this process. ECM doesn't magically fix your processes, but it can assist you when it is used intelligently.

Finally, companies are searching for ways to keep IT departments from being the bottleneck between employees who have content and other employees who need access to that content. Many times, the IT department must create a file share, Web site, or some other container for a process that slows down the momentum of the process. SharePoint Products and Technologies can be used to allow users to manage their own unstructured and structured content in a secure fashion while maintaining availability to a wider audience. When users control their own destinies without IT, it is more likely that the process will move forward and not be delayed. SharePoint Server 2007 is about giving users the ability to quickly adapt to ever-changing business requirements.

## Scenarios

You may still not be convinced that ECM is something that every company needs to be concerned about. You may be convinced that managing your structured content is all you need to do or that your company doesn't have sufficient unstructured content to make ECM a necessity. Let's look at some sample scenarios that highlight the need for ECM in most businesses.

### Small and Medium Business Market

There are between 5 and 6 million businesses in the United States that would be classed as part of the small and medium business (SMB) market segment. Traditional ECM is normally too expensive and complex for organizations in the SMB market segment. But size alone does not exempt companies from the legal requirements and competitive pressures that we have described. A glaring example of this would be a small medical practice consisting of two physicians, three nurses, an insurance billing clerk, and a receptionist. This small office must comply with the same HIPPA regulations as would the largest hospital. It also frequently produces a higher percentage of unstructured content than a larger corporation because employees work in a more open environment with fewer established standards. SharePoint Products and Technologies provides tools that make it possible for non-technical users to manage unstructured content in a proactive controlled fashion. Another example we see frequently is small engineering firms that need to prove when they created a product or fostered an idea so that litigation against a competitor can occur if necessary. Think about your business from the big picture, and plan your ECM strategy around those regulated or protected items.

## Content-Driven Internet Sites

SharePoint Server 2007 doesn't really differentiate between a Web page and an Office Word 2007 document. They are both simply items in a list. Therefore, Web pages can be managed in the same way documents are managed. Numerous studies have concluded that Internet Web sites (think pages in a list) that rarely change are sites that don't continue to draw much traffic. If companies are going to maintain a dynamic, robust presence on the Internet, it is imperative that they facilitate changing, adding, and deleting content from company Web sites. Traditionally, these Web sites have been created and maintained by the professional staff in the IT department. But usually the people who are truly responsible for Web content are not part of the IT department. Given that most IT staff are overloaded with work, often the result is company Web sites that are too expensive to maintain and that aren't updated on a regular basis.

A very common process is that users give content to Web authors, who in turn create Web pages that are approved by content creators and management. A better way is leveraging ECM within SharePoint Server 2007 to delegate the creation of these Web pages to users. This removes IT as a bottleneck to the process and simplifies the overall process. Sure, this takes some planning and causes some short-term pain, but it usually results in long-term gain through timely content on your Web site.

Before you hand off all Web authoring to your users, however, you need to understand the potential consequences. There are two common issues we see when companies give the end-user community direct authoring access to company Internet Web sites. First, end-users often lack the technical skills necessary to create and edit Web pages. This is easily overcome with education and practice. Second, even if users have the necessary skills, the result may not be a unified corporate presence. Each author will tend to develop pages using his or her own view of what the company's Web site should look like. You must provide both an easy way to add content and a context that maintains an overall consistent corporate branding. The Web content management (WCM) capabilities of SharePoint Server 2007 provide a framework for managing your Internet sites as well as your intranet sites. You needn't leverage the entire framework to get immediate results. Something as simple as cascading style sheets (CSS) with your company colors goes a long way toward maintaining a common theme in your Web sites.

## Collaborative Intranet Sites

Companies have always recognized the importance of small group collaboration, but IT tools to support this kind of collaboration have traditionally been in short supply. Most companies have settled for providing network shares for small groups to store their information. This approach has two problems. First, file-based network storage of information is appropriate only for some of the content on which small groups collaborate. Storing things such as contact information, to-do lists, and schedules in files turns what should be structured content into unstructured content.

### Notes from the Field **SharePoint Server 2007 versus Outlook 2007**

It may seem strange, but many companies view SharePoint Server 2007 as a competing technology to Microsoft Office Outlook 2007 and Microsoft Exchange Server 2007 for storing items such as calendars, tasks, and group discussions. While there is some validity that teams within Microsoft compete for platform and feature dominance, there doesn't have to be a line in the sand regarding these technologies. First, storing lists, such as tasks and meetings, in SharePoint Server 2007 brings obvious benefits such as Web viewing, information management policies, metadata and content type filtering, and limited anonymous access. For example, conference rooms can have an associated SharePoint Server 2007 calendar so people can easily see the occupation schedule. You can then synchronize this calendar list with Office Outlook 2007 so it is viewable and editable. One of the benefits of SharePoint Server 2007 and Outlook 2007 integration is that synchronization occurs over HTTP, so any SharePoint Products and Technologies server viewable on the Internet can be synchronized without VPN access. The tradeoff is that the calendar is now fragmented between two technologies: Exchange Server 2007 and SharePoint Server 2007. Many users will continue to use Outlook calendaring via Exchange while some will use SharePoint Server 2007. This represents problems such as users removing the view from Outlook 2007 and not seeing updates, or being able to update the calendar from their e-mail client. Additionally, it would require further user education about how and where to create events. The calendar example is just that–an example. Many parts of SharePoint Server 2007 integrate with Outlook 2007, and they all have tradeoffs. Your design should determine how much integration you will have between SharePoint Server 2007 and Outlook 2007 and also when that integration will occur. Be aware that functionality, such as discussions lists, work brilliantly, but others, such as document library synchronization, do not.

*Ben Curry, Microsoft MVP, Mindsharp*

A second problem is the increasing mobility of corporate workforces. To address this problem, companies have embraced Internet technologies as a way to access corporate applications and information from anywhere. With SharePoint Products and Technologies, you can create Web sites that allow small teams to store both structured and unstructured content where team members can access the information from anywhere on the Internet. This gives your users a single place to work on a project and helps govern your structure so that content isn't fragmented between Web sites, file shares, and other systems.

### Content Archiving Sites

The price of disk storage continues to decline, and the capacity of backup technologies continues to rise. But the availability of relatively inexpensive storage doesn't mean that you want to keep everyone's content online forever. When you decide to archive or delete old content, the question is, "Who is going to decide what should be removed and what should stay?" Any single answer to this question can raise significant issues. Content owners know best what should be kept online, what is to be deleted, and what should be archived to some other type of storage. But usually they don't have access to the tools necessary to archive content effectively. Content owners usually have very different views than network administrators about what should be archived and what should be deleted. But if file removal decisions are made and implemented by the central IT staff, you run the risk of archiving something that will soon be needed again. No matter who is responsible for archiving content, currently it is a manual, labor-intensive task.

To reduce the manual administrative overhead of content archival, you can use content types, information management policies, workflows, and the Records Center in SharePoint Products and Technologies to support centralized automation of archiving while still allowing for localized control. Proper use of these tools will allow you to create centralized policies on content categories that specify a retention and disposition strategy. Then local users can apply or extend these categories to manage the disposition of content.

> **Note** The Unused Site Deletion functionality in Central Administration does not work as expected. In fact, if you completely enable this functionality, you will be sending an e-mail to all site collection owners with a link to delete their site collection, whether it is in use or not! There is currently a third-party tool by Barracuda to properly enable site collection and site archival and deletion. See *http://www.deliverpoint.com* for more information and a free trial version.

## SharePoint ECM Technologies

Companies of every size, shape, and market segment need to consider how they will manage all of the unstructured content produced by their employees. ECM systems provide content management in five areas: document management, WCM, records management, forms management, and e-mail archiving. In this section, we'll review how Windows SharePoint Services 3.0 and SharePoint Server 2007 capabilities can be used to manage both the unstructured and structured content in your organization.

> **More Info** The Microsoft ECM Team blog is an excellent source of information about how to effectively use SharePoint Products and Technologies to implement ECM in your company. The blog location is *http://blogs.msdn.com/ecm.*

# Document Management

Document management is ignored by many administrators because they view it as an insurmountable summit to reach. Taking a simplistic approach in the beginning and maturing your file plan as you understand the technology is a best practice. Basically, files have usually been created by a word processing program like Word 2007, a spreadsheet program like Office Excel 2007, or a variety of other programs like Adobe Acrobat. These files contain a wealth of information that is critical to the business processes of an organization. SharePoint Products and Technologies provides a variety of features that can be used to catalog, store, and manage the retention and disposal of these documents. In this section, we'll examine the basic capabilities available for managing unstructured content stored as files in document libraries.

> **More Info** For a detailed discussion of document libraries, refer to Chapter 8, "Document Management." Only the points relevant to this discussion are included here.

## Content Types

A best practice to managing unstructured content is mandating that the appropriate metadata is collected when the file is first stored in a document library. This metadata can then be used to manage the content programmatically and leveraged by search to find unstructured content that would otherwise be lost to obscurity. In SharePoint Products and Technologies, metadata is stored in data columns, also called Site Columns in the user interface, and these are associated with the documents in a document library. The specific metadata that will be stored with a particular document is defined by the Site Columns associated with that document. There are two ways to encourage, if not enforce, this metadata collection: List Columns and Site Columns used in content types. Content types can also be used to specify the template used to create a new document, a rights management policy, or a workflow for a document.

> **More Info** For a detailed explanation of content types, see *Microsoft Office SharePoint Server 2007 Administrator's Companion* (Microsoft Press, 2007) and *Microsoft SharePoint Products and Technologies Administrator's Pocket Consultant* (Microsoft Press, 2007). This section is concerned with how to leverage content types, not what they are.

Custom content types can be created for a site or a site collection by clicking the Create button in the Site Content Type Gallery found on the Site Settings page of every SharePoint Web site. Figure 9-1 shows a Site Content Type Gallery.

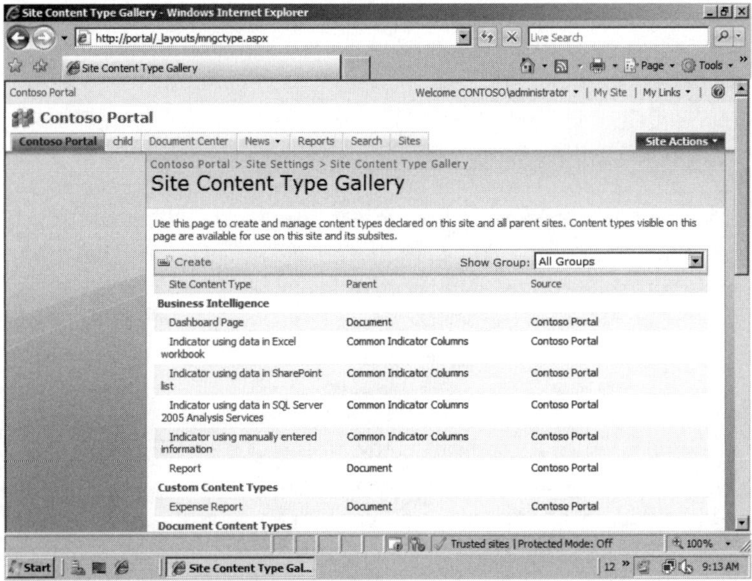

Figure 9-1 Site Content Type Gallery

These content types will be available to document libraries and lists in the site where they are created and every site below it. However, you can also define a content type as a SharePoint feature, which allows the content type to be defined centrally but also used in any site or site collection in a SharePoint farm.

> **Note** Defining a content type as a feature is a best practice for two reasons. First, features can be defined by a central IT staff and deployed to an entire farm using a solution package. This guarantees the availability of identical content types in all site collections. Second, content types deployed as features have the same definition wherever they are used, including the content type ID. This is critical when deploying content across site collection boundaries. A prime example is when you send official records to a Record Center. The inbound content type must match the record routing definition.

> **More Info** For a more detailed discussion of features and solutions, refer to Chapter 12, "Web Parts, Features, and Solutions Management."

When you create a custom content type, your first step will be to choose the content type from which it inherits. To be able to use it in a document library, a new content type must trace its inheritance back to the document content type. When a content type inherits from another content type, it automatically picks up the Site Columns, rights management policy, document template, and workflows associated with the parent content type. Then you can expand on the original definition by adding to or changing the properties of the inherited content type. Using inheritance, you can create increasingly complex content types without having to start each from scratch.

When you create a custom content type, you can also specify columns that will be required metadata when a document is saved or uploaded. By doing this, you can guarantee that specific metadata is available when users are searching for unstructured content. Be careful that you don't specify too many columns as required when creating a content type. Large amounts of required metadata will make it easier to find content but more difficult for the author to save it. If content is too difficult to save, people will store it elsewhere, and that defeats the purpose of using SharePoint Products and Technologies for ECM. A best practice is requiring no more than five metadata fields when users save documents. You can most certainly have more than five fields to be populated, but don't create them as required fields.

You should strive for a balance between easy creation and storage of content and the need to categorize it. One way to balance these goals is to edit the default DIP. This is the InfoPath form that is displayed in Office 2007 applications when users save a file. If the document is loaded into a document library or created from a content type within a documents library, a generic form is created for each content type that enforces the capture of required properties. By editing the form, you can set custom default values or add validation logic to the form that will enhance the user experience when documents are saved from Office 2007. Microsoft Office can display the DIP without the InfoPath client application, but you will need the full InfoPath 2007 client if you wish to edit a DIP. Figure 9-2 shows a DIP being edited in InfoPath 2007.

If a content type is already in use, you should be very careful about changing its definition. The best practice is to have a content type completely defined before using it. Adding required columns or removing existing columns that contain data can cause unexpected side effects. To prevent this, set content types to Read Only under Advanced Settings of the content type.

> **Note** When you see Sealed content types in the interface and documentation, it simply means Read Only.

Figure 9-3 shows the radio button that must be clicked to set a content type to Read Only.

By default, each document library is based on one content type selected when the document library was created. But, by enabling the Allow Management Of Content Types option in the advanced settings of a document library, you can add additional content types to the document library. Using multiple content types in a single document library allows the storage of related material in a single location while preserving a unique set of metadata, including Site Columns, for each document. Each content type can also contain a unique document template, information management policy, and workflow.

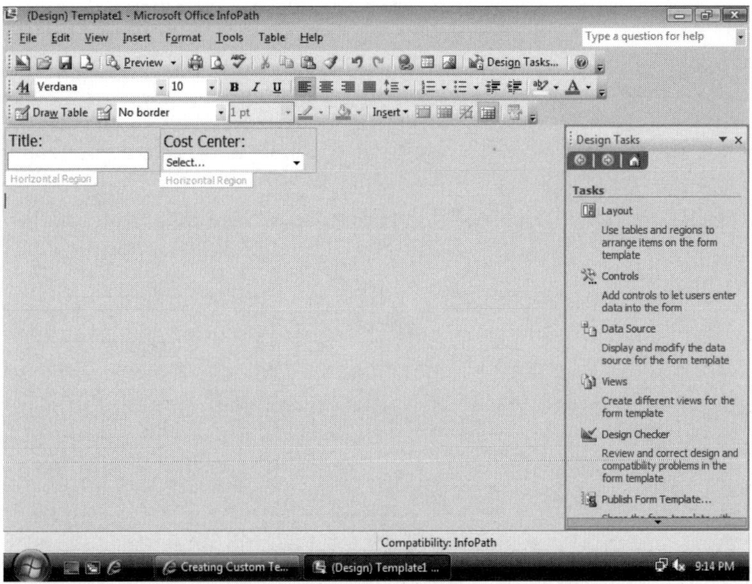


Figure 9-2 Editing a DIP requires InfoPath 2007.

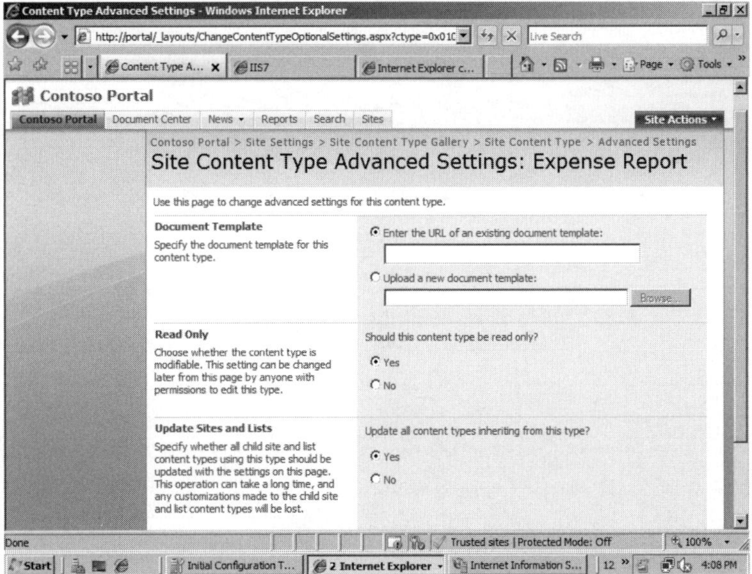


Figure 9-3 To seal a content type and prevent inheritance from above, set it to Read Only.

> **Note** If you are struggling with the concept of content types, imagine what your users will go through learning them! A good starting point for learning content types is leveraging them for multiple templates for a single document library. When your users see multiple items in the New drop-down menu of a library, they will be convinced that they need to learn more about content types. Then, continue your end-user education into workflows, Site Columns, and policies.

Later in this section, we will see that content types also provide the basis for specific auditing, labeling, and disposition information management policies. We will also examine how content types are used to file content in a Records Center.

## Versioning

Versioning is another SharePoint Products and Technologies feature that is useful when you are managing unstructured content in a document library. By default, versioning is turned off in most document libraries, but can easily be turned on and configured through the versioning settings link in the document library settings panel. In fact, some organizations create custom list definitions for their environment that specify at least one major version to support their backup and restore governance policy. SharePoint supports two different types of versioning. First, there is a simple versioning system that tracks all versions as simply another major version. There is also a second type of versioning that tracks versions as a combination of major and minor version numbers. Figure 9-4 shows the versioning settings panel in document library settings.

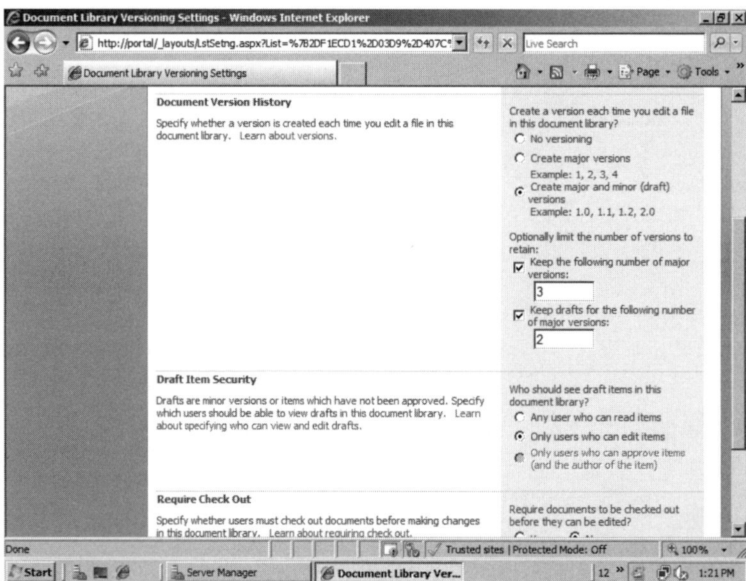


Figure 9-4 You can enable major versions only or major and minor (draft) versions.

Using either versioning type will allow you to recover previous versions of a document. If content is accidentally deleted or changed in a document, versioning can provide a quick way to get lost content back without needing to go through a lengthy backup restoration process that can be accomplished only by the server administrators. Both versioning systems also allow you to conserve storage space by limiting how many previous major versions are retained. When you use major and minor versioning, all of the minor versions for a specific major version are kept, but you can control which major versions retain all their minor versions. Versions are always retained as full copies, so make sure you have enough storage space in your SQL server to maintain all of the versions. This is often correlated with site collection quotas, so be sure to include it in your overall design.

> **Note** SharePoint Products and Technologies does not support differential versioning. A full copy is stored whether it is a major or minor version.

Major and minor version numbering adds a number of additional capabilities. Major versions are considered published versions, while minor versions are designated as draft versions. You can choose whether a document is checked in as a major or minor version. Figure 9-5 shows the panel of versioning choices available when you check in a document.

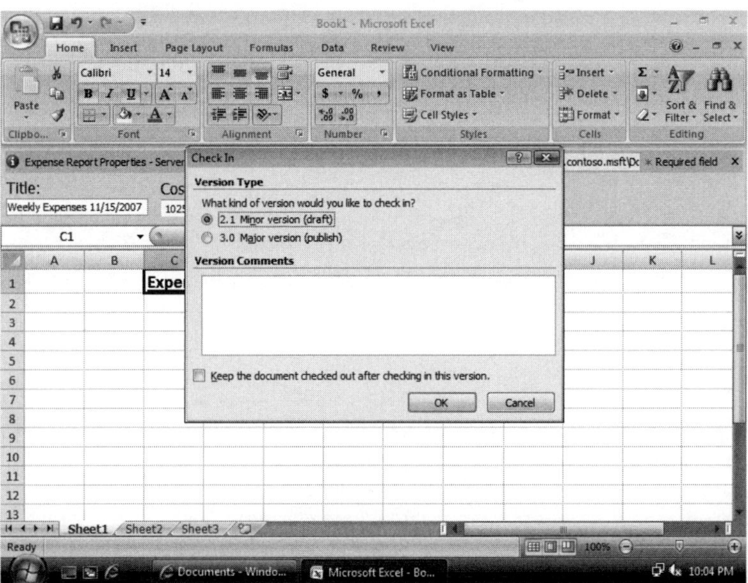


**Figure 9-5** Users select the version when checking in a document.

Only major versions are subject to the approval settings of the document library. You can also designate who can see minor versions. By default, draft versions are viewable by everyone who has access to the library. But you can limit visibility to only those who can edit a document or even to just the original author. Of course, approvers and administrators can see all of the versions. By implementing versioning, content authors can manage their own content efficiently by keeping it both up to date and available.

## Item-Level Security

Security is also a concern when you need to manage unstructured content. Many of the new legal requirements are directly related to holding companies and individuals accountable for unauthorized access to content. HIPAA and FERPA specifically deal with who should have access to medical and student records, and these records are not limited to structured content stored in databases. These records include *all* of the documentation produced while creating and maintaining that structured content. For example, the grades recorded in an Excel spreadsheet by a university professor need to be secured, just like the grade records in the university registrar's database system.

By default, security permissions granted to users or groups in SharePoint Products and Technologies at the site collection level will be inherited, but exceptions can be created by customizing security at any level down to the individual document. Best practice dictates creating a security structure in SharePoint sites that will cover most security concerns automatically and minimize the number of exceptions that must be applied at lower levels. For example, don't give all users read/write access to a site if only a subset of those users will be adding or editing content on the site. Instead, create a SharePoint group at the site level with contribute permissions, and add the users who need read/write access to that group.

Security in SharePoint Products and Technologies works by bringing together three things: a securable object like a Web site or document, a SharePoint user or group, and a permission level. Collections of individual site, list, and personal permissions–called *permission levels*–are defined at the site collection level and inherited down to the level of an individual document. The use of appropriately named permission levels such as approve, contribute, or read, makes it easy to maintain security without having to understand the more technical list of thirty-two base permissions. This makes the establishment of descriptively named permission levels and groups essential because content authors will not use what they don't understand.

> **Note** A best practice is creating permission levels with corresponding names. For example, a permission level named "professors" should be associated with a SharePoint Group named "professors." Extending this idea, name your Active Directory directory services groups accordingly as well, if you are using them in SharePoint groups. Another best practice is to *never* change the default permission levels. Doing so could cause a user to inadvertently escalate permissions for another user.

## Integrated Information Rights Management

Although SharePoint Products and Technologies provides security all the way down to the individual document level, that security protects unstructured content only on the server. But what about copies of files that are checked out of SharePoint Products and Technologies document libraries and stored on local hard drives? This is really no different than any system, but there are some tools that help encourage users to adhere to policy. A file that is downloaded is no longer subject to the security settings established in SharePoint Products and Technologies. It can be copied or edited by anyone who has access to the file. Normally this will be someone with edit access to the original file, but even someone with read-only access to a document library can download a copy of the file. That's where Microsoft Windows Rights Management Services (RMS) for Microsoft Windows Server 2003 comes into play.

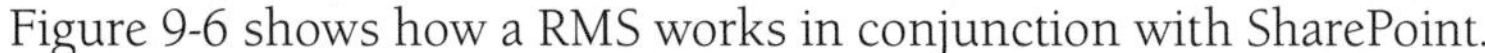

Figure 9-6 shows how a RMS works in conjunction with SharePoint.

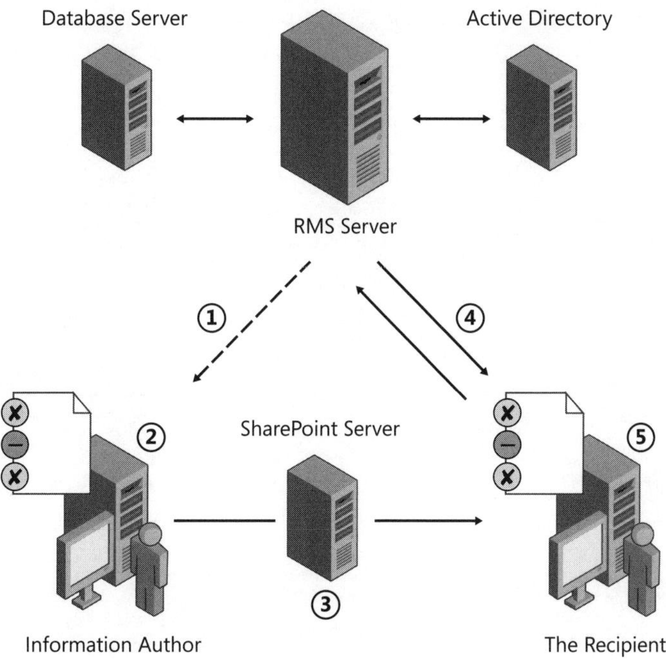


**Figure 9-6** Information Rights Management Server environment

We are slow to say that RMS is a best practice, but it is definitely an enabling technology for enterprise access control. RMS integrates with SharePoint Server 2007 to protect content even when it is downloaded from a SharePoint Products and Technologies server. Content owners can control who can open, edit, print, forward, and/or take other actions with unstructured content stored in files. RMS consists of a Windows Server service that installs on a computer running Windows Server 2003 and an RMS client application that installs on each workstation that will access protected content. Authors can use the RMS client to digitally encrypt documents that are stored in SharePoint Products and Technologies document libraries.

> **Note** To integrate with SharePoint Server 2007, your clients must be using Service Pack 2 for the RMS client.

The documents are encrypted with RSA 1024-bit Internet encryption. Included in the encrypted document are instructions that control what can be done with the document. Users at workstations that have the RMS client installed can decrypt the document but are still limited by the client regarding what they can do with the document. Common limitations include the ability to edit, copy from, e-mail, or print the document.

The following list details how an RMS client interacts with a document:

1. An author with client software installed obtains a certificate from the RMS server the first time she contacts the server.
2. The author creates a file in an RMS-enabled application such as Word 2007 and uses the RMS client software to encrypt the file, along with a "publishing" license that specifies what can be done with the file.
3. The author saves the file to a document library in SharePoint.
4. When a recipient with an RMS-enabled application and the RMS client software opens the file, the client software validates the user and issues a "use" license. If the recipient does not have an RMS client, he will be unable to open the document.
5. The RMS-enabled application displays the file but enforces any limits on usage defined in the use license. The file can now be removed from the network location, but the use license stays with the file and limits how it can be accessed.

> **More Info** You can get more information about Windows Rights Management Services, including a 180-day evaluation copy, at the Windows Server 2003 R2 Technology Center located at *http://www.microsoft.com/windowsserver2003/technologies/rightsmgmt/default.mspx.*

# Web Content Management

Windows SharePoint Services 3.0 document libraries can be used to store unstructured content, but SharePoint Server 2007 includes features that make it possible to author and display content as Web pages. The WCM capabilities of SharePoint Server 2007 can be used to create and maintain a set of content-driven Web sites. Content-driven Web sites enforce corporate standards governing the look and feel of the sites, but adding or modifying content is left in the hands of end-users. IT professionals can create the infrastructure for the Web sites, including a corporate-branded look and feel. Then users can add, modify, and change content using a variety of tools to create a dynamic, constantly changing Web site. In this section, we'll examine the features provided by SharePoint Server 2007 to create and manage content in the form of content-driven Web sites.

## Publishing and Publishing Infrastructure Features

The basis for creating a content-driven Web site is contained in a set of SharePoint features that are rolled up into two overall features. The first is a site collection scoped feature called the *Publishing Infrastructure*. It enables the publishing infrastructure "plumbing" for the site collection, but doesn't enable it in any Web site. The second is a site scoped feature called Publishing. The Publishing feature is the actual enabling of the publishing "plumbing," which allows use of the features in a given site. A best practice is using the Publishing Portal and Collaboration Portal Site Templates when requiring publishing functionality. These templates activate features automatically when a site is provisioned. It is important to note that almost any SharePoint site can be retrofitted with this capability by activating these two features later. See Chapter 13, "Creating and Managing Publishing Sites," for a complete list of best practices.

Activating the Publishing features creates an infrastructure consisting of a combination of content types, document libraries, "templatized" field controls, approval workflows, page layouts, master pages, and external document conversion services that can be used to author Web pages for a content-driven Web site. There are two primary methods for authoring content to be displayed in a publishing Web site. The first is direct editing of a new Web page through the use of a page layout that contains field controls and, possibly, Web parts. The second is by re-purposing content that was authored in a program like Word 2007 and then converted to Web content.

## Page Layouts and Field Controls

Page layouts are a combination of a content type, field controls, and an .ASPX page. When an author chooses to create a new page in a publishing site, he is required to choose from a list of pre-built layouts. These layouts confine authors to specific approved formats while allowing them complete freedom in choosing the content that can be added to a site. These layouts are as much about your governance strategy as they are about ECM. Figure 9-7 shows the dialog box for selecting a layout when you create a page for a Web site in which the Publishing feature has been activated.

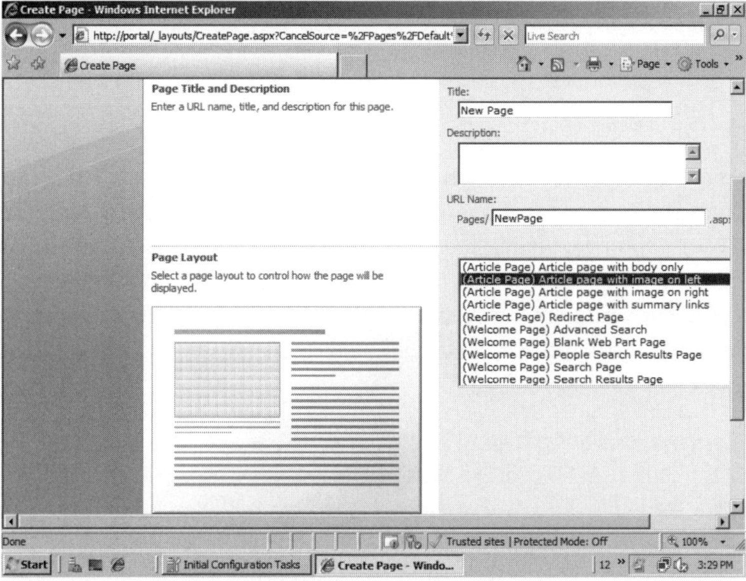


**Figure 9-7** Choosing a layout page on a publishing site

Once a layout has been chosen, an author adds the content directly to field controls that are displayed on the page. Each field control is associated with a column in a related content type that will store the information entered by the author. Because the positioning of the field controls on the page is controlled by the layout page, any layout page built on the same content type can be used to display the page. This allows the author, editor, or approver the freedom to change the layout at any time without having to re-enter the content. Custom layout pages, content types, and field controls can be created to customize the entry and display of information for any environment. Figure 9-8 shows a layout page with a Rich Text field control open for editing.

**Figure 9-8** Editing a field control

## Document Converters

Not all content to be displayed on a content-driven Web site will be entered directly onto a SharePoint layout page. Some content has already been authored in external programs and uploaded to document libraries. SharePoint Server 2007 can be used to automatically convert this unstructured content from one format to another, making it available to a wider audience. For example, you can use one of the provided document converters to automatically convert press releases written in Word 2007 and stored in a document library to a Web page for display on your site.

Several document converters are provided with SharePoint Server 2007, including DOCX or DOCM to HTML, InfoPath to HTML, and XML to HTML. Using these external services, you can easily take content authored in either Word 2007 or InfoPath 2007 and re-purpose it for display on your SharePoint Server 2007 Web site. These document converters are external applications that can be invoked from the command line with values specifying four parameters:

- **Input file** A required parameter containing the full path to the original file to be converted
- **Configuration information** An optional parameter that is the full path to the ConfigInfo file containing custom configuration settings for the document converter
- **Output files** A required parameter containing the full path where the converted file should be placed
- **Log file** An optional parameter with the full path to a log file where errors and other information can be recorded

As long as you have, or can write, a .NET console application that accepts these parameters, you can create your own document conversion services by writing a SharePoint feature that includes the application and a document converter definition file.

Although document conversion services were envisioned to be used to re-purpose previously written content for use on a Web site, they can also be used for a more general purpose for content management. You can create and deploy a custom document conversion service that will convert editable content into a read-only format like Adobe PDF, or automatically convert files from older formats like Microsoft Office 2003 to a newer standard format like Office 2007. You could even convert documents in the opposite direction to support older, non-upgraded clients or external users on different platforms.

## ASP.NET 2.0 Master Pages

One the best aspects of the design of SharePoint Products and Technologies is its support for the standards of ASP.NET 2.0. Master pages are one of the most important of these standards. When the Publishing features are turned on in SharePoint Server 2007, support is enabled for the inheritance of two master pages throughout the site collection. These two master pages are the site master and system master. The site master page is used for the pages stored in the pages library of a publishing site; the system master page is used for the default pages in a non-publishing site. You can choose these two master pages from several that are stored in the master page gallery of the site. When publishing is not enabled for a site collection, there is a single editable default master page stored in site's master page gallery. Each layout page contains a declaration at the top of the page. Custom programming can expand these limitations, so any site can support a different master page for each layout page.

> **More Info** For a more detailed discussion of master pages, refer to Chapter 11, "Branding and Customization."

Implementing a custom master page or a coordinated set of master pages separates the content on a page from the basic look and feel of the frame around the edge of the page. This allows centralized control of a corporate look and feel while still allowing localized control of the content.

## Reusable Content and Image Libraries

Another way that SharePoint provides for both central standardization and local editorial freedom is the use of document libraries to house various kinds of reusable content. When the Publishing features of SharePoint Server 2007 are activated, libraries are created at both the Web site and site collection levels to hold content that can be used over and over again in field controls on layout pages. There are two primary kinds of libraries: one to hold text and one to hold pictures.

A single reusable content library for text is created in the top-level site of the site collection when publishing is enabled. There is no reusable content library for each site. Text in the library can be either unformatted or HTML-formatted text. You can also choose whether the text will be inserted as a static or a dynamic copy when used. If the Automatic Update check box is selected, then the copy will be dynamic, and any usage of the content will be updated if the content in the library is changed. Figure 9-9 shows the dialog box for editing a reusable content entry with the Automatic Update check box selected.

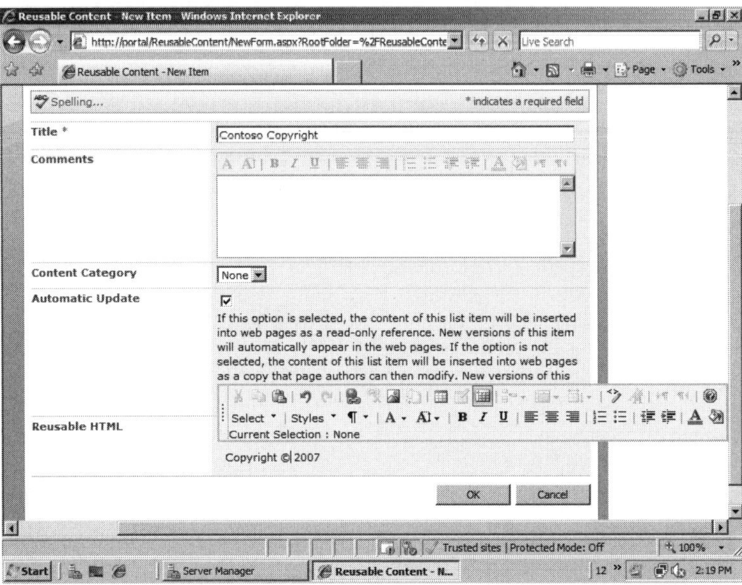


**Figure 9-9** Setting reusable content to be automatically updated

Two image libraries are created in the top-level site of a site collection: one for the entire site collection and one for that site alone. An additional image library will be created in each child site to hold graphics that are reused only in that site. A variety of image formats are supported, and metadata about the image will be collected when images are added to the library.

Reusable content libraries provide an opportunity to decrease duplication of effort by reusing commonly used words, phrases, and pictures. But it also provides a mechanism for implementing standardized versions of wording, formatting, and images at various levels in the corporation. If the content is marked as dynamic, it also provides an opportunity to update the content easily. Companies should use these facilities for things such as standardized logos, copyright statements, and perhaps even company and division names. For example, if division names are entered as HTML-formatted reusable text, then not only will their display have a uniform look and feel, but if a company reorganization occurs you will be able to quickly change important names by changing a few entries in a reusable content list.

### Approval Workflow

SharePoint Server 2007 uses a built-in, three-state workflow as the default approval process for content pages added to a publishing site. But you can also substitute your own custom workflow. There are several reasons why you might want your own custom workflow for this type of approval. First, content may need to be approved by more than one person or group. For example, you may need signoffs from several different groups, such as a marketing department or a legal group, in addition to the normal editor. A second reason might be that you have a multilingual site, and content entered in one site needs to be translated and duplicated for another site. A workflow can be used to route the content to a translation service. Yet another reason might be that you want to implement a more complex workflow that would allow for escalation of approval to another group if a lower-level editor has a question. Whatever the reason, the integration of Windows Workflow Foundations as the underlying workflow engine for SharePoint makes extensible workflows possible.

### Content Deployment

The final piece of the puzzle in a content-driven Web site is deployment. WCM is frequently used to create a read-only Internet presence Web site for a company. This kind of scenario commonly has two or even three different sites involved in creating, editing, and publishing content. A typical three-layer model would consist of an authoring site, where users create new content; a staging site, where new content is held once approved until the time is right to publish it; and a production site, which contains the finished content. SharePoint Server 2007 has a content deployment service that can be used to move content from one site or site collection to another on a scheduled basis. Although the service moves both draft and approved content, only approved content whose publishing start date has passed will be visible on the production site.

## Records Management

According to most modern universities, nonprofits, and corporations, records management is the systematic control of all records, regardless of media format, from initial creation to final disposition. The thing that makes records management different from ECM, in general, is the emphasis on preserving and destroying content. When we consider the huge amounts of unstructured content produced by most businesses on a daily basis, the real challenge is determining which documents to keep and for how long. The focus of records management in SharePoint is on the long-term preservation and disposition of content that should be considered part of the official record of a company. Preservation of this official record is increasingly important in light of new regulatory requirements such as the Sarbanes-Oxley Act of 2002. For example, if a legally required document gets buried in the mountain of unstructured content and can't be retrieved in a timely fashion, an auditing agency might consider the document discarded, which could lead to a negative audit finding or even contempt of court. If a critical document is accidentally disposed of during litigation, a company might lose its case simply because it can't produce evidence. Of course, losing a major case in court can be the downfall of a company.

> **More Info** For a more in-depth look at how SharePoint can be used to comply with new legal requirements, download the white paper titled "Compliance Features in the 2007 Microsoft Office System" by Joanna Bichsel. You can download the white paper at *http://www.microsoft.com/downloads/details.aspx?FamilyID=d64dfb49-aa29-4a4b-8f5a-32c922e850ca&displaylang=en.*

## Records Center

To accomplish the preservation and disposition of content, SharePoint Server 2007 provides a custom site template called a Records Center. Figure 9-10 shows a site created using the Records Center site definition.

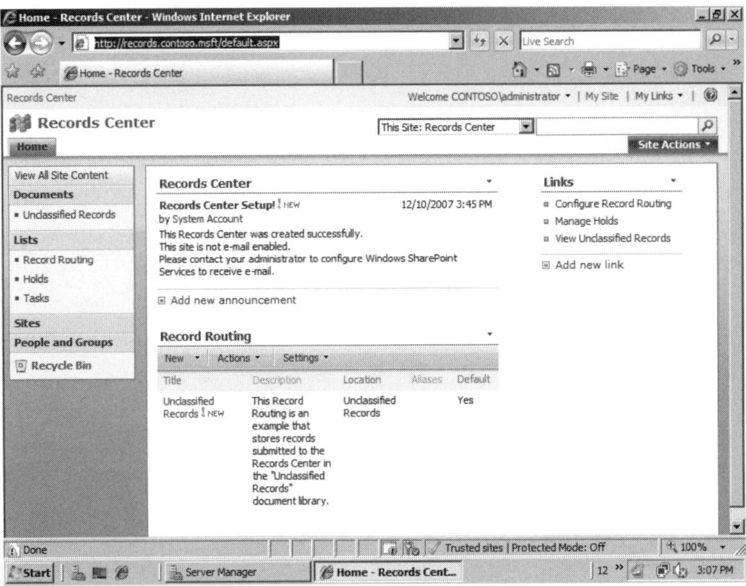


**Figure 9-10** Records Center site

There are several characteristics that make a site created from the Records Center uniquely suited for the retention and disposition of content. The first is that submission of content to a Records Center site can be done through a secure Web service. This service lets users submit content to the Records Center without having actual security rights in the Records Center. If the Records Center is created on a separate Web application with its own application pool, then it will be a secure location where access can be made audited. This secure audit trail is critical if the documents in the site will be used in any kind of legal proceeding or used to protect intellectual property. This service connection can be configured in the External Service Connections section of Application Management, in Central Administration. Note that you can have only one external service connection per farm.

## Information Management Policies

Another critical component in automating the preservation and disposition of content submitted to the Records Center site is the establishment of information management policies. Information management policies are actually a broader concept than the Records Center. They are available in every document library and can even be set for each unique content type. But the Records Center is where these policies become critical. You can define four types of information management policies. Figure 9-11 shows the configuration panel where you can choose which of the four policies to implement.

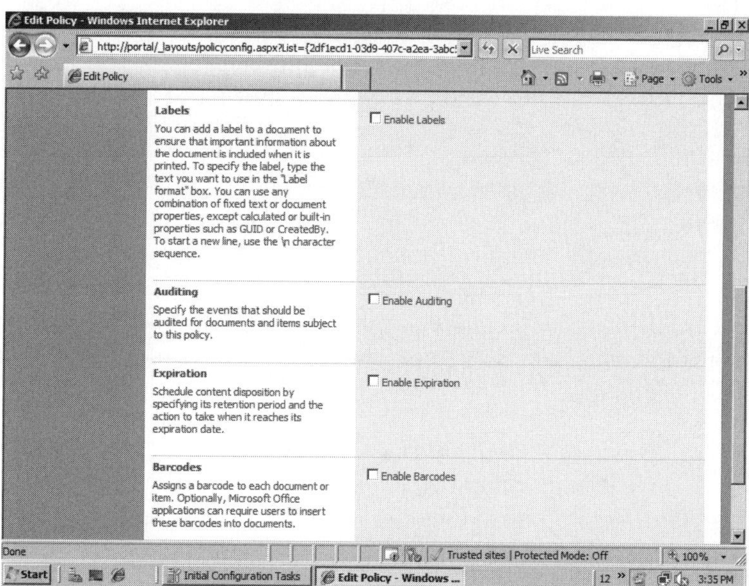


**Figure 9-11** Selecting information management policies

The first type is a labeling policy. Using this policy, you can create and print a custom label that is generated from a document's metadata whenever the document is printed.

The second type is an auditing policy. Using this policy gives you the ability to choose to track specific events in the life cycle of a document. These events include when a document is viewed in any way (including downloading), edited, checked in/out, moved/copied within the site, or deleted/restored. The audit information collected by these policies is stored in a single audit log on the server. Reports showing the audit trail can be run by site administrators, but no one can delete or modify individual audit records.

> **Note** There are no list or item permission event handlers in the SharePoint Products and Technologies object model. Therefore, you cannot see who changed permissions on a document, item, or list. Because event handlers do not exist, you cannot custom code this functionality either.

The third type is an expiration policy. This policy setting controls when content will be scheduled for automatic deletion/archiving. The timing of this disposition can be based on a formula that uses metadata stored with the document record. The action taken can be an automatic deletion of the item or a more complex workflow process that archives the document to offline storage before it is deleted. An often-overlooked capability of expiration is using these policies in lists and libraries. When an expiration policy is defined at the list level, you can create a custom policy based on any Site Column of the date type.

The final category is applying a barcode. Using the barcode feature, you can automatically assign a barcode label that will be printed whenever the document is printed. This simplifies the subsequent retrieval of related hard copy. Many individuals have found creative ways to use the barcode feature, such as labeling student records on printed forms at universities. But the primary use of the barcode feature is tracking hard copies of documents. Yes, SharePoint Server 2007 can manage documents outside of a site as well as native objects.

Information management policies include both an administrative description and a policy statement. The administrative description is used to explain the purpose of the policy to anyone thinking of altering the policy; the policy statement is displayed to users when they work on documents that have associated information management policies. This can be an invaluable way of keeping users informed about what they need to know when they work with various types of content. For example, users need to know not to discuss sensitive content stored in certain documents and that their actions are being audited. Policy statements automatically appear in the DIP in Office 2007.

Information management policies can be a critical component in the business processes of your company and can be used to either replace or enhance workflows that implement those business processes. Best practices for using information management policies include the following:

- Use expiration to reduce unnecessary content. This reduces required storage and backup capacity and increases the relevancy of other documents in your search corpus.
- Use auditing when needed based on a Site Column. Do not use auditing by default because it affects system performance.
- Use labels and barcodes sparingly. Do not use them for functions for which they were not intended. A product version change might affect your custom code.

## Record Routing

Because content added to the Records Center can be submitted anonymously, there needs to be an automated method of categorizing and storing the records when submitted. This process is accomplished by a record routing list that is created in the Records Center site. Each item in the record routing list specifies where content of a particular content type should be stored in the site. Don't make this part difficult. If an inbound content type matches a record or alias, it routes to the corresponding document library. If an entry does not exist for an incoming content type, then that content is automatically placed in a default library. Entries can also be created that send different types of content to the same final library or list. Because the Records Center will usually be created in a separate security context where regular users have no rights, it is critical for an automated procedure to exist for categorized storage of submitted content. This categorization system should be considered when planning the creation of custom content types. You should also consider implementing these content types as features to make it easy to create parallel definitions in different site collections such as the Records Center.

## Holds

So far, we've discussed how SharePoint Server 2007 supports the automated categorization and disposition of content by using information management policies and the Records Center site. But what happens when a legal question is raised? If a suite is filled, there needs to be some way to guarantee that the content will be available even if a policy calls for the content to be deleted. Like the record routing list, a holds list is created in the Records Center. You can add a new record to this list to create a hold for a specific legal case. Then you can add or remove content from a hold by selecting Manage Holds from the context menu of a document in the Records Center. Figure 9-12 shows a holds list in a Records Center with the context menu for removing a hold.

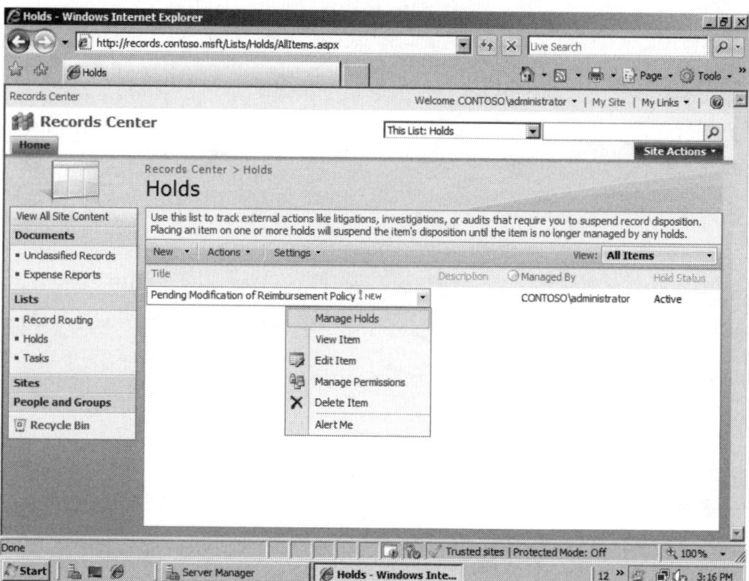


Figure 9-12 Removing a hold

As long as the link to the hold exists, any expiration policy will be delayed. Once the case is settled, removing the hold from the document will allow suspended expiration policies to be processed. Holds can be established only for content in the Records Center, so you *must* add to the Records Center any official content that needs to be retained for legal purposes.

## Forms Management

So far, we've primarily discussed best practices surrounding managing unstructured content stored in documents. But automating most business processes requires finding ways to collect structured information electronically. Creating full database projects for the collection and storage of this information can be very time and resource intensive, so many companies are turning to electronic forms packages that can simplify the collection of this information. InfoPath 2007 provides an excellent way to collect information electronically, but it allows the user to store the collected information either in a structured content repository like a database or in a library of unstructured content files. InfoPath forms libraries in Windows SharePoint Services 3.0 and InfoPath Forms Services in SharePoint Server 2007 can streamline the collection and manipulation of this kind of content.

There are a number of reasons to use InfoPath to collect business process information. InfoPath forms can be designed to include data validation and calculations without coding. This is particularly important to take pressure off scarce resources such as professional programming staff. Figure 9-13 shows data validation settings for a form designed in the InfoPath forms client.

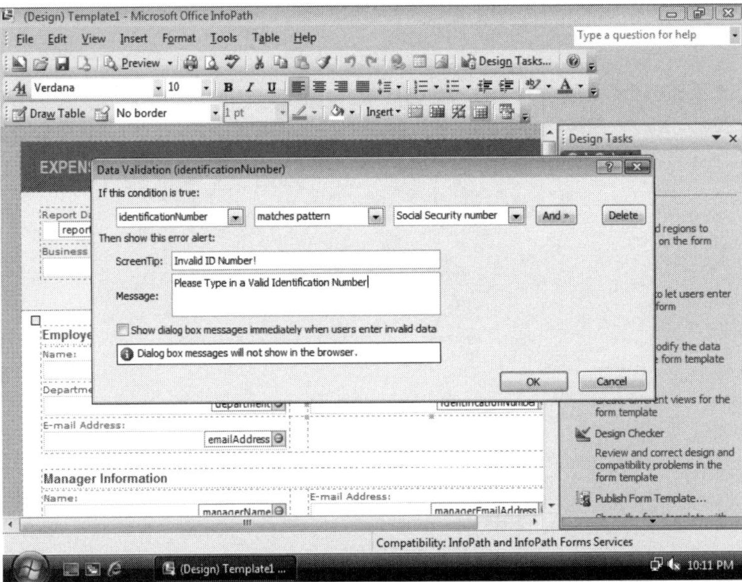


**Figure 9-13** Designing a form with data validation in InfoPath

Different views of the data can also be easily created to provide a view that better matches the usage of the data or to hide information from unauthorized viewers. For example, a professional data entry clerk may need only a streamlined view for data entry, but end-users may want a more detailed view. Figure 9-14 shows two views of the same InfoPath form.

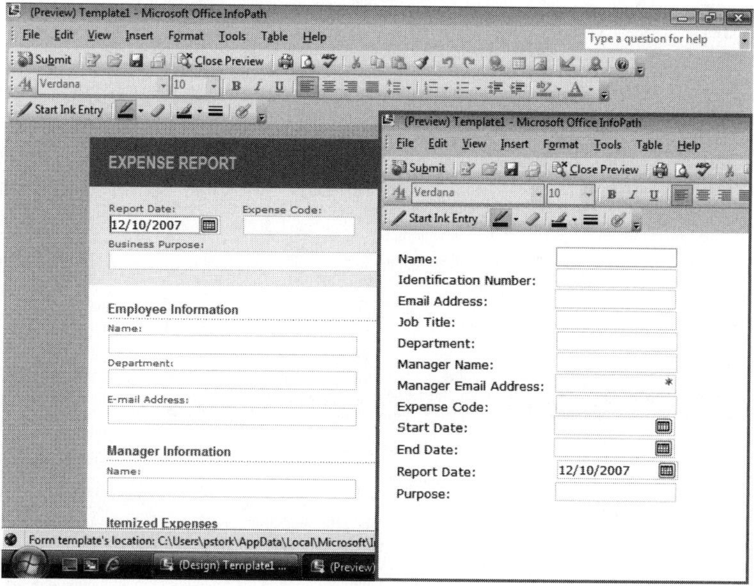


**Figure 9-14** Data entry and end-user views of an InfoPath form

Another advantage is the presence of advanced controls such as repeating tables and optional sections. These controls can solve many of the common problems associated with data entry forms. Finally, the separation of the actual data collected from the form used to collect the data means that the form can be easily modified or copied to other locations. This makes InfoPath 2007 a far better option for collecting form-based data than traditional paper-based forms.

## Forms Library

In the same way that documents can be stored in a document library, SharePoint Products and Technologies makes use of libraries to store InfoPath 2007 forms data. But in the case of InfoPath 2007, the template associated with the library is an InfoPath form template–an .XSN file. Clicking the New button in the form library will open the user's copy of the InfoPath client and load the associated form template. When the form is submitted, the XML data collected by the form will be stored as an XML document. Publishing an InfoPath form to a forms library also makes it possible to surface individual data collected by the form as metadata of the document. This makes an InfoPath 2007 form a hybrid that has characteristics of both unstructured and structured content. Figure 9-15 shows an InfoPath Form library in SharePoint with metadata columns that have been promoted from data fields on the form.

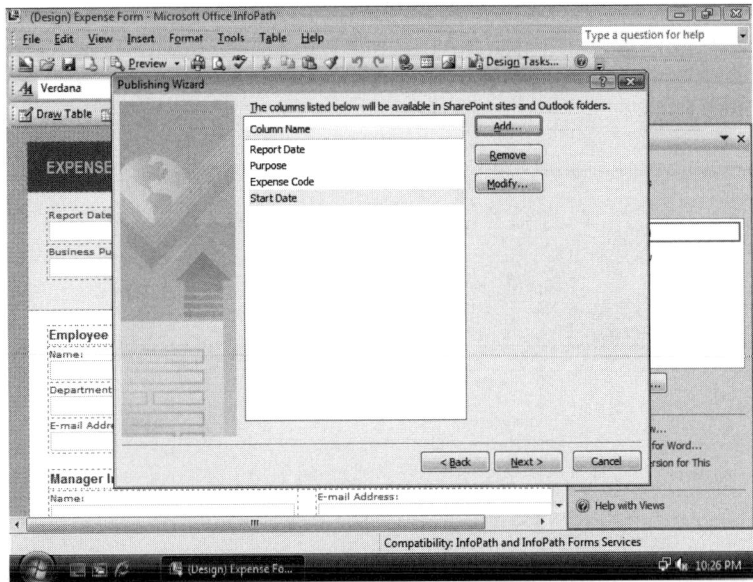


Figure 9-15 Promoting InfoPath fields as library metadata

## InfoPath Forms Services

Windows SharePoint Services 3.0–based forms libraries require that everyone who fills out a form must have the InfoPath 2007 client. SharePoint Server 2007 Enterprise Edition removes this requirement by adding InfoPath Forms Services. InfoPath Forms Services allows users to fill out InfoPath forms by using a Web browser. Forms must still be created using the InfoPath 2007 client, and there are some limitations on the features supported by the Web client. You also need to consider whether you will configure InfoPath Forms Services to use session state or Form view for storing session information. Form view stores session information in hidden fields on the InfoPath form, which increases the use of bandwidth when the form is downloaded or posted back to the server. Session state stores that information in the SharePoint database, which decreases the amount of bandwidth used between the SharePoint server and the Web browser.

> **Note** A best practice would be to configure InfoPath to default to Form view for forms that contain a small amount of session state but automatically default to session state for larger forms. That will allow you to balance SQL server load against the use of client bandwidth.

Figure 9-16 shows the configuration settings that will use Form view for forms with up to 4 KB of session data but use session state for larger forms.

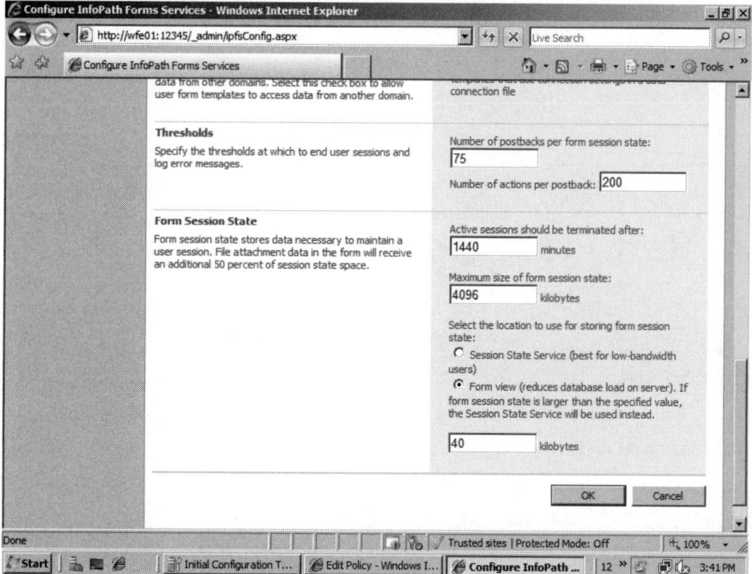


**Figure 9-16** Setting InfoPath Forms Services session state

# E-mail Management

Another form of structured content that many organizations overlook when planning an ECM strategy is electronic mail. In today's business climate, a great deal of content never makes it into formal documents but is simply passed around in the form of electronic mail messages. But this content is also covered by many of the legal initiatives mentioned earlier. For example, one element of the Sarbanes-Oxley Act states that companies must maintain an archive of e-mail messages, many of which contain sensitive information. Managing this information, including deletion of expired content, requires more than just an e-mail archive or a journaling feature installed on the user's desktop. But this archived material also needs to be protected from unauthorized access because e-mail often inadvertently contains extremely sensitive information. Consider how many recent scandals can be traced back to leaked copies of e-mail messages. But simply protecting the e-mail archive is not enough because a record must be maintained that allows retrieval of specific messages when they are needed.

To facilitate the processing of e-mail messages as records, Microsoft has implemented tight integration between Outlook 2007, SharePoint Server 2007, and Exchange Server 2007. Organizational folders can be created in Exchange Server 2007 that map to business functions and then pushed out to a user's Outlook 2007 client using group policies. This makes it possible for users to simply drag and drop e-mail messages into these folders. Then Exchange Server 2007 will automatically copy the messages to SharePoint Server 2007. If there is missing metadata, an e-mail alerts the user to fill it in.

> **More Info** Kathy Hughes, Microsoft MVP, has written a thorough white paper on using SharePoint to archive e-mail titled "E-Mail Records Management in SharePoint Server 2007." You can download a copy from the Mindsharp Premium Content area of the Mindsharp Web site at *http://www.mindsharp.com*.

# SharePoint ECM Best Practices

SharePoint Products and Technologies provides a robust set of components to implement ECM in a company. In addition to the individual best practices that have already been covered in the previous section, there are some overall best practices that should be observed. In this section, we will examine some of the best practices that apply to the general governance of SharePoint Products and Technologies.

## Combine Centralized and Local Governance

Most traditional ECM deployments concentrate on centralized management. Although this can lead to a quick return on investment, it is rarely a recipe for widespread end-user acceptance and use. One of the strengths of SharePoint Products and Technologies is that you can use a combination of centralized, regionalized, and local governance. This combination of governance can lead to an optimum balance of users feeling in control while still allowing you to maintain an overall corporate look and feel. Balancing these two outcomes will lead to an effective ECM system that will be used consistently for storage of your unstructured and structured content. That balance is the best way to guarantee a successful ECM deployment.

But which components of SharePoint Products and Technologies should be controlled centrally, regionally, or locally? Although each specific deployment will vary, there are some general guidelines that we can provide. Some SharePoint Products and Technologies components such as master pages, layout pages, Web parts, content types, Records Center, taxonomy, and permission level definition, are best controlled centrally, where they can provide a consistent set of standards and enforce a corporate branding. But other components such as versioning, site creation, check-out/in policies, and personalization of pages with Web parts, is best left to local control. In large enterprises, there may even be a need for a more regionalized set of standards. The key to SharePoint Products and Technologies governance is to balance the need for corporate standards against empowerment of local employees.

## Develop Document Plans

One of the keys to managing unstructured content stored in files is to understand what kinds of content you are storing. One of your early goals in planning for an ECM system based on SharePoint Products and Technologies should be to develop specific document plans for each specific type of content that you will be storing in your system. These document plans should include the type of content contained in the document, what type of access is needed to the document, how long the content must be available, and any legal requirements about the content. As you refine the plans, they will become the basis for designing content types, security permission levels, information management policies, and perhaps even the design of a Records Center site.

## Don't Migrate All Legacy Content

SharePoint Products and Technologies–based ECM systems are rarely created in a vacuum. Most companies will have legacy content that is currently being stored in some other fashion. It is common to want to include migration of this content into SharePoint Products and Technologies as part of your implementation plan. But legacy content should be evaluated before moving it all into SharePoint. If the content is still being modified regularly, then you should consider moving it into an appropriate location in SharePoint. But if the content is essentially read-only content, it will be much more efficient to add the location of that content as a content source in SharePoint's search and indexing system. Once the legacy content has been added to the search index, users will be able to find and open the content without the work required to migrate that content into SharePoint.

## Store Large Media Files in External Storage

In addition to the question of where to store legacy content, there is also the question of whether large files (over 500 MB) should be stored in SharePoint Products and Technologies. By default, SharePoint Products and Technologies imposes a 500-MB size limit on the upload of files. Although this limit can be increased, Microsoft warns that it is impractical to try to store individual files of more than 2 GB due to network bandwidth and timeouts. Most unstructured content will be well below the 500-MB size limit. But what if you want to include a library of multimedia presentations? Media files will often exceed the 500-MB limit and can even be larger than the 2-GB limitation. One way to overcome these restrictions is by adding the Link to Document content type to document libraries that need to store this type of large file. This content type inherits from the document content type and allows the storage of regular document metadata while storing a link to an external document rather than the document itself. Because the documents will be retrieved through a Web site, the link must be to a Web site location. But using this content type, you can add content of any size to a SharePoint Products and Technologies document library. Figure 9-17 shows a document link being added to a library containing both the document content type and the Link to Document content type.

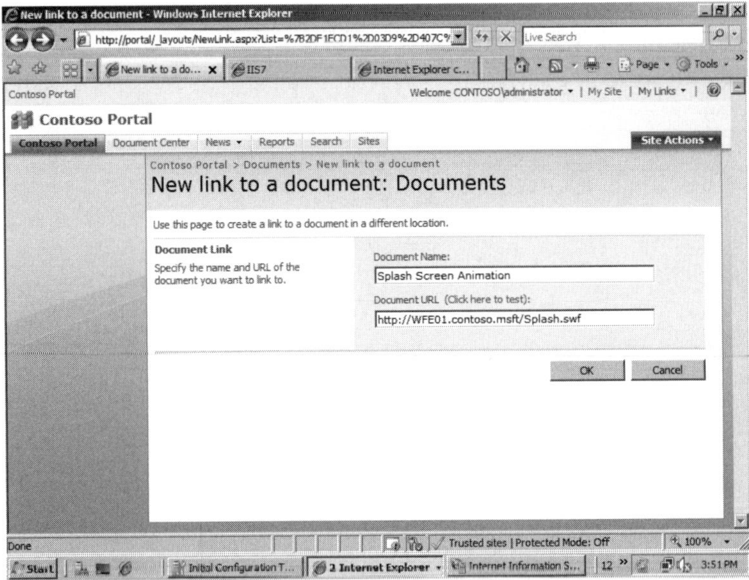


Figure 9-17 Adding linked documents to a library

## Add iFilters to Index Unstructured Content

Most unstructured content is locked up inside files. Although we can find this content by searching for metadata that was collected and indexed when the file was added to SharePoint Products and Technologies, we've already discussed how requiring too much metadata can lead users to look for other ways to store their content. One way to overcome the limitation of searching only by metadata is to index the contents of the files themselves. But to do this, you need to be able to read the contents of the file. iFilters are small programs that make it possible for SharePoint to read the contents of files so that they can be indexed. iFilters are usually made available by the company that programmed the software that creates the file. Microsoft has pre-loaded iFilters for most of its own file formats into SharePoint Products and Technologies, but there are exceptions. For example, iFilters for Microsoft Visio and Microsoft One Note are not part of the default load for SharePoint Products and Technologies. Third-party file formats like Adobe Acrobat and Open Office are also not pre-installed. If you use these programs in your environment, you should consider loading the iFilter for the appropriate format.

> **Note** Some iFilters perform better than others. Always test a new iFilter before installing it in a production environment. Use of some iFilters may necessitate the use of a dedicated Index server.

## Summary

In this chapter, we've presented several reasons why managing your content is critical to the success of your company. We've also examined how SharePoint Products and Technologies provides tools that can be used to meet these challenges in the areas of document, Web content, records, forms, and e-mail management. We also reviewed some overall best practices that should be observed when planning an ECM system using SharePoint Products and Technologies.

## Additional Resources

- DeliverPoint software and documentation: *http://www.deliverpoint.com*
- The Microsoft ECM Team blog: *http://blogs.msdn.com/ecm*
- Windows Rights Management Services 180-day evaluation copy: *http://www.microsoft.com/windowsserver2003/technologies/rightsmgmt/default.mspx*
- White paper titled "Compliance Features in the 2007 Microsoft Office System" by Joanna Bichsel: *http://www.microsoft.com/downloads/details.aspx?FamilyID=d64dfb49-aa29-4a4b-8f5a-32c922e850ca&displaylang=en*
- White paper titled "E-Mail Records Management in SharePoint Server 2007" by Kathy Hughes: *http://www.mindsharp.com*

Chapter 10
# Business Processes and Workflows

**In this chapter:**



Workflows represent a series of actions and decisions within a larger process that are committed in a particular order. The more ordered a process is, the easier it is to record that process electronically in a workflow. An example is how an expense claim is managed internally between an employee and the company. An employee submits an online expense claim, which is either approved or disapproved by her manager. This determines the next step in the workflow, such as the approved expense claim being routed to accounts so that employee reimbursement can be organized.

Workflows automate otherwise manual and repetitive business processes and add some smarts to routing processes within workflows, such as e-mailing one or more end-users during the workflow process, assigning tasks, and setting conditions that need to be met before a workflow can progress. For example, a basic workflow can be envisioned by using a flowchart like the one shown in Figure 10-1. Point A is the input stage or beginning, such as an online expense claim. This triggers a workflow. Point B is the decision point, which determines the next step or stage of the workflow. For example, Yes approves an online expense claim, while No disapproves the same claim and sends an e-mail to the submitter requesting additional information or adjustments. The workflow will end once all of the conditions within the workflow are met and an outcome is achieved.

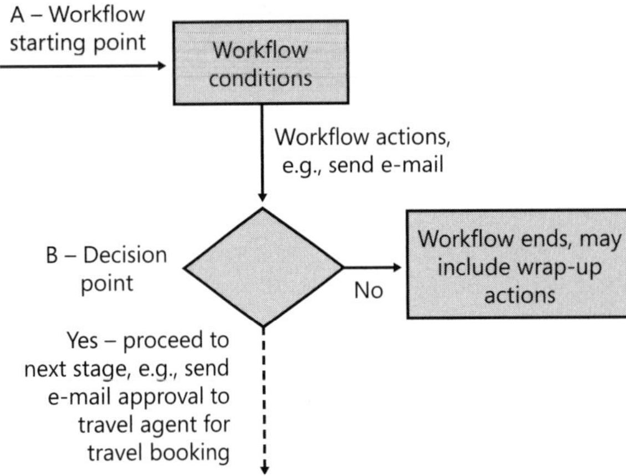


**Figure 10-1** Basic workflow process concept

Microsoft Office SharePoint Server 2007 includes a wealth of built-in workflow features, including workflows specific to documents, approvals, content expiration, user feedback, and publishing. Workflows can be associated with documents and items, document libraries and lists, as well as specific types of content, referred to as *content types*. Microsoft Office SharePoint Designer 2007 includes a workflow designer that can be used to extend the out-of-the-box workflows. In addition, enhanced workflow features can be integrated throughout SharePoint sites and site collections using Microsoft Visual Studio 2005 in conjunction with Windows Workflow Foundation, Microsoft Office InfoPath, and the SharePoint Object Model.

In this chapter, we'll focus on the out-of-the-box workflows and custom workflows created using Office SharePoint Designer 2007, and we'll discuss best practices for creating workflows throughout SharePoint deployments using these technologies.

# Identifying Workflow Candidates

An automated workflow process can potentially replace existing manual, or labor-intensive, business processes and boost productivity throughout an organization. But you must first identify where and how you can adapt workflows to best meet business requirements. For example, do you have any existing processes that demand a great deal of user-generated e-mail, or are you still using a paper-based solution that has the potential to be replaced by an online workflow?

Two examples of how companies have utilized automated workflows include the following:

- A document review and approval process; for example, project technical and functional specifications that need to be reviewed and approved by multiple team members

- A company travel system in which employees must submit a travel request to their manager and have that request approved before it can be sent to the travel agency for airline and hotel bookings

Workflows within SharePoint can be as simple as triggering an e-mail when a document is uploaded to a document library or as complex as workflows that interact with back-end Line-of-Business (LOB) systems, such as SAP.

Before creating workflows, you need to assess potential workflow candidates by reviewing your existing business processes. Best practice is to hire a good business analyst to help you assess your existing processes and consider issues such as employee productivity drain. Even 5 to 10 minutes per day, every day, for each employee can have a significant impact on overall company productivity. Workflows can also add control, consistency, and structure to business processes. But remember, embarking on an automated workflow project where the underlying processes haven't been fully identified and assessed can lead to project failure, budget blowout, and an unprofitable end solution that helps no one. For instance, if discussions focus predominantly around the workflow technology solution rather than the actual process, then the project is at risk of failing to identify correct candidates for automated workflow and doomed to failure. Best practice is to ensure that you have correctly documented the actual workflow before trying to replicate it electronically.

## Adapt the Technology to Business Requirements

Once you've identified existing and/or new candidates for automated workflow processes, you're ready to choose exactly what workflow technology you'll use. In other words, you should adapt the technology to the business requirements rather than the other way around. That is, fit the business requirements to the technology. One size doesn't fit all!

A commonly used workflow within SharePoint sites is the document approval workflow, which is available as an out-of-the-box workflow. SharePoint Designer 2007 adds the ability to create code-free custom workflows that extend out-of-the-box workflows. For example, you can use SharePoint Designer 2007 to add a multiple-step workflow to progress a document through several approval stages and move the document into another document library based on a certain condition. A more complex workflow, such as one involving integration with a LOB system like SAP, will involve using Visual Studio. Table 10-1 details the key differences between workflows created using the out-of-the-box workflows, custom workflows created in SharePoint Designer 2007, and workflows created using Visual Studio.

The degree of complexity for each method is also listed in Table 10-1. This is something else you will need to consider as part of your up-front workflow design and strategy. For example, will you need to hire additional resources to build custom workflows, or will you be able to address your workflow requirements with the out-of-the-box workflows?

Table 10-1 Comparison Between Workflow Tools

| Workflow tool | Functionality | Complexity |
|---|---|---|
| Default out-of-the-box workflows | Application Task and Issue Tracking, Routing and Approval, Review Approval, Signature Collection | Ad hoc |
| SharePoint Designer 2007 workflows | Custom Form Actions, Document Processes, Weekly Status Report, Service Requests, Asset Tracking | Ad hoc/structured |
| Visual Studio 2005 and Workflow SDK | Line of Business Integration, Purchase Order Processing, Product Lifecycle Management | Structured/requires coding |

# Overview of Out-of-the-box Workflows

Workflows are provisioned in SharePoint Server 2007 site collections as features and are built on the Windows Workflow Foundation. Each type of workflow includes a custom workflow template specific to the type of workflow activity. For instance, the template that underpins the approval routing workflow includes the ability to assign workflow tasks to all participants at the same time (parallel workflow) or one participant at a time (serial workflow). More advanced workflows, such as a disposition workflow, determine whether a document (item) is deleted (allows the item's metadata to be retained in the audit log). Workflows are enabled at the site collection level and are consumed within document libraries and lists throughout sites within a site collection. Table 10-2 defines each of the out-of-the-box workflows.

There is also a special Translation Management workflow template, not listed in Table 10-2, that works with the Translation Management library and manages source documents by creating copies of each document for specified languages. The workflow subsequently assigns tasks to translators so that each separate copy of a document can be translated into defined languages.

Table 10-2 Out-of-the-box Workflow Overview

| Template | Description |
|---|---|
| Approval | Routes a document for approval. Approval is often a prerequisite to another document management task, such as publishing a document to a Web site or submitting a business proposal to a client. Authors choose approvers, send instructions, and track workflow status. By default, Approval is a *serial* workflow, and the order in which approvers view the document is specified by the author. Approvers can approve or reject the approval task or request changes. Approvers cannot modify the document. |
| Collect Feedback | Sends a document for review. The author chooses the reviewers, sends instructions, and can check the workflow's progress. Reviewers receive e-mail notification and are assigned a task with a link to the document to review. Participants can optionally delegate their tasks or decline altogether. Reviewers provide feedback that is compiled and sent to the document owner at the workflow completion. Collect Feedback is a parallel workflow. Reviewers can provide feedback in any order. |

**Table 10-2 Out-of-the-box Workflow Overview**

| Template | Description |
|---|---|
| Collect Signatures | Gathers signatures needed to complete the document. The workflow is started from within a Microsoft Office client. Requires that signing documents be enabled on Microsoft Office 2007 applications. |
| Disposition Approval | Manages the expiration and retention of documents. Participants decide whether to retain or delete expired documents. |
| Three-state | Manages approvals in issues lists, but can also work with other lists and document libraries. In SharePoint Server 2007, this is the only out-of-the-box workflow that is *not* enabled (active) by default. You need to activate this workflow under the site collection features. |

## Workflow Configuration Options

During workflow creation, several configuration options are available, including the following:

- **Designation of a task list and a history list for the workflow** By default, this is the tasks list in sites provisioned from the team site template or the workflow tasks list in sites provisioned from a publishing site template. The workflow history list is selected by default as the history list.
- **Start options** By default, these options allow users with edit rights to a document library or list to manually start a workflow on an item (or, alternately, to lock down the ability to start a workflow to those users with Manage Lists permissions); start a workflow to approve publishing a major version of an item (enabled only where versioning and content approval is enabled on a document library); start the workflow when a new item is created; and start the workflow whenever the item is changed.
- **Workflow Tasks** This setting enables you to either assign tasks to participants included in a workflow as serial (one participant at a time) or parallel (all participants simultaneously) and allow workflow participants to reassign a task to another person and request changes before completing the task (for example, request more information or make modifications to a document before it gets approved).
- **Default Workflow Start Values** Use this setting to add the names of workflow participants (the participant names are added in the order in which you want to assign serial workflow tasks); allow changes to a participant list; enter text for the workflow request; establish due dates for both parallel and serial workflow options; and notify others about the workflow without assigning them tasks (for example, alert a team leader that a project document is currently in a workflow approval process).
- **Complete The Workflow** Use this setting to define the actions that determine when a workflow is completed (e.g., a certain number of tasks are completed) or canceled (e.g., a document is rejected or changed). Remember that when a workflow is initiated on a document (or item within a document library), that document is not automatically checked out, and other users who are not participants within a workflow can potentially modify the document.

- **Post-completion Workflow Activities** This gives you the option to update the approval status (use this workflow to control content approval). Note that if you select the Update The Approval Status (Use This Workflow To Control Content Approval) check box but don't have the document library configured to require approval, then the workflow will generate an error when it runs. An error message such as *The task was marked as complete but no approval or rejection was made* and a workflow status of Error Occurred will be logged in the workflow history once a workflow task is completed.

Figure 10-2 shows a typical workflow process within SharePoint Server 2007.

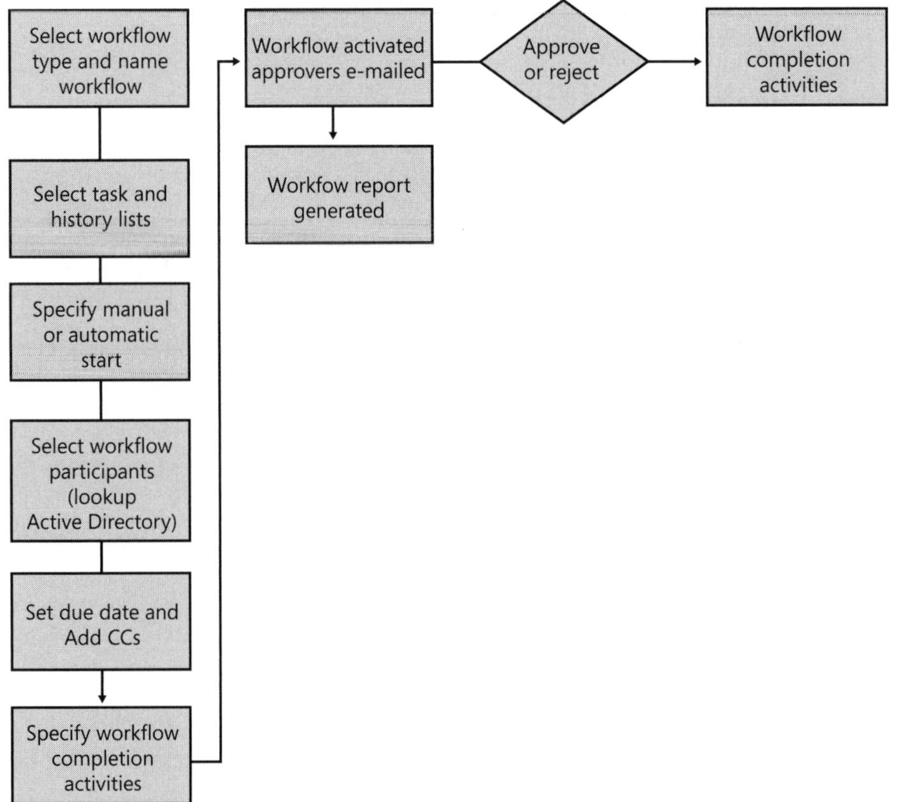


**Figure 10-2** Example of a workflow process in SharePoint Server 2007

## Tradeoff **Parallel and Serial Workflows**

One of the configuration options available with the out-of-the-box Approval workflow is the ability to assign workflow tasks as either parallel tasks or serial tasks. Let's consider when you might choose one over the other.

A typical use of a serial workflow could be a travel request, which initially involves approval by a manager or a hierarchical chain of managers. That is, one manager must approve the document before it can be passed on to the next, more senior manager. In this scenario, the workflow tasking is hierarchical. Another way of looking at it is that the task routing must go through a (point of obligatory passage (POP) before it can reach its final destination. This is a somewhat restricted and more controlled way of assigning workflow tasks, but sometimes there may be a genuine business requirement for doing this, such as with sensitive documents that require modification before they are passed on for subsequent approval.

The risk with serial workflows is that, if the first or one of the subsequent approvers is unavailable, then the workflow progress can be halted indefinitely. Even if the workflow creator selects the Allow Changes To The Participant List When This Workflow Is Started check box, this isn't going to be of much advantage if a serial workflow is triggered automatically on a document and no one realizes the initial approver is out on leave for several weeks. That is, other approvers added to the workflow task won't necessarily know about the workflow until after the initial approver has actioned his task. An additional consideration is that, in SharePoint, the maximum number of users who can participate in any one serial workflow is estimated to be around 1,000. Best practice is to minimize serialization where possible and instead create additional workflows. When serialization is utilized, best practice is to ensure that the workflow originator is using the e-mail alerts and is checking the workflow regularly to ensure that the document is moving through the serial tasks in a timely manner.

A typical use of a parallel workflow is a document-approval process for which there are multiple reviewers involved at the same level (for example, a project team reviewing a functional specification for a new project). An e-mail is sent to all approvers at the time of workflow initiation. When one identified approver okays the document, the workflow is completed. Best practice in using parallel workflows is to ensure that those placed into the parallel approvers pool are of relatively equal influence and authority. Moreover, the approvers should mutually trust one another so that the opinion of one will be respected by the others.

## Workflow History

Workflow history maintains a record of each step within a workflow, including approvals, disapprovals, updates to a workflow, and workflow errors.

By default, when you create and consume an out-of-the-box workflow or a custom workflow created in SharePoint Designer 2007, an historical record for each workflow is saved to a workflow history list within the site where the workflow is created and/or deployed. The workflow history list is either created when a content type configured with a workflow is added to a document library or when a workflow is directly created on a document library. The workflow history list is not directly visible in the site's All Site Content list, but you can access the list through a document library's workflow settings. You can also access the workflow history list in its raw form by directly entering the list URL into the browser address bar. Even if a document library workflow or content type workflow is deleted from a site, the workflow history remains in the site's designated workflow history list.

## Which Workflow History List?

When you create an out-of-the-box workflow, part of the workflow configuration process involves designating a workflow history and task list for each workflow. For instance, if you create a new approval workflow on a document library, you have the option of using the default workflow history list or creating a new history list. If you choose to create a new history list, SharePoint will create a new workflow history list and prefix the name of the list with the name of the workflow (for example, *ApprovalXYZ History*). The same applies when you choose a task list for a workflow. However, no matter how many workflow history lists you create, none of them will be directly accessible from within the site's user interface.

We believe it is usually a best practice to create new workflow history lists for each workflow that is created by your end-users. There are several reasons to create separate workflow history and task lists. First, added workflow security allows you to lock down permissions on a workflow task list and/or a workflow history list (for instance, where users with the member role can still access documents, but won't be able to access workflow details). A second reason is to keep workflow lists properly classified. Workflow task list categorization is especially relevant where a site includes several workflows and end-users are connecting the workflow task list to their Microsoft Office Outlook client. If all workflow tasks are routed to a single workflow task list, then every task will be synced to the Office Outlook client, even those tasks not relevant to the current user. Rather than routing all workflow tasks into a single task list, selecting disparate task lists for each workflow is a best practice when users sync those lists to their Outlook client.

A common workflow task list is a best practice when the workflow is invoked programmatically and the workflow tasks themselves are not reviewed frequently by your users or site administrators.

> **Note** Workflow history lists are not directly visible in a site's View All Site Content page (or via the user interface). Workflow history lists also are not visible when using WebDav (My Network Places). This can be especially troublesome when you've created multiple workflow history lists to cater to different types of workflows within a document library and want to view or access those lists directly. A non-programmatic way to see all workflow lists within a site is to open the site in SharePoint Designer 2007.

There are implications in moving workflow history, such as when you move a document currently associated with a workflow in one document library to another document library. You need to be aware of this and consider it as part of your up-front workflow design and deployment.

If you move a document to another document library within the same site or to another site, workflow history associated with that document will not be moved and will become disconnected from the document. The document's workflow history (defined when the workflow is created) will remain in the designated workflow history list in the site where the workflow was created. Why? The ID referenced in the workflow list is the list ID rather than the GUID. The association is valid only for the original document library in the site where the workflow is created, not another document library in the same site or in another site. Assigning out-of-the-box workflows to content types as opposed to a specific document library will help in terms of portability, that is, accessing workflows throughout an entire site collection as opposed to a workflow created within a document library (limited scope). However, you will still face the same issues when moving workflow documents. Saving a document library as a template, with or without the inclusion of content, will move the out-of-the-box workflows currently configured within that document library, including content types that are configured with a workflow. However, workflows currently in progress or workflow history will not be included as part of the template.

Another consideration in working with workflows and workflow history is that workflow history association is removed from documents after 60 days; that is, the workflow history list is still there but not easily accessible via the user interface, and the link to the original document is removed. So, if you are considering workflow strategies and maintaining workflow history as part of your workflow deployment, then consider the information in the following sidebar as a workaround, and implement it as part of your up-front workflow deployment strategy.

### Notes from the Field **Workflow History Is Deleted After 60 Days!**

By default, workflows will *clean* themselves up 60 days after they "end." This process doesn't delete the actual workflow history table entries but does disconnect them from the user interface, so they are harder to access.

So, there are two key things to note about this:

1. It's configurable. You can change it in your element manifest (see *http://thorprojects.com/blog/archive/2007/10/16/708.aspx* for details on how to do this). You can also change it in the Application Programming Interface (API) for every existing workflow association if you want (SPWorkflowAssociation.AutoCleanupDays). If you never want SharePoint to delete workflow history, the workaround is simple. Write a tool that runs every 59 days that goes through every site, Web, list and workflow association and sets the AutoCleanUpDays property to 9999.
2. Workflow history is not an audit log–it's not secured by default and it's not tamper proof. If you're using workflow history for audit–and the auditors are letting you–then there's something wrong. If you need an audited record, then have the workflow bundle everything up and record it in a Record Center so that it is a final record. For example, I can put an entry into the list saying that a fictitious character

approved something if I've got contributor access to the Web site (and no one has changed the default permissions of the history list). I can delete the records indicating that I did approve something. It's just not secure, so using it as an audit record when it isn't not only doesn't work, it doesn't make sense.

Ultimately, the default design of how SharePoint manages workflow history is a non-issue. It's easy to work around and it's a bad approach to start.

*Robert Bogue, Microsoft MVP, http://www.thorprojects.com*

Additional information regarding issues around workflow history can be found at the following locations: "Re: Missing Completed Workflows History" discussion thread: *http://forums.microsoft.com/MSDN/ShowPost.aspx?PostID=2272887&SiteID=1&mode=1* and "Huge MOSS Workflow Issue...What Is Microsoft Thinking!!!!" blog entry: *http://www.sharepointblogs.com/llowevad/archive/2007/09/21/huge-workflow-issue-what-is-microsoft-thinking.aspx*

# Publishing Workflows

Aside from the out-of-the-box workflows, which are used throughout site collection document libraries and lists, publishing pages throughout SharePoint Server 2007 site collections provisioned from the Publishing Portal site template include a workflow approval mechanism based on the approval workflow (parallel approval). This workflow manages the content approval process and controls the content published by content authors throughout publishing sites and site collections.

The approval workflow tied in with the publishing page will alert the owner of the page so that the owner can either accept or reject the changes, as shown in Figure 10-3.

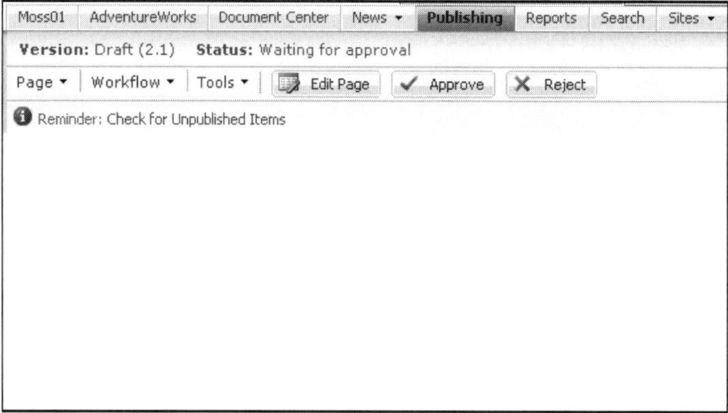


**Figure 10-3** The approval stage of the publishing workflow, as seen by the owner of a publishing page

While the publishing approval process is enabled by default in site collections provisioned from the Publishing Portal site template, site collections provisioned from the Collaboration Portal site template do not include the publishing approval process by default, and each site throughout a site collection will need to have publishing approval enabled manually. We strongly recommend that you enable approval workflows where there is a requirement for consistent content throughout publishing sites.

For top-level sites and/or subsites where publishing approval workflow is required, choose to create the site from the Publishing Site With Workflow site template, where publishing approval workflow is enabled by default.

> **More Info** For details on administrating and configuring SharePoint workflows, see *Microsoft Office SharePoint Server 2007 Administrator's Companion* by Bill English with the Microsoft SharePoint Community Experts (Microsoft Press, 2007).

# Workflow Deployment Considerations

Workflows are provisioned as features at the time of SharePoint Server 2007 installation. Out-of-the-box workflow features are controlled at the site collection level. By default, all out-of-the-box workflow features in SharePoint Server 2007 are set to active except for the Three-state workflow, which is set to inactive and needs to be activated separately. This means that workflows are enabled at all sites and subsites throughout a site collection and can be created in document libraries, lists, and as part of content types. Therefore, part of your upfront SharePoint farm design will involve deciding whether to allow workflows and locking down the ability to create workflows at the site collection level.

## Tradeoff Choosing to Implement Workflows

If you choose to deactivate workflow features at the site collection level, you can select exactly which ones to deactivate. For example, you might choose to deactivate the Collect Signatures workflow if your organization hasn't yet deployed Office 2007, which is a requirement for this particular workflow. By deactivating other workflows, such as the commonly used Routing workflows, you're removing one of the most powerful pieces of functionality throughout SharePoint sites and disempowering end-users. On the other hand, you might decide to pilot your SharePoint Server 2007 deployment and introduce workflows at a later stage when end-users have become familiar with the basic document management feature set. Another consideration may involve training, whereby you decide to roll out different functionality at staggered intervals so that you have time to train your staff and implement appropriate policies. This is the beauty of features; they allow you to introduce additional functionality at stages throughout your SharePoint deployment–plug-and-play functionality.

> Note that deactivating the Routing workflow does not disable the content publishing workflow approval functionality, which is a part of the SharePoint Server 2007 Publishing infrastructure feature. The four workflows discussed here—routing, three-state, disposition approval, and collect signatures—fall into the Document Management/ Collaboration Workflow feature set throughout SharePoint Server 2007.

Additional considerations involve when to activate/deactivate workflow features. If you choose to deactivate workflow features on a site collection *after* users have created workflows, existing workflows will be removed, including currently running workflows, excluding workflow tasks, which will remain in the designated task list throughout sites, and workflow history, which will remain indirectly accessible within the content database. Remember that if a workflow becomes separated from its associated workflow task and/or workflow history, then it's not possible to re-enable that association via the user interface. It is also difficult to accomplish programmatically.

Custom workflows, such as workflows created using SharePoint Designer 2007, are locked down at the Web application level, which you can access by opening Central Administration, clicking the Application Management tab, and then clicking the Workflow Settings (User-Defined Workflows) link. Choosing to disable user-defined workflows will stop end-users from creating custom workflows throughout site collections and sites within a Web application.

If you choose not to disable custom workflows at the Web application level, you can use Contributor settings in SharePoint Designer 2007 to stop select groups of end-users from creating, editing, and deleting custom workflows. This is a more flexible method for controlling custom workflows as opposed to choosing the lock-down option at the Web application level.

## Should You Disable Custom Workflows?

When would you consider disabling custom workflows at the Web application level? Most likely, you've decided on using the out-of-the-box workflows—the basic approval document workflow is all your organization needs right now—and, therefore, you've chosen to lock down the ability to create custom workflows to avoid any additional administrative overhead. Another good reason for locking down custom workflows at the Web application level is when your information technology department has specifically chosen not to allow SharePoint Designer 2007 workflows to be created on the production farm (that is, other features within SharePoint Designer will be allowed at a controlled level, but custom workflows will not).

On the flip side, you may choose to enable custom workflows because you need something more specific than the out-of-the-box workflows can provide. SharePoint Designer 2007 has some great workflow functionality, and information workers can easily create custom workflows, code free. Perhaps you've chosen to deactivate all out-of-the-box workflow features at the site collection level and instead only create workflows in SharePoint Designer 2007.

In the beginning of this chapter, we mentioned that the main focus would be the out-of-the-box workflows and custom workflows built in SharePoint Designer 2007. However, there are many more possibilities for extending workflow functionality using Visual Studio, features, and events. Ed Hild, a technology architect at Microsoft, has developed a novel solution for extending out-of-the-box workflows to provision sites. His solution is discussed in part in the following sidebar.

## Inside Track **Using Out-of-the-box Workflows to Provision Sites**

A large part of governance strategy is having some control on how and where SharePoint sites get created. Traditionally, people focus on whether or not to turn on Self-Service Provisioning. Unfortunately, this setting is at a Web application level and is like a big on or off switch. If you turn it on, your users can create any site, with any title, at any URL, with a selection of any installed template. In some situations, you want more control of your environment.

The solution I put together allows an organization to create forms that provision sites and to use the out-of-the-box workflows for gaining approval of the site requests. This is a big improvement over some other solutions that walk you down the path of creating a custom workflow for every type of site provisioning process you want. In fact, some developers would probably find this sidebar interesting just with the technique of adding a "twist" to the out-of-the-box workflows.

My solution is based on recognizing that an organization would likely have several different forms that could possibly go through different workflow approval steps that could result in the creation of a site collection or subsite. The trick to this solution is that it really doesn't matter what the workflow steps are; just that the form is approved. I will leverage a library's moderation feature so that forms that are saved there land with a status of Pending.

*Ed Hild, Technology Architect, Microsoft*

You can find the solution discussed here as well as additional information on the author's blog at *http://blogs.msdn.com/edhild/*.

## The Other Side of the Coin: Code-free Custom Workflows

SharePoint Designer 2007 includes a workflow wizard that can be used effectively to create code-free custom workflows for document libraries and lists throughout SharePoint sites. Workflows created in SharePoint Designer 2007 extend the out-of-the-box workflows by including the following:

- Additional workflow logic through a predefined set of workflow conditions (for example, *where "Title field contains keywords"*)
- A predefined set of workflow actions in which multiple actions can be applied based on a preceding condition being met (for example, *if [condition] "Title field contains projectX" then do [action] "Copy List Item" [to another document library or list within the site] and "Send an e-mail"*)
- Workflow (initiation) forms for capturing end-user input, which can then be used to determine certain actions throughout workflow steps
- Workflow variables (including Boolean, Date/Time, List Item ID, Number, and String data types), which can be used for calculations
- The ability to include multiple Else If conditional branches
- Multiple-step workflows (for example, breaking up a workflow into logical steps or stages and performing difference conditions and actions at each stage)
- Workflow start options, which include the option to manually start a workflow on an item, automatically start a workflow when a new item is created, and automatically start a workflow whenever an item is changed
- A Check Workflow button, which will highlight errors in a workflow before it is deployed to a document library or list

> **Note** If an e-mail is included as part of a workflow action and the e-mail form does not include any data in the Subject field, then a nondescript error will be generated. E-mail forms must include data within the Subject field.

Figure 10-4 shows an example of a basic workflow created using SharePoint Designer 2007.

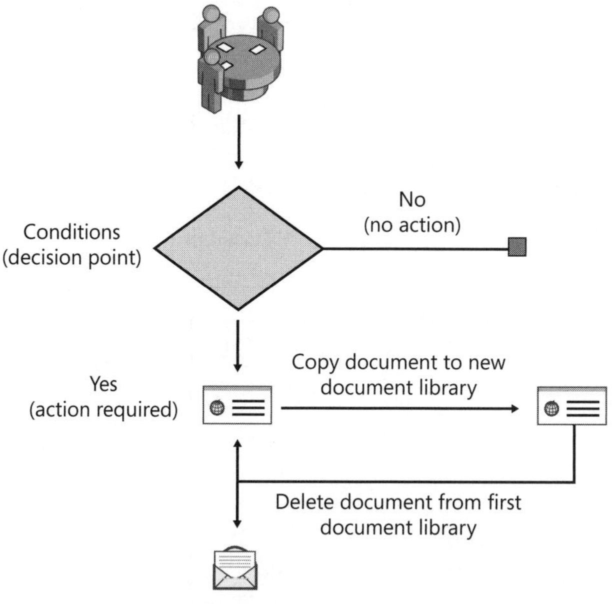


**Figure 10-4** Example of a workflow created using SharePoint Designer 2007

# Custom Workflow Considerations

There are additional considerations when using custom workflows created in SharePoint Designer 2007. For example, some companies don't like users to apply changes directly through SharePoint Designer 2007 to the production environment and may block the ability to make changes and/or additions to a site using SharePoint Designer 2007.

A major consideration in creating workflows in SharePoint Designer 2007 is that, by default, those workflows are tied to a specific list within a SharePoint site: They are not portable, cannot be copied and/or moved to another document library within a site, cannot be deployed across an entire farm, and do not get saved as part of a list or document library template. In addition, workflows created in SharePoint Designer 2007 cannot be associated with a content type, which removes the ability to centrally tie a custom workflow to content across site collections.

> **Note** While a workflow created in SharePoint Designer 2007 cannot be associated with a content type, a content type can be leveraged to meet certain conditions. For example, *"If Content Type equals <nameofContentType>" then perform the following action.*

Figure 10-5 shows an example of a workflow step within SharePoint Designer 2007 that includes two sets of conditions, each including a Compare field in the If and Else If conditional branches where each compare is based on a specific content type within the associated document library.

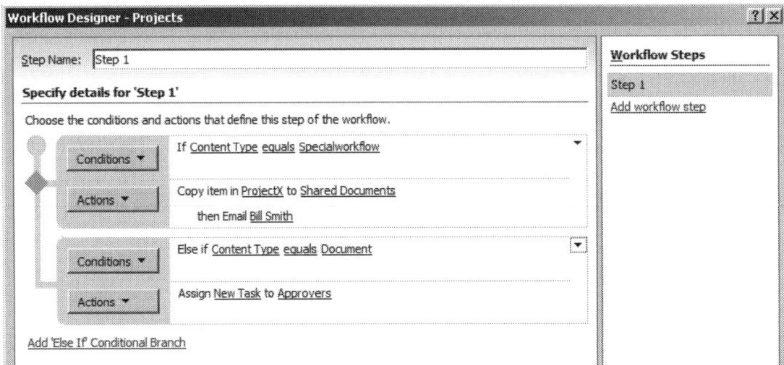


**Figure 10-5** Example of a workflow step that includes multiple conditional branches

As mentioned, a major design consideration when you deploy SharePoint Designer 2007 workflows is that those workflows are specific to a single list (or document library) within a SharePoint site. Unlike out-of-the-box workflows, it's not easy to save a custom workflow created in SharePoint Designer 2007 as part of a list template. Several files are created as part of a SharePoint Designer 2007 workflow, including the main .xoml file, which will launch in the Workflow Designer; the .xoml.rules file, which instructs the main .xoml of any specific rules within the workflow; and the .xoml.wfconfig.xml file, which includes the site and list, or library, ID where the workflow will run and also whether the workflow will start manually or run automatically as a new list item is added. In addition, if you include initiation or custom forms as part of your workflow, those forms will be saved along with the other workflow files as .aspx files. Each workflow, along with its files, is stored in a workflow folder within the site where the workflow was created and is accessible from within SharePoint Designer 2007.

Many folks have asked if it's possible to move a custom workflow created in SharePoint Designer 2007 to another document library or site. If you try to simply copy the workflow folder from one site to another (or copy a document library to another document library), the workflow may in part work but will generate errors. Trying to modify the .xoml files is tedious and will not guarantee successful results when you attempt to port a custom workflow between sites. Any forms associated with the workflow won't work if they are moved to another document library or site. In this case, and where additional workflow functionality beyond the out-of-the-box workflows is required, the obvious choice would be to create a custom workflow in Visual Studio 2005, which would then give you the flexibility to deploy that workflow throughout an entire site collection.

But there's light at the end of the tunnel. Let's assume you've created your custom workflow in SharePoint Designer 2007, but you must now apply that same workflow to multiple lists throughout your SharePoint deployment. One solution is to create a new custom workflow in Visual Studio 2005. But what if you've already done most of the workflow design in Share-

Point Designer 2007? Rather than duplicate work unnecessarily, one option is to port the SharePoint Designer 2007 workflow to a workflow template in Visual Studio. Many have asked whether it is possible to take a workflow created in SharePoint Designer 2007 and re-use it, or part of it, in Visual Studio. Until recently, this was not considered possible. However, at the SharePoint Conference 2008 held in Seattle, Washington, Todd Bleeker of Mindsharp demonstrated this very process. He will eventually detail steps to do this in a series of blog posts at *http://mindsharpblogs.com*.

> **Note** A best practice for porting SharePoint Designer 2007 workflows to Visual Studio 2005 is to ensure that the stakeholder defines the SharePoint Designer 2007 workflow before mass deployment via Features/Visual Studio 2005 to avoid unnecessary re-cording by developers. For example, ensure that any .aspx forms and custom activities are defined and documented before the handover to developers.

Finally, workflows created in SharePoint Designer 2007 cannot be edited via the browser or directly from the document library or list to which they are deployed. They must be edited in SharePoint Designer 2007. Attempting to edit a SharePoint Designer 2007 workflow in the browser will result in the dialog box shown in Figure 10-6.

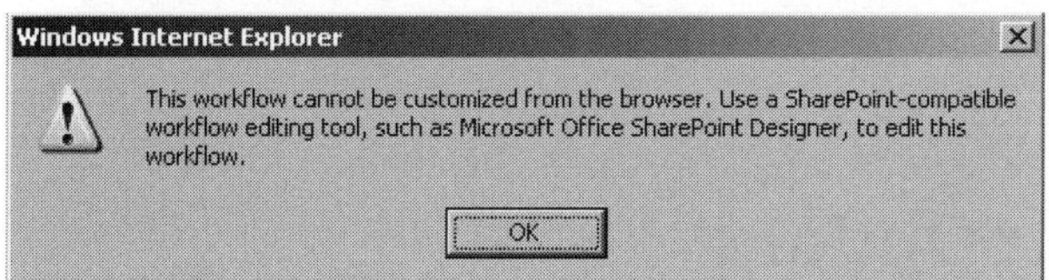


**Figure 10-6** An error dialog box appears when you attempt to edit a SharePoint Designer 2007 workflow via the browser.

## Extending SharePoint Designer 2007 Workflows

There are approximately 23 out-of-the-box workflow actions included in SharePoint Designer 2007, including custom calculation actions to logging information to a history list back in the associated SharePoint site, as well as other custom actions, such as updating list items (based on a certain condition being met). However, you are not limited to using the out-of-the-box workflow activities and can create your own custom workflow activities to suit your business processes. A number of custom workflow activities have already been created within the community and added to the CodePlex site, *http://www.codeplex.com/SPDActivities*. Numerous blog posts that include instructions on how to create your own custom workflow activities are also available.

> **More Info** A set of open-source custom workflow activities that can be installed and used in SharePoint Designer 2007 when workflows are created has been added to the CodePlex site. But remember, these are open-source activities, so use them at your own discretion. Todd Baginski, a SharePoint Server 2007 MVP, has also documented steps for creating custom workflow activities along with how to deploy custom activities to SharePoint Designer 2007. These steps are available at *http://www.sharepointblogs.com/tbaginski/archive/2007/03.aspx*.

## Deployment Configuration and Custom Workflows

Where you've branched out and chosen to create and deploy custom workflows throughout your SharePoint environment, you must consider some issues involving configuration, such as when you redeploy modified workflow assemblies.

Workflows start off in w3wp.exe, which loads the workflow assembly from the Global Assembly Cache (GAC). When the workflow hits a delay, it puts an event in the queue for OWSTimer.exe to pick up at the scheduled time. When the time comes, OWSTimer.exe loads the workflow assembly from the GAC.

However, if you modify and redeploy the workflow assembly into the GAC and do an iisreset, starting a new workflow will make w3wp.exe pick up the new workflow, while OWSTimer.exe still has the old workflow cached. Because of this mismatch, the workflow may crash and appear to hang indefinitely. Thus, when you reset the timer, it flushes the cache and, on next load, it picks up the same assembly as w3wp.exe.

> **Note** The preceding two paragraphs are attributed to Eilene Hao, Program Manager, SharePoint Workflow, Microsoft, whose original post and associated comments can be found at *http://blogs.msdn.com/sharepoint/archive/2008/01/04/issues-with-the-delay-activity-in-sharepoint-workflows-we-need-your-help.aspx*.

# Workflow Deployment Options

Out-of-the-box workflows can be added to both document libraries or lists and content types, including site and list content types. By default, document libraries (not lists) include two partly configured workflows—Approval (serial) and Collect Feedback—which can be selected from the contextual drop-down menu on documents added to a document library, as shown in Figure 10-7.

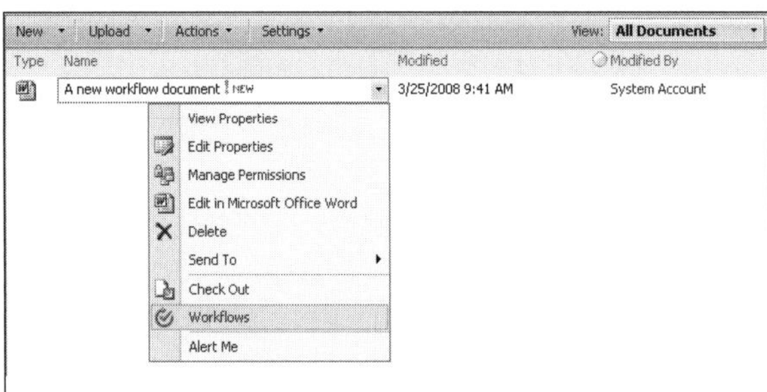


**Figure 10-7** Choosing a workflow from a document within a document library

Let's quickly review the configuration for creating workflows specific to a document library before discussing how you might choose to implement and run document library workflows.

## Workflows Deployed to a Document Library

Selecting the Workflows option from a document's contextual drop-down menu will, by default, direct you to the Workflows:[*Name Of Document*] page (that is, workflows specific to that particular document), as shown in Figure 10-8.

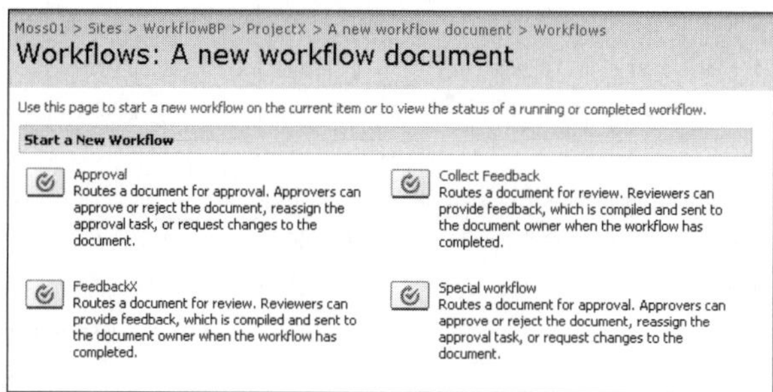


**Figure 10-8** Document-specific workflows

All available workflows within a document library or list are accessed through a document libraries/list settings page (for example, navigate from [*From The Home Page Of A Document Library*] Settings, to Document Library Settings, to Permissions and Management, and then to Workflow Settings). If you are accessing workflows through a new document library's settings page (or where no previous workflows have been configured on that document library), then the Add A Workflow:[*Name Of Document Library*] page will be shown. If you're accessing workflows through an existing document library's settings page where workflows have been configured for that document library, then the Change Workflow Settings: [*Name Of Document Library*] page will be shown, which includes the options to Add A Workflow, Remove A Workflow, and View Workflow Reports, as shown in Figure 10-9.

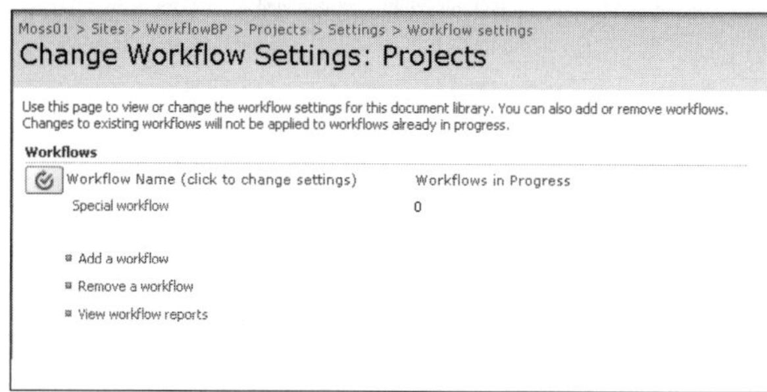


**Figure 10-9** Change Workflow Settings page for a document library

So, you can create workflows within a document library and/or list that will be accessible to all documents and/or items added to that library/list. For instance, you may have a document library that includes a generic approval workflow and have that workflow set to manual start rather than have it fire automatically when a new document or item is added to the library/

list. This is especially true when you add multiple workflows to a single document library; you wouldn't necessarily want multiple workflows on a single document/item firing concurrently.

However, some workflows may be more specific to some documents/items than to others within the same library/list. And you may want to choose to apply some workflows to some types of documents but not to others. How can this be accomplished?

## Workflows and Document Libraries: Many to One

Thankfully, SharePoint offers a workaround for this scenario, namely, by adding workflows to content types rather than to the base document library. For example, a single document library that is configured for multiple content types can have separate workflows for each document type added to that library. For instance, you may have some documents that require a different type of approval than others. In addition, each content type can have multiple workflows associated to it, and workflows can be associated to either a site or list instance of a content type.

Unfortunately, workflows created in SharePoint Designer 2007 cannot be associated to a content type, but rather are associated directly to either a document library or list within a site. Associating workflows to content types is limited to either the out-of-the-box workflows or to custom workflows created in Visual Studio.

The obvious benefit of associating workflows to content types is that those workflows are then portable throughout an entire site collection and not limited to a single document library/list. Plus, any updates to workflows associated with content types can be pushed out to all existing instances of those content types throughout a site collection. Workflows will be specific to a content type, so when a new document is created based on a specific content type, that document will have direct access to the content type's workflows. Other documents within the same library that are created from different content types will have access to any workflows associated to those content types. Both content types, and workflows associated with content types, are saved as part of a list template (when you select the Save Document Library As Template option), and new document libraries can be created from that list template.

> **Note** New workflows created on the base document library will be available by default to all content types added to a library, in addition to workflows specific to each content type. For example, Content Type A includes a workflow named FeedbackA, while the document library itself includes a workflow named FeedbackB. Both FeedbackA and FeedbackB will be available to documents created from Content Type A.

## Workflow Naming Conventions

Carefully consider workflow naming conventions when you establish workflow policies throughout an organization. For instance, imagine a scenario in which people have created a multitude of workflows throughout SharePoint sites, but the workflow names don't clearly correspond to the intentions of the actual workflows. A prime example would be when an approval for legal documents is simply named *Approval* rather than prefixed by the legal file number, such as *CaseXYZ_approval*. Another point to consider when you name workflows is when new workflow history and task lists are created for different workflows within a site. For instance, the default workflow history list is named *Workflow History* and the default task list is named *Tasks*, but you may choose to create new lists for each respective workflow within your site. In this case, you will want to consider introducing policies for creating new workflow history lists and task lists and include naming convention guidelines for each list created.

> **More Info** See the "Workflow and Approval" section of Chapter 8, "Document Management," for further information regarding workflow naming conventions. This chapter also includes consideration of naming conventions relative to workflow e-mails.

# Workflows and Client Applications

By default, workflows within document libraries and lists are invoked via the Documents/Items contextual drop-down menu, aside from workflows that fire immediately when a new document or item is added to a library/list where the workflow has been set to start automatically.

Workflows can also be accessed and started directly from Microsoft Office Word 2007 by accessing the File menu and selecting Workflows. Figure 10-10 shows the Workflows dialog box accessed directly from within Office Word 2007, which displays the workflows available to that document (or content) type. This option is available only to Word 2007, so if you're still running Microsoft Office Word 2003, then you will need to invoke the workflow back in the document library.

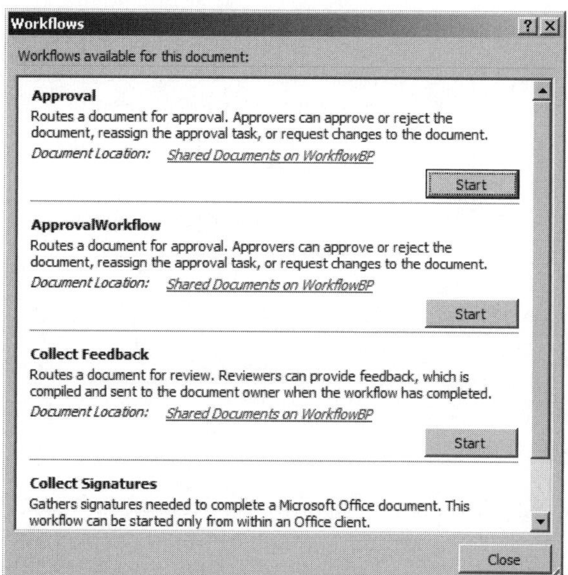


**Figure 10-10** Workflows dialog box accessed from within Word 2007

If you attempt to start a workflow from the Word 2007 Workflow dialog box, SharePoint intelligently informs you that that particular workflow is already in progress, as shown in Figure 10-11.

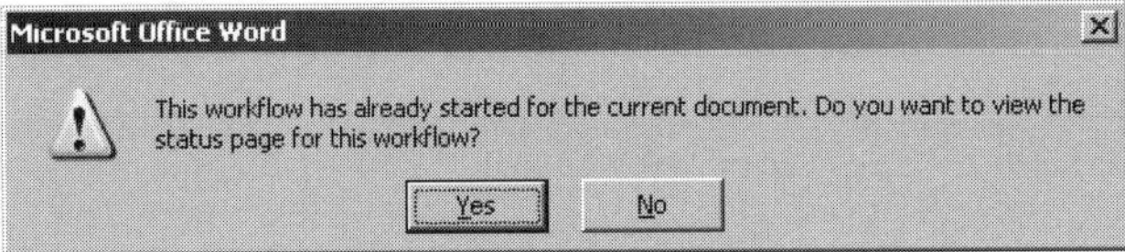


**Figure 10-11** Dialog box shown when you attempt to duplicate an existing workflow via the Workflow dialog box in Word 2007

# Invoking Workflows: Clients

The most common way users will access workflow tasks is via e-mail. For instance, when a workflow is created, the initiator of the workflow chooses which users or groups of users will participate in the workflow task. In the first place, some users may not expect to be involved in a workflow and may choose to ignore a workflow e-mail. So, part of your workflow policy should involve best practices concerning which participants to add to workflow tasks. For example, participants added to a particular project workflow should either be actively working on that project or should have a legitimate need to be informed about the project. Remember, the larger the group of approvers in either a serial or parallel workflow approval, the longer the approval process. In addition, if a workflow is cancelled, previous e-mails sent to approvers are not automatically retracted. You need to consider the entire workflow routing process as part of your end-user training strategy.

Another available option if you are running Outlook 2007 is to connect the workflow task list to Outlook. Figure 10-12 shows the Connect To Outlook option that appears when Outlook 2007 is present on the client machine accessing the SharePoint site. Workflow participants will be able to access workflow tasks directly within their Outlook 2007 Tasks pane and action those tasks directly through Outlook.

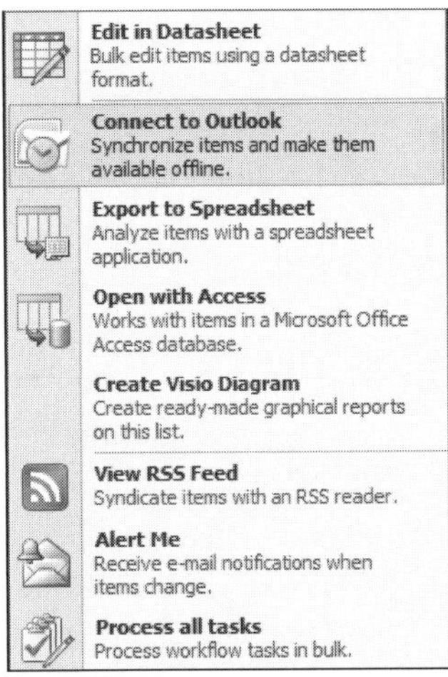


**Figure 10-12** Connecting a workflow task list to Outlook 2007

As with workflow e-mails, earlier approval tasks won't be deleted if a workflow is cancelled. However, if a workflow is terminated, then all tasks associated with that workflow will be deleted, including tasks synced between the workflow task list and Outlook clients.

## Security Considerations

There are a number of security considerations regarding implementing and deploying workflows, such as who should be able to access a workflow in the first place. For example, you may have a document library that includes multiple workflows but may want to limit who can access one particular workflow without affecting permissions on the document library itself.

Other considerations pertaining to workflow comments, which are stored as part of the workflow history. By locking down a workflow's workflow history list, you could hide those comments from non-participants.

### Notes from the Field **Workflow Security and Column Design Consideration**

By default, Workflow columns are created and added to the default view of a document library for each respective workflow created within the document library. However, you can modify the library's view or create new views specific to a workflow to avoid having multiple workflow instances showing up in the default view. First of all, when a library has multiple workflows–for instance, workflows set on the library itself and/or workflows on multiple content types added to the library–the default view will become somewhat cluttered and hard to read. Second, you may not want all users who have access to that document library to view the status of all workflows. Remember, the Workflow Status page is respective to each item (or document) within a document library and includes access to the workflow approval form. It also lists workflow history.

Users who are in the members group of a site can still access a Workflow Status page. Even if those users haven't been designated as approvers for a workflow, they can access the respective workflow approval form. However, when they attempt to approve a workflow, they will receive an error page with the message *Task update was not accepted*. The failed attempt to approve a workflow will be logged in the workflow history (for example, *Task rolled back, Task updated by <username> was rejected*). Users who are in the visitors group of a site can access a Workflow Status page, but will be challenged if they attempt to approve a workflow.

Best practice is to lock down the security on a document library when you don't want everyone with access to the parent site to access workflows and/or workflow statuses. For instance, you may have a special document library that includes workflows for patent documents. Individual documents are within the document library, but this form of storage mechanism becomes tedious when a document library contains many documents and you need to give multiple users access to a workflow created on a document. Another option is to lock down the designated workflow task list. This will prevent users in both the members and visitors site groups from accessing Workflow Status pages. When you have multiple workflows and may want to limit access to each respective workflow status, create different tasks lists for each workflow and then lock down each respective task list. You cannot apply workflows to a folder within a document library, so any permissions you add to workflows will need to be done at the document library and/or list level or the document/item level within a document library and/or list.

Remember, the default workflow history and task lists are accessible to all users who have Read access to the site where those lists reside. So, if you choose to stay with the default lists for workflow history and tasks rather than create additional history and task lists, then you will need to lock down those lists.

*Kathy Hughes, Microsoft MVP, SharePoint Server 2007*

# Summary

In this chapter, we discussed the out-of-the-box workflows included in SharePoint Server 2007 and considerations for deploying and using these workflows. We highlighted best practices for security when deploying multiple workflows to a document library, such as removing workflow columns from a library's default view and locking down permissions on workflow history and task lists. Additionally, we pinpointed issues involved in configuring the out-of-the-box workflows, such as the need to have configured content approval on a document library before choosing to update the approval status as part of a workflow's post-completion workflow activities. We also discussed how the built-in publishing workflow works on publishing pages as well as best practices for configuring publishing workflow on publishing templates that don't include this functionality by default.

We presented the two main methods for applying and working with workflows throughout document libraries and lists, including workflows set on an entire document library as opposed to a content type workflow, which can follow content throughout an entire site collection.

We examined custom workflows created in SharePoint Designer 2007 and design considerations for configuring and deploying those workflows to document libraries and lists throughout sites. Specifically, we discussed non-portability as a major limitation of workflows created in SharePoint Designer 2007 and how workflows are unique to a single document library or list to which they are deployed.

Finally, we touched on extending workflows within SharePoint Server 2007 using Visual Studio 2005 and presented an example of how other people use custom code to enhance out-of-the-box workflow functionality.

# Additional Resources

- "2007 Office System Starter Kit: Enterprise Content Management Starter Kit" includes a white paper on adding activities into SharePoint Designer 2007: *http://www.microsoft.com/downloadsdefault.aspx?familyid=38ca6b32-44be-4489-8526-f09c57cd13a5&displaylang=en*
- Visual Studio 2005 Extensions for Windows Workflow Foundation download: *http://www.microsoft.com/downloads/details.aspx?FamilyId=5D61409E-1FA3-48CF-8023-E8F38E709BA6&displaylang=en*
- "MVP-Submitted: The Power of Custom Workflow Activities (Part 1)" by Maurice de Beijer: *http://msdn2.microsoft.com/en-us/vbasic/cc351048.aspx*
- White paper "Identifying the Workflow Potential of Business Processes" by Jörg Becker, Christoph v. Uthmann, Michael zur Mühlen, and Michael Rosemann: *http://www.workflow-research.de/Publications/PDF/JOBE.CHUT.MIZU.MIRO-HICSS(1999).pdf*

Chapter 11

# Branding and Customization

**In this chapter:**



For collaborative site collections such as team sites and workspaces, we generally recommend minimal branding and customization. But sometimes your organization mandates specific branding and customization for Microsoft Office SharePoint Server 2007 sites. Conversely, when building large intranet sites and World Wide Web sites, we almost always recommend branding and customization to fit your needs. Office SharePoint Products and Technologies supports several ways for an organization to incorporate its images, logos, colors, and styles to give SharePoint Web sites a customized look and feel.

The focus of this chapter is understanding when SharePoint Server 2007 should be customized, how to customize, and the best practices to use when customizing. This chapter will explore the following methods to effectively customize the look and feel of SharePoint Products and Technologies sites:

- Methods and controls for branding and customization
- Native support for branding
- Branding with SharePoint Designer 2007
- Branding with Microsoft Visual Studio 2005
- Hybrid approaches

In this chapter, we'll cover branding for SharePoint Product and Technologies sites, specifically covering the advantages of the Microsoft Office SharePoint Server publishing infrastructure feature and related tools, and will enumerate a number of best practices for branding and customization.

# Overview of SharePoint Branding

Two concepts should be clarified before we discuss branding SharePoint Product and Technologies Web sites: customization and personalization. *Customization* is the process of making changes to the overall look and feel of the SharePoint environment or adjusting the functionality of SharePoint for all users. *Personalization* refers to instances in which users change the Web parts displayed on a site. Personalization also takes place when administrators use audiences to modify the content displayed on a site in order to adjust functionality for individual users.

## Why Customize Branding?

Every SharePoint Server 2007 site comes pre-built with a distinct look and feel that is easily recognized as SharePoint. The interface wasn't an accident and is the result of research and feedback from usability groups. This native look and feel was achieved through the careful selection of default font selections, color choices, and the placement of elements such as navigation and Web parts. Customization becomes necessary when organizational goals and requirements dictate that a given SharePoint Products and Technologies Web site adhere to corporate standards that the default site templates do not address. Politics and culture are usually the driving factors for deviating from the native look and feel.

How do you accomplish the corporate branding standards or other driving factors for branding and customization? Essentially, you can modify the layout, color scheme, graphics, and other elements of the design of a SharePoint Server 2007 page while staying in a supported installation posture. Figure 11-1 shows the home page of a site that has been customized to change its overall look and feel.

**Figure 11-1** Mindsharp home page

Changes to the basic design of a SharePoint site will often involve significant customization of a SharePoint environment. Because these customizations are extensive, it is a best practice to thoroughly document all of the customizations made. It is possible that service packs or upgrades to the next version of SharePoint Server 2007 may overwrite customizations. Keeping detailed records of these customizations will allow you to reapply customizations after an upgrade, and will assist you when troubleshooting problems possibly caused by customizations.

> **Note** Keep detailed records of customizations so that they can be reapplied if altered by a service pack or upgrade and to aid in debugging any issues that arise during the customization process.

## Who Controls Branding?

Before you begin to customize native SharePoint Server 2007 sites, you should take the time to determine who will control the various aspects of branding and customization. SharePoint Server 2007 installations can be designed to allow for branding and customization at several different levels in the environment, and the decisions defining where customizations will be performed should be included in your governance strategy. Each of these customization levels can lead to different business outcomes and affect the choices of tools and methods of branding. For example, allowing local site administrators to change visual aspects of their site, beyond simple personalization, can enhance a sense of ownership for local users. This heightened sense of ownership often leads users to make more extensive use of the site. However, this decentralized approach can quickly lead to an inconsistent look and feel. If a strict look and feel is required, you may be forced to centrally control the branding. The most successful implementations we have seen use a combination of centralized and decentralized branding, ensuring a consistent corporate identity while fostering a sense of teamwork across sites and site collection boundaries.

By establishing governance policies that selectively mix localized and centralized control, feelings of local ownership and collective identity are simultaneously enhanced. For example, an organization could establish several approved master pages and allow site administrators to select which specific master page they would like to use on their site. The level of centralized control versus decentralized freedom will depend on the business goals for your implementation. Remember that SharePoint Server 2007 is an end-user product and was intended for site collection administrators to control their destiny, including customizations.

## What Method Should I Use?

SharePoint Server 2007 includes a variety of native tools and methodologies that can be used to implement customizations. First, simple branding can be applied using the native in-browser site management tools. Site administrators can change the theme, modify navigation, and change the default logo. Second, site administrators can more extensively modify a site using Microsoft SharePoint Designer 2007. This second level of customization brings more freedom for page customization, but also allows for more governance noncompliance. It is critical that users with SharePoint Designer 2007 be adequately trained on *when* to use the tool in addition to *how* to use the tool. Third, almost any facet of SharePoint Server 2007 can be modified using Visual Studio. Visual Studio customizations can be made by modifying code and configuration files stored on the SharePoint server's file system or modifying files in the site. Choosing the appropriate mix of these tools and the associated governance policy is not a simple decision. Careful planning should be done prior to choosing any one customization approach.

## Criteria for Selecting a Customization Method

There is no single best way to customize a SharePoint installation. Several criteria should be considered when you select a particular approach to customizing a SharePoint installation. Your choice of an efficient and effective approach will depend on several factors, such as:

- Where in an organization branding and customization will be controlled
- The technical expertise of the users designing the customization
- The scope of the change
- Adherence to corporate, governmental, or international standards
- Technologies used to control the look and feel of non-SharePoint Web sites
- Performance requirements for the production site

Some of the methods we will examine are best used on individual sites and pages, while others can effect broad, sweeping changes across an entire SharePoint Farm. Some approaches require advanced training, but others can be done by relatively non-technical users. Choosing an effective strategy involves considering all of these factors and selecting a combination of tools and methodologies to implement your brand. Regardless of the chosen method, there are some underlying factors that you must understand when you decide how to customize a SharePoint site.

**Understanding Where Changes Are Stored** The first factor that must be considered is where the customization changes will be stored. Depending on the tools used, customization changes will be stored in one of four places:

1. The SharePoint farm's configuration database
2. The Web application or site collection's content database
3. The Web application's configuration (web.config) file
4. The SharePoint server's 12 hive directories

> **Note** The 12 hive is the principle file system location for SharePoint Products and Technologies resources and is located at *C:\Program Files\Common Files\Microsoft Shared\web server extensions\12*. The structure of the 12 hive is not automatically replicated on every server in the farm. The initial structure is created on each server, thus allowing each server to *initially* behave exactly as its siblings. Throughout this chapter, it should be understood that changes made to the 12 hive must be made consistently across all servers in the farm.

The location of the stored changes is important because it will have a long-term effect on the scope of future changes that may be made. For example, if SharePoint Designer 2007 is used to edit a master page, then the results will be stored directly in the content database used by that site collection. This process is called *customization*. The customization process has the negative effect of limiting the scope of any future changes to this particular site. Activating the publishing infrastructure feature can partially mitigate this limitation by allowing inheritance of changes made to a master page to all sites in a site collection. But most publishing master page modifications are made via SharePoint Designer 2007, and the publishing infrastructure feature doesn't change how SharePoint Designer 2007 works; changes are still stored at the site level in the content database. The advantage is site inheritance, and through inheritance the scope of future changes will be expanded to the site collection. Even so, the changes made with SharePoint Designer 2007 never apply beyond the level of a site collection. However, modification made with Visual Studio and deployed to the 12 hive will affect the entire farm. For instance, a master page deployed to the 12 hive with Visual Studio can be referenced by pages throughout the farm.

### Notes from the Field **Customized versus Uncustomized Pages**

When a page is added to a SharePoint site, a physical copy of the page is not immediately added to the appropriate SQL content database. Instead, a process previously named *ghosting*–now named *customization*–is used. When a page is created, a record is added to the content database that points to a file on the SharePoint server's file system in the 12 hive. In SharePoint Server 2007, these pages are called *uncustomized* pages. Pages from anywhere in a SharePoint Server 2007 farm can all point to a single page in the 12 hive. Changing that one page will change all of the uncustomized pages that point to it. This makes it possible to make sweeping global changes by modifying one file in the 12 hive.

When you change a page in a site with SharePoint Designer 2007, the file is not saved to the 12 hive. Instead, the application stores a full copy of the modified file in the content database. This effectively uncouples the file from the original stored in the 12 hive. In Microsoft SharePoint Portal Server 2003, these files were called *unghosted* files, but they are now referred to as *customized* files. The problem in Microsoft SharePoint Products and Technologies 2003 was that excessive numbers of unghosted files could pose a performance problem because of the way ASP.NET 1.1 handled page rendering. Changes made to the process in ASP.NET 2.0, which SharePoint Products and Technologies 2007 leverages, have removed this performance problem. But customized pages, particularly customized master pages, can still make branding difficult to maintain by limiting changes to a single site or site collection. Therefore, it is a best practice to train your users and limit the number of customized pages.

*Ben Curry, Microsoft MVP, Mindsharp*

**Security, Audiences, and Performance** Another factor to take into customization consideration is security. Modifying security to remove elements from the page can lead to performance issues due to a decrease in caching effectiveness. SharePoint Server 2007 pages follow a pattern in which a control is placed on the page that is always visible, but what happens or what is displayed in a submenu when that control is activated varies depending on the security of the user. For example, most SharePoint Server 2007 pages contain a Site Actions menu that is displayed for anyone who has more than read-only access to the page. But when the Site Actions menu is activated, users see only the menu entries to which they have security access. This allows the main page to be cached in only two formats, one for Read Only and one for other users. Adding code to the page that removes or hides the Site Actions menu would cause excessive invalidation of the ASP.NET Page and Fragment cache. This excessive invalidation results in an increase of trips to the SharePoint databases and a resulting decrease in Web front-end server performance. This example demonstrates why it is considered a best practice to apply security to the results of an action on a page rather than applying security to objects on the page itself.

Audience targeting is another native capability that can be leveraged to customize what a user sees on a page. Audiences are not the same as security. For example, if the contents of an existing Web part are being filtered by an audience, a user can add another instance of that Web part that is not filtered. Audiences provide a way to provide content relevance and should not be used as an alternative security mechanism. A good use of audience targeting is limiting which Web parts show up on a shared page based on audience membership.

**Publishing versus Nonpublishing** Activating the publishing infrastructure feature for a site can affect the choice of tools for branding. As we have already discussed, activating the publishing infrastructure feature provides for inheritance of master pages from the top-level site of a site collection to subsites. This inheritance increases the scope of changes made using SharePoint Designer 2007. Additionally, the use of the publishing infrastructure feature can affect branding decisions in other ways. For example, when a user creates a new page in a site where publishing has been activated, she is required to use a preapproved page layout for the new page. This extends a company's ability to control the look and feel of the pages within a site beyond the constraints applied by a master page. Master pages are used to provide a consistent framework of navigation, colors, and the basic layout of a page, but publishing layout pages provide control down to the level of content placement and formatting.

> **More Info** For a more detailed discussion of SharePoint's publishing features, refer to Chapter 13, "Creating and Managing Publishing Sites."

## Branding Methodologies

Knowing the strengths and weaknesses of each potential method for branding a SharePoint Web site will help you select the correct method for each situation. Your chosen solution should depend on the best methodology for the job, but many times will be limited by your budget and technical expertise.

**Master Pages and Content Pages** Prior to the inception of ASP.NET 2.0, Web pages usually enforced a common look and feel by using a common set of user controls or HTML *includes* files. ASP.NET 2.0 introduced the concept of a master page. Think of a master page as an HTML template that contains named regions where content from an HTML content page can be inserted. The regions on the master page are called content placeholders and are actually ASP.NET server controls. Content pages are composed of ASP.NET server content controls that encapsulate all of the content to be displayed on the rendered page. When a content page is requested from the server, the associated master page is retrieved, content is inserted into the content placeholder controls, and the resulting page is rendered and returned to the user. SharePoint Products and Technologies fully supports the use of ASP.NET 2.0 master pages.

Master pages make it easy to define the overall look and feel of pages in a site. A master page is created using HTML just like any other Web page, but in the case of a master page, spaces are left for content to be filled in by placing content placeholder controls at the appropriate locations. Because any HTML in the master page applies to all rendered pages that use it, the overall look and feel of a site can be changed by simply changing the master page. The master page also provides one file that can define how events are handled for things such as site navigation. This prevents errors that find their way into code through duplication. It's always a best practice to keep common code in a single centralized location where it's easier to manage. Figure 11-2 shows some content placeholder controls on the *default.master* master page being edited in SharePoint Designer.

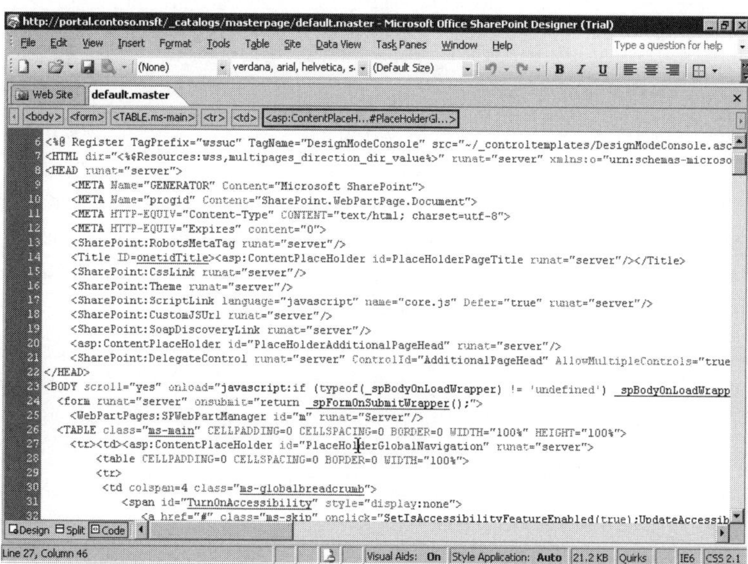


**Figure 11-2** Content placeholder controls on the *default.master* master page

Although master pages provide the promise of a single centralized file to define the branding of a SharePoint installation, how the master page is created, modified, or installed can detract from the efficiency of this approach. Master pages created or modified using SharePoint Designer can be customized and, once customized, will no longer reflect changes made to a centralized master page stored in the 12 hive. Each site where the master page was saved using SharePoint Designer will have its own unique copy of the master page. Activating the publishing infrastructure feature will expand the scope of a master page to an entire site collection, but there is no easy way to synchronize customized master pages across multiple site collections, Web applications, or an entire farm.

SharePoint Server 2007 also makes use of many pages that are not stored in the content database in either a customized or uncustomized fashion. For example, the page for uploading files into a document library is retrieved from the _Layouts virtual directory that is mapped directly to the TEMPLATE/LAYOUTS directory in the 12 hive. These pages all use a master page called *Application.master*, and it is also stored in the 12 hive. Unlike other master pages, there is no way for files in the _Layouts directory to use an alternative master page. The only way to brand the *Application.master* page is by directly editing the page on the file system. Because this page may be overridden automatically by an upgrade or service pack, it is never a good idea to change one of the default files in the 12 hive.

> **Note** *Application.master* is the master page used by most of the pages retrieved directly from the _Layouts virtual directory of a SharePoint Server 2007 site. Many of these pages are used for administrative purposes on a site. For example, the Site Settings page, settings.aspx, is accessed through _Layouts. The impact of *Application.master* on the Site Settings page is mitigated by the fact that site settings will be used only by a limited number of users with administrative privileges. Unfortunately, other pages—such as the page used to upload files to a document library, upload.aspx—are essential to almost all users and also reference *Application.master*. The problem is that there is no easy way to substitute an alternative master page for *Application.master*. There are only two possibilities for branding pages that use *Application.master*. First, you can use themes to change the basic graphics and color scheme. Although you can do this without editing *Application.master* directly, it will not affect the basic layout of the page, only the color scheme. The second way to brand pages that use *Application.master* is to edit the master page itself. Be aware that editing this file is not supported by Microsoft.

**Cascading Style Sheets** In addition to master pages, SharePoint Server 2007 makes extensive use of cascading style sheets (CSS). The default style sheet is CORE.css, which contains over 800 styles. In a default SharePoint Products and Technologies installation, styles are used to control things like the height, width, color, and fonts used by controls on the rendered page. But CSS can also be used to reformat the rendered page of a SharePoint site. When used in conjunction with HTML, <Div> and <Span> tags have the advantage of decoupling the contents of a page from its eventual layout. This can be used to create a site that is more compliant with accessibility standards for devices like screen readers because it replaces the use of tables, rows, and columns for formatting the rendering of a page.

Although custom CSS files can be used to change the layout of a Web page, there are several potential problems with this approach. First, this would require a complete rewrite of the master page to remove the hard-coded table, row, and cell elements that currently format the page. Second, this would provide no practical advantage because the page is already abstracted via the required master page. A third problem is that browser support for advanced CSS is often inconsistent. This may limit who can effectively view the customized site. Because of these issues, it is best that the use of custom CSS be limited to controlling the visibility and styling of elements on the Web page and not their layout.

> **Note** Use master pages to control the layout of HTML elements, controls, and content on SharePoint pages. Then use CSS to control the visibility and styling of those elements, controls, and content.

If CSS is used only to control styling and not layout, how will sites be made compliant with the current accessibility standards? The problem isn't that sites that use HTML tables can't be compliant with accessibility standards; it is simply more difficult. Although the default SharePoint Server 2007 sites fall short of meeting accessibility standards, Microsoft began working on a toolkit shortly after the release of Windows SharePoint Services 3.0 to extend for this functionality. The toolkit is called *The Accessibility Kit for SharePoint* (AKS) and is available as a free download. Using the templates, master pages, and controls included in the kit, accessible sites can be created without implementing custom CSS files to control the layout of SharePoint Web pages.

> **Note** Microsoft has contracted with HiSoftware to create a set of resources for making SharePoint more compliant with the accessibility standards. The freely downloadable kit provides templates, master pages, server controls, Web parts, and documentation that will help designers and developers to improve SharePoint Server 2007 and Windows SharePoint Services 3.0–based Web sites and applications for access by people with disabilities, especially those who are vision impaired. AKS can be downloaded from *http://aks.hisoftware.com*.

**Themes** Themes and CSS are often used interchangeably, but they are actually different. Themes are related to CSS because they are a collection of alternate CSS, image, and skin files that can be applied to a site. The CSS and image files replace existing files that are used by the site. Skin files define the visual properties of ASP.NET controls by overriding the default property settings. This means that themes can be used to quickly apply alternative graphics and color schemes by site administrators. For example, three corporate branded themes could be approved so that site administrators can select which one they want to use for a specific site. Themes could also be used to provide alternate sets of culturally specific graphics for use in a multilingual installation that makes use of SharePoint Variations.

The limitations inherent in the use of themes involve the way that they are applied to a site. When a user selects a theme, the directory in the 12 hive that contains the corresponding theme files is copied to a subdirectory of the site and stored in the content database. Subsequent changes to the original theme in the 12 hive are not picked up by the site. This means that any changes to a theme will need to be manually applied to each site that currently uses that theme.

Another limitation inherent in the use of themes is that they do not include a master page. Because themes contain CSS and do not contain master pages, they can be used to control graphics and color schemes but not the basic layout of the page. As noted previously, it is a best practice to control the layout of pages in a site by using master pages.

Due to their limitations, themes are not a perfect way to maintain centralized branding. But they work well in a limited fashion and are useful when the objective is to empower site owners to select approved brandings. Themes can also be used to provide approved images available for use as part of a branding effort. You should remember that changes to themes after deployment will be very laborious. Therefore, planning and quality assurance are crucial to preempting unnecessary changes to themes after they are deployed.

Themes can also be used to address one of the problems with pages that use *Application.master*. If a theme is applied to a site, that theme will affect the graphics and color scheme of pages retrieved from the _Layouts directory, just like every other page in the site. The theme will not affect the layout of the pages referencing *Application.master*, but it does provide a look-and-feel branding solution that does not involve editing the master page.

**Features, Solutions, and the Object Model** For several of the methods discussed so far, improper deployment strategies may make it difficult to maintain the customizations. These maintenance issues are usually the result of using SharePoint Designer 2007 to create a custom brand that is stored as customized files in the content database. Because these files are specific to an individual site (or site collection if publishing is enabled), using them in a broader context is problematic. A way to mitigate this problem is by creating a file in a parallel development environment, exporting it to the file system, and then deploying it to the production environment using a solution. For example, a custom master page can be created in a development environment using SharePoint Designer 2007. That customized master page can then be exported to the file system and deployed in a production environment using a solution.

Custom features can also be used to support deployment scenarios. The URL address of several key components for branding, like master pages and alternate CSS files, are stored as properties of the SPWeb object that represents a SharePoint Products and Technologies site. Custom features can be created to set these properties to point to custom master pages or CSS files that have been deployed via a solution. It is also possible to deploy and activate features as part of the solution, which automates the entire process. This combination of features and solutions is used to overcome some of the limitations of updating themes. Modifications made to themes in the 12 hive can be packaged as a solution, with the same solution containing a feature that would deploy the theme to sites. This feature could copy the theme from the 12 hive to the site's content database. Doing so allows for centrally controlled updates to existing themes.

> **More Info** For a more detailed discussion of features and solutions, refer to Chapter 12, "Web Parts, Features, and Solutions Management."

**Web Parts** Web parts aren't normally used to brand SharePoint Products and Technologies sites, but they can be an asset when leveraged intelligently. One of the issues of centrally controlled branding is a perceived lack of local control by the end-users. Allowing users to personalize the content of a specific site using Web parts may alleviate some of the problems associated with this "control" perception. Although users won't have the freedom to change the color scheme of a site or how to navigate between sites, controlling the content that is on the site itself may provide users with the independence that empowers them.

Now that you have seen some of the strengths and weaknesses of the various tools and methods available for creating a custom brand, we need to look at the different ways that they can be used. We'll examine the following four approaches:

- Using native in-browser SharePoint Products and Technologies interface
- Using SharePoint Designer 2007 to directly edit master pages and layout pages
- Using Visual Studio 2005 to edit and deploy files in the 12 hive
- Using a combination of SharePoint Designer to edit pages and Visual Studio 2005 to deploy the edited pages to the 12 hive

# Native Support for Branding

If organizational requirements mandate creating a truly custom brand for SharePoint Product and Technologies sites, then the capabilities built in to the user interface will not be sufficient. Still, you should take every advantage of built-in support before making plans to develop a custom brand using other methods. A best practice is to keep it simple and keep it native when possible. From an end-user perspective, the native options are available on the Site Settings page. Most of them appear on the page in a column with the appropriate name of *Look And Feel*. Figure 11-3 shows the Look And Feel column of a publishing site.

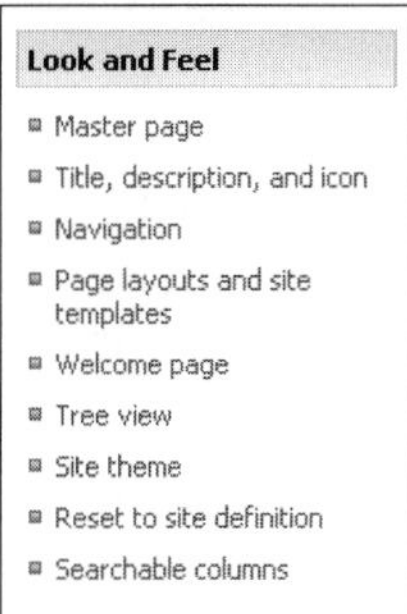


**Figure 11-3** Look And Feel options on the Site Settings page

## Title, Description, and Icon

Using the title, description, and icon settings is often an acceptable way for you to customize collaborative team sites. The current default image is loaded from the 12 hive using the following address: _Layouts/images/titlegraphic.gif. But a site administrator can define a custom site icon referenced from any Web-addressable location. Be aware that some image locations work better than others. For example, if a graphic is stored in a picture library on a different site, users will be forced to re-authenticate on the other site to retrieve the image. This can cause a performance delay and, quite honestly, an inconvenience to the user.

> **Note** Don't underestimate the importance of user perception in your implementation. The technical reasons behind any branding solution don't matter to the user. Users simply want an easy-to-use branding interface that addresses their business goals. Using graphics from another source that could possibly require authentication is a good example of a bad solution. Simple design decisions can often greatly enhance the user perception of the solution. In this example, placing all graphics in an anonymous picture library or enabling integrated authentication enhances user perception.

Another option is to load the icon from a picture library on the current site. Although this won't cause re-authentication, it won't lend itself to centralizing the graphic for a common look and feel. If a centralized graphic is desirable, you should use a solution to deploy the file to a custom subdirectory under the images directory of the 12 hive or host them in an anonymous picture library.

## Publishing Support for Branding

Additional functionality for controlling branding is added to the Site Settings page when the publishing infrastructure and publishing features are activated. These features include links to change master pages, navigation settings, and the governing of inheritance of page layouts and site templates. Don't underestimate the power of the robust navigation functionality of publishing sites. Training your users how to create and modify global and current navigation can go a long way in empowering those users.

### Master Pages in Publishing Sites

The Master Pages link on the site collection settings allows for two specific master pages to be set for an entire site collection. It also configures master page inheritance throughout the site collection. The two master pages that can be configured are the Site Master page and System Master page from the Master Page Gallery of the top-level site. The Site Master page will be used by layout pages in the pages document library of any publishing site collection. The System Master page is used by other pages in the site collection that do not use a specific master page, like the *Application.master*, and by most pages in the _Layouts virtual directory. The same Master Pages link in child sites of the site collection can be used to override the inheritance of the Site or System Master page at any level of the hierarchy. However, when you make selections at this level, the pages being chosen are stored in the top-level site's Master Page Gallery and not the current site's Master Page Gallery. When the publishing infrastructure feature is active on a site collection, all default master page requests are directed to the top-level site. The Site and System Master page settings work on both customized and uncustomized master pages. The Site and System Master page settings are critical when you plan to modify master pages using SharePoint Designer 2007 because they allow a set of customized master pages to be used throughout an entire site collection. Without these settings, any master page modified using SharePoint Designer 2007 will be available only in the site where it is stored.

> **Note** When you plan to use SharePoint Designer 2007 to modify master pages directly on production sites, consider turning on the publishing infrastructure feature for the site collection and setting the System Master page to be inherited throughout the site collection. Sites that participate in a Web content management system should also have the publishing feature enabled, and the Site Master page should be inherited.

Turning on the publishing infrastructure feature adds eight additional custom master pages to the top-level site's Master Page Gallery. Although these master pages are fully functional, they are best used as examples of how master pages can be customized to change the layout, color scheme, and default navigation in a site. They provide alternate starting points when you create a custom master page.

## Alternate CSS URL

The Master Pages link allows you to define an address for the location of an alternate CSS file. Any CSS file specified here will be the last CSS file loaded by the master page, so its styles will replace any similarly named styles in SharePoint's default CSS files. There are only three occasions when the styles in this file do not represent the last style definitions loaded:

1. Styles defined inline on the master page or content/layout page will always load last when rendering a page.
2. Links to CSS files loaded through a content placeholder control on the master page will load after the alternate CSS file, but may load before or after inline styles depending on the placement of the content placeholder control on the master page.
3. Styles can be directly defined in a Content Editor Web Part (CEWP). Again, these styles will load after the alternate CSS file, but they are otherwise dependent on the location of the CEWP.

Note that when you edit master pages in SharePoint Designer 2007, most generated styles will be created as inline styles. To preserve a predictable and scalable set of styles, take care to create all styles in an alternate CSS file or files so that they can be loaded in a predictable fashion. Inline styles provide predictable results, but they cannot be reused or centrally managed.

## Navigation

Navigation in a SharePoint Products and Technologies site collection is handled through server controls that dynamically load the addresses of pages, sites, and other links. Three types of navigation controls are used in most SharePoint master pages: the AspMenu control used for the top navigation bar and quick launch menu, the SiteMapPath control used for breadcrumb trails, and the SPTreeView used for a treeview alternative to the quick launch menu. These controls are bound either directly or through a SiteMapDataSource control to a SiteMapProvider. The Navigation link in the Site Settings page can be used to fine-tune how these navigation controls work. This is accomplished by adjusting whether they show sites or pages by default and how navigation nodes are sorted. Manual nodes can be added or existing nodes hidden from the Navigation controls. Figure 11-4 shows a portion of the Site Navigation Settings page.

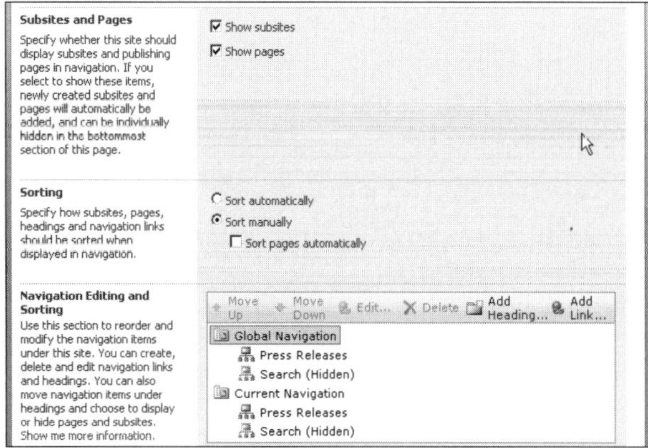


**Figure 11-4** Site Navigation Settings page

## Page Layouts

Layout pages are used in a Web content management environment to advance branding beyond the master page down to the level of a content page. In a normal SharePoint Products and Technologies site, users can create pages where the majority of the content on the page is targeted toward one content placeholder control named PlaceholderMain. In a Layout page, the contents of PlaceholderMain are further restricted through the placement of field controls. These field controls, combined with a custom content type in the pages document library, restrict the type and placement of content that an author can put on a page. When they work in a publishing site, users will be required to pick from a predefined list of Layout pages when they add a page to a site. For example, there are a set of Layout pages called Article pages. When an Article page is displayed, it contains the text of an article and a picture. There are several variations to the page, such as Article Page With Image On Left, Article Page With Image On Right, and Article Page With Body Only, but they all share one thing in common: The user building the page can display only one picture and one text body in PlaceholderMain using any of these layouts.

By defining a set of Layout pages and turning on publishing, control can be maintained over the placement of everything on the resulting rendered page. The Page Layouts and Site Templates link on the Site Settings page of a publishing site grants control over which Layout pages will be available in lower-level sites.

# Branding with SharePoint Designer 2007

SharePoint Designer 2007 is the most frequently used tool for creating many of the components involved in branding a SharePoint site. Nonetheless, there are some pages that SharePoint Designer 2007 can't modify. Because SharePoint Designer 2007 reads and writes its changes to the content database, it can't change any page or file that is not ghosted to the content database. This includes all of the application pages, which are accessed via the _Layouts directory of a SharePoint Products and Technologies site, because these files are stored in the Template/Layouts directory of the 12 hive. Although typically administrative pages, some pages in the _Layouts directory are frequently used. For example, the File Upload page is stored in _Layouts. Neither these pages nor the master page they use, *Application.master*, can be customized using SharePoint Designer.

Despite these limitations, the SharePoint Designer 2007 editor is the easiest way to customize master pages, create publishing layout pages, or build custom CSS files. The real challenges when using SharePoint Designer are scalability, deployment, and long-term maintenance. We believe a hybrid approach is a best practice when using SharePoint Designer 2007. Extend the power of SharePoint Designer 2007 by using it in conjunction with Visual Studio to provide farm-scale deployment and simplified maintenance.

## Master Pages

Most pages in a SharePoint Products and Technologies site are set to obtain their master page by using a replaceable parameter that SharePoint converts to a URL address at run time. That parameter, *~masterUrl/default.master*, will normally point to a master page called *default.master* that is ghosted from the 12 hive to the Master Page Gallery of the site when the site is created. It is the value of this parameter that is being changed when the System Master page is set on a publishing site. The first challenge involved in editing an existing master page is that most editing tools cannot access SharePoint pages or sites directly because they are stored in the content database and not the file system. For example, although Visual Studio can edit a master page, it cannot load it directly from a URL site address. In fact, there are currently no other HTML editors that can open a SharePoint master page directly from a SharePoint Products and Technologies site other than SharePoint Designer 2007. This fact alone makes SharePoint Designer 2007 a tool that must be considered when you edit or create master pages.

Although the HTML code on a master page is quite complex, it can be edited relatively easily in SharePoint Designer's WYSIWYG editor. SharePoint Designer can easily perform the following functions:

- Restructure the HTML tables, rows, and cells on the page that are being used to control the layout of page elements.
- Move content placeholder controls or server controls to different locations on the page to modify the layout of content on the page.
- Add additional controls to the master page to customize the functionality of all of the pages in a site.
- Modify attributes of server controls to extend their features (e.g., configuring the navigation controls to support dynamic flyout menus).
- Attach a specific CSS or JavaScript file to the master page so that it is available for use in all content pages linked to use this master.

There are a few actions that should be avoided. First, be very careful about removing existing controls from the page. Most of them are necessary, otherwise some of the pages built into SharePoint Products and Technologies will stop working. Instead of removing them, the controls should be moved inside an ASP:panel server control at the bottom of the page and the visible attribute set to false. Although still on the page, this effectively hides them from view.

Adding inline C# or VB code to a script tag on the page should also be strictly avoided. SharePoint Products and Technologies runs in a restricted security environment where inline code will not be parsed and compiled on master pages or content pages housed in the content database. Although this behavior can be changed by adding the location of the page to a PageParserPath tag in the web.config file, it is not recommended because this is a security risk. Note that client-side JavaScript is not a security risk and does not require a PageParserPath entry.

The SharePoint Designer 2007 editor also includes several safety net features to improve the editing experience. As previously pointed out, editing the page using SharePoint Designer 2007 will customize the page and disconnect it from the original page stored in the 12 hive. Any page that has been edited and saved by SharePoint Designer in this way will have a blue octagon icon containing a lowercase "i" next to its name. This icon denotes a customized page stored in the content database. In addition to the visible indicator, SharePoint Designer 2007 can quickly roll back the changes if you right-click the file and select Reset To Site Definition from the context menu. Doing this will store a copy of the customized page and restore the original page to its uncustomized state.

With the exception of the increase in maintenance workload caused by the limited scope of customized master pages, SharePoint Designer is the most full-featured editor available for modifying or creating new master pages.

## Publishing Layout Pages

In a publishing environment, SharePoint Designer 2007 is the best editor for creating new page layouts or modifying existing ones. In fact, when you try to edit a page in a publishing site that is based on a page layout, SharePoint Designer 2007 will inform you that these pages cannot be directly edited in SharePoint Designer. It will then give you an option to both launch the browser and edit the content using the user interface or edit the layout page upon which that the page is based in SharePoint Designer.

Once a layout page has been loaded for editing in SharePoint Designer 2007, it will operate like any other HTML page–with two exceptions. First, all HTML content in the body of the page must be encapsulated inside <ASP:content> tags that target a content placeholder on the master page. The other change is a new set of controls in the toolbox where ASP.Net server controls and HTML controls reside. There will be two new categories called *Content Fields* and *Page Fields* under the SharePoint Controls group. These content and page fields represent columns in the content type associated with this layout page. Content fields contain content that can be displayed directly on the page. Page fields contain information about the page, such as the author last modified date. This information can also be displayed on the page. Drag either type of field into a content placeholder control in the location the content should appear on the page. To use the controls to collect metadata values when the page is edited but not display that information on the page when not in editing mode, place the controls in an EditModePanel. Authors can add pages and content to pages based on layout pages, but the ability to modify the layout page themselves is reserved for designers.

## Site Templates

One of the easiest options for replicating a site with the same look and feel is to turn it into a site template and then use that template to create other sites. This has the advantage of taking all the branding changes made to the site by customizing files in SharePoint Designer 2007 and wrapping them up in a single file with an STP extension. Customized master pages, layout pages, applied themes, custom CSS files, and, optionally, content stored in site lists and libraries are all included in the STP file. This SharePoint Template Package file is then saved to the Site Template Gallery of the top-level site of the site collection. From there, it can be exported to the file system to import it into another site collection's Site Template Gallery or installed into the SharePoint farm's central Site Template Gallery using the following STSADM command:

```
stsadm.exe -o addtemplate -filename <filename> -title <template title>
   -description <description of the template>
```

There are only two real limitations to this approach. First, STP files are by default limited to no more than 10 MB in size. Including customized master pages and other content can quickly overrun this limit. This can be overcome by using the following STSADM command to increase the maximum size of an STP file:

```
stsadm.exe -o setproperty -pn max-template-document-size -pv 20000000
```

The maximum size should be guided by two considerations: First, if the resulting STP file is to be used in other sites, the size should not be increased above your maximum upload limit.

The default limit of an STP file is 500 MB. Also, understand that there is a risk that increasing the STP file size by too much may tempt users to use this as a way to make a quick backup of an existing site. STP files were not intended for this purpose, and their use in this fashion should be discouraged.

The other limitation of this approach is that it must be done before creating other sites. Once new sites have been created, you cannot make changes to them by making changes to the original. STP files are a blueprint for the creation of new sites, but changing the blueprint after the site is created has no effect on existing sites.

# Branding Using Visual Studio 2005

Creating a SharePoint branded Web site that is consistent across the entire SharePoint Server 2007 farm requires making changes to the files stored in the SharePoint server's 12 hives. Because SharePoint Designer 2007 cannot open pages directly from the file system, these pages must be edited in some other way. For many of these files, a simple editor like Notepad.exe can be used, but Visual Studio 2005 provides the best environment for these files. Using Visual Studio 2005, it is possible for you to create all of the files necessary to implement a custom brand, including master pages, layout pages, CCS, and JavaScript files. But more importantly, Visual Studio 2005 allows the creation of features, solutions, and program code that will automate the deployment of these components across an entire farm. Branding files created using SharePoint Designer 2007 are customized and stored at the site level, but files stored in the 12 hive are available to all site collections. The key to their use is developing strategies that will deploy these files from the 12 hive as uncustomized copies to the sites in the farm. Because uncustomized files always get their source from the original file in the 12 hive, this allows updates to be made simply by updating the original file stored in each server's 12 hive.

## Site Definitions

Site definitions provide the blueprints used to provision SharePoint Product and Technologies sites; they are the instructions that orchestrate site creation. You can use site definitions for branding and customization in two distinct ways: by associating features with existing site definitions or by creating custom site definitions.

### Custom Site Definitions

Site definitions are stored on the file system in the 12 hive and are a suitable method for globally deploying customizations. When a site is provisioned, a copy of the site definition is not made in the content database; rather, a pointer is created that points to the underlying definition in the 12 hive. If the site definition is deleted from the 12 hive, the sites provisioned from it will no longer function.

In addition to the site definition being stored on the file system, a site definition's resources–such as master pages, layout pages, CSS, and JavaScript files–can reside on the file system. As long as the site definition's resources are not customized, such as with SharePoint Designer 2007, changes made to those resources on the file system will be globally reflected in all sites that were provisioned from the site definition. This provides a much more manageable mechanism for consistently maintaining enterprise customizations than the process used by SharePoint Designer 2007, which is limited in scope to either sites or site collections. In the event a file system resource, such as a master page, is opened from a site using SharePoint Designer 2007 and then altered, any future changes made to the file system version will not be reflected in the site that was edited. If site definitions are used for the purpose of referencing resources located on the file system, it is important to limit any modification of sites that would result in file system resources being customized and copied to the content database.

Site definitions also allow a wide array of customizations, including the following:

- Features, scoped at either the site collection or site level, can be provisioned with the site, and features suitable for only the top level of a site can be limited to only the top level.
- List and document templates can be made available when the site is created from the custom site definition.
- Instances of lists and document libraries can be created.
- Master pages and layout pages can be added to the site's Master Page Gallery with the pages actually residing on the file system and referenced by all sites created from the site definition.
- Web parts can be added to the default page of the site and will be immediately available when the site is created.
- An external CSS resource, named AlternateCSSUrl, can be modified after the site is provisioned and will affect all sites created from the site definition. Although it is possible to set the AlternateCSSUrl property of a site after the site is provisioned, it is much simpler to do so at creation.
- An external JavaScript resource, named CustomJSUrl, can be modified after the site is provisioned and will affect all sites created from the site definition. Unlike the AlternateCSSUrl resource, the CustomJSUrl can only be set at creation via a site definition.

> **Note** Because adding CustomJSUrl or AlternateCSSUrl values to a site definition cannot affect existing sites already provisioned from the definition, always specify a value for both the CustomJSUrl and AlternateCSSUrl. If their functionality is not immediately required, then both files can be created containing only comments that describe their intended purpose and the site definition with which they are associated.

Although custom site definitions provide a tremendous resource for branding and customization, you must be aware of certain limitations. First, Microsoft has stated explicitly in Knowledge Base article 898631 that modifying site definitions after they have been deployed and sites provisioned based on them is not supported. Second, because site definitions are essentially the blueprints that detail how to create a site, altering a site definition after sites have been provisioned from it would not positively affect sites even if it *was* supported. These limitations will severely hamper your ability to maintain, support, and extend site definitions. There is a very powerful means to mitigate them by using features in conjunction with site definitions.

### Feature Site Template Association

Feature site template association, often referred to as *feature stapling*, allows a feature or features to be automatically run whenever a site is created from a given site definition, even the default Microsoft site definitions. Feature stapling does not affect sites that have already been provisioned, but it does provide a ready means of extending functionality to new sites provisioned from the associated site definition. Feature stapling provides a powerful way to maintain site definitions without modifying the site definition itself. By creating a minimalist site definition that implements as much of its functionality as possible through feature stapling, you can add or remove functionality from the site definition by altering the feature associated with it, which does not contravene Microsoft's site definition policies. Using this approach to add functionality requires that the stapled feature be modified or call other features as dependencies. If it becomes desirable to remove functionality, the appropriate features can be modified or no longer called as dependencies. Although altering the site template's associated feature will not automatically standardize existing site definitions, using this approach will make doing so easier because the alterations required will largely consist of activating and deactivating the appropriate features.

> **Note** Site definitions should be implemented as lightweight as possible and feature site template association used for as much functionality as possible.

There are some things that will require a custom site definition and should be included within one. These include any Web parts that will appear on the Welcome page, a custom Welcome page, and implementing sites with variations. Variations, which provide multilingual support in SharePoint Server 2007, provision sites for multiple languages and copy content between them. Because the variation process provisions sites and does not copy them, when a new variation target is created, it will reflect the default site as described in the site definition. It will not automatically provide custom Welcome pages, lists, libraries, documents, or images that are not part of the site definition. Although it would be possible to re-create any resources manually through the user interface, doing so would be a tedious and time-consuming process not suited to enterprise deployment. Therefore, it is generally wise to create a custom site definition when you implement variations so that new variation targets will be created with appropriate content and structure.

## Master Pages

There are many ways to specify which master page to use when you render a page in SharePoint. For example, pages in the _Layouts virtual directory reference *Application.master* directly because it is stored in the same virtual directory. But most pages in SharePoint use one of two replaceable tokens to reference a master page. These tokens are *~masterurl/default.master* and *~masterurl/custom.master*. Most pages in a SharePoint environment use the first token except for publishing pages stored in a pages document library, which use the second token. In a publishing site, these tokens represent the System and Site Master pages, respectively.

Master pages can be created using Visual Studio, but are most easily created using SharePoint Designer. However, after creation, master pages can be implemented in a custom site definition or through a feature. Because these files will be stored in the 12 hive and only ghosted to the Master Page Gallery of the Web site, any change made to the original file will be picked up the next time the page is refreshed.

## Cascading Style Sheets

The AlternateCSSUrl property of a site can be set within a site definition via the user interface or with object model code. As previously mentioned, the AlternateCSSUrl causes an external CSS resource to be referenced in addition to the base CSS used for the site. By extending and overriding the base CSS, you can modify a site's look and feel to reflect custom colors, fonts, and images associated with branding.

## Solutions

Visual Studio's tremendous strength for branding and customization is scope of deployment. Deploying resources, such as master and layout pages uncustomized to the file system, makes them much easier to manage, because multiple sites can reference the same resource and will therefore all reflect changes made to that resource. Unfortunately, unlike SharePoint Designer deployment of content database resources, deploying file system resources is not done automatically by Visual Studio. There is a specific means of overcoming this obstacle—the Windows SharePoint Services Solution Package, often referred to simply as a solution or WSP. A Windows SharePoint Services Solution Package is a SharePoint-specific CAB file that contains a manifest with instructions on how to deploy resources throughout a SharePoint Products and Technologies farm. The Windows SharePoint Services Solution Package is added to the solution store using the STSADM.EXE command ADDSOLUTION. The solution store is a single farm-wide resource that can be managed from either the command line to deploy resources throughout the farm or to specific Web applications. A Windows SharePoint Services Solution Package can be added to the solution store, making it available to operations to be deployed to the appropriate locations at scheduled times.

# Hybrid Approaches: SharePoint Designer and Visual Studio

Optimally, it would be possible to both edit resources stored on the content database and the file system and be able to deploy them globally and to the content database using a single tool.

While that is not yet possible, it is possible to utilize the strengths of both SharePoint Designer and Visual Studio when you implement customization and branding. To do so, SharePoint Designer is used to the greatest extent possible to customize resources using its graphical user interface and its ability to rapidly see the changes in an actual site. Once customizations have been completed and approved, the files generated can be saved to the file system for use with Visual Studio. Using Visual Studio, you can package the resources into a Windows SharePoint Services Solution Package for global deployment to the file system; features are used to create pointers to the files in the content database. The features involved are module features, which either make a physical copy of files to the content database or create a pointer in the content database to an uncustomized file. This approach has the very attractive benefit of utilizing the strengths of both design and development teams to the greatest extent possible.

## Summary

This chapter described how a hybrid approach to SharePoint Products and Technologies branding provides a unified set of functionality greater than the sum of the individual parts. Begin the process of branding using customizations that can be accomplished via the browser, and use them to the greatest degree possible. For requirements that cannot be met via browser-based customizations, use SharePoint Designer 2007 to leverage the experience of Web designers and to provide a rapid design and prototyping of customizations. To deploy branding content beyond the single site collection scope, use Visual Studio to create Windows SharePoint Services Solution Packages for wide-ranging deployment. No single tool provides all of the functionality required for a successful branding effort. Using the full suite of tools, paired with the appropriately skilled professionals, will provide the foundation for a successfully branded SharePoint Products and Technologies implementation.

## Additional Resources

- *The Accessibility Kit for SharePoint* (AKS) download: *http://aks.hisoftware.com*

Chapter 12

# Web Parts, Features, and Solutions Management

**In this chapter:**



This chapter will discuss best practices for using Microsoft Office SharePoint Products and Technologies for custom application development. It will outline development environment scenarios, the difference between content and infrastructure, and the three major resources that are available for custom development: Web parts, features, and solutions. Before discussing best practices for Web parts, features, and solutions, you should first understand what each is at a high level.

- **Web parts** Web parts are the most familiar aspect of Office SharePoint Products and Technologies development. Web parts are discrete modules of code that users can add to, move, and delete from pages. They are also user-configurable for their content, behavior, and appearance. From a utilitarian perspective, Web parts represent the opportunity to do *something* within a SharePoint Products and Technologies context. While they can certainly interact with and enhance SharePoint Products and Technologies, that is only a small portion of their scope of functionality. Web parts provide a means of interacting with data sources such as SQL Servers, Line-of-Business (LOB) applications like SAP, or any resource that provides a Web service interface. They are also suitable for performing tasks that have been previously accomplished with traditional page-based development.
- **Features** Features provide a number of ways for users to modify, enhance, extend, and interact with SharePoint Products and Technologies. There are several different types of features, each of which is designed to provide a particular valuable service. Features are more narrowly scoped than Web parts and are generally focused upon SharePoint Products and Technologies. They provide a means for performing tasks such as copying files

to the content database, adding or removing items from the SharePoint Products and Technologies interface, and wiring up functionality like events and workflows.

- **Solutions** Solutions are packages, specifically Windows SharePoint Services 3.0 Solution Packages, that are often referred to simply as solutions or WSPs by SharePoint Products and Technologies developers. They provide integrated deployment for SharePoint Products and Technologies artifacts. Solutions are a form of CAB files that contain instructions for consumption with a SharePoint Products and Technologies environment. They reside in a single farm-wide *solution store* and are managed from Central Administration using STSADM.exe. Solutions provide a method of bundling Web parts, features, and their dependent resources into a single object that can be managed as a unified whole by operations.

# Content and Infrastructure

The information stored and displayed in a SharePoint Server 2007 server farm can be generally divided into two categories: content and infrastructure. *Content* is the documents, list items, text, and images that are displayed on the sites in the farm. *Infrastructure* contains the definitions, templates, pages, and Web parts that are used to organize and present the content. Over time, the information displayed to users via SharePoint pages will change. Some of the information is date sensitive, such as event descriptions and announcements. Other information becomes less relevant and is therefore removed from high-traffic pages. Regardless of the reasons, it is important to have a clear, defined process for managing these changes.

Content is generally developed and reviewed by information workers using a Web browser or specific Microsoft Office application. Copying content from a development environment to a production environment can be accomplished by these same information workers using processes that are native to SharePoint Products and Technologies. The Web Content Management feature allows for the copying of content items from its source location to its destination location. These source and destination locations must be in different Web applications and will often be in different farms.

Infrastructure components are developed by software developers using typical development tools. Like all computer software, the components must be tested in an environment that is similar to the production location. Infrastructure components must be copied to test and production environments using administrative processes by users with administrative privileges; the Web Content Management feature will not copy these items. Figure 12-1 shows a proven content creation workflow.

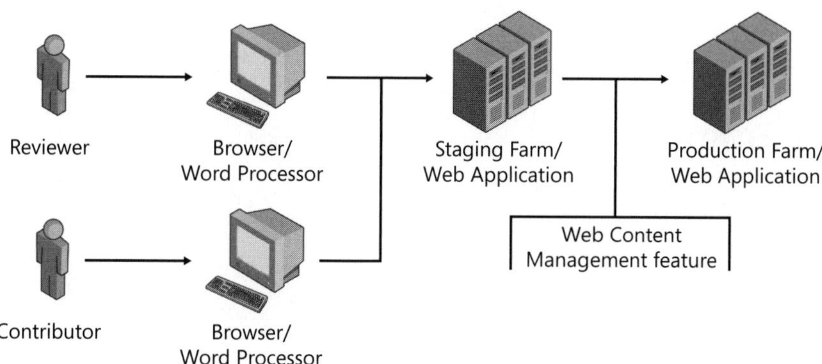


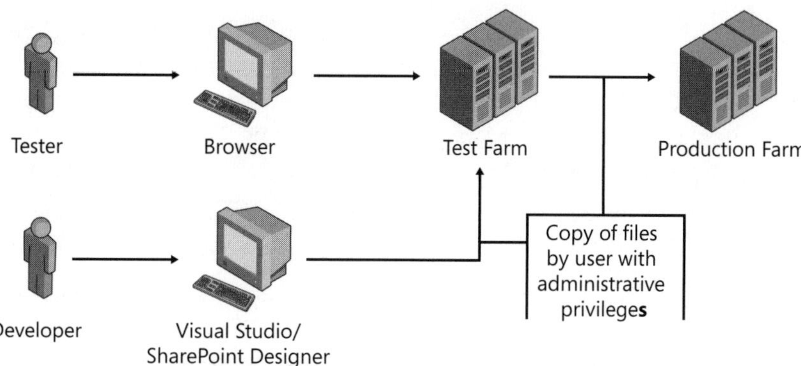


**Figure 12-1** Creation workflow diagram for content and infrastructure

# Developer's Role in SharePoint

With the separation of content from infrastructure, the developer's role in SharePoint programming is different than traditional ASP.NET Web sites. Many areas of the Web site are handled by SharePoint Products and Technologies; security, navigation, style sheets, and browser detection are the most prominent. And, as we've just discussed, the majority of the content on the Web site is created by information workers. The primary effort of developers in a SharePoint environment is the creation of infrastructure components that support the content.

# Environments

The complex nature of the dependent resources required for development and testing for SharePoint Products and Technologies creates unique challenges for the developer.

## Development Environment

Developing infrastructure components for SharePoint Server 2007 poses some unique problems. Of primary concern is the fact that the SharePoint Server 2007 platform must be run on a server operating system (Windows Server 2003 or Windows Server 2008). Most development groups have standardized on Windows XP and Windows Vista for their development workstations. While it is possible to compile programs against the SharePoint Object Model by copying the appropriate assemblies (.dll) to the development machine, virtualization technologies provide a much better solution.

By leveraging virtualization programs, such as Microsoft's Virtual PC 2007 and Windows Server 2008 Hyper-V, developers can create infrastructure components on a machine that contains both the SharePoint platform and Microsoft Visual Studio. Having both the development program and the platform on the same machine will provide many benefits, primarily fast deployment of updated artifacts and process debugging. While remote debugging is possible, local debugging is dramatically easier to set up and much faster. Having a virtual machine with the platform and the editor will provide edit/compile/debug cycles that are very close to what most developers expect.

To aid in the setup and configuration of the SharePoint platform on developer machines and to reduce the licensing cost of doing so, we recommend downloading and using the prebuilt virtual hard drive created by Microsoft and available on its download site. If you are a seasoned SharePoint Server 2007 developer, you will most likely want to build your own development virtual machine.

> **Note** When developing on a virtual machine, be sure to save your code to the host computer's hard disk. This will allow you to easily and quickly start fresh with a new virtual machine copy without losing your content.

## Test Environment

While a single virtual machine will provide a satisfactory development environment, testing infrastructure components requires an environment that is substantially similar to the production environment. Whether the test environment is virtual or physical depends on your resources, but the test environment must account for the following variables, which are not present in a single-machine default installation:

- Separate database server

- Multiple Web front-end servers
- Shared Services Provider
- Multiple user accounts and varying permissions
- Network infrastructure, such as load balancers, switches, and firewalls

## Separate Database Server

Accessing the SharePoint content and configuration databases happens automatically when coding against the SharePoint Object Model. However, custom development will often leverage other application databases. In a development environment, it is common to have a copy of these databases on the local machine. Local databases have a much simpler connection configuration than remote databases. Avoid the temptation to put test databases on the same computer as the application–the testing of the connection configuration is just as important as the rest of the application.

## Multiple Web Front-End Servers

If your production environment contains multiple Web front-end servers (WFE Servers), deploying infrastructure artifacts requires specific steps. These steps are discussed in detail later in this chapter. Replicating the server farm topology is critical in the testing of component deployment. In our experience, this aspect of the test environment causes the most friction: Developers are unfamiliar with Web load-balancing concepts, and administrators do not usually implement load balancing in a test environment. Difficulties are almost guaranteed to arise if you do not test custom code in a load-balanced environment mirroring your production implementation. Simply using software network load balancing (NLB) to test code when your production uses hardware load balancing (HLB) is not optimal for code verification.

## Shared Services for SharePoint Server 2007

You must understand the resources used by custom infrastructure components. Many of the aggregation and targeting services in SharePoint Server 2007 are provided by Shared Services. While many of the Shared Services settings are tested before being deployed to production, such as Business Data Catalog applications and Excel Services trust settings, many are tweaked in the production environment and may not be changed in a test environment, such as audience rules and profile import settings. Be sure to review the Shared Services settings before commencing test activities that depend on them.

## Multiple User Accounts and Varying Permissions

The entire SharePoint platform honors and enforces security permissions. Customization and personalization changes are dependent upon the user account used to make the changes. In order for you to properly test components, the test environment must have multiple user accounts with varying permissions. Do not test with a single account that is a site owner;

rather, create accounts that are members of all roles that exist in your production environment. Do not assume that your environment will have only owners, members, and readers. Site collection owners can create custom permission levels that differ from the standard levels.

## Test Environment Content Replication

In addition to the items discussed previously, the content in the test environment should resemble the production environment. Bugs in code are not only caused by incorrect logic; often, edge cases and other environmental settings are not considered during development. A program that runs satisfactorily with a few hundred items in a list may fail if a list has thousands of items. Similarly, the template used for a site may impact the customizations that are applied. The presence or absence of other SharePoint features, such as the publishing infrastructure, may cause failures as well. There are several strategies for replicating the production content to the test environment. Each of these strategies has its benefits and drawbacks and must be considered within the context of your organization.

### Replication via Backup and Restore

If the test environment has sufficient capacity, performing a farm restore is the best approach for replicating the production content to the test environment. However, you need to consider a few items before attempting the restore:

- The farm topology needs to match, or at least replicate, the functional basics of the production farm. For example, if you have an application server and two WFE Servers, you should have one application server and two WFE Servers for testing.
- The test environment must be a separate farm (separate configuration database) and be physically separate to prevent name and ID conflicts. The restore process assumes that the destination servers are named the same as when the backup occurred. Also, objects in the content databases (sites, lists, items) have unique identifiers that will be restored.

An additional benefit to restoring the production environment is that the backup and restore process can be tested. Most likely, some manual adjustments to the farm will be required after the restore completes (such as IIS metabase changes). Performing the restore in a test environment will uncover these changes and improve recovery time.

A farm backup and restore can be invoked via Central Administration as well as via the STSADM command-line utility. When you use Central Administration, console access to the servers hosting SharePoint Server 2007 is not required.

### Replication via Export/Import

The STSADM command-line utility has an operation to export and import content from a site or subsite. The export and import operations do not provide full fidelity. Items such as workflows, alerts, Web part personalization, Recycle Bin, and various other items are not included. But it is an acceptable approach if the requirements for a full backup are not met.

If disk space in the test environment is at a premium, the export operation can omit older file versions and compress the resulting data files. If the test environment is a separate Web application on an existing server, the export approach will allow a site to be imported to a Web application that is different than the source. The primary drawback to the export/import approach is that it is available only via the STSADM command-line tool. Console access to a WFE Server is required.

## Replication via Other Methods

The content in the test environment can be replicated or created via other means. The most popular of these utilizes the publishing features. The Web Content Deployment process can be used to schedule a one-time push of content from the production environment to the test environment. As discussed earlier, the Web Content Deployment process will not include infrastructure components, but it is an effective approach to replicating content.

The test environment content can also be created manually or via utility programs. The SPSiteBuilder program, available from CodePlex at *http://www.codeplex.com/SPSiteBuilder*, will generate hierarchies of site collections, including lists and document libraries. Another popular tool is the SPDataPopulation tool, which can be downloaded at *http://www.codeplex.com/sptdatapop*.

### Notes from the Field Development and Test Environment

SharePoint tools vendor Barracuda, LLC, has a geographically dispersed development team that consists of over a half dozen members. The software developed by Barracuda is targeted for wide distribution and therefore requires a variety of farm configurations.

Each developer is provided with a company-standard virtual hard disk (.vhd) that contains SharePoint Server 2007, Microsoft Office, and Visual Studio. The availability of this standard disk helps to facilitate the requirements and testing of the components. Mockups are easy to understand, because the base SharePoint objects (site, site collection, and so on) are easily visible by all developers. The steps to reproduce an error are guaranteed to work regardless of the computer hosting the development machine.

Orienting new team members is much faster. Not all developers are comfortable configuring the SharePoint platform, and the standard disk alleviates that issue. Developers are allowed to create their own farm configuration. In fact, this diversity is helpful when targeting external customers. However, this is not usually required for in-house development.

On development machines, the infrastructure components are usually copied to the appropriate location in the SharePoint subfolder during a post-build event. Each developer is responsible for updating the solution manifest and directive file as necessary. The automated build process creates the solution files (.wsp), which are then published to a known location. At certain milestones in the development project, the developers are encouraged to deploy the published solutions and report any discrepancies.

For testing the application, Barracuda has multiple farms that represent the most popular configurations. The application is installed on each farm using a custom configuration tool, which uses the SharePoint API to deploy the solutions and install and activate the features they contain. These varied test environments are vital in uncovering bugs in the application that do not surface in the development environment. This includes the obvious items, like files missing from the solution and permission errors, as well as edge cases, such as multiple WFE deployment problems and large farm performance.

*Keith Richie, Microsoft MVP*

# Web Parts

Web parts, at their most basic level, are a type of composite Web control called a *server control*. A Web part is a container for other Web controls, such as labels, text boxes, and buttons. In addition to containing child controls, Web parts are designed to exist on Web part pages and to allow customization and personalization of those pages. Figure 12-2 shows a basic example of a Web part page.

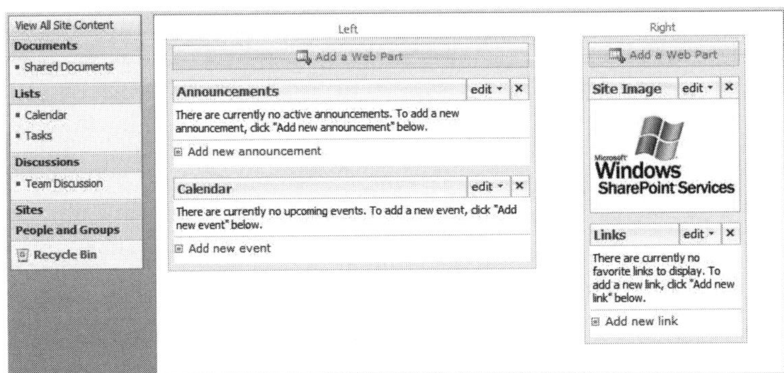


**Figure 12-2** Web part page containing Web parts

## Web Part Infrastructure

With the release of ASP.NET 2.0, Web parts moved from being exclusive to Windows SharePoint Services to becoming part of the larger .NET framework. Consequently, Windows SharePoint Services 3.0 has introduced an entirely new model for Web parts, although it maintains backward compatibility with legacy Windows SharePoint Services 2.0 Web parts. In several instances, a SharePoint Product and Technologies–specific version of the infrastructure extends the base ASP.NET implementation.

## Web Part Manager

The principal improvement in the new ASP.NET Web part infrastructure is the addition of a Web Part Manager. The Web Part Manager serves as a central hub that has awareness of all Web parts on a page. SharePoint Products and Technologies uses a Web Part Manager in the *Microsoft.SharePoint* namespace. The actual Web Part Manager class that is used is *Microsoft.SharePoint.WebPartPages.SPWebPartManager*, which is derived from the ASP.NET System.Web.UI.WebControls.WebParts.WebPartManager.

There must be one, and only one, Web Part Manager on a page that is to host Web parts. Furthermore, the Web parts should reside within Web part zones. Web parts that reside outside of a Web part zone will not provide full Web part functionality and will have limited interaction with the Web Part Manager.

The Web Part Manager provides the following functionality:

- Tracks controls, including Web parts, Web part zones, and Web part connections
- Manages adding, deleting, and closing Web parts on a page
- Creates and manages connections between Web parts
- Manages moving controls between zones
- Allows personalization of which Web parts are on a page, where they are located, and per-user settings for the Web part's properties.
- Switches page views, allowing users to edit Web parts and move them between zones
- Controls and raises all Web part life cycle events
- Imports and exports Web part property XML files (.webpart or .dwp), allowing property settings to be persisted and shared among users

The *SPWebPartManager* is able to provide a path to Web part external resource files. The *GetClassResourcePath* method will return a path that assumes successful deployment to the appropriate standard location for the resources. It will not verify that the resources exist or search for them.

The following code snippet demonstrates retrieving the appropriate external resource path for a Web part assembly:

```
string webpartResourcePath = SPWebPartManager.GetClassResourcePath
  (Microsoft.SharePoint.SPContext.Current.Web,this.GetType());
```

With the notable exception of *Application.master*, all SharePoint Products and Technologies master pages include a *SPWebPartManager*. Therefore, other than application pages and pages that reference a custom master page, it is safe to assume that a Web Part Manager will be available. Unless business requirements dictate that a master page will never be used with Web parts, it is a best practice to include a *SPWebPartManager* when creating custom master pages.

## Web Part Zone

One or more Web part zones should exist on a page that is to host Web parts. If a Web part is added to a page outside of a Web part zone, that Web part will not provide full Web part functionality. The fully qualified name of the Web part zone used by SharePoint Products and Technologies is Microsoft.SharePoint.WebPartPages.WebPartZone, and it inherits from the ASP.NET implementation System.Web.UI.WebControls.WebParts.WebPartZone. Note that, although the Web part zone does not have the SP prefix associated with many SharePoint Products and Technologies controls, it is in the *Microsoft.SharePoint* namespace. In addition to providing a container for Web parts, Web part zones work in conjunction with the Web Part Manager to serialize Web part property values to the content database. Finally, the Web part zone provides a common means for affecting the styles that frame Web parts within the zone (for instance, the appearance of borders around Web parts).

## Editor Zone and Tool Parts

In addition to Web part zones, ASP.NET also implements tool zones. There are three varieties of tool zones: editor zones, connection zones, and catalog zones. Of particular interest to SharePoint Product and Technologies developers is the editor zone, from which the tool pane derives. The tool pane allows users to specify values to customize the appearance, behavior, and content of Web parts via tool parts. Tool parts are server controls that provide an interface for displaying and editing the values of Web part properties. By default, when a Web part is edited, the tool pane will display the WebPartToolPart and the CustomPropertyToolPart. The WebPartToolPart will display all of the base class properties of the Web part. The CustomPropertyToolPart will provide a default interface to display any custom properties of the Web part. It is possible to override the *GetToolParts* method of a Web part to return a custom set of tool parts. The *GetToolParts* method returns an array of tool parts that will be displayed in the order that they occur in the array. Therefore, when you override the *GetToolParts* method, you can display custom tool parts in place of or before the defaults. The default tool parts must be explicitly added to the array of tool parts if they are to be displayed when *GetToolParts* is overridden. It is a best practice to provide editor parts to facilitate configuration of Web parts that have non-trivial combinations of properties.

## Web Parts

Web parts provide discrete, modular, reusable functionality that can be combined and connected and that allow users to configure their appearance, behavior, and content. Individual Web parts are not a replacement for either a traditional Web-based application or even most pages of an application. Web parts should be combined to provide complete Web-based solutions. It is a best practice to limit Web parts to provide a single function that is implemented as generically as possible to encourage re-use. One of the key concepts of Web parts is that they should be designed to allow as much user configuration as possible. To do so, careful consideration should be given to any requirements that may change over time and whether those requirements could be met using user-configurable properties. For instance, it might be valuable to use Web part properties to allow users to alter which columns are displayed from a database or the titles that are given to items within the Web part.

Web parts provide a tremendous maintenance advantage even when they cannot be serviced by power users. Because of their re-usable nature, an improvement to one Web part can be readily reflected in all existing instances of the Web part by updating the appropriate assemblies. To limit the scope of modifying a Web part, a new Web part can be created based on an existing one, and then selected Web parts can be replaced with the new version. Web part development should also leverage as much native SharePoint Product and Technologies capability as possible. A useful goal for Web part development is a solution that utilizes lists, views, and preexistent Web parts, whether native or custom.

## ASP.NET and Windows SharePoint Services 3.0 Web Parts

Although SharePoint Products and Technologies utilizes a new Web part infrastructure based upon ASP.NET 2.0, there are several differences between their implementations. One of the greatest differences is that ASP.NET supports hosting non-Web part controls as Web parts when they are placed in a Web part zone. When a user control or server control is placed within an ASP.NET Web part zone, it is wrapped by the *GenericWebPart* wrapper class, which provides Web part functionality. The SharePoint Products and Technologies implementation of Web parts does not support automatically wrapping non-Web part controls so that they behave as Web parts, although this can be achieved through other means. SharePoint Products and Technologies does offer a preexistent, standardized method for implementing Web part personalization. ASP.NET implements the *SQLPersonalizationProvider* class, whereas SharePoint Products and Technologies implements a personalization provider that integrates with and leverages the Windows SharePoint Services infrastructure. Finally, remember that SharePoint Products and Technologies requires specific versions of the Web part infrastructure that are located within the *Microsoft.SharePoint* namespace.

## Legacy and ASP.NET Web Parts

Within SharePoint Products and Technologies, there two different options for creating Web parts: ASP.NET 2.0 Web parts and Windows SharePoint Services 3.0–specific Web parts. To create a custom ASP.NET 2.0 Web part, a class should inherit from *System.Web.UI.WebControls.WebParts.WebPart*. Alternatively, a Windows SharePoint Services 3.0 Web part can be created by inheriting from *Microsoft.SharePoint.WebPartPages.WebPart*. It is always a best practice to fully qualify when inheriting, and the two possible Web part classes only underscore this general best practice for Web part development. Microsoft recommends using standard ASP.NET Web parts whenever possible, and you should consider that as a best practice. The Windows SharePoint Services 3.0 Web part implementation was created principally for backward compatibility, and Web parts that inherit from it will not work in a generic ASP.NET context. That said, Windows SharePoint Services 3.0 Web parts do provide functionality not included in ASP.NET Web parts, such as the following:

- Cross page connections
- Connecting Web parts outside of Web part zones
- Utilizing SharePoint content database caching

Rarely would any of the preceding functionalities justify creating a Windows SharePoint Services 3.0 Web part. If cross-page connections are desired, current ASP.NET Web parts should be engineered to provide the required functionality while remaining within the modern framework. If preexistent Web parts are to be connected across pages, you should consider modifying the existing Web parts to support the cross-page functionality. If it is not practical to modify Web parts that are already in use, then it might be possible to create proxy Web parts that would remain hidden on a page but would handle the cross-page connections.

Although Web parts can be connected outside of Web part zones, doing so is generally bad practice. Web parts that are outside of Web part zones will not provide full Web part functionality. If the layout of a page requires the placement of a Web part outside of a Web part zone, you should consider using a different page layout or altering the current layout to include a new Web part zone. Although every effort should be made to create Web parts that function efficiently, a Web part that cannot be made to perform effectively without the data caching abilities of the legacy-compliant Web part class is likely approaching the edge of current Web part technology. Such a Web part should be carefully vetted before its design is approved. It is a best practice to always create ASP.NET Web parts unless it is impossible to meet business requirements without using backward-compatible Web parts.

## Web Part Connections

One of the most useful features of Web parts is their ability to be connected together. Prior to their inclusion in the ASP.NET 2.0 framework, Web part connections were delegate based, with Web parts directly raising events on the Web parts to which they were connected. With the creation of the Web Part Manager, Web parts are now controlled in a hub-based model, and the Web Part Manager is responsible for managing all connections. One of the principal differences that will be noticed in the new implementation is that Web parts can provide a connection to as many consumers as desired, but can consume only a single connection per named connection point. The Web part class in the *Microsoft.SharePoint.WebPartPages* namespace will allow unlimited consumer connections, but this would generally not be a reason to implement a backward-compatible Web part. However, if the decision is made to implement backward-compatible Web parts for the purposes of unlimited connections, it is a best practice to ensure that the Web part consumes unlimited providers in a meaningful way. For instance, it is acceptable to create a Web part that will consume an unlimited number of images and display them as a slide show or thumbnails. It is not acceptable to create a Web part that will accept an unlimited number of images but will display only the last image provided to it.

Creating multiple connections is not difficult when you use ASP.NET Web parts. Each connection point must simply have a unique ID. Unfortunately, one possible constructor for Web parts connection consumers provides a default ID of "Default." Because this is the simplest constructor to employ and because it works for the first consumer connection, you may become confused when you try to implement a second consumer connection. Therefore, it is a best practice to give every Web part connection an explicitly defined, unique ID. It is also possible to implement connections of more than one type per Web part. The following code snippet is taken from an ASP.NET Web part that implements five connections of four different types. The first consumer connection uses the constructor that provides a default ID and is not best practice. The second and third connections implement the same interface but provide two unique connection points. The fourth connection implements an alternate custom interface, and the fifth uses the IWebPartRow interface that is the standard for legacy Web parts. The public methods have been named *NameDoesNotMatter* for illustration only. It is, of course, strictly best practice to give any method a meaningful name.

```
// This is not best practice! This should have an explicit, unique ID!
[System.Web.UI.WebControls.WebParts.ConnectionConsumer
   ("Default Connection ID=Default")]
  public void NameDoesNotMatterOne(IDefault defaultInterface)
  {
    _defaultProvider = defaultInterface;
  }

// This is best practice, this provides an explicit unique ID.
[System.Web.UI.WebControls.WebParts.ConnectionConsumer
   ("Best Practice Connection 1","UniqueID_S")]
  public void NameDoesNotMatterTwo (IBestPractice aProviderInterface)
  {
    _aProvider = aProviderInterface;
  }

// Note that the name of the methods is not important.
[System.Web.UI.WebControls.WebParts.ConnectionConsumer
   ("Best Practice Connection 2", "UniqueID_D")]
  public void NameDoesNotMatterThree(IBestPractice bProviderInterface)
  {
    _bProvider = bProviderInterface;
  }

// Don't implement an alternate connection unless it will be meaningfully
// used. If the goal is to allow a Web part to use connections of Type A or
// Type B, implement a Web part transformer from Type B to Type A instead.
[System.Web.UI.WebControls.WebParts.ConnectionConsumer
   ("Alternate Connection", "Alt_UniqueID_G")]
  public void NameDoesNotMatterFour(IAlternate altProviderInterface)
  {
    _altProvider = altProviderInterface;
  }

// This is a legacy standard interface.
[System.Web.UI.WebControls.WebParts.ConnectionConsumer
   ("Web Part Row Connection","Row_UniqueID_JJ")]
  public void NameDoesNotMatterFive(IWebPartRow rowProviderInterface)
  {
    _rowProvider = rowProviderInterface;
  }
```

Finally, Web part connection points should be used for providing separate individual connections. They should not be used to allow connections of Type A or of Type B. If requirements dictate such a scenario, you should implement a Web part transformer instead. Web part transformers provide translation between interface types, allowing Type A to be converted to Type B. The transformation process is invisible to end-users when they create Web part connections. The only effect on the connection process that end-users will notice is the possibility of connecting Web parts in a greater number of ways. Web part transformers must be registered in the Web.config file of the appropriate Web application and will silently provide connection transformation once they are added.

## Web Parts with User Controls

One of the most common requests for extended Web part functionality is the ability to host user controls (.ascx files) as Web parts. This is possible when you use Web parts in a generic ASP.NET setting, but not when you use Web parts in a SharePoint Products and Technologies context. The ability to leverage programmer experience with user controls when you create Web parts is compelling enough that generic user control Web part wrappers have been created for just that purpose. However, the process for hosting user controls within Web parts is simple enough that there is no reason that a generic wrapper must be used. To leverage user controls when creating Web parts, you should use the *Page.LoadControl* method to load the user control in the Web part's class file. Use the *this.FindControl* method to reference controls from the user control's code behind. An example of each is listed below:

```
// Use this in the Web part's class file to load the user control.
UserControl Yukon = Page.LoadControl("_controltemplates/BP/Yukon.ascx");

// Use this in the user control's code behind to reference
   // controls on the .ascx page.
Label bpLabel = this.FindControl("bestPracticeLabel") as Label;
```

If complete control over the code and security settings when creating Web parts is required, then you should consider creating Web parts that are fully owned by your organization to leverage user controls.

## Web Part Verbs

One often-overlooked aspect of Web parts is the ability to add custom Web part verbs. Web part verbs are the actions that can be performed from a Web part's menu. It is possible to add Web part verbs to a Web part by overriding the WebPartsVerbCollection of a Web part. Web part verbs can then be added to the Web part to fire either client side or server side. Web part verbs are an excellent way to allow users to perform discrete actions that integrate naturally with the SharePoint Products and Technologies look and feel. Consider using Web part verbs to perform actions such as refreshing the data in a Web part or allowing users to switch between custom display modes. Figure 12-3 shows an example of Web part verbs.

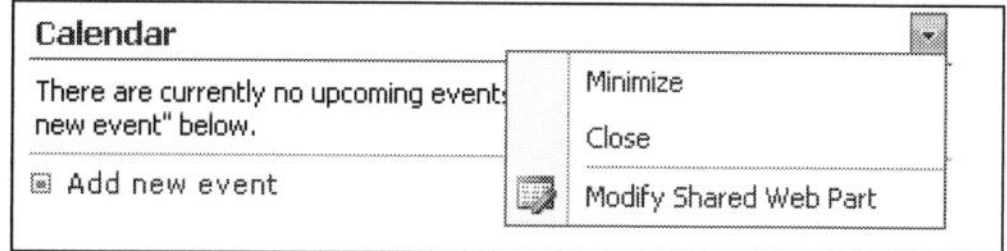


**Figure 12-3** Web part verbs

# Customization and Personalization with Web Parts

When pages in SharePoint sites are discussed, the terms *customization* and *personalization* are often used. Customization refers to changes that are visible to all site members. Personalization refers to changes that are visible only to the site member making the change. The most common method of customizing a Web part page is the addition of a Web part to the page to display additional information. Other methods include removing Web parts and changing the order (left to right, top to bottom) of Web parts. Personalization usually involves reordering Web parts in order of relevance to the specific member and closing non-relevant Web parts.

## Branding and Customization/Personalization

It is important to remember that neither customization nor personalizations are intended to change the branding of the site. When developing Web parts for use on Web part pages, you should use the class names as defined in the Microsoft Windows SharePoint Services 3.0 SDK. You can refer to the page titled *Cascading Style Sheet Class Definitions for Windows SharePoint Services* in the Reference section of the SDK.

Best practice mandates avoiding specifying style attributes directly on controls contained in a Web part if those attributes will override the branding specified in the page's cascading style sheet or master page.

## Provide a Consistent Method for Customizing and Personalizing a Web Part

Web part pages are used throughout the Windows SharePoint Services platform. Site members will be exposed to Web parts on almost every page. Users who have been exposed to the native Web part pages will have expectations about how Web parts are changed to suit their preferences. When developing custom Web parts, you should meet these expectations. For example:

- Provide access to the properties that control the placement and relative order of the Web part.
- Provide access to the properties that control the title and the page presented when the title is clicked.
- Categorize your properties to distinguish them from common Web part properties.
- Provide a custom tool part to contain your categories if you require multiple categories.

Figure 12-4 shows a Web part page in edit mode, which includes the tool pane on the right.

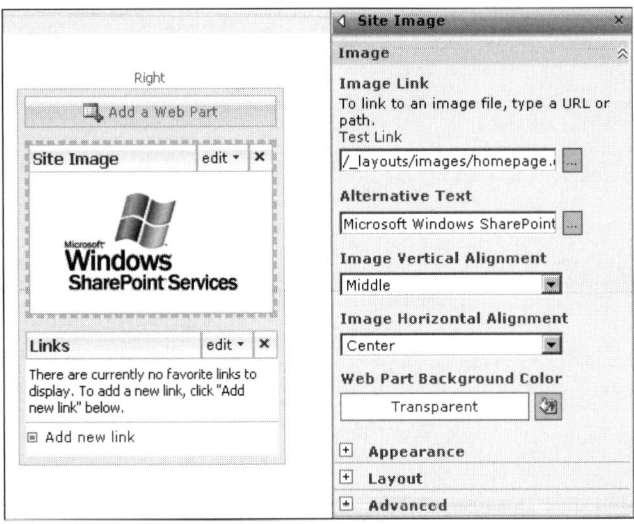


Figure 12-4 Web part tool pane

## Properties and View/Control States

The ASP.NET framework provides a property bag to store the state of a control (or page) between page requests in a session. This facility is designed to work within the stateless nature of the HTTP protocol. Many properties of a control are placed into this property bag automatically, such as the initial value of a text box. The framework can then determine if a particular control has changed and act accordingly.

Web part properties are not designed to work in the same fashion. A property on a Web part control can be stored in a long-term fashion, not just between page requests in a session. Rather, they are persisted from one browser session to the next. Web part properties are changed via an EditorPart or a ToolPart in the *Microsoft.SharePoint.WebPartPages.WebPart* class and are not automatically set based on the current state of the Web part on the page.

> **Important** You should treat Web part properties like all other user input. One often-overlooked practice in Web part development is the validation of user-provided input. In this age of malicious code and denial-of-service attacks, it is important to use defensive techniques when dealing with user-provided data. You should validate the input to ensure that it falls within expected ranges and values. Data that is not valid should be rejected, and an appropriate message should be displayed in the ErrorUI section of the tool pane template.

## Web Part Execution Environments

Web part assemblies run in a secure environment. This environment is controlled via Code Access Security (CAS) and is set on a Web application basis in the Web.config file. By default, Web applications in SharePoint are set to a minimum trust level. A medium trust level is provided in the CONFIG subfolder of the root SharePoint directory, also called the *12 hive*. By default, the root folder is located at C:\Program Files\Common Files\Microsoft Shared\Web server extensions\12.

Web parts can be deployed in two different locations: the bin folder or the Global Assembly Cache (GAC). The bin folder is a subfolder of the Web application root directory. Web parts in the bin folder are subject to the CAS policy in effect for that Web application. A different policy can be specified for the Web part assembly. Web Parts in the GAC will always run with full trust. Please refer to Chapter 17, "Optimizing Information Security," for details on creating and using CAS policies.

## Resource Locations

When programming for SharePoint Products and Technologies, you should replicate the structure of resource locations within the Visual Studio environment. Doing so provides three major advantages. First, deployment can be easily accomplished using post-build events to XCOPY the contents of folders in the Visual Studio solution to the corresponding resource locations in the development environment. This provides a very quick development, test, and edit cycle by automating deployment as part of the build process. Second, it aids in production deployment by making the creation, interpretation, and debugging of Windows SharePoint Services 3.0 solutions considerably easier. When a project is ready for production deployment, the post-build events development deployment process has largely validated the solution resource locations. These locations can be easily referenced in Solution Explorer when you create and edit the Manifest.xml and .DDF files for Windows SharePoint Services Solution Package. Finally, replicating the structure of the resource locations in Visual Studio self-documents the solution. The replicated folder structure immediately identifies that the solution is SharePoint Products and Technologies–related and clearly demonstrates what sort of artifacts are being created. This self-documentation makes maintenance considerably easier for individuals unfamiliar with the original project, or when you return to a project after a long absence. It is a best practice to replicate the structure of SharePoint Products and Technologies resource locations in Visual Studio to aid deployment and maintenance of solutions. Figure 12-5 shows an example of the best practice.

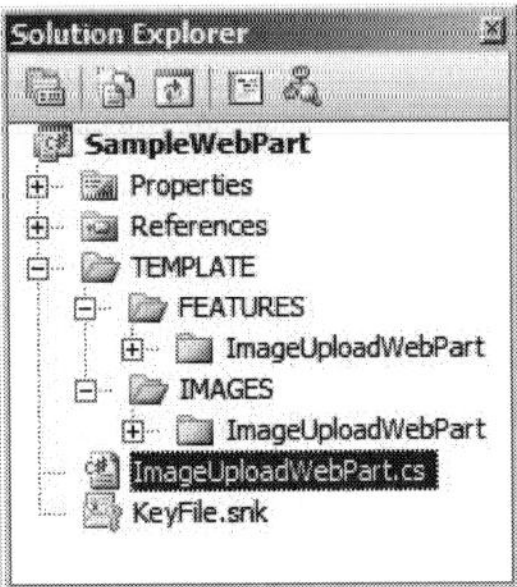


**Figure 12-5** Resource locations in Visual Studio

# Features

Version 3 of the SharePoint platform introduced the concept of features. Features are a collection of elements that modify, override, and extend the platform. These elements can contain infrastructure components (definitions, templates, and so on) and can create instances of content items (lists, pages, and so on). The feature framework is very flexible: The elements in a feature can be applied to a scope (valid scopes are the entire farm, a Web application, a site collection, and a site), and developers can run custom code when a feature is activated. Every component created by a developer should be packaged into a feature. The feature is then installed and activated in the appropriate scope by the owner of the target SharePoint object.

## Feature Element Types

The feature framework provides over a dozen different element types. This section discusses those types, providing an example of where each is used.

### Custom Action Definitions

Custom action elements are used to add, or hide, links and options to the user interface of SharePoint sites. The most frequent use of custom action elements is in the creation of custom SharePoint-based applications and the restriction of SharePoint management activities to a smaller set of site members. Figure 12-6 shows an example of a custom action.

**Figure 12-6** A custom action can be added to Site Actions.

A SharePoint-based application will usually contain custom pages. Rather than relying on users to remember the URL of these pages or using their browser Favorites, developers can provide a link to the pages within the SharePoint interface. Custom action elements allow for adding a link to many different areas in the interface. Links can be added to the Central Administration pages, to the Site Settings page (for the top-level site or all sites), to the Site Actions menu, to the toolbar of a list, and to the context menu of a list item. These links function just like any other SharePoint-provided link. They can be security trimmed to show only if the current user has the appropriate permissions, and they will inherit the look and feel of the site.

Custom action elements can be targeted to users with specific permissions (called *rights*) to the applicable object. This targeting is accomplished via two different attributes: Require-SiteAdministrator and Rights. The RequireSiteAdministrator attribute is a simple true/false value. The Rights attribute is used to provide a finer level of granularity to the action. The list of valid rights can be found in the Windows SharePoint Services SDK under SPBasePermissions.

The *HideCustomAction* element will remove the specified link from the display. This element can be used to remove links, even SharePoint-provided links, from the display. However, the *HideCustomAction* element cannot be targeted to specific users, so it should be used in conjunction with a custom action element that is targeted to the appropriate users. Otherwise, the functionality will not be visible to anyone, which may cause difficulties in the future when the functionality is necessary.

## *DelegateControl* Element

The *Control* element, also called *DelegateControl*, provides for changing the display of specific items in the SharePoint interface. Control elements are loaded inside a tag named *DelegateControl* that is included in many of the out-of-the box administrative pages.

> **Note** The display of Web part pages can be changed by adding or removing Web parts, so the *DelegateControl* is not often used on them. However, the search box at the top of Web part pages and list forms is inside a *DelegateControl*. This allows customization of the search interface and search parameters.

## *Module* Element

The *Module* element is used to create a page in a SharePoint site when the feature is activated. The page can be part of a document library or outside of a library. Any type of page supported by the SharePoint platform can be created, including Web part pages, master pages, and content pages. If the page being created is a Web part page, the *Module* element provides for the inclusion of Web parts, including views of lists, on the page as it is created.

When a file is created using the *Module* element, it will appear in the list of files in the library or in the site when viewed in SharePoint Designer 2007. However, the file is not initially copied into the content database. In order to improve performance, SharePoint Products and Technologies makes extensive use of caching on the WFE Servers. This minimizes the amount of data that must be retrieved from the database server. When a feature containing a *Module* element is activated, the content database is updated with an entry for the file that refers to the location on the server's file system, i.e. 12 \FEATURE\[Feature name]. If the file is later customized via SharePoint Designer 2007, the differences between the original and the customized version (called the *delta*) are stored in the database. When the page is rendered, SharePoint Server 2007 starts with the cached version from the file system and then applies the delta from the database.

To make these pages visible in the browser interface, the feature can contain custom action elements as discussed earlier. Also, the *Module* element can specify *NavBar* elements that specify the name and location of the new page in the site's navigation. For anything other than a non-trivial SharePoint Products and Technologies implementation, it is a best practice to limit customizations that result in copies being made in the content database. It is preferable to manage resources from the file system to the greatest extent possible.

## *Field* and *ContentType* Element

The native list templates provided by Microsoft are designed to communicate unstructured information. Announcements, events, and tasks contain information that is horizontal in nature. That is, the information applies to a wide variety of companies, departments, and groups regardless of the business activity that the group performs. These groups will likely create more specific lists that contain data that is much more structured. When these custom lists must be used in different sites, the *Field* element is used to define the individual columns, called *site columns*, and the *ContentType* element is used to define a collection of related columns. Site columns and content types created via the feature framework are included in the Galleries section of the Site Settings page.

Site columns and content types can be created via the browser instead of the feature framework. However, these items cannot be copied to other locations in the farm. Even if the exact changes are made to two different lists, they are not considered to be the same because they will have two different identifiers assigned by the SharePoint Products and Technologies platform. To ensure that the items have the same identifier, they must be created via the feature framework. This identifier discrepancy is noticed most often in the publishing infrastructure.

> **Note** Content types are bound to a list, enabling the list to store the information defined in the type. This binding can be accomplished via the browser or the *ContentTypeBinding* element.

## *ListTemplate* and *ListInstances* Elements

The *ListTemplate* element defines the properties of a list. The *ListInstance* element actually creates a list based on the specified template. The combination of these elements is very powerful for application developers.

Most applications require storage, and the SharePoint Products and Technologies platform easily provides storage of any structure. In addition, the SharePoint Products and Technologies *list forms* will dynamically create forms for creating, viewing, and editing items in a list. Including a *ListTemplate* element and a *ListInstance* element in the application's feature set will leverage the platform with minimal effort. The *ListInstance* element can also include data with which to initialize the list.

## *FeatureSiteTemplateAssociate* Element

The *FeatureSiteTemplateAssociate* element will associate a feature with a site template. This association is also known as *stapling*. When a site is provisioned using the site template, all stapled features are automatically activated on that site. This element allows developers to extend a native site template to include additional functionality without changing the files provided by Microsoft.

> **Note** Changing the provided files is not supported by Microsoft and may be overwritten in future releases of the product to include service packs.

There is a bit of overlap between stapling and site definitions. Feature stapling is the preferred approach due to its upgradability. Once a site has been provisioned based on a site definition, changing the definition is not supported. In addition, any pages that have been customized using SharePoint Designer 2007 will not reflect any changes to the definition files. However, changes to components in a feature can be applied to existing sites using a feature with the incremental changes.

## *Workflow* Element

The SharePoint platform includes support for Workflow Foundation workflows. These workflows can be created using SharePoint Designer as well as Visual Studio. Workflows created in SharePoint Designer are automatically bound to a specific list in a specific site, and do not use the feature framework. The *Workflow* element applies only to workflows created using Visual Studio.

The *Workflow* element is used to describe the components of the workflow. This includes its identifier as well as the forms used and the assembly to call at each step. Workflows that capture or generate data will likely contain *Field* and *Content Type* elements that specify the structure of the data.

### Executable Elements

The remaining elements are used to instruct the SharePoint platform to execute custom code. These are the *Receiver* and *DocumentConverter* elements. The *Receiver* element is used to specify the code to execute in response to list events. The listing of list events can be found in the Windows SharePoint Services SDK under SPEventReceiverType. The *DocumentConverter* element is used to specify the code that is used to convert documents from one format to another. The *DocumentConverter* element works in conjunction with the Document Converter Process.

## Feature Events

The feature framework provides provisioning callouts that work similarly to the executable elements described previously. By specifying a class and its strongly named assembly, custom code can be executed when features are installed, activated, deactivated, and uninstalled. It is important to note that, while these are often called events, they are in fact code callouts. In the .NET framework, events can be cancelled by returning a value to class that raised the event. The feature callouts cannot be canceled.

Feature callouts should be used to set initiation data or configuration settings that cannot be performed using feature elements. You might require a feature-activated callout if you are creating a *SPWebConfigModification* class to update the Web.config file of a Web application, populating a list with dynamic values (static values can be specified in a *ListInstance* element), or creating a timer job to perform tasks at a scheduled interval.

Any modifications made during feature installation/activation must be removed during feature deactivation/uninstallation. It is common for features to be deactivated and reactivated. This cycling of feature status should be handled correctly and tested thoroughly.

Feature callouts must be carefully written. Any unhandled exceptions will leave the feature in an invalid state. The callout code is run without a user interface, so the code should output information to the trace logs. Information about the trace logs can be found in the Windows SharePoint Services SDK under Trace Logs.

# Solutions

The nature of the SharePoint Products and Technologies platform causes files to be placed in a variety of locations. Definitions and features are copied to a folder on the WFE servers; modules and list instances are created in the content database; Web configuration files in the wwwroot folders are updated; and custom locations are used for additional files created by developers. To address this problem, the platform has a unified infrastructure for deploying components. This infrastructure uses solution files, which are compressed cabinets called *CAB files*.

The deployment of development artifacts to test or production servers must be performed using the solution framework. If you attempt to do so outside of this framework, service outages can result. For example, features are deployed to a subfolder of the root SharePoint directory. By default, the root folder is located at C:\Program Files\Common Files\Microsoft Shared\Web server extensions\12. If a folder is created manually by right-clicking on the parent folder in Windows Explorer, the new folder will not inherit permissions from its parent. This may cause the folder to be inaccessible to the Web server process, which will cause the rendering of any site that uses the feature to fail.

The creation of solution files is a detailed process. The solution file must contain a manifest file that details the source and target locations of all other files in the solution. In addition, the tool provided by Microsoft for creating the cabinet file requires an input list of files to include. There are several open-source projects on Microsoft's CodePlex site (*http://www.codeplex.com*) that will automate the creation of solution files. Use of one of these tools is recommended.

## Cabinet Directive File (.ddf)

Solution files for the SharePoint platform are created using the MAKECAB.EXE program. MAKECAB.EXE has many options, all of which are documented in the Cabinet SDK available from Microsoft at *http://suport.microsoft.com/kb/310618*. The Cabinet SDK is not required. The program is included with the operating system starting in Windows 2000. The options that are necessary for SharePoint solution files are discussed in this section.

The easiest approach for running the MAKECAB.EXE program is to create a directive file that is used as input for the program. The directive file is a plain-text file that contains commands, one per line, that dictate how the cabinet file is created. The list of commands is quite extensive, but the only commands required for SharePoint solutions are the Set Variable and File Copy commands. The file can contain comments, which are recommended. Comments are noted by a single semicolon (;) at the beginning of a line.

The File Copy command is the most frequently used and has the simplest syntax. The source file is specified, followed by the destination within the output cabinet. The destination is optional, which means the File Copy command can simply be the name of a file. The Set Variable command, as well as all other commands, is prefixed with a single period (".Set"). The Set Variable command has a large list of variables, of which only a few are necessary.

At the top of the directive file, use the following commands to specify the name of the solution file and the output directory. The single period for the DiskDirectory1 variable indicates the current directory. Using absolute paths (i.e., C:\SolutionDirectory) will cause incompatibilities between developers if they use differing development environments.

```
.Set CabinetNameTemplate="Image Upload Web Part.wsp"
.Set DiskDirectory1=.
```

> **Note** The value of the CabinetNameTemplate will be the only description available to operations when referencing the solution. It is best practice to use fully descriptive names for Windows SharePoint Services Solution Packages.

Next, add commands that override the default size settings. By default, the MAKECAB.EXE program will create as many cabinet files as necessary to hold the files provided, with each cabinet file formatted to fit on a single 3.5-inch, high-density floppy drive (1.44 MB).

```
; Override size limits for the wsp (cab) file
;
.Set CabinetFileCountThreshold=0
.Set FolderFileCountThreshold=0
.Set FolderSizeThreshold=0
.Set MaxCabinetSize=0
.Set MaxDiskFileCount=0
.Set MaxDiskSize=0
```

After these initialization commands are entered, the remainder of the file contains File Copy commands. Folders in the cabinet file are not necessary unless the cabinet file needs to contain two files with the same name (for example, if the cabinet will contain two features, each with a feature.xml file). Although this is not strictly necessary, building a folder structure in the cabinet file that matches the destination folders in the SharePoint root folder will provide a directive file that is much easier to understand in the future.

> **Note** It is a best practice to group files in a Windows SharePoint Services Solution Package within folders that mimic the deployment destination structure.

Specifying the folders in a cabinet file can be accomplished in two ways. First, the File Copy command can include the destination that includes a relative path.

```
feature.xml ImageUpload\feature.xml
```

Commands in the directive file are limited to 256 characters. As an alternative to specifying the file path in the source and destination names, the SourceDir and DestinationDir variables can be set. Then, the File Copy command needs only the file name. Using .Set is the preferred method of specifying folders in a .ddf file.

```
.Set SourceDir=.
.Set DestinationDir=ImageUpload
feature.xml
```

## Solution Manifest File

In addition to the artifacts created for a solution—assemblies, pages, and definition files—a solution must contain a manifest file. This file is an .xml file that indicates to the solution framework what is contained in the solution and where those contents should be placed. Other settings required by the contents of the solution—such as Code Access Security settings, Safe Control settings, and resources—can be specified in the solution manifest as well.

A solution manifest has elements for each of the component types that can be deployed via the solution framework. These elements have attributes that reference individual files in the solution file, which must match the destination they were assigned in the File Copy command of the MAKECAB.EXE program. The final destination of these files is determined by the element type (*FeatureManifest*, *SiteDefinitionManifest*, *TemplateFiles*, and so on) Where appropriate, the elements provide for specifying additional deployment information.

The root SharePoint folder has been mentioned throughout this chapter. Beneath the root folder are folders for the definitions and components used on the WFE servers.

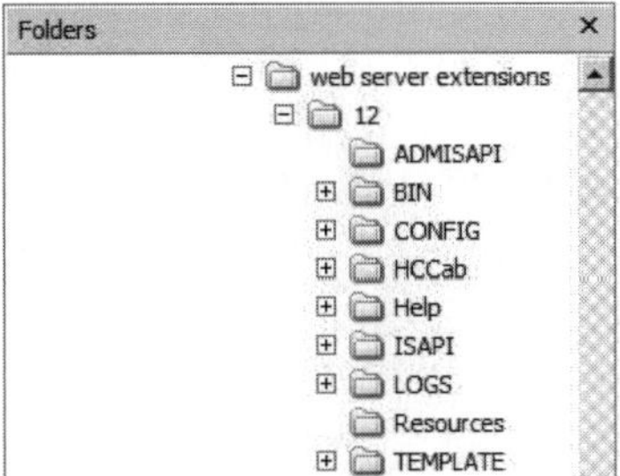


Fortunately, the solution framework has elements that match the functionality of the components rather than their final location.

## *FeatureManifests* Element

The *FeatureManifests* element and its child *FeatureManifest* are used to identify the .xml file that describes a feature. The Location attribute of the *FeatureManifest* element contains the root-relative path of the file in the solution file. It is expected that this location will contain a folder that is unique in the farm. This folder name will automatically be created in the directory 12\TEMPLATE\FEATURES.

## *SiteDefinitionManifests* Element

The *SiteDefinitionManifests* and its child *SiteDefinitionManifest* are used to identify the folder on the file system that will contain the files that make up the site definition via the Location attribute on the *SiteDefinitionManifest* element. This folder is created automatically in the directory 12\TEMPLATE\SiteDefinition. In addition, the framework creates a subfolder below this location named "xml" and puts the onet.xml file (required for a site definition) into this subfolder. The onet.xml file must exist in the solution file (in a folder named "xml"), but the onet.xml file is not referenced in the solution manifest file.

The *SiteDefinitionManifest* element has a child element named *WebTempFile*. The *WebTempFile* element specifies the location in the solution file of the webtemp*.xml file. (This is another file required in a site definition.) WebTemp files must be installed in a folder below 12\TEMPLATE that is named after the locale ID of the definition's language. The value for U.S. English is "1033\xml." Notice that it does not contain TEMPLATE. Accordingly, the source file must be in a folder with the same name in the solution cabinet file.

## *Assemblies* Element

The solution manifest specifies the location to which assemblies are deployed–the GAC or the bin folder of the Web application. This location is specified via the DeploymentTarget attribute. If the location is the bin folder, then the deployment of the solution will require the URL of the target Web application. (The STSADM command will need the -url parameter. If deployed via the Central Administration Web page, then the Deploy Solution form will display a drop-down list at the bottom.)

If the assembly being deployed contains a control that is rendered on Web pages, SharePoint will require an entry in the SafeControls section of the Web.config file. The solution framework provides for specifying the details of this Web.config file entry. When the solution is deployed to a Web application, the Web.config file will be updated automatically based on the values provided on the *SafeControl* element(s) in the solution manifest. Because Web applications can be hosted on multiple servers, using this facility is recommended instead of manually updating the Web.config files.

Similarly, any resources required by the assembly's controls can be deployed automatically by including a *ClassResources* element. These resources are external to the assembly file (.dll), such as images, browser script files, and style sheets. The physical location of assembly resources depends upon the deployment target (GAC vs. Web application) of the assembly. However, this resource location does not need to be specified in the solution manifest–the framework will deploy the files correctly.

## *TemplateFiles* and *RootFiles* Elements

The most common elements used in the solution manifest are the *TemplateFiles* and *RootFiles* elements. These elements copy the referenced file to the like-named folder on the WFE servers. These elements should be used for files that are not handled by other elements, such as application pages (those that are accessed via the _layouts address), administration pages (displayed in Central Administration), user controls, and images.

## *CodeAccessSecurity* Element

As discussed in detail in Chapter 17, "Optimizing Information Security," a custom Code Access Security policy can be set for a Web application during solution deployment. The *CodeAccessSecurity* element is required only for assemblies that are deployed to the Web application bin folder. Assemblies deployed to the GAC will execute with full trust.

# Sample Web Part (Available Online)

The out-of-the-box Image Web part can be used to display an image on a site. The Web part has a property that specifies the Web address of the image. For most site members, this is problematic: How do they get an image on the Web site? And how do they determine the Web address? Power users understand these steps, but find them time consuming to complete.

The Image Upload Web Part will allow site members to browse their local computer for the image. Once the image is selected, the Web part will automatically upload the image to a location specified by an administrator and set the Web address.

The Web part can be downloaded from *http://www.schaeflein.net/blog/ImageUploadWebPart.htm*

# Summary

This chapter outlined development environment scenarios and the three major resources that are available for custom development. Web parts are discrete modules of code that users can add to, move, and delete from pages. Web parts represent the opportunity to do something within a SharePoint Products and Technologies context. Features provide a number of ways of modifying, enhancing, extending, and interacting with SharePoint Products and Technologies. Solutions provide integrated deployment for SharePoint Products and Technologies artifacts. Solutions are a form of CAB files that contain instructions for consumption with a SharePoint Products and Technologies environment. More importantly, solutions provide a method of bundling Web parts, features, and their dependent resources into a single object that can be managed as a unified whole by operations. This improves consistency and gives administrators the ability to redeploy as needed.

# Additional Resources

- The CodePlex SPSiteBuilder program: *http://www.codeplex.com/SPSiteBuilder*
- The CodePlex SharePoint Server data population tool:*http://www.codeplex.com/sptdatapop*
- A sample Web part that illustrates the topics discussed in this chapter: *http://www.schaeflein.net/blog/ImageUploadWebPart.htm*

Chapter 13

# Creating and Managing Publishing Sites

**In this chapter:**



Previous versions of Microsoft Office SharePoint were completely centered around collaboration efforts. But the integration of Content Management Server functionality into Microsoft Office SharePoint Server 2007 has introduced a totally new approach to Web sites, known as *publishing sites*. There are several characteristics that are distinctly different in the approaches between designing collaborative sites and publishing sites. Understanding these differences is crucial to determining the best way to manage publishing.

First, you must define how the information will be shared and the location of information being shared. Collaboration sites primarily involve working with information contained within documents that Office SharePoint Server 2007 makes available in Web site lists and document libraries, whereas publishing sites involve making information available on the Web site pages themselves, although these pages may also include links to download individual documents. These pages, as well as some of their content, are stored in document libraries named, by default, the *pages library*.

Second, there is a major distinction between collaborative and publishing approaches in the balance of site user functionalities. For example, a collaborative site has users who are primarily contributors, with a balance of readers and contributors. These contributors may also manage the sites. The completed work of a collaborative site is usually copied to document storage for read-only access or is passed along to other locations as part of a larger process or workflow for that content. The audience of those locations becomes much wider than the collaborative, contributing audience that initially developed the content. This is generally considered a best practice rather than opening the collaborative environment to a wide, read-only audience. This could be considered a type of publishing, but not within the definition of publishing for SharePoint Server 2007. This chapter specifically deals with the best practice of the SharePoint Server 2007 publishing infrastructure feature as a technology.

The majority of users in a SharePoint Server 2007 publishing site will be readers, with a much smaller percentage of users contributing content and an even smaller percentage of users managing the site. Therefore, these publishing sites require mechanisms only to expose completed work to readers, while still permitting "work in progress" information to be managed by a small group of contributing users and content managers. The management of the sites will generally be separated from contributors and content managers.

The SharePoint Server 2007 publishing features are built around some basic concepts. First, published information will be presented to the public and/or business partners, as opposed to collaborative sites, which are usually intended for internal users or a select few business partners. Second, business requirements mandate that Web content be approved at various levels to reduce business liabilities. Third, there is a separation of roles between the following:

- Farm administrators to keep the services running
- Site collection administrators and site owners to maintain infrastructure
- Web designers to maintain standards of look and feel (branding)
- Content experts to publish information without involving farm managers, site managers, and Web designers
- Approvers to assure that content conforms to business policies

Every publishing environment seems to be unique in that publishing features provided by SharePoint Server 2007 are rarely used in their default configurations. As with most design decisions for SharePoint Server 2007, most publishing configurations will be driven by business requirements and politics, not technical requirements. Design decisions should always be driven by business requirements. This discussion of distinct needs for publishing sites, and the best practices therein, will be reflected throughout this chapter as we examine SharePoint Server 2007 publishing sites and features.

# Publishing Infrastructure and Publishing Features

Publishing features are available for activation in all SharePoint Server 2007 sites after they are created. These features are grouped into two categories:

- **Office SharePoint Server publishing infrastructure** This is essentially the "plumbing" to support publishing sites within a site collection. The scope of this feature is the site collection, where the activation is controlled by the site collection administrators. While activating the publishing infrastructure feature makes the publishing feature available for sites within the site collection, it does not add any functionality to existing sites. As part of the infrastructure change, however, the activation does present additional management tools in Site Settings and adds the Edit Page item to the Site Actions menu. We will discuss the new management tools in the "Publishing Infrastructure" section later in this chapter.

- **Office SharePoint Server publishing** This enables publishing for the individual site. This feature can be activated for any site in a site collection that has the publishing infrastructure enabled. Activating the publishing feature extends the functionality of some collaborative sites but also removes functionality of others. We will examine the modifications to various sites when we demonstrate how the publishing feature is activated later in this chapter.

Using a publishing site definition to create a site at the root of a site collection activates both sets of features by default because they are required for the site. Creating a publishing subsite requires that the publishing infrastructure feature be activated at the site collection level first; those subsites will have the publishing feature activated during the site creation process. Collaborative sites created within a publishing site collection do not have the publishing feature activated when they are created. It must be manually activated.

> **More Info** See Chapter 11, "Branding and Customization," for more information on site definitions.

Even after publishing features are enabled, the general approach taken by the original site definition is reflected in the design of the site. Usually, the default page of the site does not give any indication of the new features until site owners begin to modify the site, leveraging the publishing features. Before we discuss the various publishing sites that SharePoint Server 2007 offers, you need to understand how the publishing features extend the collaborative environment.

## Publishing Infrastructure

Although the scope of the publishing infrastructure feature is at the site collection level for activation, the impact of the activation is seen in the management interfaces and content available to all sites within the collection, whether or not those sites have the publishing feature activated. The best practice of applying the publishing feature set to subsites completely depends on your design. Our goal is to help you understand how to develop best practices for your implementation and how these changes will impact your specific implementation. Because the functionality is often misunderstood, a quick overview is warranted before we define best practices.

### Site Settings

For an administrator, the impact of activating the publishing infrastructure feature on a site collection is most evident on the Site Settings page and on the View All Content page. Figure 13-1 shows the Site Settings page for the root site of a site collection without any publishing features enabled. Figure 13-2 is the same page after the publishing infrastructure feature was enabled by the site collection administrator.

| Users and Permissions | Look and Feel | Galleries | Site Administration | Site Collection Administration |
|---|---|---|---|---|
| People and groups | Title, description, and icon | Master pages | Regional settings | Search settings |
| Site collection administrators | Tree view | Site content types | Site libraries and lists | Search scopes |
| Advanced permissions | Site theme | Site columns | Site usage reports | Search keywords |
| | Top link bar | Site templates | User alerts | Recycle bin |
| | Quick Launch | List templates | RSS | Site directory settings |
| | Save site as template | Web Parts | Search visibility | Site collection usage reports |
| | Reset to site definition | Workflows | Sites and workspaces | Site collection features |
| | | | Site features | Site hierarchy |
| | | | Delete this site | Portal site connection |
| | | | Related Links scope settings | Site collection audit settings |
| | | | | Audit log reports |
| | | | | Site collection policies |

**Figure 13-1** Site Settings page of the root site of a site collection with no publishing infrastructure features activated

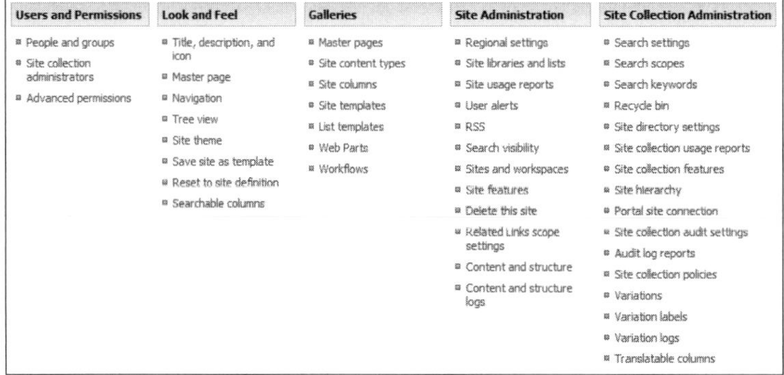


**Figure 13-2** Site Settings page of the root site of a site collection after the publishing infrastructure feature is activated

In the Site Administration column, links for the Content And Structure page and for the Content And Structure Logs page were added. Figure 13-3 shows the Content And Structure page with a context menu opened to display the management options for moving and copying a subsite within the site structure.

Site Content and Structure

Refresh all
Team 10
Team 10 SubSite1
Open Link in New Window
New
Site
List
Page
Delete
Copy...
Move...
View Recycle Bin
Site Settings
People and Groups
Advanced Permissions
General Settings
Tasks
Team Discussion
Workflow Tasks

Team 10
New · Actions · Settings · Show Related Resources · View: Default View · Show 100

| Type | Title | Modified | Created By |
|---|---|---|---|
| | Team 10 SubSite1 | 2/29/2008 | |
| | Announcements | 2/29/2008 | |
| | Calendar | 2/29/2008 | |
| | Content and Structure Reports | 2/29/2008 | |
| | Form Templates | 2/29/2008 | |
| | Links | 2/29/2008 | |
| | Reusable Content | 2/29/2008 | |
| | Shared Documents | 2/29/2008 | |
| | Site Collection Documents | 2/29/2008 | |
| | Site Collection Images | 2/29/2008 | |
| | Style Library | 2/29/2008 | |
| | Tasks | 2/29/2008 | |
| | Team Discussion | 2/29/2008 | |
| | Workflow Tasks | 2/29/2008 | |
| | default | 2/29/2008 | |

**Figure 13-3** Content And Structure page

**Note** Some administrators have learned that it is not necessary to activate the publishing infrastructure feature to access the Content And Structure page. It is available for any site by simply appending the site URL appropriately. For example, if the following URL opens your site:

*http://www.contoso.com/sites/Project%20One/default.aspx,*

then this URL would open the Content And Structure page:

*http://www.contoso.com/sites/Project%20One/_layouts/sitemanager.aspx.*

However, the ability to copy and move sites and subsites within the site collection requires the activation of the publishing infrastructure feature.

Changes in the Look And Feel column of the Site Settings page are the result of modifications to master page management and the exposure of navigational management. These were previously available only by modifying files on the Web front-end (WFE) servers directly or with SharePoint Designer 2007. A new link gives you access to a Master Page Management page where the Site Master Page, the System Master Page, and alternate cascading style sheets (CSS) can be configured for the site and those inheriting from this level. This inheritance of master pages reflects a change in the APIs used by the publishing infrastructure. We consider the use of flexible, inheritable navigation one of the deciding factors for enabling the publishing infrastructure feature. If you do not have designers branding your site with SharePoint Designer 2007 or Microsoft Visual Studio, you should consider and test activating the publishing infrastructure feature to enable your site owners to easily modify the out-of-box navigation of their sites.

In sites where the publishing infrastructure is not activated, site navigation is managed with links to pages that configure the top link bar, quick launch, tree view control, and quick launch control. With the publishing infrastructure feature activated, the tree view page remains to toggle to the quick launch control, but a new link called Navigation now opens the Site Navigation Settings page. This is where all navigation management is consolidated, as shown in Figure 13-4.

On this page, the terminology has changed, reflecting the new navigational management modifications of the publishing infrastructure feature. What previously was referred to as the top link bar is now called Global Navigation, and quick launch navigation is now called Current Navigation. Customizing the navigation elements is much easier in this interface. While the master page changed when the publishing infrastructure feature was activated, navigation really did not change. Everything that publishing exposed in the new management pages could have been accomplished in a non-publishing site by a developer writing code. SharePoint Server 2007 natively supports this functionality through the Publishing feature.

**Note** While some SharePoint administrators may want to activate the publishing infrastructure feature just to enable these new navigation and branding capabilities, the full functionality of publishing is not available without activating the publishing feature at the site level. Much of the configuration is not completely exposed in the user interface without both features activated. This is not a best practice, but just a management/business need decision. A publishing page is larger than a Web part page and thus impacts WAN performance. You need to weigh the impact to the WAN versus the functionality gained by enabling publishing. If necessary, you may decide to increase your WAN capabilities.

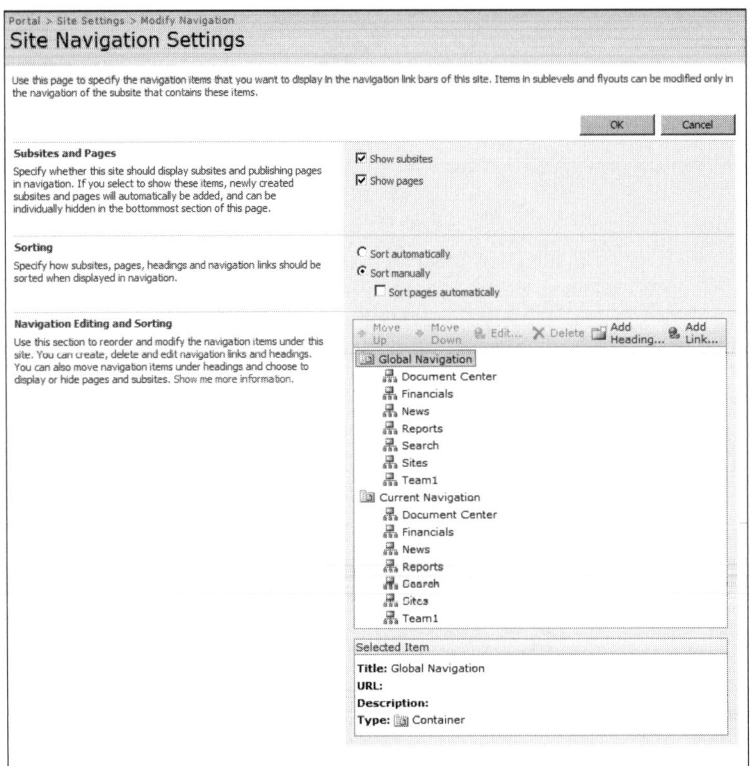


Figure 13-4 Site Navigation Settings page

## Content

Activating the publishing infrastructure feature for a site collection does much more than just expose additional management interfaces in Site Settings. Eight additional master pages are added to the top-level site's Master Page Gallery. All subsites will use one of these master pages unless a custom one is created at the site level. Several new lists and libraries are added at the site collection level as part of the "plumbing" to support publishing sites within that collection:

- A site collection documents library as a centralized storage for documents that can be used by any site within the site collection
- A site collection images library as a centralized storage for images used on pages in any site within the site collection
- A style library as a centralized storage for custom XSL styles and CSSs unique to this site collection
- A re-usable content list as a centralized storage of HTML or text content to be inserted into Web pages. This content can be inserted as references or as a copy. Referenced content will be updated on pages as the content on this list is updated.

- A workflow tasks list for publishing approval workflow tasks
- A content and structure reports list to store customized queries (views) for the content and structure tool (sitemanager.aspx).

The default configurations of check in/check out, versioning, approval, workflow, and scheduling capability of these lists and libraries are designed to meet the needs of the publishing concepts that we discussed earlier in regard to separation of roles. These centralized storage areas facilitate the introduction of content by the appropriate roles and the approval and control processes necessary to reduce the liability of exposing inappropriate content on your organization's Web site.

# Publishing Feature

Once the publishing infrastructure feature has been activated for a site collection, sites can be created using the publishing site templates, or the publishing feature can be activated for existing collaborative sites.

## Site Actions

The first obvious change created by activating the publishing feature for a site is the modification of the Site Actions menu, shown in Figure 13-5. Access to many of the common tools needed by site owners are now available directly from the menu without opening the Site Settings page.

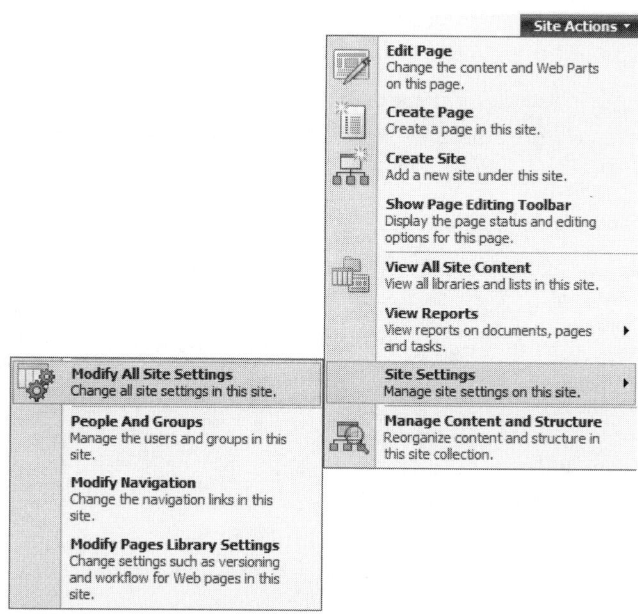


**Figure 13-5** Site Actions menu for publishing sites

## Site Settings and Caching

As with the Site Collection feature activation, activating the publishing feature adds management interface selections to Site Settings. These additional interfaces are not restricted to just the site owner's tasks, as some site collection management tools do not appear until at least one site in the site collection becomes a publishing site.

For the Site Collection Administration column, three pages were added for managing caching. Caching should be considered a best practice whenever possible. SharePoint Server 2007 caching, in conjunction with IIS binary large object (BLOB) caching, is considered a best practice for performance. The following site collection cache options are available:

- Site Collection Output Cache, where caching can be re-enabled, profiles can be selected for the site collection, unique caching settings for subsites can be enabled, and information can be added to pages to assist in troubleshooting caching.
- Site Collection Cache Profiles, where the default and custom caching profiles can be configured for use within this site collection.
- Site Collection Object Cache for configuring the file system cache of objects and list queries on the WFE Servers. This page is also used to flush or reset these cache items.

Remember that site owners may have different permissions, and site owners have separate caching management. Three management links were added to site management, one was renamed, one was relocated, and one was removed as follows:

- Under Site Administration, the Site Output Cache page was added where unique cache settings for this site can be configured.
- Under Galleries, the link to the Master Page Gallery was renamed Master Pages And Page Layouts. The publishing feature added eight default publishing layout pages to this gallery.
- Under Look And Feel, there were the following four changes:
    - The master page configuration tool was simply relocated on the menu. It still functions the same.
    - The Page Layouts And Site Templates link opens configuration options for controlling the site templates and page layouts that are available in the user interface when subsites or publishing pages are created.
    - The Welcome Page link provides a page for selecting the Welcome page (default page) for the site from the new pages library.
    - The Save Site As A Template link was removed. Publishing sites do not successfully save as a template to be used for site creation.

**Notes from the Field BLOB Caching**

While not directly a part of SharePoint Server 2007, the implementation of BLOB disk caching can substantially improve the performance of your WFE. By default, objects such as .gifs and .bmps are retrieved from the database. Enabling disk-based BLOB caching is simple and efficient. You change the BLOB cache location and enable it in the relevant Web.config file on each WFE server. Details can be found at *http://office.microsoft.com/en-us/sharepointserver/HA101762841033.aspx*. Basically, you set the location on disk, file types to cache, and change *enabled="false"* to *enabled="true"*.

This is not the same as the site collection object cache that can be configured on publishing site collections. The object cache optimizes page rendering by storing properties of sites, page layouts, and pages. Site collection administrators can specify the maximum size of the memory that can be used for the object cache. Both caching methods improve performance.

*Ben Curry, Microsoft MVP, Mindsharp*

# Portals and Publishing

Because most people equate publishing with a portal, we will begin our discussion of publishing site templates with portals. What is a portal? A portal is generally considered the entry point or area for a much larger space or continuum of spaces. A portal in our context is generally considered a site presenting a point of entry to the Internet or intranet that normally includes a collection of links to other sites arranged in some logical order and a search engine.

You may find it useful to keep in mind the original definitions of *portal* as an entrance, door, or gate to a building when you design a portal. Others analogize a vestibule, porch, or foyer of a building when they design a portal. When you enter the foyer of an office building, you will generally see a message board that includes rules of behavior as well as a directory that will help you find where you want to go.

Essentially, this is the purpose of a SharePoint Server 2007 Portal—to present information relevant to users entering the portal, as well as navigation aids to help users find information should they not be on the Welcome page of the portal. If you could not find the information you needed on the message board or directory in an office building foyer, you would ask the attendant, receptionist, or guard. Perhaps you would call a friend who worked in the building for information not readily available through normal channels. For a SharePoint Server 2007 portal, you would ask the search engine. For information that is not documented, you would ask your colleagues.

The well-designed SharePoint Server 2007 portal has one major advantage over an office building foyer: It can discern who you are and what your interests are. Using that information about you, your SharePoint Server 2007 portal can modify not only the information initially presented, but also the navigational aids available and the results of the search engine. Consider it a best practice to use audiences to present information that is useful to the user and content expiration to improve timeliness. In fact, a well-designed portal must be *timely* and *relevant* to retain the visitor's continued interest.

# Leveraging Publishing Sites

As stated in Chapter 1, "Introducing SharePoint Server 2007," there are two native portal templates in SharePoint: the Collaboration Portal and the Publishing Portal. There is a distinct conceptual and functional difference between the two portal versions. As its name indicates, the Collaboration Portal not only presents content (information) on individual pages, but it also presents the organizational structure of other sites along with the links to easily access those sites. The Publishing Portal, however, is designed to present information within the site pages themselves and possibly within subsites of the Publishing Portal. While many people in different roles may certainly be involved in producing the various pieces of content used to construct the publishing page, the process is more one of separation of roles than, for example, the collaboration of several authors writing a book. The publishing pages are stored in libraries requiring approval processes. The creation of the page is generally the work of an individual, but he or she may have used pictures and blocks of text previously submitted and approved by others.

The Collaboration Portal was envisioned for small-to-medium intranets and provides a starting point to connect people, content, and third-party systems. The Collaboration Portal functionality includes the Sites Directory, customizable Search Center, Document Center, Report Center, and all publishing features. The Publishing Portal has fewer features activated than the Collaboration Portal and was envisioned for large intranets and external public-facing Web sites.

Large implementations may use both types of portals. The Publishing Portal may represent the "daily news" site for those who are just readers and need to keep up to date on the activities of the organization. The Collaboration Portal may be used as the entry point for those going to work. Expanding the imagery of the building foyer used earlier, think of the large organization as a campus of office buildings, such as the Microsoft campus.

At the entrances to the campus, there may be informational displays describing the organization, the campus, and the activities conducted there. These displays may even have digital signage with changing messages presenting current news or mission status. This would roughly equate to the Publishing Portal.

Each building has a foyer with a receptionist, a building directory, signage, and displays that indicate the activities occurring within that building. These are all very useful to visitors and people who are working there temporarily. These features of the foyer would represent the portal portion of the Collaboration Portal. However, most employees simply go directly to their offices and work. These would be the collaborative portions of the portal or of other sites that are referenced by navigational links within the portal. Most workers know the location of their offices and go there directly without consulting the portal until they need information located outside of their offices.

With SharePoint Server 2007, users now have the search engine from within their collaboration site and may have created their own set of navigation links for frequently used sites without using the portal template. The following sections are a short description of these sites within the context of publishing. Note that the Report Center is left out because it is covered in Chapter 18, "Business Intelligence and Reporting."

## Document Center

The Document Center is available as a default subsite of the Collaboration Portal template or site definition. While it does not have the publishing feature activated at the site level, its primary function is centralized publishing of documents, announcements, and tasks stored within the default document library, announcements list, and tasks list. This document library is best used for finished documents and not for collaborative efforts. We recommend that pre-publishing collaborative efforts on these documents be performed in sites or workspaces located elsewhere and the Send To feature leveraged to copy the documents to this location when they have been approved for publication. This Send To functionality will maintain a link between the published document and its original location. Be aware that list items support only library items and not the Send To functionality, so the announcements and tasks must be maintained within the Document Center.

> **Note** Do not confuse the Document Center with the Records Center. A Document Center is best used for finished documents considered authoritative for use in daily operations of your organization. A Records Center is for storage of official records, but they are defined by your document plan and various regulations. See Chapter 8, "Document Management," for more information.

## News Site

The News Site is a standard publishing site that also has collaborative features activated. The design of the site is such that information, by default, is presented within pages created in the pages library and not within documents stored in a document library. The default Welcome or Splash page has Web parts that display news article pages and pictures from a special pictures library, as well as an RSS viewer that can be connected to any RSS feed that does not require authentication other than Kerberos. You may want to add other Web parts that present information from lists or libraries in other sites throughout your farm so that information can be produced in distributed locations but displayed centrally within your portal.

## Sites Directory

The Sites Directory is a publishing site definition specifically designed to facilitate the design of organized, logical presentation of sites within your portal and the root sites of site collections across your farm. You may have more than one approach to organizing your information containers (sites), and the Sites Directory can accommodate these multiple taxonomies on a single page or by using multiple pages.

The Sites Directory, by default, is part of a Collaboration Portal and not a Publishing Portal because the Collaboration Portal is generally the entry to your entire farm and a Publishing Portal is generally a self-contained publishing site for the public Internet or extranet partners. The Sites Directory of your top-level portal should be configured as the Master Sites Directory for your farm on the Site Directory Settings page, as shown in Figure 13-6, prior to creating any other site collections in your farm. Among your planning considerations will be whether to enforce the listing of new site collections in the Master Sites Directory and how many site categories are mandatory. The taxonomies used by that Sites Directory should also be functional prior to creating any other site collections in your farm. If these configurations are in place, then when any site collection is created within your farm, it will be listed and properly organized within the designated Master Sites Directory dynamically. Should you decide to implement a Master Sites Directory after site collections have been created, then links to those site collections must be maintained manually within the Sites Directory.

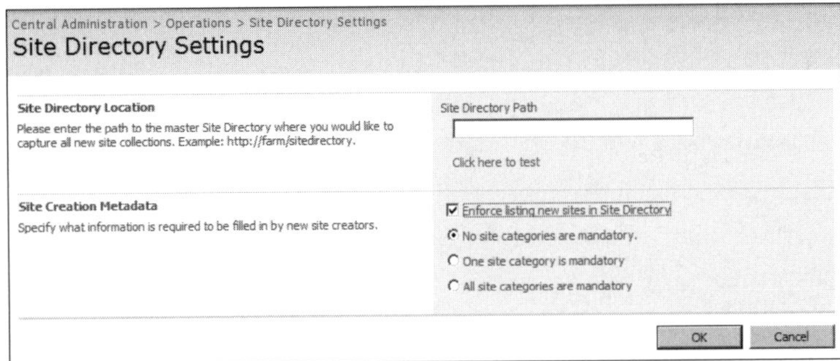


**Figure 13-6** Configuring the Master Sites Directory on the Site Directory Settings page

There are several best practices centered around the Sites Directory. The first involves planning. While the metadata used by the Web part to present your taxonomy can be changed after a site or site collection is created, you will simplify the maintenance of your presentation if design of the Sites List columns containing these metadata or attributes are planned and created prior to the creation of the sites and site collections that will be listed. If the columns and the attribute choices, along with the configuration of required columns, are available during the creation of site collections from Central Administration, the list is populated dynamically. Manual entries to the list can be added later.

> **Note** The Enforce Listing New Sites In Sites Directory option is not enabled by default on this page, and without it, selecting a Global Sites Directory has no impact when site collections are created. While the title phrase for the check box references "sites," it applies only to site collections, not subsites within a site collection. You should configure the Master Sites Directory to require one or all site categories according to your taxonomy design so that category selections are made during the site creation process.

## Choosing a Content Deployment Strategy

While we have observed many recent discussions of perceived weaknesses of the current iteration of content deployment, many of these comments seem to be products of a lack of understanding about what the process is designed to accomplish and when it is needed. The key word in understanding the process is *content*. Content deployment does not deploy any features, functionality, or code—only content from the content database. While it does require the publishing infrastructure feature to be activated for a site collection for its functionality, it will deploy both publishing and collaborative content *if* the templates for the containers are available on the destination site collection. Note that while only content is deployed, the appropriate containers will be built and the appropriate features will be activated as long as like definitions and features exist on the target servers. If you have deployed custom features as solutions to your source, then they should be deployed to your target prior to content deployment. If they are deployed after the initial content deployment, content dependent upon containers created by the custom features will not deploy correctly. Also, the custom features will need to be activated on the target site collection either as part of the solution deployment or manually.

Second, both the source and the target of a content deployment path must be site collections. Also, the root site of the target site collection should be created with a blank site template. See the Knowledge Base article at *http://support.microsoft.com/kb/923592* for details. The deployment job does not need to deploy everything within a site collection, but the root of the path on both ends must be a site collection. Also, the level of the content must be consistent. That is, a third-level site of a source cannot be deployed as a second-level site in the target. Furthermore, only content contained within the site collection is deployed. Therefore, some list views or Web part sort orders will not be deployed when they are stored as "personal" configurations, even though they appear to be "shared."

Other than the initial deployment of a site collection, content deployment of collaborative content has proven problematic and inconsistent. Some of the problem areas involve target site collections where the content has been modified locally or STSADM export/import operations have been performed. Anything that changes the object ID at the target will cause errors in the deployment job. Also, an object created in both the source and the target with the same name will cause a deployment job to fail.

Safe best practices would be to limit content deployment to pure publishing site collections and initial snapshot deployments of site collections with collaborative features for testing environments.

For additional troubleshooting tips, see Stefan Gossner's excellent six part blog series, "Deep Dive Into the SharePoint Content Deployment and Migration API," at *http://blogs.technet.com/stefan_gossner/archive/2007/08/30/deep-dive-into-the-sharepoint-content-deployment-and-migration-api-part-1.aspx*.

> **More Info** For more traditional deployment strategies (authoring, staging, production), see the Microsoft planning guide, "Design Content Deployment Topology," at *http://technet.microsoft.com/en-us/library/cc262004.aspx#section2*.

## Authoring in Place with Approval

The good news is that, like collaborative sites, publishing sites are designed for all content work to be accomplished on the production servers, effectively replacing the "authoring, staging, production" cycle for content in simple publishing scenarios. In most instances, the default tools are sufficient to permit content authors to produce, edit, and maintain their content while satisfying the most stringent requirements for content approval and branding control. While some organizations may not initially be comfortable with this scenario, SharePoint Server 2007 provides the tools necessary to effectively and securely create content directly on production sites.

The one instance in which these tools interfere with SharePoint Server 2007 functionality is the use of connecting Web parts on publishing pages that require checkout for any changes. The modification of the presentation of one Web part by another Web part is considered a modification of the page. This "new page" must be checked in before it can be presented to users. If you are going to use connected Web parts on your publishing pages, you will need to maintain control of the content creation process on a staging server and deploy content to a production site where the checkout requirement can be disabled to permit these pages to work appropriately.

Another solution would be to place connected Web parts only on standard Web part pages that are not stored in a document library that requires checkout. This solution will impact your branding because Web part pages use the System Master Page, and publishing pages use the Site Master Page. Your designers will now need to maintain consistent branding between the two different master pages.

> **Note** There are no publishing pages that use connected Web parts by default.

While content creation and management on the production site will probably reduce the need for a set of authoring, staging, and production sites for content, you will still need different farms for development and testing custom code, including master and layout pages, Web parts, content types, and custom features. The tools used to deploy code from one SharePoint farm to another are packaged into features and solutions that can be pushed to the appropriate servers via the SharePoint APIs.

The need for this staging environment for code, and not for content, commonly presents an interesting scenario in which a reverse content deployment is used to deploy content from production back to the development and testing farms so the code can be tested against "live content." Content deployment works quite well for this task as long as the production servers are established first; then content deployment is used to create the site collection structures for the testing and development farms.

## Publishing Tools

Maintaining a consistent, approved look and feel (branding) and the control of content published on a corporate site available to those outside the organization is often of major concern for most organizations. SharePoint Server 2007 has several tools enabled by default on publishing sites to alleviate those concerns:

- **Pages library** Contains all publishing pages and is configured by default to require checkout for all changes, to maintain major and minor versions, and to require approvals on all major versions with a parallel approval workflow enabled. The term "publish" is introduced here to define the action of creating a major version that then triggers the approval process. Minor versions of the images can be viewed only by users with rights to edit them.

> **Note** Do not create folders in a pages library. While it permits the creation of folders, a pages library does not support folders. New pages are always created in the root of the library, and the navigation tools do not display pages moved to a folder.

- **Documents library** Used to store documents used by publishing pages within the site. This library is configured to maintain major versions only and requires neither checkout for modifications nor approval. You may choose to change these requirements if your organization's policies require approval for any content that is used on your site or site collection.

> **Note** An alternate solution would be to control the Contribute permissions to the library. Then documents to be placed here could be developed in a collaborative environment with a custom Send To location for copying approved documents to this library by those with the appropriate permissions.

- **Images library** Not a picture library, but used to store images that are used on a publishing page within the site or site collection. Like the pages library, the default configuration of the images library requires checkout for all changes, maintains minor and major versions, and requires approval on all major versions with a parallel approval workflow enabled, as shown in Figure 13-7. Minor versions of the images can be viewed only by users with rights to edit them. Images from these libraries may be placed on a publishing page as an image that is stored with the page content or as a hyperlink so that they are retrieved from the library (or object cache) when the page is called. For images, this option is determined by the page author.

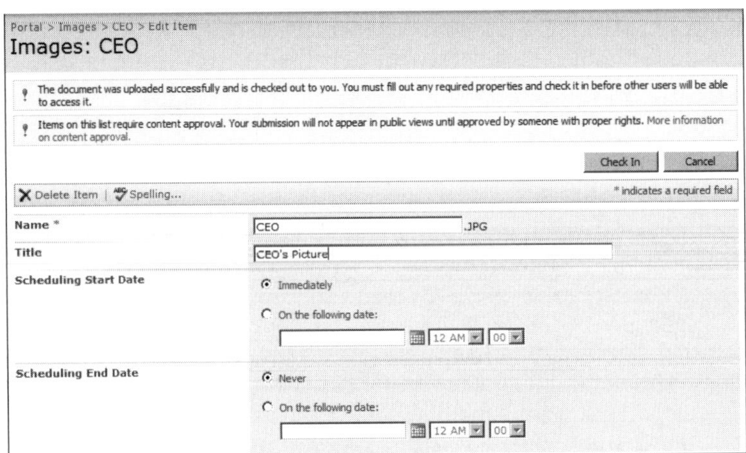


**Figure 13-7** Image library property page for an image

- **Re-usable content list** Stores HTML or text content that can be inserted into content editor controls of publishing pages as embedded text or as a reference. For re-usable content, this option is determined by the author of the re-usable text. Each list item of text has an option named *automatic update*. If this option is selected, the content is placed as a read-only reference. If it is not selected, the content of the item is copied into the Web content and stored with the page. By default, the list maintains major versions and requires approvals but does not have a workflow enabled for the approval process. There is only one re-usable content list for each site collection that is available for all sites with the publishing feature activated.

- **Style library** Stores custom XSL styles and CSS for use throughout the site collection. This library does maintain both major and minor versions of documents and requires checkout when making changes. It does not, by default, require approval of items added or modified. While everyone needs Read permission to items in this library, you will want to limit Contribute permissions to your Web designers. In many environments, approval will be required because items in this library will impact your site's branding options.

> **Note** These tools separate the roles of designer, content author, and management content approvers to safely permit content authoring directly on a production site. For increased security and peace of mind, you may choose to extend a second Web application for your site that provides anonymous read access only for public Internet users.

The option on the re-usable content list and images library to include content as a reference (or hyperlink) rather than embedded content provides the following advantages that you should carefully consider:

- Smaller databases because the content is stored only once
- Performance improvement because referenced objects are common to multiple pages delivered from the object cache
- Reduced overhead in updating content because a single update of the item in the library or list appears in the next delivery of all pages that contain the reference
- Centralized approval process for content that can be used throughout the site collection or site

> **Notes from the Field Placing Re-usable Content**
>
> You should place content in the containers at the site collection level unless it should be available only for a specific site. This is beneficial for the following reasons:
>
> - Centralized approval is more efficient.
> - Duplicate items require more space.
> - Referenced items can be changed in the single container and be reflected immediately across the site collection.
>
> The content and image pickers of publishing pages expose these site collection and site-specific publishing containers only for object selections. Therefore, if you need to centralize the storage and approval processes across multiple site collections, then you should create collaborative containers where the creation and approval processes can take place and then copy the objects to the appropriate site collection containers with custom workflows, the Send To option, or programmatically using custom code.
>
> *Daniel Webster, MCSE: Security + Internet, MCT, Senior Instructor, Mindsharp*

The scheduling option of the images and pages libraries permits the content creation and approval processes to be completed in advance of the date when an item should be displayed, in addition to stopping the presentation of content at a specific date and time. This will require planning, training, and enforcement, but will please both users and management in that your sites need not display out-of-date information ever again. Using scheduling functionality assists you in the best practice of content timeliness.

> **Note** None of the publishing containers that are configured to maintain versions have any limits on how many versions to retain. Because each version is a complete copy, retaining extraneous copies increases your database size unnecessarily. This should be a cooperative planning decision between those concerned with database size and site owners who best know the needs of their sites.

## Document Conversions

One tool provided by publishing that is frequently overlooked is the document conversion service. Once the service is enabled and configured by your farm administrators, content editors can use it under special conditions to convert Microsoft Office XML documents directly into Web pages. Because it has no page in Site Settings and appears only in the context menu of documents in document libraries of publishing sites, users must be trained on how the process works and when it is appropriate. There are some best practices and one big don't.

In a business setting, a user may create some piece of information, such as a press release in Microsoft Office Word 2007 and then need to present it in a Web page on a publishing site. Assuming the document conversion service is running and configured properly by farm administrators, the user can upload the document to a document library in the publishing site. Once in the library, the document's context menu will include an action called Convert Document that offers conversion options depending upon the configurations in Central Administration.

For the From Word Document To Web Page option, a page opens that presents entries for required metadata and a selection of the Web site where the page should be published.

Because we are concerned with the best practices, let's examine the "don't ever" caution first. Certainly you should not install a Web server on a domain controller for any number of reasons, but if you place the member of your SharePoint farm running the document conversion service on a domain controller, it will not work, at all, ever. This occurs because the converter is executed in the context of a local account, and there are no local accounts on a domain controller. Your users will be frustrated because everything will seem to work until the last step, whereupon it fails. For details, see the entry on the Microsoft Enterprise Content Management Team blog at *http://blogs.msdn.com/ecm/archive/2006/06/13/629525.aspx*.

Next, you should consider the document library to be used for documents being converted to Web pages. We recommend creating a separate library for this purpose. Because the information will be published on a Web page, there is probably no need for the documents in the library to appear in search results along with the Web page. Having a separate library, you can disable crawling for that specific library. You will not be able to disable the function in other libraries on the publishing sites, so some special training will be required to encourage users to use the appropriate library.

Finally, you should consider the page layout that will be configured for the service to use in creating the Web page from the document. You may want this type of page to offer a link to the original document so users can download it. In this case, a special page layout will be required with a field control or Web part to display the link. Also, you may want to add a Web part to store a picture from the document, should it have one, and not to show the picture as missing when there is none.

# Managing Master and Layout Pages

ASP.NET 2.0 introduced master pages, which define the look, feel, and standard behavior of Web site pages. They are designed with Microsoft Visual Studio 2005 and 2008 applications. Non-publishing pages that use master pages are referred to as content pages or Web part pages. This combination of a master page and content page, along with CSSs, separates the coding functionality of developers working with Visual Studio and the design functions of Web page designers with SharePoint Designer 2007 from the content page creation by users in the browser. Users can also add Web parts to the Web part zones provided by the content page design to increase the functionality of the pages.

Publishing adds another layer to the page-building process: the layout page. Layout pages are created in SharePoint Designer 2007 and may contain field controls, such as a master page, to control content. SharePoint Designer 2007 can also be used to create Web part zones to permit the flexibility of adding or moving Web parts. Publishing pages separate the content of the page displayed in field controls from the design of the page. Web parts normally display content that is stored separately from the page itself. So, with a publishing page in the pages library, only the content itself is stored as metadata in the columns of the library, along with other metadata that includes a reference to the page layout.

> **More Info** We do not include publishing-specific developer or designer content in this book, but instead focus on managing the parts of publishing pages. If you want detailed information on SharePoint Designer 2007, consider the book *Microsoft Office SharePoint Designer 2007 Step by Step* by Penelope Coventry (Microsoft Press, 2008) available at *http://www.microsoft.com/MSPress/books/12083.aspx*.

SharePoint Server 2007 includes a *default.master* page used by the Web part pages and several out-of-the-box *custom.master* pages designed specifically for publishing layout pages within sites. The *custom.master* page selected for a site is called the Site Master Page in the administration user interface. When pages are created in the pages library, they use both layout pages and the Site Master Page. The *default.master* page is called the System Master Page in the administration user interface. It is used by all forms and view pages in a SharePoint Server 2007 deployment. A third master page, the *application.master* page, is used by the administrative pages within SharePoint, such as those in the _Layouts directory. End users do not see these pages, so we recommend that you do not attempt to brand this page.

> **Important** Do not permit editing of any files stored in the layout folders with SharePoint Designer 2007. This will most likely corrupt them.

Activating the publishing feature for a site provides access to the Site Master Page Settings page. Under the Look And Feel column on the Site Settings page, you will find a link named Master Page, which you can use to access the Site Master Page Settings page. On the top portion of the page, shown in Figure 13-8, you can configure the Site Master Page used by layout pages and select whether to reset subsites to use this new page selection.

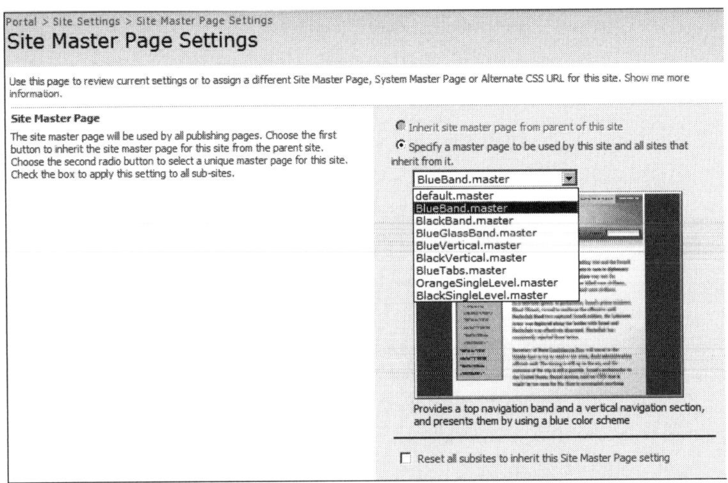


**Figure 13-8** Master page choices for the Site Master Page

Figure 13-9 shows where the System Master Page and the Alternate CSS URL options are configured. Once again, you have the option to reset subsites. In both Figure 13-9 and Figure 13-10, the option to inherit from a parent site is not available because portal was the top-level site in the site collection.

SharePoint Server 2007 leverages style rules saved in a number of default CSS files referenced within master pages. These CSS files are saved in the style library of publishing sites, discussed earlier. Images used by the master pages, such as background images, are also stored in the style library. Additional CSS files can be stored in this library and used to override or supplement those referenced in the master page. However, as shown in Figure 13-10, the URL of any centralized source of CSS files could be used instead of the local style library. Modifying and publishing CSS files could quickly change the look and feel across your entire site collection or even your farm.

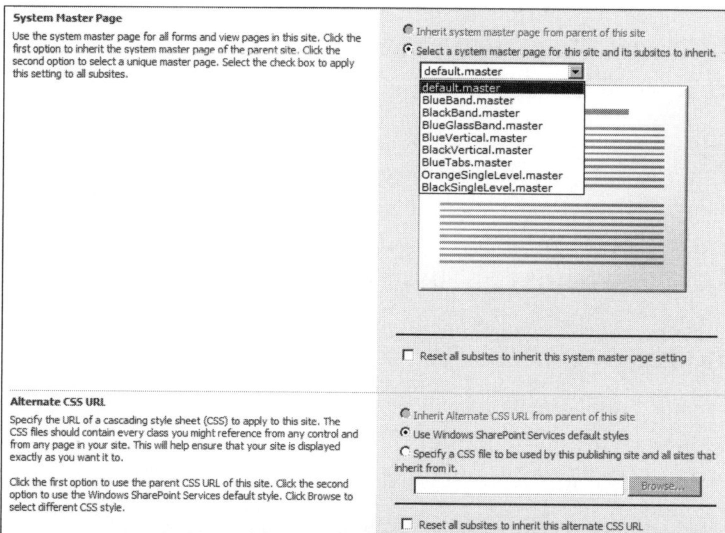


**Figure 13-9** Master page choices for System Master Page and optional CSS settings

Portal > Master Page Gallery

**Master Page Gallery**

Use the master page gallery to store master pages. The master pages in this gallery are available to this site and any sites underneath it.

New ▾ Upload ▾ Actions ▾ Settings ▾

| Name | Modified | Modified By | Checked Out To | Approval Status |
|---|---|---|---|---|
| Editing Menu | 3/17/2008 8:01 PM | TRAINSBYDAVE\administrator | | Approved |
| en-us | 3/17/2008 8:01 PM | TRAINSBYDAVE\administrator | | Approved |
| Preview Images | 3/17/2008 8:01 PM | TRAINSBYDAVE\administrator | | Approved |
| ArticleLeft.aspx | 3/17/2008 8:02 PM | TRAINSBYDAVE\administrator | | Approved |
| ArticleLinks.aspx | 3/17/2008 8:02 PM | TRAINSBYDAVE\administrator | | Approved |
| ArticleRight.aspx | 3/17/2008 8:02 PM | TRAINSBYDAVE\administrator | | Approved |
| BlackBand.master | 3/17/2008 8:02 PM | TRAINSBYDAVE\administrator | | Approved |
| BlackSingleLevel.master | 3/17/2008 8:02 PM | TRAINSBYDAVE\administrator | | Approved |
| BlackVertical.master | 3/17/2008 8:02 PM | TRAINSBYDAVE\administrator | | Approved |
| BlankWebPartPage.aspx | 3/17/2008 8:02 PM | TRAINSBYDAVE\administrator | | Approved |
| BlueBand.master | 3/17/2008 8:02 PM | TRAINSBYDAVE\administrator | | Approved |
| BlueGlassBand.master | 3/17/2008 8:02 PM | TRAINSBYDAVE\administrator | | Approved |
| BlueTabs.master | 3/17/2008 8:02 PM | TRAINSBYDAVE\administrator | | Approved |
| BlueVertical.master | 3/17/2008 8:02 PM | TRAINSBYDAVE\administrator | | Approved |
| default.master | 3/17/2008 8:01 PM | TRAINSBYDAVE\administrator | | Approved |
| OrangeSingleLevel.master | 3/17/2008 8:02 PM | TRAINSBYDAVE\administrator | | Approved |
| PageFromDocLayout.aspx | 3/17/2008 8:02 PM | TRAINSBYDAVE\administrator | | Approved |
| PageLayoutTemplate.aspx | 3/17/2008 8:01 PM | TRAINSBYDAVE\administrator | | Approved |

**Figure 13-10** Master Page Gallery

The design of these configuration pages offers both consistency and flexibility. The choices in the drop-down lists for master pages are retrieved from the Master Page Gallery shown in Figure 13-10. Your Web designers can create new master pages and page layout pages and place them in this gallery for use throughout the site collection. If you need uniformity across site collections, these new pages can be packaged with Visual Studio and deployed as solutions, where required by farm administrators. This gallery is configured to require checkout for modifications, to require approval (without a workflow), and to maintain both major and minor versions. Versioning permits rolling back to a previous version of both master pages and layout pages.

## Inside Track **Master Page and Themes on Windows SharePoint Services 3.0 Sites in SharePoint Server**

I was in a meeting one day, showing off master pages on a team site on our SharePoint Server 2007 farm, and discovered a few things. The following steps should work with any of the master pages and themes. Feel free to substitute. These steps are great for information workers, IT pros, or whoever wants to change the look and feel of a site. This is a walkthrough of my experience with trying to brand a simple team site and change it from Microsoft blue.

### Applying a Site Master

1. Create a team site (team template).
2. In Site Settings, go to Site Collection Features, and activate the Office SharePoint Server publishing infrastructure feature.
3. Under Look And Feel in Site Settings, select the Master Page link.
4. For the Site Master Page, choose BlackVertical.master. Select the Apply To Subsites check box.

After performing these steps, you may expect to go to a home page and see a fancy site with the black sides.

Wrong. Apparently, the site master applies to publishing pages only. It works for intranet or Internet portal templates, but you'll discover that it doesn't apply to subsites with Windows SharePoint Services 3.0 templates.

### Applying a System Master

1. Return to Site Settings, click the Master Page link, and for the System Master Page, choose BlackVertical.Master. Select the Apply To Subsites check box.
2. You'll notice that the Site Settings page still uses Microsoft blue.
3. Go to the home page.
4. You will see the new master page, but the bars on the Web parts are Microsoft blue.
5. On the Site Settings page under the Look And Feel column, click the Site Theme link, and then choose Obsidian. Click Apply.
6. The Site Settings page should now reflect the black Obsidian theme, but the home page and all lists still show the blue Web part bar.

So, how do you change that?

### Applying a Custom CSS from a Theme

1. On the Site Settings page, click View Source, and you'll see the reference to the theme in the style sheet just a few lines down. Look for <link rel="stylesheet" type="text/css" id="onetidThemeCSS" href="http://blogs.msdn.com/sites/tr5iw /_themes/Obsidian/Obsi1011-65001.css?rev=12%2E0%2E0%2E4518"/>.

2. Copy the href URL path of the CSS reference (minus the query string): /sites/tr5iw/_themes/Obsidian/Obsi1011-65001.css.
3. Go to Master Page, scroll to the bottom, choose Specify A CSS File To Be Used, and paste the href URL path of the CSS reference that you copied in step 2. Then select the Apply To Subsites check box.
4. Go to the home page. You did it. No blue.

Without opening any tools, you can apply a consistent user interface theme across site settings, the home page, and the list pages in your team site.

So what did you learn? There is a difference between site.master and system.master in relation to the pages and templates.

- **Site Master Page** The Site Master Page will be used by all publishing pages. That's great for the Internet and intranet publishing site, but not for many of the subsites.
- **System Master Page** The System Master Page is used for all forms and view pages in the site. These are all the site templates and pages that the Site Master Page does not apply to, including team sites, document workspaces, Web part pages, and all non-publishing pages.

*Joel Oleson, Microsoft Senior Technical Product Manager, Microsoft*

In SharePoint Server 2007, publishing content pages are referred to as *page layouts*. These special ASPX pages have predefined content type fields, Web parts, and tables. The choice of layout pages is displayed when you create a publishing page, as shown in Figure 13-11. This selection is retrieved from the Master Pages And Layout Pages Gallery at the site collection level. Sites can also have a similar gallery for pages unique to that site, but it is only available through SharePoint Designer.

The choice of layout pages can be filtered in another administration page called Page Layouts And Site Templates under the Look And Feel column of the Site Settings page for each site. The lower portion of the Page Layouts And Site Templates page enables each site owner to filter the list of page layouts from the gallery to limit the choices offered when creating a publishing page on that site, as shown in Figure 13-12. A best practice is to involve your branding team and site owners to establish the page layouts to make available for their sites. If subsites have different owners, written policies should be established to control whether owners override the settings that they inherit.

The upper portion of the same page presents the option to filter the site templates available for creating subsites in the site, as shown in Figure 13-13.

**Note** If the site owner of a subsite chooses to initiate a unique page layouts and site templates filter for the site, the full range of page layouts in the Site Collection Gallery and site templates for the site collection are available to be selected, not just those selected from the parent site filters. Only policies and training control this behavior.

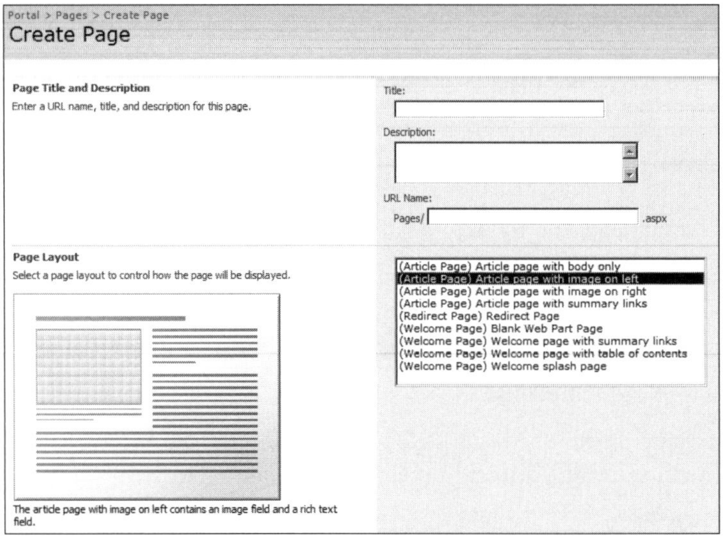

Portal > Pages > Create Page
Create Page
Page Title and Description
Enter a URL name, title, and description for this page.
Title:
Description:
URL Name:
Pages/
.aspx
Page Layout
Select a page layout to control how the page will be displayed.
(Article Page) Article page with body only
(Article Page) Article page with image on left
(Article Page) Article page with image on right
(Article Page) Article page with summary links
(Redirect Page) Redirect Page
(Welcome Page) Blank Web Part Page
(Welcome Page) Welcome page with summary links
(Welcome Page) Welcome page with table of contents
(Welcome Page) Welcome splash page
The article page with image on left contains an image field and a rich text field.

Figure 13-11 Page layout choices when creating a publishing page

Pages inherit preferred layouts from parent site
Pages in this site can use any layout
Pages in this site can only use the following layouts:
(Article Page) Article page with body only
(Article Page) Article page with image on left
(Article Page) Article page with image on right
(Article Page) Article page with summary links
(Redirect Page) Redirect Page
(Welcome Page) Blank Web Part Page
(Welcome Page) Welcome page with summary
(Welcome Page) Welcome page with table of c
(Welcome Page) Welcome splash page
Add >
< Remove
Reset all subsites to inherit these preferred page layout settings

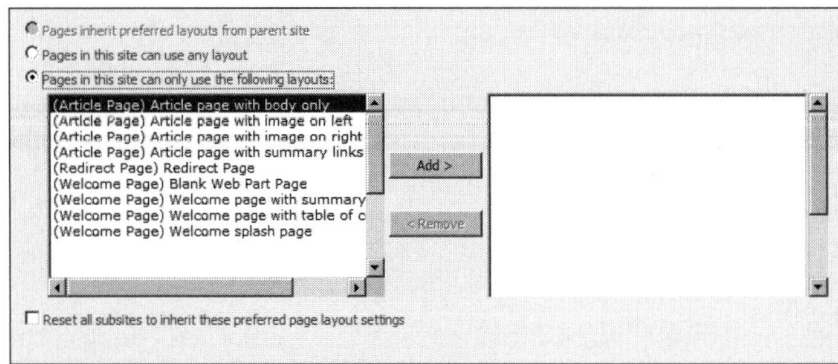

Figure 13-12 Page layout choices filter

Subsites inherit site templates from parent site
Subsites can use any site template
Subsites can only use the following site templates:
(All)
Document Center (All)
Document Workspace (All)
Mindsharp CBT Library (All)
Multipage Meeting Workspace (All)
News Site (All)
Personalization Site (All)
Publishing Site (All)
Records Center (All)
Report Center (All)
Search Center (All)
Search Center with Tabs (All)
Site Directory (All)
Social Meeting Workspace (All)
Add >
< Remove
Publishing Site with Workflow (All)
Reset all subsites to inherit these preferred subsite template settings

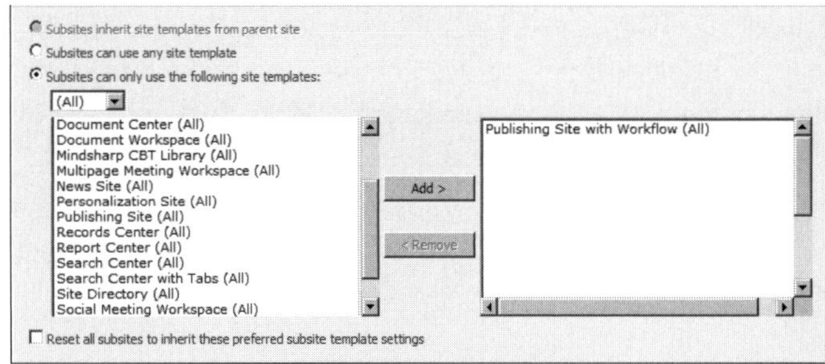

Figure 13-13 Site templates choices filter

## Search Considerations for Public Sites

Because the Publishing Portal template is frequently used for the public face of organizations, there may be special search considerations involved when creating this template. In small-to-medium environments, the Internet site may be part of the same farm as the intranet or extranet sites. If you have only a single SSP, the one index will contain information about internal sites as well as your Internet site. Despite the security trimming provided by search, if a user does not secure documents correctly, internal documents could be displayed in Internet search results. Even though the Internet user would not have access to the documents, the name, title, and author of the document could expose confidential or private information. In this scenario, you should have a separate Shared Service Provider indexing this public site so that there is isolation between the public and internal indexes. See Chapter 16, "Leveraging Shared Services Providers," for more information.

## Supporting Localization

Publishing sites have two options for presenting sites in different languages and locales. Both options require that the locales be available on all WFE servers and that the appropriate language packs be installed on all WFE servers. Because the topology of your farm can quickly be changed by simply changing roles, you should configure locales and install language packs on all members of the farm to allow the flexibility of assigning the WFE role freely and quickly without stopping for additional installations and configurations.

> **More Info** When you plan for a multilingual solution, please see *http://go.microsoft.com/fwlink/?LinkId=79322* for more information.

> **Note** Both Windows SharePoint Services 3.0 and SharePoint Server 2007 are available in numerous languages, as are the Windows operating systems. The language of farm administration pages is controlled by the language of the SharePoint Products and Technologies installation, independent of the operating system language. However, the language of the administration pages of individual sites are determined by the locale selection of the particular site. Because a site collection can contain sites of different locales, the site collection administration pages are presented in the locale of the top-level site.

### Unique Language Sites

Some scenarios will require sites in various languages that host unique content. After the appropriate locales are configured and the language packs are installed on the servers, a new site can be created at any level in any language installed on the server. Once a site is created, its locale can be changed but its language cannot.

Installing the language packs creates a complete set of site definitions, in the installed language, for all native site definitions. When you select the language on the New SharePoint Site page, as shown in Figure 13-14, the appropriate site definition is used to create the site, including the default.aspx and any other resources required. The master pages, layout pages, content page templates, and administration pages for this site are in the language selected. Translating the content will be accomplished by content and page authors and is *not* done automatically. You may need to employ translators to modify the content or train multilingual employees to create the appropriate publishing pages along with the content.

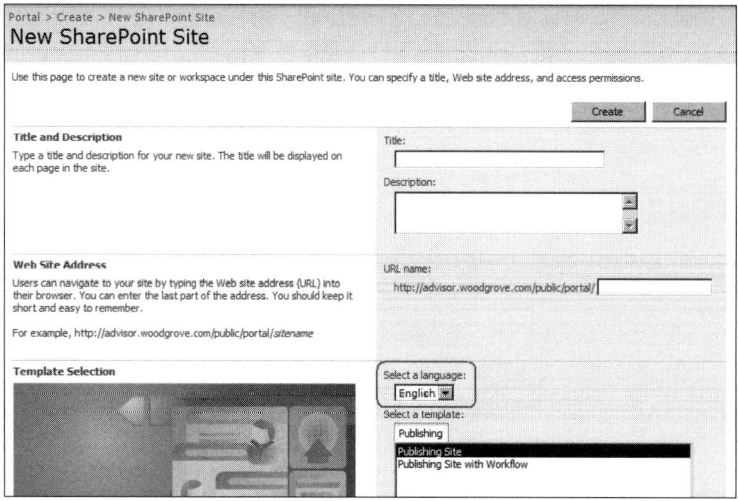


**Figure 13-14** Select A Language options for site templates

> **Important** The location of the different language sites and the navigation aids used must be designed into all surrounding sites.

> **Note** If you are going to permit users to select the language of their My Sites, the language packs must be installed before anyone creates a My Site. Remember that the language and locale of a site cannot be changed after it is created.

# Variations

Publishing also offers tools for creating sites hosting the same content in multiple languages and automatically redirecting a user to the appropriate language/locale version of the site based on the locale settings of his or her browser. This technology is grouped into a number of configurations referred to as *variations*.

> **Note** While variations are most commonly considered to be based only on languages, it can present the content in different locales of the same language, variations of the content based on browser types if some users have browsers that do not support all SharePoint Server 2007 functionalities, or variations of the site content in which some users access the site with PDA-type devices and want to have some content removed.

Because variations are largely misunderstood, we will present the basics in line with discussing best practices. The term *variations* really describes the set of sites (with some type of variation) established at the same level within a site collection. The set of sites are referred to as a *hierarchy*. While it is theoretically possible to set the root of a variation hierarchy at some point lower than the root site of the site collection, that does not seem practical because users would need to understand the language of the higher-level sites to be able to navigate to the variations root level. Thus, the best practice is to set the root of the variation hierarchy as the root of the site collection.

Variations constitute a major planning issue. All sites within the hierarchy are empty when the hierarchy is created. You want to avoid management directing you to present a SharePoint Server 2007 site in multiple languages *after* you have created the content. After you have created a site collection full of subsites and content, it is very difficult to implement variations. The variation hierarchy must be created before any content is added to a site because the source "label" is created empty as part of building the hierarchy. Yes, the best practice is to plan for variation sites and to not convert existing sites to variation sites. A common attempted workaround is creating the source label with a blank template and then using content deployment to move content, including containers, into the site. This will not work out of the box because the root site of the site collection would need to be a blank site for functional content deployment. This should reinforce the need to plan for variations.

Unlike content deployment, which requires the publishing infrastructure feature to be activated but will deploy both publishing and collaborative content, variations work only with publishing sites and content. That is, subsites without publishing activated do not get created throughout the hierarchy. Likewise, Web part pages are ignored, as are some lists and libraries. Variations were designed for Internet publishing sites, not collaboration sites with the publishing feature activated.

All sites within the hierarchy do not have to be identical. Careful planning of your choices when adding labels (sites) will permit selectively pushing content to some members of the hierarchy and not others. Also, content can be refused by site owners of members of the hierarchy. Unique content that does not exist at the source label can also be added directly to members of the hierarchy. Note that approvals, workflows, permissions, and scheduling can be configured uniquely at each member of the hierarchy and will be honored by the variations process.

Variations employ the content deployment API, which is frequently referred to as the PRIME API. Just like content deployment, Save Site As A Template, and STSADM export | import, variations use the API in its own unique method. To address some of the planning issues in configuring variations, we will examine the configuration pages.

First, all variation configurations are accomplished by the site collection administrator because they appear only in the Site Collection Administration column of the Site Settings page. The first page requiring configuration is the Variation Settings page, shown in Figure 13-15. It is accessed from the Variations link under the Site Collection Administration column on the Site Settings page. These settings are all global for the hierarchy.

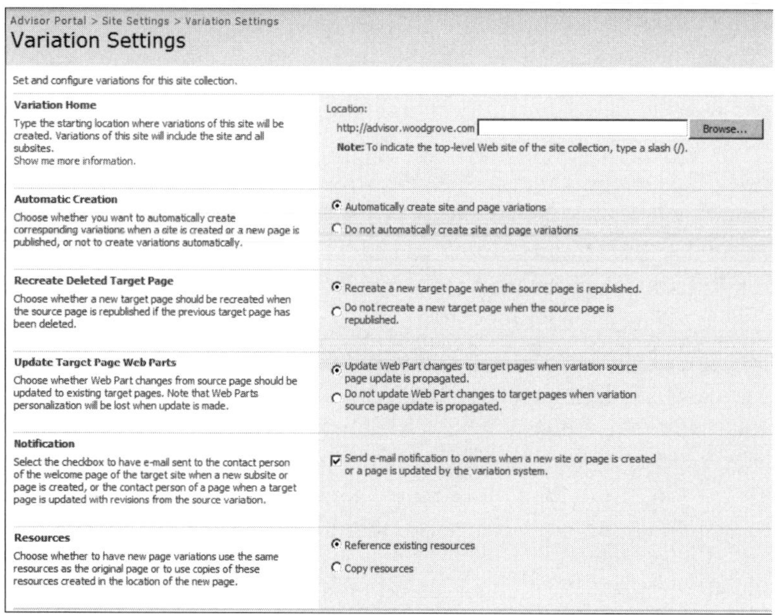


**Figure 13-15** Global Variation Settings page

The first section of the page designates the starting point (or root) of the variation hierarchy. As previously stated, we believe the best practice is to use the root site of the site collection as the starting point. If this site has any existing content, it can be accessed only with a direct URL after it is selected as the starting point. The Welcome page, or Splash page, for the site will be replaced with a page containing redirect code that evaluates the HTTP header information, determines the locale setting of the browser requesting the page, and sends the request to the correct site. This evaluation code can be modified to check other portions of the HTTP header. All variation labels will be created at the level just below the starting location.

The Automatic Creation section of the Variation Settings page determines globally whether publishing content will be pushed automatically to other labels when it is created on the source label. Choosing not to create site and page variations means that someone must create them manually for each new content piece created on the source label. You will get options for individual labels that will override the automatic option, so the best practice here would be to accept the default automatic creation.

In the Recreated Deleted Target Page section of the Variation Settings page, you must determine whether you want to override the actions of the site owner of the target label. If a page is created on the source label and pushed to all target labels (default action), individual site owners can decide to delete the page from their site if they do not need it. The decision to be made here is whether the page should be pushed to that site again just because it was modified and republished. Because this is a global setting, we recommend retaining the default setting unless the owners of all of the target sites elect to disable it.

The Update Target Page Web Parts section of the Variation Settings page deals with Web parts placed on publishing pages. This concept is perhaps unrelated, but you will need to test Web parts on pages that will be pushed out with the variation process. Some Web parts do not work well under these circumstances because they contain references to locations on the original site. They may work again if the site owner of the target label reconfigures the Web parts with a new reference that is local to the current site. Also, site owners or page managers may modify the sort order or some other customization available within the Web part. This configuration determines if you overwrite their modification just because other content on the page changed requiring that the page be republished.

In the Notification section of the Variation Settings page, you determine whether the variation process should send notifications to the site owner when changes are pushed to the target label. We suggest clearing this check box because individual site owners can subscribe to alerts or establish their own workflows to achieve the same goal.

The Resources section impacts only objects that are stored on pages as references. It is somewhat misleading because all of the variation labels are within the same site collection. If the images being referenced are in the site collection images library, there is no need to copy them because all sites use the same library. However, site owners may wish to have pictures of people on their site reflect the nationality of their site. In this case, some planning is involved. You should train your content authors to use the site images library of the source label to store referenced images. Then this configuration should be changed to Copy Resources, which will cause the referenced images to be copied to the site images library of the target label site. The site owner can then replace the image with one suitable for the target site.

On the Variation Labels page, you will create and manage the labels (sites) within the variation hierarchy. The first label that you should create is the designated source label. It is the only label required to have a variation hierarchy. In our earlier scenario, had you suspected that a particular site collection would eventually need to be published in multiple languages, you could have configured the variation hierarchy with only the source label in the default language of your farm. Everyone would have been redirected to the one site because it would be the only one available.

However, when management decided that this site should also be published in other languages, other labels could be created for those languages and the hierarchy rebuilt. Then the automatic creation of variations would have pushed publishing sites and pages to the new labels in the appropriate language(s). Other language packs could be installed, labels created at any time, and the hierarchy rebuilt, which would trigger pushing content to the new labels.

When you click New Label, the Create Variation Label page appears. The first part of this page, shown in Figure 13-16, is common to all variation labels. The label name, description, and display name is straightforward, but the names should reflect the language and locale selected for the label.

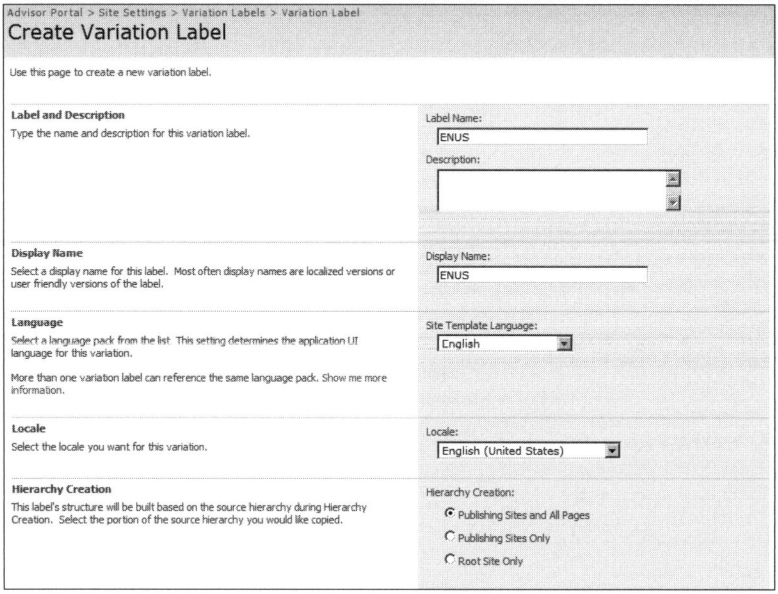

**Figure 13-16** Create Variation Label page

In the Language section, choose the language to use in selecting the template to build the site. This selection cannot be changed once configured and the site has been built. In the Locale section, select the locale corresponding to the language, and set other locale configurations such as keyboard, currency, date/time displays, and so forth. These settings cannot be changed after the site has been created.

In the Hierarchy Creation section, you will determine how much of the source variation is automatically pushed to the target label. Because the first label you are creating is the source, you should choose Publishing Sites And All Pages. On a per-label basis, your choices may differ. Remember that these choices are configuring what will automatically be created on the particular target site. Any publishing site or page can be manually configured at the source to be pushed to all or selective labels after it is created on the source. So if you have a label that will have the same structure but not all pages, select Publishing Sites Only. Then any publishing sites created on the source will be created on the label along with the default page for the site. Other pages will need to be manually configured on an individual basis to be part of the variation for this label.

If you have a label where all of the structure of the source label will not be required on the target, then choose Root Site Only. The target will receive the root site and the default Welcome page, but nothing else until the appropriate sites and pages have been manually configured to be part of the variation for this label. Once sites and pages have been created on the target with the link established back to the source, any updates will be pushed from the source to the target whether the original link was established automatically or manually.

The bottom section of the page, shown in Figure 13-17, is available only until the source label is created. Selecting this label as the source label activates the template picker for the source label. All target labels will use the corresponding template in the appropriate language.

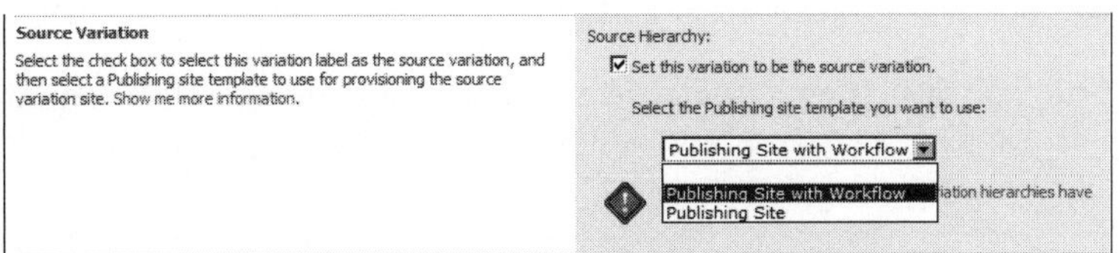


**Figure 13-17** Unique source label template choices

Once a source label has been created, the only way to remove it is to completely disable the variations hierarchy, delete all sites, and start over. Target labels can be deleted from the variation hierarchy at any time, as shown in Figure 13-18. After a target label is removed from the hierarchy, the site and its contents will still exist but will no long receive updates from the source label.

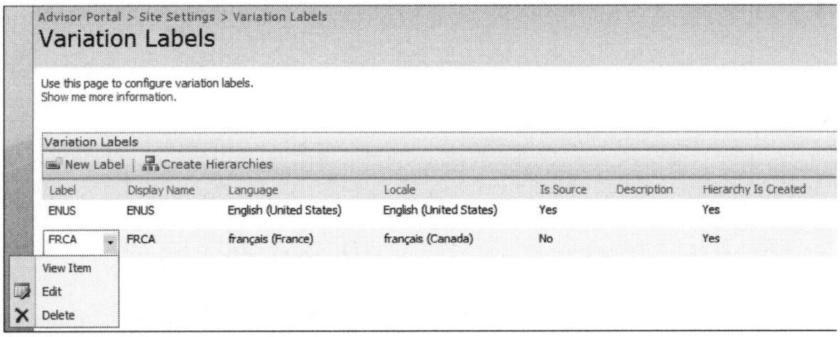

**Figure 13-18** Label management options

The Site Content And Structure tool is used to manually configure variation links, as shown in Figure 13-19. For this example, the FR_CA label was configured to receive the root site only. Therefore, Site A was not pushed to the FR_CA label. In the context menu of Site A in the Site Content And Structure page, the options New, Site Variation were available because at least one label did not have a variation of Site A.

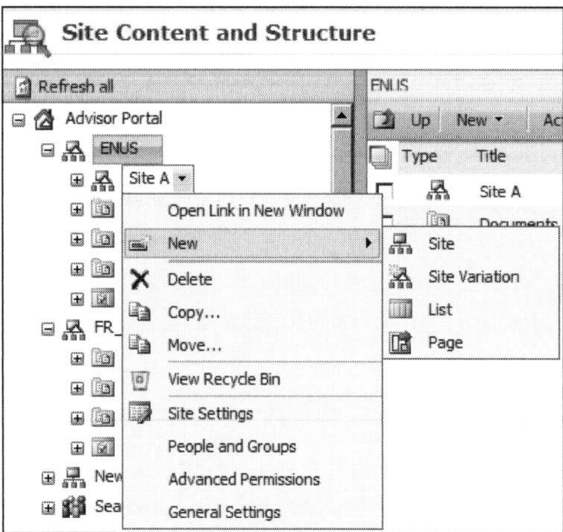


**Figure 13-19** Accessing the New Variation Site page from the Site Content And Structure page

In the New Variation Site page shown in Figure 13-20, the site title and URL can differ from the source label and still be linked for future revisions to the site. The same process could be used for pages that had not been pushed to all variation labels.

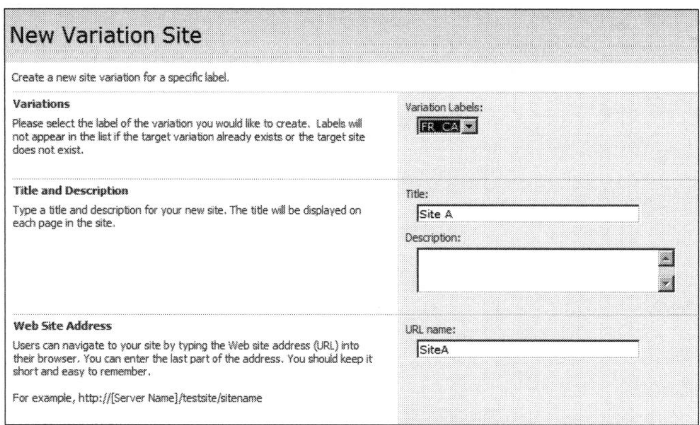


**Figure 13-20** Creating a new site variation

## Best Practices for Troubleshooting the Variation Process

The remaining page link under the Site Collection Administration column in site settings is for the Variation Logs page, shown in Figure 13-21. This page displays the log files in a very legible format with different columns for successes and failures. The log file entries give detailed information on the time started and completed, the action attempted, and the results, including the objects that are now linked for ongoing variation processes.

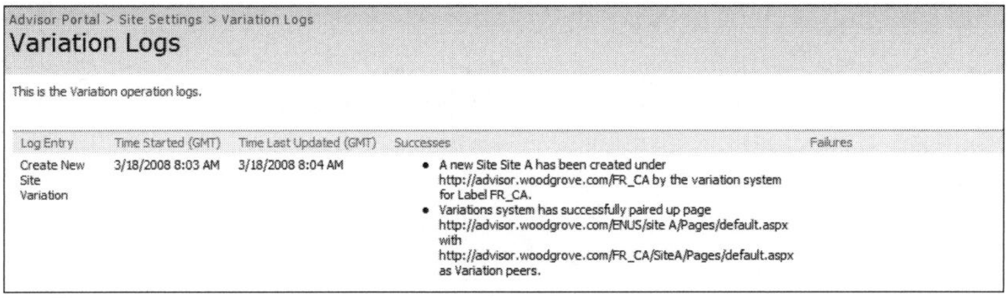

Figure 13-21 Variation Logs page

## Content Translation Management Tools

SharePoint offers no translation capabilities. The content is pushed across the variations in the original language even though the master pages and page layouts are in the target language. You have two choices for translating content: internal staff translators or external services. SharePoint Server 2007 does provide several tools to assist in managing both internal and external translation services.

**External Services** The first step involves planning what portions of your sites need translation from external translation services. Remember that all of the content of your publishing site is stored in columns of a database. On the target site in the Site Collection Administration column of site settings, the Translatable Columns link opens the Translatable Columns Settings page, which displays every column within your site collection, as shown in Figure 13-22. Here you can select the columns of your sites, libraries, and lists that contain text that needs translating. Many columns contain data, such as numbers, that will not require any translation. This relatively painful process is necessary only if you are going to use an external translation service that can utilize the SharePoint APIs to examine and expose data.

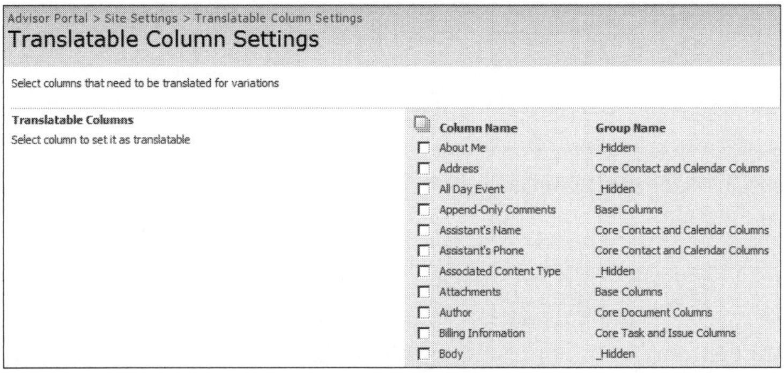

Figure 13-22 Translatable Column Settings page

The settings configured on this page are used by a process activated in the Site Content And Structure page to export the content of all columns selected into a .CAB file, as shown in Figure 13-23. This .CAB file can then be processed by an external translation service such as Idiom WorldServer (see *http://www.microsoft.com/presspass/events/sharepointconference/docs/idiom.doc*).

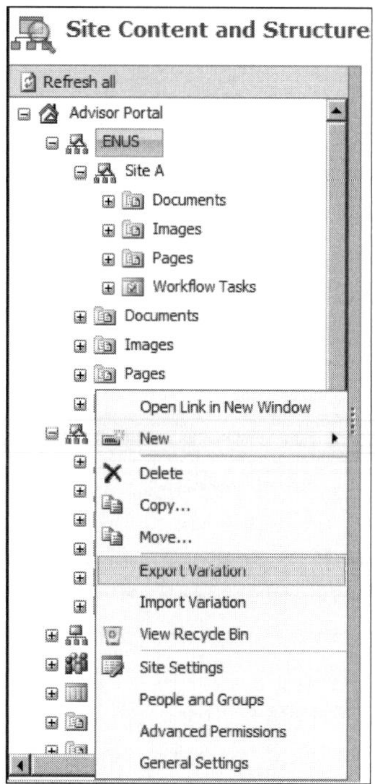


**Figure 13-23** Export Variation option on the Site Content And Structure page

After the content of the .CAB file has been translated into the appropriate language, it is repackaged by the external service and returned. Because the .CAB file retains the column storage information, it can now be imported into the appropriate language site using the Site Content And Structure page on the target site where the translated content replaces the content in the original language.

**Internal Translation Services Tools** Translation by internal teams takes a completely different approach and therefore requires different tools. For internal translation, you work with the entire page or document. Publishing provides three tools that assist in these efforts and that are functionally linked together. The Translation Management Library is a custom document library available for creation after the site feature is activated. This library provides a translation workflow that is available only from within the library. It also provides a translators list, which shows available translators and their language translation capabilities.

These three tools provide storage for pages or documents that need translating with metadata specifying the source and target languages. When the workflow is initiated, the translation requirements are retrieved from the document metadata, and one or more translators are selected from the list based on their capabilities listed and assigned the translation task. A translator accepts ownership of the task, translates the document, and returns it to the document library, which keeps separate copies of the document in the various languages into which it has been translated but maintains a link between all copies. The copy in the appropriate language can then be sent to the correct language site. These internal tools do not depend upon the variations process like the packaging tool for external translation teams.

### Notes from the Field **Managing the Translation Process**

Support for multiple languages is not restricted to content for public Internet sites. Many organizations today need to provide documents and pages in multiple languages even though access to the information is tightly controlled. With its special workflow and translators list, the Translation Management Library is an excellent tool for managing translation of this information.

However, the information still needs to be controlled during the translation process. Most administrators set the appropriate permissions on the document library but forget two other very important containers. You should control access to the task list and the history list used by the workflow just as tightly as the document library itself. In our world today, the document names themselves may contain more information than your organization wants made public. For instance, a document name such as *Feasibility Study on Purchasing the XYZ Corporation.doc* could impact the stock prices for two different organizations.

*Daniel Webster, MCSE: Security + Internet, MCT, Senior Instructor, Mindsharp*

## Summary

In this chapter, we have discussed the many features that are available under the overall umbrella of publishing. Some of them, such as publishing sites, work together to provide special functionality. These, in turn, differ greatly from collaborative sites. Others, like variations, extend the functionality of publishing sites. Due to their unique approach and structure, publishing sites require more planning in their design and architecture. Because they are generally used as the public face of your organization, branding and content control are particularly critical considerations.

## Additional Resources

- For detailed information on SharePoint Designer 2007, consider *Microsoft Office SharePoint Designer 2007 Step by Step* by Penelope Coventry (Microsoft Press, 2008): *http://www.microsoft.com/MSPress/books/12083.aspx.2.*
- For details on creating the target site collection for content deployment, see the Knowledge Base article on the topic: *http://support.microsoft.com/kb/923592.*
- For content deployment troubleshooting tips, see the blog series by Stefan Gossner, "Deep Dive Into the SharePoint Content Deployment and Migration API:" *http://blogs.technet.com/stefan_gossner/archive/2007/08/30/deep-dive-into-the-sharepoint-content-deployment-and-migration-api-part-1.aspx.*
- For a detailed white paper on planning your multilingual implementation, see "Building Multilingual Solutions by Using SharePoint Products and Technologies:" *http://go.microsoft.com/fwlink/?LinkId=79322.*
- For more information on Idiom's WorldServer translation service: *http://www.microsoft.com/presspass/events/sharepointconference/docs/idiom.doc.*

Chapter 14

# Understanding and Implementing Microsoft Search Server 2008

**In this chapter:**



What has been known as Microsoft Office SharePoint Server 2007 for Search has been rebranded to Microsoft Search Server 2008. But Search Server 2008 isn't just a new name for an existing product. Along with the new branding comes several new features, the most prominent of which is federated queries and tight integration with other Microsoft products to form a compelling business value proposition.

The search vertical is a busy, noisy vertical. Presently dominated by Google, Microsoft enters the market with an updated and improved product that is both compelling and well integrated with its online search, Live Search. The features in Search Server 2008 and Live Search will cause many who are entrenched with Google and other competitors to take pause and consider the direction Microsoft is taking search technologies and why they might want to use Search Server 2008 in their organization.

In this chapter, we'll explore Search Server 2008 and its features and benefits. We'll show you how to install and manage it. We'll discuss the OpenSearch 1.1 standard, upon which Search Server 2008 is built. In addition, we'll show you the solid integration Search Server 2008 has with Live Search, and we'll uncover the business value proposition that Search Server 2008 offers. Along the way, we'll also offer best practices for administrating and implementing Search Server 2008. We have much to discuss, so let's get going.

## Search Server 2008 Features and Benefits

Search Server 2008 is a standalone search product from Microsoft that is built on the SharePoint platform and extends the Office SharePoint Server 2007 search capabilities. When it is installed, you'll receive a Shared Services Provider and a Search Center, both of which are fully capable of all of the search functions that you've come to expect in SharePoint Server 2007. However, the Search Server 2008 implementation will lack many of the SharePoint Server 2007 farm features because it is a product focused on search and indexing.

The entire reason that a company implements a search engine is because users want to find information via a keyword query. Because we are accustomed to finding information on the Internet using an Internet search engine, it is only natural that we would want to have our own search engine on our internal corporate network to find internally hosted information. Because much of our information is not indexed by an Internet search engine, it stands to reason that having our own indexing engine that indexes our organization's internal information will help users find the information they need to be successful in their jobs.

Search Server 2008 was built for that purpose and offers the following benefits:

- Search Center, which is a Web site with a query and result set interface that can be exposed to the Internet if needed.
- Improved relevance engine, which shipped with the SharePoint Server 2007 product release and can be fine-tuned within the Search Server 2008 administration interface.
- Ability to target search Web parts with different functionality to SharePoint Server 2007 audiences.
- Ability to build customized search results pages for each scope and audience to produce a highly customized search experience.
- Ability to localize the interface in 25 languages (at the time of this writing).
- Ability to customize the search interfaces using Microsoft Visual Studio and Microsoft Office SharePoint Designer.
- Scalability to crawl any number of documents that you wish. This is important: Unlike other search engine companies, Microsoft does not impose a document limit.
- Federated queries and connectors allow you to execute queries to remote indexes in other data repositories, applications, and services using the Open Search standard.
- Reporting on user query and result activity is built-in with Search Server 2008.
- High availability and load balancing can be used through a combination of front-end and back-end server topologies, which allows you to grow your search infrastructure to meet your needs.
- Secure federated relationships by setting global- or user-level security for your federated search relationships.
- Specify unique crawl inclusion/exclusion behaviors and authentication credentials for specific content sources.

- Remove single items from the index using the single item index removal feature. This action automatically creates a new crawl rule to ensure the single item isn't crawled again.

Search Server 2008 is built on the OpenSearch 1.1 standard. This standard was developed by the folks at Amazon (*http://opensearch.a9.com*), and Internet Explorer 7 was built with an OpenSearch client embedded into it. OpenSearch was introduced by A9/Amazon at ETech in March of 2005, and a number of sites adopted the standard during the first six months after its introduction.

> **More Info** There is a growing list of Web sites that are OpenSearch compliant. A list of these sites can be found at *http://opensearch.a9.com//opensearch/searches.jsp*.

### Notes from the Field Search Providers in Internet Explorer 7 that Use OpenSearch 1.1

Because search is such an important aspect of our users' daily lives, a browser ought to do something special with search queries. In OpenSearch, the Internet Explorer 7 product team saw the foundation for making this happen.

One of the main goals of the Internet Explorer 7 product team was to make it easy for Internet Explorer 7 users to personalize their lists of search providers. Specifically, the goal was to allow users to target their search queries directly to the site of their choice, such as MSDN, an intranet portal, a SharePoint team site, or some other OpenSearch-compliant search engine. The way a user adds a search provider is similar to adding a favorite.

Site administrators can facilitate this process by providing a link to an OpenSearch definition file for the site in the head tag of the master page by using the following format:

```
<link title="Company Intranet" type="application/
opensearchdescription+xml" rel="search" href="/Style Library/
XSL Style Sheets/intranet.xml" />
```

In Internet Explorer, the Search button will respond by turning orange and listing the Intranet Search as a provider. Users may then simply add your search provider to their list of search providers.

The HREF is a link to the OpenSearch 1.1 Description Document for the search query. If the goal is to search the company's SharePoint intranet, the following XML is used:

```
<?xml version="1.0" encoding="UTF-8"?>
<OpenSearchDescription xmlns="http://a9.com/-/spec/
opensearch/1.1/">
  <ShortName>Company Intranet</ShortName>
  <Description>Company Intranet Search</Description>
  <Url type="text/html" template="http://intranet.company.com/searchcenter/pages/
results.aspx?k={searchTerms}"/>
  <SyndicationRight>open</SyndicationRight>
</OpenSearchDescription>
```

If the goal is to add a people search, the following would work for SharePoint.

```
<?xml version="1.0" encoding="UTF-8"?>
<OpenSearchDescription xmlns="http://a9.com/-/spec/
opensearch/1.1/">
  <ShortName>Company People</ShortName>
  <Description>Company People Search</Description>
  <Url type="text/html" template="http://intranet.company.com/searchcenter/
pages/peopleresults.aspx?k={searchTerms}"/>
  <SyndicationRight>open</SyndicationRight>
</OpenSearchDescription>
```

Another alternative is to advertise the availability of search on your site through a link that calls window.external.AddSearchProvider("URL"), where the URL is a link to the previously mentioned OpenSearch XML file. When the user clicks this link, code in Internet Explorer opens a dialog box asking the user if the search provider should be installed. Note that this process must be initiated by the user. If the client selects to install the search provider, Internet Explorer is configured to allow queries to the remote index using the Description Document for the search provider from the URL.

The OpenSearch options mean that you can also offer search results from other sites. Taken from the Internet Explorer 7 team blog site at MSDN, what follows is an example of a Description Document for searching on MSDN:

```
<?xml version="1.0" encoding="UTF-8"?>
<OpenSearchDescription xmlns=
"http://a9.com/-/spec/opensearchdescription/1.1/">
            <ShortName>MSDN</ShortName>
            <Description>MSDN Example Search</Description>
            <Tags>MSDN Developer</Tags>
            <Contact>admin@msdn.com</Contact>
            <Url type="text/html"
                   template="http://search.microsoft.com/search/
results.aspx?qu={searchTerms}&amp;View={language?}
&amp;p={startPage?}"/>
</OpenSearchDescription>
```

If a user searches MSDN for "Search Server 2008," the following URL is passed: *http://search.microsoft.com/search/results.aspx?qu=Search%20Server%202008&View=en-US&p=1.*

The OpenSearch standard allows the remote search engine to return results using Really Simple Syndication (RSS), Atom, HTML, or XHTML. The XML for returning the results in both RSS and HTML would look something like this (this XML is taken directly from the Internet Explorer 7 team blog site):

```
<?xml version="1.0" encoding="UTF-8"?>
<OpenSearchDescription xmlns="http://a9.com/-/spec/opensearchdescription/1.1/">
            <ShortName>MSN</ShortName>
            <Description>MSN Example Search</Description>
            <Tags>MSN Web</Tags>
```

```
            <Contact>admin@msn.com</Contact>
            <Url type="text/html"
                    template="http://search.msn.com/results.aspx?
q={searchTerms}"/>
            <Url type="application/rss+xml"
                    template="http://search.msn.com/results.aspx?
q={searchTerms}&amp;format=rss"/>
</OpenSearchDescription>
```

If the results come back with both HTML and RSS available, then the default setting in Internet Explorer is to choose the first URL specified in the Description Document. When it comes to returning results to Search Server 2008 for federation, be sure that the first URL in the Description Document is formatted to come back with RSS or Atom, not HTML or XHTML, because Search Server 2008 does not support the rendering of HTML or XHTML in the Web parts that display results from remote indexes.

*Matthew McDermott, Microsoft MVP, Principal Consultant, Catapult Systems*

Now that we've learned about some of the main features of Search Server 2008, it's time to learn about the standard with which Search Server 2008 is compliant. Part of the reason that we'll spend as much space on this as we do is because a good understanding of the command in the Description Document will help you understand how to build Federated Location Definition (FLD) files from scratch, if needed. While the Search Server 2008 interface will produce much of this XML for you when you build the FLD files from within the Search Server 2008 administration interface, the ability to read and understand the FLD files will be helpful to you when you troubleshoot Search Server 2008.

# Understanding OpenSearch Standards

What is OpenSearch? Well, the opensearch.org Web site says it best. "OpenSearch is a collection of simple formats for the sharing of search results." In OpenSearch, there are four basic parts to the standard:

- A Description Document that is used to describe the search engine
- Search client applications
- OpenSearch response elements
- A result set

In this section, we'll look at the OpenSearch 1.1 standard, focusing on the description file and some of the response elements. In Search Server 2008, the search client is the Keyword Query Web part, and the result set is the page of Web parts that displays the results from one or more indexes. When you build an FLD in your environment or when you export an FLD to a file system, you'll be working with an OpenSearch-compliant XML file.

> **Note** If you want to read the OpenSearch documents directly, you can do so at OpenSearch.org. The vast majority of this section is taken directly from the OpenSearch 1.1 documentation at the OpenSearch Web site.

## OpenSearch Description Documents

The Description Document is used to describe the Web interface of the OpenSearch-compliant search engine. The document is written in XML. The document consists of description elements that form the overall Description Document. The description elements are laid out in the OpenSearch 1.1 standard and are summarized here for your consideration.

> **Note** All XML files start with an XML declaration that specifies, among other things, which version of XML is being used. This is the first line in the XML document and normally looks like the following:
>
> ```
> <?xml version="1.0" encoding="UTF-8"?>
> ```

The grammar of the URL template used by OpenSearch 1.1 is defined by the Augmented Backus-Naur Form (ABNF) rules from RFC 2234. You can think of a parameter as a variable that will need a value supplied in order for the URL template to work. Anytime there is a parameter in the template, a value must be entered by the search client before the search request can be performed. Parameter names consist of an optional parameter name prefix followed by the local parameter name. If the parameter name prefix is present, then it will be separated from the local parameter name with the ":" character. All parameter names are associated with a parameter namespace. In the case of unqualified parameter names, the local parameter name is implicitly associated with the OpenSearch 1.1 namespace. In the case of fully qualified parameter names, the local parameter name is explicitly associated with an external namespace via the parameter name prefix.

Now, let's discuss each Description Document element individually in the follow sections.

### *OpenSearchDescription* Element

The *OpenSearchDescription* element is the first entry in the Description Document after the XML declaration statement. Hence, this element is the overall opening and closing tag for the Description Document. The following is what the opening and closing tags would look like:

```
<OpenSearchDescription xmlns="http://a9.com/-/spec/opensearch/1.1/">
</OpenSearchDescription>
```

The *OpenSearchDescription* opening and closing tags must appear once in the Description Document and cannot appear more than once. In addition, this tag is a *root* tag because it has no parents inside which it must operate.

## *ShortName* Element

The *ShortName* element allows you to assign a vanity, or easily remembered, name to the search engine that you are trying to describe. It must appear inside the *OpenSearchDescription* tags and may contain no more than 16 plain-text characters. The name may not include HTML or other markup language. This element must also appear in the Description Document. The entry would look like the following:

```
<ShortName>Web Search</ShortName>
```

## *LongName* Element

If 16 characters aren't enough, you can use the *LongName* element to assign a vanity name to the search engine that you are describing in the Description Document. The *LongName* element can contain up to 48 characters and cannot contain any HTML or other markup characters. The XML will look like the following:

```
<LongName>contoso.msft Search Engine</LongName>
```

## *Description* Element

The *Description* element allows you to describe the search engine in the Description Document. While this element has the same title as the overall document, don't confuse the two. The *Description* element is a customized text description of the search engine that the Description Document is describing. The Description Document contains many elements, and a *Description* element is one of them.

You can put up to 1,024 characters in the Description element. As with the *ShortName* element, it cannot contain any HTML or other markup language text. It also must appear within the *OpenSearchDescription* tags. The *Description* element will look something like the following:

```
<Description>Use the <name_of_Web_site> search engine
to retrieve results from this Web.</Description>
```

## *URL* Element

The *URL* element points to the URL address that clients normally use to enter search queries for the remote index that was generated by the remote search engine. The *URL* element must appear within the *OpenSearchDescription* tags and will have several required and optional attributes. Because OpenSearch supports both index-based and page-based search engines, you'll find that two of the attributes help you define offset numbers for the result sets that these two basic search engine types return. The four attributes are as follows:

- **Template** This is the actual URL template that will be processed by the remote search engine. This attribute is required as part of the *URL* element.

- **Type** This attribute specifies the Multipurpose Internet Mail Extension (MIME) type of the search result format. This attribute is also required, and the values entered must be valid MIME types.
- **Indexoffset** By default, the content items in the result set are set to start with the first content item or the integer 1. This number can be changed if needed. The offset means that, from the first content item in the result set, you can start with the first one or you can start the result set with another content item in the list. By default, the offset is set to 1, so you don't need to include this attribute unless you want to set the offset to something other than 1.
- **Pageoffset** This attribute defines which page of the result set you want displayed first. By default, the first page of the result set will be displayed. If you need to start the result set on a page other than the first page, set this attribute to a number other than 1. In Search Server 2008, you'll use this attribute most often for the next results URL when creating an FLD.

Examples of the *URL* element query template are as follows:

```
<Url type="application/rss+xml"
http://example.com/search?q={searchTerms} />
```

> **Note** When crafting the XML or the FLD file in Search Server 2008, you must capitalize the *T* in *searchTerms*. If you enter *searchterms*, the query template will fail because the OpenSearch standard is case sensitive, as is XML.

If you're unfamiliar with MIME, you can think of MIME types as an Internet standard describing different types of content that can exist on the Internet. Many of these MIME types have subtypes, which are also defined in the RFC documents. To learn more about MIME, see RFC 4288 and RFC 4289 as well as the Internet Assigned Numbers Authority (IANA) Web site about MIME types at *http://www.iana.org/assignments/media-types/*. The potential MIME types (in theory) that can be included are audio, video, example, image, message, model, multipart, and text. But for our discussion about building FLDs, you'll likely use the Application MIME type and two of its subtypes–atom+xml and rss+xml–for nearly every FLD that you create.

The Application MIME type is explained in RFC 2046, which outlines the standards for the Application MIME type. According to this RFC, "The application media type is to be used for discrete data which do not fit in any of the other categories, and particularly for data to be processed by some type of application program. This is information which must be processed by an application before it is viewable or usable by a user." The data that is transferred between the FLD file during the execution of a query and the result set that is returned fits this definition well because it is not usable until the query is executed and the result set–returned in XML–is rendered using the built-in XSL in the Federated Results Web part. Therefore, you will want to use the Application MIME type, which is why the XML will read <ULR type=application/>.

You'll also specify the subtype of content that will be returned from the remote index. When you work with Search Server 2008, your choices are atom+xml or rss+xml because Search Server 2008 can't render HTML or XHTML in the Federated Results Web part. You'll enter both the MIME type (usually Application) and its subtype into the *URL* element. Both the MIME type and its subtype are required as part of the *URL* element.

## *Contact* Element

The *Contact* element will specify the e-mail address for the person who maintains the Description Document. The e-mail address must conform to the <alias>@<domain> convention that is specified in RFC 2822. This element is not required in the Description Document, but if it does appear, it can appear only once. The XML tag would look like the following:

```
<Contact>admin@contoso.msft</Contact>
```

## *Tags* Element

The *Tags* element contains one or more words that are used as keywords to identify and categorize the search content. These words must be single words (no phrases are allowed) and are separated by a simple character space. This element is not required in the Description Document, but if it does appear, it can appear only once. The XML tag would look like the following:

```
<Tags>clothing boots</Tags>
```

## *Image* Element

If you want to associate an image with the search content, you'll want to use the *Image* element in the Description Document. The value entered must be a Uniform Resource Indicator (URI), which is described in RFC 3986.

> **Note** URIs are a standard way of identifying resources, both real and logical, on the Internet. URLs are similar to URIs in that, while they specify the location of the resource, they also include the method of finding that resource. URIs often include the method of finding the resource, but are not required to do so.

The *Image* element is not required as part of the Description Document, and it can appear from zero to *n* number of times. It must appear within the *OpenSearchDescription* tags.

There are three attributes that accompany the *Image* element, and they are as follows:

- **Height** Specifies the height of the image and must be a non-negative integer.

- **Width** Specifies the width of the image and must be a non-negative integer.
- **Type** Specifies the MIME Image subtype and must be a valid MIME type. Possible subtypes include common formats like jpeg, bmp, png, gif, or tiff. There are also vendor-specific types identified with the beginning vnd suffix, such as vnd.microsoft.icon.

A common practice is to use the 16 ×16 size for the image type "image/x-icon" or "image/vnd.microsoft.icon" and a 64 × 64 image for the image type "image/jpeg" or "image/png." Examples of the XML for this attribute are as follows:

```
<Image height="16" width="16" type="image/x-icon">http://contoso.msft/icon_name.ico</Image>

<Image height="64" width="64" type="image/png">http://contoso.msft/image_name.png</Image>
```

## *Query* Element

The *Query* element is the template or actual query that will be performed against the remote index. You can specify a specific search request or define a variable to host user-defined keyword query terms.

The *Query* element should also provide at least one element of role="example" in each OpenSearch Description Document so that search clients can test the search engine. Search engines should include a *Query* element of role="request" in each search response so that search clients can re-create the current search.

The following attributes for the *Query* element are important to understand:

- **role** Identifies how the search client should interpret the search request. This is the only attribute that is required for this element, and the specified role values are as follows:
  - **Request** Represents a search query that retrieves the same set of search results
  - **Example** Represents a search query to demonstrate the search engine
  - **Related** Represents a search query that represents similar, but different, results
  - **Correction** Represents a search query that improves the result set, such as correcting misspelled words
  - **Subset** Represents a search query that narrows an existing set of results
  - **Superset** Represents a search query that expands an existing set of results
- **title** Contains the title or name of the search query that is no longer than 256 characters. This attribute cannot contain HTML or other markup language and is optional, so it is not required as part of the *Query* element.
- **totalResults** Contains the expected number of content items in the result set that will be returned from the remote index engine. This value is optional and, if configured, must contain a non-negative integer.

- **searchTerms** This attribute is replaced with the keyword values that you want to execute against the remote index. The configuration of this value is optional; however, you'll use this attribute often when you build FLD files in Search Server 2008.
- **count** This attribute is replaced by the number of search results per page that is indicated by the search client. This is an optional attribute.
- **startIndex** This attribute is replaced by the number of the first search results specified by the client's search query. This is an optional attribute.
- **startPage** This attribute is replaced with the page number of the result set that is specified by the client's search query. This is an optional attribute.
- **language** This attribute is replaced by the name of the language in which the client wants to view the search results (see the "*Language* Element" section later in this chapter for more information). This is an optional attribute.
- **inputEncoding** This attribute is replaced by the specific character encoding that the client specifies in the query (see the "*InputEncoding* Element" section later in this chapter for more information). This is an optional attribute.
- **outputEncoding** This attribute is replaced by the specific character encoding for the result set (see the "*OutputEncoding* Element" section later in this chapter for more information). This is an optional attribute.

An example of the XML would be the following:

```
<Query role="example" searchTerms="dog" />
```

The *Query* element can be extended with additional attributes if those additional attributes are associated with a namespace. The extended attribute will have a corresponding template parameter with the same name within the specified namespace.

## *Developer* Element

The *Developer* element is similar to the *Contact* element in that it is used only to identify the person who created or maintains the Description Document. This element is optional and may contain up to 64 characters that are non-HTML or non-markup text. An example of this element would be following:

```
<Developer>Bill English bill@contoso.msft</Developer>
```

## *Attribution* Element

The *Attribution* element is used to credit the right sources for the result set content. This element can have up to 256 plain-text characters and may appear either zero or one time in the Description Document. The XML would look like the following:

```
<Attribution>Copyright contoso.msft</Attribution>
```

## *SyndicationRight* Element

The *SyndicationRight* element is included to indicate the degree to which the search engine's results or contents can be queried or redistributed. The default value is "open," and this element is not required in the Description Document.

The attributes for this element and their meanings are explained in Table 14-1.

**Table 14-1 Explanation of the *SyndicationRight* Element Attributes**

| | The search client may request search results | The search client may display the results to end-users | The search client may send the results to other search clients |
|---|---|---|---|
| Open | Yes | Yes | Yes |
| Limited | Yes | Yes | No |
| Private | Yes | No | No |
| Closed | No | No | No |

The following is what the XML would look like in the Description Document:

```
<SyndicationRight>open</SyndicationRight>
```

## *AdultContent* Element

The *AdultContent* element indicates whether the content should be displayed only to adults. There are no industry standards for what constitutes adult material, so the search engine manager must indicate if the material is adult oriented. The value for this element is Boolean, so the values of *FALSE*, *NO*, *0*, and *no* will all be accepted for the Boolean FALSE. All other character strings will be considered TRUE.

This element is not required in the Description Document, but if it does appear, it should appear only once. The XML for this element would look like the following:

```
<AdultContent>false</AdultContent>
```

## *Language* Element

The *Language* element indicates which languages the search engine supports. A value of "*" indicates that the search engine does not restrict results to any particular language. This is the default setting. The language tags must conform to the specifications for RFC 3066. The following are two examples of the XML code:

```
<Language>en-us</Language>

<Language>*</Language>
```

## *InputEncoding* Element

The *InputEncoding* element indicates the character set that will be used for entering queries into the search engine. This element is also considered an attribute of the *Query* element, described earlier. The input of this element must conform to the XML 1.0 Character Encodings that are specified by the IANA Character Set Assignments. The default is UTF-8. This element is not required in the Description Document, but may appear from zero to *n* times.

An example of the XML would be the following:

```
<InputEncoding>UTF-8</InputEncoding>
```

> **More Info** The sources for the XML 1.0 Character Encodings can be found at *http://www.w3.org/TR/2004/REC-xml-20040204/#charencoding*. You can find the IANA specifications for the Character Set Assignments at *http://www.iana.org/assignments/character-sets*.

## *OutputEncoding* Element

The *OutputEncoding* element specifies the character set with which the result set will be encoded. The default is UTF-8. The character sets must conform to the XML 1.0 Character Encodings that are specified by the IANA Character Set Assignments. This element is not required in the Description Document, but may appear from zero to *n* number of times.

An example of the XML would be the following:

```
<OutputEncoding>UTF-8</OutputEncoding>
```

## AutoDiscovery of RSS/Atom

RSS and Atom are the only supported formats in Search Server 2008 for result sets. If the remote search index isn't capable of returning the results in either RSS or Atom, then you'll need to write a custom connector page that will convert the HTML/XHTML results into RSS or Atom in order to display the results in the Federated Results Web part. Some restrictions will apply when you use this element in the Description Document.

First, the "type" attribute must contain the value "application/opensearchdescription+xml." Second, the "rel" attribute must contain the value "search." Third, the "href" attribute must contain a URI that resolves to an OpenSearch Description Document. The "title" attribute may contain a plain-text string describing the search engine, but this is not required.

An example of the XML would look like the following:

```
<link rel="search"
        href="http://example.com/opensearchdescription.xml"
        type="application/opensearchdescription+xml"
        title="Content Search" />
```

## OpenSearch Response Elements

In addition to the description elements, the OpenSearch standard also specifies some response elements, which we will briefly discuss. There are fewer response elements than description elements, and it is less likely that you'll work with them directly. In addition, you'll notice that the response elements are really just that: responses to the query elements found in the Description Document. We've pulled an example of some response XML directly from the OpenSearch 1.1 documentation and have represented it here for your consideration:

```
<?xml version="1.0" encoding="UTF-8"?>
 <rss version="2.0"
      xmlns:opensearch="http://a9.com/-/spec/opensearch/1.1/"
      xmlns:atom="http://www.w3.org/2005/Atom">
   <channel>
     <title>Example.com Search: New York history</title>
     <link>http://example.com/New+York+history</link>
     <description>Search results for "New York history" at Example.com</description>
     <opensearch:totalResults>4230000</opensearch:totalResults>
     <opensearch:startIndex>21</opensearch:startIndex>
     <opensearch:itemsPerPage>10</opensearch:itemsPerPage>
     <atom:link rel="search" type="application/
opensearchdescription+xml" href="http://example.com/opensearchdescription.xml"/>
     <opensearch:Query role="request"
searchTerms="New York History" startPage="1" />
     <item>
       <title>New York History</title>
       <link>http://www.columbia.edu/cu/lweb/eguids/
amerihist/nyc.html</link>
       <description>
         ... Harlem.NYC - A virtual tour and information on
         businesses ... with historic photos of Columbia's own New York
         neighborhood ... Internet Resources for the City's History. ...
       </description>
     </item>
   </channel>
 </rss>
```

As you read through this XML, you can see the responses to query elements that were entered into the Description Document (not illustrated here), such as *totalResults*, *startIndex*, *Query role*, *searchTerms*, and *title*.

Other response elements are part of the OpenSearch standard. The following sections outline them briefly.

### *totalResults* Element

The *totalResults* element indicates the total number of results that will come back from the search engine. Interestingly, the standard indicates that if this element doesn't appear on the result page, then the user should consider that page to be the *last* page in the result set. The value returned must be a non-negative integer. The default number will equal the offset index number of the last content item on the current page. This element is not required on the result set page, but based on the standard itself, you may find its lack of requirement a bit confusing. The XML for this element would look like the following:

```
<totalResults>492420</totalResults>
```

## *startIndex* Element

The *startIndex* element is the number of the first content item in the result set. If this element doesn't appear, then the OpenSearch standard indicates that the current page should be considered as the first page in the result set. The value must be an integer, and its default value equals the *indexOffset* value in the Description Document. This element is not required in the result set. The XML would look like the following:

```
<startIndex>1</startIndex>
```

## *itemsPerPage* Element

This element indicates the number of content items returned on each page of the result set. If this value is not set as one of the response elements, then the number of items that are returned on the first page of the result set will be considered the default number. If the value is set, the number must be a non-negative integer. The XML would look like the following:

```
<itemsPerPage>10</itemsPerPage>
```

# Installing Search Server 2008

Search Server 2008 is Microsoft's latest search engine, with improved functionality over previous versions. In this section, you'll learn how to install Search Server 2008.

Start the setup process by running setup.exe. The initial setup wizard splash screen will appear, as shown in Figure 14-1.

You'll notice that there are three sections of the install wizard:

- Prepare
- Install
- Other Information

Let's discuss each section of the installation wizard and illustrate how those sections support a successful installation.

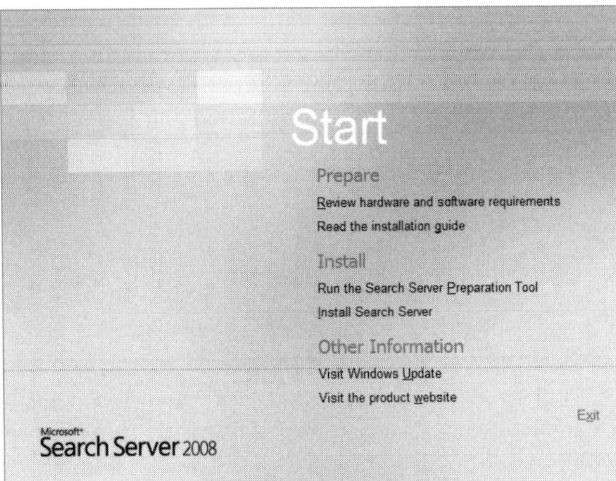


**Figure 14-1** Initial screen in the Search Server 2008 setup wizard

## Preparing for the Installation

Under the Prepare section of the Search Server 2008 installation wizard, there are two main sections:

- Review Hardware And Software Requirements
- Read The Installation Guide

If you click the Review Hardware And Software Requirements link under the Prepare section, you're taken to the minimum information in the ReadMe file for installing both the Express and the Farm version on the server's hard disk under the \program files\msecache \sserver121\folder. The hardware requirements are well in line with what most IT shops are installing today. Some of them are purposefully less powerful to support installations in parts of the world where updated hardware is more difficult to purchase. Some of the hardware requirements and recommendations are as follows:

- Minimum 2.5-GHz processors with recommended dual processors running at 3 GHz or faster
- 1 GB of RAM is required, although 4 GB of RAM for 32-bit operating systems is preferred
- 56-KB network connection is the minimum with which Search Server 2008 will work, but we obviously recommend as much bandwidth as possible.

If you click the Read The Installation Guide link, you are taken to the "Install Microsoft Search Server 2008 Express" online article.

## Other Information

The Other Information section of the installation screen includes links to the Windows Update site where you can ensure that your server is fully updated before you install Search Server 2008. If you have already turned on Automatic Updates or are using a Software Update Server (SUS), then there is little need to use this link. However, for some people, this link will be a handy way to ensure that your server is updated. There is also a link to the Search Server 2008 Web site where you can learn more about this new product.

## Conducting the Installation

Under the Install section, there are two links, both of which you'll want to use. Run The Search Server Preparation Tool invokes another wizard that will ensure that your server is ready to install Search Server 2008. Specifically, this tool checks that the following elements are downloaded and installed on your server:

- Windows Server 2003 Service Pack 1
- Windows Workflow Foundation Runtime Components and the Microsoft .NET Framework 2.0 or the .NET Framework 3.0
- Internet Information Services (IIS) ASP.NET Web Service extensions
- Application Server role (IIS and ASP.NET)

If you click Next on the Welcome screen that appears, the tool runs and checks that these elements are installed properly on your server. Moreover, if you have never installed SharePoint Server 2007 or Windows SharePoint Services, this tool will make the following changes to a default installation of the Application Server role:

- MSSharePointAppPool secured by the LocalSystem account
- Microsoft SharePoint administration Web site with a random port number and no host header
- Installation and enabling of ASP.NET 2.0 (v50727) in IIS

Clicking the Install Search Server link in the second section of the Welcome page will launch the actual installation of the Search Server 2008 bits. The first screen that will appear is the product key code screen. Enter your key code, and then click Next to read through the licensing agreement. As usual, you won't find anything in the licensing agreement that you don't agree with because you need to install the software. After reading the licensing agreement, click Next to open the Choose The Installation You Want page (see Figure 14-2).

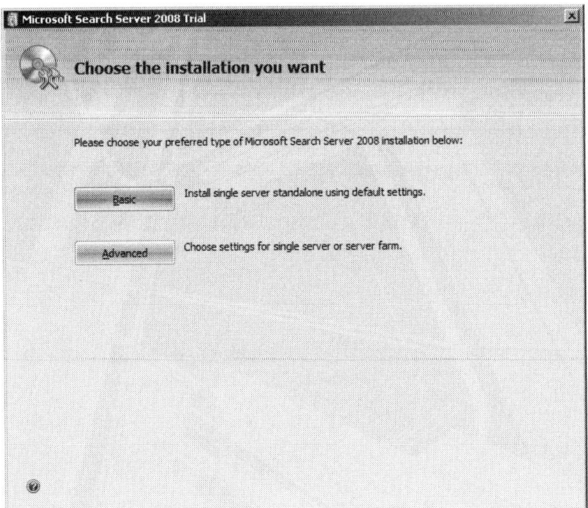


**Figure 14-2** Choosing between Basic and Advanced installation in the Search Server 2008 Installation Wizard

On this page, you'll select either the Basic or the Advanced installation. The Basic option will immediately start the installation of Search Server 2008 in a single-server environment and will install the Express version of Search Server 2008, which uses the desktop version of Microsoft SQL Server for its database and does not allow the farm to be scaled out beyond one server.

The Advanced installation option will use a remote SQL Server and will want to place its databases on that SQL Server. In addition, the Advanced option will allow you to scale out the Search Server 2008 farm with multiple Search Server 2008 servers and allow you to configure the following items (Figure 14-3):

- The type of installation you want on the server, such as Complete, Web Front End, or Stand-Alone
- The location where you want the binaries installed
- If you want to participate in the customer improvement program by giving feedback to Microsoft about its products

When you click Install Now, the binaries will be installed. Similar to SharePoint Server 2007 installations, once the binaries have finished installing, you'll have the option to start the SharePoint Products and Technologies Configuration Wizard. This wizard will allow you to create the Search Server 2008 farm in which the search engine will run.

It is important to note that you're not just installing a product Search Server 2008. You're installing an entirely new SharePoint farm that is focused on running Search Server 2008. You'll get Central Administration, a Shared Services Provider, and the ability to build out an entire collaboration environment around a Search Server 2008 installation. You'll be able to add Web front-end (WFE) servers to your farm as well as additional Query servers. At the time of this writing, Search Server 2008 does not install into a current SharePoint Server 2007 installation. It is our understanding that plans are underway to connect a Search Server 2008 installation with SharePoint Server 2007, which will extend the SharePoint Server 2007 implementation with Search Server 2008 features, such as Federated Querying.

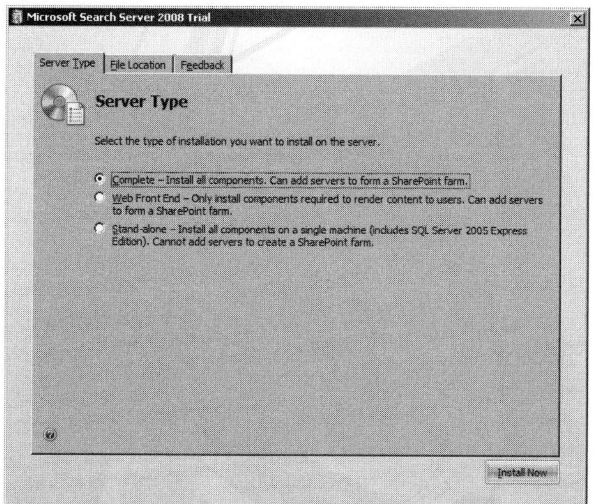


**Figure 14-3** Advanced installation configuration options in the Search Server 2008 Installation Wizard

Once you have selected the type of installation that you want, click Next to start the installation of the binaries. Once the binaries have been successfully installed, you'll be given the opportunity to run the SharePoint Products and Technologies Configuration Wizard. Run this wizard to build the new Search Server 2008 farm.

> **Note** Running the configuration wizard for a Search Server 2008 farm implementation is identical to running the wizard for a SharePoint Server 2007 installation. Refer to *Microsoft Office SharePoint Server 2007 Administrator's Companion* and *Microsoft Office SharePoint Server 2007 Administrator's Pocket Consultant*, both published by Microsoft Press, for information on how to run the SharePoint Products and Technologies Configuration Wizard.

After Search Server 2008 is installed, you'll see that a Microsoft Search Server shortcut group has been created from the Start menu. It includes the SharePoint Products and Technologies and Central Administration sites for SharePoint, plus the Search Server 2008 Administration shortcut. The Search Server 2008 shortcut will not appear on the Administrative Tools shortcut menu, but the two other SharePoint shortcuts will appear there.

After the SharePoint Products and Technologies Configuration Wizard runs, the Search Server Configuration page appears, as shown in Figure 14-4.

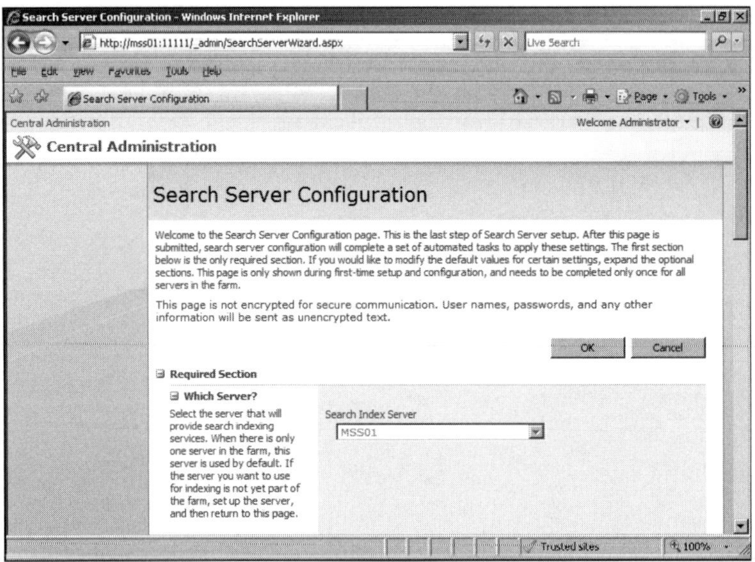


Figure 14-4 The Search Server Configuration page

On this page, you'll enter values for the following configurations:

- Search Service Account
- Search Center Account (application pool account for the Search Center site)
- Search Contact E-Mail Account

At the bottom of the Search Server Configuration page (shown in Figure 14-5), you'll be able to set configuration values for a number of different parameters, such as the Index File Location or the name of the search database.

If this effort to create a new SSP fails, you can create the SSP manually. Figure 14-6 shows the Search Server Configuration Completed With Errors page that appears if automatic configuration fails. Click the Configure Manually link and you'll be taken to the managessp.aspx page, where you can click the New SSP link in the menu bar and create the new SSP from there.

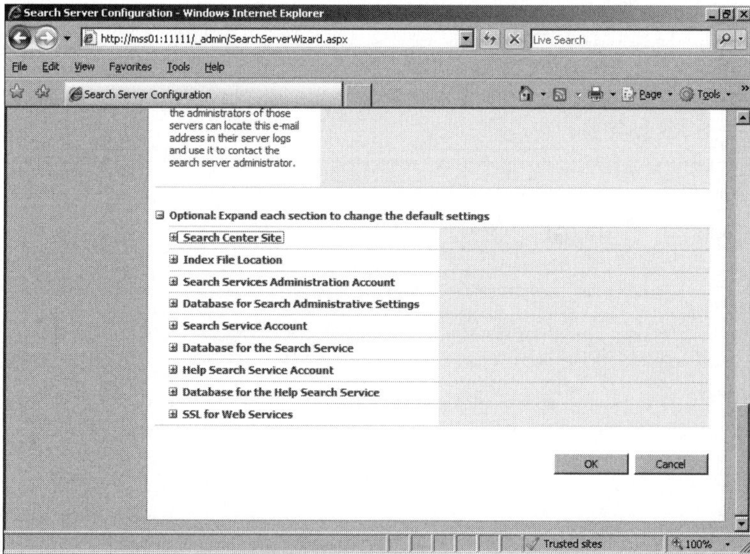


Figure 14-5 Optional configuration settings

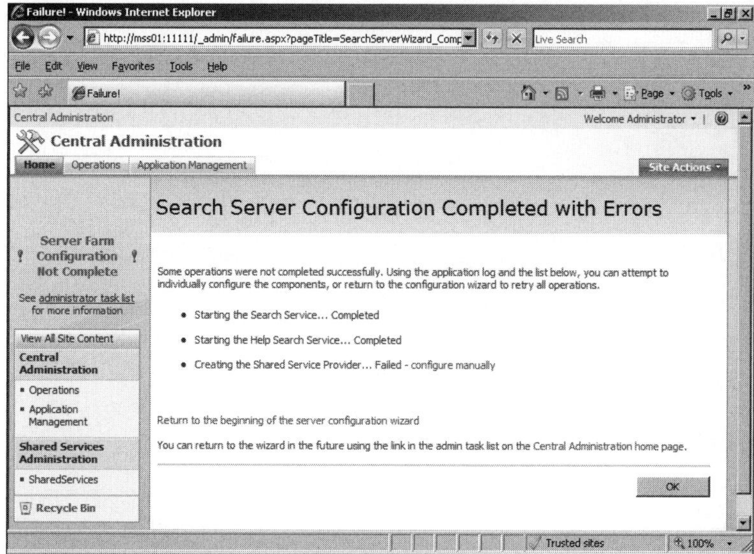


Figure 14-6 Search Server Configuration Completed With Errors page that appears if automatic configuration fails

> **Note** The part of this chapter that focuses on installing Search Server 2008 was written against the public beta that was released by the product team in the spring of 2007. We don't anticipate that the final version of the code will produce problems in creating a new SSP as part of the installation process.

## Administrating Search Server 2008

In this section, we'll discuss the basics on how to administrate Search Server 2008 so that you can begin using this emerging product. We'll look at the Search Administration interface and explain basic Search Server 2008 administrator activities. We'll also look at the Search Center, which is installed by default, using the host name of the server and port 80. (For example, if your server name is "Server1," then the Search Center's default URL would be *http://server1*.)

When you first open the administration Web site for Search Server 2008, you'll find that the administration interface is a bit different than the search interface for SharePoint Server 2007 SSP. Frankly, it is an improved interface. It is organized into several sections, which are displayed in the left, central, and right panes as illustrated in Figure 14-7. The left pane includes the following set of nested links:

- Administration
  - Search Administration
  - Central Administration
- Crawling
  - Content Sources
  - Crawl Rules
  - Crawl Logs
  - Default Content Access Account
  - File Types
  - Reset All Crawled Content
  - Crawler Impact Rules
  - Proxy And Timeout
- Queries And Results
  - Authoritative Pages
  - Federated Locations
  - Metadata Properties
  - Server Name Mappings

- Search Result Removals
- Usage Reports
  - Query Reports
  - Results Reports

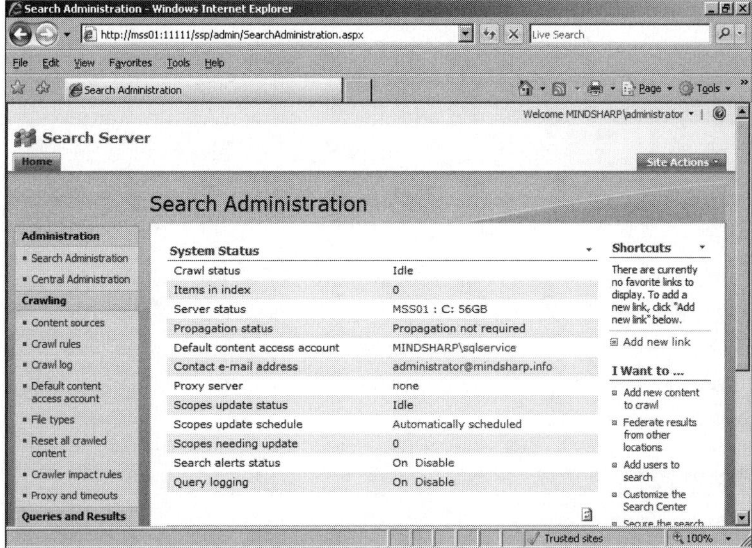


Figure 14-7 Default Search Server 2008 administration interface

In the center pane, you'll see three different Web parts, which essentially constitute a dashboard, that are not available in the SharePoint Server 2007 implementation of search:

- System Status
- Active Crawls
- Recently Completed Crawls

The right pane includes prebuilt shortcuts for the Search Server 2008 site as well as online help links to content. If you enter Edit mode for this page, the center and right panes are really Web page zones, and the left navigation pane is a set of nested links, which is consistent and expected behavior for a Windows SharePoint Services 3.0 team site page's navigation scheme.

If you click Add Web Part in Edit mode, you expose a fourth Web part that is not available by default–the Subsystems Web part. We'll look at the functions performed by this Web part later in this section.

The main administrative tasks that can be performed in Search Server 2008 include creating content sources and FLD files. There are also links in the Search Server 2008 administration interface that will help you navigate to other pages with administrative tasks. The administration links in the left pane are default links that will take you to either the home page for the Search Server 2008 administration site or the Search Server 2008 Central Administration home page for the farm. You can think of these links as two home page links–one to Search Administration and one to Central Administration.

> **Important** In this section, we assume that you have knowledge and experience in administrating search technologies in SharePoint Server 2007. If you are unfamiliar with how to administrate search in SharePoint Server 2007, please consult *Microsoft SharePoint Products and Technologies Administrator's Pocket Consultant* and *Microsoft Office SharePoint Server 2007 Administrator's Companion*, both published by Microsoft Press.

The links under the crawling section of the Search Server 2008 administration site simply re-expose Search Administration in SharePoint Server 2007 with a few improvements.

First, the Manage Content Sources page (shown in Figure 14-8) has a different set of metadata that is exposed for each content source than what we would normally see in the SharePoint Server 2007 Search Administration pages. This page includes information such as the most recent crawl duration, when the most recent completed crawl was finished, and the schedules for the next full and incremental crawl.

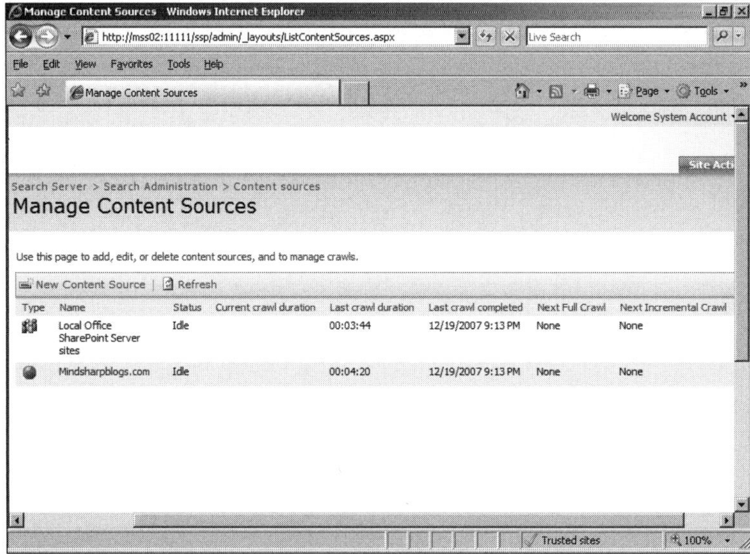


**Figure 14-8** Manage Content Sources page

One great Search Server 2008 feature not included in SharePoint Server 2007 search is the extra reporting about the content source within the content source itself. In Search Server 2008, the new Content Source Details feature (see Figure 14-9) provides a number of interesting, up-to-date details about the content source.

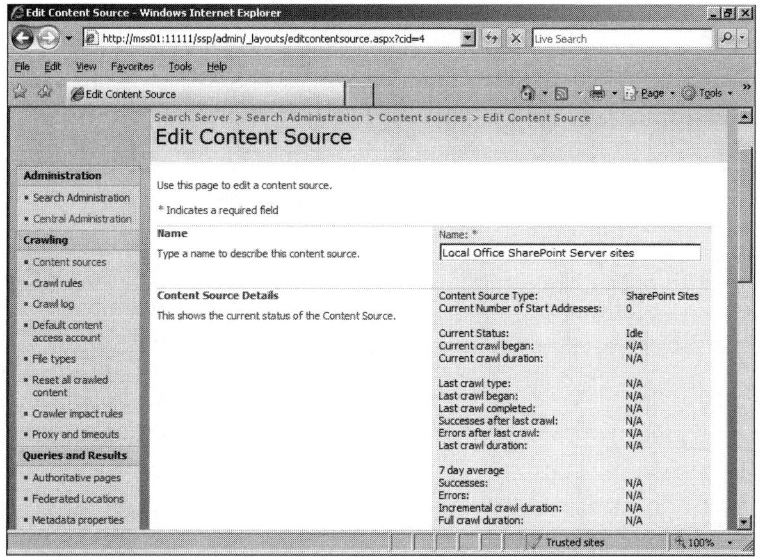


**Figure 14-9** Content Source Details interface for the default content source in Search Server 2008

Second, when it comes to creating crawl rules, there are a few additions to the rules in Search Server 2008 that are not part of SharePoint Server 2007. As you can see from Figure 14-10, you can now enter forms-based and cookie-based credentials for the crawler to connect with when crawling content that is secured through either forms-based authentication or cookies.

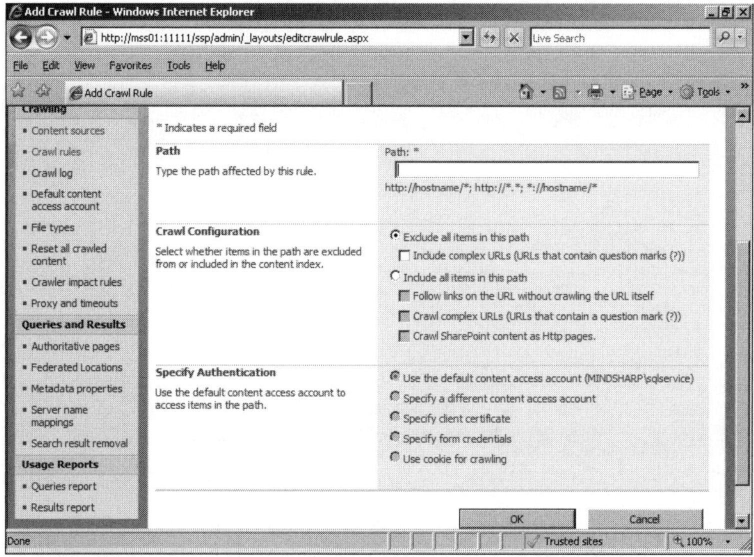


**Figure 14-10** Crawl rule improvements in Search Server 2008

Third, the Crawler Impact Rule link has been exposed in the Search Administration interface, so you are not forced to go to Central Administration to create Crawler Impact Rules. Interestingly, if you do go to Central Administration and click the Manage Search Service link on the Application Management tab, you'll be presented with a login to the Search Administration Web site. If you hover over the link, it will show the default URL location of *http://<CA_Site:port>/_admin /managesearchservice.aspx*, but clicking the link will redirect you to the Search Administration site in the SSP.

Fourth, Search Server 2008 installs fewer crawled property categories than does SharePoint Server 2007. More specifically, SharePoint Server 2007 installs 149 SharePoint-crawled properties, whereas Search Server 2008 installs only 116. This is a micro-illustration of how Search Server 2008 installs only that portion of SharePoint Server 2007 that it needs to run effectively.

There are three Web parts that ship with Search Server 2008 that do not ship with the SharePoint Server 2007 version of search. The first of these Web parts is the System Status Web part. This Web part, illustrated in Figure 14-11, contains a wealth of real-time information, including scopes update status and schedule, search alerts status, number of items in the index, and current crawl status. This is a great Web part that will give you some of the instant information you need as an administrator when you first fire up the Search Administration Web site.

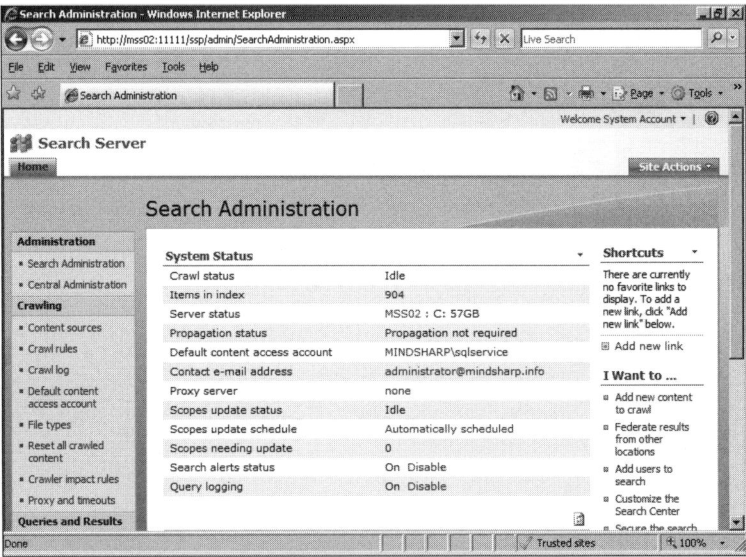


**Figure 14-11** System Status Web part in the Search Server 2008 administration interface

The next Web part is the Active Crawls Web part, which will show the status, duration, and any successes or errors for the active crawl. The nice aspect of this Web part is that it gives you the ability to see the number of successes and errors while the crawl process continues. If there are a high number of errors, you can stop the crawl, use the crawl log to troubleshoot the errors, and then restart the crawl process to ensure that you index the content while minimizing errors.

The last Web part is a companion to the Active Crawls Web part. Whereas the Active Crawls Web part shows information about the current crawls, the Recently Completed Crawls Web part (shown in Figure 14-12) shows information about the crawls that have recently been completed, including the type of crawl that was completed, when it finished, its duration, and the successes and errors encountered.

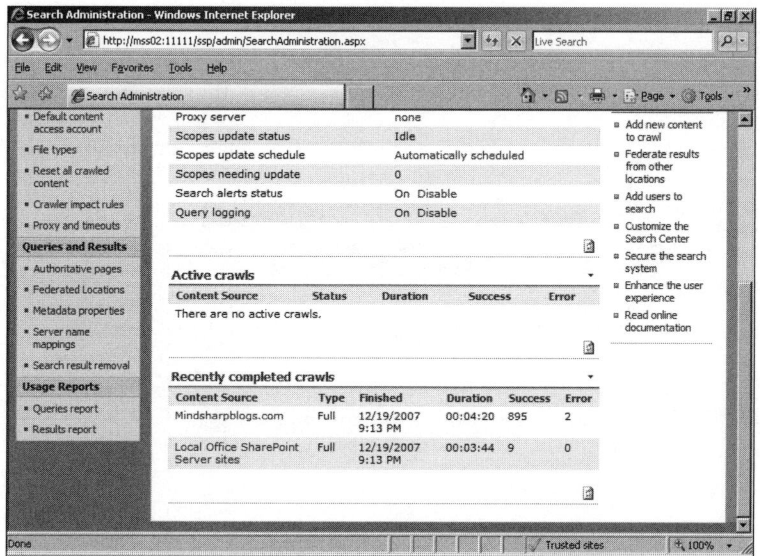


**Figure 14-12** Recently Completed Crawls and Active Crawls Web parts

The combination of these three Web parts gives you a full snapshot of your crawling efforts and environment as well as links to drill down into more administration activities if you need to troubleshoot or fine-tune your Search Server 2008 implementation.

# Building Federated Location Definition Files and Integrating Search Server 2008 with Live Search

Creating FLD files for Search Server 2008 is not as hard as you might think. In this section, we'll walk you through how to create FLDs and give you some tips on important synergies between Search Server 2008 and live.com.

The biggest effort in building an FLD using the Search Server 2008 interface is obtaining a result set from a remote indexing engine that can be transferred via RSS or Atom. Once you have that, building the FLD is very easy. If the results come back in HTML/XHTML, then you'll have to do some custom coding to get those results to appear in your Search Server 2008 Search Center. That customization work is beyond the scope of this chapter and book, so if you need to build out connector Web pages in Search Server 2008 for HTML/XHTML result sets, we suggest you check the main Search Server 2008 Web site at *http://www.microsoft.com/enterprisesearch* for more information.

Let's run through the steps that are necessary to build out a new FLD. To start, let's assume that we want to create an FLD to query MSDN online from our Search Server 2008 interface. Following are the steps we'll use to accomplish this task. First, open a browser to *msdn.microsoft.com*, as illustrated in Figure 14-13.

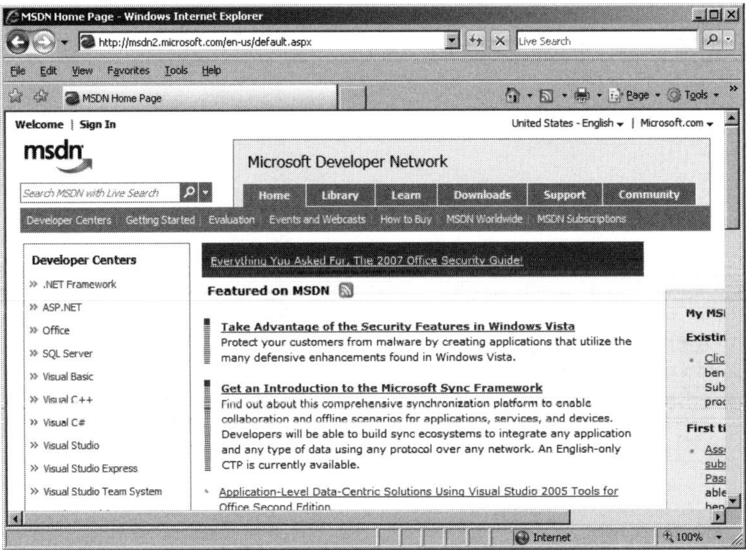


**Figure 14-13** Search interface at *msdn.microsoft.com*

Now, we'll search on a keyword. It doesn't matter what keyword we use for this illustration, so we'll use the keyword *SharePoint*. The result set URL is the most important element that we're interested in receiving. In our example, the result set URL (also illustrated in Figure 14-14) is *http://search.msdn.microsoft.com/search/default.asxp?query=sharepoint&brand=msdn*locale=&refinement=00&lang=en-us*.

At this point, Search Server 2008 couldn't use the results because they came back using HTML. The results must be converted into an RSS feed to expose the URL that will return the results using RSS. To do this, click the RSS button in Internet Explorer 7 (as shown in Figure 14-15), which will provide the required RSS URL.

The created URL is *http://search.msdn.microsoft.com/search/feed.aspx?query=sharepoint&brand=msdn&local=&refinement=00&lang=en-us&feed=rss*.

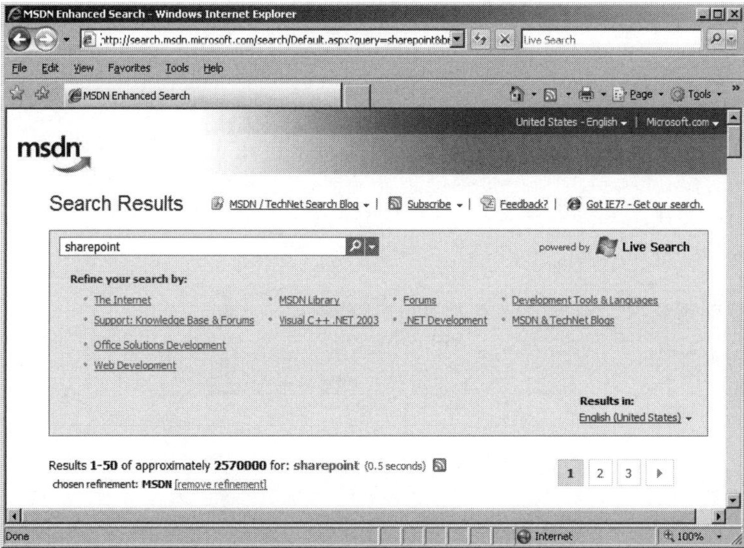


**Figure 14-14** Result set URL

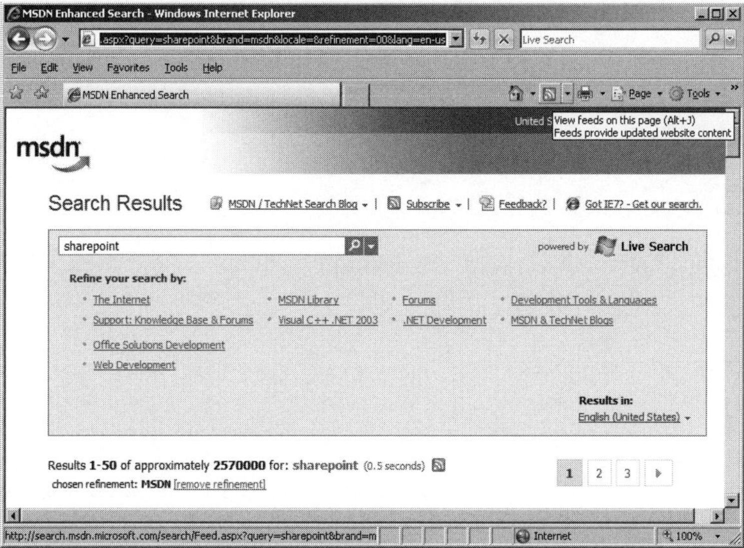


**Figure 14-15** RSS button in Internet Explorer 7 that will create the RSS feed URL

The last part of the URL, *feed=rss*, indicates that the results will be returned in the RSS format. At this point in the process, you can return to the Search Server 2008 administration interface and select New Location on the Manage Federated Locations page. In the Query Template input box, enter the RSS-based URL, replacing the search term with the query variable "{searchTerms}" (shown in Figure 14-16). Enter this same URL in the More Results Link Template input box as well. Be sure to enter a location and display name as well as a description (which is required by the OpenSearch standard). Be sure to add the same URL to the More Results input box when building the FLD.

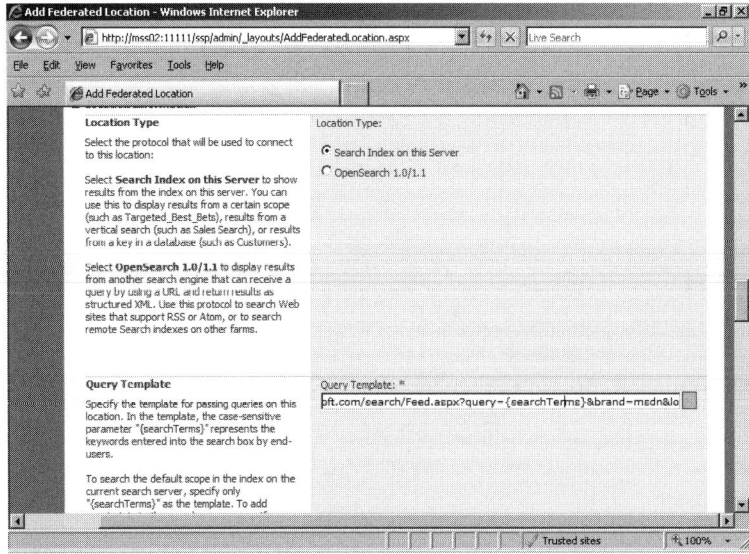


**Figure 14-16** Entering the RSS URL in the Query Template input box using the searchTerms variable

> **Note** In the Location Type of the FLD, you can select either the Search Index On This Server radio button or the OpenSearch 1.1 radio button. Even if you build out the FLD the way you want with a correct URL pointing to a remote index, if you leave the Location Type selection at Search Index On This Server, the Federated Results Web part will return results only from the local index.

Part of building out a new FLD is deciding if you want any *triggers* created with it. Triggers allow you to throttle, or define, when the FLD is invoked based on the query search terms. Your choices are as follows:

- **Always** Always be invoked regardless of what query terms are entered by the user
- **Prefix** Invoked only when an exact string of characters are entered as the first set of characters as part of the overall set of query terms

- **Pattern** Invoked only when a consistent pattern of characters is detected as the first part of the overall query search terms. This pattern option allows your developers to write custom code as the specific pattern.

At this point, accept the other defaults, then scroll to the bottom of the page and click OK. You'll now have a new FLD in your list. Once you have defined this information for the FLD, you can build it out and use it in your Search Center.

To apply this FLD to the queries that are entered by the users, you'll need to open the Search Center and edit the results.aspx page that hosts the various Results Page Web parts. The FLDs are applied to the Federated Results Web part on the results page.

Once you've entered Edit mode on the results.aspx page, navigate to the current Federated Results Web part or add another instance of this Web part on the page in one of the Web part zones. Once you've focused on the Web part, click the Edit Drop-Down button and then click Modify Shared Web Part. In the Location drop-down list, select the MSDN FLD file and then click OK (see Figure 14-17).

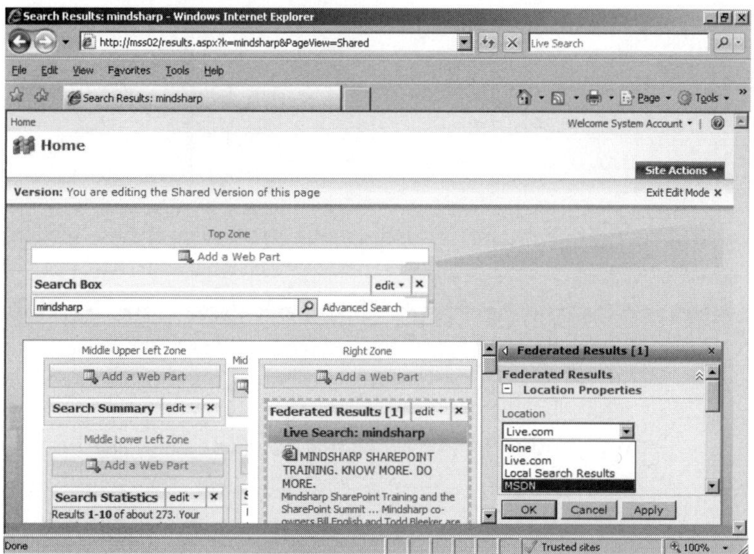


Figure 14-17 Selecting the MSDN FLD in the Federated Results Web part Location drop-down list

After the Web part has been configured, it's time to exit Edit mode and test the new FLD by executing a query. For our example, we selected *sharepoint* again as our keyword for testing the new FLD. When the query is executed by the user, the query is sent not only to the local index but also to the remote index(s) that are defined via the Federated Results Web part and the FLD that has been associated with each instance of this Web part. If you fill your results page with these Web parts, with each sending the query to a different remote index, be prepared for high latency while all of the remote indexes are queried and their results are returned to the Query server for processing and display within the interface.

In this running example, as you can see in Figure 14-18, the FLD was built accurately because it sent the query to the search engine at *msdn.microsoft.com*, and the results were successfully returned to this Search Center.

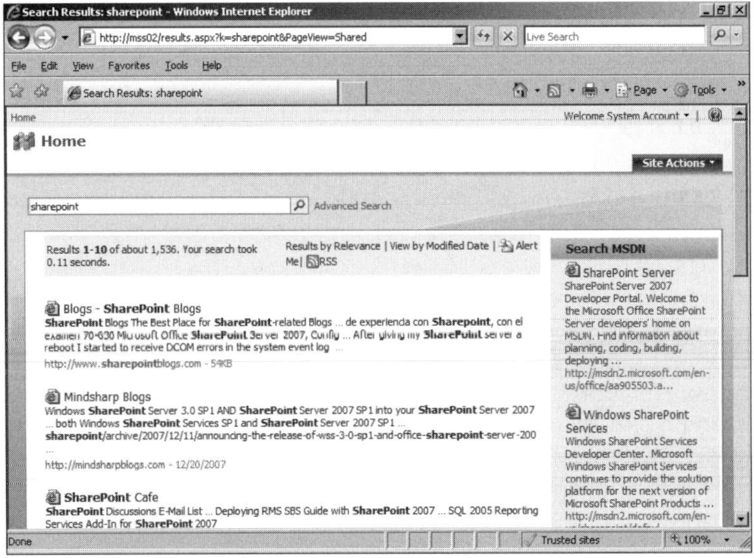


Figure 14-18 Successful query of both the local index and the remote index at *msdn.microsoft.com*

# Best Practices for Implementing Search Server 2008

So far in this chapter, we have discussed the *how* of implementing Search Server 2008. In this section, we'll outline what we believe are some best practices for a Search Server 2008 implementation. Because this product is new to the market, there is a lack of rich implementation experience, but that doesn't mean that we can't suggest several best practices for you to consider.

First, while it is possible to use Search Server 2008 to implement a new SharePoint Server 2007 farm, this is not a best practice because of the limitations inherent in the product. For example, you can't implement more than one SSP in a Search Server 2008 implementation. In addition, most of the site templates that you would expect to exist in a SharePoint Server 2007 implementation will be missing, as will some expected features. It is a best practice to stand up your Windows SharePoint Services or SharePoint Server 2007 farm and then upgrade the search services by installing Search Server 2008 into that farm.

Second, you need to decide what content you'll crawl and index and what content to which you can send a federated query to receive a result set. There are several considerations. First, you can't send a federated query to a non-existent index. If the remote content isn't being indexed by another OpenSearch 1.1–compliant indexing engine, then you'll have to crawl and index that content if you want it to appear in your result set.

Creating a large number of federated Web parts in the result set will diminish the quality of the end-user experience because of the way the result set page renders. This page renders when the Web parts are ready to render in a serial, non-dependent fashion. So, if you have five federated Web parts for a given query, each gathering results from five different remote indexes, then each Web part will render independently and in no particular order. The rendering of these Web parts can cause other parts of the page to repaint, and sometimes content shifts up or down on the page when it repaints. This can be irritating to users if a large number of federated Web parts are rendering at different times. We recommend having fewer than 10 federated Web parts involved in returning results for any given query. While it is possible to federate most of your queries, best practice is to federate only those queries that are executed the most often to the largest remote indexes. So, even though you *could* build a federated Web part and FLD to a remote index, it might not be the best course of action if you already have a large number of queries federating to other remote indexes.

Those in geographically dispersed deployments with multiple SharePoint Server 2007 farms might consider standing up a Search Server 2008 farm for the sole purpose of providing federated queries across all of your farms' indexes. SharePoint Server 2007 is OpenSearch complaint, so a Search Server 2008 implementation could provide federated queries to all of your SharePoint Server 2007 users in their respective locations. In most geographically dispersed deployments where multiple SharePoint Server 2007 farms are deployed, most of what a user needs can be found in their local SharePoint Server 2007 farm. However, there are times when a user may need to query an external farm for a content item. Search Server 2008 can provide this type of infrequent query service at very little cost.

From a staffing perspective, if you plan to implement a robust search and indexing solution for your users, you'll likely need to add additional staff to your IT department because creating, testing, and managing content sources and search scopes can be rather time consuming. Also, the opportunity to use SharePoint Server 2007 audiences with Search Web parts and the flexible customization of how results are displayed demand additional full-time staff in large search and indexing implementations. For those large implementations, it is a best practice to dedicate full-time staff to this effort.

It is also best practice to ensure that you index only the content you need in your index when you crawl public Web sites. Often, Web sites include extraneous information that is helpful to the site itself, but shouldn't appear in your index, such as a privacy policy or the Contact Us page(s). You should use the crawl rules to ensure that only those pages of content that you really need in your index appear in your index. To do this, use a combination of include and exclude rules. For example, assume a very simple Web site design with a home page and two virtual directories, or subdirectories, as follows:

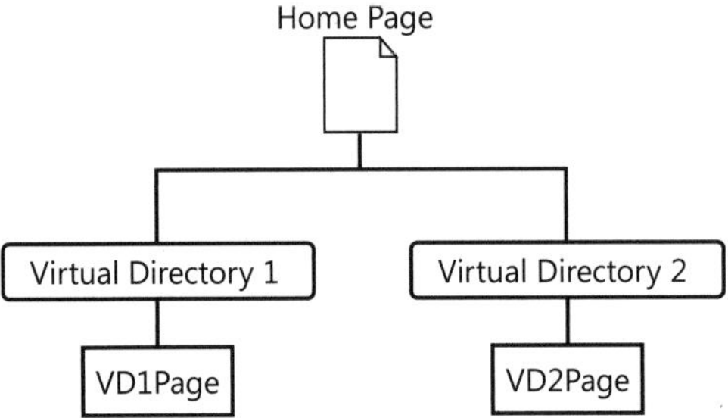


Assume that you want to crawl content only on the VD1page, and you do not want content on the VD2 page or the home page. In this case, your crawl rules would look like the following:

```
http://testweb/vd1/*            Include
http://testweb/*                Exclude
```

Order is important here, and you need to ensure that you're using the crawler rules to carve out portions of Web sites that you need to appear in your index.

As you implement Search Server 2008, you can also use the following list of questions as a checklist to ensure that you've covered many of the decision points that you'll encounter as part of a robust Search Server 2008 implementation:

- What will be the full and incremental crawl schedules for each content source?
- Do you have adequate server hardware to crawl all of the content sources in your current schedule?
- Do you have adequate bandwidth available between your index server and your content sources?
- For each content source, what crawl rules, crawler settings, and crawler impact rules are needed?
- Who will troubleshoot failed crawls or information that does not appear in the index?
- Who will evaluate the content sources so that crawl criteria are configured efficiently?
- What words should you add to the noise word file?
- What will be your search scope topology?
- Do you need additional iFilters?
- Do you need additional Protocol Handlers?
- Do you need to add File Types to SharePoint?
- Do you need to add icons to SharePoint?
- Do you need to turn on the OCR feature and adjust the size above 1 MB?

- Do you need special accounts to crawl certain content sources?
- Do you need to create any Best Bets?
- Do you need to group any Crawled Properties into Managed Properties and then expose the properties in the Advanced Search Web Part?
- Do you need any special Server Name Mappings?
- Will you use a dedicated WFE server for crawling farm resources or all of your WFE servers?
- Establish primary, secondary, tertiary, and demoted sites for relevance/ranking in the result set.
- Ensure that disks are optimized for Search and SSP databases.

## Summary

In this chapter, you have been introduced to OpenSearch 1.1 and the basics on Search Server 2008 administration. We illustrated how to install Search Server 2008 on a single server that uses a SQL Server as its database server. Finally, you have learned how to build an FLD so that your queries can be federated to remote indexes.

## Additional Resources

- On the CD: The MSDN FLD file for you to use as needed
- Microsoft's Web site for Search Server 2008, essentially a marketing site that helps explain what Search Server 2008 is all about: *http://www.microsoft.com/windowsserver2008/en/us/serverunleashed/default.html?WT.srch=1*
- Microsoft's technical Web site for Search Server 2008, filled with more technical than marketing information on Search Server 2008: *http://www.microsoft.com/enterprisesearch/serverproducts/searchserver/default.aspx*
- Search Server 2008 product team blog: *http://www.microsoft.com/enterprisesearch/serverproducts/searchserver/default.aspx*
- Search Server 2008 SDK for writing code to customize your Search Server 2008 implementation: *http://msdn2.microsoft.com/en-us/library/bb931107.aspx*

# Part III
# Deploying

**In this part:**

Chapter 15

# Implementing an Optimal Search and Findability Topology

**In this chapter:**



We search for information because we want to find it. Findability and search technologies are two parts of a larger effort to make the vast sea of content items quickly and easily findable. In this chapter, we will focus on the best practices that will support the findability and retrieval of the right data quickly, easily, and efficiently. This chapter contains three main parts:

- What is findability, and why is it important to you?
- Design for Microsoft Office SharePoint Server 2007 and Microsoft Search Server 2008 search implementations
- Findability tools that can be used within the SharePoint environment to help you and your users find the right information.

There's no time like the present to get started, so let's first discuss findability and why it is important to you.

## Findability: What Is It and Why Is It Important to You?

*Findability* is a measurement of how easy or difficult it is to find a particular object. You can also think of this concept as the degree to which an object can be found. Because objects never exist in a vacuum, the environments in which they are hosted—along with the descriptors that are used to describe the object—become part of the findability equation. This concept applies to nearly everything in life.

For example, golfers don't use green golf balls because green golf balls would be difficult to find in a sea of green grass. This is why white is a common color for golf balls—the color contrasts nicely with green grass and enables golfers to easily find the ball. Restaurant menus are another example of findability. Menus help us find the food we want to order. When it comes to office buildings, directories help us find the location of the people with whom we need to meet. Even romance can be a findability issue. Most online dating services go to great lengths to ensure that their participants are matched based on an extensive set of data elements, such as values or interests, which helps their clients find just the right person! Finding the right partner can be thought of as little more than a search problem.

> **Note** We first read about the concept of findability in a rather interesting book titled *Ambient Findability: What We Find Changes Who We Become* by Peter Morville (O'Reilly Media Inc., 2005). We would recommend that you read this book. Concepts that we learned from this book are woven into this chapter, and instead of crediting each part of this first section independently, we'll express our gratitude to Mr. Morville for his thought-provoking book and acknowledge that several key concepts from his book have found their way into this chapter.

The reason that we will place a heavy emphasis on findability is because—while it may be painful to state the obvious—the following statements are true:

- Customers cannot purchase what they cannot find.
- Decision-makers cannot include options that they don't know exist.
- Information that is hard to find is rarely used.
- Users cannot use what they cannot find.
- The number and type of sources from which we can find new information is complex, overwhelming, and tiring.
- Users have a difficult time discerning between quality, trusted information to which they should pay attention and other information that they can safely ignore.
- Many of us simply cannot keep up with the information avalanche under which we labor.
- Authority, trust, and findability are interwoven.

The truths presented in this list form the conceptual backdrop for the first part of this chapter. Let's begin by discussing information overload and why it makes findability difficult.

## Information Overload

Most of us labor under an ever-increasing glut of information that we're expected to absorb and assimilate. This glut of information is known as *information overload* (also known as *infoglut* or *data smog*). Depending on your role and workload right now, this book may or may not be contributing to your current information overload. The reasons we tolerate information overload are somewhat rational:

- We collect information to indicate a commitment to competence.

- We seek more information to verify the information already acquired.
- We need to be able to justify our decisions.
- We collect information just in case it may be useful.
- We play safe and get as much information as possible.
- We like to use information as a currency—we don't want our colleagues to leave us behind.

As the preceding list demonstrates, even though we often tolerate and perhaps contribute to our own information overload, we can't keep ourselves from experiencing the negative effects that information overload naturally brings to our lives. So while statistics can be used to make nearly any argument, there are some statistics that are helpful for us to consider.

We doubt you'll be surprised to learn that over half of us report experiencing e-mail fatigue and information overload. We simply have too many sources of information vying for our attention. Users often have cluttered inboxes containing hundreds of messages, including outstanding tasks, partially read documents, and conversational threads. Undoubtedly, e-mail is a major source of our information overload, but certainly it is not the only source of information in our lives. Consider the significant number of sources (and this is only a partial list) that can provide information to us each day:

- Blogs
- Wikis
- Newspapers
- Radio
- Television
- Conversations
- Books
- Magazines
- Web sites
- E-mail
- Letters
- Journals

In many professions, keeping up with all of the information is essential to success: Those who fall behind in assimilating new information end up out of a job or, worse, out of business. The race to keep up with all of the new information is taking a toll on us, too. We don't escape uninjured from this race. Many of us make significant sacrifices in order to keep up with customers, vendors, partners, and competitors.

A Reuters 1997 report, *Glued to the Screen,* noted that 4 out of 5 respondents felt "driven to gather as much information as possible to keep up with customers and competitors." This same report indicated that information addicts were becoming a real problem.

The 1997 reports built on a 1996 report from Reuters which noted that two-thirds of those in the test group reported that, as a result of too much information, they experienced increased tension with colleagues and a loss in job satisfaction. According to the report, 61 percent cancelled social engagements due to information overload and 60 percent were frequently too tired for social activities. In addition, research has shown that those who live in urban areas and who experience an overload of stimuli tend to become jaded and experience an increasing incapacity to respond to new situations with the appropriate energy. And to top it off, a study at King's College in London found that information overload can reduce your IQ by as much as ten points, whereas smoking marijuana reduced your IQ by only five points.

Information overload has many unintended consequences. First, decisions are often delayed as we wait for others (and perhaps ourselves) to assimilate a common base of information so the collective decision-making process can proceed. Second, decisions are often made without the right amount and quality of information. This is directly due to our inability to fully qualify the quality of information that is available to us as well as our inability to find the right information at the right time. Finally, we naturally tend to shy away from the overload. The effort to wade through all of the information to find something helpful is sometimes too much. So we stop. We ignore. We retreat from data, tolerate pushes of information, and minimize the number of information sources from which we pull. We simply can't handle it all, so we invoke filters and avoidance behaviors to keep the amount of information with which we must interact to a manageable level.

One of the problems with our (natural) retreat behavior is that we might (perhaps often?) miss or neglect important information to which we otherwise would have given time and attention. Instead, we filter out all but the most obvious and important facts and data to keep our level of information input to a manageable level. And if we go into a pull mode to do some research, we tend to find information sources that validate what we're already thinking and then congratulate ourselves on having done a marvelous job of researching a topic. This type of fast-food approach to assimilating information often leads to partially informed decisions or conclusions that might not have been made if a fuller information picture had been considered. But then again, who has time for reflection? There are another 100 e-mails in the inbox that need attention.

At a visceral, intuitive level, many administrators feel that SharePoint either can't or doesn't solve the information overload problem. In fact, many who are considering implementing SharePoint Server 2007 honestly feel that all they are really doing is moving the information chaos from e-mail and file servers to a Web-based storage system that includes several nifty technologies. From this viewpoint, they're not impressed with SharePoint nor are they excited about their prospects for success.

So, most administrators' knee-jerk reaction is to either tightly lock down SharePoint so users cannot do much of what SharePoint is intended for them to do, or they want to overlay an intuitive and enterprise-wide taxonomy on their SharePoint deployment. In other words, they want to organize their information. Why? Because they believe (to a point, correctly) that if their information is well organized, then it will be easy to find and perhaps the chaos will subside.

But finding the right information in a sea of information overload has inherent problems. It is to these problems that we now turn our attention.

## The Long Tail

The Long Tail is a marketing and business concept that asserts that the number of infrequently requested objects are larger than the number of frequently requested objects in most information retrieval systems. Online retailing provides us with great illustrations of this concept.

For example, 57 percent of Amazon's sales comes from books that are outside its top 130,000 titles. Another example is Blockbuster and NetFlix. Most Blockbuster stores carry fewer than 3,000 titles, yet 20 percent of NetFlix sales are from titles outside these 3,000 titles (and this percentage is rising). Rhapsody, an online music retail store, carries 19 times more titles than Wal-Mart's 39,000 tunes. Because Rhapsody's market is worldwide, it can carry over 735,000 tunes, and 22 percent of its sales are outside Wal-Mart's 39,000 tunes (their percentage is rising, too).

> **Note** If you're interested in reading more about this topic, you can pick up *The Long Tail: Why the Future of Business Is Selling Less of More*, by Chris Anderson (Hyperion, 2006).

When we think about the Long Tail and SharePoint, we can find two immediate applications. First, a sizable number of the queries for content items will be for niche documents or items that are rarely accessed. For these documents to be pinpointed in a retrieval system, they will need to have accurate metadata attached to them that is highly discriminatory. The better the metadata is at differentiating the niche documents from the more commonly accessed documents, the more likely it is that users who search for documents not commonly accessed will be able to find them.

Second, most of the objects that your users create will be niche objects. Consider the number of site collections and sites that your users create (or will create) in your SharePoint system. Most of those sites will be accessed by a small subset of users in your organization. And because most users will be accessing numerous sites over time, it will be important for you to provide them with findability tools to help them find the sites they don't access often. We'll discuss these tools in the last part of this chapter.

From a content item and site viewpoint, most of what will be hosted by SharePoint will be Long Tail, niche objects. As your implementation grows and users work with an increasing number of documents in an increasing number of sites, their ability to find known items will only become more difficult. Just like their inability to find documents on a shared network drive is rather high in most present-day implementations, moving those documents into SharePoint will not resolve this problem. You'll need to give them findability tools that will help them find their information quickly and easily, and those tools must be tied to metadata that is attached to the objects that users want to find.

Discriminating between documents is the result of a robust taxonomy system that returns relevant documents to the end-user. It is to this topic of relevance, along with the companion topics of precision and recall, that we now turn our attention.

## Relevance, Precision, and Recall

When we execute a query against the index, we hope to receive a result set that is relevant. But what constitutes relevant? How do we know when the result set that one user or another receives is relevant? The short answer to this question is that the more useful and usable the content items are in the result set, the more relevant it is to the user. In fact, research has shown that the content items in a relevant result set need to be the following:

- Usable
- Useful
- Accessible
- Findable
- Valuable
- Desirable
- Credible

> **Note** This list is called the *user experience honeycomb* (because it is graphically presented as a set of seven hexagons, which resemble a honeycomb) and is a great way to think about the qualities that users are looking for in the result set. The user experience honeycomb was developed by Peter Morville. You can learn more about the honeycomb at *www.findability.org*.

While *relevance* incorporates the preceding elements, *precision* refers to the information system's ability to retrieve only relevant documents. To the extent the result set has only relevant documents, the set is described as precise. Accompanying precision is *recall*, which is the system's ability to retrieve *all* of the relevant documents. So, to the extent that the system can retrieve all of the relevant documents without retrieving spurious, irrelevant documents, the retrieval system is thought to be highly precise with high recall.

The longer answer to our question, "What constitutes relevance?" has some difficulties buried inside it. For instance, what constitutes useful or usable is different for each person and is often different for the same person at different times–even if she has executed the exact same keyword query and received the same result set. In other words, while the result set might contain content items that are syntactically accurate in terms of keyword matches, the result set might not be useful at all.

For example, let's suppose you are looking for information about the history of a musical instrument, the trumpet. After doing some research, you learn that in ages past, the trumpet was called a horn. So you search on the word *horn* to learn more about the history of the trumpet. Yet when you search on the word *horn*, you receive content items that refer to the horns that go into automobiles, horns that grow on the head of rams, and horns that might have been attached to an altar in different religions. Obviously, these content items would not be relevant when doing research on the trumpet.

Furthermore, your search returns documents that describe what a trumpet is and what it looks like. Now, because you're searching on the history of the trumpet, documents that provide raw data on the present-day trumpet are probably not very helpful. In other words, the type of information you're looking for is more historical and less descriptive, so basic descriptive documents about the trumpet will not be relevant.

There are a plethora of examples of this phenomenon: words that have more than one meaning in different contexts match to dissimilar (and irrelevant) content items in the result set. Examples abound for these types of words: boot (a type of footwear) and boot (to start a computer), bonnet (a hat tied under the chin) and bonnet (the hood of a car), or ram (a male sheep) and ram (random access memory). While the result set might be syntactically accurate to the keywords entered in the query, those content items may not be *relevant* because the result set's content items are not useful. Why? Because *meaning* is very difficult to discern by the information retrieval system in a keyword query. It is impossible, for instance, to discern what is meant by entering a keyword query on *horn*. By their nature, keyword queries are matched syntactically while meaning is ignored. So, keyword queries sometimes link to documents, lists, sites, and other elements that contain content items that are not helpful at all, even though they might be syntactically accurate.

This doesn't mean that keyword queries are worthless, but it does mean that keyword queries will fail to meet most users' expectations for recall and precision. This is why the findability tools that we'll describe later in this chapter are so important to implement. While keyword searches are an important findability tool, they *must* be supplemented with other findability tools if SharePoint is to be used as an information management and retrieval system.

### Notes from the Field **Understanding Different Types of Keyword Queries**

When it comes to relevance, precision, and recall, it is helpful to note that users can commit different types of queries. For example, there are sample searches, which means that users want an introductory sampling of the types and number of documents that might exist within the information retrieval system. Within SharePoint, teach your users that they should use the Simple Search Web part with the All Sites scope selected if they want to commit this type of query.

A second type of query is an existence search, which means that users are looking for a known item and don't care about any other documents that might be similar to this known document. Precision is most important here. Within SharePoint, users who want to commit this type of query should use the Advanced Search Web part, specifying as much metadata and using as tight a search scope as possible. Note that if you have not implemented a robust taxonomy for your environment, then it is highly unlikely that successful existence searches will occur in your deployment.

A third type of query is an exhaustive search, which means that users need all of the relevant documents. Recall is most important here. Teach your users that when they commit this type of query, they should use the Advanced Search Web part plus enough metadata values to help refine the domain of documents they are looking for, as well as the All Sites search scope. Again, note that if you've not implemented a robust taxonomy in SharePoint, it will be difficult for users to successfully perform exhaustive searches.

*Woody Windischman, Microsoft MVP*

Moving on, we can't really discuss relevance without also discussing George Zipf's power law distribution concept, so we now turn our attention to this subject.

## Power Law Distribution

George Zipf, a linguist at Harvard, found that as the size of the corpus increases, the ability of the information retrieval system to retrieve relevant information will diminish. The *corpus* is the entire domain of content items against which keyword queries are executed. You can think of the corpus as the documents and Web sites that you need to crawl in your indexing topology.

For example, Zipf found that just 50 specific, high-frequency words constitute 50 percent of communication in English. In addition, he learned that, over time, individual words will begin to be used in multiple, dissimilar ways. It seems that when we need to describe something new, instead of creating a new word, we borrow words from other topic domains and use them in new ways with new meanings.

The information technology industry is adept at doing this very thing. We use spacial words to describe a number of technology concepts: *domain*, *firewall*, *network*, *windows*, and *site* are just a few examples. These words have original meanings completely outside of technology, yet we use them in very different ways to describe specific technology concepts. As the meaning of individual words moves from more specific to less specific or if a word's meaning becomes randomized in several dissimilar ways, the ability of the information retrieval system to retrieve relevant documents based on a keyword query alone becomes more and more difficult because, as we have learned, keyword queries are not good at indicating meaning on behalf of the user.

Idioms are a great example of how colloquial phrasing can refer to the same concept as a set of keywords. "Push the ball over the goal line" is an idiom for "finish." "Give it a go" is an idiom for "start" or "try." Keyword searches fall very short when it comes to meaning–retrieving documents that are *about* a subject but whose documents do not have the exact keywords contained within them to make them difficult to find. Meaning is often expressed using different words and culturally known idioms. Figuring out how to execute a keyword search that incorporates meaning and "aboutness" is rather difficult. We don't see this problem being overcome quickly by any major search engine company without a robust and pervasive implementation of a descriptive taxonomy on content items.

> **More Info** The thesaurus in SharePoint is a great way to align meaning with keywords due to its ability to create expansion sets for keyword queries. For example, the thesaurus could be configured to equate "finish" and "push the ball over the goal line." Hence, if a user enters the keyword "finish," the result set includes content items that contain the phrase "push the ball over the goal line." But the creation and maintenance of the thesaurus is a manual process lacking a graphical user interface. So, you'll need to know some XML to enter expansion sets in the thesaurus, and you'll have to build this over time based on a collaborative effort with your users. You can learn how to configure the thesaurus by referencing Chapter 12, "Configuring Search and Indexing," in the *Microsoft SharePoint Products and Technologies Administrator's Pocket Consultant* by Ben Curry (Microsoft Press, 2007).

Similar to the Long Tail, a robust metadata tagging system (often called a *taxonomy*) can help improve precision and recall if the following conditions are true:

- Metadata has been created.
- Documents and other content items have been correctly tagged.
- Users know what the metadata is.
- Users know what the metadata means.
- Users have a realistic expectation that their query will be relevant.

The problem with implementing a robust taxonomy that accurately describes all of the content items in your organization is that the development of the taxonomy is time consuming and expensive. In addition, enterprise-wide taxonomies are notoriously difficult to maintain, and they tend not to be scalable, easily expandable, or extensible. So, many organizations shy away from the initial and ongoing investments that need to be made to implement an organization-wide taxonomy. But without the taxonomy, our ability to find information based on the simple keyword diminishes, making our search and indexing system less helpful to our users.

> **Note** One of the questions to be asked—and one that is not easily answered—is what is the value of finding the right information at the right time quickly and easily? We would probably all agree, in principle, that a high value could be placed on this scenario. Yet, when it comes to actually hiring personnel, allocating budget money, and going through the pain of change to tag each document properly, most organizations end up not implementing a robust taxonomy. The indirect, incremental costs of not having the right information at the right time seem to be more acceptable in the short run.

When users are searching for meaning, we find that keyword queries often fall short of what we need them to do. In addition, relevance can be impaired if users receive content items in result sets that don't match the level of information that they were seeking. So, we need to discuss what the users are really looking for, not only in terms of meaning, but in terms of an information maturity gradation.

## What Are Users Really Seeking?

The answer to this question is answered by looking at the keywords that users input into the search Web part, right? Well, not really.

First, we have found that users are not seeking information that will make their jobs harder. And second, users can search for different *levels* of information, which are rarely reflected in a keyword query. To get us where we need to go in this discussion, we first need to consider Mooers' Law. Second, we'll consider information maturity gradations.

### Mooers' Law: The People Problem

To begin, we need to understand what users are *not* seeking. This brings us to Calvin Mooers, a computer scientist best known for his work about information retrieval, who learned that users will tend not to use an information retrieval system whenever it is more painful for the user to have the information than to not have the information. In other words, even though we might *need* the information, we may not *want* the information and, therefore, will not try to *find* that information. Moreover, if unwanted information is presented to us, we'll tend to ignore it if it makes our lives more painful to have it than to not have it.

Why would people not want information? Because, when you have information, you have to read it, understand it, and then act on it. Reading, comprehending, and assimilating details takes time. And time, for many workers, is a rare commodity these days. Another reason to not use information is because that information may contradict the beliefs, conclusions, or assumptions upon which your work is built.

Also, research has shown that people will tend to give the least amount of effort to accomplish their goal. When it comes to SharePoint, what this means is that users will not work hard to find information, even if they know it is in the SharePoint system. Even though they know the information exists and they need it, if their perceived need is surpassed by the pain they experience in trying to find that information, the chances are good that they will give up and not use the information. And, in most scenarios like this, users will blame the software for their inability to find information rather than their lack of persistence. In the absence of good findability tools, their criticism will be accurate.

One of the organizing principles for your SharePoint implementation should be to make it simple for your users to find and use information. A SharePoint implementation needs to subtract from, not add to, the information overload problem and needs to help place people in touch with information that they need, want, and will use. Your SharePoint implementation needs to make the findability of information easier, not harder.

## Understanding Information Maturity Gradations

The other aspect to understanding what people are really looking for when they execute keyword queries is to understand that there are different levels of information maturity that can reasonably be mapped out in the following telescope of concepts:

Data ⇨Information⇨Knowledge⇨Understanding⇨Wisdom

The five levels of information maturity build on one another and can be used as a type of classification to describe what your users are really seeking. Table 15-1 describes how this classification can work and the technologies in SharePoint that support each level in the classification scheme.

**Table 15-1 Classification Levels and Supporting SharePoint Technology**

| Classification level | Description | Questions asked at this level | Supporting SharePoint technology |
|---|---|---|---|
| Data | Symbols that represent objects, events, elements, and properties that are often measurable and discrete. For example, the speed of a car while being driven or the symbols *c*, *o*, and *l* that can form the word *cool* are instances of data. | What? | Lists hold data and metadata. Libraries hold documents, which usually contain both data and information. |
| Information | Data that can be used. Information represents a coherent whole of the data and can be related to other information. | Who?<br>Where?<br>When? | Lists and libraries can hold information. |
| Knowledge | When information is put into action or is acted upon, the thought that precedes the action is called knowledge. Information that is integrated with other information is also referred to as knowledge and provides a basis for making decisions and planning actions. | How? | Documents that contain records of what others have done in the past could offer knowledge in a written form. In addition, using the social networking part of SharePoint will enable users to find others who might have been in their situation who can also give advice on how to plan and make decisions. |

**Table 15-1 Classification Levels and Supporting SharePoint Technology**

| Classification level | Description | Questions asked at this level | Supporting SharePoint technology |
|---|---|---|---|
| Understanding | Understanding explains the knowledge and helps people figure it out. Understanding also helps people make judgments about what can and cannot be done. | Why? | The social networking features of My Sites will enable users to find the right people who can help them understand a particular situation. Documents that describe past actions as well as a thought history of a recurring topic or issue will also be of value here. Documents that can explain a process to arrive at a level of understanding on the topic will be helpful too. |
| Wisdom | Wisdom brings meaning, values, ethics, and principles to this process, allowing people to make cost/benefit and/or value-based judgments and predictions about the future based on the knowledge and understanding gained from insight and experience. | Why? | Wisdom-level topics can be found in both documents and the experiences of people. Finding the right people as well as the right documents are key to finding wisdom-level thinking. |

It's very possible that when a user enters a query, she isn't just looking for documents with the exact query words. She is also looking for integrative knowledge or documents that can help her understand the topic(s) that are represented by her queries. For example, if a user enters the phrase "document management" as a query in SharePoint, in the absence of further query refinements, SharePoint is going to return all documents and user profiles that contain the phrase "document management." But the person executing the search query may not be looking for data-level or even information-level documents: the user might be looking for knowledge or understanding about the topic of document management.

This is where finding the right people becomes important. *Tacit* knowledge–the knowledge that is difficult to record and that is usually the result of people's experiences, intelligence, intuitions, talents, and the facts of a scenario–is obtained by finding the right people. The reason that instructor-led education is still highly valued is because students are looking for more than raw data. Research has shown that, for some of us, close to 80 percent of the information we need to do our jobs is found through people, not through reading documents. Often, we'll find understanding or wisdom by talking with people as opposed to finding raw data or information. Sometimes, wisdom is written down in a document, but more often, it is found by interacting with people.

This is why we believe that most SharePoint Server 2007 deployments should include the Personal Features functionalities that are part of a larger My Site implementation. Collaborative My Sites include elementary built-in social networking software to help you find the right people, not just the right documents. Of course, user profiles in SharePoint are just another object and really represent a predefined set of metadata for the SharePoint user account. Understand that if the profiles' metadata is not consistently and properly tagged and configured, finding people will be like finding documents and will be subject to all of the same problems we have been discussing with keyword queries. It's no easier to find the right people than it is to find the right information, unless you already know the people and know something about them. So, this leads us directly to a discussion about the pros and cons of developing both taxonomies and *social networks*, which are dynamic social groups that emerge at the initiation of users who need to work with other users.

## Taxonomies and Social Networks

A *taxonomy* is a set of centrally controlled metadata hierarchies that are top-down and predetermined. A taxonomy's purpose is to describe data. It is used to create keyword hierarchies, equivalencies, and relationships. For example, a taxonomy can be used to create the keyword hierarchy as shown in the following figure:

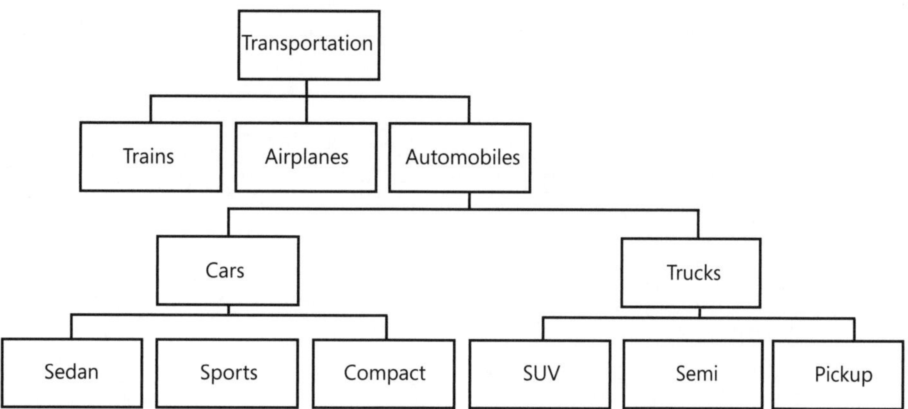


Keyword hierarchies and equivalencies are essential in building out an enterprise-wide taxonomy. Ensuring that descriptors are used in only one way throughout the enterprise is foundational to the development of a taxonomy. In addition, a robust taxonomy would enter synonyms for various keywords, creating equivalencies within the hierarchy. For example, *motorcar* could be a synonym for *automobile,* and it is conceivable that *sedan* could be a synonym for *car*. Keyword equivalencies are managed through the thesaurus file in SharePoint using the expansion set feature. Using this scenario, if a user entered the word *sedan* in his keyword query, through the use of expansion sets, we could force the query to execute for the word *car* as well. Content type metadata fields are used to describe and differentiate between documents in an enterprise wide taxonomy; when used with the thesaurus, both hierarchy and equivalence can be obtained for keyword queries.

*Social networks* are Web-based locations that are used for collaboration and are self organizing with a low transaction cost. These sites have user-defined labels and tags to organize and share information. The focus in social networks is not on organization, but on relating, sharing, and collaborating.

Later in this chapter, we'll discuss social networking as one of the findability tools in more detail, but suffice it to say here that if findability is an organizing principle of your SharePoint Server 2007 deployment, you won't use social networking as one of your main findability tools. Why? Because social networks, by their very nature, lack organization. This isn't to say that social networks lack *navigation* to meander to the person or group that you might need to find, but it is to say that the lack of consistent metadata that describes people and groups results in a chaotic type of meandering to find the right people or group.

## Governance, Search, and Findability

So, how does SharePoint Search support and fit into our findability discussion? Well, the obvious answer is that without a search technology that creates an index of content, keyword queries become a moot point. In other words, without content being indexed, all you'll have left are social networks and no method of querying your taxonomy.

The following factors affect how you will design your search and indexing topology:

- Credibility of the source of the information: Obviously, you'll want to crawl only those sources that are credible.
- Authority of the source of the information: The source of the information needs to be reliable and trustworthy.
- Mobility of accessing devices and context of use of the information: To the extent that mobile devices will access the information, you'll want to consider how that information will display on the screens of mobile devices.
- How to execute a discriminatory query: This is a user education issue. The more discriminatory the query, the better the result set.
- The characteristics of the information that is found need to contain the following qualities:
    - Relevance
    - Precision
    - Recall
    - Existence
    - Exhaustion

You'll need to develop business criteria for these elements and then articulate the conditions and criteria for when you'll build a content source by crawling the content source. Let's discuss this topic more fully.

# Business Requirements and Search

In order to know which content sources you'll need to crawl and the sources for which you'll need to build Federated Location Definition (FLD) files, you'll need to understand your business requirements for your search implementation. Your business requirements for search will drive how you implement SharePoint Server 2007 search or Search Server 2008 via the SharePoint Server 2007 interface.

For example, if you need the most recent crawl of data to be available from the index even if the content source goes offline, then you'll need to crawl that content source instead of just building an FLD to that source. Even if the links in the result set point to a site that is down, there may be a requirement to know that the content is available under normal circumstances.

The business requirements for a search topology will contain both logical requirements and physical or deployment requirements. Obviously, the logical requirements are driven by the need to have certain content appear in the result sets. The business requirements will likely revolve around needs to aggregate content and make it easily findable. These requirements will overlap with your metadata and taxonomy requirements—requirements that will help make your data more easily findable using search technologies.

# Designing Crawl and Query Topologies

We'll discuss two basic parts in this section. The first is how and when you need to scale out your index and query server topology. The second is understanding the differential assessment points for when you'll want to make information findable by using the federated query feature in Search Server 2008 and when you'll want to have that content crawled and indexed locally by SharePoint Server 2007 (if you don't implement Search Server 2008) or via your Search Server 2008 implementation.

## Scaling Out Your Index and Query Servers

In SharePoint Server 2007, you have the option of separating out the index and query server roles to different servers. The index server role performs the crawling and indexing functions. Specifically, it is the index server that connects to a content source, reads the content and metadata out of the documents hosted at the content source, and then places the metadata in the SQL property store and the content in the full text index. The Query role accepts search queries that users enter in the default or customized search Web parts and returns results that are based on its local index. So, it is the Query role that builds the result set, ensures it is security trimmed accurately, and then returns the result set to the user for rendering in the user's browser.

As you might know, there is hardware scalability and software scalability. Software scalability deals with gaining the right mix of functionalities and services based on your business and technical requirements. The software scalability limitations are imposed by the product itself: There are certain things that you can and cannot do with Index and Query role scaling in SharePoint Server 2007. The following are the actions you can and cannot perform when it comes to scaling the Index and Query roles in SharePoint Server 2007:

- The same physical server can host both the Index role and the Query role.
- If you need two query servers, then neither of them can serve as the index server.
- Multiple Shared Service Providers (SSPs) can use the same index server for crawling content sources.
- You cannot assign multiple index servers to a single SSP for crawling content sources.
- You cannot map a query server to an SSP for query purposes, so each query server has a local copy of all indexes from all SSPs in the SharePoint Server 2007 farm.

Keep in mind that most environments will not bump up against the software limitations, and a fairly simple search topology should suit most organizations well. A best practice for implementing SharePoint Server 2007 search is incrementally adding content sources so you can easily monitor the performance and capacity and adjust your design accordingly.

In addition, the only time that the index is copied from the index server to the query server is when the query server is first added to the farm. Thereafter, continuous propagation will update the query server's copy of the index each time the copy on the index server is updated.

Hardware scalability does not change software scalability or modify software behavior. Instead, we scale out hardware because we need to increase the overall throughput of the farm and to achieve acceptable performance as the number of objects in the farm and the number of client requests increases.

Microsoft has recommended that you not crawl more than 50 million documents per index because the company will not support an index that contains more than 50 million documents. (This number includes user profiles where each user profile is considered one document.) Microsoft has tested the index's performance up to 100 million documents, but its recommendation remains at 50 million. Now, if we recall that each SSP has only one index and can use only one index server, then we quickly realize that Microsoft's recommendation is to not crawl more than 50 million documents per SSP. If you do crawl that many documents for a single SSP/index, then you'll be doing so using a single index server.

It's worth noting that, if you are crawling somewhere close to 50 million documents, the chances are very, very high that you'll experience high query demand as well. If your crawl topology is to crawl millions of documents, best practice would suggest that you start with several query servers to meet user demand. Usually, user demand is the number one reason to scale out your query servers.

In addition, Microsoft's own tests found that it took nearly 35 days to do a full crawl of 50 million documents. For most environments, this is an unacceptable time frame in which to perform a complete crawl of data. So one of the factors in knowing when to scale out your index server role is the timing of crawl jobs and whether those jobs are completing in a timely fashion. So, let's turn our attention to the specific discussion of when to scale out index and query server roles.

## When to Scale Out with More Index Servers

Several elements may come to exist in your environment that will cause you to scale out your index servers. In short, these elements are as follows:

- You need to crawl an excess of 50 million documents. We don't recommend that you place more than the supported number of documents in your index. If you need to crawl more than 50 million documents, best practice is to create a second SSP, build out another index server, and crawl your corpus from two different index servers. We would further recommend that you balance, as much as possible, the number of documents crawled by each index server so that one server is not performing most of the crawling load. Finally, we would also recommend that you use federated queries to show content items in a single result set page to form a better result set experience for the end-user.
- Your crawl times are too long. We've seen scenarios where the incremental crawls were taking so long that they didn't finish before the next incremental crawl on the same content source was scheduled to start. If you can't finish all of the crawling efforts within a defined time frame, you need to consider off-loading the crawling to a second index server or balance the crawl processes over multiple content sources that can start and stop in a more timely manner. If you choose a second index server, this will mean a second SSP, of course, but there are tradeoffs in nearly every decision with SharePoint. The defined time frame may not relate to the crawl times, per se, but instead may relate to a combination of two factors: how often the content changes at the content source and the level of urgency that those changes appear in your index. If the content changes frequently and the level of urgency is high, but the crawler can't crawl the content fast enough to meet your needs because the index server is busy crawling other content sources, then you'll need to lower the priority of the crawl schedule for other content sources, scale out to a second index server, or consider using a federated query (assuming the content can be indexed by another indexing engine).
- If you need a second SSP for legal or design reasons, you may also decide to crawl the content sources for the second SSP using a separate index server. This is, of course, optional because two SSPs can use the same index server. The indexing load on the first index server will help inform your decision about scaling out to a second index server.

> **Note** If you scale out to additional index servers, you're necessarily choosing to have multiple SSPs in your environment because each SSP can use only one index server to crawl its content. Hence, for every index server you to which you scale, you'll be doing so (at least in part) because you need another SSP in your SharePoint Server 2007 environment.

You should also bear in mind that, if you move the index server role, you'll be forced to re-crawl all of your content sources in order to rebuild your index. The index does not move with changes in the index server role, but because the content sources and their accompanying configurations are stored in the configuration database, you won't need to re-create the content sources or other crawl configurations. The next index server will pick up that information from the configuration database, but then it will need to perform full crawls on all of your content sources in order to rebuild the index.

## When to Scale Out with More Query Servers

Like the index server scaling scenarios, scenarios may arise in your environment that will indicate it's time to scale out your query servers. These scenarios can be described as follows:

- You need to include content items in the result set that you cannot crawl. In this case, you'll need to use the federated query topology of Search Server 2008 and, in some cases, that may indicate a need for additional query servers to service the federated query demand in your environment.
- Query demand is rising, while indexing levels remain constant. This is a good problem to have because it means that your users are executing an increasing number of queries in your SharePoint implementation, which also means that the result sets they are receiving are relevant and wanted. As query demand increases, you may need to scale out to multiple query servers in order to meet user demand.
- If you scale to more than one index server, best practice will be to scale to multiple query servers.

You should also know that, if you move the query server role off of the index server, you'll need to stop and start the index server services to re-establish a proper connection with the query server for continuous propagation.

## Planning the Thesaurus and Noise Word Files

When an SSP is first configured, the thesaurus and noise word files are copied from C:\Program Files\Microsoft Office Servers\12.0\Data\Office Server\Config\ to %Index File Location%\SSPNAME\GUID\Config\. Each Web application has its own set of thesaurus and noise word files. This allows you to customize your thesaurus implementation for each SSP in your environment.

If you edit the C:\Program Files\Microsoft Office Servers\12.0\Data\Config\ noise and/or thesaurus files before configuring the SSP, then they are copied to the %Index File Location*\SSPNAME\GUID\Config\ directory and for every SSP thereafter.

When adding a query server to the farm, these files are copied from Index File Location* \SSPNAME\GUID\Config\ to the query server's index location, but only at Query Share Creation time. After the initial files are copied, any updates made to the files on the index server are not propagated to the query server. The thesaurus and noise word files are utilized during crawls, and they are invoked at query time, so keeping all copies of these files up to date is important. If you have multiple query servers, you'll need to update each thesaurus and noise word file manually with those updates.

Best practice will be to set your global noise word and thesaurus settings at the time that you create the first server in your farm. Thereafter, you can modify the files on all of the index and query servers and keep them updated.

## When to Use the Federated Query Features

In this section, we need to differentiate between those content sources that we need to crawl and those sources that we should simply query using the FLD technology.

From our perspective, your decision about whether to use traditional crawl technologies or the new FLD technology should be based on (a) whether the source's content *needs* to extracted and placed in your SharePoint index and (b) your determination of which content does not need to be indexed or cannot be adequately indexed by Search Server 2008.

> **Note** If you have not read Chapter 14, "Understanding and Implementing Microsoft Office Search Server 2008," then you should read that chapter before reading this section on designing a query topology.

Designing these topologies has tradeoffs that represent positives and negatives. In most instances, no single choice will be only positive or negative–there will usually be a combination of both.

> **Note** The design for Search Server 2008 is rather simple in one sense. Instead of having SharePoint Server 2007 crawl all of the locations that might have content that your users will need to see in the result sets, you can opt to have the query simultaneously and automatically send to those search engines or Web sites to execute the search query. By creating Federated Locations, you can offer your users the chance to execute their query in other search engines that have already indexed their own content.

There are several advantages to querying other Web sites from the client end rather than attempting to index their content using SharePoint Server 2007, such as the following:

- You conserve bandwidth and resources by crawling and indexing only that content which is highly necessary to host in your index. Because you now have the option to include content at query time rather than first crawling the data, your need to query Web sites with dynamic or constantly changing content is significantly reduced.
- You can include content in the overall result set that cannot be crawled because it is either restricted in the robots.txt file on the target Web site or the content is not exposed in a way that is easily crawled, such as hosting the content in a database that is not exposed via normal HTML pages.
- You can use the triggers in the FLD files to invoke certain content sources only when the query matches one of the triggers. For example, if you have a database of contact information, one of your triggers for that FLD file might be a client name that is triggered by the word "company" or "client" before the client's name. Hence, the query might be "client Microsoft," and this query string would send the query to the contact's database and return results that only include Microsoft contacts from the database. This is different from scopes in that scopes carve out logical partitions within a single index in SharePoint against which the query is executed. Triggers send the query to certain content sources only when there is a match in the query string.
- You're able to leverage the latest information from different content sources by relying on their search engines to return the latest results from their own index.
- You can still crawl content that isn't exposed via a local search engine at the content source.

But like most things in life, there are disadvantages as well. Some of the disadvantages to using federated queries to show results from remote indexes include the following:

- You are unable to configure ranking within the result set from the remote index because the Authoritative Pages feature in Search Server 2008 does not apply to results that are returned from the remote index.
- You are not able to control which results appear in the result set. In Search Server 2008, you can remove individual content items from the index, which automatically creates an exclusion rule for that individual content item. If objectionable content comes through using an FLD, your only option is to limit the result set through the use of triggers, to add search terms to the FLD, or to cease using the FLD completely.
- You cannot scope FLD results using the scopes option at the site collection level.
- You cannot combine into a single result set any of the results from FLDs with the results that are returned from the local index.

- You will find that many FLDs in the same result page will result in usability issues. As the number of Web parts on any Web part page increases, the time to load the page and the ability to use the information on the pages gradually diminishes. Loading up twenty or more FLDs onto a single result set page will likely result in information overload for that result set page.

Given these advantages and disadvantages for implementing FLDs in your search topology, we offer the following scenarios and design decisions about when to crawl content and when to query a remote index.

## Scenario: You need to conserve bandwidth.

The crawl process consumes a significant amount of bandwidth resources when you're crawling content sources outside the local SharePoint farm. Routers and WAN connections can quickly become consumed by the crawling thread.

For those sites that are heavily queried, and assuming the remote site's index is OpenSearch 1.1 compliant, an FLD might be a better solution because you can have the results appear in the result set without having to build an index for that content source.

> **Note** Scheduling crawl processes is a significant part of your overall search design, in part because the crawl should be committed during times when your farm is not being backed up and when there is sufficient bandwidth to efficiently commit the crawl.

## Scenario: You need to display the content in the results set, but the remote index's robots.txt file blocks SharePoint's crawler.

SharePoint's architecture honors the robots.txt file and the robots meta tag element. If it finds these blocking instructions, the crawler honors them and does not crawl the content.

FLDs bypass any robots.txt and robots meta tag elements by submitting the query directly to the remote index's query engine. If the remote index's crawling engine ignores the robots.txt file and meta tags, then using an FLD is the right decision.

## Scenario: You need to see results from a content source only when certain keywords and/or keyword patterns are entered by the user.

The common example is that, when a user enters a phone number, the query is sent to a contacts database that returns contact information that is associated with that phone number. This is a great example of when you'd want to create and use FLD files.

### Scenario: Content at the content source changes very often, and those changes must immediately be reflected in the result set. You can crawl and index the content source.

In this scenario, you need to think through the implications of crawling that information frequently and compare that with the benefits of having that content in your index. For example, while you can crawl the remote content source frequently, the use of the bandwidth for that purpose may be less urgent than the use of the bandwidth for other purposes, such as sending e-mail. Depending on your scenario, it may or may not be best to have that information appear in your index. FLDs will display the latest update of the remote index in the result set without being crawled by your index server. There is a tradeoff here, and the variables that play into this tradeoff will be different for each scenario.

> **Note** Note that you gain updated information in your result set only when the remote index is updated. If the remote index updates less frequently than the frequency at which you're able to update your own index using SharePoint's crawler, then you should crawl the content directly.

### Scenario: Content at the content source changes frequently, but those changes need not be reflected quickly in the result set. You can crawl and index the content source.

In this scenario, crawling the index makes sense because the urgency to have those content items in the result set is low, so a low-frequency crawl schedule will likely meet your needs and can be more easily planned into your overall crawl schedule. You could build one or more FLD files to represent this content in the result set. But given the lack of urgency to display content items in the result set, building one or more FLD files for this content source would be optional, not a best practice.

As you can see in this scenario, either option would work. The choice you make here would likely depend on other factors that are considered along with this factor.

### Scenario: You need to tightly define which URLs from the remote index will appear in the result set.

The ability to remove individual URLs can be important when you need to display selected results from a content source. You can surgically remove content items from your index by using the Remove URLs from Search Resultsfeature. This feature creates an exclusion crawl rule that the crawler obeys and that content will be removed from the index after the next crawl on that content source. FLD files will display all of the content items that are returned from the remote index. In this scenario, building FLD files to the content source will not meet your needs and best practice would be to crawl the content source directly.

### Scenario: You need to have queries executed under different security contexts to different remote indexes to receive security-trimmed results within the FLD's result Web part.

SharePoint Server 2007 search doesn't provide client-side security trimming that is pre-configured by the Search Administrator before the query is executed. Search Server 2008 provides this feature by assigning a security context in which the FLD query will be executed.

> **Note** Potentially, this could hold significant ramifications on how search results are presented to the users of the Search Center. Note that this is security trimming and not an audience-based feature.

### Scenario: You need to have content in the result set that is not indexed locally at the remote site or server.

For this need, you must crawl the content source because there is no remote index against which to build FLD files. FLD files will run only against remote indexes that have been built by another engine and whose query language is OpenSearch 1.1 compliant.

### Scenario: The remote index is intermittently available when users execute queries. You are able to crawl and index the content source's content.

In this scenario, you must crawl and index the content from the source because an intermittently available index does your users no good when they execute a query if the query is executed when the remote index is not available. Even though the FLD file could be generated and built for this type of content source, the unreliability of the remote index to always be available will lead you to crawl and index the content directly. Of course, you'll likely have problems crawling and indexing the remote content, but that can be resolved through a more aggressive crawl schedule.

### Scenario: The remote index does not return results in RSS or Atom or the presentation of the results is not usable within the FLD Web part.

In this scenario, you'll need to crawl and index the content directly. Search Server 2008, by default, works only with results that are returned in RSS/ATOM. HTML or XHTML results are not supported in this version of Search Server 2008.

> **Note** Connector .aspx pages can be written to overcome this obstacle. Look for third-party vendors to write these types of connectors so that results returned in HTML or XHTML will be presentable within the Search Center. Of course, you can also write your own connector pages to display results from non-OpenSearch–compliant indexes.

### Scenario: The content needs to be available in the result set, but the query frequency of the content is not sufficient to justify the resources needed to crawl and index that content.

Users will often search for items that are not often queried, but they'll expect your search implementation to return relevant, useful results anyway. If the content they infrequently desire is hosted within a large content source, using an FLD to return results from that source's index will likely be a good solution. Monitor the frequency of the queries that invoke this content source and, if the frequency increases, consider crawling and indexing the content directly. FLDs would work well here if there are triggers that will differentiate whether this content source is frequently accessed or not.

> **Note** Be aware that with a high number of content items in a remote index, the chances of an FLD returning irrelevant result sets is very likely. And without triggers, the FLD will always be queried, leading to an overly high number of queries to an infrequently accessed content source.

### Scenario: You have more than 250,000 start addresses and/or 500 content sources that you need to include in the result set, and you do not want to or cannot build a second Shared Services Provider in SharePoint Server 2007.

There is a limit of 500 content sources with a total of 250,000 start addresses across those 500 content sources in SharePoint Server 2007. After you reach this limitation, your only option to crawl more content is to build another SSP. FLDs can be a good workaround in this situation if you have only a handful of additional content sources or start addresses from which you need content items in a result set.

Because of usability issues in the interface, we don't see more than 14-20 FLDs per Search Center being realistic. So, if your need to crawl content well exceeds the 500/250,000 limit, building another SSP is really your only option.

### Scenario: You have too many FLDs in your result set, and the usability of the result set interface has diminished significantly.

We believe that usability begins to break down after roughly 14-20 FLD Web parts on an individual result set page. This is obviously open to interpretation and personal choices. If you need to return results from more than 10 content sources, we recommend that you crawl and index the content directly. FLDs work well if you're only going to coalesce a few remote indexes into the result set interface. Anything over 14-20 FLDs will likely result in diminished usability.

### Scenario: Best Bet–type results have several content items and are easily displayed within either the Best Bet Web part or the FLD Web part.

In SharePoint Server 2007, Best Bets are pre-configured and are merely links to resources that are called out based on the query keyword and its synonyms that you've configured within the Search Administration interface. However, if the content changes, is moved, or is updated at the content source, you'll need to manually update your keyword Best Bet.

FLD files can act like Best Bet solutions, except their results are generated by the remote index server instead of being pre-configured by you, the SharePoint Server 2007 Search Administrator. FLDs will work well here if the remote index is often queried and there are certain keywords for which content items would rise to the level of being a Best Bet. You'll use keyword triggers as part of the FLD. In addition, if the content is updated, moved, or modified, the FLD will act as a dynamic update of the Best Bet information.

### Scenario: Scoping effects are needed on a remote content source that you are not crawling and indexing.

While scopes can be created within SharePoint Server 2007, this feature applies only to content that is crawled and indexed directly by SharePoint Server 2007. Through the use of triggers, you can effectively scope content items at the keyword level that are returned from the remote index. You cannot create triggers that will mimic a scope at the property (metadata), folder, content source, domain name, or host name level.

### Scenario: You have created FLD files to federate queries in your SharePoint Server 2007 implementation, but the results are returned too slowly from the remote index and users are complaining.

If latency is too high to return the results from the remote index, then it will be better to crawl the content directly and place it in your local index for faster retrieval. One additional advantage of this approach is that you'll also have SharePoint's ranking applied to content items from that content source when they appear in the result set. One of the elements that SharePoint can't resolve is latency in returning results from a remote index when you use the FLD feature. Latency can be caused by a number of factors, including bandwidth latency or slow response time from the remote index.

In the next section, we'll turn our attention to the findability tools that ship with SharePoint Server 2007.

## Findability Tools in SharePoint Server 2007

In this section, we'll look at the SharePoint Server 2007 findability tools from both the push/taxonomy perspective and the pull/social network perspective.

## Findability Tools that Support Taxonomies and Push Needs for Administrators

A great findability solution involves a combination of administrator-created access vectors that remain relatively constant to the content plus user-created access vectors that are dynamically created. In this section, we'll outline the findability tools in SharePoint Server 2007 that exist to help you, the administrator, create methods of finding information. These methods will remain relatively static and will change over time, but will not necessarily be dynamically responsive to the ebb and flow of users' daily tastes and desires. Instead, these methods will change, but only after there is a clear, demonstrated need for the change to occur, accompanied by a clear understanding of what the change will implement and look like after it has been implemented.

### Master Site Directory

It stands to reason that, in a collaborative and information management product like SharePoint Server 2007, we would find a method of organizing URL-addressable locations. If you're running only Windows SharePoint Services, then you'll have the Summary Links Web part available to you. But if you're running SharePoint Server 2007, then you'll have the added benefit of the Master Site Directory to organize your site collections and any URL-addressable location.

The Master Site Directory setting is in Central Administration (Figure 15-1) and works with the Categories Web part in the Sites Directory site that is installed, by default, with a Collaboration Portal site template. The purpose of this configuration is to automatically enable (or force, depending on the settings you select) the categorization and organization of all of the site collections that are created in your farm.

Once enabled, the Sites Directory site that is specified as the Master Site Directory will become the hub for the taxonomization of all of your site collections. The category structure that is created within the Sites list and the Categories Web part in this Sites Directory site will be important to plan because as the site collection is created, the links to the Top-Level Site (TLS) are automatically created within the category structure. If that structure is modified (by modifying the Site Columns for the Categories Web part), then the links will persist in the root list for this Web part, but the metadata assignments previously given to the link may or may not persist depending on the modifications made. Even more difficult would be the situation in which the metadata persists in a column but doesn't match the new column name or data type.

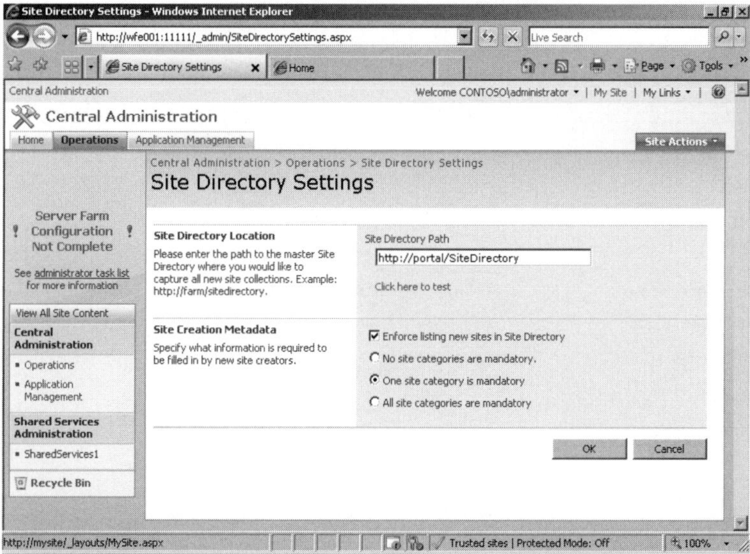


**Figure 15-1** Master Site Directory setting in SharePoint Server 2007 Central Administration

For example, as illustrated in Figure 15-2, you can see that the categories that appear in the Categories Web part are merely columns on the list of links to the root TLS for each site collection (Figure 15-3).

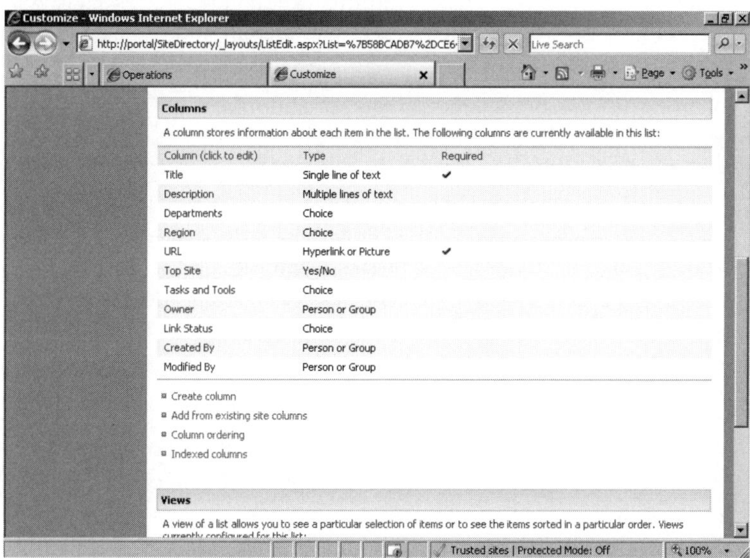


**Figure 15-2** Default view of the Category's List Columns that form the categories displayed when users create new site collections if the Master Site Directory settings are enabled

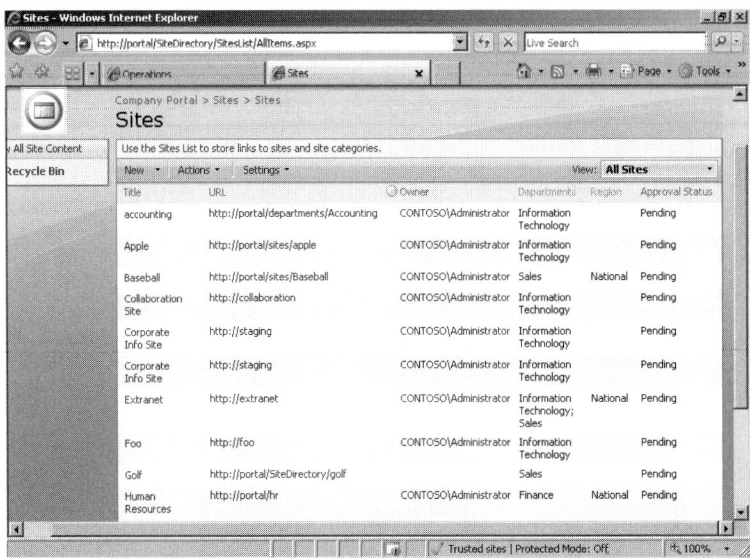


**Figure 15-3** List view of the links in the Categories Web part. Note that the categories are merely Site Columns on this list.

One of the pain points with Self-Service Site Creation (SSSC) is the lack of inherent organization of the newly created site collections. When SSSC is enabled and made available to a wide audience of users, organizations have found that users take advantage of this feature. Most organizations with whom we have worked have not liked the results of everyone being able to create new site collections whenever they feel like it. In addition, most IT administrators feel that their SharePoint deployment is out of control, and their urge to lock it down intensifies, sometimes souring their attitude toward SharePoint in general.

> **Note** Self-Service Site Creation in Central Administration should be thought of as *Self-Service Site Collection Management* because this feature actually allows users to create new site collections, not just new sites. Users given this permission should be well trained in how to effectively administrate and manage a site collection before they create their first site collection.

What IT administrators want out of their SharePoint implementation, among other things, is a better organization of unstructured and tacit knowledge. Without an ability to organize newly created site collections, administrators are left to conclude that the collaboration chaos they manage in e-mail, shared network drives, and file servers is merely being transferred to a Web-based platform.

But the Master Site Directory is not all that it appears to be. One of the main drawbacks is that it only enforces the categorization of the root TLS in each site collection. Subsites within a site collection are not categorized with this feature. So, you'll need to think of the Master Site Directory settings as a method of categorizing groups of Web sites within SharePoint. Aside from a manual process or workflow that asks users to categorize each site they create within the Master Site Directory, you'll find that the majority of the sites that are created will still not be categorized or associated with your Web site taxonomy.

Given all this, what are the best practices for implementing a Sites Directory? Well, here are some thoughts and ideas that should help you implement this technology. First, like any taxonomy, be sure to select quality, persistent metadata to describe your site collections. This list can be used for a number of different taxonomies in SharePoint, and it is applicable here. This list is not exhaustive. You'll likely come up with other ways that add to this list to describe and categorize site collections within SharePoint:

- Subject
- Author
- Customer
- Project
- Product
- Department
- Division
- Security level
- Team
- Process stage

Second, be sure to plan and implement this taxonomy as early as possible. The more site collections that are created without this feature being used, the higher the number of site collections in your deployment that will not be categorized for easier findability or the higher the number of site collections that you'll need to manually add to the Sites Directory after this feature is enabled.

Third, train your users on how to categorize their sites within SharePoint so that they don't wrongly tag a newly created site collection. Getting everyone on the same page regarding the tagging or taxonomization of site collections is important if you plan to offer a browsable way to find site collections within your organization.

Fourth, enter descriptive keywords in the Description input box for each new site collection and site to help make the site collection and site more findable via the search technologies.

> **Note** The Sites Directory feature in SharePoint Server 2007 is a logical feature whose links map to physical locations. In the next section, we'll discuss the best practices and decision points regarding where information should physically reside within your SharePoint Server 2007 deployment. But please do not become confused regarding the logical taxonomization of those site collections using the Sites Directory and the physical hosting of the information in the URL taxonomy.

## URL/Managed Paths

No other feature more directly answers the question "where does stuff go?" than this feature. Where you decide information should reside within your SharePoint deployment both directly impacts and is impacted by your URL naming conventions.

> **More Info** To learn what managed paths are and how to implement them, please reference Chapter 3 in the *Microsoft SharePoint Products and Technologies Administrator's Pocket Consultant* by Ben Curry (Microsoft Press, 2007).

How to design for URLs and managed paths could (and often does) require hours of conversations with clients. In a nutshell, however, there are essentially two concepts to bear in mind when designing for where stuff goes in SharePoint. First, you can decide which levels of the URL you want users engaged in collaboration. Table 15-2 nicely illustrates your choices.

**Table 15-2 Advantages and Disadvantages of Collaboration at Different URL Levels**

| URL Level | URL Example | Advantages | Disadvantages |
|---|---|---|---|
| Root site collection in a Web application at which a new site collection can be created | http://*sales* | ■ URL independence<br>■ Most collaboration flexibility and scalability for creating more site collections<br>■ Highly secure<br>■ Default method for database isolation<br>■ Best for very large groups whose members work together<br>■ Can have multiple site collections beneath it by using explicit and wildcard managed paths | ■ Highest resource consumption if created for a single site collection<br>■ Needs a distinct URL<br>■ Must be created by IT personnel<br>■ Requires a new Web application |

**Table 15-2 Advantages and Disadvantages of Collaboration at Different URL Levels**

| URL Level | URL Example | Advantages | Disadvantages |
|---|---|---|---|
| Explicit managed path that creates a virtual root beneath the Web application's root site collection at which a single site collection per namespace can be created | http://sales/*customers* | ■ You can economize URL namespaces by not using wildcard managed paths<br>■ You can give the appearance of nesting a site collection within a site collection | ■ You cannot create other site collections beneath this one, so SSSC will not work within a site collection created in an explicit managed path<br>■ IT must create the managed path, although either the end-users or IT can create the site collection |
| Virtual root beneath a wildcard managed path at which (potentially) thousands of new site collections can be created | http://sales/customers/*contoso* | ■ Organize your collaboration spaces by intuitively naming the wildcard managed paths<br>■ This is the only location at which end-users can use SSSC to create new site collections independent of contacting the SharePoint Administrator<br>■ Best when there are small groups who need an entire site collection within which to collaborate and also for groups who need to create it quickly and easily using SSSC | ■ Wildcard managed paths need to be intuitively named in order for them to be effective in helping users know where they are in the overall deployment<br>■ Longer URL namespaces may contribute to violation of the 256 character URL limit in SharePoint |

As you can see, you can create site collections at any of the first three layers in the URL namespace, http://<layer1>\<layer2>\<layer3>. Where you want different site collections depends on the decision criteria listed in Table 15-2 plus other criteria you add to the matrix from your own environment. Note that layer 2 can act as either an explicit managed path that can host site collections or as a wildcard managed path that creates a virtual root in layer 3. You'll create this in Central Administration, and, once the namespace is set in Central Administration, it cannot be used for other purposes. For example, if you create an explicit managed path called *customers* (as illustrated in the second row of Table 15-2), then you can't have a subsite in the root site collection called *customers* nor can you create a wildcard managed path called *customers*. By creating the explicit managed path called *customers*, you've reserved that namespace for that purpose only and, by default, have excluded that namespace from being used in the root site collection as a subsite or as a wildcard managed path.

Second, you need to decide when to use explicit versus wildcard managed paths. Explicit managed paths are created at layer 2 and create a virtual root at which only one site collection can be created. Wildcard managed paths are created at layer 2 as well, but they create a virtual root at layer 3 and allow for the creation of thousands of site collections at layer 3. Wildcard managed paths simply reserve the namespace to create a categorized location in which many new site collections can be created. In a sense, although not technically accurate, you can think of wildcard managed paths as forming categories into which collaboration spaces can be taxonomized.

Explicit managed paths are great for one-off or ad hoc site collections that need a place to reside without having to create a new Web application for them. Wildcard managed paths are great for series of collaboration spaces that need to be disparate at the site collection level but need to be grouped together under a common namespace.

As part of your overall taxonomy efforts when implementing SharePoint, you need to use the preceding suggestions to supplement your own decision-making criteria for when you'll want to create new Web applications versus new site collections in explicit managed paths versus new site collections within a wildcard managed path.To the extent that you need unique configurations for the following configuration items, you'll need a new site collection:

- Different site collection ownership
- Different site quota assignment
- Different lock assignment
- Different custom scope assignment
- Unique search scope assignments
- Unique keyword/Best Bet assignments
- Unique site directory settings
- Disparate site collection feature enablement matrix
- Unique portal site connection
- Unique audit settings
- Different site collection policy settings
- Unique output cache settings
- Unique cache profiles
- Unique object cache configurations
- Unique variation settings

Everything in this list is a site collection setting that would be configured by the site collection administrator.

As part of the where-stuff-goes conversation, don't forget to consider the use of Alternate Access Mappings (AAM). AAMs allow you to provide alternate URL names for access to the same content. These different names can be the result of using Secure Sockets Layer (SSL) for extranet access and using normal HTTP for intranet access, or they can be the result of needing vanity names for access to content that is initially created using a Fully Qualified Domain Name (FQDN). For example, your FQDN might be research.contoso.msft, whereas your vanity name might be *research* or *RandD* or just *RD*. Usually, vanity names are not intended to be routed on the Internet and are used mainly for easy, quick access to a Web application's root site collection.

AAMs provide the ability to rename content that reflects a re-organization of your company without requiring you to physically move all of the content around within your Web applications. For example, if your organization today calls your sales department *Sales* and tomorrow wants to subsume sales inside of *Marketing*, then you can use an AAM to overlay the *http://sales with http://marketing* without having to physically move the content into a new Web application. The best practice for the use of AAMs is to supplement different authenticated methods of access to the same content (in conjunction with extending the original Web application) and to provide content vanity names that are easy for your intranet user to remember and use.

Finally, as part of the where-stuff-goes conversation, help your users understand when it is better to create a new site collection and when it is better to create a new site within an existing site collection.

The main differential decisions are about security and collaboration. First, if the site collection owners should not have access to the new content, then it should go into a new site collection. Second, to follow the first point more fully, both the site collection owners and the site administrators should be the owners of the content. If they are not the owners of the content, then the content has been placed in the wrong location. Content owners should be responsible for the creation, maintenance, security, and distribution of the content. In SharePoint Server 2007, both the site collection owners and the site administrators can exercise these administrative functions over content within their purview. Best practice is to map the content to its owners, both at the site collection and site levels.

Finally, new sites should be created within site collections when the overall project or collaborative effort can be broken into subparts or subefforts that realistically form a new, distinct collaboration effort. New sites can be used within the site collection to accomplish part of the larger project or collaboration effort on which the site collection is focused.

From a findability perspective, it is a best practice to ensure that the object's display names include spaces and that the descriptions contain appropriate keywords to help make the objects more findable.

## Content Types and the Document Information Panel

Because this topic is covered in such depth in Chapter 9, "Enterprise Content Management," all we need to do in this section is mention that content types and the Document Information Panel (DIP) provide you with a way of ensuring that your content items are tagged or described appropriately to fit your taxonomy needs. You can require certain metadata to be supplied before a document can be saved to a SharePoint location. This is an excellent way to obtain consistent, enterprise-wide tagging of documents in your environment.

## Summary Links Web Part

The Summary Links Web part (Figure 15-4) is a basic Web part to give you the ability to create a browsable set of links to content items or their locations, such as lists or libraries. But because it is a nested list of URLs, you can include any URL-addressable location.

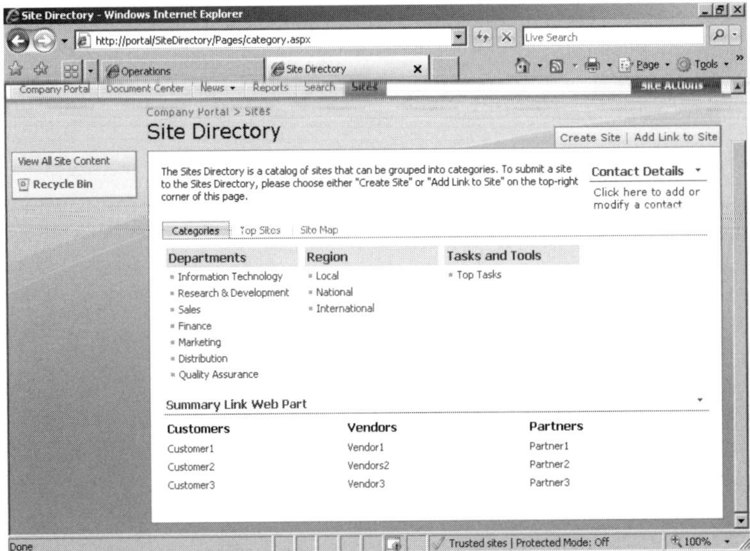


**Figure 15-4** The Summary Links Web part on the Sites Directory page. Note how both the Categories and the Summary Links Web parts are similar, yet serve different functions.

Similar to the Categories Web part, you can use the Summary Links Web part to create categories into which links to URL locations can be created. In concept, the Summary Links Web part is similar to the Categories Web part, but it isn't tied to the creation of a new site collection. Links are created and placed within the overall taxonomy of the Summary Links Web part.

Using multiple Summary Links Web parts, you can create a federated group of Web parts across multiple sites that can provide users a browsable set of links to find information. If you plan to generate a nested set of links that can help you navigate to content items, then using multiple Summary Links Web parts is a good way to achieve this in SharePoint Server 2007.

## My Site and My Site Personalization

In SharePoint Server 2007, you have the option of allowing users to use non-collaborative My Sites by turning on the Use Personal Features right without turning on the Create Personal Sites right. You grant this right through the Personalization Service Permissions in the SSP.

When you use this feature, users retain their My Links personal features. When a user invokes her My Links, the Manage Links option appears at the bottom of the menu list. If the Manage Links option is selected, a My Profile tab appears, along with the links that the user has created for her My Links list.

What's interesting about this feature is that you can grant users the ability to perform the following actions without the ability to collaborate through their My Sites:

- Complete user profiles to increase findability through people search
- Work with their My Links lists to find URL-addressable locations of interest
- Develop their My Colleagues lists to add and edit their colleague information
- Use a Memberships Web part to find the sites and groups in which they are members

In a non-collaborative personal site, what is missing is all of the collaboration tools, such as the following:

- Shared documents
- Shared pictures
- Surveys
- Discussions
- Blogs
- Ability to create new sites and objects

In a collaborative personal site, what many refer to as a *My Site*, users can share information and ideas and can use it as a collaborative platform. Collaborative personal site users also manage most site collection administrative functions. Collaborative personal sites are full-fledged site collections, whereas non-collaborative personal sites are merely pages that host information for a particular user. A site collection does not exist until the user is allowed to use the Create Personal Sites feature to create a collaborative personal site.

The design choices and best practices that arise from this discussion are as follows. First, use non-collaborative personal sites to give users important findability tools without giving them the ability to collaborate through their personal sites. If you decide to wait until phase two or phase three of your deployment before rolling out collaborative personal sites, it is a best practice to turn on the Use Personal Features right so that users can describe themselves, build their user profiles, be findable via search, and use the findability tools that ship with the non-collaborative personal site.

Second, it is a best practice to create two global groups in Active Directory and use those groups to gradually grant users the ability to create collaborative personal sites. If you plan to wait until later phases of your deployment to open up the full functionality of My Site to the users, then first place all of your users in one global group that is assigned only the Use Personal Features right. As individual users are ready to receive a collaborative personal site, move them to another global group that has been given both the Create Personal Sites right and the Use Personal Features right. Using this method, you can slowly introduce collaborative personal sites into your SharePoint deployment.

Third, don't underestimate your users' abilities to get around a non-collaborative personal site. Once they have the ability to create sites at any location, there is nothing to stop them from creating a team site and inviting their peers to the site to share information and ideas. It is a best practice to embrace, manage, and train your users in the use of all of the collaboration tools, including collaborative personal sites.

Finally, you never want to turn off personal sites entirely because you will lose the findability tools that are inherent in the personal features portion of the personal sites. We find that the loss of these tools is worse than whatever pain might be associated with allowing users to use their personal features within SharePoint Server 2007.

My Site Personalization extends the personal features in a non-collaborative or collaborative personal site and is a way to expose disparate URL-addressable locations in their own tabbed interfaces within the My Site interface. Figure 15-5 illustrates how this can be done. Note that both a connection to Windows Live, Fox News, and the BBC News can be coalesced into the same interface. SharePoint locations, such as the home page of your corporate intranet or portal, can be placed here, too. In addition, team sites for defined audiences can be created because these views can be limited to viewing by audience members. Adding frequently accessed sites to the tabbed interface is a great findability feature that can be pushed to the user by you, the administrator.

You'll configure the links to personalization sites in the SSP using the Personalization Site Links menu option, but they will be displayed in the interface of your users' My Sites. Creating these links to personalization sites is not difficult. Simply enter a name for the location, the URL of the location, the owner of the link, and the audience information (if any).

There are some differences in how this feature works. If you link to an external source, such as *www.live.com*, then the new site will take over the entire window in the browser, and your users will not really be in My Site anymore. If you link to the home page of a corporate portal or any publishing site (refer to Figure 15-5), then the navigation bar of the portal will appear, but the tabbed interface of the My Site will be retained, and the tabbed interface of the portal will not appear. If you link to an individual document library or site, you'll be able to work within that list or library while not having to navigate there (Figure 15-6).

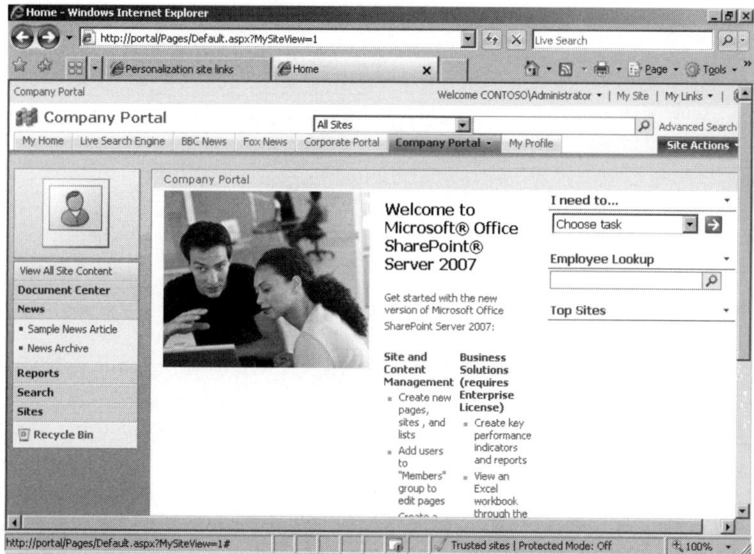


**Figure 15-5** My Site page showing the tabbed interfaces for various public Web sites plus the home page of the corporate portal

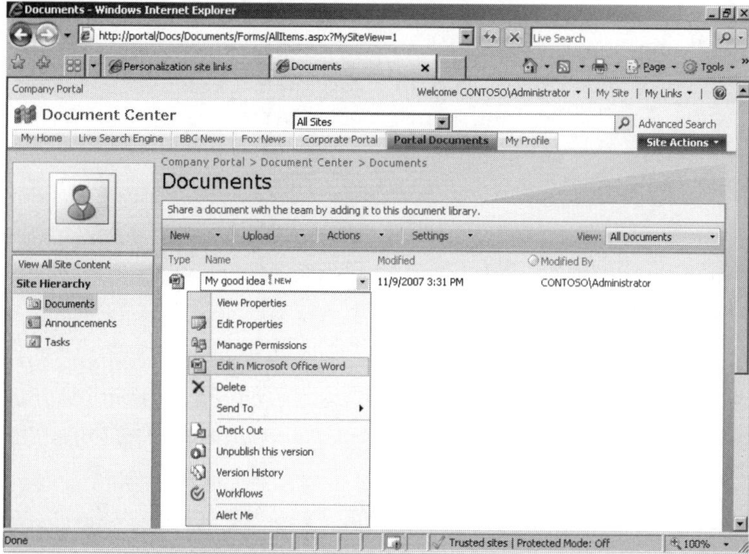


**Figure 15-6** Document library functionality exposed in the Personalization Site feature in a My Site

## Audiences

Audiences are a way to define who can view a list item or Web part on a page. They are not a security feature. You can think of audiences as a way to hide certain content based on who you are when you come to a site or a list. So why would audiences be thought of as a way to do findability in a push method? Because audiences will allow you to make a list item or Web part appear or disappear based on the identity of the user who has connected to the site. So you could, in theory, hide a Web part from most users while allowing a select group of users to see it, thereby pushing the Web part into view when certain people arrive at that site.

There are other, more direct ways to push information to your users, but audiences can certainly be a way to make information appear or disappear based on user characteristics.

## Scopes

From a findability perspective, scopes give users the opportunity to refine their queries so that the result set contains fewer irrelevant content items that it would otherwise have contained had the entire index been queried. This increases findability within the result set because those items that could be realistically classified as false positives are not included in the result set.

From a governance perspective, you need to realize that, while scopes can be created at the SSP level, they can also be created at the site collection level by the site collection administrator. In addition, their creation doesn't mean that they are utilized. It is the site collection administrator who decides which scopes appear in the drop-down lists in the search Web parts. So, from a findability perspective, the site collection administrators are responsible for enabling this feature that will aid your users in obtaining a more refined result set. If you think certain scopes should appear in the search Web parts, you'll need to either work with your site collection administrators to make this happen or make yourself a site collection administrator and implement the scopes topology yourself.

## Records Centers

Closely tied to content types, Records Centers become the repository for official communication that appears in different types of content items, such as documents, e-mails, or other types of communications.

You can enable the findability of official records by using the Records Center feature and creating a farm-wide official Records Center. This center is configured in Central Administration using the Records Center link under the External Service Connections settings on the Application Management tab (Figure 15-7).

Because the successful classification of documents in the Records Center entirely depends on a robust content type deployment, the findability of official documents is greatly enhanced. Not only can you find documents from their metadata assignments, but you can also search the Records Center directly if you've placed that center in its own Web application and then associated it with its own SSP.

When you combine the ability to commit an advanced search on specific metadata that is focused on an individual Web application, the ability to find specific known items increases substantially.

Figure 15-7 Configuring the Records Center in Central Administration

## Galleries

Galleries are special lists that hold objects that are needed in order for a site to work properly. Galleries are ways to organize elements, including the following:

- Site content types
- Site Columns
- Web parts
- Site templates
- List templates
- Workflows
- Master pages and page layouts

Many of these objects are not content items, so they don't appear in the result set when a user executes a query. If you need to find these objects, first focus on the site in which you need to find the object, and then use the appropriate gallery to find what you're after.

# Findability Tools that Support Social Networks and Pull Needs for Users

In this section, we'll discuss some of the findability tools that ship with SharePoint Server 2007 that users can use directly to increase their ability to find certain pieces of information. Note that these tools are nearly all focused on a user's ability to find a specific document or set of documents, whereas the push tools nearly all focus on categorization and the provision of a flexible findability solution across a wide range of content items. In other words, push findability tools tend to be more global in nature, whereas pull findability tools tend to be more limited in nature.

## Microsoft Office Groove

Microsoft Office Groove is a product that can help synchronize document libraries and lists to a local computer, such as a desktop or laptop. Office Groove allows users to synchronize entire document libraries–often in the gigabyte range–to a Groove workspace that is created on the users' local desktop or laptop. The workspace can contain more than one list from the corresponding SharePoint site and can enable those who are often disconnected from their SharePoint farms with the ability to find important information within the Groove workspaces.

Before users can synchronize documents from a SharePoint document library to a Groove workspace, the workspace must first be created. To do this, open Groove 2007 and click the New Workspace link (Figure 15-8).

Give the workspace a name and, for our purposes here, select the Standard Workspace radio button (not illustrated), then click OK. The new workspace will appear automatically. At this point, you'll want to add the SharePoint document library to the workspace. In Groove 2007 terms, this SharePoint document library will be a tool that you can add to the workspace. You'll start that process by clicking the Add Tool link (Figure 15-9) in the Common Tasks section of the workspace.

When you click the Add Tool link, the More Tools selection box will appear. Select the SharePoint Files check box (not illustrated), and then click OK. Once you do this, the SharePoint Files Wizard will appear, and you will click the Setup button (not illustrated) to start the wizard.

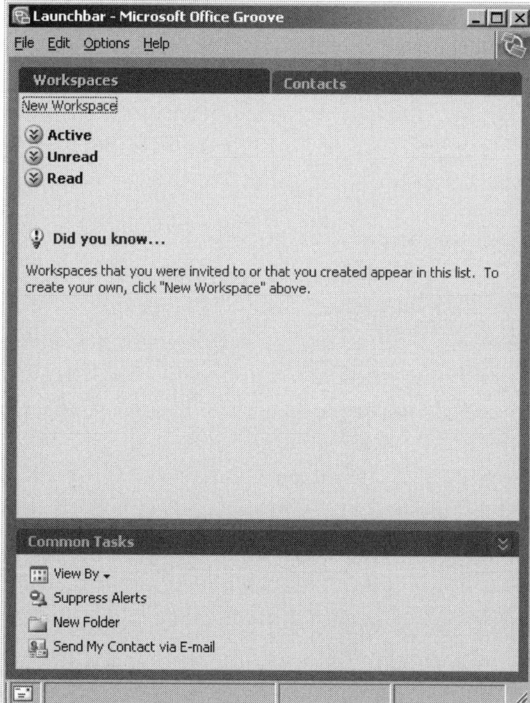


**Figure 15-8** New workspaces in Groove result when you click the New Workspace link from the default Groove 2007 interface.

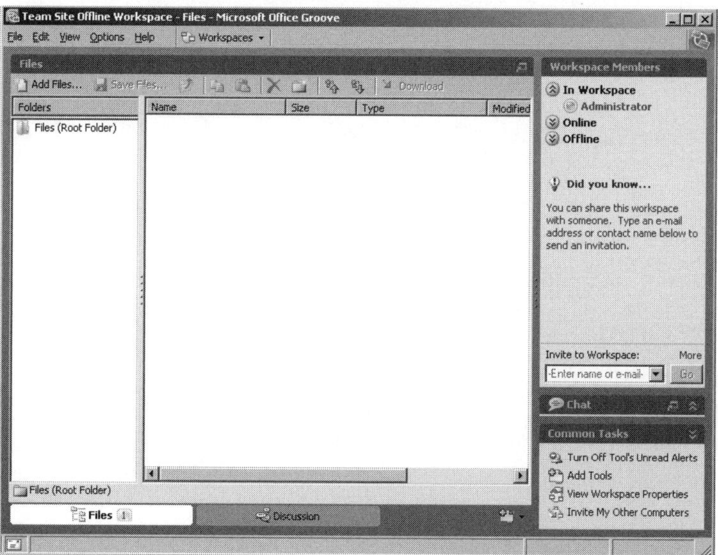


**Figure 15-9** Add Tools link in the Common Tasks section of the standard Groove workspace

The wizard will present you with the Select A Document Library Or Folder dialog box. This is the interface that you'll use to connect to the SharePoint site from which you want to synchronize one or more lists or libraries into your Groove workspace. If this is the first time you're stepping through this wizard, it will focus on the local \windows\system32 folder. To refocus the wizard to a SharePoint site, simply enter the URL of the site (not including the *default.aspx* portion of the URL), and then click the Select button (Figure 15-10).

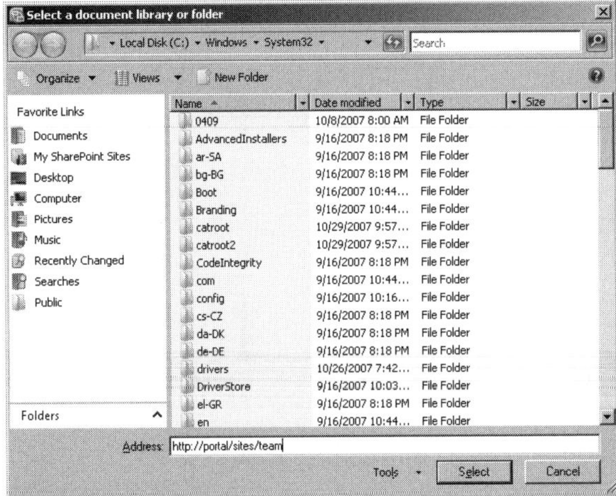


**Figure 15-10** Select A Document Library Or Folder dialog box

The document libraries within the SharePoint site will appear in the dialog box, and the name of the site will appear in the Address input box, as illustrated in Figure 15-11. Highlight the document library you want to synchronize to your local Groove workspace, and then click the Select button.

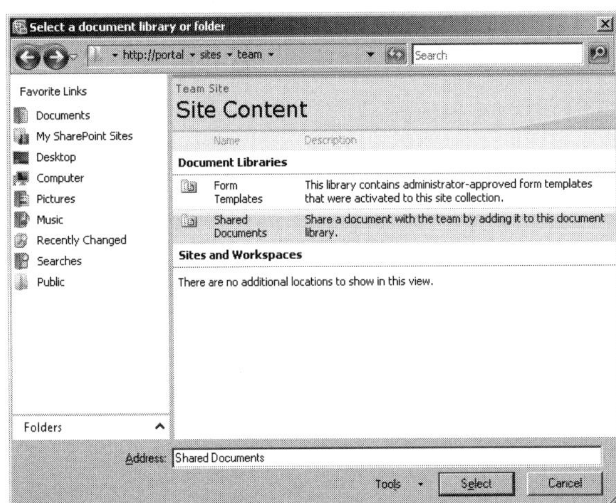


**Figure 15-11** The available document libraries in the SharePoint site appear in the Select A Document Library Or Folder dialog box of the Add Tools Wizard.

After you click the Select button, the documents will synchronize and the workspace tool will open, showing the documents (Figure 15-12). Note that all of the documents were synchronized to the workspace (Figure 15-13).

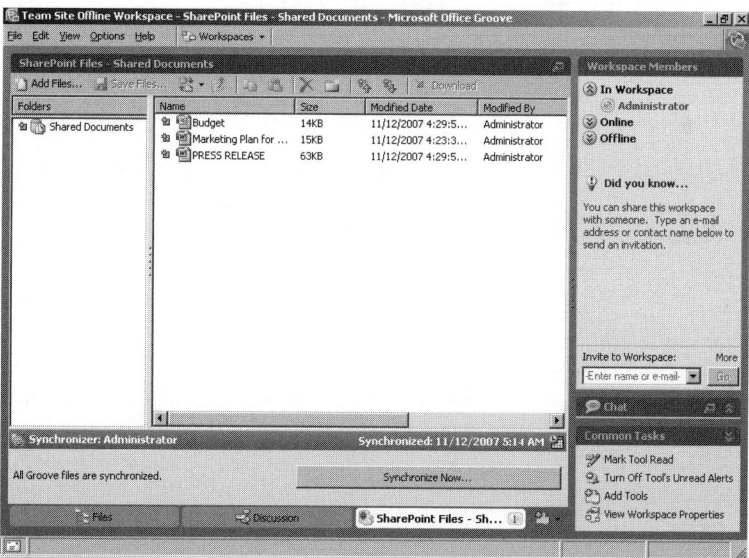


**Figure 15-12** Groove workspace opened to the SharePoint files that were synchronized from the SharePoint server to the Groove workspace

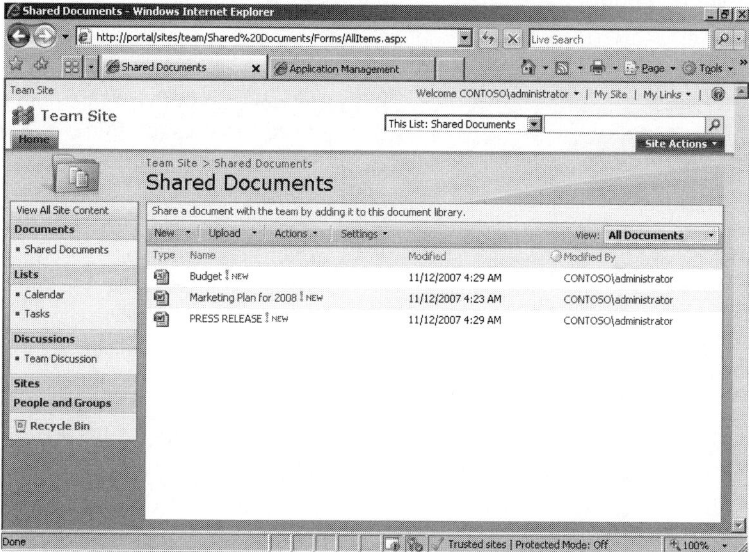


**Figure 15-13** SharePoint document library from which the documents were synchronized to the Groove workspace

Once the documents are synchronized to Groove, you can work with those documents offline and synchronize them back to the SharePoint document library. If the library requires that documents must first be checked out before they are modified, then you'll need to check out the documents in SharePoint before synchronizing them. This action can be performed through the Groove interface if you're able to connect to your SharePoint farm.

> **More Info** There is much more that can be written about using Groove in conjunction with SharePoint installations. If you need additional information about integrating SharePoint and Groove, please consult *Microsoft Office Groove 2007 Step by Step* (Microsoft Press, 2008).

## Wikis and Blogs

Wikis enable users to organize unstructured data into a format that fits their needs because the organization of the data is created entirely by them. Users can create their own Wikis to act as a navigation interface that allows them to organize links, documents, and content based on the ways that they view and work with that information.

Blogs represent one of several ways for a user to collaborate with a large number of people. In SharePoint, there are basically four different collaboration paths, as illustrated in Table 15-3. As you can see, blogs represent a preferred way for an individual to collaborate with the enterprise.

**Table 15-3 Collaboration Paths in SharePoint**

| Collaboration Path | Supporting Technologies | Notes |
|---|---|---|
| 1:1 | ■ E-mail<br>■ Workspaces | In the 1:1 collaboration path, one individual collaborates with one other individual. This path may be fluid as others need to be added to the collaboration group in order for the project or effort to be completed. |
| Many:1 | ■ Portals<br>■ Team Sites<br>■ Wikis | In this path, multiple individuals and teams present their information in a common location for the consumption of an individual user. |
| 1:Many | ■ Blogs<br>■ My Sites<br>■ Wikis | In this path, the individual user offers up ideas, thoughts, insights, and other content to the enterprise, although it is usually consumed by individuals. |
| Many:Many | ■ Blogs<br>■ Wikis<br>■ Team Sites | Here, team blogs, team Wikis, and team sites can offer to other individuals and teams what a particular team is thinking about or planning. |

Blogs give users the opportunity to share their thoughts in an *ad hoc* format with others inside (or outside) the organization. Blogs can also be authored by project teams as a way to keep others in the organization up to date on how their team's work is progressing. But blog sites cannot be tagged with metadata easily, so any search efforts at finding a blog will need to be executed against the blog's content, the content's metadata, the content writer's names, or the blog owner.

Both blogs and Wikis are the best ways to capture tacit knowledge because they can be used to record ideas and thoughts as they occur.

## Social Networking, My Site, and User Profiles

Social networking is the hot focus right now when it comes to findability. People often look to other people to find information, especially when the user is looking for tacit information. By definition, tacit knowledge is knowledge that people carry in their minds and is, therefore, difficult to access and seldom recorded. Sometimes, people can't explain how they know something, yet we find that their intuition or ability to connect seemingly disparate pieces of information relative to a given context renders highly valuable conclusions or insights. This type of information is very difficult to write down or record in some permanent way. Effective transfer of tacit knowledge generally requires extensive personal contact and trust and is not easily shared. By contrast, explicit knowledge is easily shared and recorded. Documents and Web pages are common forms of explicit knowledge.

Social networks are a good way to find people who have tacit knowledge–*if* the people are described properly. This is why the accurate tagging of people via their user profiles is so important. If you can't find the right people to gain the right information, then social networking becomes nearly irrelevant unless the value of interacting with people online seems to aid your organization's overall culture, which could be true in organizations in which the user base is highly dispersed.

### Notes from the Field **Taxonomy and Social Networking Coexistence**

In most of the designs that we do for our customers, we find that many want to push out their implementation of My Site to the second or third phase of the overall rollout. Not only do most of our customers release SharePoint in small doses to their user base, but they also incrementally release SharePoint's features and functions to their user base as the users become more familiar and trained on the new functionality.

Most customers seem to value collaboration and understand how a solid taxonomy can help them achieve findability of their information within their SharePoint Server 2007 implementation. Sometimes, however, there is a lack of understanding about how My Site and, more generally, social networking fit into the overall picture.

We often remind customers that social networks are good indicators of users' interests and can serve as effective locations in which ad hoc collaboration can exist. We need social networking in our environments to connect people with people. For example, users who manage company social clubs can easily host a site in their My Site for the members to collaborate on agendas, location maps, attendees, and so on. But if there is a lack of taxonomy, social networking can become chaotic. For example, if we don't use a consistent set of descriptors to build our user profiles, then users will be left to describe themselves, and their choice of descriptors will be random and inconsistent. This will reduce the findability of people in your organization.

Best practice is to embrace both social networks and taxonomies, understanding that the first will move quickly and fluidly while the latter will provide stability and continuity for your collaboration environment. Also, use the SharePoint Server 2007 administrative tools, such as User Profile Policy Management, to your advantage for social networking.

*Steve Smith, Microsoft MVP, Combined Knowledge*

My Site and Groove represent the two best methods of enabling social networking in today's version of SharePoint Server 2007. My Site gives your users the ability to collaborate with the enterprise, sharing documents, preferences, and ideas with those who might be interested. Groove gives your users the ability to dynamically create communities of interest, whether those communities are offline or online. One of the hallmarks of social networking solutions is the ability of users to dynamically create collaboration spaces that can represent communities of interest in a peer-to-peer environment. While SSSC enables users to create these communities within SharePoint, SharePoint sites are not peer-to-peer. In addition, if those communities require offline or outside user (users who need to belong to the social community but who are not allowed to log in to your SharePoint environment) capabilities, Groove is a good solution to implement.

In addition, social networks have one strong inherent problem to overcome: They are based on *people* who behave in inconsistent ways and who can do a lot of things to hinder a great social networking deployment. For example, let's say that you're learning about shooting digital cameras in low-light situations. Let's assume that you've tried and tried to get high-quality photos in low-light situations, but you're simply unable to figure out how to shoot the type of photos that you desire to shoot. So you go online and find a social network that is dedicated to shooting photos in low-light situations. You try to join the site, only to find that the person running the site is an old enemy of yours from days gone by, and you are denied access to the group. So, in this case, past human interactions block you from working with people who could help you.

Or consider the situation in which you can't find the right social network to help you find the information you need, so you start your own social network in the hopes of attracting people who possess the tacit knowledge you're after. But after working with your group for a while and attracting some people, you find that other groups *do* exist that could have connected you to the right information, but you were unable to find them. The solution to this kind of scenario would be to ensure that the social networks are consistently described and tagged so that redundant groups are not needlessly created. So, now we're back to building a taxonomy.

In the end, findability of people and social groups will require a taxonomy of some sort, whether you're tagging user profiles, content types, or some other hierarchy. If you want to make findability the organizing principle of your SharePoint deployment, then you'll end up building at least one–and probably several–taxonomies.

## Membership Web Part

One of the cool findability tools that ships with the SharePoint Server 2007 My Site is the Membership Web part (Figure 15-14). This Web part appears by default on both the private view and the public view of a user's My Site.

**Figure 15-14** Membership Web part in a user's My Site

What the Membership Web part does, essentially, is list users' memberships in sites and distribution groups so that users can find the sites and groups in which they are members. Users can then use the list to navigate to individual sites. As users work in an increasing number of sites, the usefulness of this Web part becomes more apparent, allowing users to find Web sites they have forgotten about or cannot find quickly.

In terms of findability training, best practice would be to train your users on how to use the Membership Web part to find sites in which they are members quickly and easily.

## Summary

In this chapter, we have learned about findability and the inherent problems that findability and search present when you try to implement them in a SharePoint environment. Best practices on how to manage the index and query server roles have been presented, as well as some ideas on when you'll want to use the federated query features in Search Server 2008. Finally, we briefly reviewed the findability tools that ship with SharePoint Server 2007, with a view to helping you understand what you'll need to implement a robust findability solution in SharePoint Server 2007.

## Additional Resources


- *Ambient Findability: What We Find Changes Who We Become.* Peter Morville (O'Reilly Media Inc., 2005).
- *The Long Tail: Why the Future of Business is Selling Less of More.* Chris Anderson (Hyperion, 2006).
- *Information First: Integrating Knowledge and Information Architecture for Business Advantage.* Roger Evernden and Elaine Evernden (Butterworth-Heinemann, 2003).
- Microsoft's social computing site, full of ideas from Microsoft on how to plan, build, and implement social networking using SharePoint Server 2007: *http://www.microsoft.com/sharepoint/capabilities/collaboration/social.mspx.*

Chapter 16

# Leveraging Shared Services Providers

**In this chapter:**



Microsoft Office SharePoint Server 2007 Shared Services are a set of centralized utilities or services that are consumed at the site collection layer while their association with a Shared Services Provider (SSP) is accomplished at the Web application layer. A good analogy for Shared Services is your local utility provider. While you could burn coal to generate the needed electricity for your home or business, it is almost always more cost efficient to purchase a shared utility from a public provider. Usually, all of your public utilities are provided by a single entity, but sometimes you might consume water and sewage service from one public utility provider and electricity from another. Office SharePoint Server 2007 Shared Services can work in much the same way. Figure 16-1 shows a rough analogy between Shared Services and a local utility provider.

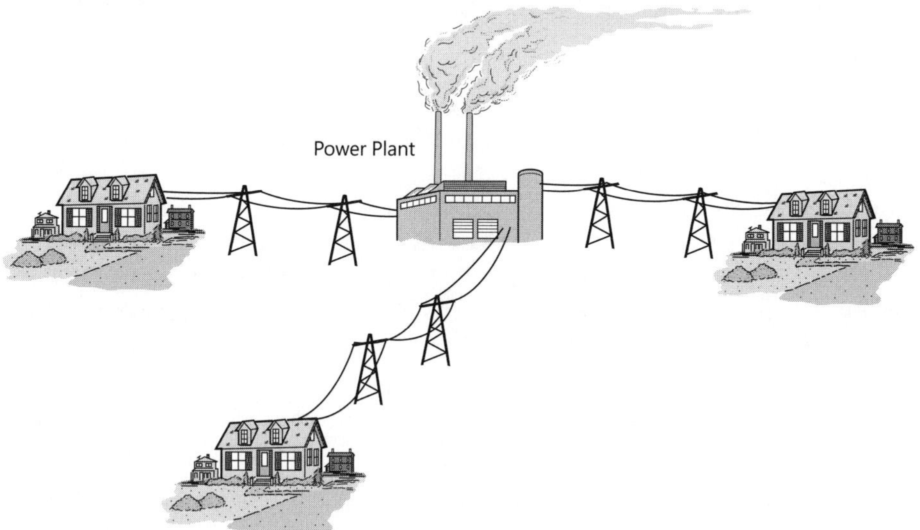


**Figure 16-1** Shared Services are much like your public utilities provider.

For example, you could consume Excel Services from your local SSP, yet consume a My Site Provider from a different SSP, and everything else from a third. While most Shared Services must be consumed from a single provider, the previous example shows what is possible. Obviously, multiple SSPs complicate your design and will not be commonly implemented. We merely want to show you the flexibility of SharePoint Server 2007 Shared Services. This chapter will discuss the Shared Services provided by SharePoint Server 2007 and methods for implementing them in intranet, extranet, and Internet scenarios. Specifically, this chapter will cover the following:

- Best practices using the Shared Services
- Intra-farm versus Inter-farm Shared Services
- Designing Shared Services
- Geographically dispersed Shared Services implementations

This chapter will assist you with commonly asked questions, such as:

- Why do I create an SSP?
- How do I leverage Shared Services?
- When should I use Shared Services?

Whatever your focus is with SharePoint Server 2007, whether it is automating business processes, document management, collaboration, or content-driven Web sites, SharePoint Server 2007 Shared Services provide a centralized set of utilities to be consumed by all of your Web applications that will reduce your total cost of ownership (TCO) and enhance the user experience.

# What Shared Services Are Provided with SharePoint Server 2007?

If you are looking for technical specifics on installing Shard Services Providers, you should reference either the *Microsoft SharePoint Products and Technologies Administrator's Pocket Consultant* (Microsoft Press, 2007) or the *Microsoft Office SharePoint Server 2007 Administrator's Companion* (Microsoft Press, 2007) for details. Both cover details of SSP installation and configuration. This best practices chapter will answer more high-level questions and design points, showing detailed implementation examples only where necessary. Depending on which version of SharePoint Server 2007 you installed, either Standard or Enterprise, your Shared Services will vary slightly. Those differences are pointed out respectively in the following sections. There will first be an overview of individual best practices with Shared Services and then deployment best practices as a whole.

## Search

Search is easily the "hot" Shared Service and drives many customers to purchase SharePoint Server 2007. SharePoint Server 2007 Search services provides the standard indexing and basic querying one would expect from any vendor, but adds many services such as search scopes, managed properties, and advanced search capabilities. These services are provided to any site collection that is hosted in a Web application that is associated with a specific SSP. While this association may sound complicated, it really isn't. Figure 16-2 shows how the Search service is consumed by a site.

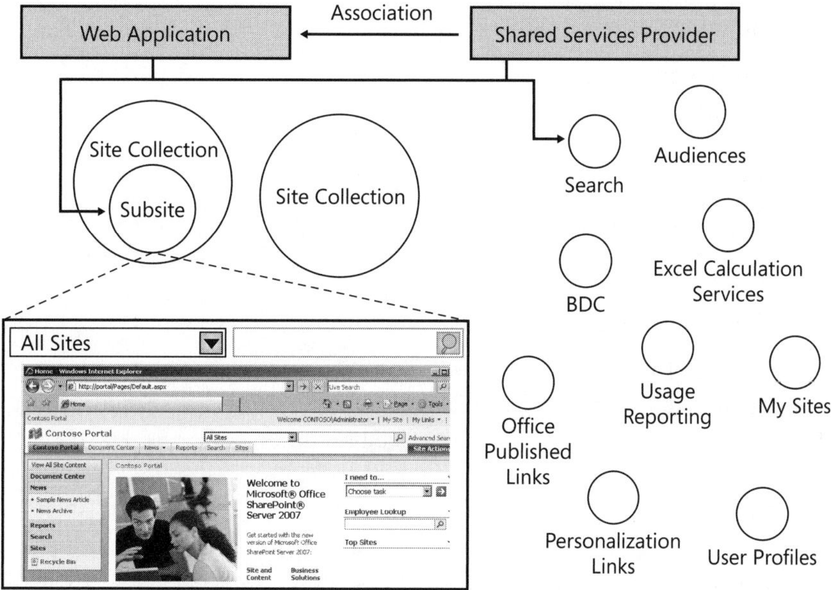


**Figure 16-2** Sites consume Search Shared Services from the hosting Web application's association with an SSP.

Search design best practices are detailed in Chapter 15, "Implementing an Optimal Search and Findability Topology," so we will only discuss Search in this chapter as it applies to a Shared Services design best practices. It is important to understand the difference in this context: We need to design an SSP using best practices that in turn hosts a Search provider. It is a best practice to implement a single SSP and therefore a single Search provider. Because an SSP can host only a single Search provider, the requirement of multiple Search providers greatly complicates your SSP design. If you are not sure if you should create a second SSP to support a second Search provider, don't! If you decide not to heed this advice, let us give you an example of what the outcome could be.

Let's assume you created a second SSP to support another Search provider. Let's also assume you had a robust default SSP implementation that included Search, audiences, personalization site links, and My Sites. After creating your second SSP and Search provider, you realize you cannot consume that provider unless you change the hosting Web application's association with the default SSP (see Figure 16-2), so you change the association and can now consume your new SSP provider. But you quickly realize all of your audience targeted Web parts fail, My Sites cease to work, user profiles (think People Search) doesn't work, and the next day Microsoft Office 2007 applications start losing their custom "Save To" locations! Because you re-associated with a new SSP, you have lost all of the functionality of the previous SSP. Now you have a mess to clean up that will not be an easy task. So we will restate the best practice of carefully planning for multiple SSPs.

## User Profiles

User profiles are a strong selling point in SharePoint Server 2007. User profiles are not used for authentication; they are used for exposing descriptive information about people. Many times we are looking for *someone* who possesses knowledge about a subject, and not simply a keyword search for documents. This is the first benefit of user profiles in your environment—finding people who possess *tacit* knowledge about a subject by using the information that describes them.

> **Note** Tacit knowledge was discussed briefly in Chapter 1. Tacit knowledge is generalized as "know-how" or "institutional knowledge." It is the undocumented knowledge that people have in their heads.

This profile information is gained through either importing the content from an LDAP (Lightweight Directory Access Protocol), or through direct input from the users themselves. While the best practice is usually to obtain this information from an LDAP import, there are times when gathering this information directly from the user is beneficial. First, let's look at information imported from an LDAP. You can import metadata about a user directly from any LDAP, such as Active Directory, but that content is limited to what is stored in that LDAP. For example, SharePoint Server 2007 can leverage the hierarchal management structure in your organization for audiences and search scopes. For that information to be valid and applicable, you must have populated the "reports to" field correctly in your Active Directory. In general, your imported information is only as good as the source. SharePoint Server 2007 doesn't magically find information about people in your environment; it would cost substantially more if it did! The second method we have for populating properties about a user is directly from the users themselves. This input is gathered through personal feature pages, as shown in Figure 16-3, or My Site User details shown in Figure 16-4. Notice the URL is the same in both of the following figures, but the entry point is different.

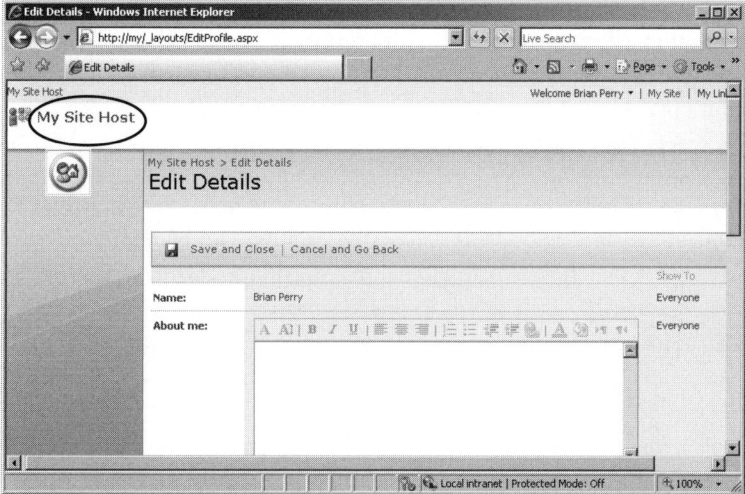


Figure 16-3 Users who do not have a My Site can edit profile details in a personalization page.

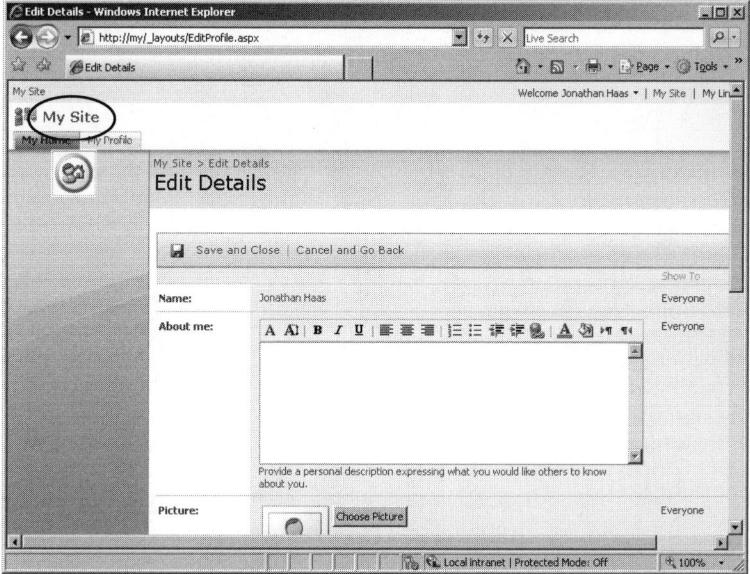


Figure 16-4 My Site users can edit their profile details from within their respective My Site.

Through both of the personal details pages, we can collect user information such as technical skill set, likes and dislikes, and any other discriminating information about that person. These properties can then be used to define audiences for targeting content or to create custom search scopes. Think about the possibility of searching the content of all users whose specialty is database design, circuit design, or any specific technology about which they are experts. This allows your organization to identify *who knows what* in your organization. Consider it a best practice to *immediately* start using personal details pages, even if you will not implement My Sites. You can always leverage the same content in their My Sites later. Users will quickly begin using People Search against these profiles if the correct metadata exists.

## Published Links to Office Applications

Published Links to Office Applications assists you in the arena of relevance. Remember, two of your primary goals with SharePoint Server 2007 are timeliness and relevance. Publishing links to Office applications such as Word, Excel, or PowerPoint allows you to populate the "Save As" locations in Office 2007 applications based on *who* a user is. For example, you could have the public document library in the accounting site collection be available in the Office client for every person in the *Accounting* Active Directory group. This is very powerful and tailors SharePoint Server 2007 functionality for groups within your organization. Figure 16-5 shows where this link will appear in your Office 2007 client.

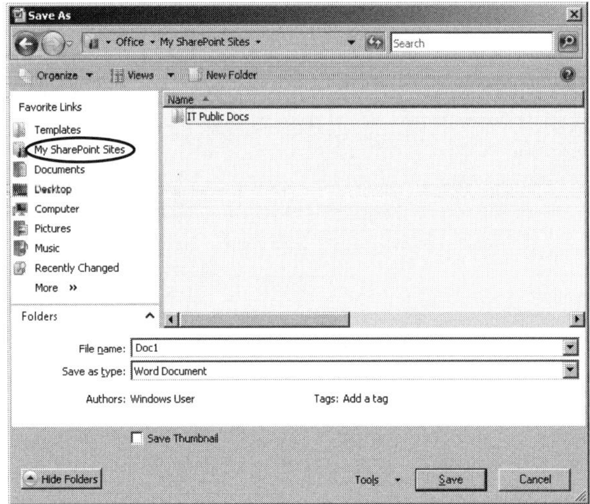


**Figure 16-5** You must have Office 2007 or higher to see the "Save As" locations correctly.

The best practices here are rather simple. Do not publish numerous links to the same person. Too many links usually get ignored, thus negating their functionality. Ten to twenty links would be a good maximum target number, unless you have specific requirements to do otherwise.

By default, the Office client gets these links updates via its association with an SSP. When a client first visits his or her My Site, they are asked if they want to make it their default, or they can select the link in their My Site home page, as demonstrated in the following images.

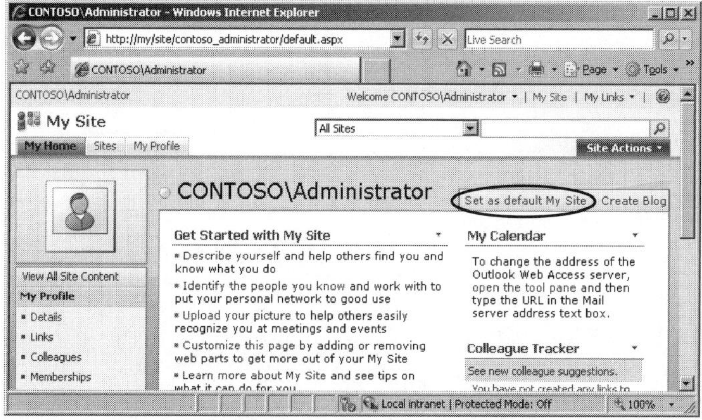


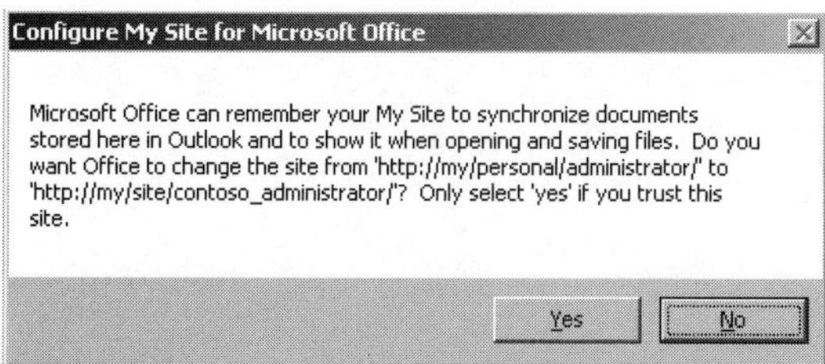


By choosing this My Site to be their default, they will now pull information from the SSP that hosts the My Site Provider every 24 hours. Figure 16-6 shows a logical diagram of how a client gets information from published links.

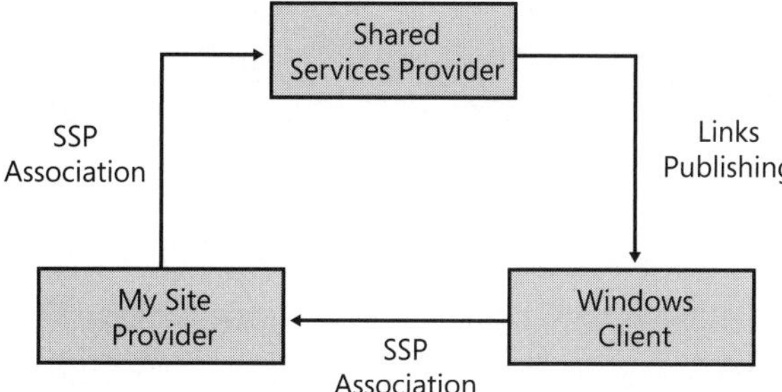


**Figure 16-6** A Windows client gets published links via its My Site Provider information.

In most implementations, it is a best practice to leave the scheduling defaults alone for this setting. Changing the defaults to a more frequent schedule can substantially increase the traffic to your SSPs and decrease performance. The more clients you have pulling these updates, the more apparent the performance decrease will be.

> **Note** You can change the frequency that your Windows clients pull this setting by adding "LinkPublishingFrequency" to *HKEY_CURRENT_USER\Software\Microsoft\Office\12.0\Common\Portal* with a value in seconds.

# Personalization Site Links

Personalization Site Links are very different than Published Links, but are often confused. Personalization Site Links allows you to target content to My Site Global navigation, also called *top link bars*, en masse or by targeting users and groups. For example, let's assume you have Active Directory groups that are organized by Building Number. You can then target information based on the building a user is located in. Figure 16-7 shows an example of targeting an activity only to users in a specific building using Site Links.

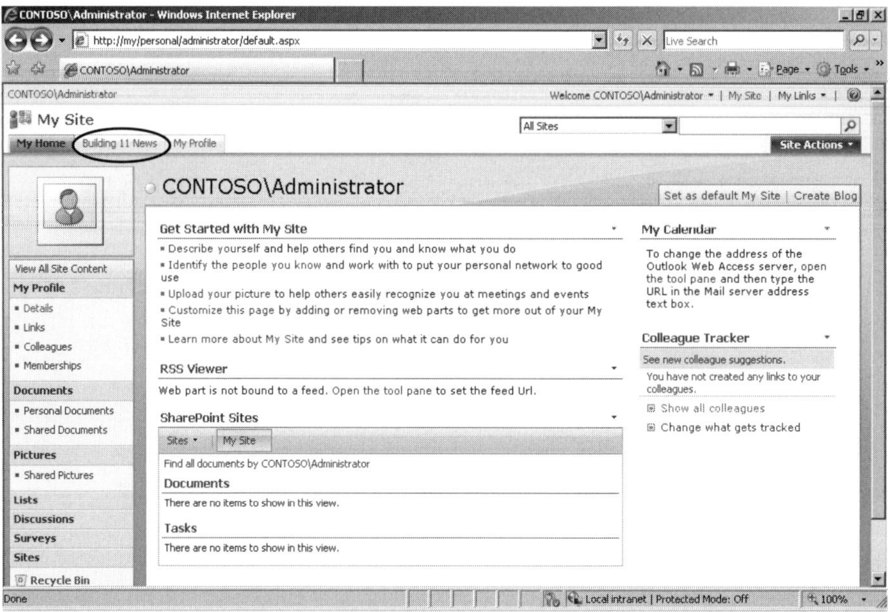


**Figure 16-7** You can target information on top link bars to specific users, based on the Active Directory group.

Once again, the best practice is that fewer links are better. The fewer links a user has on their top link bars, the more likely they are to use them.

## Exposing Publishing Portal Sites in the My Site Global Navigation

An often overlooked option of personalization site links is the ability to view Publishing site links in the My Site. When configured, the My Site navigation is retained even after browsing to the Publishing site. Figure 16-8 shows how a link to the *Sites* directory of a collaboration portal would appear when targeted to a My Site. Figure 16-9 shows the navigation structure *after* browsing to the Sites directory.

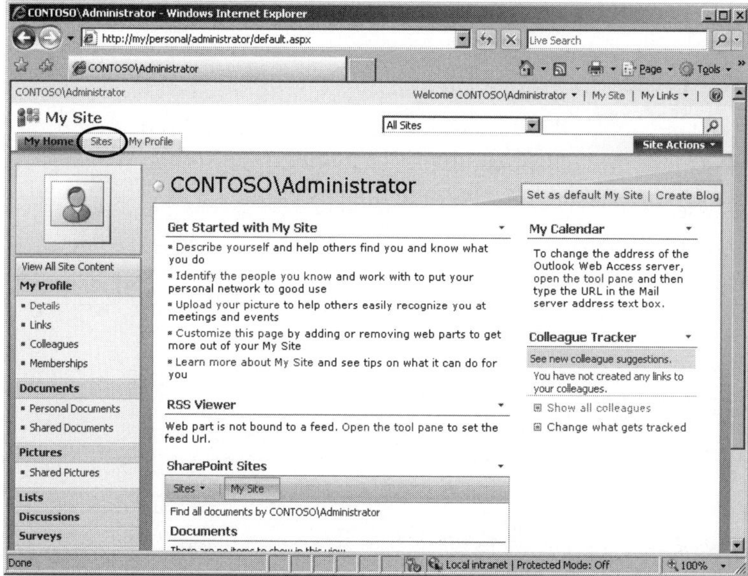


**Figure 16-8** You can expose Publishing site navigation to your My Sites.

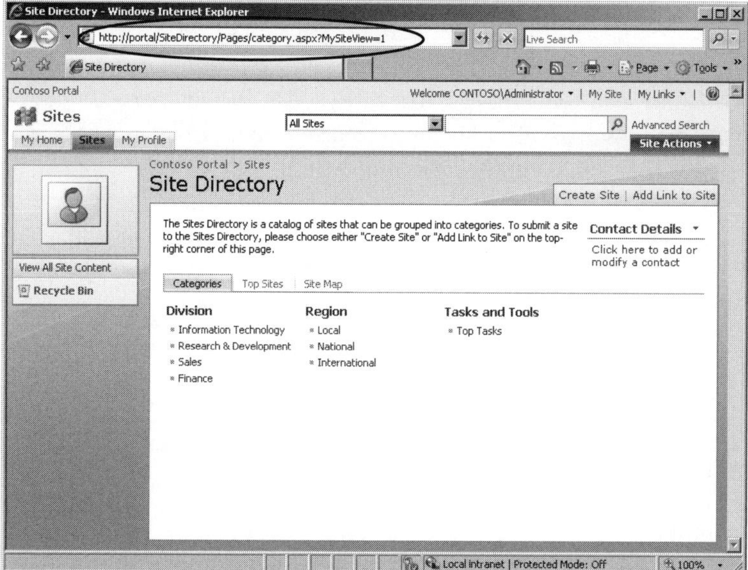


**Figure 16-9** After browsing to the Publishing site, you will still see the My Site global navigation.

If you want your users to start with a combined view of their environment—both personal and corporate—then have them start with their own My Site and expose the key corporate sites they need to visit on their My Site tab structure using this Personalization Sites Link feature.

## Audiences

As was discussed in the previous two sections, *audiences* are a very powerful piece of functionality in your SharePoint Server 2007 design. Audiences allow you to target information to users based on their Active Directory groups, SharePoint groups (when synchronized with Directory Management Services), or user profile information.

> **Note** At the time this book was published, using Active Directory Universal groups for audiences was a best practice. Universal groups expand differently on the Global Catalog server and provide a more consistent experience for the users. Be aware that SharePoint Server 2007 creates global groups, by default, when implementing Directory Management Services. Some organizations have also had success with local groups. Be sure to check Technet for the most up-to-date information.

From a big picture point of view, think about audiences as increasing relevance. Let's look at the following scenario. You are a SharePoint Server 2007 administrator at a university. Your users are university staff and students, and everyone visits the same portal URL. You want to provide a relevant portal experience so that students see student news, and the staff sees staff news. You would first create two audiences, one for staff members, and one for students. Then, place two News Web parts on your portal home page. In the Web part properties, target the audiences in the advanced settings. Now, students will see student news, and staff will see staff news. What if a user is in both groups? They will see both Web parts. Audiences can be used on individual objects in a list also, *but only the default content type can be targeted.* Audiences can also be used to tweak your Search configuration. For example, you could have several search Web parts in your Search center, each with different functionality, targeted to groups in your organization. A problem audiences do not solve easily, however, is the ability to have users *choose* their audience "on the fly."

> **Note** To use SharePoint groups as audience members in Shared Services administration, you must first e-mail-enable those SharePoint groups at the site level. Then, those synchronized distribution lists are available when building global audiences in SSP administration.

## My Sites

My Site functionality is detailed in Microsoft Press books and TechNet extensively. Therefore, the following section is an overview of the implementation best practices. First, My Sites provide a personal portal, or a one-to-many collaboration site. Besides the advantages of providing an easily accessible and portable personal workspace for your users, we can collect user profile information, surface critical information in the global navigation, and provide further integration with Microsoft Outlook through Meeting Workspaces.

For most organizations, a single My Site provider is sufficient. A key to Shared Services implementation is that simpler is better. Unless you are geographically dispersed or have some other specific requirement, you only need a single provider. A My Site provider is simply a Web application that will host My Sites. The first best practice is to always create a My Host site collection in the root managed path of a Web application dedicated to hosting My Sites. Figure 16-10 shows the configuration screen in Central Administration to create this site collection.

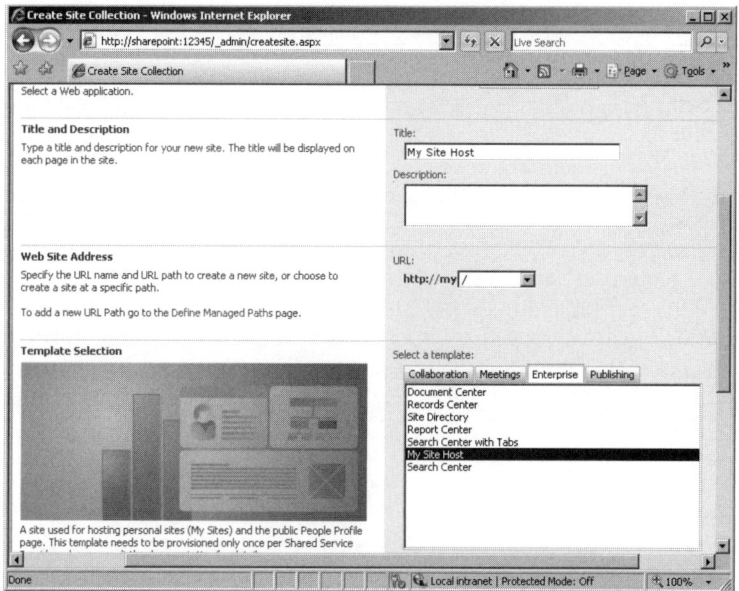


**Figure 16-10** Create a My Site Host site collection in the provider's root managed path.

This My Site Host provides two primary functions. First, users can simply browse to the root of this Web application and be redirected to their individual My Site automatically. For our example scenario we will use *http://MY* as the My Site provider, which is simply a Web application. Second, it provides the entry point to crawl user profile information. Using the *sps3://* protocol handler in Search content sources, you can index user profile information to make it available to queries. Be sure to name the My Site Host site collection something meaningful because the name will be seen by users without My Sites.

> **Note** Remember that you are using the crawling engine to import user profile information. This is important when troubleshooting errors, because user profile import errors are usually *Search* errors.

When creating an SSP, you are asked to select a My Site location. This location is referred to as a Provider, Web application, and location. The naming convention in SharePoint Server 2007 is fairly inconsistent in regard to My Site providers. Just remember that all three define the same object. Unless you have a specific requirement, always create a dedicated Web application to host My Sites. Why, you ask?

- You can easily leverage Web application policies to define security levels for all My Sites in a given Web application.
- You can change the available permission levels to all My Sites from Central Administration.
- You can more easily define content database design.
- Backup and Restore is simplified because portal and team sites are not in the same Web application as My Sites.
- You can create zones for the My Site Web application to allow modified access externally, via a different URL.
- Your users can browse to the root (like *http://my*) and automatically be redirected to their respective My Site.

  You are given the option to create a My Site provider during SSP creation. Figure 16-11 shows where you create the My Site provider.

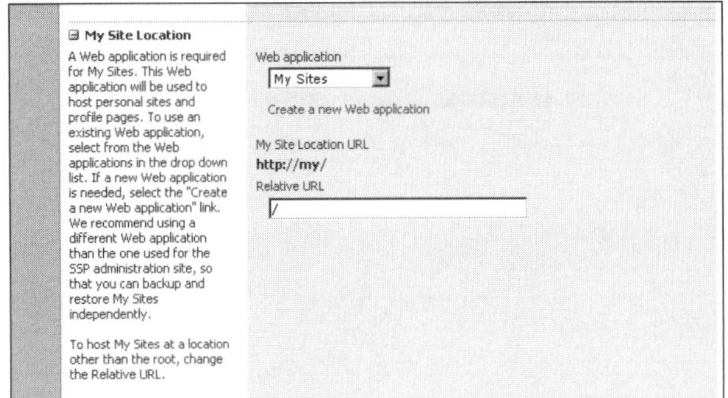


**Figure 16-11** You have the option to create a My Site provider during SSP creation time.

> **Note** Always have at least one indexer started before beginning the SSP creation process. If not, you will not be able to finish the SSP creation.

While this location can be overridden by configuring Trusted My Site Locations, it is best to get it right the first time. Another interesting note about the creation of a My Site location is the *relative URL*. This is simply a managed path that is named *personal* by default. You can create a managed path named anything you want and use it. A common My Site managed path is *site*. If your My Site provider was created as *http://MY*, then the complete path will be *http://my/site/username*. This is user friendly and makes it easy to do bulk maintenance on My Sites. The globalization of My Sites is covered later in this chapter for large deployments.

## Excel Services

Excel Services provide many functions, such as in-browser viewing of workbooks and worksheets, centralized processing and caching, and abstraction of spreadsheets without exposing proprietary formulas. Excel Services best practices are covered in-depth in Chapter 18, "Business Intelligence and Reporting." This section is merely for your implementation and design best practices.

First, Excel services can be consumed only by the local SharePoint Server 2007 farm. That is, you cannot share Excel Services between farms. Second, Excel Services self load-balances when the service is started on multiple machines. If you require configuration information, you should reference the Microsoft Press administrator guides and companions, or MSDN and TechNet.

## Business Data Catalog

When planning and designing for the Business Data Catalog, it's all about entities and methods. The Business Data Catalog relies on an application definition file to connect to almost any structured content. When generating your application definition file, you are going to be creating things called *entities*. For programmers who are used to object-orientated programming, entities will make sense. You need to think of the entities that you define as being real-world objects that people want to display data about, for example customers, products, or orders. If you are lucky, these entities will be unique tables from your database; however, in more complex scenarios, you may be constructing joins across tables with SQL statements.

Once you have decided upon your entities, you need to create methods for them. Which methods you define depends on what you want to do with your Line-of-Business data in SharePoint. If you want to display the information in the BDC List Web Part, you need to create a finder method. For using Business Data Columns in your lists or document libraries, you need a Finder and SpecificFinder method. For MOSS to be able to crawl your entity so you can search the data, you'll need to create an IdEnumerator and SpecificFinder method. Also, for searching make sure your default content access account has the necessary permissions to execute Business Data Catalog applications and entities.

If you are looking to make use of your Line-of-Business data through Web services, you need to ensure your Web services are presenting data in a way in which MOSS 2007 can use it. As our entities have Finder, SpecificFinder and IdEnumerator methods, we must have Web services for each entity that presents data for these methods. For example, if we want to create a Product entity that we will access through Web services, we would create Web methods:

- **GetProducts-Finder** Returns a list of product data.
- **GetProductById-SpecificFinder** Will accept the entity identifier as a parameter and return the data for a single product.
- **GetProductIds-IdEnumerator** Simply returns a list of product IDs.

Quite often, it is easier to wrap third-party Web services with your own custom Web service methods to present the data in a way that the Business Data Catalog can use.

> **Note** Microsoft has released a free tool to assist in generating the XML for your application definition file, but it requires many manual steps of editing XML and understanding the underlying schema in great detail. The BDC Meta Man tool has been developed to help you generate your application definition files with a wizard style interface, meaning you don't have to edit XML by hand. You can download BDC Meta Man and watch many screencasts of the Business Data Catalog in action at *http://www.lightningtools.com/bdc-meta-man/default.aspx*.

## Intra-Farm versus Inter-Farm Shared Services

Assuming you have a solid understanding of Shared Services in SharePoint Server 2007, and what they provide, we next investigate the differences of Inter-farm SSPs and Intra-farm SSPs. *Intra-farm* SSPs are multiple SSPs within the same SharePoint Server 2007 farm. Remember that *farm = configuration database,* so Intra-farm SSPs will all share a common configuration database. First, most installations should have a single SSP. The best practice is to have as few as possible. While it is feasible to have up to 20 SSPs in a single farm, it overcomplicates your configuration and management and is rarely needed. Index and query functions are the primary reasons to create a second SSP in a single farm. Real-world experience has shown four SSPs to be the real performance limit in a SharePoint Server 2007 farm.

*Inter-farm* SSPs are created for several reasons, but usually for performance increases or process isolation. First, large implementations sometimes build entire SharePoint Server 2007 server farms for the sole purpose of providing Shared Services. This allows dedicated hardware and software for things like searching, queries, Business Data Catalog, and truly global audiences. Second, creating a second SSP can create a boundary between the Shared Services being provided and the consuming SharePoint Server 2007 farm.

There are limitations to Inter-farm Shared Services, however. The first limitation is that Excel Calculation Services cannot be provided or consumed between server farms. This is rarely an issue, but it is one that must be planned for. Second, you cannot consume Shared Services over a Wide Area Network. There is a lot of gray area between a local gigabit network and a regional network, such as a campus area network. A good rule of thumb for Inter-farm service design is that you must control the fiber that connects two server hosting points. So dark fiber that you light, connections between campus buildings, and high-speed regional links might work. You should consult Microsoft with your specific design if you will cross network connections that are not on the same Local Area Network (LAN). It probably depends on who you ask at Microsoft whether you will be supported or not. Whatever the answer–get it in writing.

## Designing Intra-Farm Shared Services

As previously mentioned, one SSP is sufficient for most installations. The following are some requirements that might force multiple Intra-farm SSPs:

- Hosting multiple Web applications in a charge-back mode for internal customers. Each customer may require a different set of Shared Services.
- Sarbanes-Oxley (SOX) or HIPPA regulations might require a separate SSP for Records Management.
- Specialized organization units such as legal or human resources.

Multiple Intra-farm SSPs should not be considered when absolute isolation is required for security. Some server roles, such as Excel Calculation Services and Search queries, cannot be isolated to a specific SSP. If you require absolute isolation for security, you should consider hosting Shared Services in an entirely different server farm.

> **Note** You cannot associate query servers with a specify index server. Each query server in the farm will build indexes, and return query results, for all SSPs in the farm. If you require query server isolation, you must build a second SharePoint Server 2007 server farm. You also cannot associate Excel Calculation Services servers with a specific SSP.

Multiple SSPs in the same farm allow for dedicated Shared Services for one or many Web applications. Figure 16-12 shows a possible logical architecture of a SharePoint Server 2007 server farm using three SSPs.

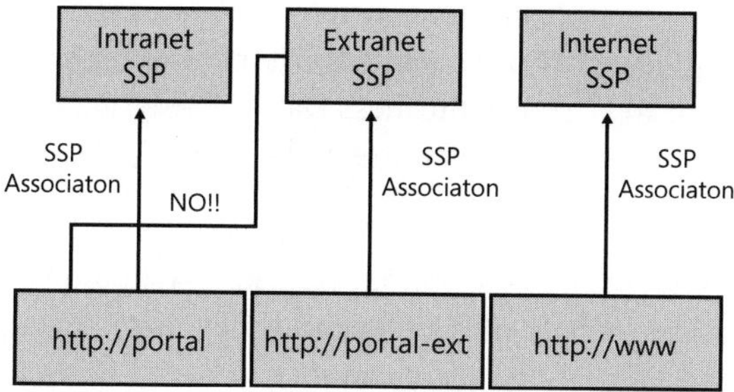


**Figure 16-12** Each Web application can be associated with one SSP.

Each farm must have a default SSP. You may have multiple Intra-farm SSPs, but one of those must be the default. The default SSP is associated, by default, with all new Web applications in the farm. You can change the association later if desired.

> **Note** You cannot delete the default SSP. If you want to replace the default SSP, you must create another SSP, make it the default, and then delete the original.

> **Important** Use caution when re-associating Web applications with SSPs. All site settings that are inherited from an SSP, such as search scopes, audiences, Excel Calculation Services, and My Site settings, will be lost.

## Designing Inter-Farm Shared Services

Inter-farm Shared Services implementations are much rarer than Intra-farm Shared Services, but can still serve a useful purpose when there are requirements for process isolation for the reasons of performance and security. Inter-farm Shared Services are the consuming of Shared Services from another SharePoint Server 2007 server farm. There are some limitations when consuming Shared Services from another farm, such as:

1. Cannot be consumed over a WAN.
2. Excel Calculation Services cannot be shared Inter-farm.
3. You must provide authentication between farms.
4. You cannot consume another Shared Service, such as Search or Audiences, on a per-service basis. With the exception of My Sites, you must consume the entire provider's Shared Services, or none.

At first glance, many administrators have planned to use a centralized farm for organizational Shared Services, and then provide these services to geographically dispersed SharePoint Server 2007 server farms. Because the consuming farm is actually making a SQL connection to the provider's Shared Services database, WAN connections are not possible. It is very likely you could make it work with a low latency, high-speed connection. Be aware that it is not supported by Microsoft. If you have a geographically dispersed environment, read the last section in this chapter, "Geographically Dispersed Deployments."

So why implement Inter-farm Shared Services? If you create a dedicated, centralized SSP, you can offload the overhead of these services from your production collaboration and publishing farms. The following scenario assumes the purpose of multiple farms is for performance, but the same logical designs will work for security as well. Figure 16-13 shows an example of a dedicated server farm for a centralized SSP.

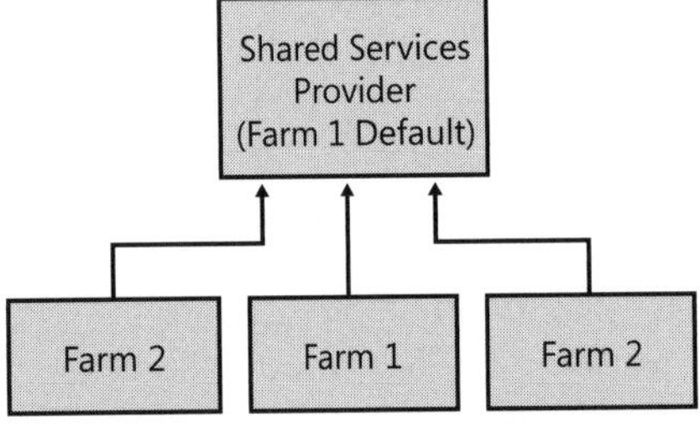


**Figure 16-13** A centralized SSP offloads processing from busy collaboration farms.

When creating a central SSP, it is best to do so in the beginning. It is not required, however, and in fact we can change the SSP consumption at any time in SharePoint Server 2007. As is discussed in the *Microsoft SharePoint Products and Technologies Administrator's Pocket Consultant* (Microsoft Press, 2007), you can associate and un-associate with providers at any time. There are some limitations when providing Shared Services to another farm:

- Only one Intra-farm SSP can provide Shared Services to other farms.
- A farm can only consume Shared Services from a single provider.
- When re-associating with another SSP or creating a local SSP, all site customizations based on the previous provider will be lost. Search scopes, audiences, and BDC connections are the most common.

## Inside Track **Using Inter-Farm SSPs**

If Intra-farm Shared Services are Web applications consuming from SSPs within the same farm, then Inter-farm Shared Services are Web applications consuming from SSPs outside the farm. Because of the WAN limitation (can't consume SSP across the WAN), many people discount a solution with more than one farm. Consider this: It really isn't that strange to create two farms in the same region. Why, you may ask? You may decide that you want to do collaboration with out-of-the-box functionality—for example, custom master pages and layouts—but pretty much no custom assemblies or custom site definitions or Web parts. On the other farm, you create your intranet portal with custom Web applications for your business and it becomes much more application-centric.

### Why Have the SSP in a Separate Farm?

- If you have multiple farms, then creating an SSP in a dedicated farm consolidates management for Search, Profiles, My Sites, and so on.
- The number of servers and disk space for Query can be reduced. If high availability of the site is important, but search isn't, you could save considerable disk space by having your Index/Query/WFE SSP farm all on one box, thus reducing the storage needed for Query since it would be on the same box. You could even use the same SQL environment for the two farms.
- Political reasons can be important. The SSP is a very hot commodity. By putting it in its own farm, you can optimize the disks, SQL, and the management from top to bottom could then be managed in a vacuum.

### What You May Not Know

- You may want to run Search in a separate farm with the Search SKU (Microsoft Office SharePoint for Search Standard or Enterprise) and have it provide Shared Services. Unfortunately, this won't work. Both parent and child farms need to be the same SKU (hence same features).

- Excel Calculation Services show up as a Shared Service. It's basically just configuration for the safe locations. The Excel Calculation Services are still with the consuming farm for rendering and calculation purposes.
- Forms services are always on the front ends for rendering. There's actually no real way of offloading the forms rendering to an application tier server. You can offload document conversions, however.
- Contrary to some rumors, there is no magic latency calculation to consuming Shared Services over the WAN.

Shared Services Providers can be configured to provide services to multiple SharePoint Server 2007 farms. Utilizing Shared Services Providers across farms has the following benefits:

- Reduces the number of services that provide the same role.
- Dramatically reduces hardware, resource, and network bandwidth use.
- Centralizes administration of Shared Services Providers.

### Shared Services Design Notes

- Intra-farm Shared Services are offered by a parent farm to one or more child farms.
- A provider farm is configured to provide Shared Services to other consumer farms.
- Consumer farms are configured to consume Shared Services from the parent farm.
- A farm cannot be both a parent farm and a child farm.
- Only one SSP can participate in Inter-farm Shared Services.
- Parent farms can only share one SSP to child farms. However, a parent farm can include more than one SSP for its own use.
- Child farms can only consume services from one SSP. However, a child farm can include more than one SSP for its own use.
- Shared services consumption for child farms can be reconfigured at any time, and can disassociate from a parent farm and be configured to either consume Shared Services from a different parent farm or use its own SSP.
- Parent farms can be re-configured as stand-alone farms at any time. Parent farm administrators should alert administrators of affected child farms before reconfiguring the SSP as a stand-alone SSP.

The following limitations apply to Intra-farm Shared Services:

- Parent and child farms must reside within the same Active Directory forest. If the farms reside in different domains, there must be a trust relationship configured between the domains.

- Intra-farm Shared Services are not supported across a WAN. A child farm cannot be associated with an SSP at a parent farm if the two farms are separated by WAN links.
- Parent farms must have all Office server products installed that are used by child farms. For example, if a child farm includes Microsoft Office Project Server, then Office Project Server must be installed on the parent farm for Shared Services to work correctly. If a child farm uses the Enterprise CAL of Office SharePoint Server, then the parent farm must also use the Enterprise CAL (as opposed to the Standard CAL).

*Joel Oleson, Senior Technical Product Manager, Microsoft*

# Designing Shared Services

This section is intended to give you the commonly asked questions and answers when designing Shared Services for an intranet. The following scenario uses a single Intra-farm SSP, with a single index server. Most Intranet SharePoint Server 2007 deployments will leverage the functionality of My Sites, user profiles, search, and audiences.

## My Sites

My Sites provide a one-to-many collaboration space for your users. Many organizations shy away from My Site deployment because they want control over all of the collaborative space, and My Sites are not easily policed. Be aware that users tend to create a personal collaboration space, whether you allow it through a My Site or not. For example, any site collection administrator can create a subsite and grant access to that site. We have seen this many times when My Sites weren't allowed. Site collection administrators simply created their own. Now you can't find these personal collaboration sites because there is no standard in the creation or management. A better way is to embrace the technology and what is most likely a permanent shift in content management. That is, most technology is moving toward the data owner (the user) managing the life cycle of documents, including the creation of containers to host that content, and the delegation of authorization through permissions. Administrators will be tasked with building the high-level buckets that will contain this information. It is even possible that administrators may eventually control authentication only, and all authorization will be performed by the data owners themselves. Of course, there is something we can do to govern these personal collaboration spaces.

First, we can control the available permission to all My Sites by modifying the hosting Web application's user permissions for Web application, as seen in Figure 16-14. This is possible only if you have followed the best practice of creating a My Site provider (Web application) for the sole purpose of hosting My Sites. Otherwise, changing permission levels and policies will affect your collaboration sites as well.

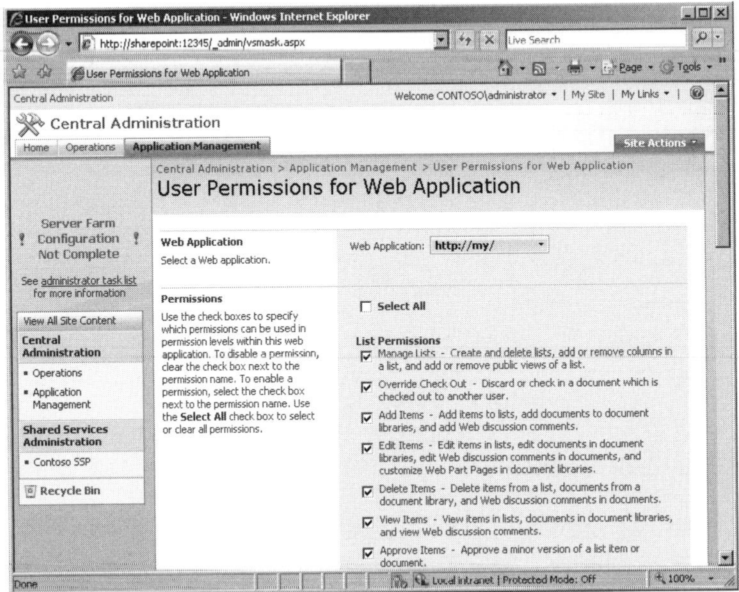


**Figure 16-14** You can remove available permission levels from the My Site provider in Central Administration.

Second, and more powerful, is the ability to *grant* or *deny* permission explicitly to a set of users' My Sites in a Web application. For example, you can remove the ability for contractors and temporary workers from creating subsites, using Web parts, and using the explorer view on libraries. Figure 16-15 shows the interface in Central Administration for creating Web application policies. Once again, you must have put My Sites in a dedicated Web application(s) to prevent modification of permissions on other site collections.

As you can see in Figure 16-15, you don't have to apply permission changes to every user; you apply policy to users individually or via groups. You can also grant permissions to users, such as the Service Desk, that will override site collection permissions. You could create an auditing account that has read permissions on all My Sites. This account can then be used to monitor site collection usage and adherence to your Information Technology governance policy.

Third, you can extend and map the My Site provider to another *zone*. A zone is another URL that is associated with the same content databases. This allows you to modify permissions based on the entering URL, authentication, protocol scheme, and encryption. For example, you could extend the My Site provider *http://my.contoso.msft* to *https://my-external.contoso.msft* for Internet access to users' My Sites. Based on the URL entered in the browser, you can grant or deny permissions such as SharePoint Designer usage and managing lists. The possibilities are almost endless for policy-based customizations using zones.

Fourth, you can have custom My Site definitions. In these custom site definitions, you can trim out functionality you do not want available in the My Site. Conversely, you can add functionality needed to meet requirements on a large scale.

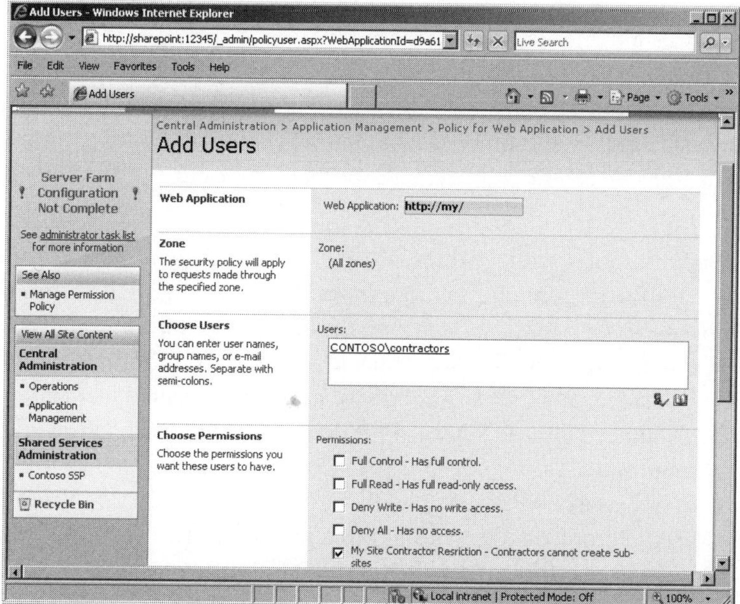

Figure 16-15 You can explicitly grant or deny permission to users' My Sites.

## Surfacing User Information via Profiles

You can surface information about your users through user profiles and the properties contained therein. These properties can contain any type of information, from a specific skill set to a user's phone number. These properties can be imported directly from an LDAP, such as Active Directory, or gathered from the user in his or her My Site. An often overlooked option is gathering this profile information through a personal profile page when a user does not have a My Site. If a user doesn't have a My Site, you can still see these properties via a people search.

### Notes from the Field **Profile Imports in the Real World**

In a perfect world, when it comes to Importing AD Profiles into SharePoint, you could simply choose to pull information from "Entire Forest" and be done with it. It's a simple query and does what you're looking for, but we don't live in a perfect world, and your AD domain may be scattered with a lot of information (Accounts) that you don't want in your profile index. These would include service accounts, duplicate user accounts, disabled accounts and administrative accounts which would cause a people search to return more than one account for the same person and invalid accounts. Query results cluttered with inaccurate information can confuse your users.

This is due in large part to poorly planned AD organizational units (OUs) where domain administrators will lump all of their accounts in a User OU. This isn't a rant on domain administrators; I was one once upon a time. But most well-running Active Directories have an OU set up for Service accounts, another for Administrative accounts, and a third for User accounts. A lot of this depends on the Active Directory structure, but when I walk into an engagement the first thing I want to know is how the OU structure is set up. With this information, we can fine tune your imports to a specific set of users that you want to target.

When targeting your import you have three options: current domain, entire forest, and custom. I tend to use the custom option more times than not because I can granularly drill down to target my user import. When using the custom option, you will be taken to a "View Import Connections" page; it's here you will see the various options such as your Search Base query. As an example, let's assume we have an OU called SharePoint, and the FQDN (Fully Qualified Domain Name) of the domain is*contoso.net*. This is where my users reside, so I simply add "OU=SharePoint,DC=Contoso, DC=net". When this import runs, it will import only the contents of that OU into your profile import. What if you have sub-OUs? Microsoft took care of this and provides the means to choose the level at which you can grab your users. It can be One Level or Sub-tree Levels.

Where is this applicable? Say you have designed a SharePoint Server 2007 environment to use three farms, each in a separate region of the world. You want your regional profiles to hold only the users from these regions. Depending on your AD farm structure, you can accomplish this by adding a custom import connection for each domain. What if you wanted to pull user profile information from a LOB (Line-of-Business) application such as PeopleSoft as well? That is also covered with the use of the option to use the Business Data Catalog, which is part of the Profile Import Source drop-down type.

One other critical mistake that people often make is running a full search crawl before importing their profile, then looking at their crawl logs and seeing that no people are showing up. The Default Search Crawl includes all SharePoint sites and the people crawl. So make sure you run a user profile import before you attempt to run a search crawl or the profile will not be in the index.

Profile imports are a critical piece of the SharePoint Server 2007 puzzle and, although not difficult to set up, they do require some careful planning. So do your homework and include this in your initial planning.

*Bob Fox, Microsoft MVP, B&R Business Solutions*

A common misconception is that user profiles are used for authentication. They are not. User profiles are associated via the SID so that information can be surfaced in a site collection. You surface this information in a site collection by marking a property as *replicable*. To mark a property as replicable, go to the property from Shared Services Provider Administration/User Profiles and Properties/View/Add Profile Properties, then check Replicable on the pertinent property. To mark a property as replicable, it must be viewable by Everyone, and the user can not change the privacy setting. Figure 16-16 shows where to select the Replicable option.

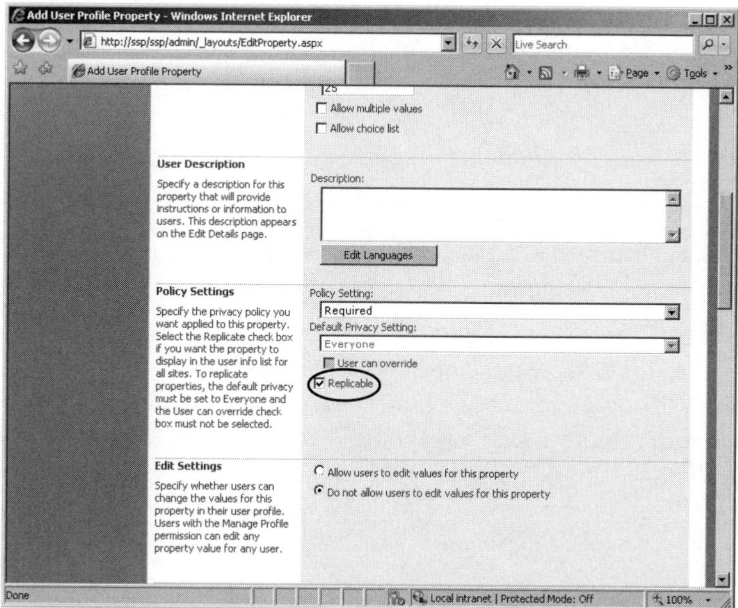

**Figure 16-16** To copy a property to sites when a user is added, select the Replicable option.

A best practice for user profile properties that are being linked to an external source is not to allow users to change it on their details page. Allowing them to do so can be frustrating because they think they are permanently changing the property, but it is overwritten during the next import. Additionally, be sure to expose the property on the users' details page if you want to collect information from them. Requiring them to fill out a property field but not exposing it on the details page is fruitless.

> **Note** Many properties do not import correctly with an incremental profile import. A best practice is to perform only full imports of user profiles. Profile information is lightweight, but you may need to dedicate a Domain Controller in very large environments.

There are some limitations to user profile imports. One of the most obvious, and quite limiting, is that you may have only one rule per LDAP import source. So, for example, you cannot import from two separate OUs in Active Directory. To target specific users in your Active Directory, you must use import filtering and Active Directory security. Simply remove access from the default content access to those objects you do not want imported into SharePoint Server 2007. When connecting to multiple LDAPs, be sure you have a common unique ID, or you could have multiple profiles per individual.

## Audience Targeting

The earlier example of audiences was targeting News information to users who are in a specific group. This can be expanded in an enterprise to include almost anything. Here are some ideas for audience targeting:

- Target content to users based on their division.
- Target content to users based on their department or manager.
- Alert users in specific buildings or geographic locations through audientized Web parts.
- Target objects in a list, such as a calendar, to specific users. You can combine content type and site column filtering for a very relevant view to a group of users.

Remember that much of SharePoint Server 2007 is already security trimmed. So, for example, when users visit a site, they will see only the items in the quick launch that they can access. Similarly, users only see sites on a publishing top link bar that they have permissions to view. Take caution when adding links to the navigation manually as they are separate objects from the sites to which they link and therefore have unique security settings. Unless you create those links in a publishing site and leverage audiences, all users will see the link regardless of their ability to authenticate to the hyperlinked source.

## SSPs in the Extranet

When using SSP resources in the extranet, you should always thoroughly test your design. For example, anonymous users cannot use audiences, nor can you target only anonymous users. When creating extranet and Internet Web sites, it is wise to think through the design of your Search infrastructure. With all but a few Internet sites, and many extranet sites, you will want to create a second index to host information for the sole purpose of exposing content to the Internet. Note that you will need a second SSP to manage your external Index. You may also want to create different BDC connections for external users.

# Geographically Dispersed Deployments

SharePoint Server 2007 does not support geo-replication of content. There are third-party products that support parts of SharePoint Server 2007, but none replicate all of it. Additionally, Shared Services over a WAN is not supported. A farm in Chicago cannot consume Shared Services from a farm in New York. What is supported, however, is the ability to localize My Sites for users in a geographic region. Additionally, you can create a centralized Search center that is consumed via Federated Location Definitions with Microsoft Search Server 2008.

## Regional My Site Providers

You have the ability to create multiple My Site Providers (Web applications) and assign users to a particular Web application based on their inclusion in an Active Directory group or Global audience. While this can be done in a LAN environment, this section specifically discusses options for geographically dispersed locations. Regional My Site providers are sometimes referred to as *Global My Site Providers*. This is primarily based on the setting in SSP Administration, My Site Settings, Multiple Deployments, as seen in Figure 16-17. The recommendation in the Note on this page cannot be implemented as the "profile replication solution" tool has not been released as of the date this book was published. The intention is to replicate profiles among multiple SSPs, therefore removing the need for *every* SSP in an enterprise to perform an individual import.

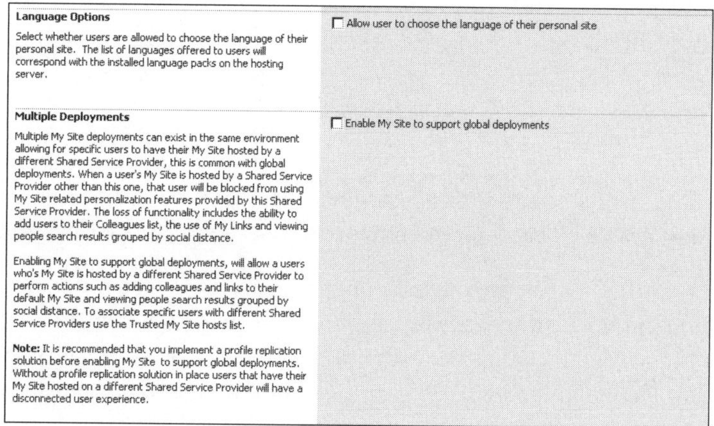


**Figure 16-17** You must write custom code to replicate user profiles.

> **Note** If you allow users to choose the language of their My Site, as seen in Figure 16-17, you must load the language pack on the WFE Servers that host the My Site Provider for those users.

You can enable personal features across multiple My Site providers. To enable the usage of personal features across multiple My Site providers, you must enable support for global deployments, as seen in Figure 16-17, on *every* SSP that manages a My Site provider that is listed in Trusted My Site Locations, as seen in Figure 16-18 on the next page.

To add a Trusted My Site Host Location, select New, New Item from the list menu shown in Figure 16-18. You should list the Web application's root managed path site collection, or wherever the My Site Host template was applied for the Web address field. When selecting the *select here to test* hyperlink, you should be redirected to your My Site on that Web application.

> **Note** Once you define a Trusted My Site Host Location, the default My Site settings are ignored. For this reason, always add your default My Site host location to the list of Trusted My Site Hosts first with no target audience. Then, define each additional My Site provider and target that provider with an audience.

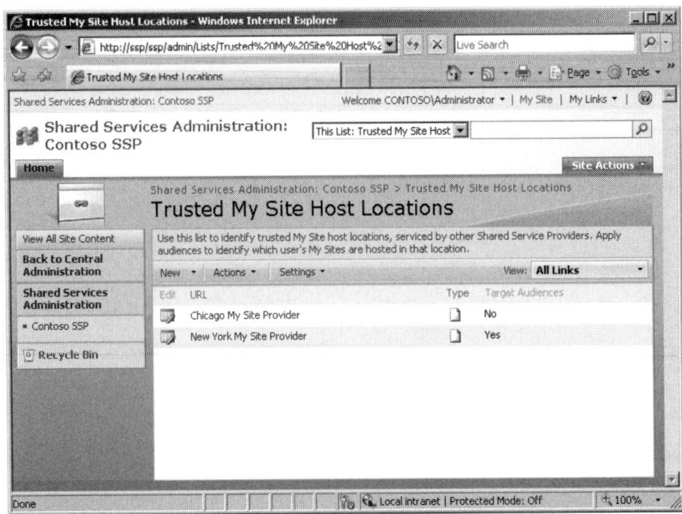


**Figure 16-18** You must enable global deployment support for every My Site location.

If you want to have a default My Site provider, do not select an audience for the first provider in the list. If a user is in multiple audiences associated with My Site Providers, that user will be directed to the first in the list. To change the order of the My Site Providers, select Actions, then Change Order, as shown in Figure 16-19. The exception to this rule is when a user is in more than one group, but the first Web application isn't available. The user will be created in the first available My Site Provider in the list.

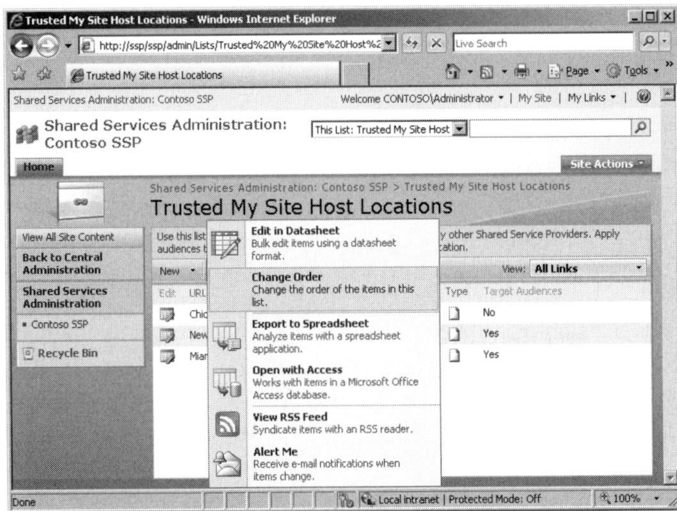


**Figure 16-19** Change Order of Trusted My Site Hosts

## Search and Indexing

In geographically dispersed environments, there is often a need to have a single index that is referenced across the enterprise so that users in each geographic location can find all of the documentation and all of the right people they need to successfully perform their job. Unfortunately, what is not in this version of SharePoint Server 2007 is the ability to build portions of the overall index at each regional center, then aggregate those indexes into a common index and then distribute the full, enterprise index back to each regional center.

Upon closer examination, what we have found in working with clients who are geographically dispersed is that the users in one geographic location often do not need to find information in the other locations simply because most of the information they need to be successful is hosted locally within their own location. Sometimes, a user's lack of need to see information that is hosted in other locations is due to language differences or dissimilar job foci or perhaps as a result of the different roles each location performs for the company, such as different product lines being produced at different geographic locations.

The need for an overall enterprise index is really built on the assumption that if a company has a single index, then all of its information will be quickly *findable*. Indeed, the reason most companies desire to implement a taxonomy coupled with a robust search and indexing topology is due to the (sometimes mistaken) assumption that if their information is organized and indexed, then it will be easy to *find* it. The market is quickly learning that findability is not solved simply because a solid search engine is implemented into one's environment. In fact, if the result sets are not meaningful to the end-users, then the chances are good that the search implementation will fail due to lack of popularity.

Search Server 2008 helps resolve this problem through its Federated Location Definition feature. The ability to send the query to remote indexes and receive back results from multiple, dissimilar indexes *simultaneously* gives you the ability to receive results back from a remote index without having to crawl its content. Because Search Server 2008 can federate its query to multiple SharePoint indexes, Search Server 2008 now gives you the prospect of enjoying the experience of an enterprise index across geographically dispersed environments without the necessity of having to re-crawl that information at the enterprise level to create the enterprise index. Instead, you get the best of both worlds: you don't create an enterprise index and your users get to enjoy a result set that has enterprise breadth and depth. When you consider that Search Server 2008 Express is free without any document limitation, the prospect of using Search Server 2008 becomes even more compelling.

## Summary

In this chapter, we have connected the many Shared Services for SharePoint Server 2007, and some best practices for implementing. Remember to use only the services required to meet your immediate technical requirements in the beginning, and install additional Shared Services as you need them. Start with the basics, such as Search, Personalization Top Links, My Sites, and Office Save As locations. As your implementation matures, consider adding Excel Services, Business Data Catalog connections, and leveraging audiences.

## Additional Resources

- BDC Meta Man, which can be used to create and manage the necessary XML for creating BDC connections: *http://www.lightningtools.com/bdc-meta-man/default.aspx*

Chapter 17

# Optimizing Information Security

**In this chapter:**



Information security is an important consideration when you decide to deploy any technology solution, and Microsoft Office SharePoint Server 2007 is certainly no exception. Protecting information and information systems from unauthorized use, modification, disruption, and destruction is fundamental to the success of your implementation. This chapter is not meant to be an exhaustive review of information security concepts and related theory, but rather an overview of key information security concepts and practical application of best practices within Office SharePoint Server 2007.

*Confidentiality*, *integrity*, and *authenticity* are core principals of information security. As we explore these key concepts and their related common objectives, it will be become apparent that many of the implementation vectors discussed here are mutually exclusive within the context of customer requirements and system constraints. Therefore, it's important to consider both the policy and infrastructure ramifications of selecting a given alternative. We will discuss ways to approach each, so that you can make an objective comparison. Specifically, we will touch on the following:

- Confidentiality
  - Information classification
- Integrity
  - SharePoint groups versus Active Directory groups
  - Access control and permissions levels
- Authenticity
  - User authentication
  - Code Access Security

## Confidentiality

Protection of confidential information has become an increasingly hot topic as our appetite for information exchange continues to grow in both volume and speed. But what does it mean to say that a given piece of information is confidential? When conditions exist, such as the expectation that provided information will be kept in confidence or made available only to a limited group, the information is generally considered confidential. This occurs every time we provide vendors, partners, or other individuals with information for a shared purpose, under the expectation that the information provided will be accessed only by persons who are authorized and only when they have a genuine need to do so.

Losing control of information provided in confidence can be disastrous! Recent security breaches involving the loss of confidential customer information have attracted the attention of both the general public and the media. Often, these events constitute a violation of privacy law, with far-reaching and often costly implications. Protection of private or confidential information is a priority concern of organizations working with such information.

The underlying motivators, which often create the expectation of confidentiality, are *value* and *risk*. When information is industrially sensitive, proprietary, or concerns matters of national security, it is often considered high-value information. Likewise, when information is considered private, or shared with the expectation of privacy or confidentiality, it is often considered high-risk information. In both cases, the information must be managed and secured commensurate to its value or risk.

Let's assume that a confidential contract agreement with a strategic partner was intentionally or inadvertently made available on an Internet-facing Web site, thereby disclosing the detailed terms to the media or competition. Or perhaps the document was left open on an unattended computer display or thrown away without being shredded. What if a conniving caller managed to squeeze the details out of an employee? In each of these cases, sensitive information is now in the hands of someone who is not authorized to have it, which constitutes a breach of confidentiality.

SharePoint Server 2007 provides a multitude of security features which, when implemented in concert with well-understood information security policies, provide significant protection of confidential information. All content is rendered via a security-trimmed interface, which greatly reduces the potential exposure of confidential information. Users are allowed to read only information for which they have authorization. SharePoint Server 2007 also provides the capability to secure individual documents with unique permissions, which allows for more granular control of information throughout its life cycle. Information can be easily identified as confidential, secured accordingly, and audited as appropriate.

## Information Classification

In order to properly secure information, we must first be able to identify its information classification. There are many different information classification schemes. Often, an organization already has a policy with predetermined information classes in place. These concepts are common to most information classification schemes as follows:

- All information has an owner.
- All information is classified as *confidential* by default.
- The owner is responsible for updating the classification.
- The owner is responsible for declaring who is allowed access to the information.
- The owner is responsible for securing the information or for seeing that it is properly secured by the administrator.

The following classes are common to most information classification schemes:

- Public
- Internal
- Confidential
- Secret

Each of these classes would have its own policy for the storage, transmission, and disposal of information. The point of this section is not to prescribe any single set of classification definitions, but rather to convey that it is a best practice to implement a well-understood data classification scheme. This allows content being developed in the system to be readily classified and identified by users, who will in turn be able to handle the information appropriate to its sensitivity.

## Content Types

Content types are a central building block in SharePoint Server 2007 and provide the basis for the classification of data. Content types, as they relate to creating detailed information taxonomies, were covered earlier in this book in more detail. They are identified here as a preferred method for providing a simple yet extendable information classification capability to information owners. Let's suppose we want to achieve the objectives outlined in the example classification policy described in the previous section.

> **More Info** For additional information regarding information architecture, refer to Chapter 7, "Developing an Information Architecture."

In order to implement the classification policy, we must set up the system so it can be used as would normally be expected, without requiring additional document library configuration steps on the behalf of end-users. Information owners should be required to fill or update a new field, "IP Classification" (shown in Figure 17-1), when adding or uploading a document. It should not be possible to store any document in the system without proper classification. Finally, all documents should be classified as *confidential* unless specified otherwise.

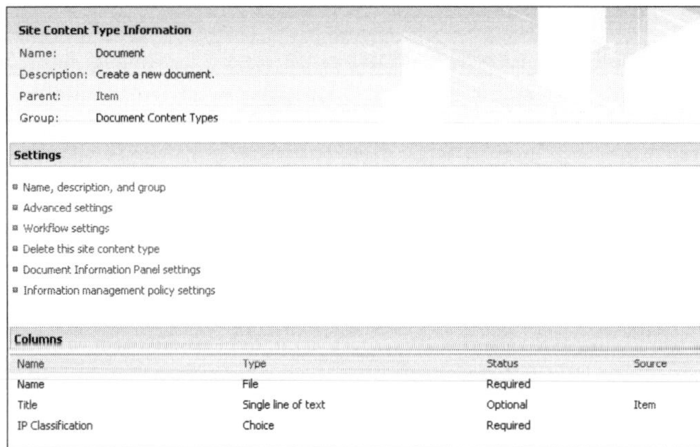


**Figure 17-1** Settings for the newly created Top-Level site

Content types provide an elegant alternative to making list column modifications to individual libraries. In addition to being unenforceable, traditional list column modifications would place an additional burden on users creating new libraries. By making similar settings changes to the pre-provided root Document content type (shown in Figure 17-2), we achieve multiple implementation advantages. Because the root Document content type is located at the top of the site collection, it can easily be protected from unwanted tampering by end-users. Such is the case for the additional site column we need to create as well. Additionally, changes made to the root Document content type can easily be rolled down to both existing and yet-to-be-created document libraries. This is important because it removes any need to customize these libraries or provide alternate custom list definitions (shown in Figure 17-3). Lastly, it ensures that any newly derived-content types created by subsite owners or users will also include the additional required field, which will be inherited from the Top-Level site, thereby protecting the content from modification or removal.

Lastly, let us consider how we might best achieve this effect on all new sites created within the implementation. This is a common goal of larger implementations where site collections are being created and disposed of on an ongoing basis. In order to accomplish this, we must create a new custom feature that can be activated through stapling. This ensures that creation of each new site includes activation of the new feature. We will then use the feature event receivers to perform the same activities in our code that we performed manually in the example.

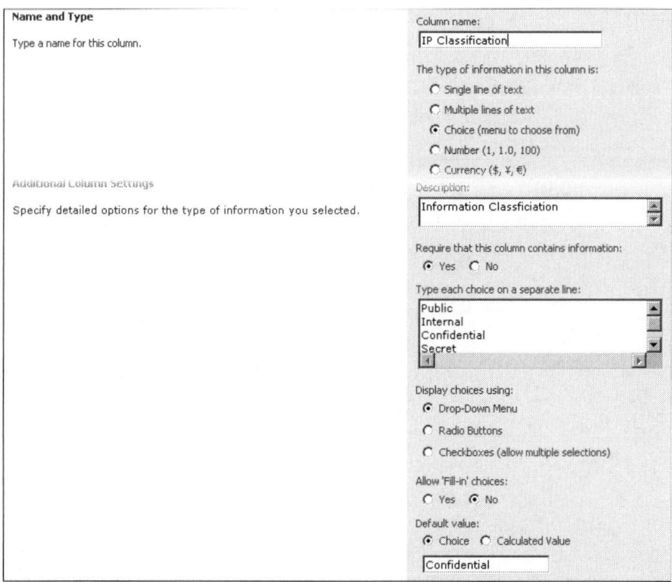


**Figure 17-2** Settings updates made to the root Document content type at the Top-Level site

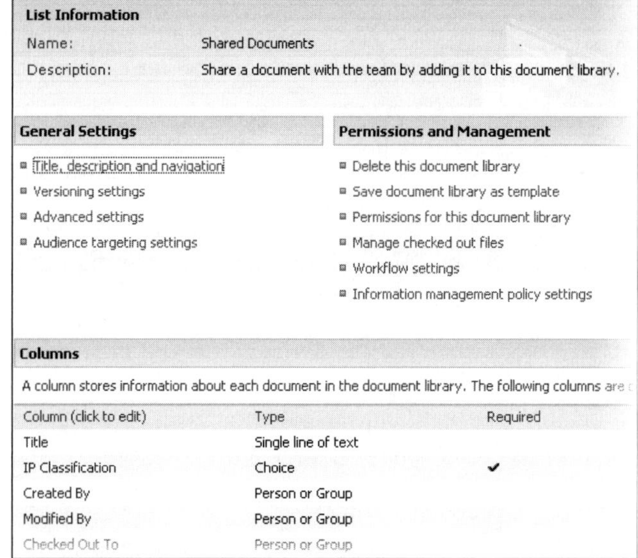


**Figure 17-3** Changes made to a document library

> **Note** Stapling a feature is also known as *Feature Site Template Association* and allows for the activation of newly created custom features upon site creation when you use the associated template. You can also perform what is referred to as a *Global Stapler*, in which you associate to the Global template, thereby effectively stapling your new feature to all site types.

# Integrity

Proper information integrity involves ensuring that data cannot be added, deleted, or changed without proper authorization. The enforcement of integrity within information systems is generally provided via access control and permissions. *Access controls* allow well-identified users access to a given information resource. If the user is defined as having access to the resource, permissions will define what activities that user may perform on the information resource. SharePoint Server 2007 provides the opportunity to define access controls and security permissions at various configuration levels for different reasons and to accomplish different goals. With few exceptions, SharePoint Server 2007 provides access controls by granting access to a user based on the entries defined for a given object instance. Once an entry has been found, SharePoint Server 2007 uses the associated role definition or specific assigned permissions to determine what a user can and cannot do. Because access is largely controlled via the granting of access, SharePoint Server 2007 is able to provide a security-trimmed user experience in which users see only objects within the system for which they have been given access.

## SharePoint Groups versus Active Directory Groups

SharePoint Server 2007 changes the way groups are handled compared to prior versions. Central to this change is the introduction of the SharePoint group, which is essentially a single-object type that can represent either a group of individual users who have been defined within SharePoint or an Active Directory directory services role group. The significance of this change is that it provides a single mechanism for defining a group of users, regardless of where that group of users is actually defined. This provides clear advantages over the distinction made between groups and cross-site groups in previous versions.

Many organizations have adopted Active Directory and Active Directory groups as a central element of their overall authentication strategy. As a result, they often attempt to mandate the usage of Active Directory groups when provisioning user access within SharePoint Server 2007. Although this appears to be a reasonable requirement that would be well supported by the new features, it often isn't possible.

The following are some of the primary challenges to enforcing the strict usage of Active Directory groups within SharePoint:

- Active Directory groups cannot be used to assign site collection administrators.
- Active Directory group membership cannot be displayed and/or managed.
- Active Directory groups for members restrict specific My Site functionality.

The choice to use Active Directory groups or SharePoint groups really depends on your specific requirements. Most likely, you will use a combination of both. Thus, the best practice is consistency in your design. Whether you primarily use Active Directory groups or SharePoint groups, deviating from your standard should be an exception and not the rule.

## Site Collection Administrators

Active Directory groups cannot be used to provide site collection administrator access. Although it is generally considered a best practice to limit the granting of site collection administrator access to users who are directly responsible for the management of content within a specific site, this often creates difficulties when you attempt to provide support to those individuals. Consider the scenario where, in order to provide support to a site collection administrator, an individual central IT support user must have explicit site collection administrator access. This creates a problem because, in order for the central IT support user to be granted this level of access, one of two things must occur—either the site collection administrator requesting support must grant this access or the central IT support user must have farm administrator access to self-grant the needed access. In either case, there is a significant risk that the access needed to provide support may not be removed once it is no longer needed. Where the central IT support user has farm administrative access, we have created an obvious risk in that the user providing support most likely does not need such far-reaching privileges in order to accomplish his task.

If it were possible, providing the needed access via membership in an Active Directory group would provide shelter from these described risks. It would also be far easier to manage in that the group memberships used for granting users access for performing specific tasks could provide them the needed access by simply adding them to a single, predefined Active Directory group which, through automation or process, could be added to each new site collection upon creation. When a user no longer needed this level of access, it would be easy to have her removed from all site collections in the enterprise, ensuring such access did not persist beyond her justifiable need for it. Fortunately, there is a way to provide this level of access while leveraging Active Directory groups through the use of Web application security policies. Simply put, these policies provide the ability to grant access privileges to members of an Active Directory group throughout all site collections within a given Web application. To implement this, simply add a new security policy for the target Web application, and select the Full Control check box (shown in Figure 17-4). Although not exactly intuitive, this effectively makes all members of the specified Active Directory group site collection administrators for all site collections within that Web application.

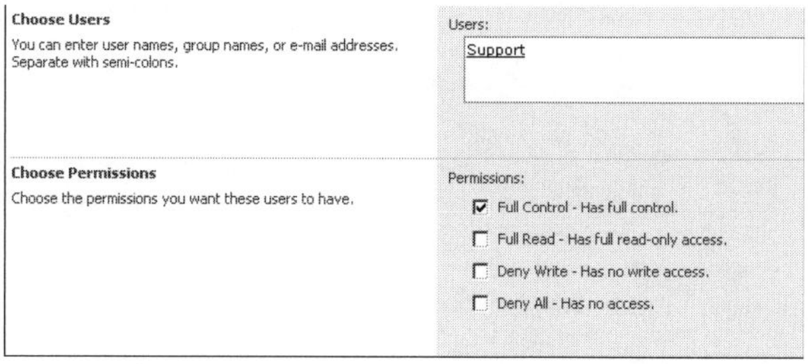

Choose Users
You can enter user names, group names, or e-mail addresses. Separate with semi-colons.
Users:
Support
Choose Permissions
Choose the permissions you want these users to have.
Permissions:
Full Control - Has full control.
Full Read - Has full read-only access.
Deny Write - Has no write access.
Deny All - Has no access.

**Figure 17-4** The permission selections for a new Web application security policy

## Active Directory Group Membership

Because the individual members of an Active Directory group cannot be displayed within SharePoint Server 2007, many site administrators face a challenge when attempting to find the correct group and verify its membership. This makes it difficult for information owners to ensure that the information contained in their sites is secure from unauthorized access. Compounding this challenge, it is not possible to manage the membership of an Active Directory group from within the SharePoint Server 2007 interface. This means that information owners must rely on the effective execution of proper Active Directory group management to ensure that intended users are granted access to information in a timely manner. Because inline access requests handled by SharePoint Server 2007 grant access by adding a member directly to a SharePoint Group, this access is often seen as residual because it takes no account of the membership of any Active Directory group. These challenges make it difficult to mandate the use of Active Directory groups. The inherent delays and procedures associated with doing so make management of a fluid, collaborative environment difficult and often result in a breach of the mandate, further complicating the goal of maintaining information integrity.

## My Site Functionality Limitations

My Site provides many new features that, when properly implemented, offer a convenient user experience, both within the Web interface as well as within Microsoft Office 2007 applications. One new feature provides users with a convenient list of sites in which they are members. This list is available via the My Links button available on all pages within the system, as well as via the My SharePoint Sites folder found in all Office 2007 file dialogs. In order for a site to be displayed in this list for a given user, the user must be defined explicitly in the SharePoint group that is defined as the site's associated members group (shown in Figure 17-5). In order for this highly popular feature to work, a user cannot be granted member access to a site via membership in an Active Directory group. This means users who are members must have their access provided directly from within SharePoint.

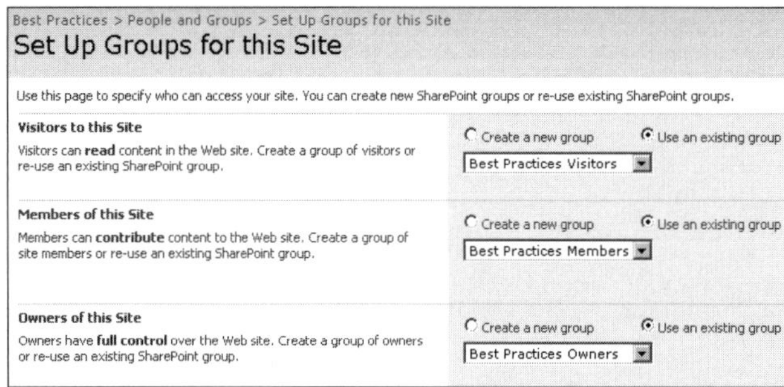


**Figure 17-5** Settings page within a site where the associated members group is defined

The significance of the associated members group is not limited to My Site functionality. Many common features, such as the Site Members Web part and user presence, are negatively affected should a member user be granted access to a site through Active Directory group membership.

## Access Control and Permissions Levels

Access to information can be controlled at many different levels within SharePoint Server 2007. The question of where best to implement control of user access is answered only with a thorough understanding of available options and implementation requirements. In this section, we will review a few best practices for taking advantage of the options available, as well as a few scenarios that place these best practices in context. The best practices are as follows:

- Consider the audience and intended use of a specific site or site type when deciding how to assign permissions.
- As a general rule, use SharePoint security and explicit group membership for management of site members.
- As a general rule, grant access at the lowest possible level without breaking permission inheritance.
- Use Web application security policies for granting broad access via tightly controlled Active Directory groups.
- Create a global deny group for use when retiring user accounts.

### Defining Access Scenarios

Table 17-1 shows common site type audience/usage combinations. It's important to understand how a site will be used and by whom. Without this information, it becomes difficult to make intelligent decisions about how to best secure the information contained within the site. It also becomes far more likely that a given site and its defined user access will morph over time, creating a scenario in which unintentional access and even participation might occur.

**Table 17-1 Common Audience/Usage Combinations**

| Audience | Usage |
|---|---|
| Member audience (equal viewers/contributors) | Team collaboration, Document collaboration, Meeting collaboration |
| Wide audience (many viewers, few contributors) | Publishing site, Collaboration Portal |
| Managed audience (controlled, role-specific access) | Records Center |

Collaboration sites tend to be used for the creation and development of content. More often than not, the only people who need access to these sites are those individuals directly involved in the content development process. This is especially true in the case of ad hoc collaboration sites. It is generally a best practice to limit access to collaboration sites to members, as explicitly defined within the standards those groups provided. When broad audience viewer access is granted to collaboration sites, it often results in viewer access to incomplete or confidential information.

Publishing sites tend to be used for the dissemination of approved content to a wider audience. Because most of the users accessing the site will be viewers rather than contributors, it is considered a best practice to use Active Directory groups whenever possible to grant viewer access. The rationale behind using Active Directory groups is that, because the membership of these groups is managed outside of SharePoint Server 2007, users being added to these groups over time will automatically be granted access to these sites. Ad hoc viewer access for specific individuals can optionally be added and removed as deemed necessary by site administrators.

Records Center sites have specific role groups for processing content according to the defined retention and hold policies. In most cases, the membership of these groups is tightly controlled and involves a limited number of users.

## Web Application Security Policies

The Web application security policy settings provided through Central Administration (shown in Figure 17-6) is the only place from which you can deny access. The preconfigured role definitions created for any given Web application provide the ability to assign specific users/groups Full Control or Full Read over all objects within the Web application. You may also set access to Deny All, which effectively locks the specified user/group out of all sites located within the Web application. Once an assignment has been made at the Web application security policy level, it effectively trumps all security permission assignments on all objects within the Web application unless the specific assignment provides a higher level of permissions than those granted via the Web application level policy.

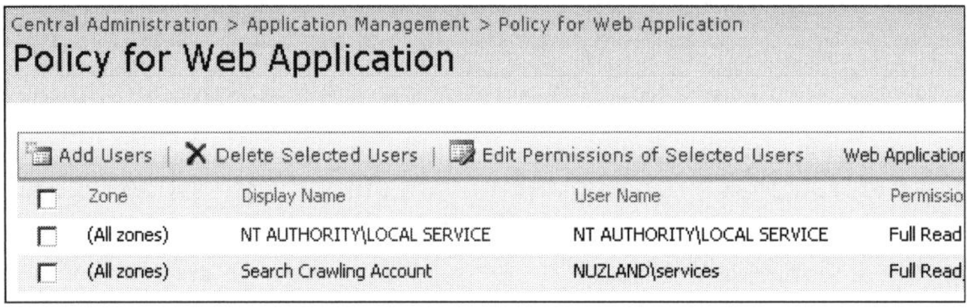

Central Administration > Application Management > Policy for Web Application

Policy for Web Application

Add Users | Delete Selected Users | Edit Permissions of Selected Users Web Applicatio

| Zone | Display Name | User Name | Permissio |
|---|---|---|---|
| (All zones) | NT AUTHORITY\LOCAL SERVICE | NT AUTHORITY\LOCAL SERVICE | Full Read |
| (All zones) | Search Crawling Account | NUZLAND\services | Full Read |

**Figure 17-6** Web application security policy management area in Central Administration

A common usage scenario for taking advantage of Web application security policies occurs when a legal or audit group needs access to an entire Web application. In most cases, these types of groups need Full Read access to information. There are three main advantages to providing this access at the Web application level rather than at the site level.

First, users in these groups can access all of the information stored within the entire Web application with Full Read permissions. In addition, they can access any information with Edit or Manage permissions located in sites for which they are specified as a user and assigned such permissions.

Second, by configuring read access at the Web application level, the ability to manage and control this access from a footprint perspective is significantly reduced because you only need to grant users access at the Web application level, whereas before you may have had to grant this group access to specific site collections or sites. Should you ever need to remove their access rights, there is only one place where you must make a settings change.

The last advantage, but not the least by any stretch, is the ability to mask the activity of users in these groups as activity performed by the system account. This eliminates audit log entries and item versions from being created by users performing discovery activities on information they do not intend to disturb, as doing so may result in altering an item's disposition, versioning, and so on.

## Site Collection Administrators

Site collection administrators are the most privileged administrative users within a site collection. As discussed earlier, it is not possible to use Active Directory groups to provision site collection administrator access. It is a best practice to tightly control this level of access and to limit it to individuals who will be performing specific activities that require such access. Such activities include master page customization and the management of site collection level settings for search, auditing, and object caching. Lastly, it should be noted that site collection administrators have no administrative powers above the site collection level. The risk footprint for these users is high within the site collection, but does not extend to other site collections or up into the Web application or farm levels.

## Permission Levels and Inheritance

Within each Microsoft Windows SharePoint Services 3.0 object, such as a site, list, or list item, at least two key pieces of information determine how that object is handled during a request. The first key piece of information is a single-object property that specifies whether the object inherits its security from its parent object. In the case of a site, this could be a subsite inheriting its security permissions from its parent site. In the case of a list, this would be the site in which the list was located, unless that site itself was inheriting its security permissions.

The second key piece of information a given object holds is an array of permission assignments. For each entry in this array, information is stored that indicates that a specific security principal (e.g., SharePoint user, Windows NT user/group) has access to the object and what specific permissions are granted to that security principal. Remember, the only place you can effectively deny access is at the Web application level; each object stored at the site collection level and below will have only grant permissions for specific users and/or groups. This is important to remember because there isn't an easy way to grant access to a parent object (e.g., site or list) and then deny access to a specific child object (e.g., list or list item) without breaking the security inheritance for that object. Once the security inheritance is broken for a given object, its manageability is significantly reduced, as changes to the permission assignments of its parent object have no effect on it. The addition of new users/groups to the parent will not automatically grant access to the child object.

As shown in Figure 17-7, security permissions are applied within Windows SharePoint Services 3.0 at an object type level, with each level in the tree representing the object exposed through the object model. For each request of an object, the highest level of applied permissions is determined by checking assignments made at the Web application level and below. The highest level of permission available to the requestor, based on the system's review of the permission assignments, is the permission level granted. For example, if a user has read-only access to a document but the same user is listed as a site collection administrator, the user will be granted site collection administrator access to the document, which includes the ability to both edit and delete the item.

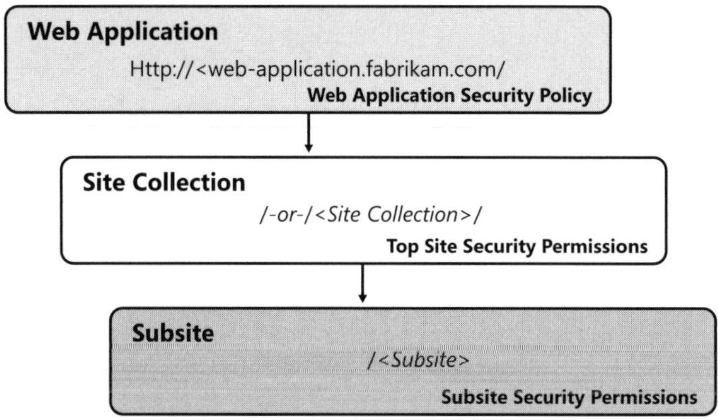


**Figure 17-7** Object level security permissions model

> **Note** Determining user permissions can be challenging because no one interface allows for an administrator to easily check what objects a user has access to within a SharePoint site hierarchy. The *SharePoint Access Checker Web Part*, which is available on *CodePlex*, provides one option for getting some of this information. Vendor partner solutions are also available and provide a wider range of capabilities for both assessment and management of user and group security assignments.

# Authenticity

Determining the validity of user activity and information in the system is critical to ensuring authenticity. In order to achieve these goals, we must ensure that information entered is genuine and that users performing the actions associated with this information have been properly identified. This includes all information and communications into and out of the system, including both process and user identification.

> ### Notes from the Field **Default Web Application Policies and Determining Number of Service Accounts**
>
> In the past, we used to run everything as a local administrator account. This really isn't a best practice anymore. The worst-case scenario is to run everything with domain

administrator privileges, which unnecessarily exposes your environment. Let me compare and contrast some different strategies.

Strategy one: All one account in the local administrator group (worst strategy). This unnecessarily gives the account that is running everything access to everything. If that account gets hacked, the intruders will have read access to everything. Because this single account has so much access, someone hacking into this account will have full read privileges to the content and can get into Central Administration to assume a full control policy. If you use this strategy with SQL rights as well, you're exposing that box info, too. A hacker needs only dbcreator and securityadmin and the entire system can be compromised.

Strategy two: One account for the crawl account and one service account for everything else (a bit better). In many environments, this strategy meets most needs, and at least the crawl account isn't unnecessarily exposing information.

Strategy three: One account for crawl, one for Central Administration service/SSP, one for SSP administration and Farm Service/Management, and one for content Web application pool (much better). This is a much smarter farm than the previous two. As long as the people who own the content Web applications have common interests, this scenario trades off management and security. For those looking to simplify their lives without compromising security, this is my recommendation. I really don't think WSSSearch and MOSS Search (the crawl or content access) accounts need to be different unless you have two different crawlers. Obviously, you're looking to divide your content between SSPs to separate the indexes or BDC access. When it's about search, I recommend paying specific attention to the crawl account(s). As a best practice, *never* make the crawl account a local administrator.

Strategy four: One for SharePoint Setup (install SP_Admin), one for WSS Search Help crawl (SP_WSSSearch), one for MOSS crawl (SP_MOSSSearch), one for Central Administration (SP_Farm), one for SSP service account (SP_SSPService), an SSP App Pool account for the SSP Admin Web app (SP_SSPAppPool), one for My Site content Web app for the app pool (SP_MyAppPool), and one for Portal App Pool (SP_PortalAppPool). This configuration is the most secure because it is speaking only to the front end. You're going to have a separate SQL Service Account (SQL_Service) and a cluster service account in a cluster (Cluster_Service). Most of these accounts really don't need any special rights. SharePoint will take care of setting up the rights. The Setup account (SP_Admin) and Central Administration (SP_Farm) do need local admin during the install, as well as dbcreator and securityadmin. This way, it works to create the databases during installation. After the Central Administration exists, new databases can be created from the Web user interface. The Setup account (SP_Admin), which is the only account with both local admin and the relevant SQL access, would be used to install hotfixes and service packs, deploy packages, and run STSADM commands. It could be disabled when you're not doing these things because it is not run as a service account. It should *never* be deleted because it is required for performing these special farm configuration activities. Remember, this account has complete access to all farm content and cannot be denied, so it should *never* be used as a logon account or for other administration.

With so many accounts, you're secure, right? But what about managing these with a 60- or 90-day password expiration policy? A handy reference for STSADM password management can be found at *http://blogs.msdn.com/joelo/archive/2006/08/22/712945.aspx.*

In testing, we created a new farm with more than eight unique accounts (many details of which is covered above). In doing so, we saw some interesting default Web application policies. You'll notice that these accounts spanned all zones with full read rights.

- NT AUTHORITY\LOCAL SERVICE NT AUTHORITY\LOCAL SERVICE
- Search Crawling Account Domain\SP_MOSSSearch
- Search Crawling Account Domain\SP_WSSCrawl
- Domain\sp_sspservice Domain\SP_SSPService

First, you can see that the built-in group local service is given full read rights. Both the Office SharePoint Search (content access account) crawl account and the Windows SharePoint Services Help Search crawl account are individually given a policy of full read. This gives the crawl accounts access to the content in the Web applications.

Note that you don't want the crawl account to have more than read rights. So, when you are creating accounts, it pays off to create this as a second account. If you remove this policy, you'll likely get errors.

The SSP service account is also given full read rights. Interesting. If you think about it, it does need to share information with the Web applications. If you have BDC, this is one example of the SSP needing to share information across Web applications.

Are you curious about local service? I was. So I looked around and found Microsoft's Service Account Planning Guide at *http://www.microsoft.com/technet/security/guidance/serversecurity/serviceaccount/sspgch02.mspx*. The planning guide has great recommendations on how to make sure you're being consistent when planning your service accounts, with some recommendations for limiting access.

The following is information on Network Service and Local Service accounts from the planning guide.

### Local Service Account

The Local Service account is a special, built-in account that has reduced privileges, similar to an authenticated local user account. This limited access helps safeguard the computer if an attacker compromises individual services or processes. A service that runs as the Local Service account accesses network resources as a null session; that is, it uses anonymous credentials. The actual name of the account is NT AUTHORITY\LocalService, and it does not have a password that an administrator needs to manage.

**Network Service Account**

The Network Service account is a special, built-in account that has reduced privileges, similar to an authenticated user account. This limited access helps safeguard the computer if an attacker compromises individual services or processes. A service that runs as the Network Service account accesses network resources using the credentials of the computer account in the same manner as a Local System service does. The actual name of the account is NT AUTHORITY\NetworkService, and it does not have a password that an administrator needs to manage.

You need to be aware that if you change the default service settings, you might prevent key services from running correctly. It is especially important to use caution when you change the Startup Type and Log On As settings for services that are set to start automatically by default.

*Joel Oleson, Senior Technical Product Manager, Microsoft*

## User Authentication

User authentication meets the fundamentally critical requirement of *authenticity* by determining the identity of the user making a request. SharePoint Server 2007 supports a variety of authentication options, including Anonymous-, Integrated-, and Forms-based authentication, as well as newly added support for pluggable authentication providers. Because authentication options are configured at the Web application level, it's important to consider goals for providing access prior to creating new site collections within a Web application. This is especially true when configuring anonymous access. Although it is not uncommon for a single farm to serve data for both internal and external users, it is a best practice to use separate Web applications. In the next section, we will review a few of the best practices regarding the configuration of authentication. Windows authentication is the default authentication mechanism for the default zone of each Web application upon creation. Windows authentication is provided using the following authentication protocols: Kerberos, Integrated, and Basic.

Kerberos is the recommended protocol for intranet users because it is more secure than traditional NTLM/Challenge. In addition, it reduces the load on the domain controllers because each session does not require checking with the directory service. It is widely accepted that in order for NTLM/Challenge authentication to be considered secure, a minimum password length of 14 characters is required.

Integrated authentication allows the use of the current user context, which is based on workstation login, to authenticate. It is considered a best practice to leverage Integrated authentication for the authentication of intranet users who access sites from a shared or trusted activity directory domain.

Basic authentication should only be used in cases in which Integrated authentication is not possible, such as extranet access scenarios.

> **Important** Use SSL whenever using Basic authentication.

# Code Access Security

Code Access Security (CAS) deals with the permissions provided to the code executing in a partially trusted domain. SharePoint Server 2007 provides a partially trusted application environment where extended functionality of SharePoint CAS provides only the level of security required for a code to perform its operations. This ensures that the code is not being misused by other applications.

SharePoint Server 2007, by default, operates on a minimum trust level of ensuring that no malicious code is executed. This is important because SharePoint Server 2007 is an information management system and would contain sensitive information. But if the assembly is placed in Global Assembly Cache (GAC), the assembly is considered to be a Full Trust assembly and gets all privileges. Also note that only signed assemblies can be placed in the GAC.

## Assembly Signing

Signing an assembly ensures that the assembly is coming from a trusted source and is not tampered with once the assembly has been signed. There are two ways to sign an assembly: strong name signing and authenticode signing.

Strong name signing is based on the strong name keys generated using .NET tool SN.exe. Strong name consists of the public key portion of a key pair used for signing the assembly and the friendly name, version, and culture of the assembly. It is also possible to delay sign assemblies using strong name. In an enterprise development scenario, the strong name key will be protected from the developers, but for the developers to test the assembly, .NET allows delay signing. In this scenario, the .NET assembly will be signed using a temporary key during development and will be signed using a proper strong name key just before deployment.

Authenticode signing uses a digital certificate issued by a certificate authority, such as VeriSign. Also, it is possible to sign the assembly with both authenticode and strong name. In this scenario, the assembly must be signed using strong name first, then the authenticode. As strong name signing excludes the signature slot generated by the authenticode, a sequence of authenticode followed by strong name will not work. Hence, the assembly must be signed with strong name, then by authenticode.

Both authenticode and strong name are cryptographically powerful ways to identify the publisher of the assembly. This ensures that the assembly has not been tampered with. Authenticode provides a way to verify the publisher of code as the certificate is issued by third-party certificate authorities. The certificates associated with authenticode signing can be revoked, thus making the assembly invalid; this option is not available in strong name signing.

**What Should Be Strong Named** Shared dynamic-link libraries (DLLs) should be strong named. Regardless of whether a DLL will be deployed to the GAC, a strong name is recommended when the DLL is not a private implementation detail of the application, but a general service that can be used by more than one application.

**What Must Be Strong Named** You must strong name the following:

- DLLs, if you wish to deploy them to the GAC.
- ClickOnce application and deployment manifests. The Microsoft Visual Studio project system enables this by default for ClickOnce-deployed applications.
- Primary interop assemblies, which are used for component object model (COM) interoperability. The TLBIMP utility enforces strong naming when you create a primary interop assembly from a COM type library.

**What Should Not Be Strong Named** In general, you should avoid strong naming application EXE assemblies. A strongly named application or component cannot reference a weak-named component, so strong-naming an EXE prevents the EXE from referencing weak-named DLLs that are deployed with the application.

For this reason, the Visual Studio project system does not strong name application EXEs. Instead, it strong names the application manifest, which internally points to the weak named application EXE.

In addition, you may want to avoid strong naming components that are private to your application. In this case, strong naming can make it harder to manage dependencies and add unnecessary overhead for private components.

**Delay Signing Assemblies** An organization can have a closely guarded key pair that developers do not have access to on a daily basis. The public key is often available, but access to the private key is restricted to only a few individuals. When you develop assemblies with strong names, each assembly that references the strong-named target assembly contains the token of the public key used to give the target assembly a strong name. This requires that the public key be available during the development process.

You can use delayed or partial signing at build time to reserve space in the portable executable (PE) file for the strong name signature, but defer the actual signing until some later stage (typically just before shipping the assembly).

The following procedure outlines the process of using delay signing for an assembly:

1. Obtain the public key part of the key pair that will be used for delay signing. The public key is in the form of a .snk file.
2. In the Visual Studio, use the .snk file to sign the assembly. Select the Delay Sign Only check box in the Signing tab of Project Properties, as shown in Figure 17-8.

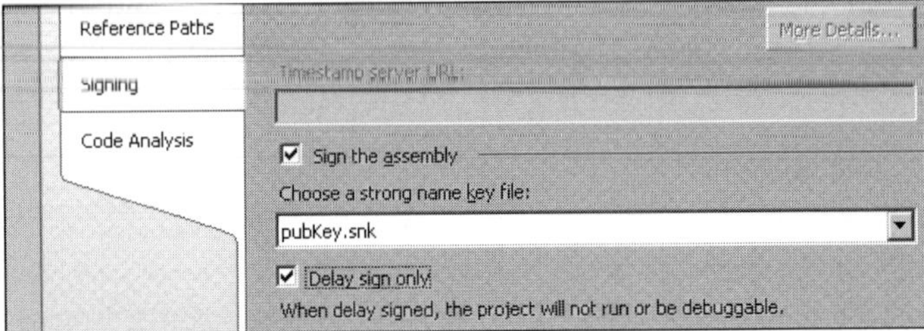


**Figure 17-8** Delay Signing Settings option within a Visual Studio project

3. As the assembly does not have a valid strong name signature, the verification of the signature must be turned off. Do this by using the –Vr option with the Strong Name tool.

```
sn -Vr DelaySignedAssembly.dll
```

4. Just before shipping the assembly, sign it using the actual key pair using the Strong Name tool with –R option.

```
sn -R DelaySignedAssembly.dll actualKey.snk
```

## Safe Controls

Safe controls are a way to specify that a class or a Web control in the assembly can be executed within the SharePoint partially trusted environment. The safe control definitions are made in the Web.config of each SharePoint Web application. The following is the syntax for declaring safe controls:

```
<SafeControl Assembly="AssemblyName, Version=1.0.0.0,
Culture=neutral, PublicKeyToken=222111222111aaab"
Namespace="Fully.Qualified.Assembly.Namespace"
TypeName="* | ClassName" Safe="True" />
```

The assembly that contains the safe control classes can be placed either in the GAC or in the bin folder of the Web application. If the assembly is placed in the GAC, it is executed with the Full Trust mode; if the assembly is placed in the bin folder, a partially trusted location, it is executed with the security trust level set in the Web.config.

**Adding Safe Control Entry Manually** The safe control definition can be manually set in Web.config of the Web application. The issues with defining safe control entries manually are the following:

- Each Web application's Web.config needs to be updated individually.
- Any inadvertent change to Web.config can crash the Web application.

**Adding Safe Control Entry Using WSP** Alternatively, safe control definitions can be made part of the WSP (SharePoint Solution) deployment for the associated custom component. In this method, the safe control entries are added into the Web.config automatically when the WSP package is deployed onto Web applications in the SharePoint 2007 Server. The deployment of the WSP can be done using the STSADM tool or using the Central Administration Web site of the SharePoint 2007 Server. This method is the preferred approach for deploying the Web parts and the safe control entries into the SharePoint server.

> **More Info** For additional information regarding the development and packaging of custom components, refer to Chapter 12, "Web Parts, Features, and Solutions Management."

The manifest.xml of the WSP should contain the safe control entries as follows:

```
<Assembly DeploymentTarget="GlobalAssemblyCache"
Location="WebPartAssembly.dll">
   <SafeControls>
         <SafeControl
               Assembly=" WebPartAssembly, Version=1.0.0.0,
 Culture=neutral, PublicKeyToken=5a5a5a5b5b5b6c6c"
               Namespace="WebPart.Assembly"
               TypeName="*" Safe="True" />
   </SafeControls>
</Assembly>
```

## Code Access Security Trust Levels in SharePoint

SharePoint Server 2007 defines two trust levels: WSS_Minimal and WSS_Medium. The default trust level for the Web application is WSS_Minimal. The default trust level can be raised to WSS_Medium, which will provide more permission for the code to execute. There is no guarantee that either of these trust levels will give the necessary permissions to your code. An alternative is to create a custom trust level, add it to the SharePoint server, and then set the default trust level in Web.config to the new trust level.

**Default Security Permissions in SharePoint** Windows SharePoint Services defines two security permissions, by default, as part of the *Microsoft.SharePoint.Security* namespace that is located in the Microsoft.SharePoint.Security.dll. Each permission contains one or more attributes, as follows:

- **SharePointPermission** Controls rights to access resources used by Windows SharePoint Services (see Table 17-2).

**Table 17-2 SharePoint Permission Attributes**

| Attribute | Description |
|---|---|
| ObjectModel | Set to TRUE to use the Microsoft.SharePoint object model |
| UnsafeSaveOnGet | Set to TRUE to save data on HTTP-GET requests |
| Unrestricted | Set to TRUE to enable all rights associated with this permission |

- **WebPartPermission** Controls rights to access Web part resources (see Table 17-3).

**Table 17-3 Web Part Permission Attributes**

| Attribute | Description |
|---|---|
| Connections | Set to TRUE to participate in Web-part-to-Web-part communications |
| Unrestricted | Set to TRUE to enable all rights associated with this permission |

**Default Trust Levels in SharePoint** As explained earlier, SharePoint defines two trust levels: WSS_Minimal and WSS_Medium.

Table 17-4 lists various permissions associated with these two trust levels.

**Table 17-4 Default Trust Level Permissions**

| Permission | WSS_Medium trust level | WSS_Minimal trust level |
|---|---|---|
| AspNetHostingPermission | Medium | Minimal |
| Environment | Read: TEMP, TMP, OS, USERNAME, COMPUTERNAME | |
| FileIO | Read, Write, Append, PathDiscovery:Application Directory | |
| IsolatedStorage | AssemblyIsolationByUser, Unrestricted UserQuota | |
| Reflection | | |
| Registry | | |
| Security | Execution, Assertion, ControlPrincipal, ControlThread, RemotingConfiguration | Execution |
| Socket | | |
| WebPermission | Connect to origin host (if configured) | |
| DNS | Unrestricted | |
| Printing | Default printing | |
| OleDBPermission | | |
| SqlClientPermission | AllowBlankPassword=false | |
| EventLog | | |
| Message Queue | | |
| Service Controller | | |
| Performance Counters | | |
| Directory Service | | |
| SharePointPermission | ObjectModel = true | |
| WebPartPermission | Connections = true | Connections = true |

**Setting the Trust Level for a Web Application** You can determine the trust level for a Web application by the value of the level attribute of the <trust> tag in the Web.config file. By default, Windows SharePoint Services sets the trust level to WSS_Minimal. In the Web.config file of a Web application extended with Windows SharePoint Services, you can find the following <trust>:

```
<trust level="WSS_Minimal" originUrl="" />
```

The following are the possible trust levels that can be applied to the Web application. These are either defined by ASP.NET (first five) or by SharePoint 2007 server (last two). You can also specify custom trust level configurations and then specify them as the trust level, as explained in the next section.

- Full
- High
- Medium
- Low
- Minimal
- WSS_Minimal (default setting)
- WSS_Medium

After specifying the trust level, Internet Information Services (IIS) must be recycled for the new trust level to take effect. Specifying a trust level in the Web.config file results in the following:

- The trust level specified in the Web.config file applies to all assemblies used by the specified Web application.
- All SharePoint sites associated with the specified Web application apply the same trust level.

**Adding a Custom Trust Level Configuration** The following steps outline the process of adding a custom trust level configuration to the SharePoint server and setting it up as the default trust level.

1. Go to the following location on the SharePoint 2007 Server LocalDrive:\Program Files\Common Files\Microsoft Shared\Web server Extensions\12\Config.
2. Make a copy of wss_minimaltrust.config to wss_customtrust.config.
3. Open the wss_customtrust.config in any text editor.
4. Add a reference to SharePointPermissions reference under <SecurityClasses> as follows:

   ```
   <SecurityClass Name="SharePointPermission"
   Description="Microsoft.SharePoint.Security.SharePointPermission,
   Microsoft.SharePoint.Security, Version=12.0.0.0, Culture=neutral,
   PublicKeyToken=71e9bce111e9429c." />
   ```

5. Search for the <PermissionSet> tags for an element with the name *SPRestricted.*
6. Copy the tag and all of its children, and paste it at the end of this tag definition.
7. Change the name property of the pasted PermissionSet tag from *SPRestricted* to CustomTrust. The changed tag will look like this:

```
<PermissionSet class="NamedPermissionSet" version="1" Name="CustomTrust">
```

8. Add the following <IPermission> node to the *<PermissionSet>* element where the name attribute equals CustomTrust:

```
<IPermission class="SharePointPermission" version="1" ObjectModel="True" />
```

Once you define the customized element, you must create a code group to specify when the common language runtime (CLR) should apply the permission set.

1. Locate the <CodeGroup> tag where the class attribute equals FirstMatchCodeGroup, and copy the following CodeGroup immediately below it. The membership condition for this code group is based on URL and the URL points bin directory. The permission is applicable to all assemblies in the bin directory. It is also possible to use the strong name membership condition, but this will restrict the permission to be applied only to one assembly.

```
<CodeGroup class="UnionCodeGroup" version="1"
PermissionSetName="CustomTrust">
   <IMembershipCondition class="UrlMembershipCondition" version="1"
   Url="$AppDirUrl$/bin/*" />
</CodeGroup>
```

2. Save and close the file.

This file now needs to be referenced in the Web.config of the Web application. To manually update the Web.config, follow these steps:

1. Open the Web.config for the Web application, and add the following trustlevel tag under the *SecurityPolicy* element:

```
<trustLevel name="WSS_Custom" policyFile="LocalDrive:\Program Files\Common
Files\Microsoft Shared\Web Server
Extensions\12\config\wss_customtrust.config" />
```

2. Change the trust tag as follows to point to the new custom policy file:

```
<trust level="WSS_Custom" originUrl="" />
```

3. Save and close the Web.config.
4. Recycle the IIS.

The new policy setting is now applied to all .dll files in the bin directory.

Note that the changes to the Web.config should be made using WSP. The changes to the Web.config can be added to an XML file and deployed to the 12\Config folder. The changes will automatically be added to the Web.config file when a new Web application is created.

**Adding Policy Definitions During Deployment** This option is the recommended approach for specifying the security permissions applicable to an assembly. In this approach, you specify the security permissions applicable to each assembly individually as part of the manifest.xml of WSP. The CAS specified in the manifest.xml is appended to the currently used trust level of the Web application. The following is an example of the *CodeAccessSecurity* element in the manifest.xml file.

```
<CodeAccessSecurity>
 <PolicyItem>
  <PermissionSet class="NamedPermissionSet" version="1"
Description="Permission set for custom assembly">
        <IPermission class="AspNetHostingPermission" version="1"
Level="Minimal" />
         <IPermission class="SecurityPermission" version="1"
Flags="Execution" />
         <IPermission
class="Microsoft.SharePoint.Security.SharePointPermission, Microsoft.SharePoint.Security,
version=12.0.0.0, Culture=neutral,
PublicKeyToken=71e9bce111e9429c" version="1" ObjectModel="True" />
   </PermissionSet>
   <Assemblies>
        <Assembly Name="CustomAssembly"/>
   </Assemblies>
 </PolicyItem>
</CodeAccessSecurity>
```

You must determine the exact set of permissions that are applicable to your custom assembly. You can use Permcalc.exe, provided as part of the .NET 2.0 framework, to determine the necessary permissions required for an assembly. Permcalc can be used as follows to determine the permission sets applicable to an assembly:

```
permcalc AnyAssembly.dll
```

This will generate an XML file of name AnyAssembly.dll.PermCalc.xml, which contains the detailed set of permissions applicable to each method. Using this, you can calculate the necessary permission set applicable to the assembly.

> **Note** Code Access Security can seem complex at first. Once the procedural changes are in place and you become comfortable using CAS, you will be thankful you made the effort. Learn more about CAS and additional best practices for using CAS by visiting the MSDN Library.

## Web Part Permissions

Web parts are user-facing components and must be executed with the least possible permission. As a Web part developer, if you install assemblies into the bin directory of the Web application, you must ensure that your code provides error handling in the event that required permissions are not available. Otherwise, unhandled security exceptions may cause your Web part to fail and may affect page rendering on the page where the Web part appears.

As stated previously, the WSS_Minimal trust level does not grant permission to the SharePointPermission.ObjectModel to assemblies in the bin directory for an application. Therefore, if your code attempts to use the Microsoft SharePoint object model, the common language runtime throws an exception.

Because the minimal permission set provides the smallest set of permissions required for code to execute, the likelihood of additional security exceptions increases.

Table 17-5 shows various options available to raise the trust level of the assemblies installed in the bin directory.

**Table 17-5 Options for Granting Trust**

| Option | Pros | Cons |
|---|---|---|
| Increase the trust level for the entire Web application. For more information, see the "Setting the Trust Level for a Web Application" section earlier in the chapter. Raising the trust level can also be achieved by adding a custom trust level configuration file to the SharePoint 2007 Server. For more information, see the "Adding a Custom Trust Level Configuration" section earlier in the chapter. | ■ Easy to implement.<br>■ In a development environment, increasing the trust level allows you to test an assembly with increased permissions while allowing you to recompile assemblies directly into the bin directory without resetting IIS. | ■ This option is the least secure.<br>■ This option affects all assemblies used by the Web application.<br>■ There is no guarantee that the destination server has the required trust level. Therefore, Web parts may not work once they are installed on the destination server. |
| Install your assemblies in the GAC. | ■ Easy to implement.<br>■ This grants Full Trust to your assembly without affecting the trust level of assemblies installed in the bin directory. | ■ This option is the least secure among the provided alternatives.<br>■ Assemblies installed in the GAC are available to all Web applications and applications on a server running Windows SharePoint Services. This could represent a potential security risk, as it potentially grants a higher level of permission to your assembly across a larger scope than necessary.<br>■ In a development environment, you must reset IIS every time you recompile assemblies.<br>■ Licensing issues may arise due to the global availability of your assembly. |

**Table 17-5 Options for Granting Trust**

| Option | Pros | Cons |
|---|---|---|
| Create custom policy definitions for the Web part assembly, and add them to the current trust configuration file during deployment. See the "Adding Policy Definitions During Deployment" section earlier in the chapter. | ■ Recommended approach.<br>■ This option is the most secure.<br>■ An assembly can operate with a unique policy that meets the minimum permission requirements for the assembly.<br>■ By creating a custom security policy, you can ensure that the destination server can run your Web parts. | ■ Requires the most effort of all three options because the required permission set needs to be determined for the Web part assembly. |

# Summary

In this chapter, we have highlighted the importance of information security in your SharePoint Server 2007 implementation. We have reviewed and discussed the concepts of confidentiality, integrity, and authenticity. We also reviewed capabilities provided within SharePoint Server 2007, such as information classification, access controls, and permissions. Lastly, we reviewed some specific security mechanisms that can be used to minimize the risks associated with the execution of custom code.

# Additional Resources

- Feature Stapling (MSDN Library): *http://msdn2.microsoft.com/en-us/library/bb861862.aspx*
- SharePoint Access Checker Web Part (CodePlex): *http://www.codeplex.com/AccessChecker*
- Code Access Security in Practice (MSDN Library–Patterns & Practices): *http://msdn2.microsoft.com/en-us/library/aa302424.aspx*

Chapter 18

# Business Intelligence and Reporting

**In this chapter:**



According to Microsoft, business intelligence (BI) can be summarized as "the aggregation, storage, analysis, and reporting of data for the purpose of informing business decision makers." And let's face it—today's business decision-makers have a distinct advantage over their predecessors when it comes to BI tools to assist in the analysis, trending, and presentation of data. A good BI strategy, supported by a solid base of BI technologies, can streamline business processes and boost productivity and profit.

Microsoft's overall BI strategy comprises a suite of server and client-side data integration tools. Powerful analytical and reporting tools in Microsoft SQL Server 2005 provide the backbone data management infrastructure, while end-user Microsoft Office applications, specifically Microsoft Office Excel, provide the flexibility for information workers to remotely interact with centralized and secure data sources.

This chapter focuses primarily on introducing the BI capabilities within Microsoft Office SharePoint Server 2007 and discusses how you can present and surface BI-critical data within SharePoint sites. This chapter discusses the best practices for using BI integration tools, such as when you might choose to use one BI tool or integration method over another. It is important to realize that there is limited information available from the field at this point; however, it's appropriate to start the discussion with what is available at this time and build on this information in the future.

**Note** Some features discussed throughout this chapter, such as data connection libraries, are offered only with SharePoint Server 2007 Enterprise licensing. For a comparison of features between the different SharePoint versions, see *http://office.microsoft.com/en-us/sharepointserver/HA101978031033.aspx*.

There are many different ways to analyze and publish external data to SharePoint sites, such as using Excel Services–a thin client delivery mechanism for viewing Office Excel spreadsheets without the need of the Excel client–and Report Center, a custom SharePoint site template with special built-in reporting BI functional Web parts, document libraries, and reporting content types. Depending on business requirements, you may choose a data integration method that will allow an administrator to more selectively create and deploy data reports and minimize end-user control, or you may choose to empower end-users by enabling them to access data sources and build custom reports directly inside of SharePoint. The Microsoft BI suite includes the flexibility to secure and selectively deploy data based on user credentials.

Two recent additions to the BI suite of products have seen richer BI integration with SharePoint Server 2007 and Windows SharePoint Services 3.0:

- Microsoft Office PerformancePoint Server 2007, which is a budgeting, forecasting, and monitoring tool
- Reporting Services SharePoint integration, which is part of the SQL Server 2005 Service Pack 2 enhancements

Both products are specifically geared toward a distributed data reporting approach. You'll learn how you can work with both of these products as part of your SharePoint Server 2007 BI solution in Chapter 19, "Extending Business Intelligence."

> **Note** In this chapter and in Chapter 19, we focus on BI integration with SharePoint Server 2007 as opposed to Windows SharePoint Services 3.0.

In this chapter, we'll cover additional considerations, such as topology and the complexity of establishing your BI solution. You may already have deployed SharePoint Server 2007 and are now at the point of introducing additional BI components to enhance data analysis throughout your company. There are several considerations for data security and data authentication modes that should form part of your overall BI planning and architecture (for example, a distributed server configuration and multiple Office client versions). Authentication and client-side dependencies are two of the major considerations in architecting a BI deployment strategy.

In the following sections, we'll review the core Microsoft BI strategy, the components that support the overall BI approach, and solutions so that you can understand the fundamentals behind the data-integration and presentation methods, such as the following:

- The Microsoft BI big picture
- Core BI features in SharePoint Server 2007 and Microsoft Office applications
- BI integration with SharePoint Services

# The Microsoft BI Big Picture

The Microsoft BI strategy includes three main components:

- BI platform
- End-user tools and performance management applications
- Delivery mechanisms

The BI platform contains the various database and data warehousing components for data storage and schema. SQL Server 2005 Analysis Services (SSAS) provides a semantic model, referred to as a unified dimensional model (UDM). The UDM defines business entities, business logic, calculations, and metrics and provides a bridge between end-users and data sources. End-users can run queries directly against the UDM using BI tools, such as Excel and Office PerformancePoint Server 2007. Figure 18-1 demonstrates how an end-user queries SQL Server data sources via the UDM.

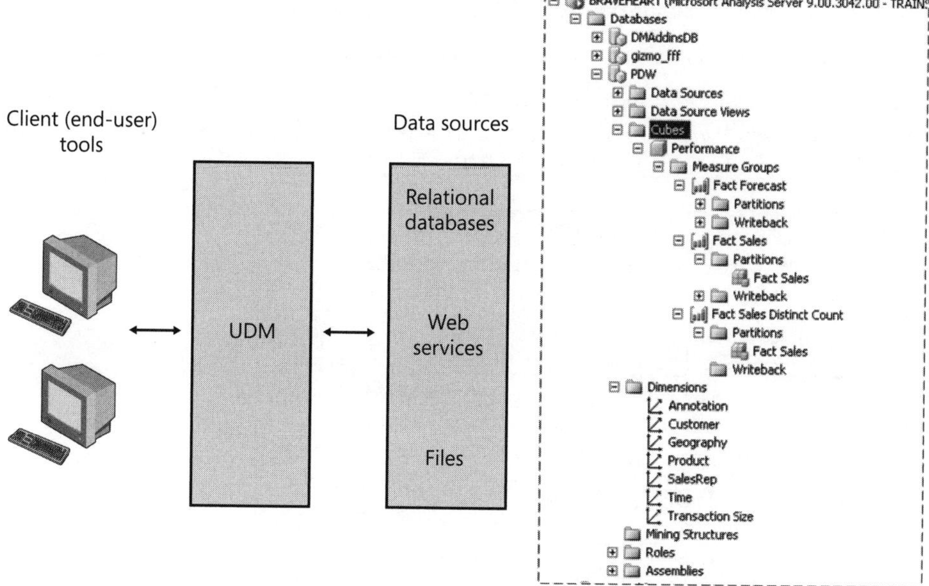


**Figure 18-1** Interaction between end-user tools and the BI platform

> **More Info** You can find further details about the UDM and the behind-the-scenes SQL Server 2005 architecture at *http://technet.microsoft.com/en-us/library/ms345143.aspx*.

Table 18-1 breaks down each of the BI components and outlines properties and details for each component.

Table 18-1 BI Components

| Component | Properties | Details |
|---|---|---|
| BI platform | ■ SQL Server 2005 Reporting Services (SSRS)<br>■ SQL Server 2005 Analysis Services (SSAS)<br>■ SQL Server Database Management System (DBMS)<br>■ SQL Server Integration Services (SSIS) | ■ Managed reporting solution.<br>■ On-line analytical processing (OLAP) for high-performance analysis.<br>■ Relational database engine that provides the database for storage of databases, including data warehouses.<br>■ Build data integration solutions including extraction, transformation, and load (ETL) packages for data warehousing. |
| End-user tools and performance management applications | Excel and PerformancePoint Server 2007/Dashboard Designer | Connect to data sources, perform in-depth data analysis, and provide a secure, distributive data-authoring environment. Create key performance indicators (KPI) and scorecard dashboards and deploy to SharePoint sites. |
| Delivery mechanisms | SharePoint Server 2007 | Centrally deploy and display real-time data, reports, and charts. |

Figure 18-2 shows a graphical representation of Microsoft's integrated BI offering. SharePoint Server 2007 is at the top of the stack and acts as the hub through which information workers can collaboratively access and analyze data.

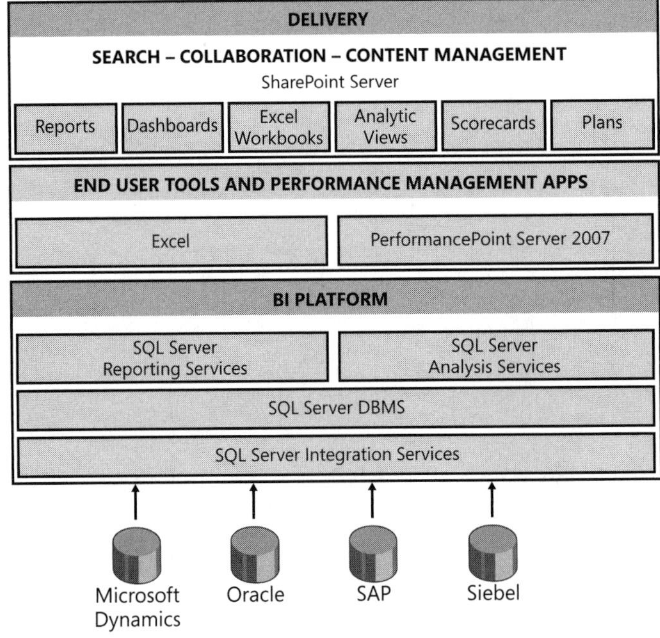


**Figure 18-2** Microsoft's integrated BI offering

Throughout this chapter and Chapter 19, we refer to reports, dashboards, scorecards, and key performance indicators (KPIs) as the means for analyzing, preparing, and presenting data within SharePoint Server 2007.

# BI Integration with SharePoint Server 2007

Excel, Excel Services, SharePoint Report Center, and the Business Data Catalog (BDC) are the default, or core, BI features within the Office suite of products. SQL Server 2005 Reporting Services, Analysis Services, and PerformancePoint Server 2007 extend the core BI functionality by offering enhanced reporting capabilities, data warehousing, in-depth data analysis, and real-time monitoring. Figure 18-3 shows the overall relationship between the various BI applications. Note how pivotal SharePoint Server 2007 is as the negotiation point for data between server and client applications.

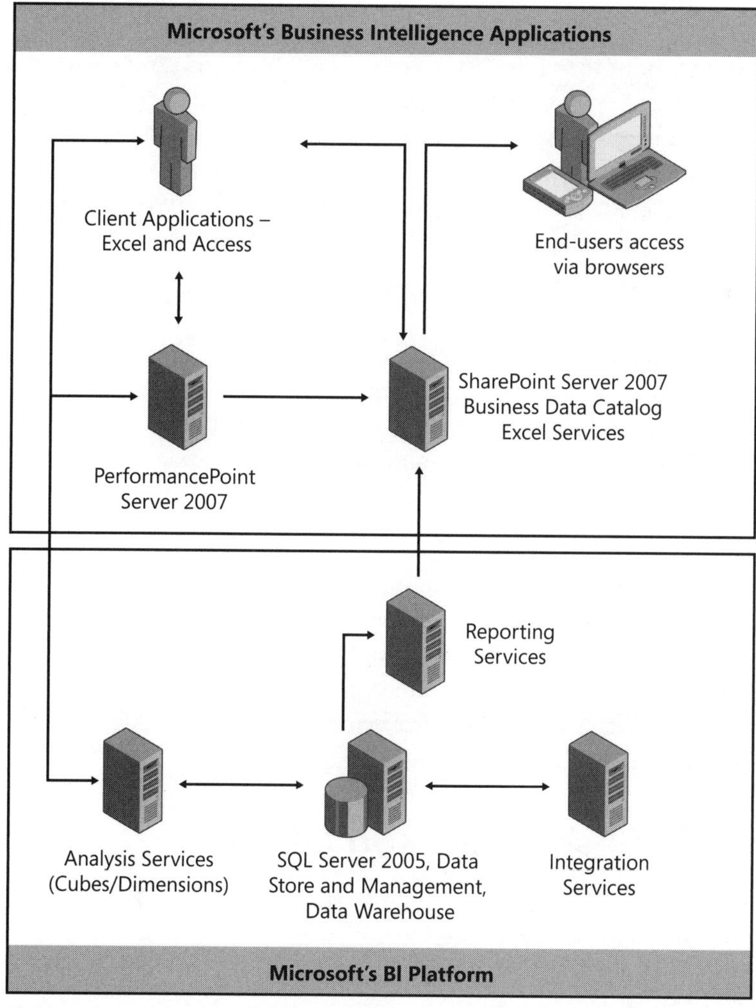


**Figure 18-3** SharePoint Server 2007 in the grand scheme of BI applications

Two other products—Microsoft Office Business Scorecard Manager 2005 and ProClarity Analytics—also form part of the Microsoft BI solution set. However, because these products have been either superseded by or integrated as part of the mainstream BI products, we won't cover them in detail. Instead, we have summarized each, as follows:

- Office Business Scorecard Manager 2005, while still supported, is superseded by PerformancePoint Server 2007—that is, there is no Business Scorecard Manager 2007. PerformancePoint Server 2007 includes functionality provided by Business Scorecard Manager 2005 plus additional analytical and trending capabilities. If you are currently using Business Scorecard Manager 2005 and are considering upgrading to PerformancePoint Server 2007, a PerformancePoint Server 2007 Scorecard Migration Tool is available. Details can be found at *http://technet.microsoft.com/en-us/library/bb838761.aspx*. Further details regarding the move from Business Scorecard Manager 2005 to PerformancePoint Server 2007 can be found at *http://www.microsoft.com/business/performancepoint/productinfo/previousversions.aspx*.
- ProClarity was introduced to the Microsoft suite of BI products through acquisition in 2006. ProClarity extends the analytical capabilities of PerformancePoint Server 2007, such as the ability to drill down further into KPIs, and can be included along with PerformancePoint Server 2007 in a BI solution for in-depth analysis and reporting. Further details about ProClarity, including purchasing details, can be found at *http://www.microsoft.com/business/performancepoint/productinfo/proclarity/proclarity-overview2.aspx*.

Other BI solutions include programmatically creating integration between external data sources (for example, using Microsoft Visual Studio 2005 and SQL Server 2005 Integration Services [SSIS] to create and format a custom connector for SAP) or utilizing the Excel Services API and/or Web services to build and deploy custom solutions. Using Microsoft Office SharePoint Designer 2007, you can integrate custom data sources, including data from SQL Server 2005 and Microsoft Office Access databases, and leverage Data View and Data Form Web parts to format and present the data within SharePoint Server 2007 sites, including the ability to both retrieve and write data back to the data source.

There are also third-party data integration products, such as Dundas Chart for SharePoint, which includes tools for creating custom dashboards and plotting data against SharePoint lists. The Microsoft Dynamics CRM Analytics Foundation, an open-source project, was released on CodePlex (*http://www.codeplex.com/crmanalytics*) early in 2007 and includes support for creating and surfacing reports from Microsoft Dynamics CRM 3.0 into SharePoint sites, such as sales dashboards.

# Core BI Features in SharePoint and Office

This section discusses the core BI features built into SharePoint Server 2007 and Office:

- Excel

- Excel Services
- SharePoint Report Center
- BDC

# Excel

Excel integrates well with SQL Server 2005 and SharePoint Server 2007 and plays a pivotal role in providing end-users with the tools for data analysis, data-mining construction, and the creation of PivotTables. Microsoft Office Excel 2007 enhances the end-user's ability to access and analyze data from SSAS cubes using PivotTables and PivotCharts. Analysis Services data can also be accessed with Microsoft Office Excel 2003 via PivotTables, but involves additional configuration. Office Excel 2007 provides new features, such as the ability to view and work with Analysis Services KPIs, and flexibility for building KPI scorecards.

Figure 18-4 shows an Excel PivotTable. The workbook is directly linked to an SSAS cube. Fields from the PivotTable Field List, shown to the right of the figure, can be dragged and dropped onto the main workspace to create scorecards, including KPIs.

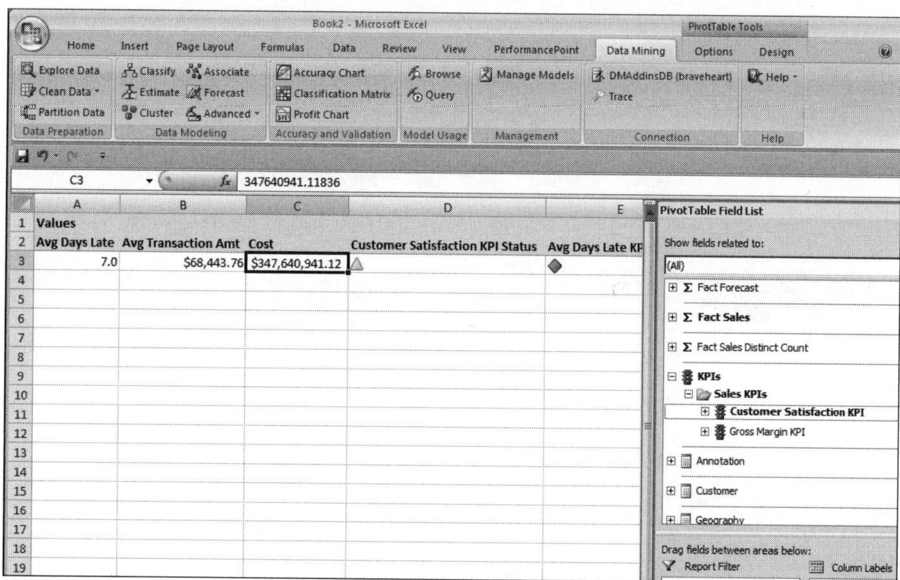


**Figure 18-4** Excel workbook connected directly to SSAS showing PivotTable functionality

Excel workbooks can be stored within SharePoint document libraries, where they can be shared and versioned; historical details can be dynamically captured and stored for each workbook. More importantly, Excel workbooks containing active connections to Analysis Services can be published to Excel Services and made available for viewing via a Web browser without the need for an Excel client.

## Excel Add-ins

Two Excel BI add-ins assist with remote data analysis and end-to-end data submission. The Microsoft SQL Server 2005 Data Mining add-ins for Microsoft Office 2007 include custom data mining and forecasting tools for Excel, such as the ability to estimate and predict based on certain patterns within selected data fields. Figure 18-5 shows the Data Mining menu on the Excel 2007 Ribbon.

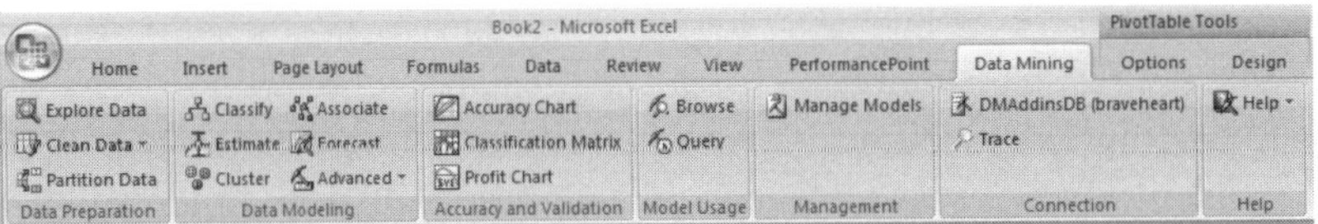


Figure 18-5 Excel 2007 Ribbon showing the Data Mining menu options

A data mining Visio template is also included as part of the Data Mining add-in, and you can easily generate dependency network, cluster, and decision trees based on mining models from SSAS. The data mining add-in can be used to create data mining models on existing analysis server data or to perform additional queries in Excel workbooks. Figure 18-6 shows an example of a predictive model based on existing analysis server data.

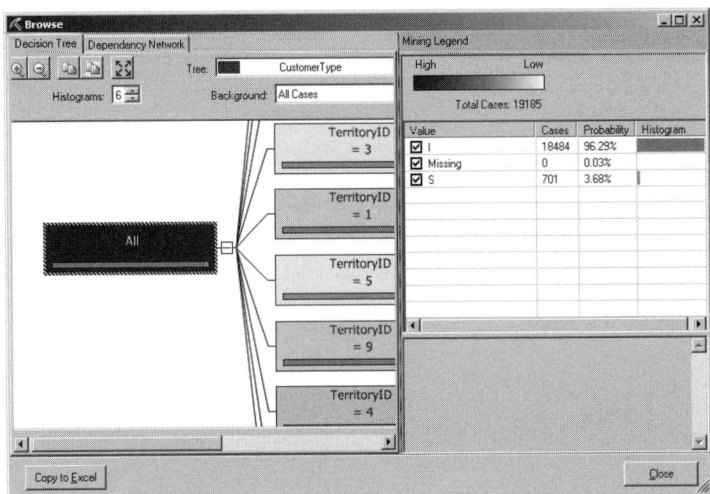


Figure 18-6 Data-mining model decision tree based on an existing Excel 2007 workbook analysis server connection

## Notes from the Field Consequences of Excel Add-ins

Be aware that certain Excel add-ins may cause an issue when you attempt to integrate Excel with SharePoint lists. Specifically, if you're attempting to create a new SharePoint (SharePoint Server 2007 or Windows SharePoint Services 3.0) list from either an Excel 2007 or Excel 2003 spreadsheet and you receive the error "Method 'post' of object 'IOWSPostData' failed," this could be due to one or more Excel add-ins. I experienced a problem specifically with the Analysis ToolPack add-in, which is included as part of Excel 2007 out-of-the-box add-in options. There is a client-side solution to this problem, which involves editing the EXPTOOWS.XLA file on the client and editing the file in Excel using the Visual Basic code editor. For details on how to accomplish this, see my blog post located at *http://mindsharpblogs.com/kathy/archive/2008/03/16/4450.aspx.*

*Kathy Hughes, Microsoft MVP*

As a best practice, use the PerformancePoint add-in for Excel to enable end-users to remotely access assigned tasks using Excel and submit updated worksheets to PerformancePoint Server for approval. The add-in provides equivalent functionality in both Excel 2007 and Excel 2003, with the exception that some formatting features specifically related to pivot styles will not be available in Excel 2003. Chapter 19 expands on the PerformancePoint add-in for Excel, delves into PerformancePoint Server 2007, and explains the end-to-end BI association between the add-in and PerformancePoint Monitoring Server.

**Note** The PerformancePoint add-in for Excel requires an existing installation of either Excel 2003 (SP2) or Excel 2007. Further information about prerequisites can be found at *http://technet.microsoft.com/en-us/library/bb838749.aspx.*

Figure 18-7 shows the PerformancePoint add-in for Excel actively selected in the Excel 2007 Ribbon.

**Figure 18-7** Excel 2007 Ribbon showing the PerformancePoint menu options

## Office BI Integration with SharePoint Lists

Both Excel and Access continue to play a key role in the negotiation between client and server BI functionality within SharePoint Server 2007 and provide the ability to expose data within SharePoint sites. For example, Excel worksheets can be published as a SharePoint list in which the data can be accessed and updated by multiple users.

The following are a few scenarios you should consider when using Access databases and assessing your data analysis needs:

- You can publish an Access database as a SharePoint list and perform additional data analysis in SharePoint; other key benefits include filtering and sorting.
- Access 2007 databases can also be upgraded to SQL Server 2005 databases using the Access 2007 Upsizing Wizard. For instance, you could upsize an existing Access 2007 database to SQL Server 2005 for a scalable database solution and then use Reporting Services to create custom reports, which you could then publish directly to SharePoint Server 2007.
- Alternatively, you could leverage Access 2007 as the front-end reporting mechanism for SharePoint lists. Access 2007 includes the ability to import a SharePoint list, or multiple SharePoint lists, into an Access 2007 database to perform additional reporting while maintaining an active link back to the list on the SharePoint server.

There are some key differences between working with data between Excel 2003 and Excel 2007, which are covered in the following sections.

**Excel-to-SharePoint and Data Synchronization** New lists within SharePoint sites can be created directly from existing Excel spreadsheets (for example, select Create, Custom Lists, Import Spreadsheet). SharePoint will import all columns and any existing data, or you can specify a range of cells to import, including a range of cells, a table range, or a named range. Existing formulas within the source Excel worksheet will be converted to calculated columns.

If you are using Excel 2003, you can create a SharePoint list directly from within Excel by clicking a single cell in the Excel spreadsheet and selecting List, Publish List. This creates a new SharePoint list in Datasheet view.

> **Note** When you are publishing from Excel 2003 to a SharePoint list, only a single worksheet will be published—that is, if you have an Excel workbook with multiple worksheets, not all worksheets will be published.

Linkage can be maintained between the original Excel 2003 file and the newly created SharePoint list, and synchronization can be performed both ways. That is, you can add new rows to the source Excel 2003 worksheet and have the linked SharePoint list updated, and you can also update the SharePoint list and have the source Excel worksheet updated.

Using Excel 2007, you have two options to publish data to SharePoint:

- **Publish to Excel Services** If Excel Services is installed as part of your SharePoint Server 2007 deployment, a one-way sync will exist between the source Excel 2007 file and the published server version. In other words, updates to the source file can be pushed to an existing published version and changes reflected within a Web page.
- **Export a table within Excel 2007 to a SharePoint list** Once a table has been exported, no linkage remains between the source and destination data. That is, updating the original Excel file will not update data in the SharePoint list, and data updated in the SharePoint list will not update the original Excel 2007 file.

The main difference between publishing from Excel 2003 and publishing from Excel 2007 to a SharePoint site is that you can publish not only a single Excel worksheet but an entire Excel workbook if you are using Excel 2007 with Excel Services installed. In Excel 2007, the publishing option has been built into the main File menu and will publish an entire Excel workbook to Excel Services.

**SharePoint-to-Excel and Data Synchronization** Lists within SharePoint sites can be exported to Excel, and you can choose to maintain a link between the exported data and the original SharePoint list. Updates to the SharePoint list will be synced to the external Excel spreadsheet. This is a one-way sync—updates to the exported Excel spreadsheet will not replicate to the original SharePoint list.

> **Note** Using the Export To Excel option from the Actions menu within a SharePoint Server 2007 document library or list, either in Standard or Datasheet view, requires the presence of the Excel 2007 client.

Using the Datasheet view, you can directly interact with and manipulate data within the Datasheet view in the browser, such as selecting and deleting multiple rows of data. Datasheet views also enable you to perform additional data analysis, such as exporting and reporting on list data within Access and using Excel to query, print, chart, and create PivotTables, as shown in the right task pane in Figure 18-8. Both Excel 2003 and Excel 2007 are supported when you select the Query List With Excel task pane option within Datasheet view.

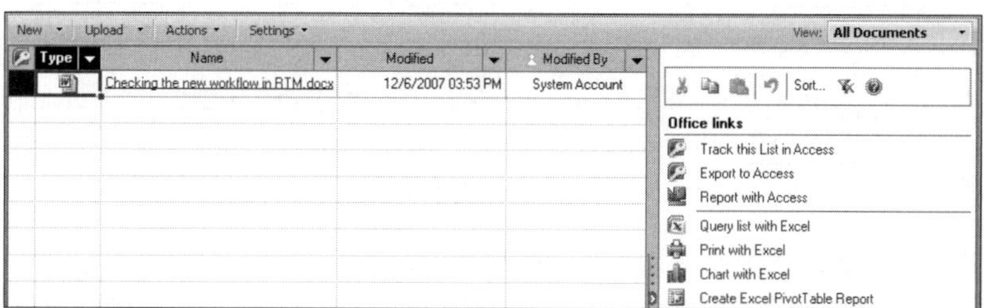


**Figure 18-8** Available data tools included in the Datasheet view task pane

> **Note** The Datasheet view requires the presence of a client-side Windows SharePoint Services–compatible list datasheet control, such as Excel 2003/Excel 2007 or Access 2003/Access 2007, and ActiveX control support. This differs from the Excel Web Access Web part, which is used in conjunction with Excel Services and does not require ActiveX and does not have client-side dependencies.

## Excel Services

Excel Services is part of the SharePoint Server 2007 Enterprise Edition. A benefit of this edition is that you can publish an Excel workbook to a Web page, and end-users can view workbook contents without the presence of the Excel client. However, for users to interact with Excel Services, clients require the Office SharePoint 2007 Enterprise Client Access License (CAL).

The published workbook is effectively a read-only version of the source Excel workbook. It provides a good way to share information while protecting the integrity of the data–a published Excel workbook, such as an annual or fiscal budget, is a centralized, single version accessed by all. This section summarizes the key features of Excel Services.

> **Note** Unlike creating a new SharePoint list by importing an Excel spreadsheet or publishing an Excel 2003 worksheet, you can use Excel 2007 to publish an entire Excel workbook to Excel Services. You can choose to limit the number of worksheets within a workbook to be published or elect to have all worksheets published.

There are three main Excel Services components:

- **Excel Calculation Services (ECS)** This component loads the Excel workbook into a Web page, performs server-side calculations, and refreshes external data.
- **Excel Web Access (EWA)** This Web part displays a workbook or interconnecting parts of a workbook on a Web page or dashboard. It leverages DHTML and JavaScript for Web page interaction, thus avoiding the need to download ActiveX controls to the client. EWA Web parts can be configured to filter on specific values. EWA is unlike the Datasheet view available in SharePoint lists, which is dependent upon ActiveX controls along with the Excel or Access client. EWA offers additional features, such as the ability to snapshot an Excel workbook.
- **Excel Web Services (EWS)** Excel Services exposes a Web service API that developers can use to develop custom or add-on applications for Excel Services. The typical address to access the Excel Services Web services is *http://server_site_name/_vti_bin/excelservice.asmx*.

Numerous configuration options are available when you deploy Excel Services. Typically, Excel Services installs EWA and EWS on the Web front-end server and one ECS on the application server. In a single-server deployment, the EWA, EWS, and ECS are installed on the same server. In multiple-server deployments, the components could be installed on separate servers. A major consideration in deploying Excel Services, and one you will want to carefully plan, is how the authentication between servers and clients is negotiated.

## Authentication Between Client and Server

In a distributed server environment where SQL Server 2005 and Analysis Services is on a separate machine from SharePoint Server 2007 and Excel Services and where you are leveraging external data connections–that is, an Office Data Connection (ODC) file–to your SSAS as the basis for your published Excel workbook, you need to configure Kerberos to impersonate the user accessing the database server and trust/delegation between servers. The same also applies when you are implementing Reporting Services integration where SQL Server 2005 and Reporting Services are on a different machine than SharePoint Server 2007.

> **Note** If you experience problems accessing data sources when you attempt to view a published Excel workbook, check the Unified Logging Service (ULS) log for external data errors. The ULS log is typically located at %SystemDrive%:\Program Files\Common Files\Microsoft Shared\Web Server Extensions\12\LOGS.

### Notes from the Field **Using Analysis Services Data in Excel Services**

I started working with Excel Services, in combination with Analysis Services data, in my virtual environment, which basically meant that everything including client, SQL Server 2005, SharePoint Server 2007, and Excel Services were all configured on the one virtual machine. The Web application was configured to use NTLM, and everything worked seamlessly. However, enter a real-world scenario where the customer's deployment consists of a multiple-server environment–for instance, where SharePoint Server 2007 and Excel Services are hosted on one server and SQL Server 2005 and Analysis Services are hosted on another–and you suddenly realize that NTLM just won't cut it! In order for Excel Services to successfully access a separate SQL server, you need to impersonate and delegate the user account. You can do this by implementing Kerberos authentication (or single sign-on [SSO]). Simply using NTLM is not sufficient because the Web server cannot delegate the current user to the SQL server, also referred to as a double hop.

Best practice when testing an Excel Services and Analysis Services scenario is to test within a multiple-server environment so you can accurately test authentication and ensure that clients and servers can successfully access back-end Analysis Services cubes and data. This will better prepare you for real-world scenarios and deployments.

*Kathy Hughes, Microsoft MVP*

The following sources provide related information:

- For a comprehensive overview on configuring Kerberos in an Active Directory directory services environment, refer to *http://www.sharepointblogs.com/tonstegeman/archive/2007/03/11/using-analysis-services-data-in-excel-services-part-1-preparing-the-ad-for-kerberos.aspx*.
- For additional information on configuring Excel Services and data connections, see "Plan External Data Connections for Excel Services" at *http://technet2.microsoft.com/Office/en-us/library/7e6ce086-57b6-4ef2-8117-e725de18f2401033.mspx?mfr=true*.
- Additional information on configuring SSO as the authentication mode for Excel Services can be found in Document 2 ("Step 2: Configuring Single Sign-On for Excel Services") at *http://office.microsoft.com/en-us/excel/HA102203821033.aspx*.

## Publishing Excel Workbooks

As a best practice, make sure you establish trusted file locations and trusted data connection libraries, as defined in the Excel Services Settings in Shared Services, before publishing your Excel workbooks. They form the basis for successfully publishing Excel workbooks, such as publishing an online analysis processing (OLAP) PivotTable, which uses an ODC file located within a Trusted Data Connections Library. Excel 2007 includes an option within the main File menu to publish to Excel Services. The Excel workbook must first be saved to a trusted file location before it can be successfully loaded by Excel Services.

> **Note** If you do not see the Publish command in the Excel client menu, this most likely means that you do not have Microsoft Office Professional Plus 2007 installed. See *http://office.microsoft.com/en-us/excel/HA101650601033.aspx* for details regarding Office version requirements when you are working with Excel Services.

ECS performs calculations included within the source Excel workbook on the server, which means that actual functions and formulas are not directly accessible to end-users.

The main inference in utilizing Excel Services is that an Excel workbook can be published to a Web page, but the published version is not editable because users cannot make edits or enter new data and then save the changes to the source Excel file/workbook. Instead, end-users can perform run-time calculations via the browser based on parameters created in the source Excel workbook. Once a Web page containing EWA is refreshed or an end-user ends her browser session, any calculated changes made to a published Excel worksheet/workbook are lost.

Snapshots of Excel workbooks can be captured and saved as separate Excel files to the client machine. A snapshot includes the data values within the published Excel workbook and excludes any formulas or other business logic from the source workbook. End-users with viewer permissions to the document library containing the source Excel file and location of the published Excel file will be able to both copy the published Excel workbook to an Excel file, including data values and formulas, and open a snapshot of an Excel workbook. Figure 18-9 shows both the Open In Excel and Open Snapshot In Excel options available from the EWA Web part toolbar.

> **Note** In Figure 18-9, although the colors are not distinguishable in this book, colors are used to highlight the variances in available stock within each column. This is based on conditional formatting within the source Excel workbook and is supported within Excel Services. For example, you could use red to highlight unfavorable figures and green to highlight favorable figures. This feature is also referred to as *heat maps*.

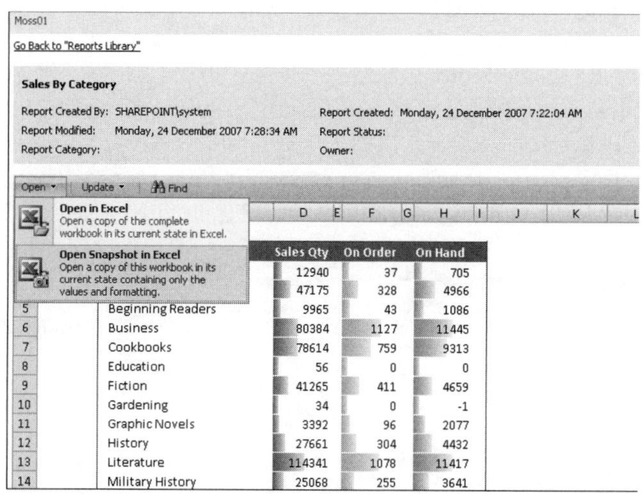


**Figure 18-9** Excel export options available within the EWA Web part toolbar

> **Note** Excel 2007 is required for Excel snapshots and Excel copies from an EWA Web part. If Excel 2007 is not installed on the client machine where a snapshot or copy is being attempted, the following message is displayed within a dialog box: "The workbook cannot be opened. Excel may not be installed properly (or was set to install on first use), the path to the document may be incorrect, or your session may have timed out. Try opening the workbook again, or clicking Reload on the Excel Web Access toolbar."

Excel 2007 workbooks containing multiple worksheets can be published to Excel Services. The person publishing the workbook can choose which worksheets within a workbook to display at the time of saving and publishing to Excel Services. Portions of an Excel worksheet can also be published based on named cells, or parameters, defined within the source Excel workbook.

A best practice is to enable auditing, versioning, and content approval on the Reports document library (or the nominated document library location) for published Excel workbooks to monitor edits and updates to the source Excel workbooks.

## Configuring Excel Web Access Web Parts

Once an Excel 2007 workbook is published to Excel Services, the EWA Web part provides the mechanism for viewing and manipulating the published workbook within the browser.

> **Note** The EWA does not have client-side dependencies, nor does it require ActiveX download to the client.

An entire Excel workbook can be displayed in a single EWA. End-users can navigate worksheets within a published workbook just as they would when using the Excel client. Sections of Excel workbooks can also be divided into individual EWA Web parts on a Web page (also referred to as a *dashboard*) based on named parameters within the source Excel 2007 workbook. For example, Figure 18-10 shows several EWA Web parts on a single Web page, which includes filtering and Web part connections between each EWA Web part to dynamically refresh and display data based on the name of the account representative selected.

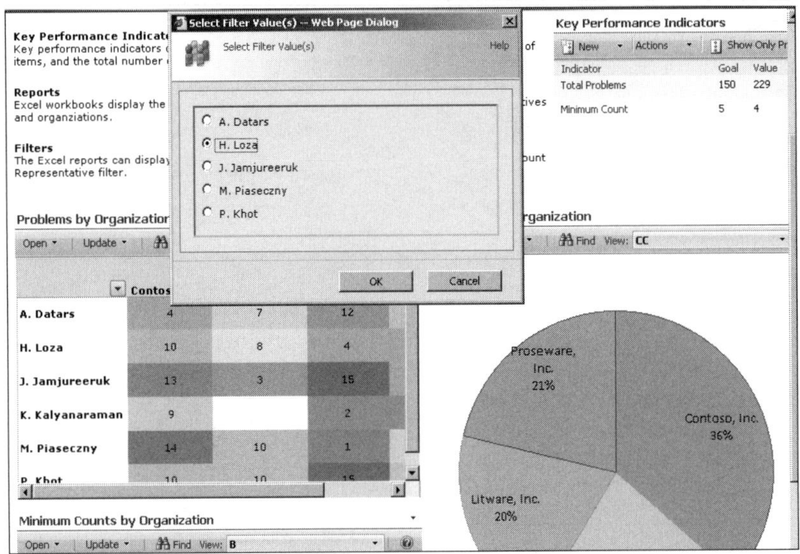


**Figure 18-10** Dashboard showing multiple instances of EWA Web parts

> **Note** Try setting the session time a bit higher in Excel Services configuration if you see the message "Session Timeout, Your session has timed out because of inactivity. To reload workbook, click OK."

Using filtering, Excel parameters, and Web part connections between EWA Web parts, you can generate powerful and intuitive dashboards within SharePoint Server 2007.

> **More Info** For additional information regarding using parameters in dashboards (and Excel) see, "Using Parameters in Dashboards" at *http://blogs.msdn.com/excel/archive/2006/09/25/770961.aspx.*

## Unsupported Features in Excel Services

Not all Excel client-application features are supported in Excel Services. For example, attempting to publish Excel files that contain code, such as Visual Basic for Applications macros, embedded pictures, or clip art, will result in failure to publish. Other non-supported client-side functionality includes, but is not limited to, comments, data validation, and external references to linked workbooks.

Unfortunately, it is not always apparent whether an Excel workbook is compatible with Excel Services until you try to publish it. However, an open source Excel Services Compatibility Checker has been developed. You can find details about it at *http://blogs.msdn.com/cumgranosalis/archive/2007/06/29/excel-services-compatibility-checker-addin-beta.aspx.* The executable file is located at *http://blogs.msdn.com/cumgranosalis/pages/excel-services-compatibility-checker-download-page.aspx.*

### Tradeoff Value-Added Solutions and Cost

If you currently have the standard version of SharePoint Server 2007 and are considering integrating Excel workbooks with SharePoint sites as part of your overall BI solution, you might consider the following two options:

1. Upgrade to SharePoint Server 2007 Enterprise Edition and use Excel Services.
2. Keep the SharePoint Server 2007 Standard Edition and do the following:
    a. Use the built-in document management features within SharePoint document libraries to store, version, and share Excel workbooks in their native format.
    b. Create a new SharePoint list from an existing Excel spreadsheet.

Option 1 incurs additional costs and deployment considerations, such as changing to Kerberos (if you're not already running in Kerberos mode) and upgrading to Excel 2007 (if you're currently using Excel 2003). However, it provides a more scalable Excel solution without the need for the Excel client or ActiveX.

Option 2(a) means that the Excel workbook will be retained in its original native format and can be checked out and edited by authorized users. However, the Excel client must be present on those clients responsible for updating Excel workbooks. Excel workbooks uploaded to a SharePoint document library can be secured using Excel's security features, but there is a risk that end-users will still be able to access any embedded formulas and republish the workbook elsewhere, resulting in duplicate copies of the same workbooks.

Option 2(b) means that, although a new list will be created from an Excel worksheet, there are implications in continuing to update the list from an Excel client or the portability of data within the list. SharePoint lists have limitations for data types and Excel functions, and it is difficult to append updates to an existing list from an Excel workbook. Also, if your organization is currently running Excel 2003, then users will experience compatibility issues when you upgrade to Excel 2007. Unlike Excel 2003, there is no two-way synchronization between SharePoint lists and Excel 2007.

If you plan to stay with the Standard Edition *and* you are using multiple Excel workbooks throughout your organization (which may also include custom formulas), then we recommend that you maintain the existing Excel workbooks in their native Excel format and utilize the document management features within SharePoint document libraries, such as versioning and approval, so you can monitor who has updated what and when. In addition, we recommend you lock down access to Excel workbooks using the built-in SharePoint security model and give edit rights only to those users who will ultimately update existing workbooks and upload new workbooks.

If you are contemplating upgrading at a later stage and the basis of that upgrade is BI—specifically, Excel features—then before you upgrade to the Enterprise Edition to adopt Excel Services, carefully consider the business requirements. For instance, are you planning to deploy a read-only version of Excel workbooks, or are you planning to have a distributed Excel authoring environment? If you're considering the latter, then you may consider purchasing PerformancePoint Server 2007 instead. Remember, while Excel Services enables you to publish an entire Excel 2007 workbook as a Web page in which end-users can access Excel data and perform run-time calculations, but cannot save data back to the source Excel workbook, the onus of updating and republishing an Excel workbook falls upon one or several people. PerformancePoint Server 2007, on the other hand, offers you the ability to distribute Excel tasks to end-users, including centralized and secure control over user access and Excel templates.

## SharePoint Report Center

The SharePoint Report Center is a BI SharePoint site template that includes document libraries specifically geared for storage of Excel workbooks, data connections to external SSAS, and creation of KPIs and dashboards. The Report Center site is provisioned as part of the SharePoint Server 2007 Collaboration Portal (publishing) site collection, although additional Report Center sites can be created throughout site collections. For example, you could create Report Center sites for storage of BI assets for each respective organizational business unit.

> **Note** The Report Center site template is available only as part of the SharePoint Server 2007 Enterprise Edition.

Figure 18-11 shows the home page of the Report Center.

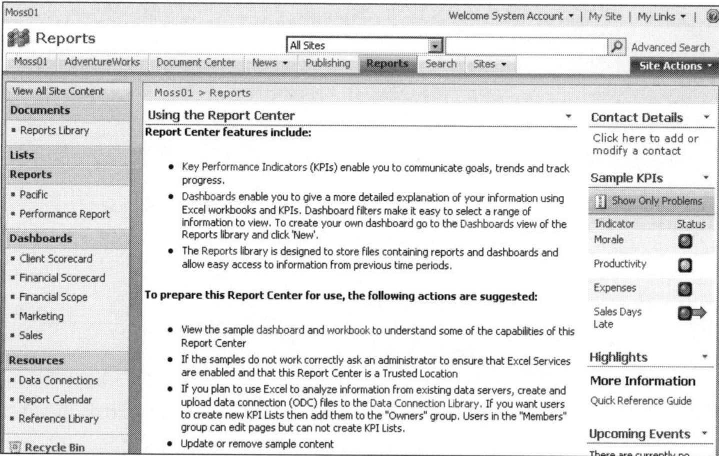


**Figure 18-11** Report Center site home page

Three main BI functional libraries/lists are created as part of the Report Center:

- Reports Library
- Data Connection Library
- KPI list

## Reports Library

The Reports Library (document library) is created as part of the Report Center site template and includes two content types: a Report content type (for creation of Excel workbooks) and a Dashboard Page content type (for creation of dashboard pages designed to contain published Excel workbooks and KPIs). Reports Libraries can be created within any site throughout a site collection. A best practice is to maintain a central Reports Library, such as in the Report Center, which will prove easier to maintain from a security perspective when you are creating and publishing multiple reports.

The Reports Library is configured by default to launch documents stored within the library in the browser; any Excel 2007 files saved or published to the Reports Library will automatically launch in the browser regardless of whether the Excel 2007 client is installed on the client machine. This excludes Excel 2003 files uploaded to the Reports Library, which will launch within the Excel client or fail to launch if the Excel client is not present.

> **Note** Reports Libraries will need to be added to the trusted file locations in the respective Web application's Shared Services to enable Excel Services access to the Excel workbooks contained within the Reports Libraries. To add a Reports Library to a trusted file location, go to the Shared Services home page, click Excel Services Settings, then click Trusted File Locations.

**Creating Reports** You can create new and edit existing reports in the Reports Library. Selecting to create a new report will generate an Excel 2007 (.xlsx) file. Optional metadata is included as part of the report creation, including the option to Save To Report History, which will record any changes to the report after creation and will remain attached to the respective report.

### Working with BI Content Types

The Report content type, included by default in the Reports Library, is one of the default site collection BI content types and can be added to any document library throughout a site collection that has been enabled for management of content types.

However, remember that document libraries other than the Reports Library will handle the Report content type slightly differently. For instance, when the Report content type is added to a document library other than the Reports Library, report history files will be saved in the root of the library along with report files rather than tied separately to each respective report file. The View History hyperlink column will not be present, and the library will not be configured by default to launch documents in the browser. This will need to be enabled separately. Best practice, therefore, is to create a Reports Library as opposed to adding the Report content type to a regular document library.

**Dashboards** Dashboards within SharePoint Server 2007 are Web pages that display BI parts, such as KPIs, scorecards, reports, and special filters (for example, a filter to display one or more parameters within a published Excel workbook).

Dashboards are created within the Reports Library using preconfigured page templates, either as a three-column horizontal, one-column vertical, or two-column vertical page. Each page is populated with Web parts, including Filter, KPI (optional at time of creating the dashboard page), and EWA Web parts. Dashboard Web parts can be configured post-page creation, and new Web parts can be added. Choosing a one- or two-column vertical layout will create a dashboard inclusive of a left-hand site menu and Filter Web part, as shown in Figure 18-12.

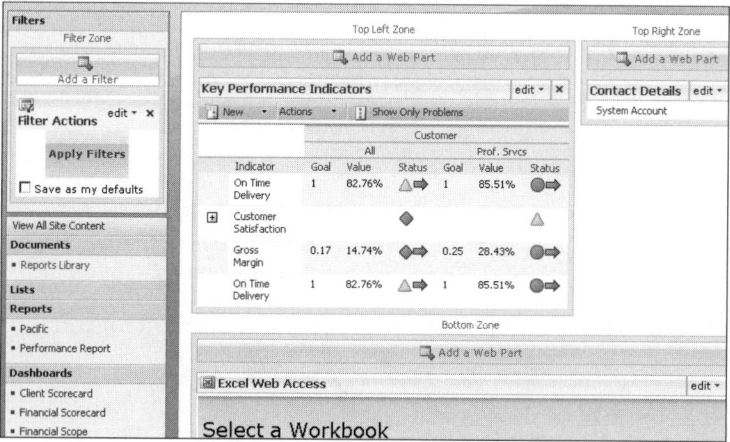


**Figure 18-12** Newly created SharePoint dashboard using a two-column vertical layout

EWA Web parts and custom filtering Web parts can also be added to non-dashboard pages, such as publishing pages and Web part pages, but the same rules apply to associated source Excel workbooks, which must be added to a trusted file location specified within the respective Web application Shared Service/Excel Services Trusted File Locations.

## Data Connection Library

Data connections stored within data connection libraries enable users to centrally connect to external data sources, such as SSAS, and create custom reports, analyze data, and create KPIs within SharePoint sites. Data connection libraries store two content types of data connection files: Office Data Connection (ODC) files and Universal Data Connection (UDC) files.

Data connection libraries are included by default in sites provisioned from the Report Center site template, but they can be created in any site within a site collection. The lone stipulation regarding data connection libraries is that the location of each one must be added to the Excel Services Trusted Data Connection Libraries list in SharePoint Shared Services so that published Excel workbooks can successfully access ODC files (external data). For example, this must be done where you've published an Excel workbook to Excel Services and that workbook is linked to a SSAS ODC. You can find more details on how to add a trusted data connection library at *http://technet2.microsoft.com/Office/en-us/library/63e9cc2b-3cb7-4c92-a549-d823d5844f011033.mspx?mfr=true*.

ODC and UDC files added to data connection libraries by default are subject to the built-in publishing approval process and must be approved before they are accessible to end-users and applications, such as Excel Services and Microsoft InfoPath browser forms.

**ODC Files** ODC files enable you to connect to external data, such as a SQL Server 2005 database or SSAS. ODC files are created by Windows Explorer, typically under the path %SystemDrive%:\Documents and Settings\userprofile\My Documents\My Data Source, and uploaded to a trusted data connection library within a SharePoint site.

There are two options for creating ODC files:

- **Connect to New Data Source.odc** This gives you the option to configure a data connection to SQL Server, SQL Server OLAP Services, ODBC DSN, Oracle, Microsoft Business Solutions, data retrieval services, or other/advanced sources.
- **New SQL Server Connection.odc** This option provides a wizard for connecting to an SQL database server and database/data warehouse tables.

**UDC Files** UDC files are special data source files that can be used by InfoPath forms to access data and overcome cross-domain browsing security issues. The format of UDC files is XML, and they can be generated using InfoPath. When you design a new InfoPath form, you have the option to connect to a UDC stored within a SharePoint data connection library.

You can find details on how to create UDC files, along with a sample download file to assist you in authoring and editing UDC files, at *http://blogs.msdn.com/infopath/archive/2007/02/12/udc-file-authoring-tool.aspx.*

UDC files can be created in data connection libraries throughout site collections. A best practice is to create UDC files in Central Administration for farm-wide access and greater security—that is, only a user with access to Central Administration will be able to upload UDC files. UDC files are added to Central Administration. To add a UDC file to Central Administration, access the Application Management page in Central Administration, click InfoPath Forms Services, and then click Manage Data Connection Files.

## KPI List

KPIs visually indicate and track progress and goals and illustrate trends. Key risks and opportunities can be quickly visualized through the use of status indicator icons, such as the traffic light icon. By default, four types of display icons are available when you create SharePoint KPI lists: default (slightly risen shapes), checkmarks, flat (similar to default but no depth), and traditional traffic light indicators.

KPIs within SharePoint can be created based on the following options:

- Indicator using data in SharePoint list
- Indicator using data in Excel workbook
- Indicator using data in SSAS
- Indicator using manually entered information

For example, in Figure 18-13, we've created a KPI based on an existing ODC file that we've uploaded to a Trusted Data Connections Library. The ODC file is connected to the Adventure-Works Data Warehouse database on SSAS. SharePoint has exposed existing KPIs as defined within the Data Warehouse cube. Selecting any one of the KPIs reveals the respective values. There is also an option to enable child indicators.

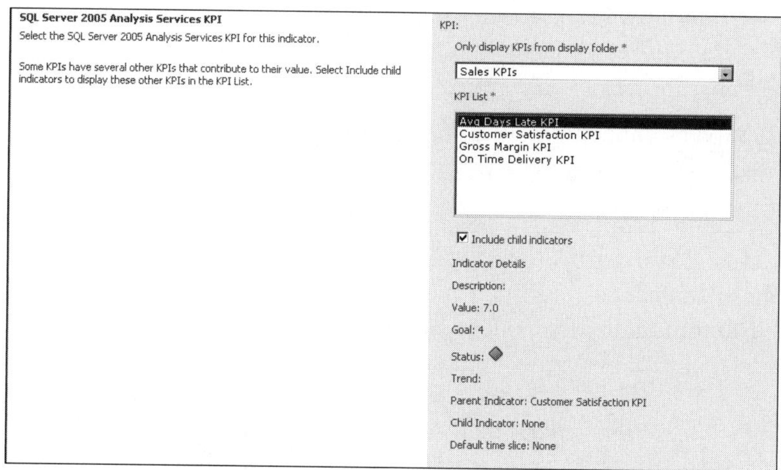


**Figure 18-13** Configuring an SSAS KPI within a SharePoint site

Figure 18-14 shows the four KPIs added to the newly created KPI list.

Sample Key Performance Indicators which are displayed by default on the home page of this Report Center.

New ▾ Actions ▾ Settings ▾ View: KPI List

| Indicator | Goal | Value | Status |
|---|---|---|---|
| Morale | 7 | 9 | |
| Productivity | 85 | 73 | |
| Expenses | 50000 | 80000 | |
| Sales Days Late | 4 | 7.0 | |

**Figure 18-14** New Sales Days Late KPI added to a sample KPI list

KPI lists can be created on any site throughout a site collection, and SSAS KPIs can source a centrally Trusted Data Connections Library within the current site collection. KPIs based on a SharePoint list or Excel workbook can source the list or workbook from within the current site or site collection, but bear in mind that users will also need access to the source in order to view the KPI results on the destination list and/or Web part.

You also have the option of drilling down into specific KPIs to reveal KPI properties, for example, comments and related data connection. In Figure 18-15, we've selected the On Time Delivery KPI, which has revealed the location of the data connection.

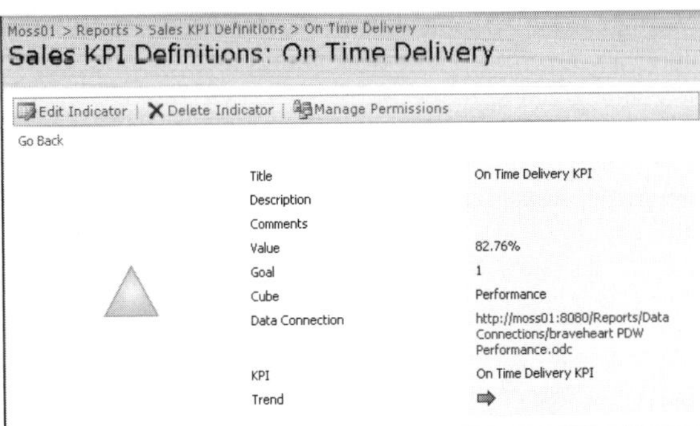


**Figure 18-15** Individual KPI view, which reveals any associated properties not exposed in the default view of the SharePoint list

There are two default Web parts for displaying KPIs within dashboards and Web pages throughout SharePoint sites: the KPI Web part and KPI Details Web part. KPI Web parts offer additional formatting and filtering options to the related KPI list, such as the ability to drill down into additional KPI assets, such as dimension and hierarchy, and filters based on members within a given hierarchy. Figure 18-16 shows an example of configuring the KPI Web part, where filtering has been set against the customer type Professional Services.

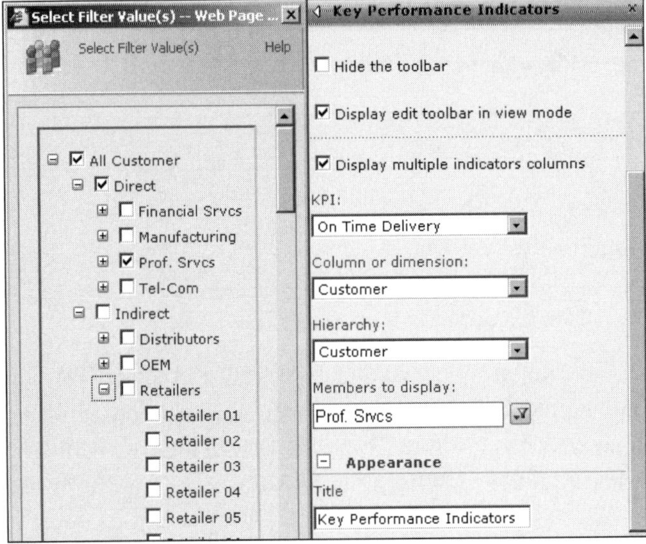


**Figure 18-16** Configuration options within the KPI Web part

Finally, KPI Web parts can be added to a dashboard to represent alternative views of a KPI list. Figure 18-17 shows the resultant KPI Web part with the additional Customer/Prof. Srvcs filter included.

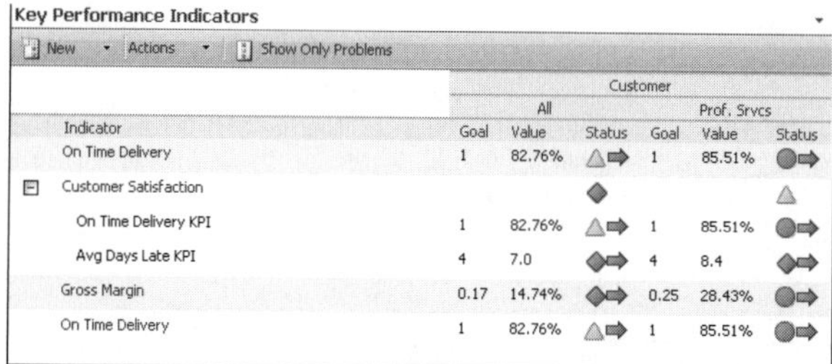


**Figure 18-17** KPI Web part including filtered values

# Business Data Catalog

The BDC is part of the SharePoint Server 2007 Enterprise Edition and enables you to integrate data with SharePoint sites from line of business (LOB) systems, such as SAP, Oracle, and SQL Server databases. A graphical user interface enables administrators to upload and configure BDC applications, set security, and include LOB data as part of SharePoint Server 2007 indexing and search. BDC Web parts can be easily configured to display and filter against imported BDC data, allowing end-users to quickly access critical LOB data in a structured fashion.

> **More Info** In this section, we consider several best practices for deploying and working with the BDC. For details on administrating and deploying the BDC, please refer to *Microsoft Office SharePoint Server 2007 Administrator's Companion* by Bill English and the Microsoft SharePoint Community Experts (Microsoft Press, 2007).

## BDC Web Parts

There are several out-of-the-box BDC Web parts, including Business Data List and Business Data Item Web parts, that interact with, present, and filter BDC data. Figure 18-18 shows the BDC Web parts listed within the Add Web Parts dialog box.

Figure 18-19 shows the Business Data List Web part, which displays the items from the Product List Entity.

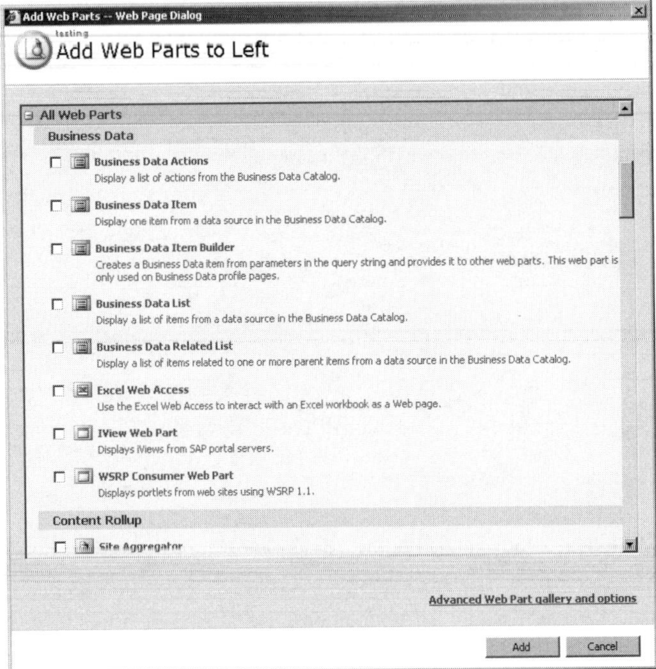


**Figure 18-18** BDC Web parts

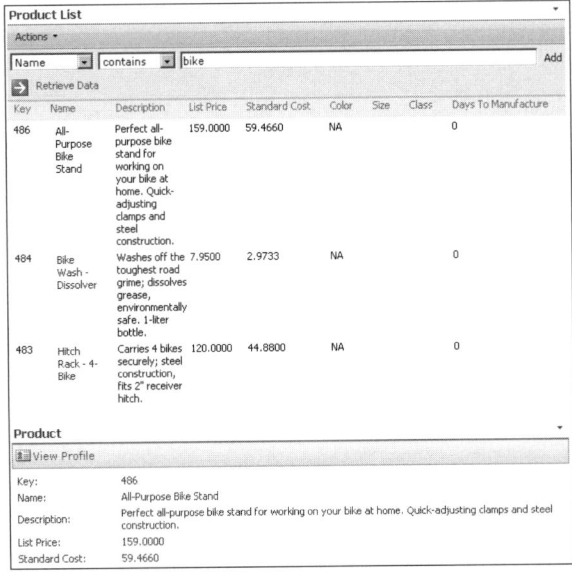


**Figure 18-19** Example of a Business Data List Web part

> **Note** When using the Business Data List Web part and attempting to select an entity from the data source, you may receive the message, "There are no Business Data Types loaded in the Catalog." This is most likely because you have not defined a Finder method in the Application Definition File. To consume the BDC connections through BDC Web parts, you must add a Finder method.

## Creating Application Definition Files

To successfully connect to LOB systems, you will need to create an application definition file (ADF). The ADF is an XML file based on the BDCMetadata.xsd schema and is located at %SystemDrive%:\Program Files\ Microsoft Office Servers\12.0\Bin. It defines the name of the BDC application, entity (database table you are connecting to, columns, and methods, including Finder methods which allow for search), filters and protocols, ID enumerators, and authentication mode. In layman terms, the information in the ADF instructs SharePoint how to retrieve data from a data source. The data source itself can be any ADO.NET data source (for example, a SQL Server database) or Web service. Figure 18-20 shows an example of an ADF.

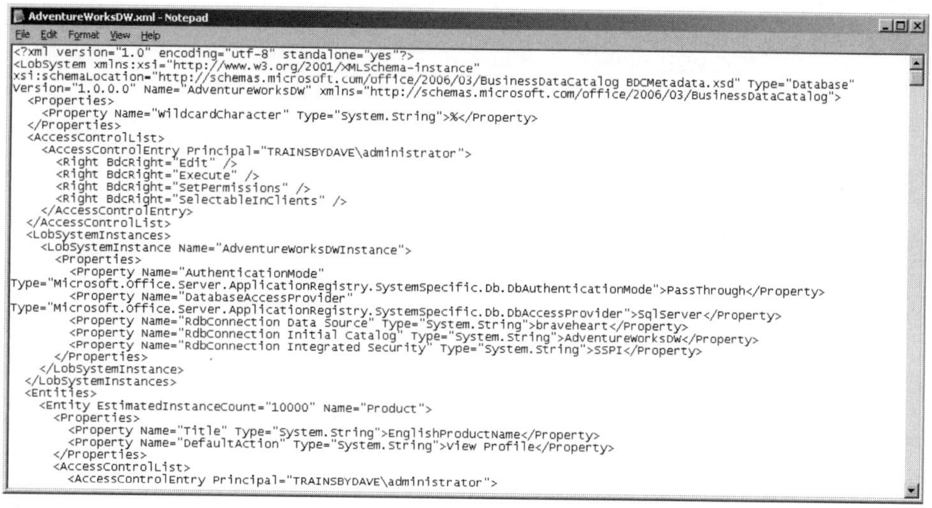

AdventureWorksDW.xml - Notepad

File Edit Format View Help


```xml
<?xml version="1.0" encoding="utf-8" standalone="yes"?>
<LobSystem xmlns:xsi="http://www.w3.org/2001/XMLSchema-instance"
xsi:schemaLocation="http://schemas.microsoft.com/office/2006/03/BusinessDataCatalog BDCMetadata.xsd" Type="Database"
Version="1.0.0.0" Name="AdventureWorksDW" xmlns="http://schemas.microsoft.com/office/2006/03/BusinessDataCatalog">
  <Properties>
    <Property Name="WildcardCharacter" Type="System.String">%</Property>
  </Properties>
  <AccessControlList>
    <AccessControlEntry Principal="TRAINSBYDAVE\administrator">
      <Right BdcRight="Edit" />
      <Right BdcRight="Execute" />
      <Right BdcRight="SetPermissions" />
      <Right BdcRight="SelectableInClients" />
    </AccessControlEntry>
  </AccessControlList>
  <LobSystemInstances>
    <LobSystemInstance Name="AdventureWorksDWInstance">
      <Properties>
        <Property Name="AuthenticationMode"
Type="Microsoft.Office.Server.ApplicationRegistry.SystemSpecific.Db.DbAuthenticationMode">PassThrough</Property>
        <Property Name="DatabaseAccessProvider"
Type="Microsoft.Office.Server.ApplicationRegistry.SystemSpecific.Db.DbAccessProvider">SqlServer</Property>
        <Property Name="RdbConnection Data Source" Type="System.String">braveheart</Property>
        <Property Name="RdbConnection Initial Catalog" Type="System.String">AdventureWorksDW</Property>
        <Property Name="RdbConnection Integrated Security" Type="System.String">SSPI</Property>
      </Properties>
    </LobSystemInstance>
  </LobSystemInstances>
  <Entities>
    <Entity EstimatedInstanceCount="10000" Name="Product">
      <Properties>
        <Property Name="Title" Type="System.String">EnglishProductName</Property>
        <Property Name="DefaultAction" Type="System.String">View Profile</Property>
      </Properties>
      <AccessControlList>
        <AccessControlEntry Principal="TRAINSBYDAVE\administrator">
```


**Figure 18-20** Sample ADF

After you've created the ADF, an administrator will need to import it into the Business Data Catalog Applications section via the Import Application Definition in the Business Data Catalog section of the Shared Services Provider (SSP), shown in Figure 18-21.

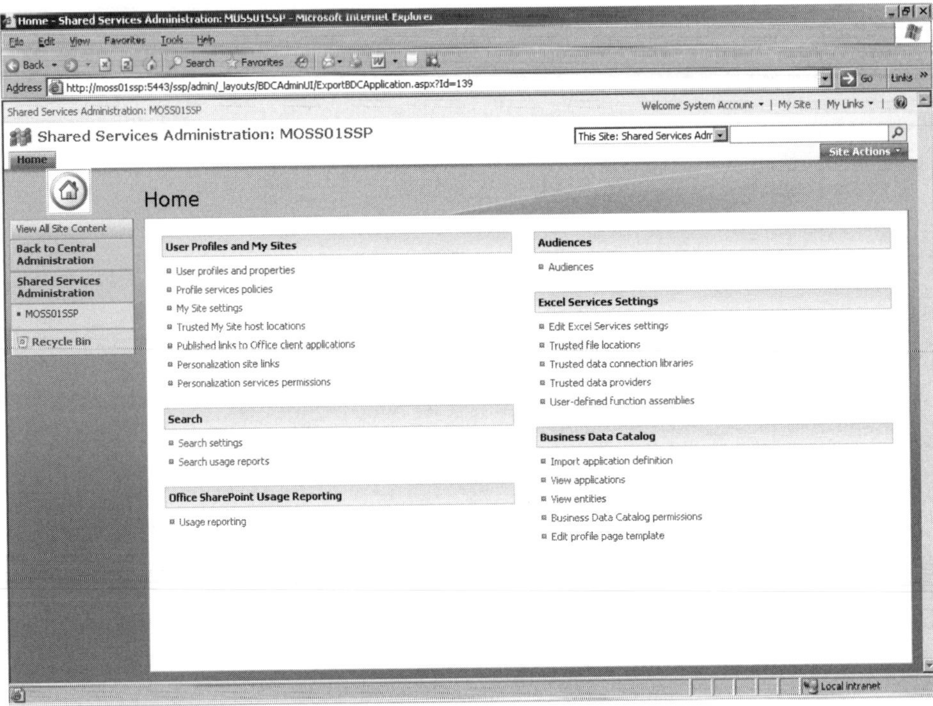


**Figure 18-21** SSP showing BDC options

Figure 18-22 shows the resultant BDC application successfully added to the Business Data Catalog Applications section of the SSP.

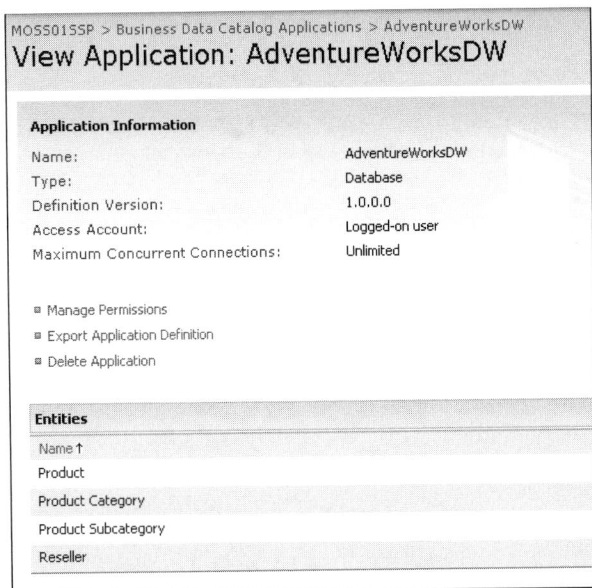


**Figure 18-22** AdventureWorksDW application successfully imported to the Business Data Catalog Applications section in SSP

> **Note** Beware of mixed case when working with ADFs. See the SharePoint Server 2007 SDK for further details.

Creating an ADF from scratch is a developer-intensive exercise. However, there are several tools to help you in configuring and creating ADFs. We list several of these here:

- BDC Editor as part of the SharePoint Server 2007 SDK. "SharePoint Server 2007 SDK: Software Development Kit" includes a BDC Definition Editor for SharePoint Server 2007: *http://www.microsoft.com/downloads/details.aspx?familyid=6d94e307-67d9-41ac-b2d6-0074d6286fa9&displaylang=en*
- Details about the Microsoft Business Data Catalog Definition Editor: *http://msdn2.microsoft.com/en-us/library/bb736296.aspx*
- BDC Meta Man for application definition (.xml) file creation: *http://www.lightningtools.com/bdc-meta-man/default.aspx*

## Authentication and Security

The authentication method you set for BDC applications will determine (1) how the BDC will access back-end data systems and (2) how clients will negotiate permissions to access BDC information throughout SharePoint sites and via BDC Web parts and search. Table 18-2 provides a snapshot of BDC authentication modes.

**Table 18-2 Snapshot of BDC Authentication Modes**

| Authentication mode | Description | Dependencies |
|---|---|---|
| Pass-through | This method is a less secure authentication mode, ideal for use in testing environments. | Kerberos to maintain logged-on user's identity between the BDC and back-end server |
| RevertToSelf | When a user logs on using Windows authentication, IIS impersonates that user account. | Kerberos recommended |
| WindowsCredentials | This method authenticates by using Microsoft Windows credentials from the default SSO service | SSO |
| RdbCredentials | This method authenticates by using database credentials from the default SSO service. | SSO |
| Credentials | This method authenticates Web service systems by using credentials other than those from Windows authentication from its default SSO service. These credentials are used for basic or digest authentication, depending on the configuration of the Web services server. | SSO<br>Because Basic and Digest authentication do not adequately protect credentials, we recommend you use SSL or IPSec or both to secure communication between the Web services server and the server running BDC. |

If you are using forms-based authentication and the BDC and you want to grant privileges to forms authentication users, you will also need to extend the SSP site and add the authentication provider to the extended SSP location.

> **More Info** For more details regarding BDC authentication methods, see "Business Data Catalog Authentication" at *http://msdn2.microsoft.com/en-us/library/ms566523.aspx*.

## Securing Entities

In addition to setting authentication on the actual BDC application, you can secure individual application entities, including Edit, Execute, Select In Clients, and Set Permissions, as shown in Figure 18-23.

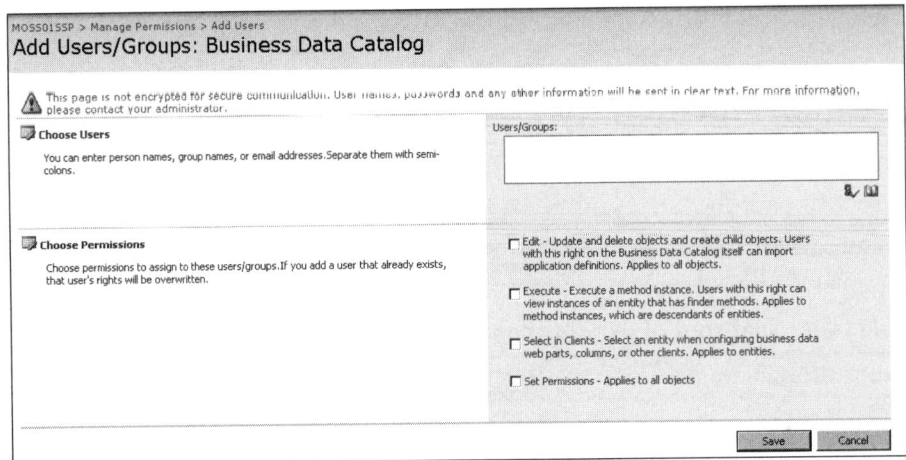


**Figure 18-23** Setting permissions on BDC entities

However, remember that the Execute permission is equivalent to a view permission. So, users who don't have Execute permission on a particular entity will not be able to search or view data related to that entity, either in search or within BDC Web parts.

# BDC Columns

BDC columns can be added to document libraries and lists throughout SharePoint sites to help describe list and library content. Figure 18-24 shows an example of a BDC column that has been added to a document library.

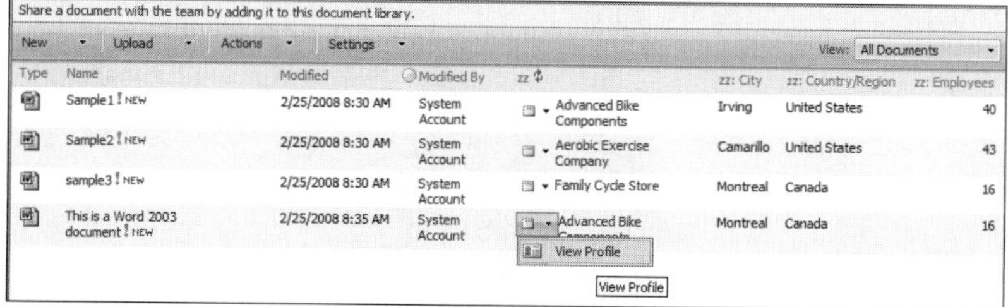


Figure 18-24 Example of BDC column data added to a SharePoint document library

> **Note** A limitation of BDC data columns is that they cannot be added to content types.

## BDC List Columns and Alternate Access Mappings

In a list or library view, you can click a BDC column to select View Profile from a drop-down menu for each BDC record. However, if you use alternate access mappings (AAM), then clicking *directly* on the Record link results in a blank page. This is a known issue related to the ProfileRedirect.aspx page, and the workaround, if you are using AAM, is to access the profile using the contextual drop-down menu instead (as shown in Figure 18-24).

## Client Interaction: Document Information Panel

BDC column data is also exposed in the Office 2007 Document Information Panel (DIP), and users can enter BDC data into the DIP, as shown in Figure 18-25.

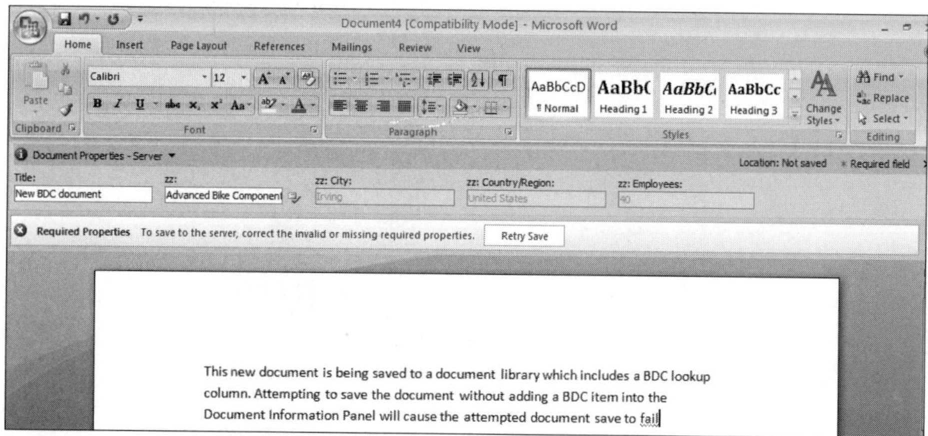


Figure 18-25 Example of entering a BDC entity into DIP

However, searching for and resolving entities via the DIP is a different experience than adding entities directly within the document library user interface via the browser. The Business Data Picker form that appears when you add data to BDC columns in a document library and allows users to select an entity from a list does not appear when you attempt to add data via the DIP. Instead, you must guess what to add. As a result, you may receive the following error when attempting to resolve entities from within the DIP:

Expected token 'EOF' found ':'. //ns2-->:<-- File:script.js Line:170

One solution (discussed at *http://blogs.code-counsel.net/Wouter/Lists/Posts/Post.aspx?List=c04a88a9-d138-4ac3-a2bb-b95c9fdd114e&ID=49&Source=http://blogs.code-counsel.net/Wouter/Lists/Posts/AllPosts.aspx*) suggests including more than one field from the BDC in your business data field. We suggest you avoid populating BDC entities/data via the DIP, either by removing the option to show the DIP or by educating users on how to add BDC entities and edit BDC column data directly via the document library.

## Summary

This chapter introduced Microsoft's overall BI platform and components. It covered the out-of-the-box BI solutions within SharePoint Server 2007, including Excel Services, Reports Center, and the BDC. You've learned how you can share Excel workbooks and perform additional reporting using the built-in KPIs. You've also learned about best practices for deploying Excel Services in conjunction with SSAS and the relevance of using Kerberos throughout your BI and SharePoint deployments.

In Chapter 19, you'll move on to SQL Server 2005 Reporting Services and PerformancePoint Server 2005. You will learn how you can extend the BI features discussed in this chapter, such as enhanced KPI and dashboard creation.

## Additional Resources

- A comparison of features between the different SharePoint versions: *http://office.microsoft.com/en-us/sharepointserver/HA101978031033.aspx.*
- Further details about the UDM and the behind-the-scenes SQL Server 2005 architecture: *http://technet.microsoft.com/en-us/library/ms345143.aspx.*
- Further details about ProClarity, including purchasing details: *http://www.microsoft.com/business/performancepoint/productinfo/proclarity/proclarity-overview2.aspx.*
- Information about prerequisites for the PerformancePoint Add-in for Excel: *http://technet.microsoft.com/en-us/library/bb838749.aspx.*
- Information about the PerformancePoint Server 2007 Scorecard Migration Tool: *http://technet.microsoft.com/en-us/library/bb838761.aspx.*

- Information about the move from BSM to PerformancePoint Server 2007: *http://www.microsoft.com/business/performancepoint/productinfo/previousversions.aspx.*
- A comprehensive overview on configuring Kerberos in an Active Directory environment: *http://www.sharepointblogs.com/tonstegeman/archive/2007/03/11/using-analysis-services-data-in-excel-services-part-1-preparing-the-ad-for-kerberos.aspx.*
- "Plan External Data cConnections for Excel Services" provides additional considerations for configuring Excel Services and data connections: *http://technet2.microsoft.com/Office/en-us/library/7e6ce086-57b6-4ef2-8117-e725de18f2401033.mspx?mfr=true.*
- Document 2 ("Step 2: Configuring Single Sign-On for Excel Services") provides additional information on configuring SSO as the authentication mode for Excel Services: *http://office.microsoft.com/en-us/excel/HA102203821033.aspx.*
- Details about Office version requirements when working with Excel Services: *http://office.microsoft.com/en-us/excel/HA101650601033.aspx.*
- Information about an open source Excel Services Compatibility Checker: *http://blogs.msdn.com/cumgranosalis/archive/2007/06/29/excel-services-compatibility-checker-addin-beta.aspx.* The actual executable file is located at *http://blogs.msdn.com/cumgranosalis/pages/excel-services-compatibility-checker-download-page.aspx.*
- Details on how to add a Trusted Data Connection Library: *http://technet2.microsoft.com/Office/en-us/library/63e9cc2b-3cb7-4c92-a549-d823d5844f011033.mspx?mfr=true.*
- Details on how to create UDC files, along with a sample download file to assist you in authoring and editing UDC files: *http://blogs.msdn.com/infopath/archive/2007/02/12/udc-file-authoring-tool.aspx.*
- "Walkthrough: Configuring Search for the AdventureWorks Business Data Application Sample:" *http://msdn.microsoft.com/en-us/library/ms493671.aspx.*
- AdventureWorksDW SQL Server 2005 (definition file [XML] for BDC): *http://msdn2.microsoft.com/en-us/library/ms494876.aspx.*

Chapter 19

# Extending Business Intelligence

**In this chapter:**



In this chapter, we'll expand on the core Microsoft Office SharePoint business intelligence (BI) features discussed in Chapter 18, "Business Intelligence and Reporting," to include discussion and best practices for enhanced functionality offered through Microsoft SQL Server 2005 Reporting Services and Microsoft Office PerformancePoint Server 2007. You'll realize additional BI capabilities such as the ability to export Web-based reports to Microsoft Office applications as well as additional formatting and drill-down features for reports and KPIs, and central management for distributed Microsoft Office Excel authoring environments.

First, let's review the BI functionality within Office SharePoint sites offered through integration with SQL Server 2005 Reporting Services.

## Reporting Services

Reporting Services was initially introduced with Microsoft SQL Server 2000 as a tool to centrally create and publish reports against database data. It leveraged Microsoft Visual Studio 2003 as the report designer and authoring environment. SQL Server 2005 has seen Reporting Services reporting capabilities extend to include reporting against multiple data sources, including

SQL Server, Object Linking and Embedding Database (OLE DB), SQL Server Analysis Services, Oracle, Open Database Connectivity (ODBC), XML, Report Server Model, SAP NetWeaver BI, and–included with Microsoft SQL Server 2005 Service Pack 2–Hyperion Essbase. SQL Server 2005 Business Intelligence Development Studio, an integrated development environment (IDE) that is hosted within Microsoft Visual Studio 2005 and installed as part of SQL Server 2005, includes Business Intelligence Project templates that developers can use to create custom reports and model data for back-end databases. A Report Designer enables developers to design and deploy reports to either Reporting Services or SharePoint document libraries.

Reporting Services has evolved to include extended functionality within SharePoint sites and direct integration with SharePoint permission sets. Information workers are now able to work directly with Reporting Services from within SharePoint document libraries. Configuration is dependent upon two main server components: SQL Server 2005 Service Pack 2 Reporting Services and SharePoint Server 2007 (or Microsoft Windows SharePoint Services 3.0). We will evaluate the numerous options in the following sections.

## How Does Reporting Services Work with SharePoint?

There are two modes in which Reporting Services can be configured and integrated with SharePoint Server 2007 sites. One is the default mode, namely, native mode. The other, SharePoint Integrated mode, was introduced in SQL Server 2005 Service Pack 2 and enables Reporting Services reports to be deployed directly to SharePoint document libraries. SharePoint Integrated mode also provides information workers with the ability to directly create and author Reporting Services reports from within document libraries.

In this chapter, we predominantly focus on using Reporting Services configured in SharePoint Integrated mode. However, we will show you the alternatives for including Reporting Services reports in SharePoint sites where the SQL Server 2005 Reporting Services can remain in native mode.

Two main components support Reporting Services running in SharePoint Integrated mode: SQL Server 2005 Service Pack 2 and Microsoft Reporting Services add-in for Microsoft SharePoint Technologies.

### SQL Server 2005 Service Pack 2

When you install Service Pack 2 for SQL Server 2005, a Reporting Services Configuration Manager is installed, which includes an additional configuration toolset (SharePoint Integrated) specifically for integrating Reporting Services with SharePoint. When a Reporting Services server is changed from native mode to SharePoint Integrated mode, additional functionality is added to the Reporting Services server, including security extensions to work directly with SharePoint permissions to control access to Reporting Services reports. Figure 19-1 shows the Reporting Services Configuration Manager dialog box where Reporting Services has been changed from its default native mode to run in SharePoint Integrated mode.

> **Note** Some screens within the Reporting Services Configuration Manager specifically reference Windows SharePoint Services, such as the screen shown in Figure 19-1, as opposed to SharePoint Server 2007, which we're discussing here. However, be aware that the configuration applies to both Windows SharePoint Services 3.0 and SharePoint Server 2007.

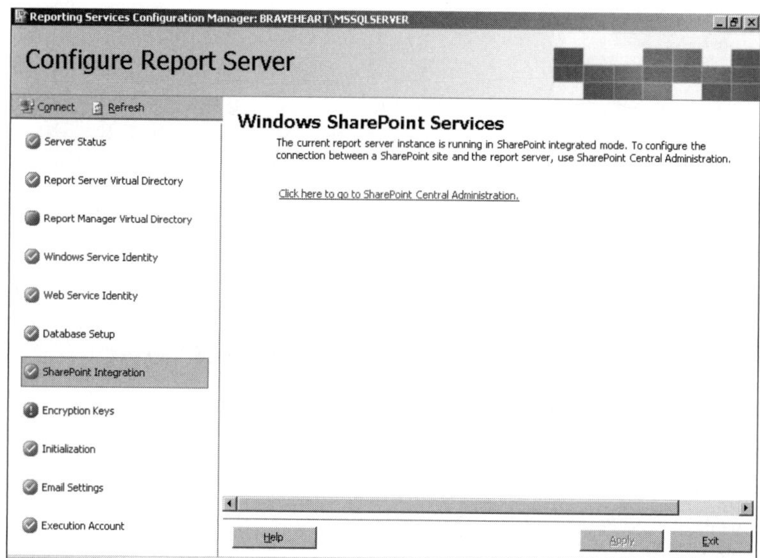


**Figure 19-1** Switching Reporting Services mode from native mode to SharePoint Integrated mode

> **Note** Any single instance of Reporting Services can run only in either native mode or SharePoint Integrated mode. Consider the impact of changing your SQL Server 2005 Reporting Services instance from native mode to SharePoint Integrated mode. For instance, you may already have existing applications that use the default native mode, or you may eventually roll out other applications that will work only with an instance of Reporting Services in native mode. An example is the PerformancePoint 2007 server reporting storage of operational and business reports, which is supported only on a Reporting Services instance running in native mode. One way to accomplish both native and SharePoint Integrated mode while minimizing licensing costs might be to create an additional *instance* of SQL / Reporting Services on the same SQL server. See the following blog post: *http://mindsharpblogs.com/kathy/archive/2007/12/10/3788.aspx*.

> **Note** You can download Service Pack 2 for SQL Server 2005 at *http://www.microsoft.com/downloads/details.aspx?FamilyId=d07219b2-1e23-49c8-8f0c-63fa18f26d3a&displaylang=en*.

By switching Reporting Services from native mode to SharePoint Integrated mode, you can combine with the Reporting Services add-in for SharePoint Technologies, which is an add-in specifically architected to work with Reporting Services running in SharePoint Integrated mode to add additional reporting functionality in both SharePoint Server 2007 and Windows SharePoint Services 3.0.

### Reporting Services Add-in for Microsoft SharePoint Technologies

To coincide with the earlier release of Service Pack 2 for SQL Server 2005, Microsoft released a Reporting Services add-in for SharePoint Server 2007 and Windows SharePoint Services 3.0 in early 2007 to take advantage of the additional functionality and Reporting Services integration throughout SharePoint sites and document libraries. The add-in, combined with Reporting Services running in SharePoint Integrated mode, provides powerful reporting features within SharePoint document libraries and gives information workers the ability to create and author Reporting Services reports using a special Report Builder application. This removes the reliance on developers to create and maintain Reporting Services reports. You can download the add-in at *http://www.microsoft.com/downloads/details.aspx?FamilyID=1E53F882-0C16-4847-B331-132274AE8C84&display=en*.

## Integrating Reporting Services with SharePoint

Reporting Services offers several flexible deployment scenarios depending on your existing infrastructure and requirements for SQL Server 2005 Reporting Services, such as whether you switch Reporting Services from native to SharePoint Integrated mode to take full advantage of integration features. It is possible to include Reporting Services reports in SharePoint sites in which the Reporting Services mode is set to native mode by using Reporting Services Viewer Web parts, which are installed as part of SQL Server 2005. However, this will not produce the rich experience you'll get when you use SharePoint Integrated mode. Let's consider the following options:

1. **SQL Server 2005 Reporting Services SharePoint Integrated mode** This is available with SQL Server 2005 Service Pack 2. It combines with a Reporting Services add-in for SharePoint Technologies to provide added functionality within SharePoint sites and document libraries, such as the ability to create reports directly within SharePoint document libraries.

   - **Pros** Full Reporting Services integration in SharePoint Server 2007 and Windows SharePoint Service 3.0 sites. Less reliance on developers to create Reporting Services reports. Flexibility in authoring of reports–you can either create reports in Visual Studio 2005 Report Designer and deploy to SharePoint document libraries or create reports directly from within SharePoint document libraries using the SQL Server 2005 Reporting Services Report Builder.

   - **Cons** If you haven't already done so, you'll need to upgrade SQL Server 2005 to Service Pack 2. You need to change the Reporting Services mode from native to SharePoint Integrated mode, which means that you need to consider other applications also accessing the same instance of Reporting Services that may have dependencies on Reporting Services running in native mode. The Reporting Services add-in works only with SharePoint Server 2007 and Windows SharePoint Services 3.0. It does not work with earlier versions of SharePoint.

2. **SQL Server 2005 Reporting Services native (default) mode** Installs two Reporting Services viewer Web parts, which can be deployed to SharePoint sites to view Reporting Services reports.

   - **Pros** You don't need to change your Reporting Services from native to SharePoint Integrated mode, which means that this doesn't add complexities for any existing applications that use the same instance of Reporting Services in native mode. The Reporting Services Viewer Web parts can be deployed to SharePoint sites, including SharePoint Server 2007, Windows SharePoint Services 3.0, SharePoint Portal Server 2003, and Windows SharePoint Services 2.0.

   - **Cons** You won't get the same rich integration experience you'll get with SharePoint Integrated mode and the Reporting Services add-in in SharePoint Server 2007 and Windows SharePoint Service 3.0 sites, such as the ability to drill down into reports. You will also be unable to create and author reports directly from within SharePoint document libraries, resulting in greater dependency on developers to create reports on SQL Server 2005 Reporting Services using Visual Studio 2005.

3. **PerformancePoint Server 2007** Using the Dashboard Designer, you can create reports against a Reporting Services server that is set to either SharePoint Integrated or native mode. We discuss PerformancePoint Server 2007 and BI integration within SharePoint later in this chapter.

   - **Pros** You have the flexibility to report against both Reporting Services modes, native and SharePoint Integrated, and then deploy the report directly to a SharePoint site.

   - **Cons** If you haven't already deployed PerformancePoint Server 2007, then you will need to purchase and deploy it. You do not get the rich report authoring environment you get using the SharePoint Integrated mode/Reporting Services add-in.

To assist readers who are running Reporting Services in native mode, we've summarized options regarding the integration of Reporting Services with SharePoint sites in the next section. Then we'll discuss the benefits of how Reporting Services integrates with SharePoint sites using SharePoint Integrated mode.

## SQL Server 2005 Reporting Services Native (Default) Mode

If Reporting Services is configured in native mode or where earlier versions of SharePoint (such as SharePoint Portal Server 2003 or Windows SharePoint Server 2.0) are deployed, Reporting Services reports can be integrated within SharePoint sites using two custom Reporting Services Web parts that are included as part of the SQL Server 2005 installation: Report Explorer Web part and Report Viewer Web part. On SQL Server 2005, these Web parts are installed as a CAB, named RSWebParts.cab, which is typically located at %SystemDrive%:\Program Files\Microsoft SQL Server\90\Tools\Reporting Services\SharePoint\RSWebParts.cab.

The Web parts will need to be installed and registered in the SharePoint Global Assembly Cache (GAC) using the SharePoint command-line editor STSADM.EXE. For example, where a SharePoint Web front-end server is installed on the SQL server, you would use the following:

```
Stsadm.exe -o addwppack -filename "c:\program files\microsoft sql server\90\tools\reporting
services\sharepoint\rswebparts.cab" -globalinstall
```

Alternatively, where SharePoint resides on a separate server, copy the CAB file to the SharePoint Web front-end server and then install the CAB using the SharePoint STSADM.EXE command-line tool.

The RSWebParts.cab can be deployed on a SharePoint Web front-end server where the Reporting Services add-in (the add-in that supports SQL Server 2005 Service Pack 2, SharePoint Server 2007, and Windows SharePoint Services 3.0) is also deployed. For instance, you may want to pull in Reporting Services reports from an additional instance of Reporting Services that is running in native mode. However, after installing the RSWebParts.cab, you will need to adjust the trust level within the Web site's Web.config file to WSS_Medium (<trust level = "WSS_Medium" originalUrl="" />) to successfully add the installed Report Viewer and Report Explorer Web parts to a SharePoint Web page.

The trust level defined in a site's Web.config file determines the permissions for Code Access Security (CAS), which ultimately limits what Web part Dynamic-Link librarys (DLLs) deployed to the bin directory can do. For example, it determines access (or level of access to) a file system. By default, the trust level is set to WSS_Minimal, which is the tightest level of restriction for a Web part DLL.

However, when developers and administrators deploy Web parts to the bin directory as opposed to the GAC, the Web.config trust level may be increased to either WSS_Medium or WSS_Full to allow Web parts further privileges or to help with testing and debugging Web parts. Changes to the trust level in the Web.config file bear no effect on those Web parts deployed to the GAC, which are given full trust by default.

## SQL Server 2005 Reporting Services SharePoint Integrated Mode

If you've installed Service Pack 2 on SQL Server 2005 and changed Reporting Services to run in SharePoint Integrated mode, you're well on the way to benefiting from the full suite of Reporting Services integration features within SharePoint sites. But to take full advantage of the integration features, you'll need to install the SQL Server 2005 Reporting Services add-in for SharePoint Technologies on each Web front-end server within your SharePoint farm.

> **Note** SharePoint Server 2007 Standard or Enterprise Edition is required for Reporting Services in SharePoint Integrated mode.

Once you've installed the add-in, you'll need to configure additional Reporting Services features within the SharePoint Central Administration and SharePoint sites and document libraries. A major factor in configuring Reporting Services within SharePoint is the authentication and security mode in which reports will be created and accessed by end-users.

## Configure Reporting Services in Central Administration

The initial part of configuring Reporting Services within SharePoint is in SharePoint Central Administration. When you install the Reporting Services add-in, a new Reporting Services configuration section is added to the Application Management part of Central Administration, shown in Figure 19-2.

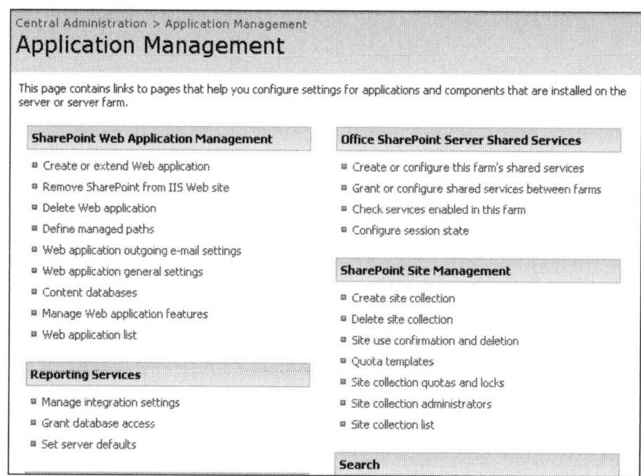


**Figure 19-2** Reporting Services configuration settings in SharePoint Central Administration

> **On the Companion Media** See the document titled "Microsoft SQL Server Reporting Services—Installation and Configuration Guide for SharePoint Integration Mode," which includes a detailed walkthrough on installing the Reporting Services add-in, including considerations for multiple Web front-end deployments.

The following settings will need to be configured before Reporting Services can be used successfully throughout SharePoint sites and document libraries:

- **Manage Integration Settings** Include the Report Server Web Service URL (for example, *http://server_name/reportserver*) and the authentication mode that will be used by SharePoint to access Reporting Services, which is either Windows Authentication or Trusted Account. Trusted Account is used where Kerberos is configured, including Kerberos for the SharePoint Web applications. Windows Authentication is used where SharePoint Web applications are using NT LAN Manager (NTLM). See the "Authentication Between Client and Server" section in Chapter 18.
- **Grant Database Access** Add the name of the server containing Report Server, and identify either a default or named instance.

- **Set Server Defaults** Configure the default server settings for Reporting Services, including Report History Default (number of snapshots to keep in history), Report Processing Timeout, Report Processing Log, Enable Windows Integrated Security for data source connections (this setting is typically checked by default), and Enable Ad Hoc Reporting.

> **Note** If you are unable to access the Set Server Defaults page, the most likely reason is that you have incorrectly set the authentication mode in Manage Integration Settings.

## Configure Reporting Services in Site Settings

Once you've configured Reporting Services in SharePoint Central Administration, you can then begin to configure additional Reporting Services settings throughout SharePoint sites and document libraries. The Reporting Services add-in adds additional configuration to the Site Settings page for each site throughout a site collection (as shown in Figure 19-3) specifically to configure Reporting Services schedules.

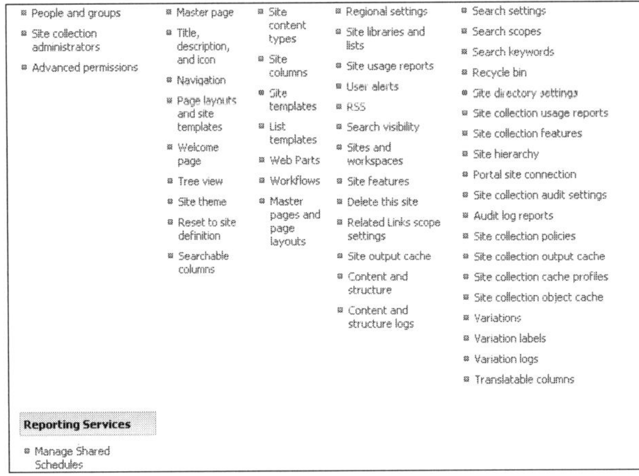


**Figure 19-3** A Reporting Services configuration is added to the Site Settings page within each site throughout a site collection.

Schedules are created against Reporting Services reports stored within SharePoint document libraries when an administrator creates a *subscription* against a specific report. Subscriptions allow for additional report workflow processes, such as e-mailing users when a report changes, or publishing additional copies of reports in alternate formats to storage locations, such as a SharePoint document library or network share.

The Manage Shared Schedules page, shown in Figure 19-4, is where any existing schedules against reports within a site's document libraries can be run or edited. For example, you can change the frequency or day(s) when a sales report update is e-mailed to the sales department on this page.

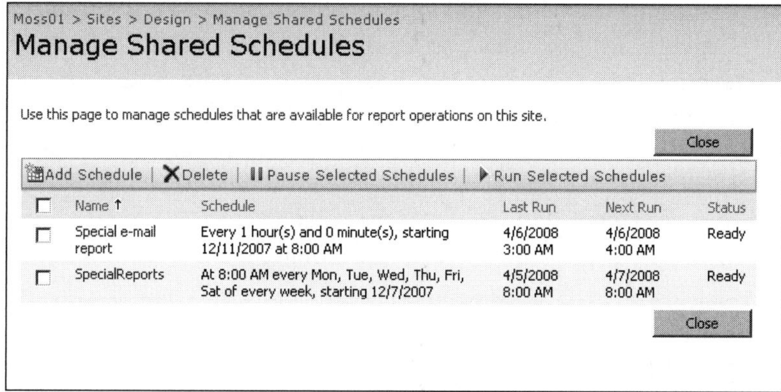


**Figure 19-4** Manage Shared Schedules page

## Managing Report Subscriptions

Administrators can configure subscriptions against Reporting Services reports stored within SharePoint document libraries. Figure 19-5 shows the Manage Subscriptions menu item selected in the contextual drop-down menu against an existing report named *salesordersreport* within the Sales Reports document library.

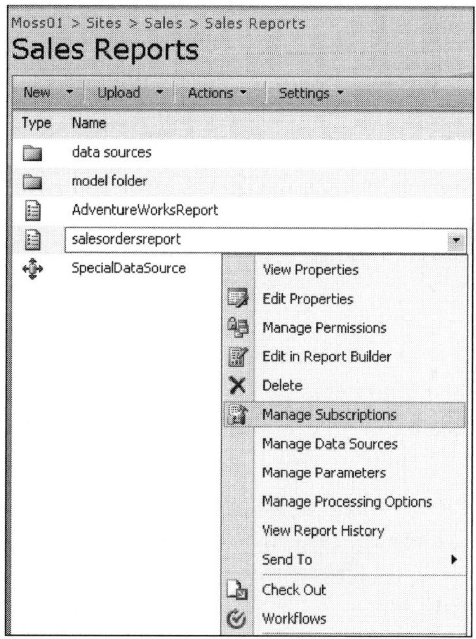


**Figure 19-5** Selecting Manage Subscriptions for a Reporting Services report within a SharePoint document library

Selecting Manage Subscriptions will direct you to the Manage Subscriptions page for the selected report, where you can then configure the subscription properties. The delivery type for report subscriptions can be configured as e-mail, Windows File Share, Null Delivery Provider or SharePoint Document Library. Report Format options include Excel, Acrobat (PDF) file, TIFF file, Web Archive, CSV (comma delimited), Web page for IE 5.0 or later (.htm), Web page for most Web browsers (.htm), or XML file with report data. Subscriptions can trigger based on either an event or a schedule. For example, you could configure a subscription to generate a report to be sent to a document library as a .pdf based on when a snapshot of the report is taken or every Sunday of the year. Figure 19-6 shows the Subscription Properties for the *salesordersreport* report where the Delivery Type is set to a SharePoint Document Library, Output Format is set to Acrobat (PDF) File, and a custom schedule has been set to have the report subscription generated every Sunday at 8:00 A.M.

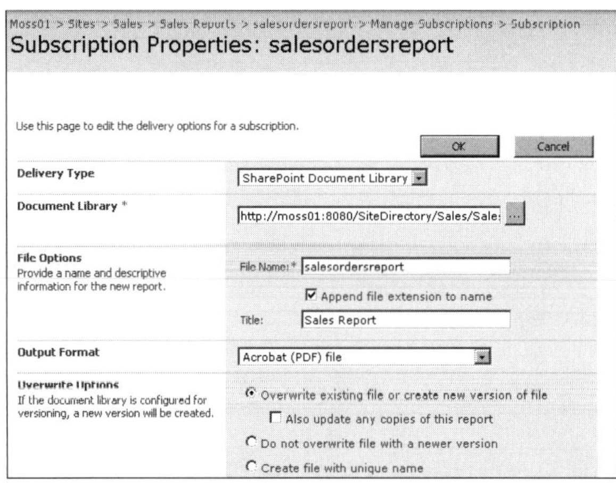


**Figure 19-6** Subscription Properties for the *salesordersreport* report

## Reporting Services Content Types

The Reporting Services add-in installs three Report Server content types to the Site Collection Site Content Type Gallery:

- **Report Builder Model** A data construct, or model, against which a report is based. Choosing to create new content based on the Report Builder Model content type will create a file with the extension .smdl.
- **Report Builder Report** A formatted representation of a data model, such as the number of outstanding inventory items or customers within a particular region, including filtering and other customized data-formatting options. Choosing to create new content based on the Report Builder Report content type will create a file with the extension .rdl.
- **Report Data Source** The actual data source upon which the report model and subsequent reports are created based on a report model, such as an SQL Server 2005 database, OLE DB, Microsoft SQL Server Analysis Services, Oracle, ODBC, XML, SAP NetWeaver BI, Oracle Hyperion Essbase, and, where Microsoft Office PerformancePoint Server 2005 is installed, Microsoft Office PerformancePoint Scorecard. Choosing to create new content based on the Report Data Source content type will create a file with the extension .rsds.

The Reporting Services content types can be added to document libraries throughout site collections but *not* to lists because the Reporting Services content types are directly inherited from the Document content type. That is, the Document content type is the parent content type. Add Reporting Services content types to document libraries when you want to give information workers the ability to create new report models, data sources, and reports. The Report Builder Report content type associates directly with a Report Builder application that launches directly from within a document library and includes an IDE for building and designing Reporting Services reports. Reports are created independently of Visual Studio 2005 and are saved directly to either the current document library or another document library within a site collection.

Another reason for adding Reporting Services content types to document libraries is to establish search scopes against one or more of the Reporting Services content types. For instance, you might have several document libraries containing reports throughout your SharePoint farm and you want to be able to search centrally to locate all Report Builder Reports (Report Definition Language [.rdl] files). If you add the Reporting Services content types to document libraries and configure the Report Builder Report content type as the default content type, any report files added to that document library will automatically be associated with the Report Builder Report content type or files with the .rdl extension.

> **Note** To successfully implement search on Reporting Services content types, we recommend establishing search scopes on one or more of the content types to coincide with the deployment of Reporting Services content types throughout sites and document libraries. Remember, by default, content types are not configured for use in search scopes, so you will need to configure the Metadata property mappings in the Shared Services Administration (Search Settings) before you can create a new search scope(s) for Reporting Services content types.

Figure 19-7 shows the Sales Reports document library where the Reporting Services content types have been added. Each content type has an associated template, which is available from the New button on the Document Library toolbar.

**Figure 19-7** Reporting Services content types added to the Sales Reports document library

## Adding Reporting Services Content Types to Document Libraries

Where Reporting Services content types are not added to a document library, developers are still able to deploy Reporting Services reports, models, and data sources to that document library from Visual Studio 2005, assuming (in this case) that Reporting Services is running in SharePoint Integrated mode. Remember, the main reason for adding Reporting Services content types to a document library is so that information workers can create new reports directly from within SharePoint, independent of a developer, and so as not to limit the ability to add or upload Reporting Services reports. Even if Reporting Services content types are added to document libraries at a later stage, they won't affect existing reports contained within those libraries.

However, whichever content type is set as the default content type within a document library is the content type with which any reports deployed from Visual Studio 2005 Report Designer will be associated. For instance, if the Document content type is the default content type, then any reports deployed to that library will be associated with the Document content type. If you want to structure your search around scopes specific to the Reporting Services content types and want to capture all reports, including those deployed from Visual Studio 2005 and those created from within SharePoint, then you should add Reporting Services content types to document libraries and configure the default content type before deploying reports. This will save you having to re-index later.

There are other design considerations when working with Reporting Services reports deployed from Visual Studio 2005 and reports created using the Report Builder from within SharePoint. For instance, reports created in Visual Studio 2005 and deployed to SharePoint cannot be edited in the Report Builder within SharePoint. We discuss this further—and other considerations about authoring Reporting Services reports—later in this chapter.

## Reporting Services Web Parts

The SQL Server Reporting Services Report Viewer is installed on the SharePoint Server 2007 Web front-end servers as part of the Reporting Services add-in installation and is used for displaying Reporting Services reports located within a SharePoint document library within SharePoint Web pages.

> **Note** The SQL Server Reporting Services Report Viewer discussed here is different than the Report Viewer included in the RSWebParts.cab, which is installed as part of the default SQL Server 2005 installation and can be used where Reporting Services is running in native mode as well as with the earlier versions of SharePoint, SharePoint Portal Server 2003, and Windows SharePoint Services 2.0. You could potentially use the RSWebPart.cab Web parts in SharePoint Integrated mode, but, ultimately, those Web parts are designed for use with native mode. You might choose to use the RSWebPart.cab Web parts if you're experiencing performance degradation in SharePoint Integrated mode and need to switch back to native mode to test performance or if performance/page load far outweighs features offered by SharePoint Integrated mode. Remember, the RSWebPart.cab Web parts will not give you the same rich features that come with the Reporting Services add-in Web parts used in SharePoint Integrated mode.

Figure 19-8 shows the available Reporting Services Web parts selected, including the SQL Server Reporting Services Report Viewer, which clearly indicates its purpose for Reporting Services report server configured in SharePoint Integrated mode. In this case, the other two Reporting Services Web parts included in the RSWebParts.cab, Report Explorer and Report Viewer, have been installed on the Web front-end server and are the two Web parts you would choose to use where Reporting Services was set to run in native mode.

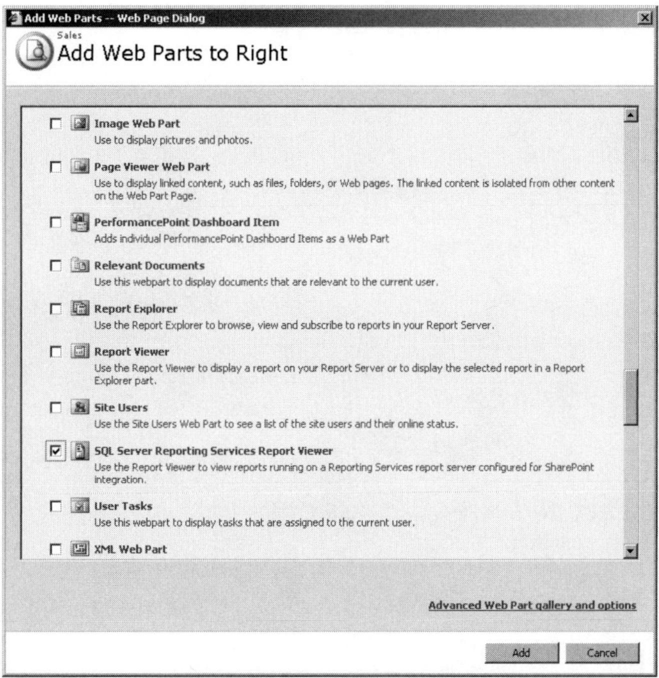


**Figure 19-8** Adding Reporting Services Web parts to a SharePoint site

The Reporting Services Web part includes custom formatting options specifically for Reporting Services functions, such as a toolbar that includes items for navigating multiple-page reports, search, zoom, and an Actions button for subscribing to, printing, and exporting reports. Reports displayed within a SharePoint Web page can be exported to XML files with report data, CSV (comma delimited), TIFF file, Acrobat (PDF) file, Web archive, and Excel.

Figure 19-9 shows the SQL Server Reporting Services Report Viewer Web part displaying a sales order report. The report itself is stored within a Sales Reports document library within the Sales site.

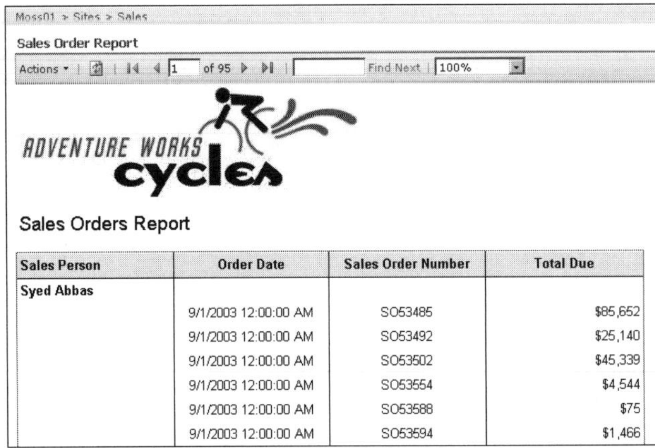


| Sales Person | Order Date | Sales Order Number | Total Due |
|---|---|---|---|
| Syed Abbas | | | |
| | 9/1/2003 12:00:00 AM | SO53485 | $85,652 |
| | 9/1/2003 12:00:00 AM | SO53492 | $25,140 |
| | 9/1/2003 12:00:00 AM | SO53502 | $45,339 |
| | 9/1/2003 12:00:00 AM | SO53554 | $4,544 |
| | 9/1/2003 12:00:00 AM | SO53588 | $75 |
| | 9/1/2003 12:00:00 AM | SO53594 | $1,466 |

**Figure 19-9** Reporting Services Web part added to a SharePoint Web page displaying a sales order report

Selecting Print from the Actions menu on the Web part toolbar will invoke a Print dialog box. When there is no physical printer port on the client, the option to print to Microsoft XPS Document Writer will be offered by default. Where there is an installation of Microsoft Office 2003, an additional print option will be included for Microsoft Office Document Image Writer.

## Report Viewer Web Part and User Permissions

When working with and configuring the Report Viewer Web part, note that the Action button on the Web part does not honor user permissions. For instance, the Action button's contextual drop-down menu within the Report Viewer Web part will display the Open With Report Builder option to a user with read-only permissions to the site and/or document library containing the report. By contrast, the contextual drop-down menu against a report within an actual document library will honor SharePoint user permissions and will offer the Open With Report Builder menu option only to users with a member role or higher.

Users with read-only permission will be able to launch the report within Report Builder from the Report Viewer Web Part Actions menu, but when they attempt to save a report, they will be confronted with a message indicating that the item cannot be saved. This is by design and, if you want users to be able to export and print reports, then you'll need to enable the toolbar as part of the Report Viewer Web part deployment and make users aware of this issue, assuming that some users accessing reports throughout SharePoint sites will have read-only access. If you choose to disable the Web part toolbar, an alternative is to implement a document map as part of the report deployment. Document maps are configured as part of the report table navigational properties in Visual Studio 2005 Report Designer and enable users to navigate through sections or pages within reports.

### Configuring the Report Viewer Web Part

The SQL Server Reporting Services Report Viewer Web part includes several formatting options, including an option to specify the URL of the report (that is, the report location within a document library in SharePoint Integrated mode). In addition, if you've included parameters or document maps within your report, you can configure how those attributes will be formatted within the Report Viewer Web part. Configuration settings also include the option to hide both the Web part title and the Report Viewer toolbar. Figure 19-10 shows the Report Viewer opened in configuration mode.

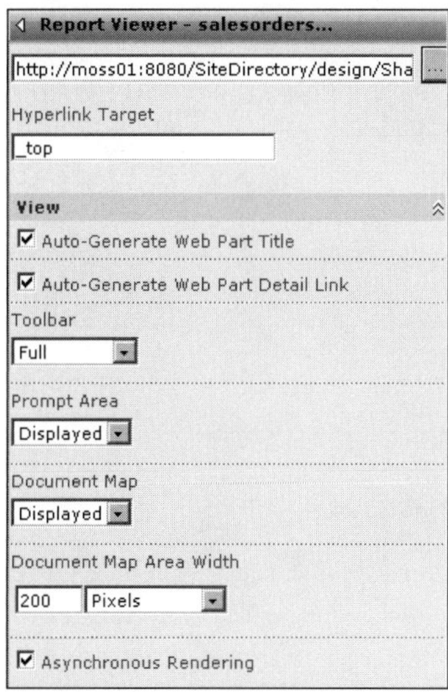


**Figure 19-10** Configuring the SQL Server Reporting Services Report Viewer

> **Note** To avoid the prefix Report Viewer and the default report name generated by Reporting Services in the Web part title (for example, Report Viewer – salesordersreport), clear the Auto-Generate Web Part Title check box in the View section of the Report Viewer Web part configuration. Then, under Appearance, add your own title before clicking OK or Apply to save changes to the Web part on the Web page.

## Other Reporting Services Features Within SharePoint

The Reporting Services add-in adds specific configuration and administrative settings for each of the Reporting Services content types—the Report file (.RDL), the Report Model file (.SMDL), and the Report Data Source (.RSDS)—which are accessible from a contextual drop-down menu against each respective Reporting Services content type stored within SharePoint document libraries.

> **Note** Reporting Services content type contextual menus are security trimmed, and only end-users with the member/contributor role and higher will see some or all configuration options relating to the administration of each content type. The exception is the Report Viewer Web part toolbar, explained earlier. For general information on securing Reporting Services reports, see the end of this section.

Next, we will list the configuration and administrative settings for each content type, along with considerations for security configuration of each type.

## Data Source Configuration

The Reporting Services data source file is the source from which the report model and actual report will be based. The data source identifies the data source *type*, such as SQL Server, and comprises a data source connection string and the credentials that will be used by the Report Server to access the data source when generating reports based on that data source. The configuration options available for a Reporting Services data source are shown in Figure 19-11.

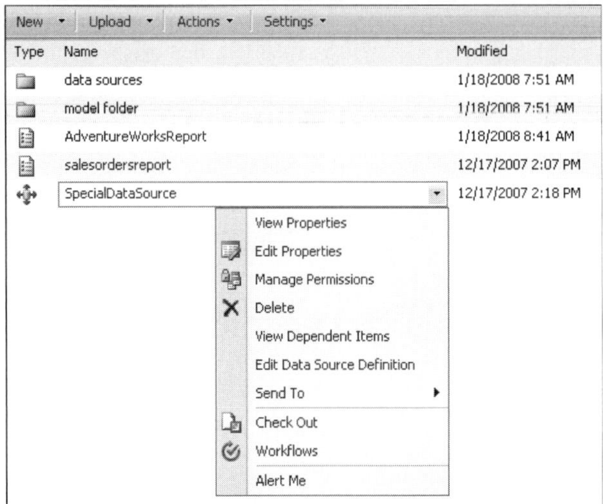


**Figure 19-11** Reporting Services data source contextual menu showing configuration options

The View Dependent Items option will display both the site and document library location of any reports or report models related to the data source, while the Edit Data Source Definition option allows modifications to the data source type and data source credentials.

## Reporting Services, Authentication, and Data Sources

The most important consideration in configuring a data source is the credentials, which will be used by Reporting Services to access the data source when running reports and report models, as shown in Figure 19-12.

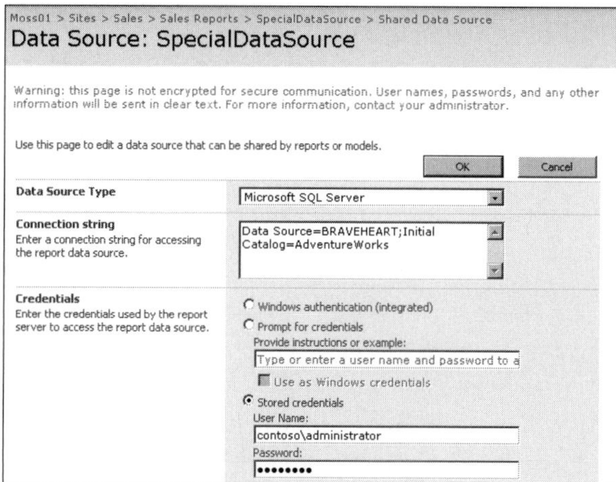


**Figure 19-12** Shared Data Sources configuration page

The credential settings applied to a data source will depend on how you've configured Reporting Services, specifically, the authentication mode you've chosen within the Manage Integration Settings section of the Reporting Services settings contained within SharePoint Central Administration, Application Management, either Trusted Account or Windows Authentication. In our environment, we configured the authentication mode as Windows Authentication and then found we needed to use stored credentials for our data source connections throughout SharePoint document libraries. If we had configured the authentication mode as Trusted Account, where Kerberos was fully enabled throughout the server environment, then the two options–Windows Authentication (Integrated) and Unattended Report Process Account–would be an alternative.

> **Note** The Unattended Report Processing account is a special account that can be configured on the SQL Server 2005 Reporting Server.

## Report Model Configuration

The report model is based on a data source. A data source can have many models, but each model can have only one data source. Reports are created from the report model. At least one report model must exist within a SharePoint site before reports can be created with the SQL Server 2005 Reporting Services Report Builder. A report model can have many reports. A report model can determine exactly the items made available for creating a report, such as particular tables and fields within a database, and can be secured using the Manage Model Item Security option in the Report Model configuration options shown in Figure 19-13.

> **Note** For further information on creating report models, see "Developing a Report Model and Designing a Report Builder Report" at *http://channel9.msdn.com/ShowPost.aspx?PostID=365619.*

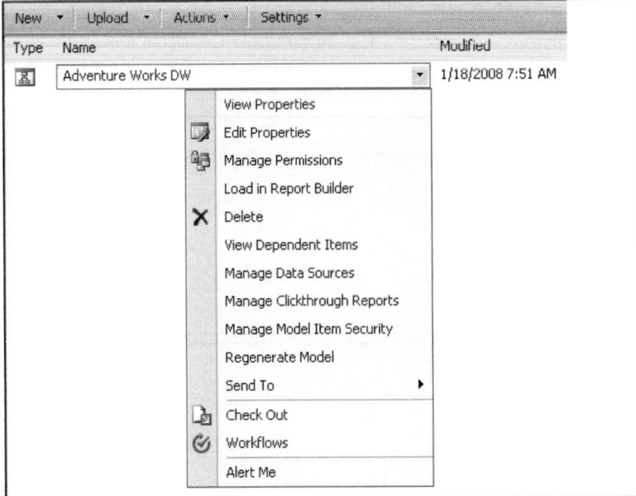


**Figure 19-13** Report model configuration options

The Manage Model Item Security option enables an administrator to lock down individual model items to specific users and/or groups of users. In other words, the data source defines a database, whereas the model tailors items within the database. This option limits the type of reports end-users can create based on their permission to each of the secured model items. For example, you may choose to allow only users within the Sales Group access to create reports against the Customer table. Figure 19-14 shows the Model Item Security page for the Adventure Works DW data source connection where access to the Dim Customer has been locked down. Other users accessing the Adventure Works DW model will not see the Dim Customer item and will not be able to create reports against that item.

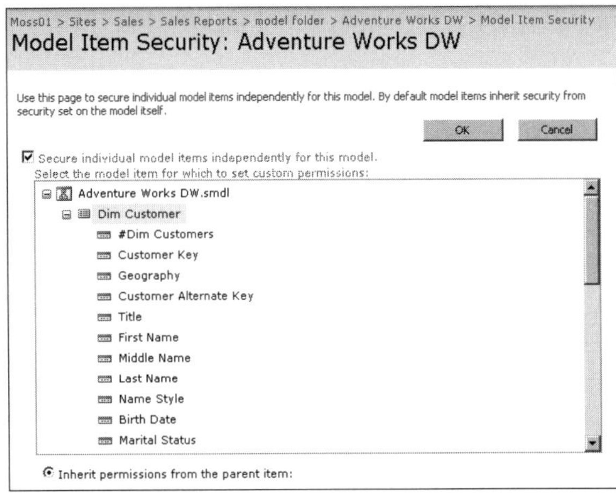


**Figure 19-14** Secure individual report model items

Permissions on the report model in entirety can be managed by selecting Manage Permissions. For instance, you may want to limit who can create reports based on the overall model. End-users who do not have access to a report model will not be able to view that report model when creating new reports.

The Load In Report Builder option will launch the SQL Server 2005 Reporting Services Report Builder to create a new report based on the current report model. Clickthrough reports relate to Reporting Services drillthrough reports. For details on how to create a drillthrough report, see *http://msdn2.microsoft.com/en-us/library/aa337439.aspx*. The Regenerate Model option is used where the source database schema has been modified. If this is the case, the model will need to be regenerated to view and access changes.

## Report File Configuration

Reports are created from a report model. In SharePoint Integrated mode in combination with the Reporting Services add-in, reports can be created and deployed to SharePoint sites using either Visual Studio 2005 or the SQL Server 2005 Reporting Services Report Builder, which is directly launched from SharePoint document libraries. Figure 19-15 shows the configuration options available for reports stored in SharePoint document libraries.

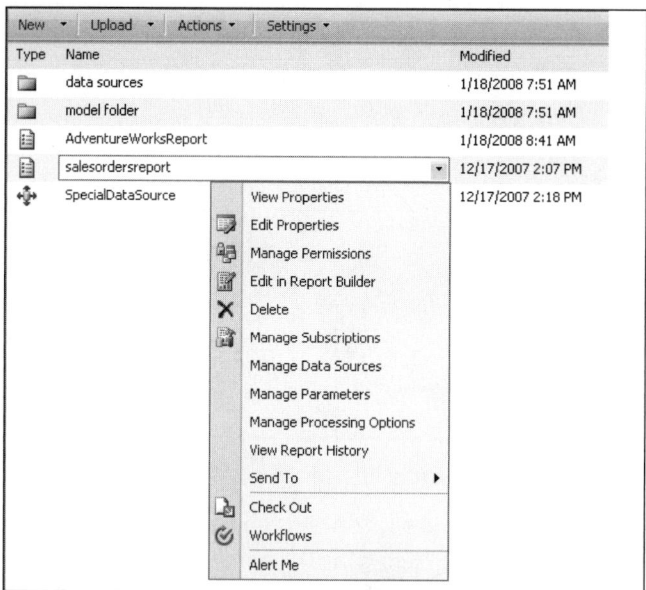


**Figure 19-15** Configuration options for a Reporting Services report stored in a SharePoint document library

The Edit option in Report Builder will launch the report in SQL Server 2005 Reporting Services Report Builder. However, if the report has been created in Visual Studio 2005 and deployed to a SharePoint document library, then you cannot edit that report in Report Builder, even though Report Builder will attempt to open it.

The View Report History option is invaluable. It allows you to view a copy of a report at a given point in time. Snapshots can be taken of reports either manually or automatically based on a schedule, which can be configured under Manage Processing Options.

> **Note** We recommend you set up scheduling for report history, especially where multiple users are editing reports and making changes. The history will provide you with a way to roll back and/or check cumulative changes in the case of errors or issues with existing reports.

The Manage Processing Options page, shown in Figure 19-16, also allow you to configure the data refresh options, such as Use Live Data, Cached Data, or Snapshot Data. Consider the size of reports throughout your SharePoint deployment and bandwidth limitations. For instance, if you are running a global deployment where end-users are browsing reports from remote parts of the world and have multiple page reports, you may want to consider leveraging the Cached Data or Snapshot Data refresh options. You could configure a schedule for report snapshots each day, or twice per day, depending on the update frequency of the report data (data source).

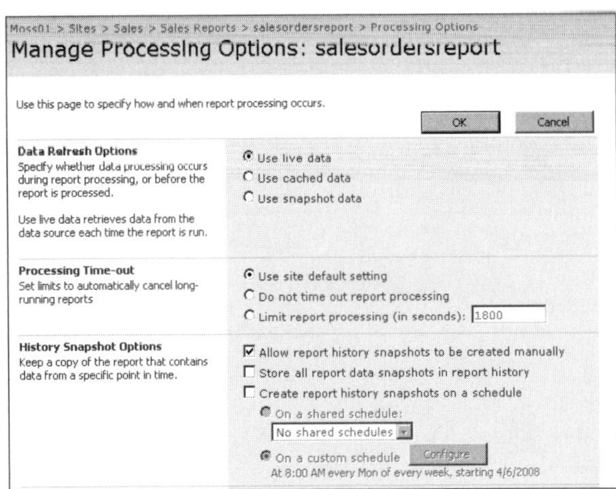


**Figure 19-16** Manage Processing Options page

> ## Notes from the Field **Performance Issues**
>
> Where there is degradation in page load performance when clients are accessing reports throughout SharePoint sites or timeouts, then consider using the Cached or Snapshot Data refresh options. Remember too that other factors may cause a report to load slowly, such as document maps or parameters added to the report, the size of the report itself, or client access points, such as global or local access and underlying model size and/or complexity. Another option is to increase the SQLCommandTimeoutSeconds and DatabaseQueryTimeout key values in the rsreportserver.config file (located in the ReportServer folder on the server hosting Reporting Services, which is typically in the path %SystemDrive%:\Program Files\Microsoft SQL Server\MSSQL\Reporting

Services\ReportServer). A full list of RSReportServer.config settings is outlined at *http://msdn2.microsoft.com/en-us/library/ms157273.aspx*. Be very careful when modifying the RSReportServer.config file–a number of configuration entries, such as the WebServiceAccount, will already have been added, and modifying some entries could cause connections to Reporting Services to fail.

But remember: While increasing timeout values may result in successful report rendering and delivery, specifically when working with larger reports, this may not necessarily satisfy end-user expectations in terms of page-load performance. You may need to revisit the design of the report and/or model to minimize its size or segment the report into several smaller reports. Another option is to try running the same report in native mode as opposed to SharePoint Integrated mode to see if there is any difference in performance. If there is significant improvement in performance when running the report in native mode *and* performance is the driving factor, then you may consider using the Web parts included in the RSWebParts.cab, which is installed as part of SQL Server 2005. The Web parts included in the RSWebParts.cab do not offer as slick a solution as the SharePoint Integrated mode/Reporting Services add-in solution, but they enable integration of reports with SharePoint Server 2007 when the SQL Server 2005 Reporting Services is running in native mode.

*Kathy Hughes, Microsoft MVP*

**Note** When moving Reporting Services reports between SharePoint document libraries, remember that you will need to resurrect the report's data source link, ensuring that the report can find its associated data source at the original location. Another consideration when moving reports is the associated report history (snapshot) files. You will need to determine whether to leave snapshots in the original location or move them, but you will also need to check that any snapshots can locate their original data sources.

# Security Considerations

Reports published to SharePoint document libraries are secured using the SharePoint permission sets. This includes user access via user roles, such as reader, member, and administrator, and the ability to lock reports down either at the site, document library, folder, or item level. Report editing capabilities are subject to end-user permission (for example, a user with read only permission will not view the Edit In Report Builder menu option from a report contextual menu within a document library, but an end-user with member role and higher will).

**Note** This capability differs from accessing Reporting Services reports via the SQL Server Reporting Services Viewer Web part where the menu item Edit In Report Builder is accessible from the toolbar Actions menu, regardless of user permission.

## Securing Reporting Services—Native Mode and SharePoint Integrated Mode

When Reporting Services in configured in native mode, you would ordinarily set users' security and access to Reporting Services reports via the SQL Server Management Studio Object Explorer. However, once you've switched your Reporting Services to SharePoint Integration mode, you will no longer be able to access Reporting Services via the SQL Server Management Studio Object Explorer to modify security. Instead, you will set security within the SharePoint document library where the reports and associated files are stored.

# Creating, Publishing, and Deploying Reports to SharePoint Sites

So far, we've looked at how to work with Reporting Services reports already within SharePoint document libraries, such as configuring the Reporting Services Viewer Web part, subscribing to reports, and using the vast array of options available to configure the Reporting Services content types stored within document libraries. But how are reports published to a document library location? Using the combination of Reporting Services configured in SharePoint Integrated mode and the Reporting Services add-in, you have the flexibility to author and publish Reporting Services reports to SharePoint document libraries using either Visual Studio 2005 or the SQL Server 2005 Reporting Services Report Builder, which is directly accessible from SharePoint document libraries. However, there are some differences between how reports are published from Visual Studio 2005 and how they are published from within SharePoint document libraries using the Report Builder, which we'll outline in the next sections.

> **Note** Between Visual Studio 2005 and the SQL Server 2005 Reporting Services Report Builder, there is a wealth of report-authoring capability. But remember that the strength of published reports will come down to the design, such as the queries and filtering to produce desired data and results. Other factors, such as assigning dedicated report editors to create and author reports, will help to gain a more consistent and successful result. Visual Studio 2005 offers greater authoring capabilities than Report Builder, but you should evaluate both options to see which one will best suit your organization and your resources. In this chapter, we snapshot both the Visual Studio 2005 and Report Builder authoring tools as a grounding for further evaluation.

## Reporting Against SharePoint Lists with Reporting Services

One often-asked question is whether it is possible in Reporting Services to report against a SharePoint list. A Reporting Services extension that enables reporting against SharePoint lists is available from Enesys (*http://www.enesyssoftware.com*). However, if you're contemplating deploying, or have already deployed, PerformancePoint Server 2007, then you can create reports against SharePoint lists using the PerformancePoint Dashboard Designer. For an overview of reporting capabilities, see the "PerformancePoint Server 2007" section later in this chapter.

Another option is the open source Reporting Services Extension for SharePoint Lists developed by Teun Duynstee. The SQL Server 2005 version is available at *http://www.teuntostring.net/blog/2007/08/finally-fixed-problem-w-reporting-over.html.*

## Use Visual Studio 2005 to Create and Author Reports

Developers can create Reporting Services reports within Visual Studio 2005 and deploy those reports to SharePoint document libraries in one of two ways:

1. Create the foundation for creating new reports within a SharePoint document library–You can create a new project based on the Report Model Project template and create a data source (for example, to a SQL database and data model), which can then be deployed to a SharePoint document library. Once this is deployed to the SharePoint document library, end-users can create new reports based on the deployed data model using the SQL Server 2005 Reporting Services Report Builder.
2. Create the actual report in Visual Studio 2005–You can also create a new project based on either the Report Server Project Wizard or the Report Server Project template and create an actual report using the Visual Studio 2005 Report Designer. In this scenario, the report (.rdl) file and associated data source file are deployed to the SharePoint document library

### Option 1: Deploy a Report Model and Data Source to SharePoint

This option provides the most flexible solution for creating subsequent reports within SharePoint document libraries and removes the dependency on the developer to create and maintain reports. Use this option when you want to have more control over the actual model properties–Visual Studio 2005 gives you the tools to granularly define a database model–and when you want to remove the need for a developer to create the actual reports, which can be done in SharePoint.

Once a data model has been created in Visual Studio 2005 and deployed to a SharePoint document library, the model can be further secured (for example, by using the Manage Model Item Security option to lock down model items). or the model can be updated in Visual Studio 2005 and redeployed. The benefit of creating the report model within Visual Studio 2005 is that the developer can more granularly control the model attributes before deploying the model to a SharePoint document library and can also deploy more than one model at a time. Figure 19-17 shows the AdventureWorksModel in Visual Studio 2005.

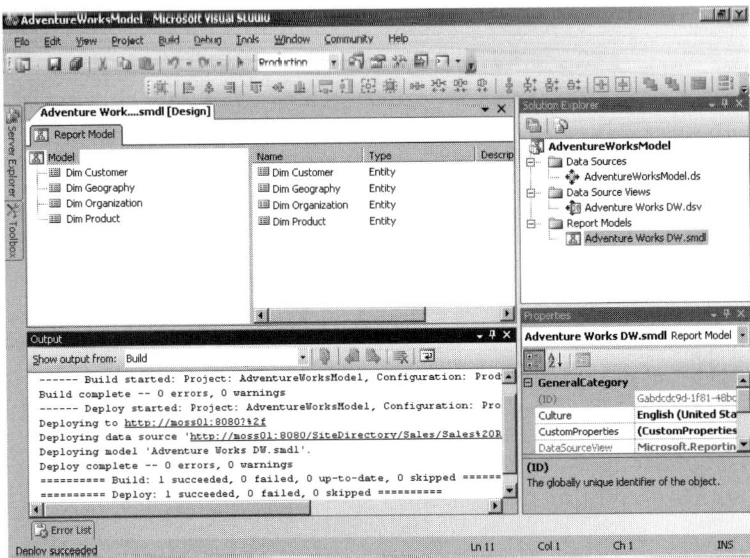

Figure 19-17 AdventureWorksModel creation in Visual Studio 2005

The properties shown in Table 19-1 must be configured when you deploy a data source and report model from Visual Studio 2005 to a SharePoint document library.

**Table 19-1 Deploying a Data Source and Report Model from Visual Studio 2005 to a SharePoint Document Library**

| Target | Example path |
|---|---|
| TargetDataSourceFolder | *http://moss01:8080/SiteDirectory/Sales /Sales Reports/data sources* |
| TargetModelFolder | *http://moss01:8080/SiteDirectory/Sales /Sales Reports/model folder* |
| TargetServerURL | *http://moss01:8080* |

## Option 2: Deploy a Report to a SharePoint Document Library

This option limits updates to the actual report to the developer. Use this option when you do not want end-users to edit a report in SharePoint. Reports (.RDL files) deployed from Visual Studio 2005 cannot be edited in the Report Builder in SharePoint. However, when a report is deployed from Visual Studio 2005, the report's data source is also included as part of that deployment, and new report models created in SharePoint can be based on that data source. Figure 19-18 shows the *salesordersreport* in Preview mode within the Visual Studio 2005 Report Designer.

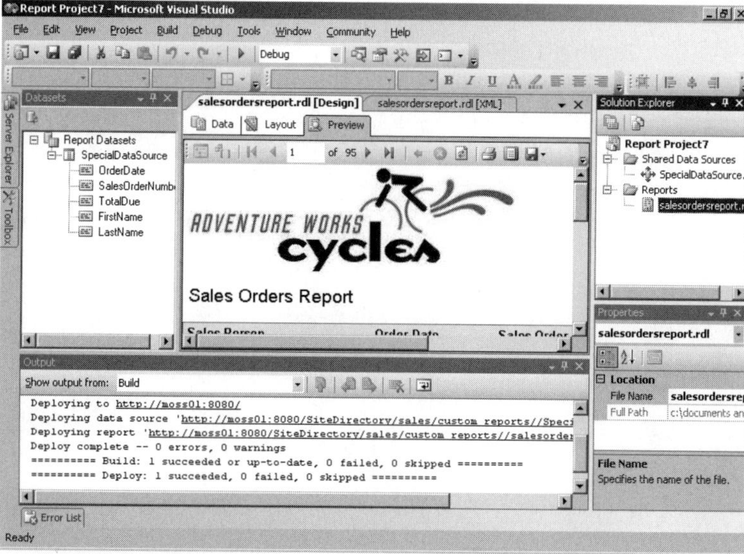


Figure 19-18 Visual Studio 2005 Report Designer

The Report Designer includes three views: Data view to define the data sources, Layout view to format the report, and Preview to preview the report before deploying it to a SharePoint document library. The Data view, shown in Figure 19-19, provides a classic designer interface for constructing data queries.

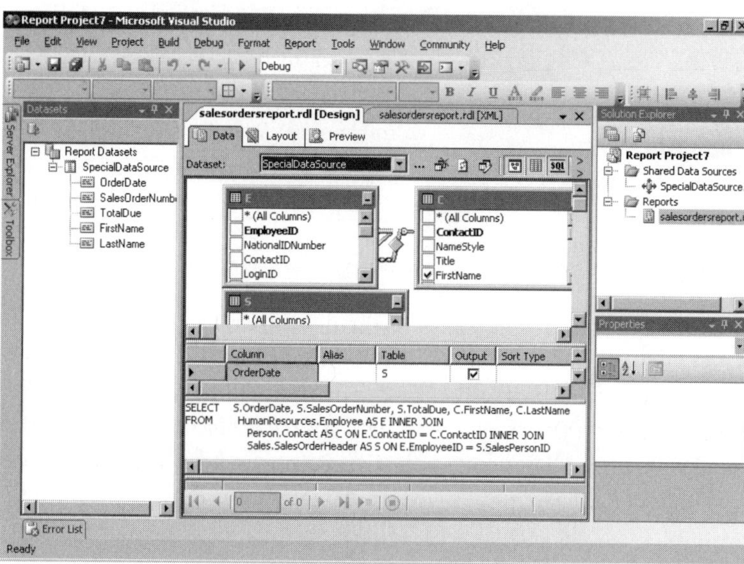


Figure 19-19 Visual Studio 2005 Report Designer in Data view

It will not be possible to modify the deployed report file using the Report Builder. Instead, modifications to the report will need to be performed by the developer using the Visual Studio 2005 Report Designer and redeployed to the SharePoint document library. An attempt to launch a report provisioned from Visual Studio 2005 in the Report Builder will result in an error dialog box similar to that shown in Figure 19-20. Unfortunately, there are no obvious differences between reports created in Visual Studio 2005 Report Designer and those created using the SQL Server 2005 Reporting Services Report Builder until an attempt is actually made to launch the report file in Report Builder. Therefore, best practice would be to determine policies based on ownership of report creation, and separate those reports created in Visual Studio 2005 from those created in Report Builder.

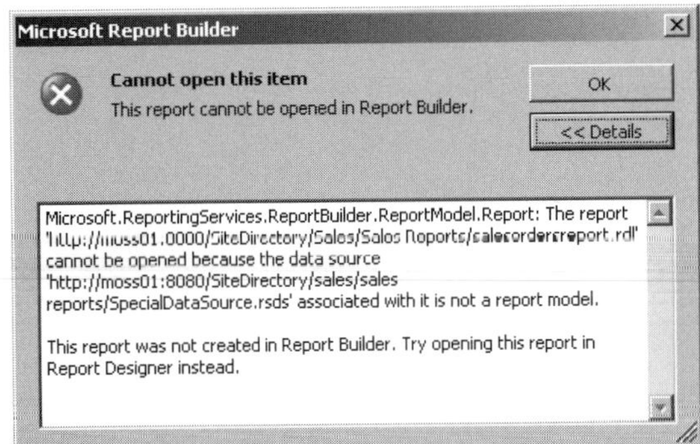


**Figure 19-20** Error dialog box in Report Builder

The properties shown in Table 19-2 must be configured when you deploy a data source and report model from the Visual Studio 2005 Report Designer to a SharePoint document library.

**Table 19-2 Deploying a Data Source and Report from Visual Studio 2005 to a SharePoint Document Library**

| Target | Example path |
|---|---|
| TargetDataSourceFolder | *http://moss01:8080/SiteDirectory/sales/sales reports/* |
| TargetReportFolder | *http://moss01:8080/SiteDirectory/sales/sales reports* |
| TargetServerURL | *http://moss01:8080/* |

### Notes from the Field **Working with Currencies in Reports**

When you author Reporting Services reports in either Visual Studio 2005 Report Designer or SQL Server 2005 Reporting Services Report Builder and you are working with currencies, use the .NET culture to auto-adapt the decimal place in currencies to regional settings. Figure 19-21 shows the custom format of C0 (C{zero}), which .NET will use to display decimal place format based on locale.

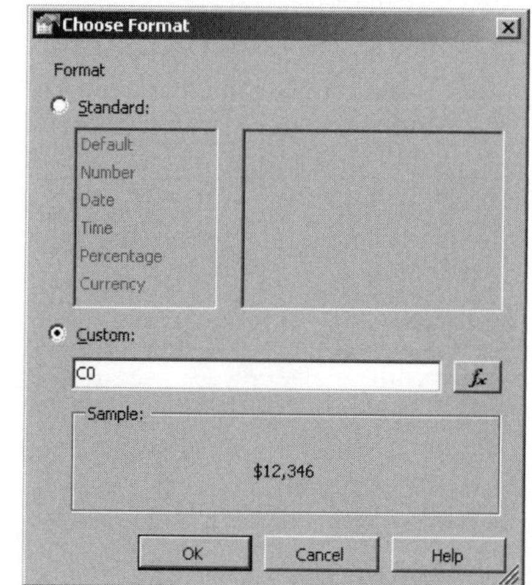


**Figure 19-21** Auto-adapting the decimal place in currencies to regional settings

See the article, "SSW Rules to Better SQL Reporting Services 2005" at *http://www.ssw.com/ssw/Standards/Rules/RulesToBetterSQLReportingServices.aspx*, for additional best practices specific to working with Reporting Services.

*Adam Cogan, Microsoft MVP, Microsoft Visual Studio Team Systems*

## Authoring Reports with SQL Server 2005 Reporting Services Report Builder

The SQL Server 2005 Reporting Services Report Builder is installed on the SharePoint Web front-end server as part of the Reporting Services add-in/SQL Server 2005 Reporting Services Integrated mode combination. The Report Builder is a ClickOnce application that will run as a temporary install when a client accesses a SharePoint document library and attempts to edit an existing report or create a new report using the Report Builder. Figure 19-22 shows the download dialog box.

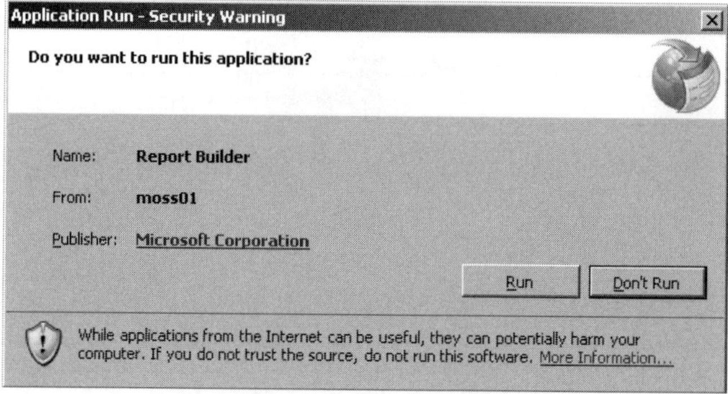


**Figure 19-22** Application Run Security Warning presented when a user tries to edit an existing report or create a new report using the Report Builder

Using the Report Builder, you can create new reports and new report models as well as edit existing reports and report models, including those report models provisioned to a SharePoint document library from Visual Studio 2005. The following demonstrates the process for creating a report using the Report Builder:

1. From a SharePoint document library where the Reporting Services content types have been installed and there is at least one report model already created in the SharePoint site collection, hover over the New Toolbar button, and select Report Builder Report. This will launch the Report Builder application.
2. Once the Report Builder application has launched, select a source of data for the report (that is, the report model against which you wish to create your report).
3. Choose your Report Layout: Table, Matrix, or Chart.
4. Transfer the fields you want to include in your report into the workspace area.
5. Add a filter, format the report, and then click Run Report to test the report.
6. Finally, click Save to save the report to the SharePoint document library, and add the report to a Web page within the SharePoint site using the Reporting Services (SharePoint Integrated mode) Web part.

Figure 19-23 shows the AdventureWorks DW data model reference (Adventure Works DW.smdl) in the upper-left corner, which was originally created in and deployed from Visual Studio 2005 to a SharePoint document library, that was launched in the SQL Server 2005 Reporting Services Report Builder in Design mode. A new report is created based on the AdventureWorks DW model.

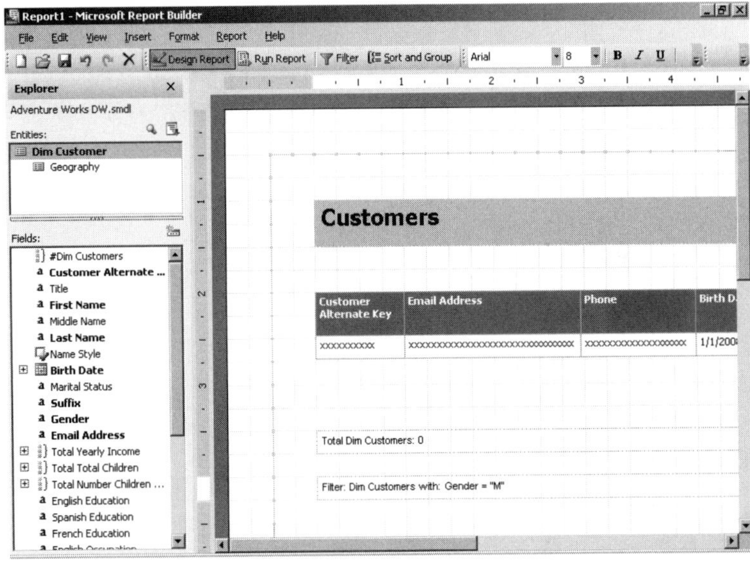


Figure 19-23 Available report model from which to create new reports

## Report Versioning

It is vital for you to understand that, when you choose to edit a report in Report Builder, choosing Edit In Report Builder from the contextual drop-down menu does not automatically check out the report (.rdl) file. This means that you could end up with multiple users editing the same file and saving changes to the file concurrently. Best practice is to either ensure that users check out any report files *before* editing reports in Report Builder or lock down permissions on individual report files to minimize edit access.

Even after a user checks out a report file for editing, the SharePoint versioning protocol will not be strictly followed. Another user will still be able to select Edit In Report Builder against a checked-out file and will not be challenged until she attempts to save changes to the checked-out report. Figure 19-24 shows the result of attempting to save changes to a report in Report Builder when the report is currently checked out to another user.

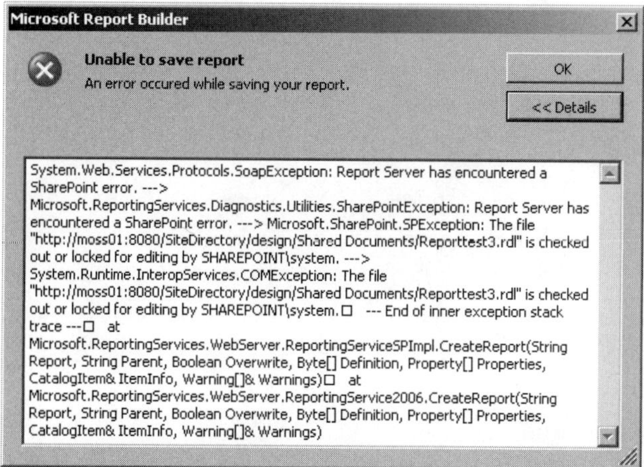


**Figure 19-24** An error dialog box appears when a user attempts to save a report in Report Builder that is currently checked out to another user.

# Distributed Server Environment Consideration

Best practice is to run Reporting Services on a separate server to the SharePoint server. In a multiple-server environment (that is, where SQL Server 2005 and Reporting Services are on separate servers to SharePoint Server 2007 Web front-end servers), you will need to configure Kerberos to enable impersonation of the user account accessing the database server, also referred to as delegation or double hop. Each server will need to be trusted as part of the delegation. Other considerations include configuring a common domain user service account for application pools on Web front-end Reporting Services servers and correctly configuring the Web Service and Windows identity as part of the Reporting Services Configuration tool.

**Note** When reviewing Reporting Services, you may choose to run everything on a single-server instance. For details on how to configure Reporting Services and SharePoint on a single server, see "How to: Configure SharePoint Integration on a Standalone Server" at *http://msdn2.microsoft.com/en-us/library/bb677368.aspx*.

Additionally, the SQL Server 2005 Reporting Services add-in for SharePoint Technologies must be installed on *each* Web front-end server within a farm. The Reporting Services add-in only supports SharePoint Server 2007 and Windows SharePoint Services 3.0; the 32-bit and 64-bit versions can be downloaded from *http://www.microsoft.com/downloads/details.aspx?FamilyID=1E53F882-0C16-4847-B331-132274AE8C84&display=en*.

**On the Companion Media** See the companion CD for a document titled "Microsoft SQL Server Reporting Services–Installation and Configuration Guide for SharePoint Integration Mode." In addition, see the Additional Resources section at the end of this chapter for more references.

## Running Reporting Services on a Domain Controller

If you are running Reporting Services on a Windows 2003 server that is configured as a domain controller, you may see the following error message when attempting to grant database access: A New Member Could Not Be Added To A Local Group Because The Member Has The Wrong Account Type. Further details can be found at *http://connect.microsoft.com/SQLServer/feedback/ViewFeedback.aspx?FeedbackID=259473*.

**Note** We definitely don't recommend deploying Reporting Services on a domain controller in a production environment. Most likely, you'll experience the above issue when you are configuring test environments on a standalone server.

# PerformancePoint Server 2007

PerformancePoint Server 2007 is the latest BI offering from Microsoft–part of the Office suite of applications–for planning, managing, and deploying BI throughout organizations. It is designed to monitor, analyze, and plan organizational business performance around budgeting and forecasting cycles and to manage performance management.

PerformancePoint Server 2007 enables information workers to seamlessly interact with key business applications and centrally author and disseminate information in real time. It removes obstacles introduced by non-automated processes, such as lack of visibility and delay in delivery of key decision-making data, prediction of future trends, manual collation of multiple Excel workbooks, and inflexible reporting. Additionally, PerformancePoint enables information workers to continue using those applications with which they are already familiar, such as Excel 2003 and Excel 2007, to author and update data. It also includes a server-based model to centrally manage roles and access to individual Excel worksheets and templates.

One question posed at a recent Microsoft BI conference was: When would you consider using PerformancePoint Server 2007 instead of Reporting Services? Two possible scenarios were suggested:

1. When you want a controlled and secured distributed Excel workbook-authoring environment
2. When you want the ability to provide greater flexibility when deploying scorecards and KPIs, including the ability to create reports against SharePoint lists, and to drill down into specific organization budget and forecasting sectors

In this section, we'll highlight the main features and components of PerformancePoint Server 2007, describe how it works with SharePoint Server 2007, and help you understand how you can best work with the product to streamline budgeting, forecasting, and reporting throughout your organization.

> **More Info** Remember, the success of a PerformancePoint Server 2007 deployment rests on solid planning around an organization's budgeting and forecasting, such as revenue and operating budgets. For further information and best practices for planning and reporting, see *Best Practices in Planning and Management Reporting* by David Axon (Wiley, 2003), available at *http://www.amazon.com/gp/product/0471224081/102-8129517-3654545?ie=UTF8*. For details on planning and architecting PerformancePoint Server 2007, see the Planning and Architecture Guide at *http://technet.microsoft.com/library/bb838746.aspx*. Also see the Deployment Guide at *http://technet.microsoft.com/library/bb794637.aspx*.

## PerformancePoint Server 2007 Components in a Nutshell

There are two main PerformancePoint components. One component comprises the budgeting and forecasting functionality, while the other comprises a Dashboard Designer for creating KPIs, scorecards, and reports. While each component performs a separate set of tasks, the two combine, or *collaborate*, to present and distribute information to key stakeholders and information workers throughout an organization.

The budgeting and forecasting component includes two planning applications–the Planning Administration Console (PAC) and the Planning Business Modeler (PBM)–which construct budgeting applications, application security (including user roles), user membership, user assignments, and business rules. Excel 2003 and Excel 2007 compliment the overall planning picture by allowing information workers to remotely author and centrally save budgeting and forecasting data based on their access as defined in the membership in the PAC and PBM.

The Dashboard Designer is the fusion of data sources, such as the data submitted to the central PerformancePoint database for an organizational budget or a SQL Server 2005 analysis services cube, and the Web front-end presentation, such as visual representation of a budgetary or forecasting period like KPIs and scorecards.

Figure 19-25 summarizes the overall functionality of PerformancePoint Server 2007 and the relationship with SharePoint Server 2007. The Dashboard Designer can act independently of the roles and assignments configured by the PAC and PBM and can be used to create dashboards, KPIs, and scorecards against multiple sources of data such as SQL Server 2005, Analysis Services, and ODBC.

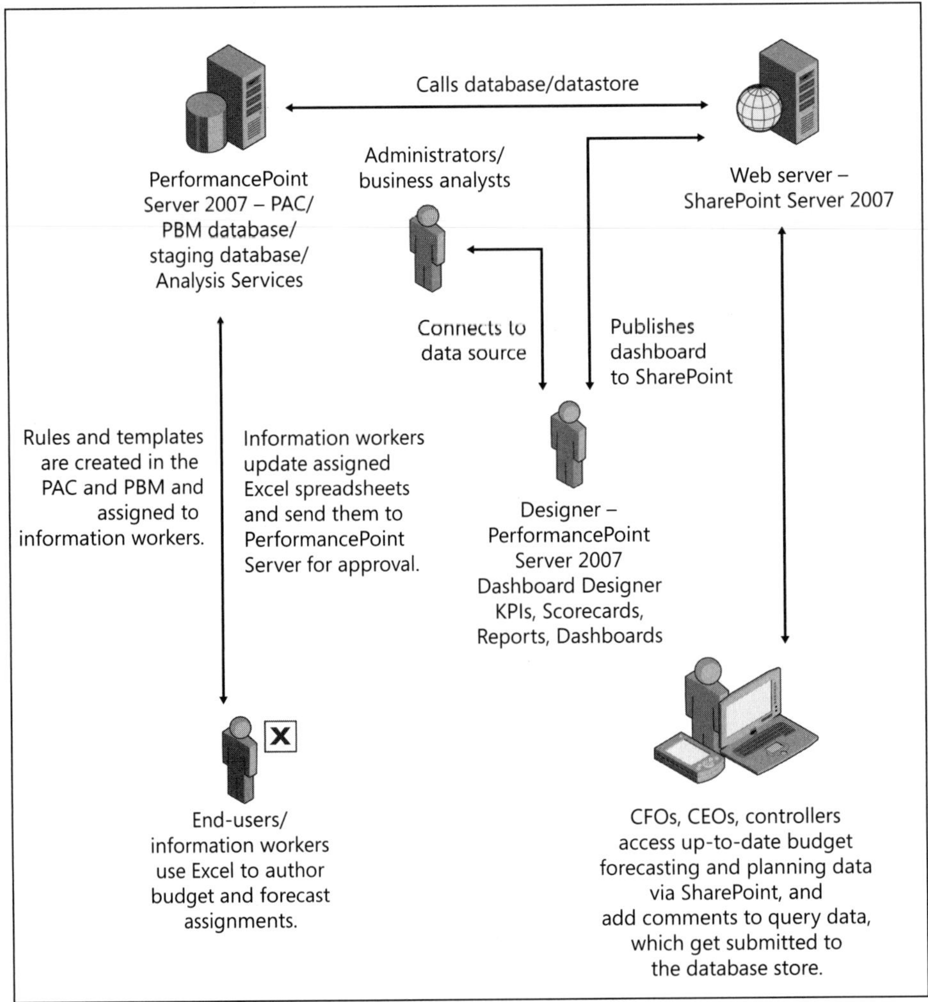


**Figure 19-25** PerformancePoint Server 2007 overall functionality

> **Note** SQL Server 2005 Enterprise version is recommended for PerformancePoint Server 2007 deployments. See *http://technet.microsoft.com/en-us/library/bb838707.aspx* for further details and best practices for deploying and configuring SQL Server 2005 for PerformancePoint Server 2007.

## Planning Administration Console

The PAC is a Web-based tool for managing the framework for budgeting applications and is the initial configuration stage when implementing an organizational performance management solution in PerformancePoint Server 2007. The PAC is where you create Planning Server applications and model sites as well as configure auditing and overall reporting storage.

An application is a container for hosting model sites, data sources, dimensions (such as Account or Currency), user roles, and other administrative settings, such as auditing and workflow. When a new application is created in the PAC, two databases are created on the SQL Server 2005 database server: one for the application database and the other for the application staging database. Figure 19-26 shows the PAC Application Configuration page. The PAC includes a master user list that will be used for setting permissions throughout model sites and models.

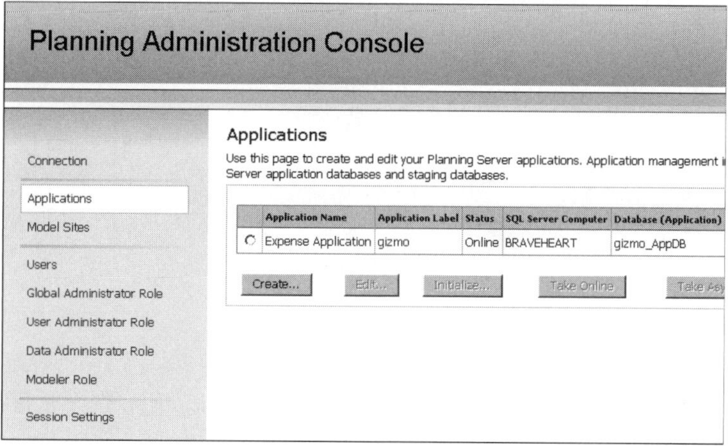


**Figure 19-26** PAC Application Configuration page

Model sites are hosted by a parent application and include a hierarchy of model subsites and models (cubes). When a model site is created, a database in SQL Server 2005 Analysis Services stores the models created under each model site. Figure 19-27 shows the hierarchy in constructing a PerformancePoint application.

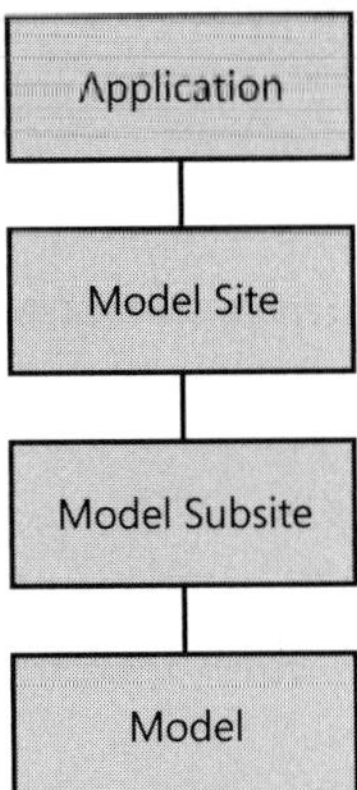


**Figure 19-27** PerformancePoint planning application, site model, and model hierarchy

> **Note** We refer to model *sites*. However, we are not referring to sites in the sense of Web sites or IIS. A site in the context of model sites is a SQL Server 2005 Analysis Services database and houses the subsequent models (cubes) created under each model site.

For instance, you may create a specific application to monitor company expenses and then create model sites and subsites under that application to define expenses by region and department. For large organizations, you may consider creating a separate application for monitoring expenses for each geography. Applications also form a physical security boundary based on user administration, as well as workflow and reporting. Figure 19-28 shows an example model site hierarchy.

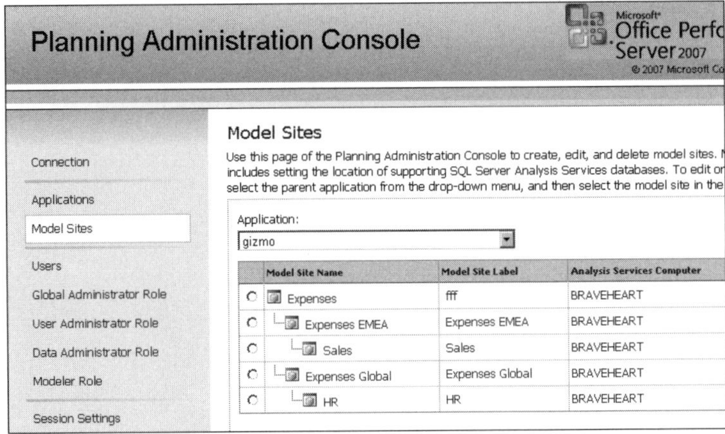


**Figure 19-28** Model sites created in the PAC

## PerformancePoint Planning Server Operational and Business Reports Requirements

SQL 2005 Server Reporting Services will need to be configured in native mode for the PerformancePoint Planning Server operational and business reports. If you have already configured Reporting Services in SharePoint Integrated mode, then you'll need to create a separate instance of SQL 2005 Reporting Services and configure that instance in native mode. If you attempt to configure operational and business reports against a Reporting Services server that is configured in SharePoint Integrated mode, then you may receive the dialog box shown in Figure 19-29.

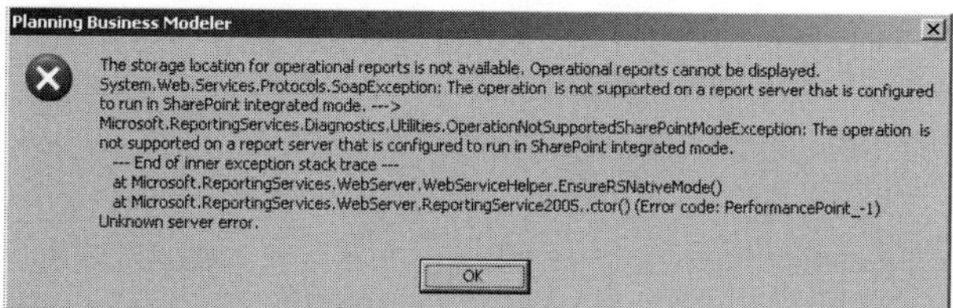


**Figure 19-29** Planning Business Modeler error dialog box

## Planning Business Modeler

The PBM is a Windows tool that runs on the PerformancePoint server. It connects to the PerformancePoint Planning server to retrieve existing applications and model sites and is used to build and configure models within model sites. Figure 19-30 shows the initial page of the PBM connected to the Expenses model site.

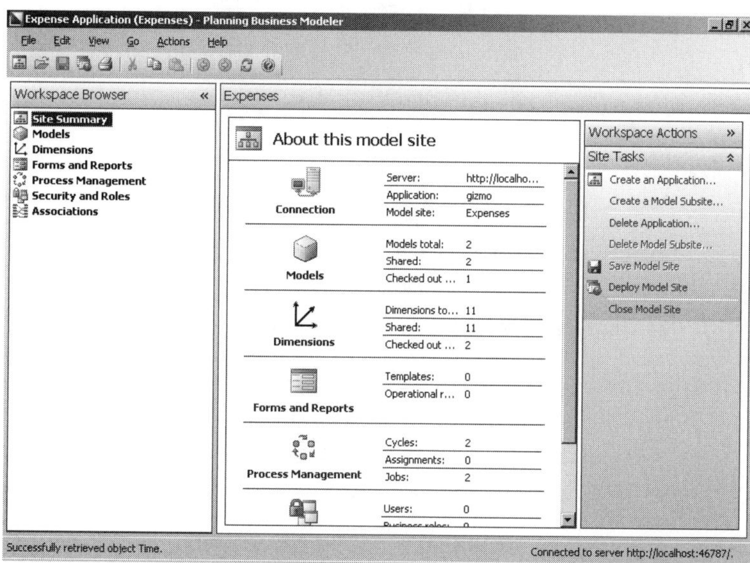


**Figure 19-30** PBM initial page

The PBM includes a number of pre-populated dimensions and pre-defined model templates that you can use when creating new models within a model site, including stock scenario and time dimension types, as well as models that support assumptions. Figure 19-31 shows the default dimensions available when accessing a model site in the PBM. The option to create a new dimension is included under the Dimension Tasks pane.

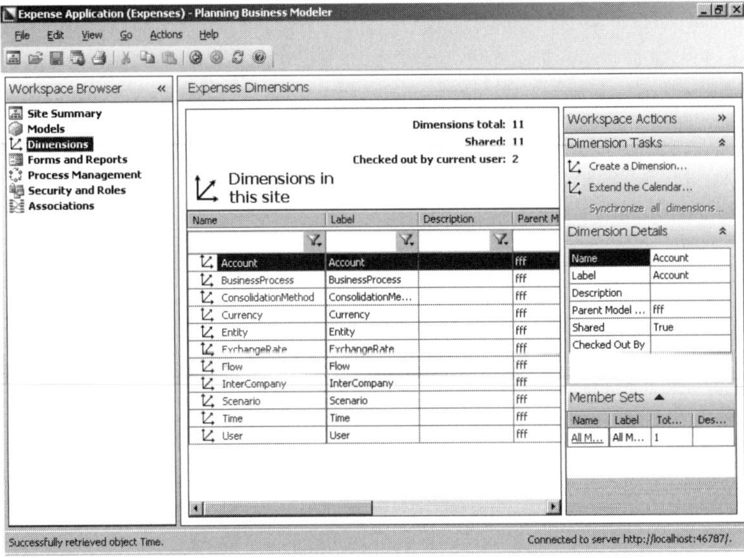


**Figure 19-31** Out-of-the-box dimensions in a model site

Other configurations in the PBM include the following:

- Defining model business rules
- Managing form templates and reports submitted to the PerformancePoint Planning server
- Process Management, which includes scheduling jobs and creating user assignments
- Configuring Security and Roles and the current model site
- Saving, deploying, and scheduling updates to models

## PerformancePoint Add-in for Excel

The PerformancePoint add-in for Excel enables *targeted* users and information workers to update budget and forecasting data using Excel and submit data to the PerformancePoint Planning server for approval and update. Access to data is secured by the user roles and by the access defined back in the model site in the PBM, as are specific data rules.

The add-in also allows administrators to create form (Excel) templates and reports for submission to the PerformancePoint Planning server. For example, an Excel template is created based on the business rules and dimensions created back in the model site, and the template is then deployed to a select group of users for data entry and subsequent data analysis. Figure 19-32 shows an Excel workbook with the PerformancePoint add-in for Excel active. The left pane is where user assignments are displayed for the current logged-in user as well as an authoring tab for creating wizard-based matrices and reports.

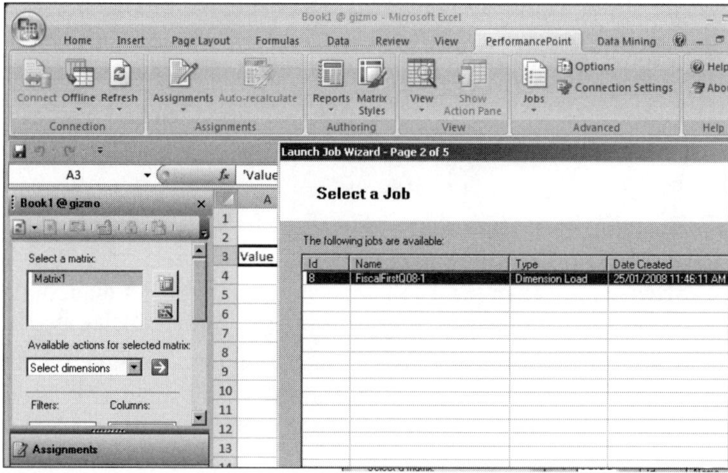


Figure 19-32 PerformancePoint add-in for Excel

A data Connection Status dialog box, shown in Figure 19-33, shows the current connection status and completed activities for the current Excel workbook connection.

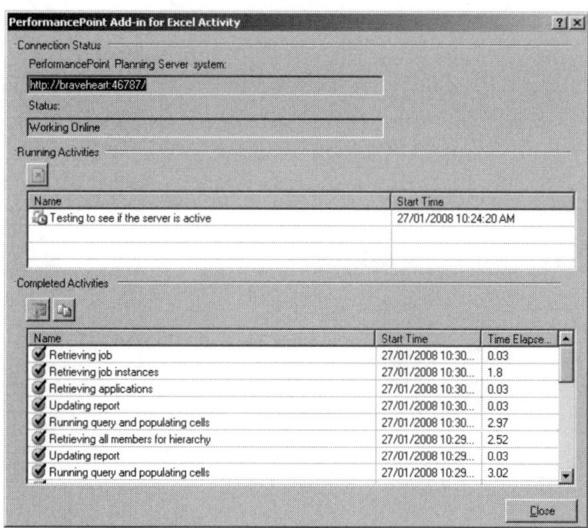


Figure 19-33 PerformancePoint Add-In For Excel Activity dialog box

A key factor in deploying the PerformancePoint add-in for Excel is how you will deploy it. The add-in is a required client installation for those users who will be sent assignments and tasks from the PBM. One possible solution is to use Active Directory directory services group policy to selectively deploy the add-in to users.

> **Note** In Excel 2007, the PerformancePoint Server 2007 add-in items appear in the Ribbon menu. In Excel 2003, the PerformancePoint Server 2007 add-in items appear in a tree-view style menu at the left of the page.

## Dashboard Designer: Presenting PerformancePoint Server 2007

PerformancePoint Dashboard Designer is a client-side tool for creating and managing dashboards, scorecards, KPIs, and reports and is included as part of the PerformancePoint Server 2007 installation. Dashboard Designer bridges the presentation gap between SQL Server 2005 Analysis Services and numerous other data sources, SharePoint Server 2007, and Windows SharePoint Services 3.0. For example, in the previous, section we provided an overview of how applications, site models, and models can be built and configured on PerformancePoint Server 2007. The logical next step would be to use Dashboard Designer to connect to the model's data source, build KPIs and scorecards, and then publish an associated dashboard to a SharePoint site for visual representation.

Using Dashboard Designer, you can build an entire dashboard solution on Windows XP or Windows Vista. A Preview mode means there is no need for a server until you're ready to deploy a dashboard to SharePoint, which makes Dashboard Designer ideal for demonstrations and proof of concepts. If you are using, or had previously used, Business Scorecard Manager 2005, an option to preview scorecards was not available; instead, you had to deploy a scorecard to a SharePoint site in order to preview it.

> **On the Companion Media** See the companion CD for dashboard planning worksheets, specifically the files titled "PerformancePoint_DashboardPlanningWorksheets."

### Deploying the Dashboard Designer Executable

End-users will need to install the Dashboard Designer in order to view, edit, manage, publish, and deploy dashboards. The Dashboard Designer is deployed to end-users via the Monitoring Central Web site, which is configured at the time of installing PerformancePoint Server 2007 and typically accessed from *http://server_name:40000/central/*. Monitoring Central, shown in Figure 19-34, includes the option to download (run) the Dashboard Designer installation as well as a Preview option to view dashboards currently submitted for preview. The Dashboard Designer download, also referred to as a ClickOnce application, is installed on a per-user profile basis on the client machine.

Figure 19-34 Monitoring Central Web site

# Working with Dashboard Designer

The Dashboard Designer is just that—a tool for creating and deploying dashboards to SharePoint document libraries. It offers an incredible degree of flexibility between working with data sources and creating and formatting dashboards, KPIs, scorecards, and reports. The look and feel of Dashboard Designer blends in with the rest of the Office 2007 suite of products, including the ribbon-style menus. Figure 19-35 shows the Dashboard Designer in action. The left pane is the Workspace Browser, which shows each type of function available within a current dashboard. The middle section is where dashboards are built and configured. The right pane displays the Details or available items to the currently opened dashboard. Items shown in the Details pane, such as KPIs and scorecards, can be directly dragged and dropped into an opened dashboard within the middle editing section. You also have the ability to create filters.

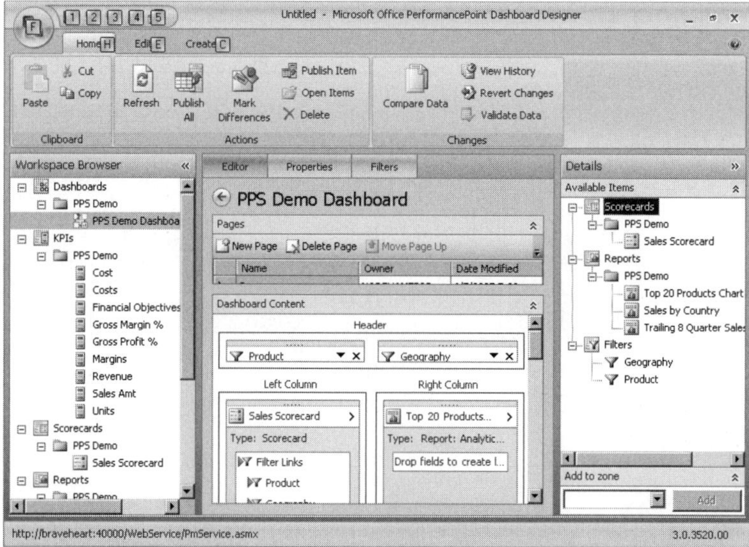


Figure 19-35 Dashboard Designer workspace

Let's consider the various components and stages involved in creating and configuring dashboards up to the eventual deployment to SharePoint document libraries.

## Dashboards

Dashboards are effectively Web part pages, which include Web part zones, and are the containers for visually presenting KPIs, scorecards, and reports. A dashboard is created based on a dashboard page template, as shown in Figure 19-36.

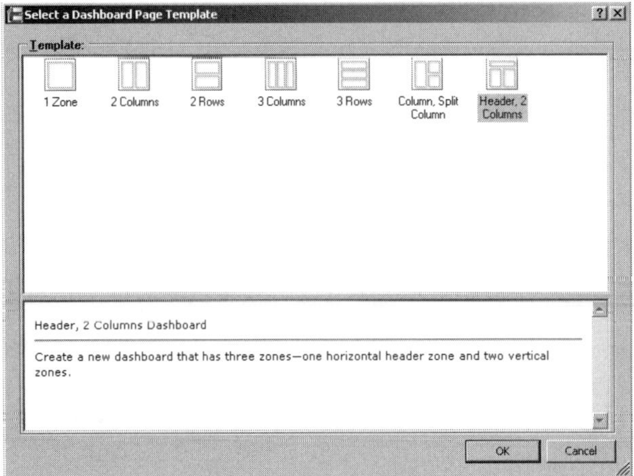


**Figure 19-36** Select A Dashboard Page Template dialog box

Dashboards can also include multiple pages. For instance, you may choose to create a multiple-page dashboard when you want a different page template (layout) or when you want to break up KPIs by business unit and place each on a separate page. Or, you may choose to create multiple pages to declutter a dashboard. Applying filters to dashboards can also assist in showing the end-user specific information on demand.

> **Note** A major consideration in creating dashboards is in the actual design—for example, how to effectively use visual indicators for KPIs and best practices for displaying graphical objects. You can find a great reference on dashboard design at *http://www.perceptualedge.com/articles/Whitepapers/Common_Pitfalls.pdf*.

The formatting features included in dashboard pages allow for Web zone changes after page creation, as shown in Figure 19-37. For example, if you've chosen to create a dashboard page based on a two-column (or two Web part zone) layout, you can choose to add additional zones and modify settings in the existing zones.

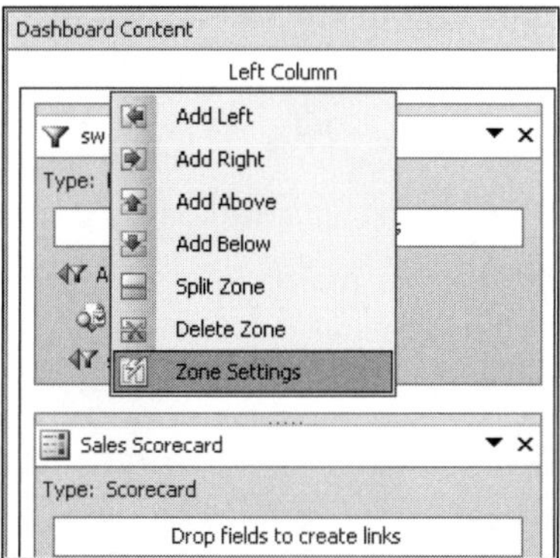


**Figure 19-37** Configuring Web part zones in dashboard pages

KPIs, scorecards, and reports are referred to as dashboard *items*. Effectively, each item is a Web part when it is added to a Web part zone within a dashboard. Once a dashboard is deployed to a SharePoint site, this is exactly how SharePoint will interpret a dashboard item–as a Web part. For example, each item within a deployed dashboard will include Web part properties and be editable when the dashboard page is in Edit mode. There is limited Web part/item configuration within Dashboard Designer, such as setting the Cache option for each item to be cached, and the width and height of each item, which is typically set to Auto-size. Dashboard item properties can be adjusted and configured further once they are deployed to a SharePoint site.

> **Note** Typical post-deployment dashboard configuration may include adjusting item/Web part properties, such as the Allow Minimize and Allow Close settings, which by default are deployed unchecked. You may also want to modify the audience settings on Web parts. We speak further about dashboard security and deployment later in this section.

## Configure Data Sources

A number of pre-defined data source templates are included in Designer Dashboard, including Analysis Services, ODBC, Excel Services, fixed values from an Excel 2007 workbook, SQL Server tables, and SharePoint lists. A major benefit of Dashboard Designer is that you can report against SharePoint lists! Previously, reporting against SharePoint lists was limited to exporting list data to Access or Excel and conducting reporting within those client applications, using a third-party add-on to Reporting Services (such as the Enesys add-on/connector) to create SharePoint list reports, or creating a custom solution in Visual Studio 2005. For example, imagine you had created a new SharePoint list based on an existing Access database or imported Excel spreadsheet that contained budget or forecasting data, and you were required to implement a reporting solution as part of that data transition. Using the SharePoint List Data Source in Dashboard Designer, shown selected in Figure 19-38, you could report against that SharePoint list, map KPIs to columns within the list to measure Actuals and Targets, and visually expose the results in a dashboard published to a SharePoint site.

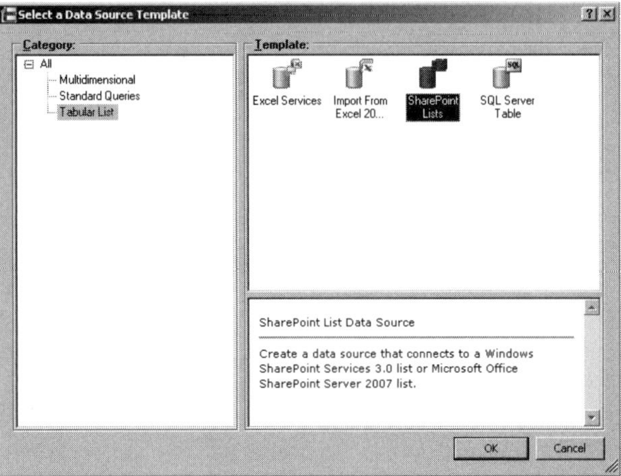


**Figure 19-38** Create data sources in Dashboard Designer, including SharePoint List data sources

# Creating Reports

Dashboard Designer includes several report templates that you can use to create new reports for plotting and listing data views, analysis, trending, and projections against data sources, including SQL Server 2005 Analysis Services. The following report templates are available:

- **Analytic Chart** Creates a chart view of OLAP data. Chart types include bar and line charts. This view requires a server-defined Analysis Services 2005 data source.
- **Analytic Grid** Creates a grid view of OLAP data. This view requires a server-defined Analysis Services 2005 data source.
- **Excel Services** Creates a new view of an Excel Services workbook. This view requires that Excel Services be installed.
- **PivotChart** Creates a PivotChart report that is stored in PerformancePoint Monitoring Server. PivotChart types include bar, column, line, smoothline, pie, XY (scatter), bubble, area, doughnut, radar, stock, and polar charts.
- **PivotTable** Creates a PivotTable report that is stored in PerformancePoint Monitoring Server.
- **ProClarity Analytics Server Page** Creates a reference to an existing ProClarity Analytics Server page.
- **Spreadsheet** Creates a spreadsheet report that is stored in PerformancePoint Monitoring Server.
- **SQL Server Report** Creates a reference to an existing SQL Server 2005 Reporting Services report.

- **Strategy Map** Creates a strategy map report that is connected to KPIs by using Microsoft Office Visio 2007.
- **Trend Analysis Chart** Creates a trend analysis report that shows the historical performance of data in a scorecard. This report includes the option to use SQL Server data-mining algorithms to generate projections that are based on future values of data.
- **Web Page** Creates a reference to an existing Web page.

Figure 19-39 shows an analytic chart report that has been created to display quarterly sales based on one or more dimensions configured in the AdventureWorks Data Warehouse Analysis Services database/cube. In this case, the Product dimension is shown plotted in a line-style chart.

**Figure 19-39** Dashboard Designer analytic chart report connected to an Analysis Services cube

# Excel Services Report

The Excel Services Report will allow you to create an additional *view* on an existing published Excel workbook stored within a SharePoint site, but it remains as a "thin" client view and does not enable end-users to edit and save changes to the source workbook.

# Reporting Services Reports

You can create a reference to Reporting Services reports using the Dashboard Designer, where SQL Server Reporting Services is set to either native or SharePoint Integrated mode. You might consider using Dashboard Designer to create and publish reports to a SharePoint site when you are unable to switch your Reporting Services report server to SharePoint Integrated mode. For instance, you may have other applications also using the report server that require Reporting Services to run in native mode.

Once a reference is made to an existing Reporting Services report, you can configure the various settings, such as enabling or disabling the toolbar. Figure 19-40 shows the Report Settings workspace when configuring a report, including options to Show Toolbar, Show Parameters, and Show Docmap. A selection of formats, including HTML4.0, HTMLOWC, MHTML, IMAGE, EXCEL, CSV, PDF, and XML, are also included that will determine how the report is presented once it is deployed to a SharePoint site.

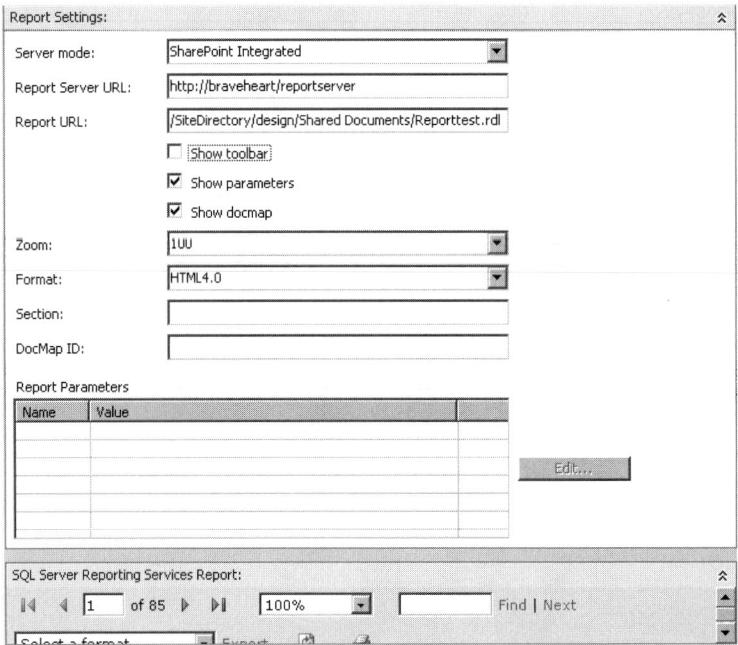


**Figure 19-40** Configuring a Reporting Services Report in Dashboard Designer

> **Note** Note that when you configure Reporting Services reports within Dashboard Designer, the control to enable or disable the Report toolbar is included in the actual Designer as opposed to the PerformancePoint View Display Web part and configured pre-deployment. This differs from using the SharePoint Integrated-SQL Server Reporting Services Report Viewer Web part, where the toolbar and parameter configuration is done within the Web part in Edit mode.

Figure 19-41 shows Reporting Services reports rendered within a SharePoint Web page. The top report is rendered in the SQL Server Reporting Services Report Viewer Web part (SharePoint Integrated mode), while the bottom report is rendered in the PerformancePoint Dashboard Item Web part.

**Figure 19-41** Reporting Services reports added to a SharePoint Web page

## Strategy Map Reports

Strategy maps are a great way to visually enhance KPI and scorecard data within a dashboard. Any Visio object can be attached to a KPI. Figure 19-42 shows an example of where a strategy map has been associated to a scorecard within a published dashboard. Clicking on each shape within the strategy map reveals additional details about the respective KPI.

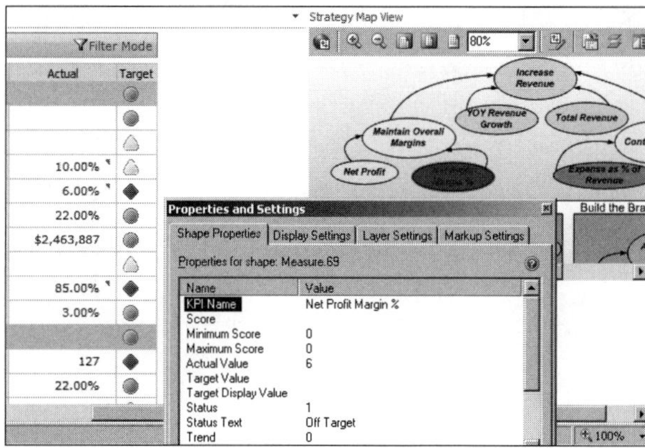


**Figure 19-42** Strategy map included as part of a scorecard dashboard and deployed to a SharePoint site

You should be aware that an installation of Visio Viewer for Office 2007 or Visio 2007 is required on clients accessing dashboards, or PerformancePoint Dashboard Item Web parts, which include strategy map reports. Where Visio 2007 or the Visio Viewer for Office 2007 is not present on the client, an error dialog box such as the one shown in Figure 19-43, may be displayed, or you may simply see a blank screen.

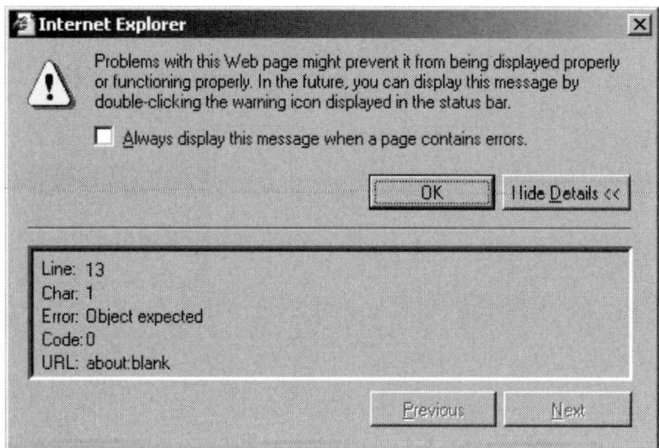


**Figure 19-43** Error dialog box when Visio 2007 or Visio Viewer for Office 2007 is not installed

> **More Info** For further information on integrating Visio with SharePoint lists, see "Integrating Visio 2007 and SharePoint Products and Technologies" at *http://msdn2.microsoft.com/en-gb/library/bb229690.aspx*.

## Using MDX Queries

If you're creating a report based on an Analysis Services data source, you can create and edit queries using Multidimensional Expression (MDX) language. If you've previously worked with MDX, then you may already be familiar with its ability to work directly with Analysis Services cubes, such as the ability to create conditional formatting based on certain measures within a cube like changing the color of rows within a report based on a particular set of values. Visual Studio 2005 Business Intelligence Development Studio includes special toolsets for working with Analysis Services, including a Cube Designer that allows you to directly manipulate a cube's properties using an MDX editor. Figure 19-44 shows the MDX query window in Dashboard Designer. The items in the right side of the Details pane can be dragged and dropped directly into the Code Editor section.

> **More Info** For further information on working with MDX, see *http://msdn2.micrsoft.com/en-us/library/ms145506.aspx*.

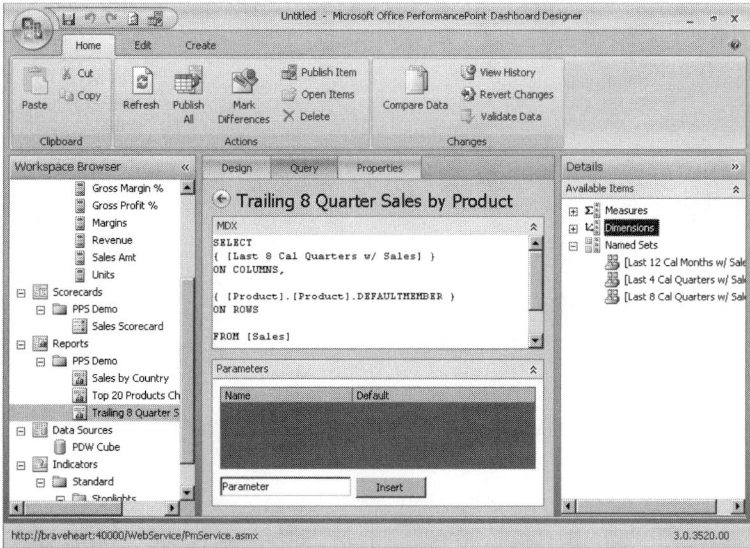

**Figure 19-44** Writing MDX queries in Dashboard Designer when reporting against Analysis Services

# KPIs

The concept of KPIs is to visually reflect the status of a given set of data using some kind of graphical indicator, like a green traffic light indicator for favorable sales figures based on a specific measure. Dashboard Designer includes an impressive set of tools for creating and designing KPIs, including the following:

- Indicators for visual representation, including traditional stoplights as well as gauges, progress bars, smiley faces, thermometers, trends, roadsigns, and weather symbols. You can also choose to upload your own custom symbol!
- The option of allowing users to edit existing targets or set custom targets in addition to using the default Actual and Target.
- Number formatting, including decimal places, symbols, and tooltips.
- Thresholds (e.g., best, in-between, worst) based on percentages, and a scoring pattern and indicator tool for determining the scoring and banding method for thresholds, such as "Increasing is Better" and "Band by numeric value of Actual."
- Data mappings for mapping each KPI to a specific data set (for example, a specific dimension within an Analysis Services cube or a fixed value). Figure 19-45 shows a Sales Amt KPI that is mapped to the Sales Amt dimension in the PDW Cube. The thresholds are also displayed in the lower half of the screen. The colored indicators to the right reveal the percentage ratios that determine the best, in-between and worst thresholds. For instance, less than 100 percent of the Target will show "red" while anything greater than 120 percent of the Target will show green.

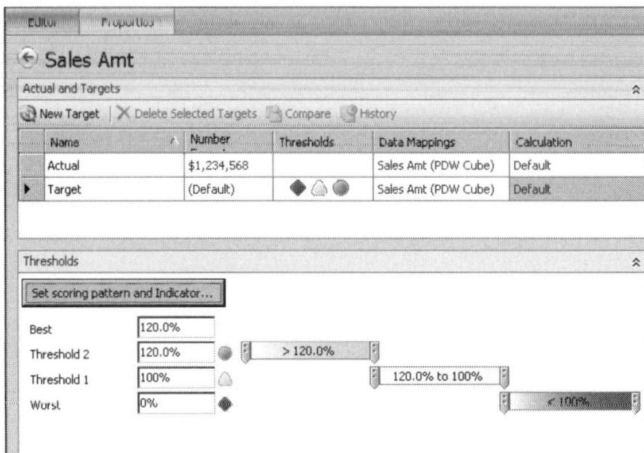


**Figure 19-45** KPI created in Dashboard Designer mapped to the Sales Amt dimension in the PDW Cube (Analysis Services)

- Calculations, such as the Average Of Children calculation, which takes the corresponding target score for each of the child KPIs immediately below the current KPI and uses the average as the input value for this KPI.

> **Note** You should use calculations only with Standard KPIs (non-leaf level); accept the default values for Standard KPIs (leaf level) and Objective KPIs. For best practices on KPI calculations, refer to *http://blogs.msdn.com/performancepoint/archive/2007/07/20/kpi-calculations-best-practices.aspx.*

# Security and Dashboard Designer

A user must have access to a data source to be able to connect to and configure the data source within Dashboard Designer. There are four types of permissions: Administrator (complete control over the Monitoring Server and dashboard data); Data Source Manager (create and delete data sources and publish data sources to the Monitoring Server); Creator (create KPIs, scorecards, and indicators and publish to the Monitoring Server); and Power Reader (read-only access to all dashboard elements). Figure 19-46 shows the Dashboard Designer Permission options.

Each dashboard includes a permission set, which by default will typically include the Administrator as the Editor role and the NT AUTHORITY\Authenticated Users group as a Reader role. Those permissions are set within a dashboard's properties within the Dashboard Designer workspace. Users who do not have access to a dashboard will not be able to successfully view the dashboard within the Dashboard Designer or within a SharePoint site. That is, the permissions set on the actual dashboard in part are honored once the dashboard is deployed to SharePoint. Figure 19-47 shows the result when a user has attempted to access a dashboard published within a SharePoint site. While the user is still able to access the dashboard page via the SharePoint document library, the dashboard items, or Web parts, fail to correctly render, and it is not clear why this has happened. Therefore, as part of your planning, you will need to consider carefully the security aspects of your Dashboard Designer deployment. For example, you may want to segregate dashboards based on user permission to SharePoint document libraries with equivalent sets of user permissions.

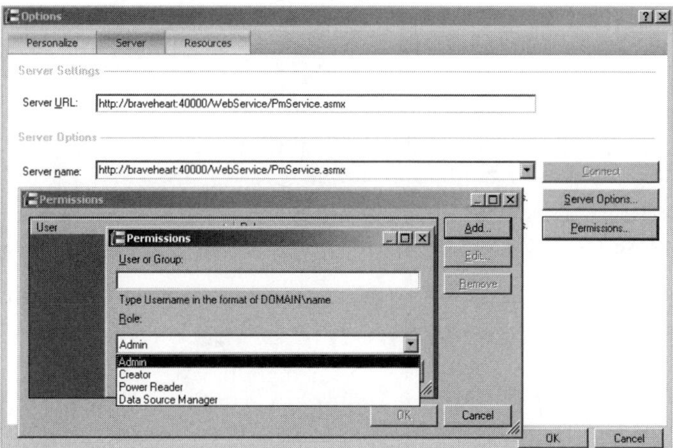


Figure 19-46 Setting Dashboard Designer user permissions and roles

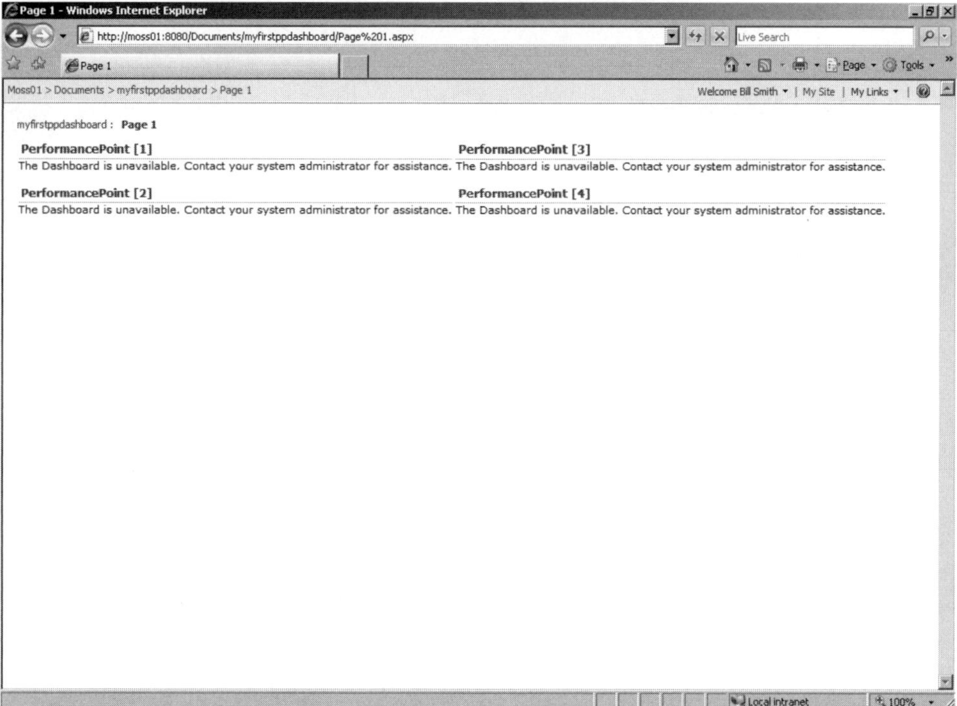


Figure 19-47 Published dashboard page within a SharePoint document library where content within each Web part has failed due to insufficient user permission

> **Note** If an administrator chooses to modify the permission set on an existing dashboard, then she must republish the dashboard to have the adjusted permission set take effect. Until a modified dashboard is republished, other users who had previously had read access to that dashboard will still be able to see the dashboard when refreshing their Dashboard Designer workspace.

If a user attempts to deploy an existing dashboard to a SharePoint site to which he has only read or visitor access, then the dashboard deploy will fail with a nondescript message: Dashboard 'myfirstppdashboard' Was Not Deployed. This applies in cases where the user has access to the actual dashboard within Dashboard Designer, but requires member role or contributor rights or higher on the actual SharePoint Site to successfully publish a dashboard.

## Deploying Dashboards to SharePoint Sites

Three main publishing and deploy modes are available in Dashboard Designer. One is the Publish mode, which is used to publish dashboards and dashboard items to the Performance Point Monitoring Server. The two *deploy* modes include a Preview mode for previewing dashboards before finally deploying to a SharePoint site and a SharePoint Site mode for finally deploying a dashboard to a SharePoint document library.

When you choose to deploy to a SharePoint Site, you are deploying an actual dashboard, as shown in the first screen of the Deploy A Dashboard To A SharePoint Site Wizard in Figure 19-48. The wizard will prompt you for a SharePoint Site URL as well as a document library within the specified URL.

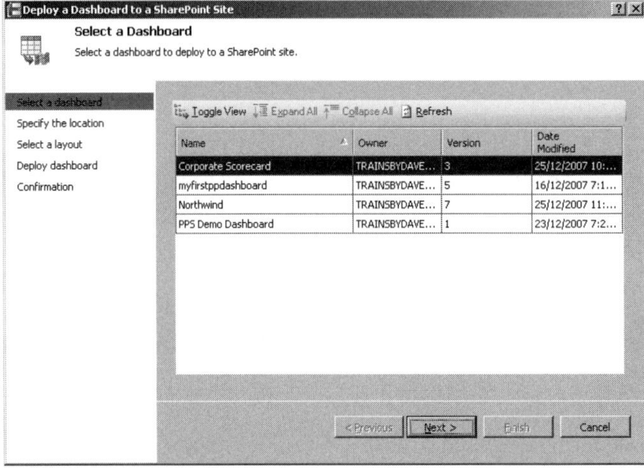


**Figure 19-48** Deploy A Dashboard To A SharePoint Site Wizard in Dashboard Designer

As part of the deployment process, you can choose to deploy your dashboard using either the default PerformancePoint master page or a master page from the Master Page Gallery of the SharePoint site to which you are deploying the dashboard.

> **Note** The default PerformancePoint master page is stored separately from the SharePoint master pages and is located on the PerformancePoint Server at %SystemDrive%:\Program Files\Microsoft Office PerformancePoint Server\3.0\Monitoring\Assemblies.

For example, you may choose to associate a different master page to departmental dashboards to help differentiate each type of scorecard. Note that the dashboard is stored within a SharePoint document library as an ASPX Web part page and does not include publishing functionality. The dashboard also does not inherit publishing functionality within a site where the SharePoint Server publishing feature is activated. Therefore, we suggest you enable versioning and auditing for document libraries where dashboards are deployed so you can more easily monitor activity and manage dashboards throughout SharePoint deployments.

Figure 19-49 shows the master page, or layout, selection when you deploy a dashboard from Dashboard Designer to a SharePoint site.

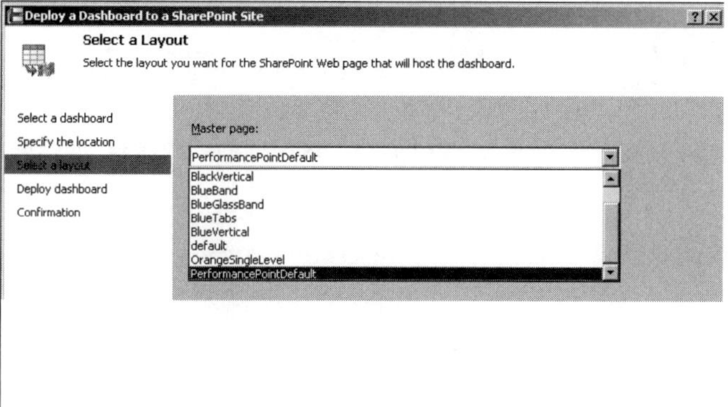


**Figure 19-49** Master page selection when you deploy a dashboard to a SharePoint site

## Adding PerformancePoint Dashboard Items to SharePoint Sites

When a dashboard is deployed to a SharePoint Site, the items within the dashboard are made available as Web parts throughout a site collection. For example, if you've deployed a dashboard that includes a scorecard and a strategy map report, then you may choose to add either of those items separately. Dashboard items can be added to SharePoint Web pages using the PerformancePoint Dashboard Item Web part. Figure 19-50 shows the Select Dashboard Item dialog box where the Corporate Scorecard dashboard is selected and the contents of the dashboard are expanded.

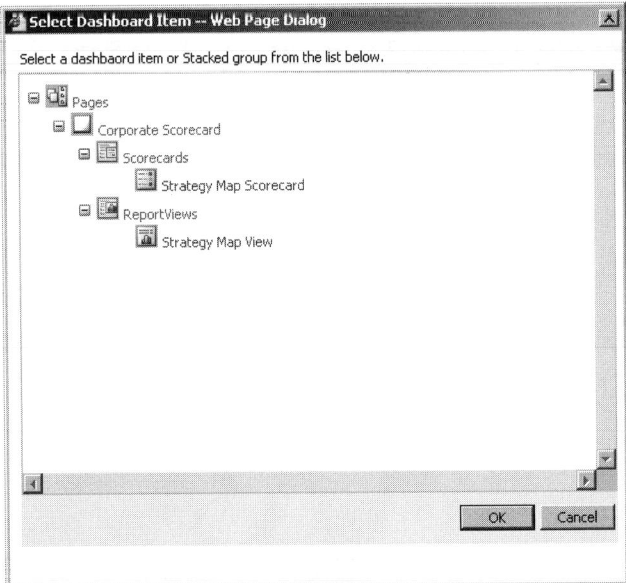


**Figure 19-50** Selecting individual dashboard items throughout a site collection

Dashboard items added separately throughout a site collection will continue to be updated as updates are redeployed to a SharePoint site from Dashboard Designer.

# Interacting with Dashboards Within SharePoint Sites

Depending on how you've configured a dashboard within Dashboard Designer, end-users will be able to drill down into data sets, filter, add comments to items within published dashboards, and export dashboard data to Excel and Microsoft Office PowerPoint.

Figure 19-51 shows a dashboard that includes a Sales Scorecard, an analysis chart report (Trailing 8 Quarter Sales By Product), a Top 20 Products Chart Report, and a Sales By Country report.

Items within dashboards can be filtered and connected. In other words, when you choose to filter by North America, all items included in the dashboard will update to reflect data specifically relating to North America. Figure 19-52 shows the available filtering options for both the All Product and All Geography filters.

A major strength of published dashboards is the ability to drill down into data sets. Figure 19-53 shows the available drill options available in one of the report items within a dashboard. In this case, the data is being pulled from an Analysis Services cube that includes the dimensions Geography, Product, SalesRep, and Time. In the current selection, Geography, each quarter can also be expanded to reveal quarter-specific data.

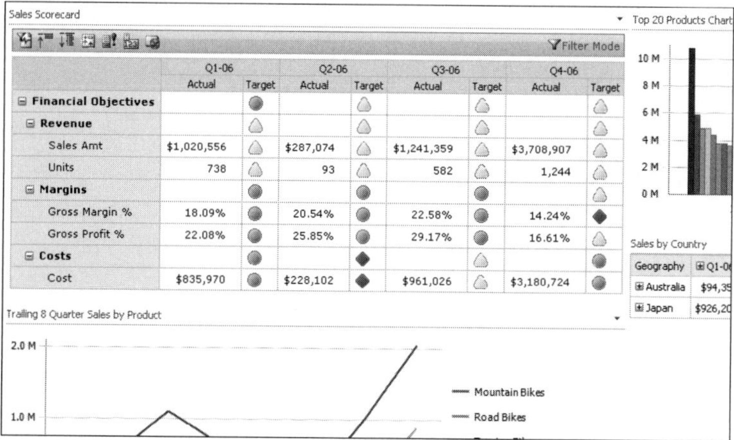


**Figure 19-51** Dashboard shown within a SharePoint site

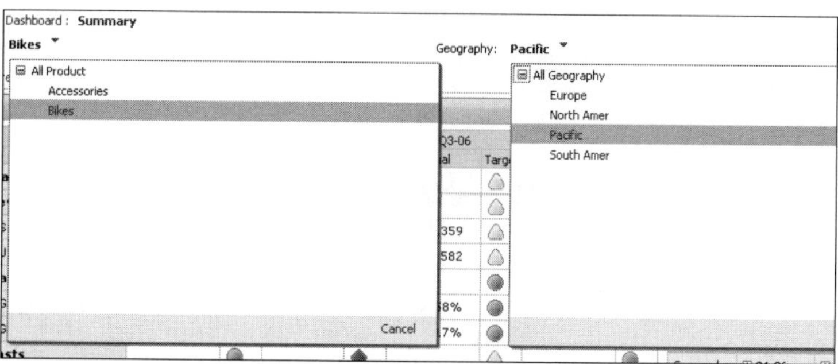


**Figure 19-52** Filtering options within dashboards

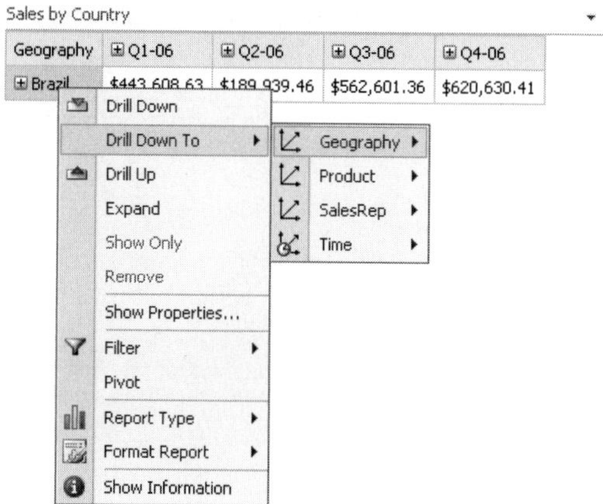


**Figure 19-53** Drill down into dashboard items

Another valuable feature of dashboard items is the ability to add comments to individual cells within scorecards (for example, querying a specific sales figure). Figure 19-54 shows the Comments dialog box.

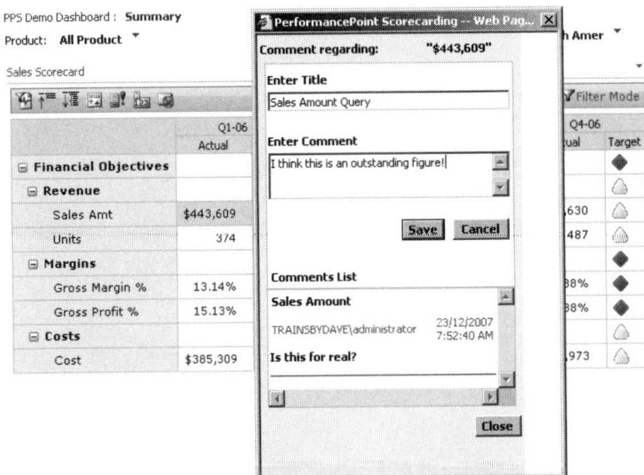


Figure 19-54 Adding a comment to an individual cell within a scorecard

# Saving a Dashboard Designer Workspace

Dashboard Designer workspaces can be saved locally and ported to other clients and servers. Workspaces are saved in a .bswx file format, which is understood by Dashboard Designer. Any currently opened dashboards or dashboard items will be saved as part of the .bswx file. One stipulation in saving workspaces locally and porting to other servers is that the recipient user/server will need to ensure that any data source connections saved as part of the .bswx file are valid in terms of connection database server and administrative user rights included in the .bswx file.

> **On the Companion Media** When opening the sample .bswx workspaces that are installed as part of the PerformancePoint Server 2007 installation, you will need to adjust the server properties to include your own server URL and administrative user ID. We've added a sample guide to the book's companion CD—see PerformancePoint_Monitoring_Samples.doc. See the "Additional Resources" section at the end of this chapter for more PerformancePoint Server 2007 resources.

If you do not save the workspace before closing it, content can be retrieved from the Monitoring Server the next time you launch and refresh the workspace (provided you've published any active content to the Monitoring Server). Figure 19-55 shows a dashboard refresh in operation within the Designer Dashboard workspace.

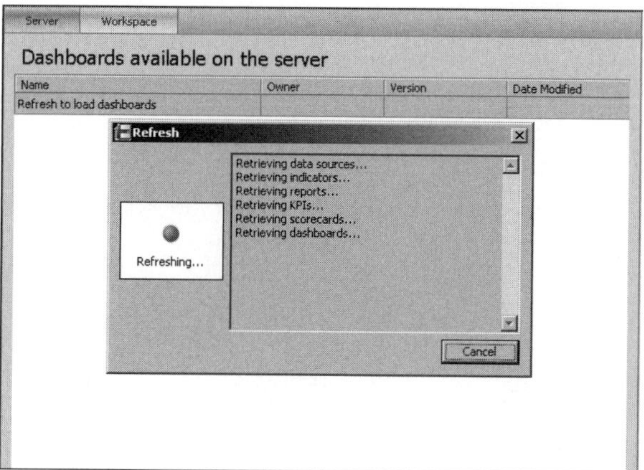


**Figure 19-55** Dashboards being refreshed from the Monitoring Server and made available within a local Dashboard Designer

> **Note** Refreshing (retrieving) data from the Monitoring Server will overwrite any equivalent items within the workspace. For example, if you have items within a local Dashboard Designer workspace that you've edited and that haven't been saved back to the Monitoring Server, then the Monitoring Server will overwrite those items when you next refresh from the server. Best practice is to always publish updated items back to the Monitoring Server to avoid having local workspace copies overwritten.

## Behind the Microsoft Firewall **Microsoft's Performance Management Solution**

PerformancePoint Server 2007 has been in use at Microsoft for approximately two years. Some of the challenges faced by Microsoft before implementing PerformancePoint Server 2007 included disconnected processes and tools, inconsistent data definitions, overlapping accountability, and manual and inefficient data gathering. Added to this was the fact that data had to be accounted for across multiple geographies, including APAC, EMEA, and Americas. There was a requirement for ongoing monitoring and analysis, depicted in Figure 19-56, which shows Microsoft's overall performance management process. This included a strategic plan with a three- to five-year outlook, including key investments and performance status at mid-year review.

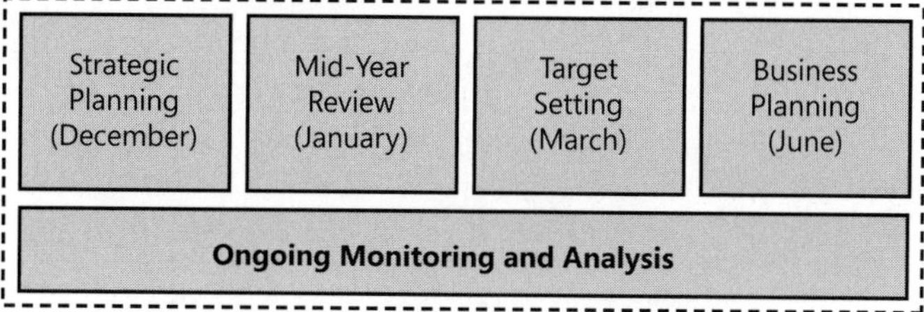


**Figure 19-56** Microsoft's overall performance management process

The PerformancePoint Server 2007 deployment included a two-fold solution: a performance management solution for Microsoft Business Divisions and a planning and forecasting solution for Microsoft worldwide.

The performance management solution involved implementing PerformancePoint Server 2007 for scorecarding, drill down, and workflow; SharePoint for Web presentation; Excel Services for thin spreadsheets; and SQL Server 2005 for sound data. This resulted in consolidated and simplified processes, data sources, and reports; consistent and accurate data rules and data transformation; and a much-reduced business administrative overhead.

The existing planning and forecasting process faced challenges such as multiple legacy tools, offline modeling and manual reporting, and data transformation. This was addressed with a solution that included PerformancePoint Server 2007 for planning and forecasting, Excel for the end-user interface/tool, SharePoint for Web presentation, and SQL Server 2005 for sound and integrated data. This resulted in an integrated planning, forecasting, and reporting solution, including time-saving real-time delivery, one data model, and a single and consistent user experience, which cut back on training.

*Chris Caren, General Manager, Microsoft Business Division*

# Business Intelligence Use Case Scenarios

Now that you've had a chance to understand the vast array of BI features—both those built into SharePoint Server 2007 and those additional BI products that can be integrated into SharePoint Server 2007 for enhanced data analysis and reporting—let's consider which features you should use in specific scenarios and how to use them properly.

**Note** The following recommendations do not include programmable solutions, such as using the SharePoint Server 2007 SDK or other XML/Web service–based solutions.

- **Scenario I** I have existing Reporting Services reports I want to have exposed in SharePoint Server 2007.

  How you do this depends on your existing SQL Server version. If you are running SQL Server 2005 Service Pack 2, then one option is to switch Reporting Services to SharePoint Integrated mode and install the Reporting Services add-in on each SharePoint Web front-end server. If you are running SQL Server 2000, then consider installing the Web parts included within the RSWebParts.cab.

  **Note** RSWebParts.cab was introduced and made available as part of SQL Server 2000 Reporting Services Service Pack 2 and is also available as part of SQL Server 2005 Service Pack 2.

- **Scenario II** I have an existing Access 2007 database I want to send to my SharePoint site.

  One option would be to create a new SharePoint list from an existing Access 2007 database, using the External Data > Export to SharePoint List Wizard, but this creates complications when you have multiple tables and queries. A more viable option would be to upgrade the Access 2007 database to SQL Server 2005 and then use Reporting Services in either SharePoint Integrated or native mode to create and deploy reports to SharePoint.

- **Scenario III** I have a multiple worksheet Excel Workbook(s) and I want to have end-users update only certain sections of the workbook. I also want the data to be exposed in my SharePoint sites real-time, including charts.

  This is an ideal-use case for PerformancePoint Server 2007.

- **Scenario IV** I want to do some additional reporting against my SharePoint lists.

  It depends what you're trying to report against—actuals, forecast? You could potentially use the built-in KPIs. You could export lists (or import lists) to Access 2007 and use Access as the front-end reporting tool. If you're currently running SQL Server 2005 Reporting Services, then you could consider using a third-party tool such as Enesys.

- **Scenario V** I want to do some in-depth analysis based on my SQL Server 2005 Analysis Services and have the ability to expose that analysis within my SharePoint site.

  You could use Excel 2007 to create an Office Data Connection (ODC) to Analysis Services and then create PivotTables and PivotCharts directly using Excel. If you're running Excel Services, you could publish the workbook while maintaining an active link to Analysis Services, providing the ODC is added to the Trusted Data Connections library within Report Center.

- **Scenario VI** I want to create views of my database within my SharePoint site and also have the ability to search the imported data.

  In this scenario, the Business Data Catalog (BDC) would be an ideal solution. Data imported via the BDC can be integrated into SharePoint search, and document libraries using BDC data columns.

## Scorecards: Which Technology Works Best?

A few years ago, if you had asked developers at Microsoft how to build a scorecard, they may have shrugged. Then Microsoft released the Business Scorecard Accelerator, a free technology mainly designed to showcase SQL Server Analysis Services.

The Business Scorecard Accelerator was so popular that Microsoft made a product out of it—Business Scorecard Manager (BSM) 2005. While BSM could pull data from ODBC data sources, its best buddy was still Analysis Services. With the right cube, you could throw together a scorecard in under a day. Of course, BSM still had its quirks.

After Microsoft bought ProClarity in 2006, the BI vision coalesced. BSM v2, ProClarity, and Biz# (a multidimensional planning application) were unified into PerformancePoint. At the same time, SharePoint Server 2007 has "KPI lists"—a special type of document list that can display collections of KPIs. This can be distracting as a type of "scorecard." SharePoint also adds Excel Services, which can allow users to build scorecards in Excel and display them inside SharePoint.

## Inside Track **Scorecard Technologies Overview**

Here is a brief overview of scorecard technologies and the pros and cons of using each technology.

### SharePoint Server 2007 KPI Lists

Pros

- Easy to use
- Integrated with SharePoint Server 2007 (Web parts and lists)
- Can show multiple data sources
- Can show KPIs from SQL Server Analysis Services

Cons

- Does not scale across the organization
- Limited functionality

Basically, SharePoint Server 2007 KPI lists are a good way to pull KPI functionality on to a SharePoint page—surface some business intelligence on a portal page or shared site. They make a good companion to a BI effort, but this is not the way to start a BI or scorecard initiative. You will quickly be frustrated by some of the limited functionality (formatting, lack of drill down, and so on).

### Business Scorecard Manager (BSM) 2005

Pros

- Strategic
- Scalable
- Linked to analytic charts
- Annotations
- Alerts

Cons

- Requires SQL Server 2000 Notification Services for alerts
- Builder is quirky
- Working with ODBC data sources is labor intensive

The best thing about BSM is how easy it is to set up a manual scorecard and publish it in SharePoint. Once you learn your way around the Builder, you can create a manual scorecard in a few hours. This is powerful because, in a scorecard initiative, putting an ad hoc scorecard on the Web can wake up stakeholders and get their attention while you start wiring it to back-end sources.

Having said that, wiring BSM to those back-end sources can be labor intensive. Each current value, target, and trend has to be wired as an independent query. Again, using SQL Server Analysis Services can make this far easier because dimensions automatically display across the scorecard.

#### Excel Services Scorecard

Pros

- Easy to use
- Ad hoc

Cons

- No drill down
- May not scale
- No linked charts

Creating a scorecard in Excel and publishing it to Excel Services is a nice way to publish an ad hoc scorecard. However, it lacks the linked ad hoc charting and drill-down capabilities. It also may be difficult to maintain due to its nature as an Excel spreadsheet. (This is not meant as a limitation of Excel, but rather how Excel .xls files often invite sloppy processes.)

#### ProClarity Dashboard Server

ProClarity had a Dashboard Server Product, which is being discontinued.

#### PerformancePoint Monitoring

Pros

- Designed for the enterprise
- Annotations
- Linked analytic reports
- Drill down
- Dashboard builder
- Extensible

Cons

- A more expensive option
- No alerts

> Honestly, PerformancePoint Dashboard and Scorecard Builder is awesome. The designer is drag-and-drop, and it is intuitive. It still works best with multidimensional data, but it can also show data from other data sources, such as SharePoint lists, Excel spreadsheets, ODBC data sources, and so on. In addition, PerformancePoint includes powerful analytics from ProClarity and the new planning engine for what-if and forecast modeling.
>
> In conclusion, SharePoint KPI lists and Excel Services are good introductions to scorecards, but for real scorecard/dashboard/BI initiatives, PerformancePoint is the way to go.
>
> *Philo Janus, Senior Technology Specialist, Microsoft*

# Summary

In this chapter, we've discussed how to extend BI functionality through the introduction of Reporting Services integration and PerformancePoint Server 2007. We've outlined the core functionality within each product and discussed authentication and security considerations, as well as best practices for integrating both products as part of an overall BI solution.

In both this chapter and Chapter 18, we discussed authentication requirements for creating connections to SQL Server 2005, specifically, using Kerberos to impersonate the user and delegation between servers in a distributed server environment. If you are in the process of designing your SharePoint Server 2007 deployment or upgrading your existing deployment to include BI solutions, such as Excel Services or Reporting Services integration, then ensure that you configure Web applications to use Kerberos as opposed to NTLM. Why? Apart from the authentication considerations discussed in this chapter and in Chapter 18, it is our firm belief that future Microsoft applications, especially those applications leveraging SQL Server, will require Kerberos by default. Making the shift now will help avoid issues later. We've included a list of references on Kerberos configuration–including configuration for Active Directory, SQL Server, and SharePoint Server 2007–on this book's companion CD. See the document titled "BI References."

Second to authentication considerations, the other key consideration in planning and deploying BI solutions is the client-side dependencies, such as the PerformancePoint Excel add-in and Office 2003 or 2007. Why? Because you will need to consider (1) how you will roll out product-dependent add-ins to clients; (2) future product upgrades for both server and client-side; and (3) bandwidth and WAN for clients accessing back-end SQL data stores and client-side applications synchronizing data from a data store, such as the PerformancePoint Server 2007 Excel add-in.

Finally, we've suggested some possible scenarios from which you might choose to use one or more of the BI solutions and products discussed in both this chapter and in Chapter 18.

## Additional Resources

- On the CD: "SQL Server Reporting Services–Installation and Configuration Guide for SharePoint Integration Mode," blog entry by Raju Sakthivel. Also available at *http://blogs.msdn.com/sharepoint/archive/2007/08/02/microsoft-sql-server-reporting-services-installation-and-configuration-guide-for-sharepoint-integration-mode.aspx*
- Microsoft SQL Server 2005 Reporting Services Add-in for Microsoft SharePoint Technologies download: *http://www.microsoft.com/downloads/details.aspx?FamilyID=1E53F882-0C16-4847-B331-132274AE8C84&displaylang=en*
- *SQL Server 2005 Reporting Services in Action*. Bret Updegraff (Manning Publications Co., 2006): *http://www.manning.com/updegraff/*
- "Tutorial: Creating a Basic Report:" *http://msdn2.microsoft.com/en-us/library/ms167305.aspx*
- "How To: Schedule Report and Subscription Processing (SharePoint Integrated Mode)" covers a SharePoint-specific configuration that enables the user to access report versioning and scheduling. Important: Faulty configuration will result in errors, including report-specific parameter errors: *http://msdn2.microsoft.com/en-us/library/bb283320.aspx*
- "Configuring an Account for Unattended Report Processing," covers using the Reporting Services Configuration tool and adding an account to the Execution Account page. It allows the report server to perform unattended operations at a very low security level; some functionality is disabled if an account if not specified: *http://msdn2.microsoft.com/en-us/library/ms156302.aspx*
- List of best practices for Reporting Services authoring/reports: *http://www.ssw.com.au/ssw/Standards/Rules/RulesToBetterSQLReportingServices.aspx*
- Microsoft Knowledge Base article "FIX: You receive an error message when you try to access a report after you configure SQL Server 2005 Reporting Services to run under the SharePoint Integrated mode:" *http://support.microsoft.com/kb/939942/*
- Office PerformancePoint Server technical library: *http://technet.microsoft.com/en-au/library/bb794633.aspx*. (Note that SP2 is required for Excel 2003 for .net support and ASP.NET 2.0 AJAX Extensions 1.0 is required for Monitoring Server installation. Also, cumulative update 3 is required for SQL Server 2005 SP2 as of December 2007.)
- On the CD: PerformancePoint_Monitoring_Samples.doc, a PerformancePoint monitoring sample guide that includes details on configuring sample .bswx workspaces. Also available at *http://office.microsoft.com/download/afile.aspx?AssetID=AM102421831033*
- "Project REAL–Business Intelligence in Practice," an overview of Project REAL: *http://www.microsoft.com/sql/solutions/bi/projectreal.mspx*

- Project REAL Reference Implementation download: *http://www.microsoft.com/downloads/details.aspx?FamilyID=b61a37b6-5852-4018-bba9-795a34123ed0&displaylang=en*
- PerformancePoint Team MSDN blog: *http://blogs.msdn.com/performancepoint/default.aspx*
- PerformancePoint 2007 Alpine Ski House Sample: *http://office.microsoft.com/download/afile.aspx?AssetID=AM102421841033*

Chapter 20

# Intranet, Extranet, and Internet Scenarios

**In this chapter:**



Microsoft Office SharePoint Server 2007 has blurred the lines between legacy file sharing and Web sites. No longer must content exist in one or the other. In fact, we believe this is a natural progression of Web technologies. Web technologies started out as simple content that was published in static .html pages. Likewise, file shares were simple file storage. Office SharePoint Server 2007 brings us the ability to store all of this in one place and aggregate via search that which is not stored in SharePoint Products and Technologies. SharePoint Server 2007 provides these capabilities through Web applications, and therefore Web applications are foundational to the design of any intranet, extranet, or Internet Web site. We divide and define three types of SharePoint Server 2007 Web application solutions as follows:

- **Internet** In 1985, Merriam-Webster Dictionary defined the Internet as "an electronic communications network that connects computer networks and organizational computer facilities around the world." Wow. We can see how far technology has come since 1985! Originally, the Internet was consumed only by government agencies, universities, and large businesses. It has matured to the point that it now connects almost any device imaginable, from your refrigerator to the largest business servers in the world. In fact, many multibillion-dollar companies exist solely because of the Internet. When information technology security professionals hear the word *Internet*, however, fear and panic often consume them. Seriously, we all know how dangerous the Internet can be; our financial data can be lost, our personal data can be stolen, and our children can be exposed to unsavory content. But the Internet also allows us to easily transmit data to cell phones and coffee shop Wi-Fi networks, enabling employees to work more and more efficiently. Lastly, we assume Internet users are an unknown identity.
- **Intranet** An intranet is essentially the Internet behind closed doors that provides services to known entities. The same protocols and basic technologies are leveraged, but the content is available only behind the corporate firewall. This allows companies to more stringently control the access to content that could be damaging if compromised. Until

recently, the intranet was thought of as only a Web technology. However, advances in technology have allowed intranets to store almost any type of content and effectively give users a one-stop shop for information. Many companies refer to their intranet Web sites as *portals* because that's what they are—a gateway to find anything in a company. Others view intranets as the entire corporate network behind the firewall. However, we do not refer to an intranet as such in this chapter. An intranet is one or more Web applications used to aggregate, organize, present, and collaborate within an organization's internal network.

- **Extranet** A network that lives in a company's perimeter network, also called a screened subnet, is usually referred to as an *extranet*. What generally differentiates an extranet from an intranet is access from third parties, such as partners and vendors. The two differentiating characteristics of an extranet over the Internet are (1) the extranet user is a known identity and (2) there are usually better security controls in place. Otherwise, extranets and the Internet are much alike. Be aware that when sharing your intranet with external partners, you should probably treat it as an extranet because your data security risk will increase.

We realize you may define these differently, and that's okay. We just need to define them here as a reference for conceptual designs. You may call these Web applications something different in your organization, but the best practices in this chapter will easily map to whatever naming convention you choose. Be aware that the following assumption was made throughout this chapter: Intranet users are trusted users only, extranets include trusted users and semi-trusted users (dedicated/unique authentication source for semi-trusted users), and Internet consumers are primarily untrusted (anonymous) users.

### Notes from the Field **Trusted versus Semi-trusted Users**

Once a user is given an account and logs in, there is little pragmatic difference between employees and non-employees or trusted and semi-trusted users. While many systems have technical controls that govern these types of users, SharePoint Server 2007 does not. Users are granted access to site collections, and SharePoint Server 2007 doesn't differentiate between them at the site level. The only place we can restrict access, and thus differentiate between trusted and semi-trusted users, is at the Web application level. We can apply Web application policies to users and groups, with those users and groups authenticated against different authentication sources. While extremely powerful, leveraging zones in this manner can create a complex security posture that is difficult to maintain.

*Bill English, Microsoft MVP, Mindsharp*

# Web Applications: The Foundation

Because Web applications are foundational to any SharePoint Server 2007 implementation, this chapter begins the best practices for implementing Web applications and then continues into possible scenarios for your intranet, extranet, or Internet solutions.

A SharePoint Server 2007 Web application is an Internet Information Services (IIS) Web site associated with at least one content database to store information for that site. We say *SharePoint Web application* because other Web applications may not require a database for content storage. Classically, Web applications were fairly simple servers where files on the hard drive of the physical server were consumed by clients via the HTTP protocol. SharePoint Server 2007 stores only the minimum set of files necessary to participate in a SharePoint Server 2007 server farm and render content to users from databases, hence the name *content database*. These Web applications are addressed by a URL, such as *http://portal.contoso.msft* or *http://www.contoso.msft*. Figure 20-1 shows the anatomy of a SharePoint Web application.

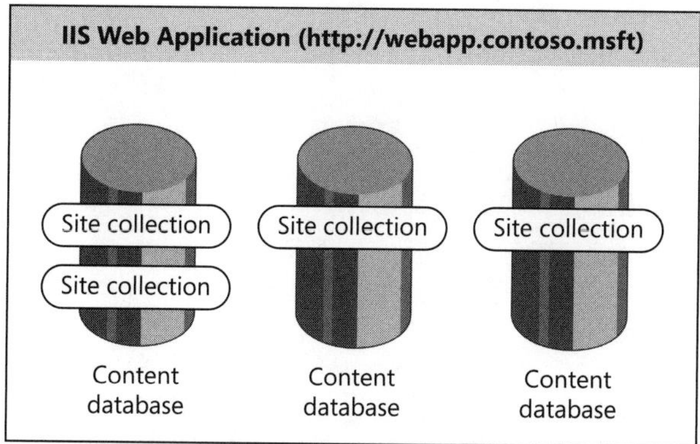


**Figure 20-1** Anatomy of a SharePoint Web application

So why store content in a database? First, it allows you to scale farms to multiple servers without the need to replicate content on the back-end. Multiple Web front-end (WFE) servers can connect to a single content database and serve content from within the database. Second, it allows for real-time collaboration via lists, libraries, workflows, and policies, and it provides robust backup, restore, and database mirroring and log shipping capabilities.

A Web application by itself is essentially useless, however. If you built a SharePoint Server 2007 Web application and stopped there, you would receive a *404 page not found* error message because a Web application is essentially an empty shell with an associated URL. Think about this URL as an entry point to the database content. You must create site collections in the Web application before it becomes functional. A site collection is just that—a collection of sites. But the sites are not randomly organized; a site collection is a group of *structured* sites with a top-level site (TLS) and a hierarchal subsite structure underneath. When you design and implement SharePoint Products and Technologies, a best practice is to use either the terms *site collections* and *subsites* or *top-level sites* and *subsites*. Note that developers often refer to these as the *root* web and *subwebs*. Avoiding the generic term *site* reduces the amount of confusion within your organization about what type of site is being referenced. Figure 20-2 is an overview of a site collection.

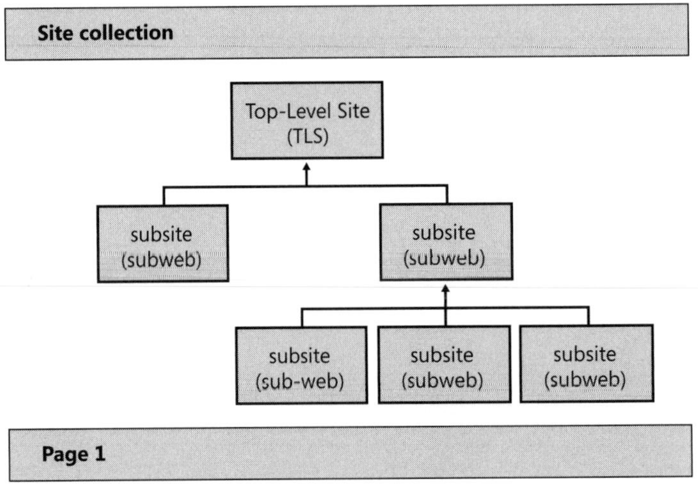


**Figure 20-2** The anatomy of a site collection

Site collections aren't randomly created in a Web application; they must be created in a managed path. There are two types of managed paths: explicit and wildcard. What's the difference between an explicit managed path and a wildcard managed path? By default, the root '/' managed path is explicit, meaning only one site collection can be in it and the site collection assumes the identity of the managed path. That's how you browse to *http://portal.contoso.msft* and get a Web page. A Web application without a site collection in the root managed path will return a 404 error when a user browses to the root. Therefore, a SharePoint Server 2007 best practice is to *always* create a site collection in the root managed path, even if it is a simple information or redirect page. You could always create another explicit managed path for multiple portal support in a Web application, such as *http://portal.contoso.msft/HR*. HR is a peer to '/'. But when doing so, you can no longer have an HR subsite in the root site collection. You will get a security validation error because the URL space is already taken by the explicit managed path *HR*.

> **More Info** Managed paths are also discussed in Chapter 15, "Implementing an Optimal Search and Findability Topology."

A wildcard managed path is basically 180 degrees in the opposite direction. A wildcard managed path can support hundreds or thousands of site collections, but the site collections are appended to the managed path, as in *http://portal.contoso.msft/sites/team*, with *sites* being the wildcard managed path. This path will always return a 404 error when a user browses directly to a wildcard managed path. Figure 20-3 shows an example of an explicit managed path during site collection creation, and Figure 20-4 shows an example of a wildcard managed path during site collection creation.

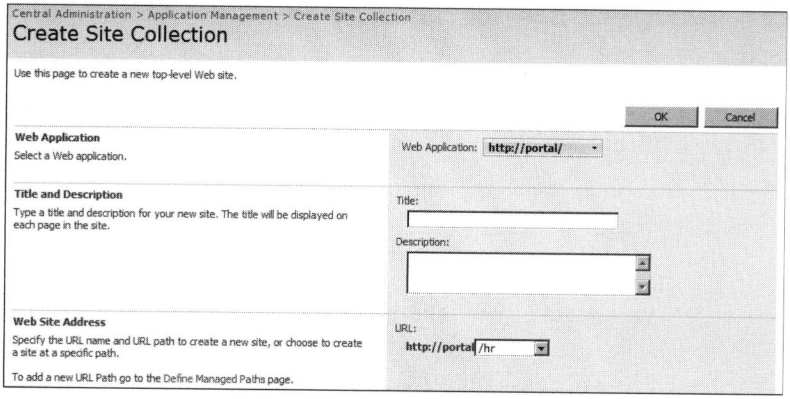

**Figure 20-3** You cannot define the URL of an explicit managed path site collection.

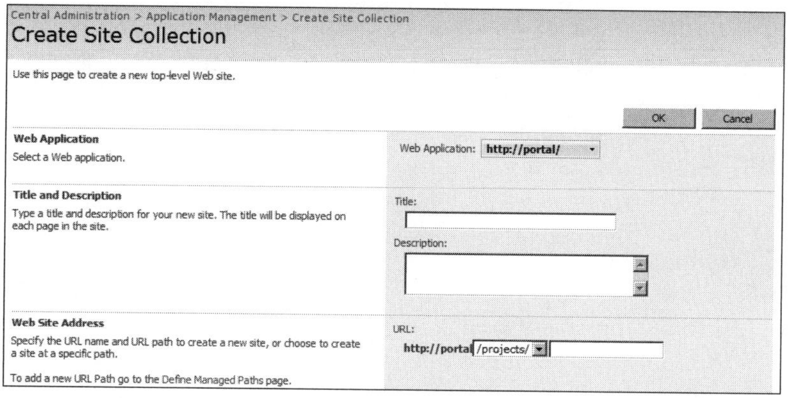

**Figure 20-4** You must define the URL of a wildcard managed path site collection.

You can create many wildcard managed paths, such as *teams* or *projects,* as shown in Figure 20-4. Wildcard managed paths are like a categorizing mechanism for site collections. It is a best practice to *not* get fancy and change the browsability of wildcard managed paths. Many have tried manipulating the native behavior via the file system or by writing ISAPI filters. It is best to use the product as designed and keep it simple.

When to use a particular type of managed path depends mainly on your information architecture decisions. As a general rule, team sites and project sites are created in wildcard managed paths. In fact, self-service site management exclusively uses wildcard managed paths and cannot leverage explicit managed paths. Organization-wide processes, such as information technology and human resources, are often created as explicit managed paths in the root of a portal. Explicit managed paths can also allow you to create multiple site collections in your WWW Web application without the need for a wildcard managed path, such as *sites*.

## Application Pool Best Practices

Web applications require dedicated memory space on the WFE servers to function. These memory spaces are called *application pools* in IIS and are simply dedicated memory for one or more Web applications. Application pools also require a username and password as an identity because there is no unauthenticated access in IIS. This application pool username is how Web applications authenticate and connect to the associated content databases. While it is possible through a great deal of effort to change an application pool identity after installation, it is not advisable to do so. In fact, it is a best practice to decide on the username for a given Web application and never change it.

How many application pools do you need? This question could be argued amongst SharePoint Server 2007 professionals, but here are what we think are the best practices. If you are running 32-bit hardware, the answer is fairly simple. Because a 32-bit SharePoint Server 2007 system is essentially limited to 1024 MB of usable memory for .NET, you should use as few application pools as possible. Why? A 32-bit system cannot directly address more than 4 GB of memory, and 2 GB is reserved for the system. A common workaround once was to use the /3GB switch to enable 3 GB for applications, leaving 1 GB for the operating system. However, the /3GB switch is not supported in Microsoft Windows SharePoint Services 3.0 or SharePoint Server 2007. Therefore, only 2 GB is available to applications, and the .NET CLR reserves at least 50 percent of that memory for other services. With a 64-bit system, you have much greater flexibility in that up to 500 GB are available for .NET applications. Whether you are using a 32-bit or 64-bit system, you will need at least three application pools:

1. **Central Administration** This application pool provides the memory space for the Central Administration Web application and root site collection. Because it has full control access in the configuration database, you should never share this application pool with another Web application. Additionally, you should never use the application pool identity for Central Administration for another application pool identity. The Central Administration Web application pool identity is the "farm account" and effectively has full control in the entire SharePoint farm.
2. **Shared Services** Your Shared Services Provider (SSP) Web application should have a dedicated application pool. A dedicated application pool assists with security and manageability of Shared Services. It also serves as isolation from other Web applications should a corrupt piece of code crash the application pool.
3. **Community** You should have at least one application pool to be used by collaborative Web applications. If security and process isolation aren't paramount in your organization, you can probably design with a single application pool.

The driving factor for creating a fourth application pool is process isolation. This isolation can be used for reliability or security. First, let's look at an example in which two Web applications share the Community application pool. Let's use *http://portal.contoso.msft* and *http://intranetapp.contoso.msft* for this scenario. An error in *http://intranetapp.contoso.msft* would also crash *http://portal.contoso.msft*. Creating a single application pool for each Web application would most likely prevent the demise of the other should one fail. The second reason for another application pool is security. We believe that using multiple application pools for security generally creates a false sense of security. It does provide some isolation from the average user in gaining access to another Web application, but a talented hacker can easily gain access to an entire server farm once a single Web application in the farm is compromised.

## Content Database Best Practices

We previously learned that the size of your content database is mostly limited to your ability to restore in a reasonable time frame, which solely depends on your SQL server implementation and backup/restore capabilities. What we present here are the best practices for creating and managing content databases.

> **Note** While we generally design databases based on availability and recovery, there are software limitations, such as five million items in a site collection, which could be a limiting factor. Browse to *http://technet.microsoft.com/en-us/library/cc262787.aspx* for more information on SharePoint Server 2007 software boundaries.

First, you should always use database names that correlate to the Web application and function of the database. If the database will be simply one of many in a round-robin style of site collection creation, then using 1, 2, 3, and so on makes perfect sense. But if the database will host a specific site collection, then name it accordingly. Some organizations will create a one-to-one site collection to content database association for critical sites. Be aware that doing so will not scale well and is not supported on a large-scale basis. Reserve dedicated content databases for very important site collections. Table 20-1 shows a naming example for a Web application named *http://portal.contoso.msft*.

**Table 20-1 Example Database Naming Convention**

| Site collection URL | Purpose | Database name | # of site collections |
|---|---|---|---|
| http://portal/ | Root site collection, hosting the primary Web application portal | WSS_Portal_Root | 1 |
| http://portal/sites/team1 | General team sites database | WSS_Portal_1 | Many |
| http://portal/sites/team2 | General team sites | WSS_Portal_2 | Many |
| http://portal/sites/CEO | Dedicated to critical site collection | WSS_Portal_CEO | 1 |

The naming convention needs to be easily identifiable within Microsoft SQL Server Management Studio as to its purpose.

Another best practice is to create multiple content databases to support multiple site collections. A very common mistake we see is when customers create all site collections in a single content database. This usually results from a lack of understanding about how the product should be architected and partially from the process of rapid deployments. All is not lost, however, if you have implemented in this way. Before we present the methodologies to fix this erroneous database design, we need to explain an almost-always misunderstood Central Administration interface. Figure 20-5 shows a screen in Central Administration, Application Management, Content Databases to take a database *offline*. Figure 20-6 shows the status of the database as stopped after it has been taken offline.

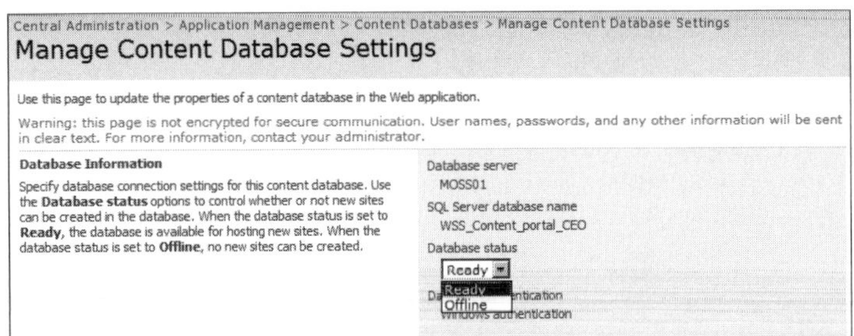


**Figure 20-5** Taking a database offline

Central Administration > Application Management > Content Databases

Manage Content Databases

Use this page to manage content databases for this web application. Click a content database name to change its properties.

Add a content database    Web Application: http://portal/

| Database Name | Database Status | Current Number of Sites | Site Level Warning | Maximum Number of Sites |
|---|---|---|---|---|
| wss_content_portal_01 | Started | 2 | 10 | 12 |
| WSS_Content_portal_CEO | Stopped | 0 | 1 | 2 |

**Figure 20-6** After taking a database offline, the status shows Stopped.

Figures 20-5 and 20-6 do not mean what they appear to mean. Taking a database offline merely blocks any new site collections from being created in it. It does not take the database offline as one might think. Users can still upload and download content, view Web pages, and process workflows. The content database status will also show as stopped. Once again, this means only that new site collections cannot be created in this database. If you want a one-to-one site collection to content database association, taking the hosting database offline is the best method to accomplish this end.

> **Note** If multiple content databases for a given Web application are online, new site collections will be created in the database with the greatest remaining capacity, not the fewest current number of sites. If the capacity is the same, it will "round-robin" the creation of site collections among the content databases.

### Notes from the Field **Script Site Collection Creation in a Dedicated Content Database**

You can use stsadm.exe to create a new site collection in its own database. Stsadm.exe –o createsiteinnewdb –url <site collection URL> -owneremail <e-mail address> -ownerlogin <SC admin> -databasename <DB Name> allows you to create a site collection in a dedicated content database. Don't forget to take the database offline after creation, or future sites could be created in the new database. The following additional parameters can also be specified:

- -secondaryemail <someone@example.com>
- -secondarylogin <DOMAIN\name>
- -secondaryname <display name>
- -lcid <language>
- -sitetemplate <site template>
- -title <site title>
- -description <site description>
- -quota <quota template>
- -databaseuser <database username>
- -databasepassword <database password>
- -databaseserver <database server name>
- -databasename <database name>

*Ben Curry, Microsoft MVP, Mindsharp*

Now that you understand what *offline* and *stopped* really mean, it is fairly easy to move site collections between content databases. There are basically two ways to do this:

1. Back up the site collection using <stsadm.exe –o backup –url>, delete the site collection, create a new content database, take all online databases offline except the target database, and restore the site collection. It *must* go into the only online database.
2. Use the *mergecontentdbs* stsadm.exe operation to move site collections between content databases.

## Moving Site Collections

> **Note** This section written by Todd Klindt, Microsoft MVP, Solanite Consulting.

Rrequently it is necessary to move a site collection from one content database to another. In the past, this process was very painful and very manual. Why would you need to move a site collection to a different content database? This comes up for a variety of reasons. For instance, because of restore times, you should keep databases under a certain size. While you try to work with site collection owners to plan accordingly, sometimes the content databases grow larger than you had imagined. When this happens, you need to shuffle site collections around to keep databases in harmony. There are other times when you would shuffle site collections if it were more convenient. For example, if site collections are not growing as expected, you might want to consolidate several into smaller databases. You might also want to move less active site collections to databases on slower discs or move site collections to databases that reflect geographic regions. Whatever the reason, in the past, you had to go through the following time-consuming steps to move a site collection.

1. Lock the site collection.
2. Back up the site collection.
3. Delete the site collection.
4. Set all the content databases' maximum allowed sites to the number of current sites.
5. Set the content database you want the site collection to go into to allow one more site collection.
6. Restore the site collection.
7. Unlock the site collection.
8. Adjust the content database maximums to allow new sites to be created.

Today, however, all of these steps can be done with stsadm.exe, so you can build scripts and move through the process quickly. In one of the security updates (KB934525) for Windows SharePoint Services 3.0 and SharePoint Server 2007, Microsoft slipped in a new stsadm.exe operation, *mergecontentdbs*. We assume this operation was added with the intention of merging content databases, but it can also be used to split them. This section will walk you through both uses. Let's start with the following configuration:

```
<Sites Count="3">
  <Site Url=http://portal Owner="BARCELONA\administrator"
ContentDatabase="WSS_Content" StorageUserMB="2.1" StoreWarningMB="0"
StorageMaxMB="0" />
  <Site Url=http://portal/MySite Owner="NT AUTHORITY\network service"
 SecondaryOwner=""BARCELONA\administrator"  ContentDatabase="WSS_Content2"
 StorageUserMB="0.2" StoreWarningMB="0" StorageMaxMB="0" />
  <Site Url=http://portal/sites/stsadm Owner="BARCELONA\administrator"
 ContentDatabase="WSS_Content" StorageUserMB="0.8" StoreWarningMB="0"
 StorageMaxMB="0" />
</Sites>
```

You can see that we have three site collections in two content databases: WSSContent and WSSContent2. We want to move *http://portal/sites/stsadm* from WSS_Content to WSS_Content2. You can prefix *–h* for any stsadm.exe and get help, as shown below:

```
C:\>stsadm -help mergecontentdbs

stsadm.exe -o mergecontentdbs
           -url <url>
           -sourcedatabasename <source database name>
           -destinationdatabasename <destination database name>
           [-operation <1-3>
                1 - Analyze (default)
                2 - Full Database Merge
                3 - Read from file]
           [-filename <file generated from stsadm -o enumsites>]
See also:
     stsadm -o enumcontentdbs -url <url>
     stsadm -o enumsites -url <url> -databasename <database>
```

For this example, we use operation 3, *Read from file*. stsadm.exe provides a clue about the file needed; it is generated from stsadm –o enumsites. Let's run that and pipe it to a file as follows:

```
stsadm -o enumsites -url http://portal > mysites.xml
```

This operation will produce a file, *mysites.xml,* which contains my site collections. To move *http://portal/sites/stsadm,* We will remove all of the other site collections except for that one from *mysites.xml* and save it. There is no need to worry about changing the site count at the top or any of the other site collection information in the file. stsadm.exe retrieves only the URLs. WE have only two content databases, so determining the target database for the site collection is easy. But what if we had many content databases? In that case, we could use the first operation, *Analyze*, to get an idea of how the content databases are laid out. Let's see how that looks:

```
Stsadm -o mergecontentdbs -url http://portal -sourcedatabasename
 WSS_Content -destinationdatabasename WSS_Content2 -operation 1
WSS_Content:
  Disk Size: 43 MB.
  Sites: 2.
  Maximum sites: 15000.
  Maximum number of sites that can be added : 14998.
WSS_Content2:
  Disk Size: 20 MB.
  Sites: 1.
  Maximum sites: 15000.
  Maximum number of sites that can be added : 14999.
```

The source database WSS_Content is larger than then the destination database WSS_Content2. It may be more performant to move from WSS_Content2 to WSS_Content. Here are the steps:

1. Retrieve all the site collections from the source.

```
Stsadm -o enumsites -url http://portal/ -databasename
WSS_Content > mysites.xml
```

2. Remove unneeded site collections by editing *mysites.xml* in notepad.exe.
3. Merge the databases:

```
Stsadm -o mergecontentdbs -url http://portal/ -sourcedatabasename
WSS_Content -destinationdatabasename WSS_Content2 -operation 3 -filename mysites.xml
```

You can see here where we got the idea to use the filename *mysites.xml*. The great thing about this screen is that you can just cut and paste the final command into the command prompt. Microsoft did a great job with the usage on this command, other than a couple of typos. One thing to note is that the –url parameter is *not* the URL of the site collection you want to move—it's the URL of the Web application that the site collection is in. Since we've already created the file and edited it, we now can run the command:

```
Stsadm -o mergecontentdbs -url http://portal/ -sourcedatabasename
 WSS_Content -destinatindatabasename WSS_Content2 -operation 3
 -filename mysites.xml
http://portal/sites/stsadm
```

**Note** IIS must be restarted before this change will take effect.

That's all there is to it. After an iisreset, the site collection *http://portal/sites/stsadm* appears in WSS_Content2. You can confirm a database move by looking in Central Administration, Applications, Content Databases before and after you run the command or by using *stsadm.exe –o enumsites.*

We also want to show you the intended usage of *mergecontentdbs*, which merges two content databases. When you use the second operation, stsadm.exe will simply move all the site collections from the source database to the destination database. To move all of the sites in WSS_Content2 back into WSS_Content use this command:

```
Stsadm -o mergecontentdbs -url http://portal/ -sourcedatabasename
 WSS_Content -destinatindatabasename WSS_Content2 -operation 2
```

Again, you can confirm the move by looking in Central Administration > Applications > Content Databases before and after you run the command, or by using *stsadm.exe–o enumsites*:

```
<Sites Count="3">
  <Site Url=http://portal Owner="BARCELONA\administrator"
 ContentDatabase="WSS_Content" StorageUserMB="2.1" StoreWarningMB="0"
 StorageMaxMB="0" />
  <Site Url=http://portal/MySite Owner="NT AUTHORITY\network service"
 SecondaryOwner="BARCELONA\administrator"  ContentDatabase="WSS_Content"
 StorageUserMB="0.2" StoreWarningMB="0" StorageMaxMB="0" />
  <Site Url=http://portal/sites/stsadm Owner="BARCELONA\administrator"
 ContentDatabase="WSS_Content" StorageUserMB="0.8" StoreWarningMB="0" StorageMaxMB="0" />
</Sites>
```

At this point, all of the site collections in the *http://portal* Web application are in the WSS_Content database, right where we want them. We think you'll enjoy this addition to stsadm.exe.

Use common sense when creating and managing content databases. SharePoint Server 2007 is very flexible and will allow more functionality than you probably need. A good example is hosting content databases on multiple SQL server instances. While this is most certainly supported, it is rarely needed. You could host a very large and very busy site collection in its own content database and associated SQL server instance to reduce the impact to other site collections in the farm. Generally, you will need only a single SQL server instance to host all farm databases.

> **Note** Site collections cannot span content databases. A site collection can exist only in a single content database, but a content database can host many site collections. For critical site collections, a best practice is to create a single site collection in an associated content database for the purposes of speedy content recovery. Be sure to take this advice with caution—creating a content database for every site collection simply will not scale. Use this architecture sparingly, and reserve its use for those site collections that require extra care.

## What's in a Zone?

Before we move into applying the technology to real-world scenarios, let's discuss the best practices for SharePoint Server 2007 zones. A *zone* is simply a policy-naming convention for SharePoint Server 2007 IIS Web sites. A zone does not infer a Web application. While a new Web application is always defined as the default zone, an extended zone of the default Web application is *not* another Web application. Think of them this way: SharePoint Server 2007 wants to associate any incoming traffic on a URL with a known farm Web application. Extending and mapping a Web application to another zone does not create another Web application. Instead, it creates another entry point for an existing Web application. This correlation is important to understand or zones become confusing. For example, if you extended *http://portal* to *https://portal-ext* for external access using Secured Sockets Layer (SSL), you still have one Web application, http://portal. The URL *https://portal-ext* is an extended zone, but it is associated with http://portal's content database. Remember that a Web application, by definition, must have its own content database. A zone does not have its own content database.

There are several things you must know about zones to adhere to best practices. First, SharePoint Server 2007 zones have nothing to do with the zones defined in the client's Internet Explorer. While they have the same basic naming convention, they are not the same thing. The five zones included with SharePoint Server 2007 are Default, Intranet, Internet, Custom, and Extranet. While you can associate any URL in your farm with any zone name, the best practice is to align zones with their desired usage. For example, if your intranet portal is *http://portal.contoso.msft* and you want to extend its usage to Internet users via another URL (*https://extranet.contoso.msft*, for example), you would put it on the extranet zone. Defining it as another zone type would just be confusing. Second, you cannot create your own zone names; you must use one of the five included with SharePoint Server 2007. Third, you should always document the URL for every zone because you are not often given the full URL when policies are applied. An example of this can be seen in Figure 20-7, which shows the Zones options. The Web application URL is visible, but the actual URL of 'Extranet' is *http://extranet*, and is not shown in the interface. If you need to find the URL to Zone association, these are viewable in Central Administration, Operations, Alternate Access Mappings.

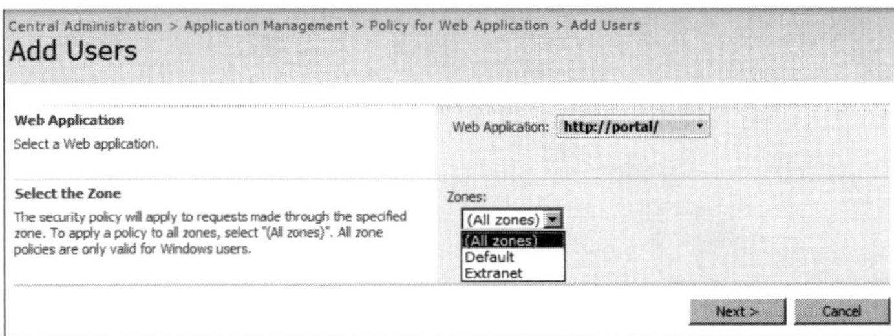


**Figure 20-7** The URL for a particular zone is not shown during policy application.

Fourth, zones are the hosting mechanism for applying security policies to a group of users using the Policy For Web Applications feature in Central Administration. When correctly configured, you can tightly define which group of users can enjoy which list, site, and personal permissions. In addition, you can give Site collection owners explicit full control in their site collections and give site collection auditors full read access without having to manually grant them access to each site within the collection individually.

Because these policies allow for explicit grant and deny permission levels, you can effectively control the exact permissions that each user or group has to the same content and ensure that different groups are either explicitly granted or denied certain permissions.

A common example of how to use this feature is when you're allowing contractors to work in your production environment. Let's assume your design is such that all non-employees must connect to SharePoint Server using SSL and must use a unique URL for which you have created an Alternate Access Mapping (AAM) in Central Administration. In addition, you place those contractors in a separate Active Directory directory service Global Group (GG) and then assign a unique permissions policy to that group in Central Administration.

That unique permission policy may grant users all kinds of collaborative permissions but deny them the ability to create subsites or personal sites. You might also want to ensure that they cannot delete information, so you deny that permission level too. Finally, to ensure that contractors always use the URL, zone, and permission levels you've assigned to them, you deny all permissions to the contractors group for the default zone for that Web application, thereby ensuring that all contractors must come through the URL you've specified in order to access content within that Web application.

Several best practices immediately present themselves as part of this discussion. First, to create highly secure and controlled extranet access to your content, use the combination of the AAMs, extending Web applications, zones, policy for Web applications, and authentication providers. These five features, when combined properly, will enable you to highly secure and control extranet access to your content.

Second, it is a best practice to use the explicit Deny feature in the Policy for Web Applications configuration if you're under compliance laws and regulations that require you to explicitly deny permissions to certain groups of users in certain conditions.

> **More Info** AAMs are discussed more fully in Chapter 15, "Implementing an Optimal Search and Findability Solution."

Last, notifications from workflows and site confirmation and deletion are always sent with the default zone URL in e-mails. Carefully think this last point through before creating the first Web application in your server farm. If you created *http://portal.contoso.msft* on the default zone and then extended it to *https://portal.constoso.msft* on the extranet zone, workflows and site confirmation and deletion notifications would be sent with the *http:// scheme*. If your firewall is denying HTTP requests, your users would not be able to browse to alerts embedded in e-mails externally. Therefore, the best practice is to always have the most secure zone as the default. In this example, *https://portal.contoso.msft* would be the default zone, and *http://portal.contoso.msft* could be on the intranet zone.

> **Note** With the release of the Microsoft SharePoint Administration Toolkit, you can change the URL used for alerts. Because it was in Beta at the time of this writing, we cannot provide a download URL. Instead, browse to *http://technet.microsoft.com/sharepointserver* and search for the toolkit by name.

# Scenarios

Building farm topologies really isn't an exact science, whether they are intranet solutions, extranet solutions, Internet solutions, or some combination thereof. It greatly depends on the infrastructure you already have in place. It depends on your firewalls, routers, switches, Active Directory, SQL Server, and—to be honest—the technical ability of the staff that manages each of those. It also depends on your organization's culture and politics, as well as governmental regulations such as the National Institute of Standards and Technology (NIST), Sarbanes-Oxley (SOX), and Health Insurance Portability and Accountability Act (HIPAA).

The following section will present to you seven possible scenarios for SharePoint Server 2007 farm configurations:

- Intranet in the private network

- Intranet in a split-farm topology
- Intranet in the screened subnet
- Extranet secured by zones
- Extranet secured by physical network
- Internet in the intranet server farm
- Internet in a dedicated server farm

These scenarios do not represent all possible variations, the inclusion of which would be lengthy and dilute the information specific to SharePoint Server 2007. As you read through the scenarios, you will quickly notice the driving factor behind most designs is securing the content. But what is insecure for one organization might prohibit another from staying in business. In our opinion, a security policy that puts your company out of business is a bad policy. You have to account for all of your implementation-specific requirements and balance the security of your farm. Keep in mind that security and usability are inversely proportional. We have never seen a secured—and we mean truly secured—environment that was very user friendly. What you can expect to find in the following sections are the most common successful scenarios and a few questionable scenarios.

## Intranet Scenarios

This is arguably the simplest farm topology to install. Installing an intranet farm is essentially like installing a file server into your network. We believe an intranet SharePoint Server 2007 installation is a good place to begin. Building a SharePoint Server 2007 server farm that is available only to the internal, private network allows you to focus on the core of the technology rather than securing it from the outside world. But be forewarned: If you need to expose and share this installation later, you will most likely be moving some, if not all, of the farm into another subnet for security. The following scenarios are possible ways you can provide this functionality, each having its own advantages and tradeoffs.

### Private Network

If you were to build a SharePoint Server 2007 server farm that in no way was connected to the Internet, it would be very secure. Sure, there could be compromises by people who have physical access or access via modems, but that wouldn't be an issue fixed by a specific farm topology. What if you build a farm that is accessible only on your private, internal network protected by a firewall? Isn't that the same? Don't get a false sense of security because you have a firewall. A private network is only as secure as its weakest link. If you had another service on this private network that was compromised, your SharePoint Server 2007 installation would be at risk. Therefore, we are assuming that you have adequately secured your private network and did not create firewall rules to the Internet for SharePoint Server 2007. It should be reasonably secured.

The first step in allowing remote access to SharePoint Server 2007 would be to set up a VPN client. Because the only remote access to the servers would be via corporate VPN, this is considered a secure solution by even the most skeptical information technology security professionals. Figure 20-8 shows a private server farm and three ways of securely accessing the content therein.

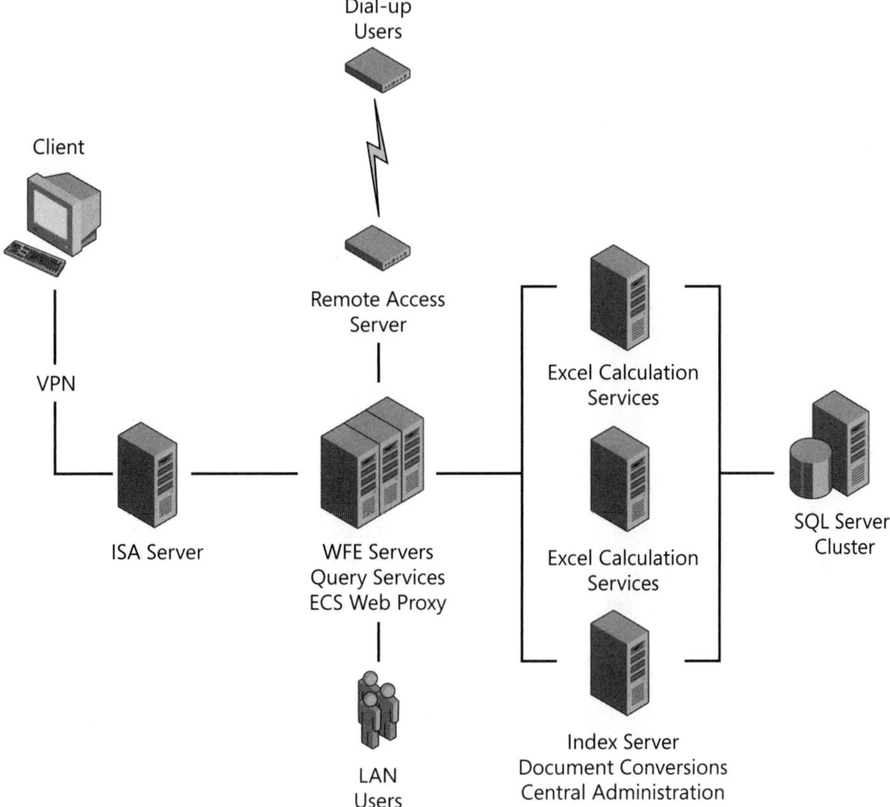


**Figure 20-8** A secure server farm would allow only local, VPN, or dial-up access.

Figure 20-8 also shows the example of using dial-up connections for secure access. This is quickly being replaced with VPN technology but is still a viable remote solution when security is paramount.

> **Note** VPNs have matured and can now be leveraged without thick clients, but that discussion is beyond the scope of this book. You should include your information technology security team in the entire farm design, but especially when determining remote access.

The upside to a private network implementation is that you can rest assured that your valuable content is safe. The tradeoff is loss of functionality. Because SharePoint Server 2007 is often an organization's core for collaboration, a private network limits the accessibility of collaborative information. If you need a more robust intranet sharing topology, you should consider allowing external access over SSL.

> **Important** It is generally considered bad practice to allow direct access to an internal application from the Internet. A compromise of such a system could result in a compromise of all privately stored content on your private network.

## Split Farm

A split-farm topology places a firewall between members of the farm to include the SQL server. This gets into an advanced implementation because a number of factors affect the functionality of the farm. The primary reason for splitting the farm into different subnets is to secure the SQL server. Figure 20-9 is a logical representation of a common farm topology when splitting subnets.

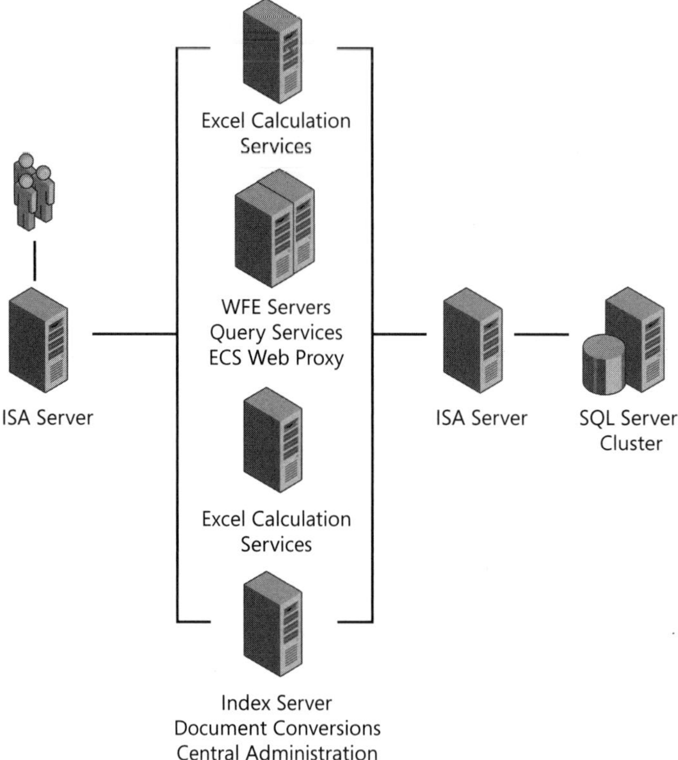


**Figure 20-9** The SQL server is commonly behind the primary firewall.

The practice of placing the SQL server behind the primary firewall is to protect it from threats, such as the Slammer Worm. In reality, we often see it placed behind the primary firewall because less attention is spent securing the perimeter firewall than the internal firewall. Yes, both firewalls *should* be secured to the same level, but the real-world fact is that they are not. Placing the SQL server in a more secure subnet isn't a perfect solution, however. If a hacker were to obtain access to your SharePoint Server 2007 farm from the Internet, he is now a short hop away from gaining access to your entire private network. We believe the best practice is to place the entire farm in the screened subnet.

Another common approach is to place an application server behind the primary firewall, thus securing your indexing functions and, more importantly, Central Administration. This does provide benefits, such as securing Web applications (e.g., the Records Center and Central Administration) and negating the need for indexing firewall rules (don't forget, the indexer still needs to be able to connect to content sources!). But you may actually be opening up more vulnerability to your network than if you left the application server in the screened subnet. The risk may not be worth the extra security provided because NetBIOS traffic, or possibly server message block (SMB), still exists in most farm topologies. A prime example of this is query propagation. As can be seen in Figure 20-9, the WFE servers are also hosting the query role. Indexes are propagated continuously via file shares on the WFE servers. So, if you put the application server (hosting the index role) behind the primary firewall, you must now open firewall ports to allow file share access. This is generally bad practice, and most security professionals would advise strongly against it. For this reason, we think only the SQL server should be split from the farm if needed; in most cases, all members of the farm should be in the same subnet.

If you have a technically talented security team and you thoroughly understand firewall rules, auditing, and SharePoint Server 2007, you could most certainly implement your farm in a more advanced topology. Just remember to keep your installation as simple as possible while still meeting your technical requirements. The more barriers you raise between farm member servers, the more you will struggle with administrating that farm.

> **Important** This section does not discuss authentication. But if you use Basic and Digest authentication or are transmitting secure data over a public network, you should seriously consider using SSL to encrypt your traffic.

## Screened Subnet

Another possibility for those who need Internet access to their intranet Web applications is to place the entire farm in the screened subnet. This simplifies the external access to your SharePoint Server 2007 server farm, but it does come at a price. First, you will need a SQL server dedicated to your screened subnet, if not to your SharePoint Server 2007 server farm. Many installations leverage an existing SQL server instance internally. There is the additional cost of hardware and software for that SQL server instance. Second, SharePoint Server 2007 is often used to connect to valuable corporate information that is stored in back-end systems, such as enterprise resource planning (ERP) or enterprise resource management (ERM) systems. If the entire farm is in the screened subnet, you will most likely need to create holes in the primary firewall to allow this access. A screened subnet intranet farm is shown in Figure 20-10.

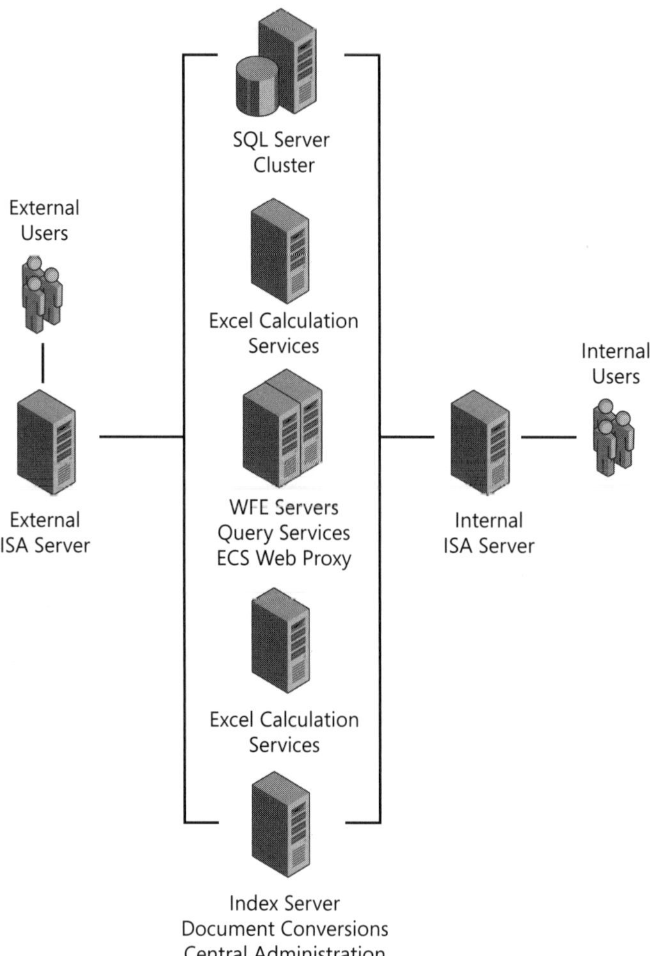


**Figure 20-10** Placing all members of the farm in the same subnet simplifies administration.

The bottom line to implementing collaborative Web applications with Internet access is that, eventually, data must traverse between the private network and the Internet. It is both good and bad. The Internet provides a medium to easily collaborate, but it also provides a medium that offers others access to that data. Your goal should be designing, implementing, and testing an intranet environment that takes the most secure route. Only you can know the route for you through research and testing.

## Extranet Scenarios

Extranets are basically intranets that allow external third parties access to information and therefore are generally considered less secure. Common third-party users are partners, vendors, and contractors. We will refer to these third-party users as *semi-trusted* users. Any time you share data with semi-trusted or untrusted users, you increase the risk of data compromise. Many times this content isn't intentionally compromised, so keep that in mind.

> **Note** An organization's intranet which permits members of the organization to access the intranet via the Internet via port 80 or 443 is normally also considered an extranet.

We are frequently asked by executives and administrators to show them how to share sensitive corporate information to others–risk free. Unfortunately, you cannot share information without the risk of it being passed to an unwanted party. Building an extranet or not building an extranet won't make this problem go away. *Dumpster diving*–the practice of going through a business's garbage looking for information–happens frequently. Employees sometimes print company information and dispose of it in public waste receptacles. So while sharing information on the Internet via an extranet might increase the electronic transfer risk, it sometimes lowers the risk of other data compromise threats by reducing content that is in printed form. When we build extranets for the purpose of sharing information, we try to build them in the most secure manner possible.

First, no matter what type of farm topology you choose, you will probably want to separate your extranet users from your intranet users. There are several ways to do this, and you must decide the best way. Here are a few ideas to get you started:

- Organizational unit in Active Directory
- Second Active Directory
- Third-party LDAP
- ASP.NET SQL database

Your extranet security will only be as good as the training and expertise that you and the other administrators have. As this discussion progresses into more complex farm configurations, leveraging zones and policies, "getting it right" becomes critical.

### Zone Isolation

We don't think zones give you absolute isolation, but they do provide a reasonable amount of protection from intentional data compromise. Most extranets are a good place for zones and policies. Because most of your extranet users are basically trusted users, the level of security can probably be less than if users were not trusted. Essentially, you are designing a "best effort" Web-sharing platform when you leverage zones.

So what does a zone-leveraged farm topology look like? It will most likely have a single collaborative Web application that is accessed by one or more URLs. In addition, each of these URLs may be rendered by different servers, as seen in Figure 20-11.

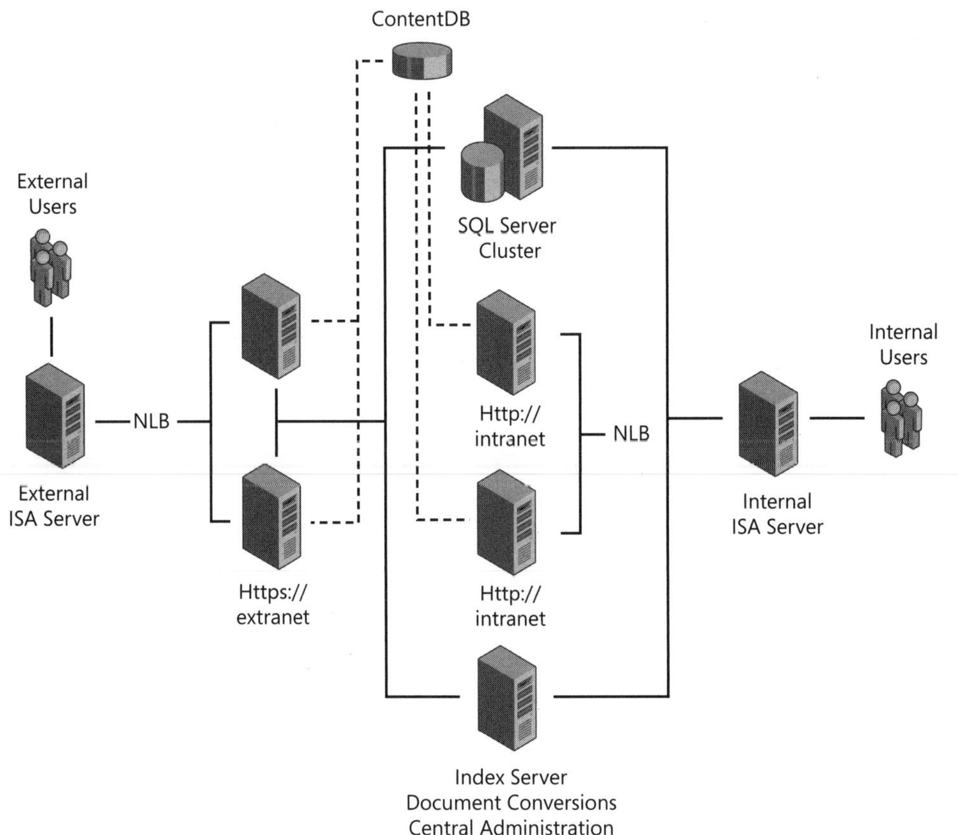


**Figure 20-11** You can publish different URLs of the same Web application on separate hardware.

Using multiple URLs will complicate things, there's no doubt about it. Remember that, in the Web application best practices section of this chapter, we discussed that all alerts are sent on the default zone. By default, this zone is the first URL created for a Web application. In a zone-leveraged farm topology, you want to carefully design around this fact. The best practice is usually to create the most secure zone as the default zone. This allows the embedded URL in e-mails to be accessible by anyone from anywhere on the Internet. A common mistake is creating the default URL as the internal address. That usually is not accessible from the Internet, so embedded alert URLs for remote users will fail. The most secure zone in an extranet topology should probably be an SSL-enabled application and also the default internal URL.

> **Note** Do not try to graphically show the logical Web application architecture and your physical farm architecture on the same diagram. This is very confusing and almost impossible to do. Remember that every server in the farm can host every Web application by default. Therefore, any server in the farm is capable of serving your entire logical architecture.

Recall that zone names have nothing to do with security by themselves; they are simply a naming convention for you. The advantages to using multiple extended and mapped Web applications, leveraging zones, is that you can apply security polices to a set of users for a given URL. This allows you to create and define policies for a URL. In this scenario, it is common to deny Manage Lists And Browse Folders for extranet users. This is thoroughly documented on TechNet, but you can see an example of the Central Administration setting in Figure 20-12.

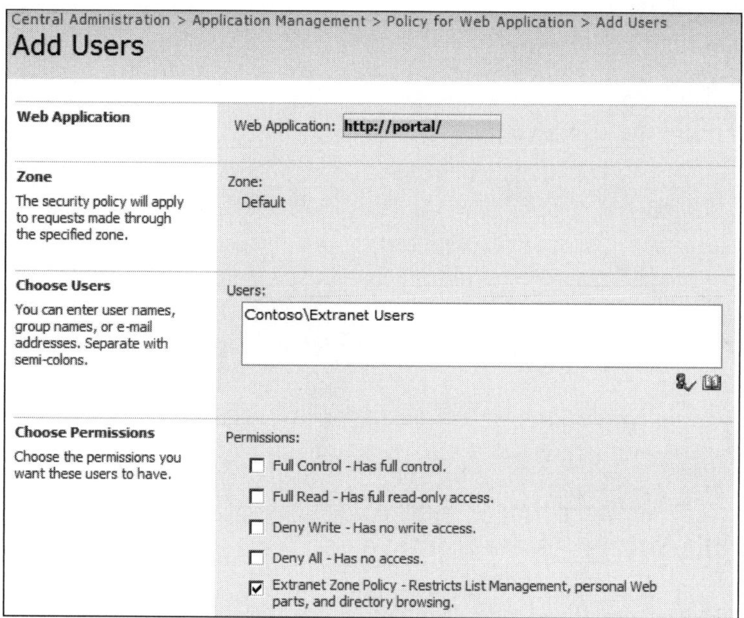


**Figure 20-12** You apply policies to Web application zones for users or groups.

Part of your solution's overall design will be determining the minimum set of rights for extranet users. We usually err on the side of being too restrictive and then loosen permissions as needed and approved. You probably won't apply any policies to your trusted users because they already have full access on another URL. We have seen customers, with mixed success, apply more restrictive policies for their trusted users, but only on the external URL. For those customers, it provided a way to restrict and scope the management of SharePoint Server 2007 to users while they are only on the intranet LAN.

## Physical Isolation

If security is paramount in your extranet design, you will probably want to create a server farm, including a dedicated SQL server instance and Active Directory, that is dedicated to your extranet. This design simplifies the creation of the farm, but often complicates the connections to other systems. Extranets almost always need connections to internal systems for reasons such as accounting or inventory, and they create more issues in the firewall connections and authentication to those sources. Carefully think through the following when you design your extranet solution:

- Who will need access to the system?
- From where will they access it?
- How will they access it?
- What content needs to be shared?
- Who will manage the content?
- Who will manage the access?

One definite advantage to a physically isolated extranet solution is a single URL on a single zone. You can still leverage Web application policies to restrict extranet users. You can also mix the scenarios and split the extranet farm topology *and* leverage zones. Be warned: The complexity of your design increases dramatically when you do this. For example, extending your portal to the extranet via a different URL seems like a good idea, but how will users now get to their My Sites? Carefully plan and test any design that leverages both zones and physical isolation. Figure 20-13 shows an example of an extranet server farm consuming shared services from the internal provider. You would need to open external access to *http://mysites* or render it on the external server for full My Site functionality to external users.

### Tradeoff Split Subnet Farm Topologies

Splitting your farm across multiple subnets allows you to isolate inbound traffic to the farm. This allows you to more easily audit for an unauthorized intruder because the destination traffic is in another subnet, and you can be reasonably assured of the source of the traffic for a given URL. The tradeoff is that you potentially could be compromised on the more secure zone, and access to your entire farm could be gained. We sometimes accept this risk when the need for corporate information is required on the extranet, such as catalogs, inventory, or other transactional data. Remember, zones and their related policies are only as good as the folks who create them. You cannot protect against two things in your design–uninformed administrators/developers and rogue administrators/developers. Attention to detail is critical when you leverage zones so that you are protected from outside attackers. A frequent audit of your Web applications and zones is considered a best practice.

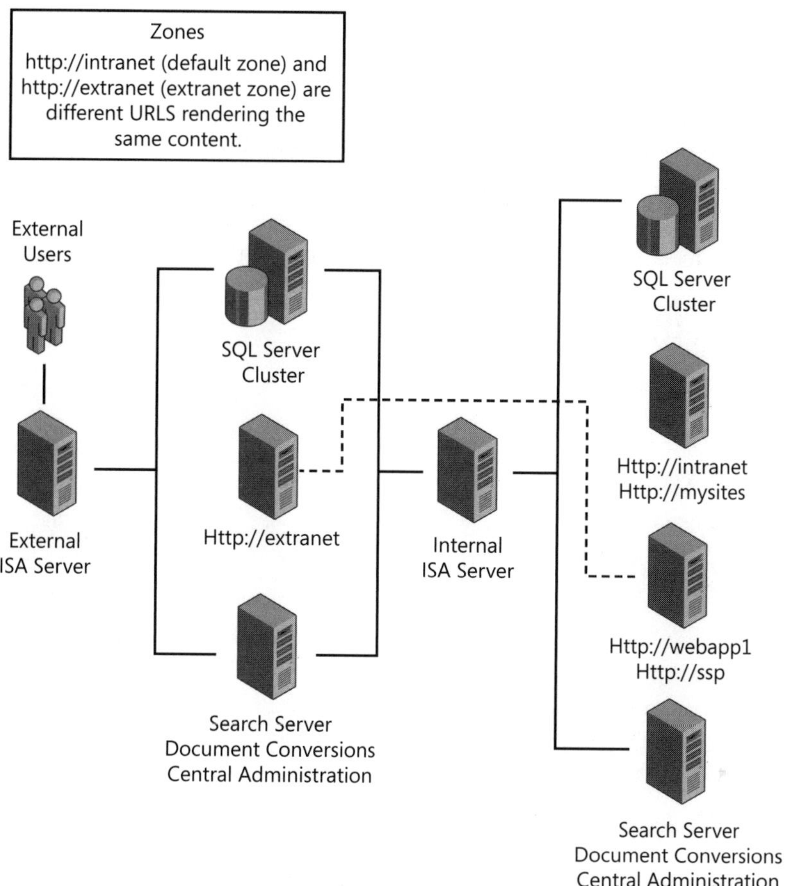


**Figure 20-13** You can build a second farm for isolation and still leverage interfarm shared services.

## Internet Scenarios

The final two scenarios we present concern the use of SharePoint Server 2007 for your Internet-facing Web site, most commonly your WWW site. To review the best practices for building Internet-facing SharePoint Server 2007 sites, refer to Chapter 13, "Creating and Managing Publishing Sites." This section simply covers the farm topology and Web application configuration for those sites. There are two basic choices when building WWW applications on SharePoint Server 2007: sharing an existing farm or building a new, dedicated farm.

### Shared Farm

We find that a wrong example often instructs better than a good example. Therefore, we will begin with a *wrong* way to do Internet sites. Many organizations that are under budget constraints or simply lack the resources to build a second farm consider putting their WWW site into their collaborative farm. We can affirm that this is almost always a really bad idea. Figure 20-14 shows an example of what this would look like.

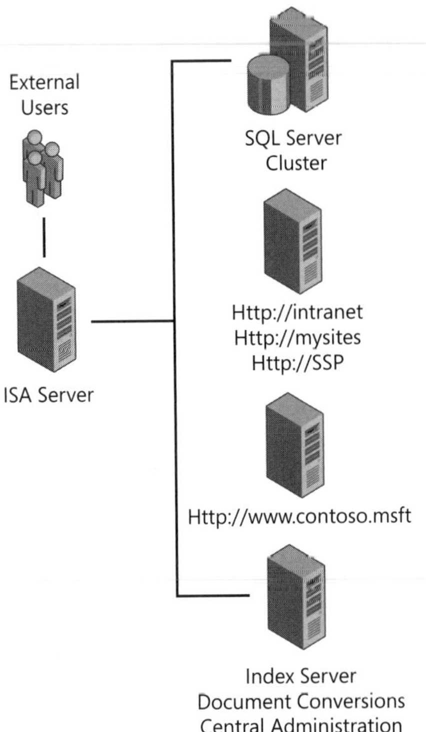


**Figure 20-14** Multiple Web applications sharing a common configuration database in the same farm

This solution is appealing because many administrators plan to use a split-farm topology to secure their WWW traffic from their collaborative traffic. Figure 20-14 shows a split-farm topology. So what's the problem? First, you would need to create another SSP to host services consumed by your WWW site, such as search. This seems simple enough and would provide modest content isolation if you ignore this cautionary scenario. But both your intranet and WWW Web applications must share a common configuration database, even if they have their own content databases and associated SSPs. Second, you should remember that all servers in the farm serve all Web applications. To isolate traffic, you should direct users to the correct box via DNS and disable the unneeded IIS applications on the appropriate server. Third, there is no method to granularly define Search and Excel Calculation Services server roles within a farm. Yes, you can define which servers perform these roles, but you cannot limit the use of these services for a specific service. Figure 20-15 shows a graphical representation of this limitation with search. Once again, Figure 20-15 shows you what *cannot* be done in a farm topology.

Using Figure 20-15 as an example, both WFE1 and WFE2 would have a complete index copy and service queries for SSP1 *and* SSP1 Indexers. Because of this topology limitation, and the fact all Web applications must share a configuration database, you should not use the same server farm for intranet and WWW Web applications. A better design, when resources are an issue, is to use your private, collaborative server farm to develop content and deploy to a dedicated SharePoint Server 2007 server farm for WWW consumption.

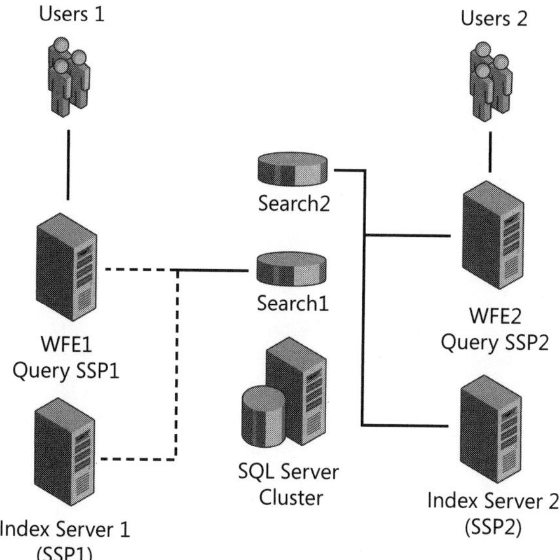


**Figure 20-15** You cannot associate specific query servers with a specific Index server.

## Dedicated Farm

The best practice of developing code on a Dev system, testing it on a Test system, and deploying it to a Production system should be followed when possible. This section refers to an *internal farm,* and that farm can be your collaborative farm or a dedicated Test farm. The latter is preferable, but we do not know your resource limitations or organizational culture.

Most Dev systems for SharePoint Server 2007 are virtual machines that can be easily deleted and rebuilt, but you need to test that code and preview any content before deployment. To accomplish this, you will need a test SharePoint Server 2007 server farm. As was previously mentioned, you do not want to use your internal farm for WWW traffic. Therefore, you must create a new server farm, which will probably reside in your screened subnet. Leveraging the Publishing Infrastructure, many companies simply edit content in-place while using development systems for custom code. This reduces the involvement of information technology for custom WWW content. But many organizations require private viewing of WWW content by managers, executives, and their legal department before deployment on the Internet-facing Web site. We recommend content deployment from one of your internal server farms to your external, dedicated WWW server farm. Figure 20-16 shows an example of two distinct server farms with content deployment between them.

Because it is a one-way connection during content deployment, the security risk of transferring content is very low. Be aware that this mechanism of content deployment is meant for Web content and not customizations such as Web parts, workflows, and policies. In fact, it should probably be used only for pages and images. But pages and images constitute the majority of updates on most WWW servers, so this method of content deployment is still a very viable solution for most companies.

**More Info** See Chapter 13 for more information on content deployment.

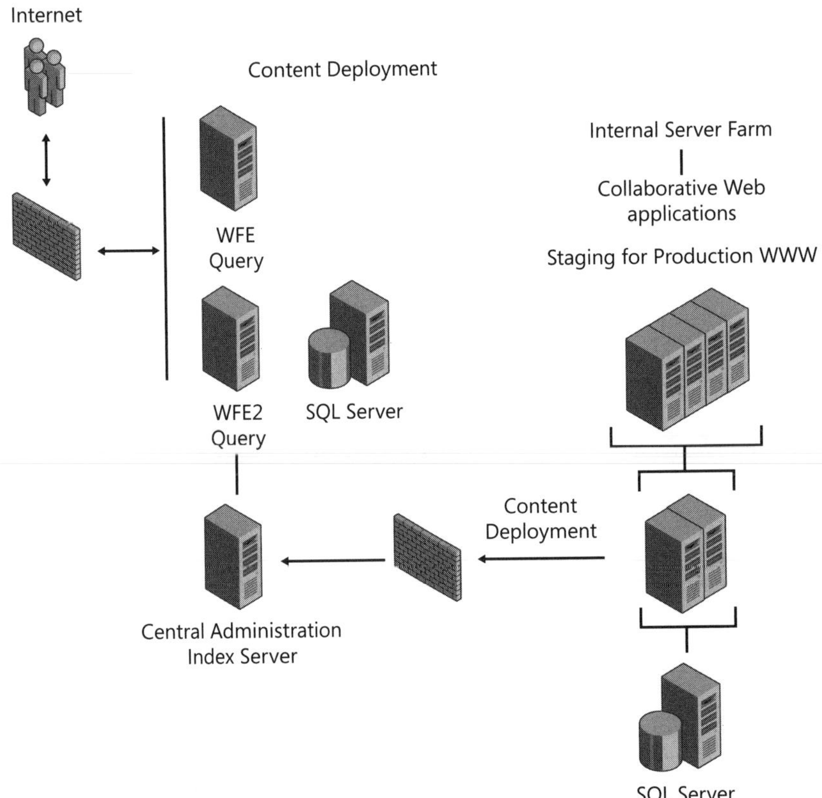


**Figure 20-16** You can deploy content from a secure farm to a less secure farm.

# Summary

There are probably many Web application designs that could appropriately mitigate risks and meet your requirements. Consider the logical scenarios discussed in this chapter and begin your design with one of those. You will most assuredly need to modify the chosen design to meet your specific requirements. Understand these are high-level scenarios that are meant to get you started in the right direction. Also, be realistic about your ability to support your solution. Just because you have the ability to support what you implement doesn't mean the rest of the information technology staff has the ability. Remember to keep your design as simple as possible while still meeting the business requirements.

## Additional Resources

- Designing your logical architecture: *http://technet2.microsoft.com/WindowsServer/WSS/en/library/5ffab48a-47bc-406f-bb8a-0825a516c55e1033.mspx*
- Plan for site creation and maintenance: *http://technet2.microsoft.com WindowsServer/WSS/en/library/b2f92589-bdca-434c-ba62-1d264b576fbb1033.mspx*
- Downloadable Book: Planning an Extranet Environment: *http://technet2.microsoft.com/WindowsServer/WSS/en/library/86e85915-7f73-4e0a-b2fc-72293757b7581033.mspx*
- Plan Web site structure and publishing: *http://technet2.microsoft.com/WindowsServer/WSS/en/library/aa456629-8de8-4328-873b-2e2db96714011033.mspx*

# Part IV
# Operating

**In this part:**

Chapter 21

# Data Protection, Recovery, and Availability

**In this chapter:**



In our experience, a great deal of critical business data is being steadily migrated to Microsoft Office SharePoint Server 2007, whether by the administrators or the users. This is primarily because Office SharePoint Server 2007 is easy to use and familiar to the end-users and is thus a logical place to store and process data. Sometimes, SharePoint Server 2007 is used to access content on a third-party system such as SAP, Siebel, or PeopleSoft. Either way, SharePoint Server 2007 usually becomes a critical component in an organization's infrastructure. As such, it is imperative to properly plan, design, implement, and maintain a data protection, recovery, and availability plan. Simply backing up and restoring via Central Administration is insufficient to fully restore data in all but the simplest implementations.

Because SharePoint Server 2007 usually consists of multiple, interconnected systems and dependencies, this chapter will focus on the planning and designing processes first and then focus on the individual components that make up a SharePoint Server 2007 server farm. The following topics will be presented in this chapter:

- Planning for recovery and availability
- Designing for high availability (HA)
- Backup and restore strategies
- Recovering from disasters

You should understand that there isn't a silver bullet when you plan and implement data protection and availability solutions for SharePoint Server 2007. Therefore, you need to internalize the concepts presented in this chapter and design a solution for your specific environment.

## Planning for Recovery

The best time to plan for content recovery is *before* you implement SharePoint Server 2007. Much of your content recovery plan depends on how your SharePoint Server 2007 server farm is implemented. A common bad practice is trying to force stringent recovery objectives from system that was poorly installed. Doing so is a lot like trying to get a Yugo to perform like a Ferrari! If you installed via the default options, use native backup tools, and ignore Microsoft SQL Server transaction logs, you are most likely assuming a 24-hour data loss in the event of SQL Server failure. If you aren't moving your backup media off-site, then you are assuming a total loss of data. Can your company sustain a total loss of data? 24 hours? These are some of the questions you need to answer before implementing SharePoint Server 2007 or at least before moving business-critical content into SharePoint Server 2007.

First, you must define where the valuable content resides or will reside. If SharePoint Server 2007 is simply a front-end dashboard for back-end business data, then you will be more concerned with getting SharePoint Server 2007 back online in a failure and less concerned with the loss of SharePoint Server 2007 content. In this example, your primary recovery target would be the back-end business data. Likewise, you must design for accessing your content. If you require immediate access to your data, then solid backups to tape may not be sufficient. Instead, you may need to plan for disk-to-disk backups or create a mirrored instance of your farm altogether.

Unless you have a very simple installation, your data protection and recovery plan will require some preparation. Often, it isn't a planning process that you can do alone. It will require discussions with the data owners and stakeholders to understand the criticality of the data, and what the expected availability is. Two key concepts are presented throughout this chapter:

- **Recovery time objective** The recovery time objective (RTO) defines how long your system can be down before it is back online after a disruption. The disruption could be due to anything from a SQL Server outage to a Web front-end (WFE) server failure. You don't need to have the same RTO all of the time. For example, a bank might have a very short RTO from Monday through Friday, 9 A.M. until 5 P.M., but a longer RTO for all other times. The RTO should include data recovery at the server, farm, database, site, list, and item levels.
- **Recovery point objective** The recovery point objective (RPO) defines your data loss threshold, measured in time. If you run daily backups only and ignore the SQL Server transaction logs, then your RPO is 23 hours, 59 minutes, and 59 seconds. Any data written to SharePoint Server 2007 after you ran the backup cannot be restored via native tools until after the next backup. Many organizations assume this risk without fully understanding the impact of losing 24 hours of data.

Keep these two concepts in mind as you plan your design and as you read through this chapter. Whenever you plan and install a new farm component, such as a Web application or databases, be sure to plan for the appropriate RTO and RPO as defined by the stakeholders.

## What Are You Protecting?

You must first decide *what* SharePoint Server 2007 content you will protect before you decide *how* you will protect it. As part of your planning process, you should define the criticality of your SharePoint Server 2007 content. Many organizations will calculate the value of the content by lost revenues or the cost to reproduce the content. If you have content within the same server farm and segments of the data have a drastically different value, then you might consider different levels of protection commensurate with the value of the content. A good example is business-critical content, such as architectural drawings, contracts, and designs, versus historical human resources documents, such as vacation requests. The business-critical content should probably be better protected, while the organization could probably withstand a greater data loss to the generic human resources information. You would probably spend more money to protect the business-critical content. Basically, you must decide the value of the content and then the cost to protect it. If a business-critical site collection costs $100,000 to reproduce, then an extra $5,000 spent on your SharePoint Server 2007 design to protect that data would be reasonable.

Putting a price on your content is easier said than done. It can be very difficult to define at what point the cost outweighs the risk. This is really a discussion in risk management, and there is simply not room to discuss it here. Instead, we will discuss those areas directly related to SharePoint Server 2007. Suffice it to say that you alone cannot define acceptable thresholds in data loss and downtime. You need to first educate your stakeholders in the costs of protecting content, gather data loss requirements, and then plan and design accordingly.

**More Info** For a good overview of risk management within the Microsoft Solutions Framework, browse to *http://www.microsoft.com/technet/solutionaccelerators/cits/mo/mof/mofrisk.mspx.*

## Stakeholder Education

Many stakeholders do not fully appreciate the complexity of fault tolerance and data recovery. In fact, many executives want all of the data, all of the time. You need to have an honest discussion with several people, but especially the users, data owners, and executives. You should ask them what their acceptable data loss is and how long the system can be down. Now, they will probably say that they cannot accept *any* data loss and that the system must always be up. Your job is to educate these stakeholders about the actual expense of achieving this. Moving to a 99.999 percent availability posture is very, very expensive. When stakeholders are presented with the costs of such HA, they often come back to reality and a compromise takes place. The compromise is between what you can design, implement, and support and what they are willing to pay.

Remember that not all data must always be online, and not all data must have recent backups. Think of it this way: Records management content usually doesn't have to be online immediately, but it must always be recoverable. Your design using this scenario might have only a single primary SQL Server system, but leverage transaction log shipping to a second SQL Server instance so a copy can always be recovered that is close to the point of failure. Conversely, some content needs to be online all of the time, but not necessarily fault tolerant to the point of never losing a byte of data. A good example of this is data warehousing and business intelligence. It might be critical to always have a Report Center online, but it might not hurt to lose a small amount of warehoused data because the online transaction processing (OLTP) content still exists. These examples show you how designing for availability doesn't always mean designing for recoverability.

Ask your stakeholders questions, and be prepared to give rough estimates of costs during these discussions. Here are a few stakeholder questions to get you started:

- What content must always be online?
- What is your pain threshold regarding RPO data loss?
- What role will users play in the recovery process?
- Do you really need 100 percent of the content in the event of a disruption?
- Must the system honestly be up *all* of the time?
- What is the lost labor cost per hour in the event of a system outage?
- What is the lost revenue?
- Will we lose customers in the event of an outage?
- Will we have to compensate for the outage in marketing costs and sales?
- Will we be legally liable for lost content?

Did you notice the last question? If you are a publicly traded company, your CFO might be a very good ally in getting overall executive support. Because the CFO is responsible for data that could be Sarbanes-Oxley or HIPAA regulated, it is in his or her best interest to always have the data available. Think about who can help you design the system you know you should build, regardless of what the stakeholders say. You may ultimately be on the hook for losses from a system outage. Keep a record of all data recovery and availability discussions for future use, and to prove your recommendations should the need arise.

## Service Level Agreements

Service Level Agreements (SLAs) set the expectations of recoverability and availability. These can be informal documents within your organization or legal contracts with and between service providers. A good SLA should be easy to read, easy to follow, and easy to apply. An overly complex SLA makes your job difficult when you implement SharePoint Server 2007. So what is the anatomy of an SLA? The International Engineering Consortium defines an SLA as "an informal contract between a carrier and a customer that defines the terms of the carrier's responsibility to the customer and the type and extent of remuneration if those responsibilities are not met." That definition obviously was originally defined for telecom carriers, but generally states what has become the standard for most SLAs.

An SLA will vary greatly depending on your operating environment, business type, and business requirements. There are some common elements of any SLA, and you should include the following at a minimum:

- System availability
- Transactional reliability of the actual data
- Acceptable performance
- Mean time to respond to problem requests
- Mean time to restore service and/or content

When discussing SLAs and availability, we usually talk about the 9s. This is actually a fairly simple concept and can help you educate your stakeholders. We sometimes associate rough design costs with each level of 9s. Table 21-1 shows Microsoft's 9s table.

**Table 21-1 Number of 9s to Calendar Time Equivalents**

| Acceptable uptime percentage | Downtime per day | Downtime per month | Downtime per year |
|---|---|---|---|
| 95 | 72.00 minutes | 36 hours | 18.26 days |
| 99 | 14.40 minutes | 7 hours | 3.65 days |
| 99.9 | 86.40 seconds | 43 minutes | 8.77 hours |
| 99.99 | 8.64 seconds | 4 minutes | 52.60 minutes |
| 99.999 | 0.86 seconds | 26 seconds | 5.26 minutes |

Most SharePoint Server 2007 installations we have seen were architected to the 99-percent availability level. Most of these were not intentionally built to two 9s, but this is the natural path for most organizations. A two-9s design would allow the occasional outage due to system failure and a regular window for updates and hardware maintenance. Why aren't most installations of such critical data designed to three 9s or higher? A rough estimate of moving from a 99-percent uptime posture (3.65 days of downtime per year) to a 99.9-percent uptime posture (8.77 hours per year) is a 100-percent increase in cost! Most likely, the 99-percent service level will be a good compromise between availability and cost.

Remember that you have many dependencies with SharePoint Server 2007, including SQL Server, networking, Active Directory directory services, operating systems, and hardware. Simply building a SharePoint Server 2007 server farm to provide 99-percent uptime doesn't guarantee the solution actually provides 99-percent uptime. If you do not own the dependencies, you should obtain an SLA from the service vendor or consider building the dependency yourself. When defining these SLAs with vendors, don't assume you need 24-hour coverage, seven days per week. If you are doing business only 12 hours a day, then your organization might need extreme availability only during that window. This would leave plenty of time for software updates, hardware fixes, and testing without the unnecessary design of failover server farms and additional server farm members. It will also reduce the cost of your design.

We recommend the creation and maintenance of SLA, even if your customer is your employer. SLAs provide a documented method for defining acceptable data loss and system availability. They also provide a way to define multiple tiers of recoverability and availability.

SharePoint Server 2007 can adapt to a multi-tiered SLA arrangement at the farm, Web application, and content database levels. Your SLA needn't be a blanket agreement covering all facets of your installation. Table 21-2 shows how SharePoint Server 2007 can be architected to support different service levels.

**Table 21-2 Tiered SLA Levels for SharePoint Server 2007**

| Component | Accomplished how? |
|---|---|
| Farm | Different farm servers, different SQL Server instance, dedicated network hardware |
| Web application | Dedicated content databases, isolated application pools, dedicated WFE servers, dedicated network hardware |
| Content database | Group site collections by SLA in their respective content databases; manage SLAs at the SQL Server instance level |
| Site Collection | Critical site collections can be in a dedicated content database and the SLA managed at the SQL Server instance level |

Obviously, a multi-tiered SLA within a single farm can complicate things quite a bit. But if you are an experienced systems administrator and comfortable with SharePoint Server 2007, it might be more cost efficient than building a second server farm. While you can design a multi-tiered farm after the fact, it is much easier to do in the very beginning before implementation.

# Designing for High Availability

While the exercise of designing for HA does not have to be complex, it does need to be thorough. We usually whiteboard our HA designs with customers, detailing all components of a SharePoint Server 2007 server farm including dependencies such as Active Directory, load balancers, SQL Server, storage, and network components. Whether you whiteboard this design or use another method, creating a visual representation of your overall architecture allows you to quickly see what you are trying to protect and make available. It also allows you to see where the most likely bottlenecks and faults will be in your design.

A basic HA SharePoint Server 2007 design might use Windows network load balancing (NLB) with two WFE servers, a single application server, and a SQL Server cluster. This is commonly referred to as a medium server farm and is the most commonly implemented architecture. Figure 21-1 is an example of a medium server farm.

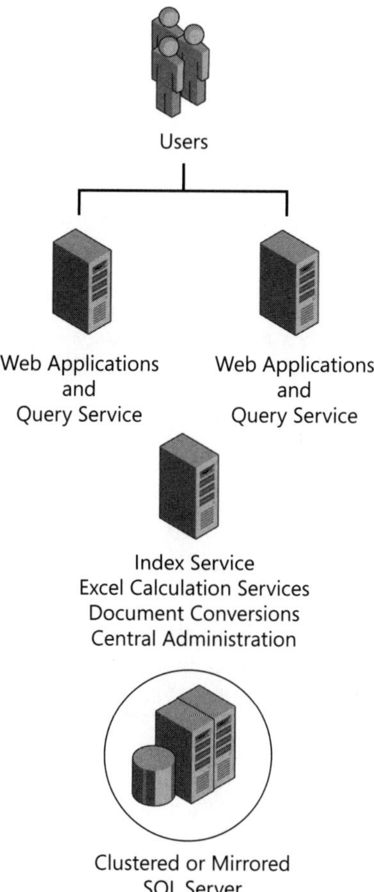


**Figure 21-1** Two WFE servers provide fault tolerance for Web and search within the server farm.

Using the medium server farm as a base topology, you can continue your design to meet your business needs. You could continue to add WFE servers, SQL Servers, multiple hardware load balancers (HLBs), switches, routers, Internet service providers (ISPs), or even failover datacenters! Some point between the medium server farm and the failover datacenter is where most medium-to-large implementations compromise. Your risk management plan and your organization's willingness to invest in technology usually define at what point your implementation will be available. When designing for availability, it is helpful to design your server farm in components. You can then ensure HA as a whole by designing the components to be fault tolerant individually.

## Fault Tolerance and High Availability

So, what's the difference between fault tolerance and high availability? ITIL v3 defines *fault tolerance* as "the ability of an IT service or configuration item to continue to operate correctly after failure of a component part." Hard disk drive arrays, such as Random Array of Independent Disks (RAID), are a good example of fault tolerance. The disk array as a whole presents a single volume to the operating system. In most RAID configurations, a single disk failure within the array does not impact the entity presented to the operating system. See? The operating system has no knowledge that a disk failed. The volume presented to the operating system is *fault tolerant.*

*HA* is designing a service that hides or minimized the effect of a configuration item failure. ITIL v3 defines it as:

> *An approach or design that minimizes or hides the effects of configuration item failure on the users of an IT service. High availability solutions are designed to achieve an agreed level of availability and make use of techniques such as fault tolerance, resilience, and fast recovery to reduce the number of incidents, and the impact of incidents.*

HA depends on the individual components of the system being fault tolerant. Remember that your SharePoint Server 2007 server farm is actually a *system of systems* (SoS). Your WFE server consists of many parts, such as memory, CPU, and disks. Your SQL Server instance may consist of multiple servers in a cluster. Each of these major components in your farm needs to be adequately fault tolerant, individually, to meet your overall system availability goals. The combination of each of these fault-tolerant components into a whole serves to form a unified service that can be highly available.

> **More Info** See Chapter 3, "SharePoint Server 2007 Design Life Cycle," for more information on designing an SoS.

## SQL Server

We consider your SQL Server components to be the most critical in your design. First, essentially all of your valuable content is stored in databases–the configuration database, Shared Services database, and all of your content databases. Second, without SQL Server, no number of WFE servers and applications servers will keep your solution available. There are several methods to architect SQL Server to be highly available, and each method comes with its own advantages and disadvantages.

### Clustering

One of the most common methods to provide fault tolerance of all databases at the SQL Server instance level is SQL Server clustering. Microsoft defines SQL Server failover clustering as follows:

*A failover cluster is a combination of one or more nodes (servers) with two or more shared disks, known as a resource group. The combination of a resource group, along with its network name, and an internet protocol (IP) address that makes up the clustered application or server, is referred to as a failover cluster or a failover cluster instance. A SQL Server failover cluster appears on the network as if it were a single computer, but has functionality that provides failover from one node to another if the current node becomes unavailable. A failover cluster appears on the network as a normal application or single computer, but it has additional functionality that increases its availability.*

SQL Server clustering provides one or more servers in groups of active and passive nodes. The *active* node acts as the current SQL Server for SharePoint Server 2007. You can have multiple active nodes in a cluster, but a smart implementation will have a single active node and single passive node for SharePoint Server 2007. The *passive* node is a warm standby SQL Server that can assume responsibility for the instance name. If you have experienced database administrators (DBAs) on staff or are a DBA yourself, you can implement your cluster any way you like as long as you test your solution.

To properly test a clustered SQL Server instance, we recommend loading a copy of your production data on the SQL Server instance to test, but never to test using live production data. If you do not yet have production SharePoint Server 2007 data, then use a tool such as SPSiteBuilder (available from CodePlex at *http://www.codeplex.com/SPSiteBuilder*) to pre-populate your farm with a sample amount of planned content. It is not enough to simply test active to passive node failover with small databases. Many of the complexities of SQL Server clustering appear with populated databases. Don't forget to also test the failover of busy databases. SharePoint Server 2007 content databases often host very dynamic content, and the transaction logs can become quite large. This can negatively affect the failover of the SQL Server instance from the active node to the passive node. When the passive node takes control of the shared clustered disk, it must replay the transaction logs to bring the SQL Server instance content up to date. We have seen large content databases, whose logs are only truncated on a daily basis during backups, take several hours to come online. For this reason, you should carefully consider how often you are truncating logs. If you need a minimal RPO and a short RTO, you should consider SQL Server mirroring.

> **More Info** For more information on SQL Server clustering, including the operating system requirements, see *http://technet.microsoft.com/en-us/library/ms189134.aspx*.

## Database Mirroring

Database mirroring is new to Microsoft SQL Server 2005 and requires Service Pack 1 or later. SQL Server mirroring sends transactions from the *principal* SQL Server to the *mirror* SQL

Server, with these two servers called *partners*. Database mirroring has the primary advantage over SQL Server clustering in that logs do not have to replay. Basically, you can have automatic failover of data in almost real time. A witness server can monitor the principal SQL Server instance and automatically failover to the mirrored SQL Server instance for a principal failure.

> **More Info** For detailed information on SQL Server mirroring with SharePoint Server 2007, see *http://go.microsoft.com/fwlink/?LinkId=83725&clcid=0x409*. For detailed information on SQL Server 2005 mirroring, see *http://www.microsoft.com/technet/prodtechnol/sql/2005/dbmirror.mspx*.

But there is a disadvantage in that you must alias the SQL Server instance name, which was not supported when this book was published, or you must manually execute the stsadm.exe –o renameserver command *and* IISReset in every server in the farm. We expect aliasing the SQL Server instance to be supported, so it is covered here briefly. Most enterprise mirroring implementations (and there weren't many when this was written) are using an alias to the SQL Server instance. Using an alias allows you to install SharePoint Server 2007 to a name such as SQLSP, with the actual SQL Server instance names being SQL01 and SQL02, as an example. Figure 21-2 shows a logical example what this mirroring looks like.

Why use an alias? SharePoint Server 2007 stores the database connection information in the configuration database. It contains a record of each content database and on what SQL Server instance that database is hosted. Additionally, each server in the farm has record of where the configuration database is stored and all content databases. If you choose to script your server farm to failover, you must IISReset all servers in the farm to update the application pool to content database association. This will read the new information from the previously executed stsadm.exe –o renameserver command and bring your Web applications back online.

> **More Info** For a free white paper on how to use the stsadm.exe command, visit the premium content area of Mindsharp's Web site at *http://www.mindsharp.com*.

Unfortunately, at this time, Microsoft supports only a full farm replication from one instance to a mirrored instance. Microsoft does not support mirroring multiple principal SQL Server instances to multiple mirrored instances. While this may be a short-term limitation and outdated when you read this, we must state it. This means that you cannot leverage multiple SQL Server mirroring technologies to address a multi-tiered SLA, as shown in Table 21-2. While it is most certainly possible, you may have difficulty obtaining support from Microsoft Customer Support Services. Check TechNet to see the most recently supported SQL Server mirroring topologies.

Additionally, mirroring more than 20 databases may not be possible without a substantial hardware investment. Once again, be sure to test your solution with real data. If you need to test your solution with hundreds or thousands of user requests, refer to Chapter 23, "Capacity

Planning and Performance Monitoring," for information on using Microsoft Visual Studio Team System 2008 for stress testing.

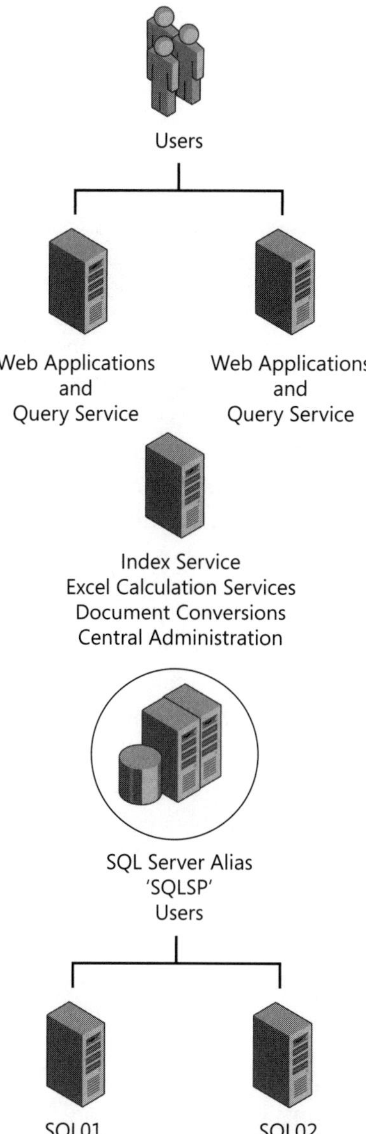


**Figure 21-2** With an alias, you don't need to use stsadm.exe –o renameserver when failover occurs.

> **Note** If you choose not to use aliasing and do not want to use stsadm.exe –o renameserver, modifying the HOSTS file or DNS to force failover is always an option. We do not recommend using Windows NLB for SQL Server failover.

### Transaction Log Shipping

Transaction log shipping differs from database mirroring in that the SQL Server agent takes backups of the logs from the *primary* SQL Server instance and ships them to the *secondary* SQL Server instance. SQL Server mirroring is constant replication and done at the database engine level, not the agent level. This presents advantages and disadvantages with SQL Server mirroring. The obvious disadvantage is the lag in RPO between the two SQL Server instances. If the logs are only being shipped every 15 minutes, then you could lose the content in that time span. Second, you cannot have a witness server as you do with mirroring. So, there is not automatic failover. To failover a log-shipped server farm, you must manually update the server farm's configuration for every content database. There are many others, but the last primary concern is that you cannot log-ship the configuration database, Central Administration content database, or Shared Services database. Yes, this has been done successfully, but it was not supported at the time this book was written.

Transaction log shipping does have some advantages. First, you can introduce an intentional delay for log shipping to provide a backup of user data. Second, you have the possibility of stopping replication during your introduced delay before a known database corruption is shipped. With SQL Server mirroring, everything is mirrored immediately, including data corruption and user errors. Third, multiple secondary SQL Server instances are supported when log shipping. This gives you the ability to send your content to more than one failover SQL Server instance and possibly support a multi-tiered SQL Server failover posture.

You should understand that this section was not meant to be a complete reference guide for SQL Server failover strategies. Depending on your business requirements, budget, and technical expertise, your solution will vary greatly. Remember, the most important part of your design is testing your solution before production use. Also remember to update your failover solution when your farm architecture changes. Examples of farm changes that require updates to your SQL Server failover solution include new Web applications, content databases, and Shared Services Providers (SSPs).

## SharePoint Servers

Once you have designed your SQL Server availability solution, you should next design availability for SharePoint Server 2007 farm members. Keep in mind that it is relatively easy to add new servers to a SharePoint Server 2007 farm. The farm = the configuration database, so simply install the binaries on a Windows Server system and connect to the server farm via the SharePoint Products and Technologies Configuration Wizard. We sometimes architect solutions with a warm server installed into a farm, with no server roles enabled, for the explicit purpose of rapid provisioning in the event that another farm member fails. The following section will cover some of the best practices for designing farm roles for high availability. Notice that we are designing for roles availability, such as Query, Index, and Web, and not individual servers. Because we can transfer roles between farm members, the physical location is not usually as important as the role itself.

## Windows SharePoint Services Web Application

The most visible server role to your users is the Windows SharePoint Services Web Application role, and a server with that role is a WFE server. This role provides the content-rendering capability of content from the database through Internet Information Services (IIS). When you create Web applications, this server role is responsible for copying the metabase and inetpub information contained in the configuration database to the WFE server.

If you stop this server role on a WFE server, you will notice that all SharePoint Server 2007–specific IIS Web applications and associated inetpub directories are automatically deleted. This is a double-edged sword. It is bad because any customizations directly in IIS, such as multiple host headers, assigned IP addresses, and secure sockets layer (SSL) certificate associations, are lost. Additionally, because the inetpub directories for those Web applications are also deleted, you lose any customizations to files contained therein, such as the commonly modified Web.config file. But we also use this to our advantage. If you really foul up your IIS configuration for a given Web application, restarting the Windows SharePoint Services Web application server will delete your IIS configuration for the farm and copy a new one back. Don't forget to reassign IP addresses, add host headers, update modifications to the web.config, and reassociate SSL certificates when doing so.

To provide HA for the WFE server role, you need more than one server hosting this role. You then must provide fault tolerance through either Windows NLB or HLB. If you have a small implementation, Windows NLB may work fine for you.

> **More Info** Refer to *http://technet2.microsoft.com/windowsserver/en/technologies/nlb.mspx* for Windows Server 2003 NLB information, and *http://technet2.microsoft.com/windowsserver2008/en/library/30eeb2ff-47ce-4a78-bf22-34b8db1967211033.mspx?mfr=true* for Windows Server 2008 updated information.

If you have a non-trivial SharePoint Server 2007 implementation, you should strongly consider using HLB. HLB has proven to be more stable than NLB and a feature-rich platform for providing fault tolerance at the Web tier. Be careful not to design in single points of failure with your HLB solution. We have seen more than one customer with a single HLB appliance load balancing multiple WFE SharePoint Server 2007 servers. This single HLB hardware may provide better performance, but it will cause the entire Web tier to fail if the appliance breaks. Figure 21-3 shows a common enterprise example of load balancing the WFE server tier.

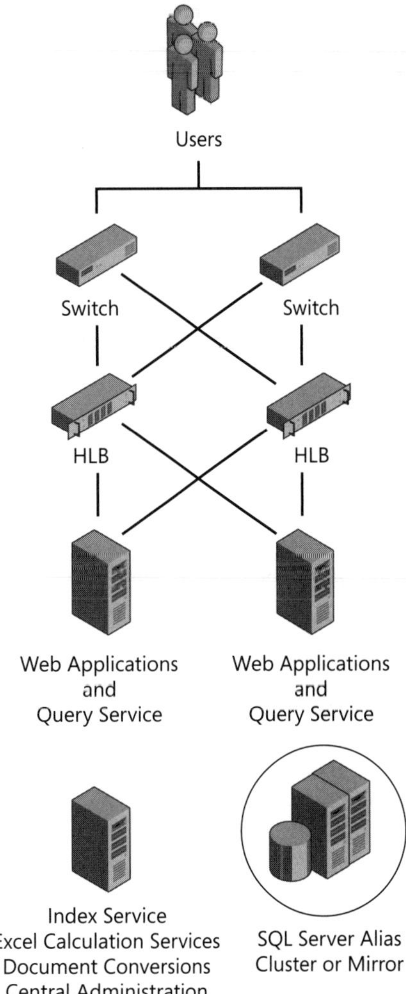


**Figure 21-3** Use multiple switches, load balancers, and a WFE server for a truly redundant Web tier.

Somewhere, every organization must draw the line in its redundancy. You could have multiple routes to the Internet, supported by multiple routers and ISPs, multiple switches, datacenters, hardware load balancers, SQL Server instances, power grids, and storage frames. Only those that require multiple 9s will require such extreme HA measures. Be forewarned that large datacenter HA solutions are *very* expensive to build, and usually more expensive to maintain. In fact, unless all appropriate staff managing their respective components are well trained, you could actually make your solution *less* available due to administrative errors. Once again, thoroughly test your solution for failover and capacity before production deployment.

## Index

The index server role is the least flexible role in a SharePoint Server 2007 server farm. You cannot cluster the index server, and you can have only one copy of the index. For this reason, you should carefully choose and monitor the hardware you install for an Index role. One possible way to create a failover strategy might be hosting the Index role on a Windows Server 2008 Hyper-V system as a virtual machine. You can then fail the virtual machine to another host should there be a hardware failure. Be aware that this is not yet officially supported, so be sure to check before implementing!

If you design your farm for availability, however, losing the index server isn't usually a catastrophic event. We usually install Central Administration on the index server, along with Excel Calculation Services and Document Conversions in a medium server farm. The most important service in your farm is often rendering Web content, so losing your index server isn't immediately noticed. While you might lose the functionality of the application services on the server, your users can still access their valuable user content. If you host the query role on your WFE servers, users' searches will work as well. Be aware that user queries will become stale rather quickly, so restoring your index server should be a priority. For this reason, query roles are not "true" fault tolerance for the index.

Be thoughtful when designing for search. First, we highly recommend moving the index to a dedicated drive or at least one other than the system disk. Your index can grow quite large and might fill up the system disk, causing a service outage. We often create an I:\ drive on index servers, with the index directory located in I:\SSPName. You also need to carefully design for the search database. In fact, it is usually one of the two busiest databases in your farm, with the SSP database being the other. If you have a large or enterprise search strategy, you should create a dedicated spindle set on your SQL Server instance that will be dedicated to the search database.

If you lose your index server due to corruption or hardware failure, the best way to return to service is by restoring from backups. When requiring a speedy return to service, you should consider using disk-to-disk backups for your indexes. The best practice is to always use the native catastrophic backup tool [stsadm.exe –o backup –directory] to back up and restore your SSPs. You cannot back up only the search components. You must back up the entire SSP that manages that index. Therefore, the only way to restore the index is by restoring the SSP that managed it. While third-party tools might be able to back up and restore much of the farm, the only way we have found to reliably return indexing to its previous state was through the native tools. This isn't to say that there isn't a third-party tool that will do it successfully; there just wasn't when this book was written. You can safely assume a best practice is testing the restoral of your SSPs.

## Query

The query role can he hosted on any server in the farm, including the index server. But if you will have more than one query server, you *cannot* host the query role on the index server. If you do, your index will never propagate to the other query servers in the farm. Other than this limitation, you can technically place the query role where you want. But, there are some design considerations to think about.

First, the index is continuously propagated from the index server to the query servers via a file share on the query servers. When you scale out to multiple query servers, you are prompted for this file share creation on the Service Initiation page. Thus, you must have the correct network ports open between the index server and all query servers for file sharing. Otherwise, the shadow index will never propagate. If you will build large indexes, then consider gigabit Ethernet as a design requirement between server farm members. Second, with two or three WFE servers, we generally place the query role on all WFE servers. Be aware that query servers also communicate with the search database and can generate a substantial amount of SQL Server traffic on a busy farm.

It is quite possible to have servers in your SharePoint Server 2007 server farm that only host the query role. This is rare and is usually done to support a Web tier of more than three servers or when you have very large indexes. Figure 21-4 shows an example of an enterprise server farm with dedicated query servers.

In medium and large server farms, you will usually create a substantial amount of network traffic and negate the processing advantages of dedicated query role hosting. We primarily move the query role to dedicated servers to reduce the replication of the content index. If you have a very large content index, it is now replicated to all query servers in the farm, as well as being hosted on the index server. If you have five WFE servers and all the servers host the query role, you now have the index on disk six times. Offloading this disk storage from all WFEs is the primary reason for using dedicated query servers.

## Excel Calculation Services

Excel Calculation Services is basically self configuring when it comes to HA. The act of starting the service in Central Administration notifies the configuration database that the server hosts the role. The other farm members will see that configuration update and automatically use the server for Excel Services processing. In fact, multiple Excel Calculation Services servers will load balance with no input from you. That's nice. Be aware, however, that a heavily used Excel Calculations Services configuration will quickly consume hardware resources. If you are planning for HA and know you will need Excel Calculations Services, carefully monitor the CPU on those servers hosting the role. If you were to implement a warm server that is not hosting any roles but is joined to the server farm, you can quickly and easily add additional Excel Calculation Services horsepower to your solution.

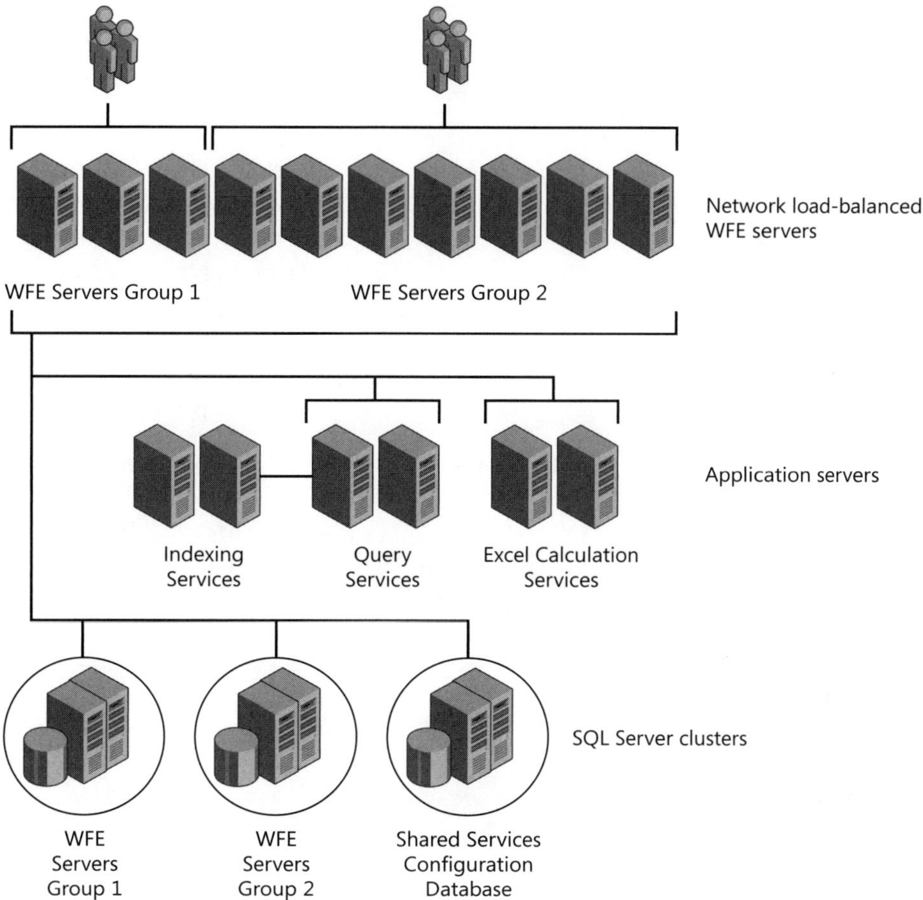


**Figure 21-4** Dedicate the query role when you have large indexes and multiple WFE servers.

## Document Conversions

Document conversions are also straightforward when you design for availability. You should first define an application server as the load balancer for the farm. This is not required when defining a single server to the document conversions role. Only those organizations that will heavily use the document conversion process will need multiple application servers for that role. If required, you must first assign the document conversions load balancer role, as seen in Figure 21-5.

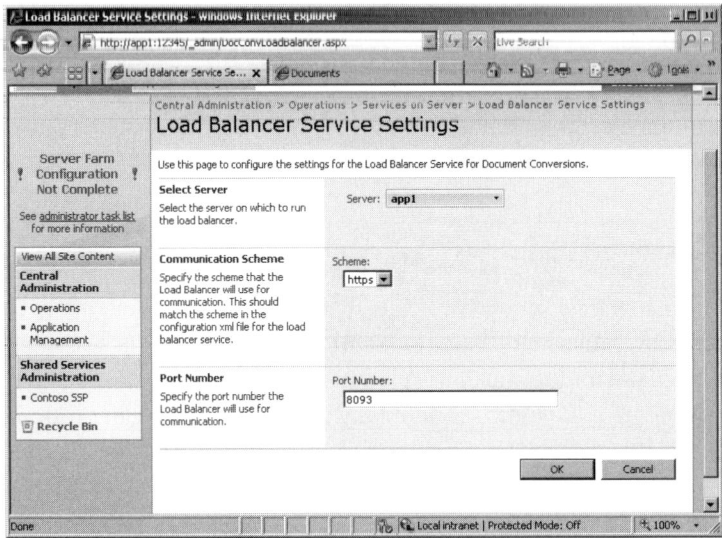


**Figure 21-5** You must define the load balancer before starting the conversions service.

After you have started the load balancer service, you can then enable multiple servers in the farm with the role. While we almost never start the role on WFE servers, the WFE server *must* have communications opened to the document conversions load balancer, and document conversions servers.

> **Note** The document conversions service runs as a local machine account. While we never recommend running SharePoint Server 2007 on a domain controller for production use, many developers and administrators test applications in a virtualized, single-server environment. Be aware whether this single-server environment includes a domain controller; if it does, you will not be able to test or use document conversions.

## Central Administration

Central Administration is not required for your farm to be available. It is basically a graphical tool to manage your farm. Central Administration is a dedicated Web application, with a site collection in the root managed path. In other words, it exists in the content database. You can quickly enable any server in the farm to host the visual interface, an IIS Web application, to render the site collection. Therefore, its placement completely depends on your design.

For security purposes, we generally do not place Central Administration on servers that render Web content to users. But you can quickly provision Central Administration on any farm member by running the SharePoint Products and Technologies Configuration Wizard (psconfigui.exe) or via psconfig.exe.

> **Note** The command to provision Central Administration is *psconfig.exe -cmd adminvs -provision -port <TCP Port> -windowsauthprovider onlyusentlm*. Psconfig.exe is in the SharePoint Root directory, also called the 12 hive. Note that this example uses NTLM as the Windows authentication provider. You may need to change the syntax to suit your environment.

# Backup and Restore Strategies

Your backup and restore strategy should be defined before your system design is completed. The availability and recoverability levels of your SharePoint Server 2007 content can greatly affect how you architect and implement your solution. If you haven't backed up your content, you won't be able to restore it. If you are running nightly backups, you can't restore content deleted mid-day. If you are reading this after you have already installed, then you need to understand that your backup and restore strategies depend upon how you installed SharePoint Server 2007. After detailing your restore strategy, you may find it necessary to re-architect portions of your server farm.

## Recovery Time Objective

RTO was briefly mentioned earlier as the interval between when a system fails, and when it should come back online. A best practice is defining multiple RTOs when a critical system is in question. For example, you may have a shorter RTO for server failure or database corruption, but a much longer RTO to deal with natural disasters. You may define a four-hour return to service for anything but the worst disaster. Trying to design a short RTO for a true disaster can spiral costs out of control and may be practically impossible. In addition, it is likely that customers and partners will be more understanding of a 24-hour (or longer) outage due to a natural disaster.

There are exceptions to this, however. Large Internet companies like Amazon and Microsoft have failover datacenters that can provide seamless service switching in the event of a major disaster. But a small engineering firm may simply have backup tapes in a vault that must be restored in a new location on new hardware. The latter might take days to complete, but would be more in line with the risk. Once again, there is no perfect answer for what your RTO should be. Most return-to-service times are in the four-hour range for critical business systems and 24 hours and longer for generic business systems. While we would all like for service restoral times to be shorter, it is rarely practical or cost effective to provide them. The sweet spot for your service restoral should be directly based on the criticality of the service. If your company will go out of business if it is down for 24 hours, then you will require a much more complex system design and failover strategy.

## Recovery Point Objective

The RPO defines your data loss threshold, measured in time. That is, how much data can you lose when SQL Server fails? Daily backups start becoming obsolete as soon as they begin. If a piece of data changes after it was backed up, you cannot restore that change until after the next backup cycle. If you must minimize the loss of any transactional data, then you must design and maintain for that minimal loss in SQL Server. You must leverage your transaction logs for restore points, and you will probably need to consider SQL Server mirroring or transaction log shipping to protect your content. RPO does not mean you have a minimal RTO. You may log ship *all* content off-site for protection, but it might take you hours or days to return that content to service. That may be perfectly acceptable for many businesses. Losing data may not be acceptable. Be very direct with the stakeholders about the expected RPO for your SharePoint Server 2007 design.

# Recovering Content

The bulk of your content recovery will probably be at the list or item level. But there are times when you must restore a lower-level component, such as a content database, to restore this content. Additionally, you need to know the best practices for recovering content at many levels in the farm, including the following:

- Web applications
- SSPs
- Site collections
- Lists, libraries, and items

This section will give you an overview of restoring failed, corrupted, or deleted content and some best practices for doing so.

## Web Applications

Honestly, we rarely see entire Web applications fail. Usually, it is a component of a Web application, such as a content database or IIS Web application, that fails. But understanding how to restore a Web application from content databases is necessary because most medium and larger organizations will rely on SQL Server backups for their SharePoint Server 2007 content. But it is important to understand some of the best practices when you use the native tools, so they will be covered also.

### Restoring Web Applications via SQL Server Restore

First, Web applications primarily consist of content databases. The configuration of the content database is stored in the configuration database, but the user data is stored in one or more content databases. In a worst-case scenario, you can rebuild a Web application with nothing but a good set of content database backups. Remember, you cannot restore what you do not back up. The following directions will assist you in a plain Web application restore using only the content databases:

1. Restore the content databases associated with the Web application in question
2. Create a new Web application using exactly the previous settings. Be sure to use the same URLs, add zones, and re-create policies if necessary. A better way would be scripting the addition of these extra items. A scripted farm install is covered at the end of this chapter.
3. When creating a new Web application, you must create a new default content database; you cannot select an existing database. Therefore, delete the newly created content database after creation. We know this sounds backward, but it works.
4. Next, add a new content database. Instead of actually creating a new database, enter the name of your restored content database. This will associate your restored content databases with the new Web application.

The preceding steps might be much more complex, depending on your installation, but should serve as the basics for restoring a Web application. When you created the new Web application in Central Administration, it forced the creation of new IIS Web applications, even if you used the same name. Therefore, you lost any direct customizations to IIS. In this case, you must reconfigure IIS customizations such as multiple host headers, Web.config changes, and SSL certificates. If you lost the WFE servers as well, be sure to restore any 12 hive customizations from your server backups.

## Restoring Web Applications via Central Administration

Restoring a Web application via Central Administration is common when the native tools for backups are used. Be sure to use host headers when building Web applications when you use the native tools for restores. Doing so ensures a painless restore process. Not doing so may cause a situation where multiple Web applications are trying to be instantiated in IIS to the same IP address, which can cause your Web application restores to fail.

> **More Info** For detailed information on backing up and restoring farm components, browse to *http://technet.microsoft.com/en-us/library/cc263053.aspx.*

Remember that you cannot restore what is not backed up. We consider it a best practice to back up IIS individually, even though it is included in the operating system backups. This gives us the ability to do a lightweight IIS restore and removes the need to restore the entire system state when we only need IIS. If you are using SSL certificates, it is a good idea to back them up in the same location as your farm or IIS backups–and don't forget to back them up with the private key! Otherwise, your SSL certificates cannot be reinstalled in a disaster.

## Shared Services Providers

Whether you are using SQL Server tools or SharePoint Server 2007 tools to back up your content databases, you should use SharePoint Server 2007 tools for SSPs backups. The primary reason we use the native backup tool is to provide a reliable way to back up and restore the index files and search database. Much like the configuration database and Central Administration content database, these are intrinsically linked and should never be backed up or restored separately. Figure 21-6 shows the restoration screen and an example of how you must restore the hosting SSP to restore the index files and search database.

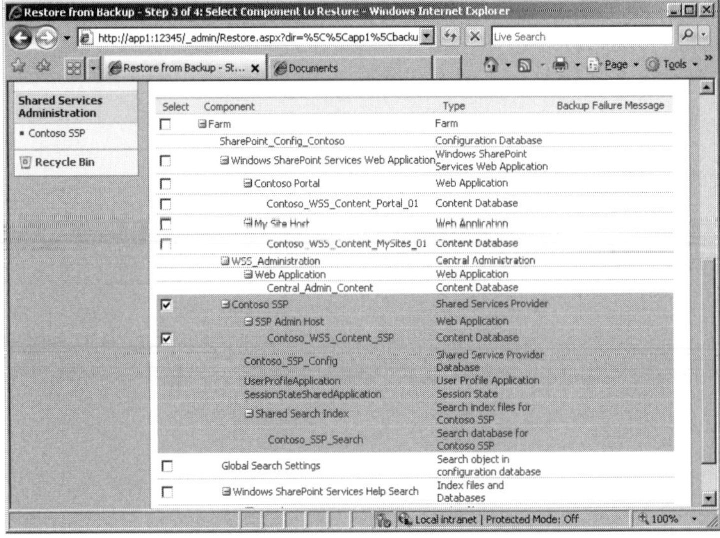


**Figure 21-6** You should select the hosting SSP to restore search.

There are other reasons to use the native tools, such as preservation of audiences, Excel Services settings, search scopes, managed properties, My Site settings, Business Data Catalog settings, and personalization features. Complete documentation for choosing backup and restore tools can be found at *http://technet.microsoft.com/en-us/library/cc263427.aspx*. This link is frequently updated and may supersede information found in this chapter.

> **Note** If you are using only the native tools to back up your SSPs, you might consider a local hard disk on the index server for your backup point. Doing so allows your SSP backups to be moved to your permanent operating system backup media. Be sure you have enough disk space to hold your Shared Services backups, and remove unneeded backups to preserve space. We recommend that this backup point *not* be the system (boot) disk or index files disk. Alternatively, you could back up to a shared drive that is then independently backed up to media.

## Site Collections

It is important to remember how SharePoint Server 2007 is architected. A single site collection is stored in a single content database. Multiple site collections can be contained in a single content database, but site collections cannot span content databases. The discussion about site collection backup and restore should begin with how you designed your database structure. If you randomly create site collections in content databases, you won't have granular control over site collection backup and restore. In fact, some administrators have difficulty determining which content database hosts a specific site collection. The Site Collection List option in Central Administration will show you the site-collection-to-content-database association, as shown in Figure 21-7

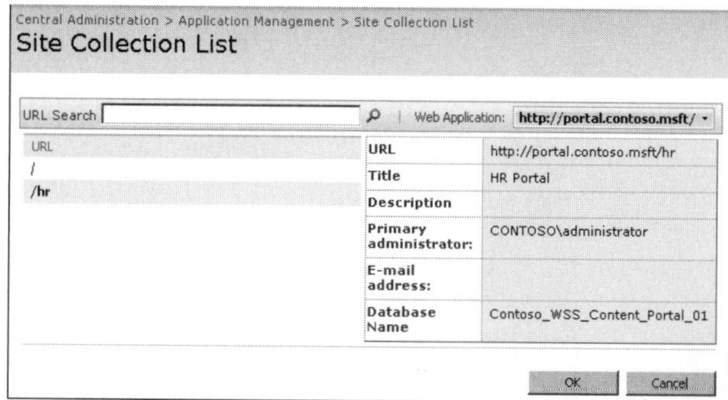


**Figure 21-7** Use the Site Collection List menu in Central Administration to determine the hosting content database.

If, however, you grouped site collections by their criticality in corresponding content databases, you can then use SQL Server tools to manage them to different support levels. Figure 21-8 shows a possible database design for hosting three different SLA levels within a single farm.

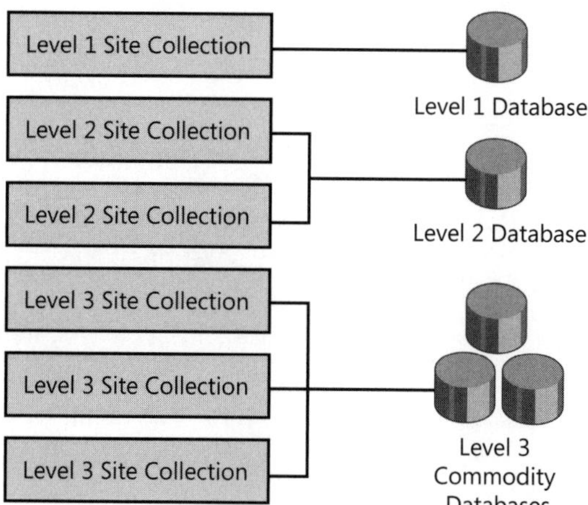


**Figure 21-8** Group site collections in corresponding content databases by SLA level

If you group site collections similar to what is shown in Figure 21-8, then you can manage them accordingly. Level 1 site collections could have frequent SQL level backups and be mirrored to another SQL instance. Level 2 site collections might be transaction log shipped, and Level 3 site collections might be in simple recovery mode and backed up only once a day. Additionally, every level of content database could be on a different SQL Server instance, and on different disk subsystems. Note that Figure 21-8 depicts a one-to-one relationship between a Level 1 site collection and a Level 1 content database. While this provides robust recovery and performance options, it does not scale well. This option should be reserved for the most critical site collections in your server farm.

So how can you manage recovery of content via the native tools? The only tool specifically scoped to site collections is stsadm.exe –o backup –url. This command set allows for the backup and restore of site collections, but not sites. There is no native tool for site-level backup and restore. While you could use stsadm.exe –o import | export for some content, it is a content migration tool and is *not* full fidelity. In fact, using stsadm.exe isn't full fidelity either unless you have locked the site collection in Central Administration or via stsadm.exe. There is always the possibility of an open object during the backup. Figure 21-9 shows how to lock a site collection in Central Administration for full fidelity backups via stsadm.exe.

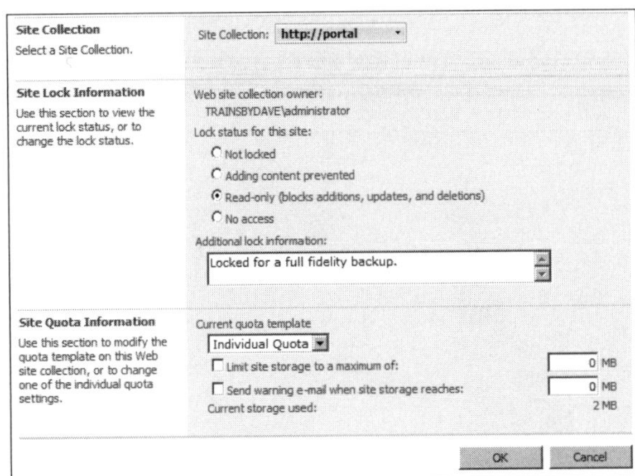


**Figure 21-9** For full-fidelity site collection backups, you should first lock the site collection.

If you require site collection backup and restore, you should consider dedicated databases for those site collections or research third-party backup and restore solutions. One advantage to using the native tools over third-party tools is that they are directly supported by Microsoft. Be sure to verify that your backups are actually working. In our conversations with Microsoft support, we were surprised to hear that many customers thought their backups were working but, after a farm failure, found out they weren't. Don't let this happen to you. While we recommend the use of native backup and restore tools, there are definitely implementations that will require third-party tools for immediate item-level restores that the native tools will not do. If you decide to use a third-party tool, be sure to thoroughly test your solution.

## Lists and Items

So, how will you protect the content at the list and item level? While we have mainly focused on larger components of your design, content recovery can be delegated to provide shorter SLAs and even remove the responsibility from you altogether. You could simply state that you will not retrieve single items that are deleted from lists or deleted lists themselves. It is more common now than you might think for organizations to *not* restore entire databases to retrieve a single item in SharePoint Server 2007. Why? Because we have a two-stage Recycle Bin. Much has been written about the Recycle Bin on TechNet and in Microsoft Press books, so please refer to them for technical questions. What we want to discuss here are the best practices for configuring the Recycle Bin and how to include its use in your SLAs.

As you write your SLAs, remember the impact that the Recycle Bin can have on your design. The second stage of the Recycle Bin doesn't count against site quota and therefore *adds* to your planned content database size. If the Recycle Bin is frequently used by your users, you could find yourself in a position to support 50-percent larger content databases than you had planned. Your SLA should define the size of the second-stage Recycle Bin, and the default 50 percent seems a bit much. But only you can define the second-stage size, and that size should be based on business requirements. If your requirements were that all deleted data should be kept for 90 days, you would need to disable the second stage completely, as seen in Figure 21-10. Be sure to educate your users when you turn off the second stage, as this will not remove the second stage management interface for site collections contained within the Web application. Objects emptied from the first stage are simply expunged.

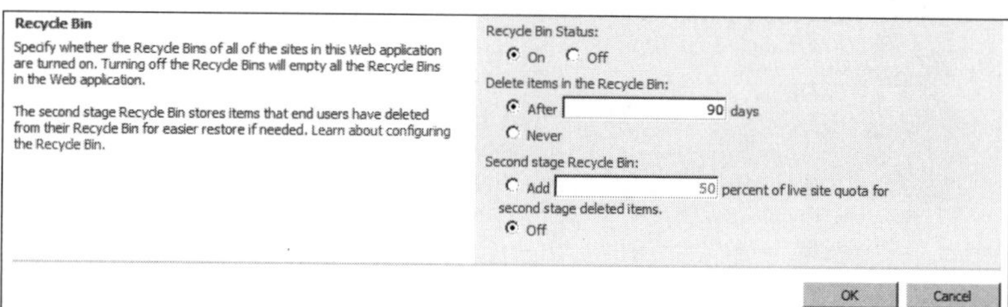


**Figure 21-10** You can manipulate time-based expiration and second-stage limits in Web application general settings.

Take care when configuring the Recycle Bin because the process isn't as straightforward as it appears. First, turning off the Recycle Bin on an active Web application will empty both the first and second stages on all Recycle Bins, and that action is not easily reversed. Second, the time-based expiration setting is a global setting. Therefore, items do not expire from the first stage to the second stage. When the time-based limit is reached, the item is expunged. Think of it this way: If the time-based setting was 90 days and a user emptied her Recycle Bin 60 days after initially deleting an item, the item will remain in the second stage for 30 days. Third, if you turn off time-based expiration and do not use site quotas, the second stage will have no limit. Because the second stage is based on the site quota, site collections without a quota will essentially have no second-stage storage limit.

As you can see, the Recycle Bin should be carefully thought out, and it should be part of the RTO and RPO requirements. If you haven't noticed, the Recycle Bin roughly maps to the RTO and the RPO. The time-based deletion setting defines how long you will keep the data (RTO), and the second stage defines how long you will keep the data online (RPO).

> **Note** While versioning can provide some protection for corrupted and deleted data, it isn't robust enough to include in most SLAs for content protection. You could create a custom list definition that always has at least one major version enabled. This would add a layer of fault tolerance should a file become corrupted. Be aware that the list administrator could simply turn this definition off. For this last reason, it has been left out of this section.

## Recovering from Disasters

Because SharePoint Server 2007 is a multi-tiered solution and cannot be backed up via a single interface, you shouldn't base your recovery plan on backups; you should base it on *restores*. You should first decide what you need to restore and in what time frame. As you progress through your plan, don't forget to leave time for dependencies, such as SQL Server. Let's use a four-hour SLA as an example. If it takes you the entire four hours to restore your SharePoint Server 2007 content, that doesn't leave you time to restore SQL Server if needed. To totally restore a server farm, the following SharePoint Server 2007 components must be backed up, scripted, or thoroughly documented:

- Configuration database and Central Administration content database via the native tools
- Content databases
- 12 hive customizations
- Inetpub customizations, such as Web.config
- Alternate Access Mappings (cannot be restored via native tools)
- IIS for every WFE server
- SSPs using native tools

Using the native farm backup tools in Central Administration, you will back up the majority of the preceding content with the exception of manually edited 12 hive customizations, Alternate Access Mappings, and unique IIS settings such as host headers, assigned IP addresses, and SSL certificates.

You cannot simply restore the native backups, however. You must first build a new farm. The new farm will create a new configuration database and Central Administration content database. The settings used for those two items will persist after a full restore. What actually happens is that the old configuration database is merged with the new one you created. Why not do a complete restore? You cannot restore the farm to full fidelity because you don't have the SharePoint Server 2007 tools to perform the restore. Essentially, you must build a new farm to use the native restore tools. For small installations, the native tools work well. For larger installations, you may consider SQL Server backups of all content databases and use the native tools only for SSPs backups. Most large organizations are already performing SQL Server backups and would like to continue doing so for SharePoint Server 2007.

### Notes from the Field **Recovering Content Databases Using SQL Server Tools**

In a worst-case scenario, we have used SQL Server Management Studio to restore content database backups created with the native SharePoint Server 2007 tools. In your SharePoint Server 2007 backup directory, look for large files, such as *00000015.bak*, as shown in the following graphic.

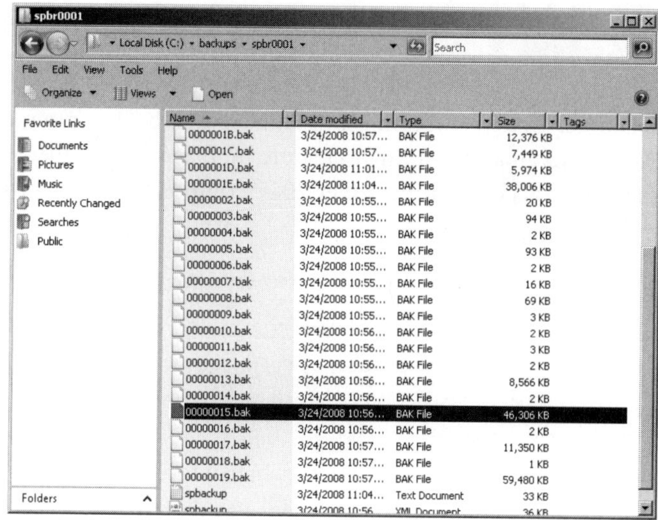


If you have a great deal of content databases, you can either use guesswork and old-fashioned trial and error or refer to your backup logs. In the relevant spbr00nn directory, open the spbackup.txt file. In this file, search and find the content database you want to restore. The content database and backup file association is defined like the following example:

```
@db_name=Contoso_WSS_Portal_01, @db_loc=\\app1\back\spbr0001\00000015.bak
```

Using SQL Server Management Studio, you should restore using the device location and selecting the .bak file previously documented. After selecting the backup file, you will be presented with the backup set selection, as shown in the following graphic.

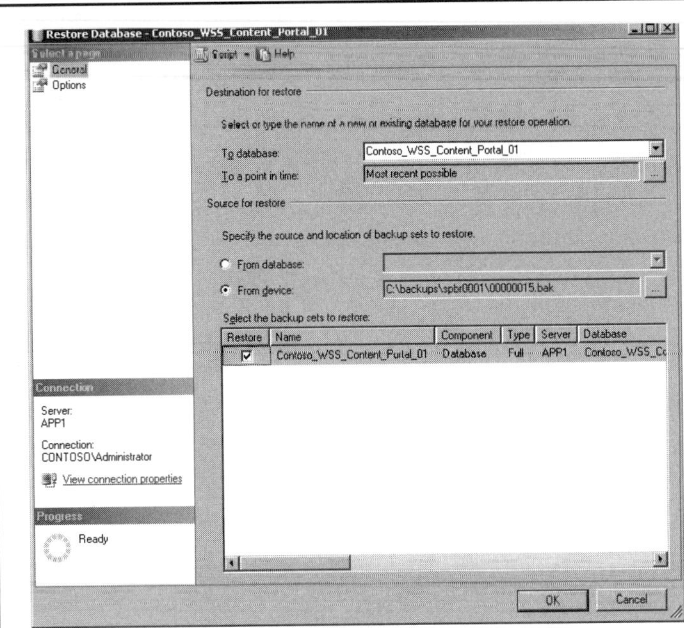


After restoring the content database, you can attach it either to a temporary Web application built for restores or associate it once again with your production Web application.

*Ben Curry, Microsoft MVP, Mindsharp*

You may also decide to script all or part of your farm restoration. This is quickly becoming commonplace and will allow an exact reproduction of your farm while using SQL Server to back up and restore your content databases. You will still need to back up the file systems on all servers in the farm and back up your SSPs using the native tools. To restore a server farm using scripted backups, the best practice is to first *build* a farm using scripted backups. In a perfect scenario, your production farm is completely built using your farm recovery scripts. This ensures that the scripts can be used to restore the farm in the event of a disaster.

**Note** To script a SharePoint Server 2007 farm installation, you need to thoroughly understand how to use *config.xml* for the binaries installation and *psconfig.exe* for farm provisioning. They are documented at *http://technet.microsoft.com/en-us/library/cc261668.asp* and *http://technet.microsoft.com/en-us/library/cc263093.aspx*, respectively.

Second, you need to use the native tools to back up your SSPs. Third, you will use SQL Server tools to back up your content databases. We have included a sample farm build script on the companion CD with instructions.

## Summary

There is no one content recovery and protection plan that will work for everyone. Instead, we have presented some general best practices and shared some lessons learned. You should take this information and integrate your implementation's specific requirements to design a plan that works. We have never seen a disaster recovery plan work the first time. So, take our advice, and be sure the first time you use your plan isn't when you need it.

## Additional Resources

- *Microsoft Office SharePoint Server 2007 Administrator's Companion* (Microsoft Press, 2007)
- *Microsoft SharePoint Products and Technologies Administrator's Pocket Consultant* (Microsoft Press, 2007)
- Protecting and Recovering Office SharePoint Server 2007: *http://technet.microsoft.com/en-us/library/cc263053.aspx*
- SQL Mirroring with SharePoint Server 2007 white paper: *http://go.microsoft.com/fwlink/?LinkId=83725&clcid=0x409*
- Database Maintenance white paper: *http://go.microsoft.com/fwlink/?LinkId=111531&clcid=0x409*
- SharePoint Server 2007 Storage Recommendations white paper: *http://technet2.microsoft.com/Office/f/?en-us/library/ca472046-7d4a-4f17-92b1-c88a743a5e3c1033.mspx*

Chapter 22

# Upgrading from SharePoint Portal Server 2003 to SharePoint Server 2007

**In this chapter:**



Upgrading from one platform to another is always a chore, but this chore has been made somewhat easier by the development of several migration paths from Microsoft Office SharePoint Portal Server 2003 to Microsoft Office SharePoint Server 2007. These paths provide different ways of migrating information from the old platform to the new. In addition, these paths have significant tradeoffs that we'll discuss; you'll find that no one path will be a perfect solution for you.

In our work with customers, we have found that roughly half of those who migrate don't use any of the three migration methods given to them by the Office SharePoint Server 2007 product team. Instead, they simply stand up a new SharePoint Server 2007 farm and then instruct people on how to copy information from the old platform to the new platform. This is usually due to the customer's dissatisfaction with their current 2003 implementation and the feeling that starting over is less painful than migrating and fixing the mistakes that they made in their Office SharePoint Portal Server 2003 implementation. In addition, SharePoint Server 2007 maps to technical requirements that SharePoint Portal Server 2003 never could. That's why we advise our customers to plan their SharePoint Server 2007 installation first to meet new requirements, then figure out how to migrate the old content into it. Good examples are those organizations that architected SharePoint Portal Server 2003 taxonomies based on their organizational chart and therefore stove-piped their processes. We're finding that many organizations let the old SharePoint Portal Server 2003 site die on the vine due to the pain of moving from a broken design. They leave it up to the users to migrate critical data to the new SharePoint Server 2007 implementation.

Most of the mistakes that customers report to us relate to their URL topology, where information was hosted within their SharePoint Portal Server 2003 implementation, and/or the poor navigation (SharePoint Portal Server 2003 areas) that was developed. Many who implemented SharePoint Portal Server 2003 liked the product and its features, but the vast majority of users with whom we have worked did not like how it was implemented in their environment. Based on this, they have a strong desire to start over in a fresh, new environment.

Unfortunately, all three of the Microsoft migration methods that were developed by the product team retain the information taxonomy that was implemented in SharePoint Portal Server 2003. While site collections and sites can be moved after they are upgraded to SharePoint Server 2007, the sheer number of sites and site collections that might need to be moved can outweigh the benefits of using one of the three migration methods. By contrast, the reason so many customers are selecting the user copy migration method (which is really just engaging the end-users to copy over their information from the SharePoint Portal Server 2003 platform to the SharePoint Server 2007 platform) is because this is often the easiest way in which a clean, new information taxonomy can be implemented in SharePoint Server 2007 while moving over the SharePoint Portal Server 2003 information using the least amount of effort.

In this chapter, we'll discuss the best practices for the three Microsoft migration methods and also include the user copy method that we've seen adopted by customers more often than any of the other three methods. While the user copy method is not a product team–originated method, we feel it is selected often enough by customers that it warrants inclusion in this chapter.

> **Note** Because of the complexities introduced by migrations from one platform to another, this chapter will focus on the upgrade or migration path from SharePoint Portal Server 2003 to SharePoint Server 2007. We will not discuss upgrades from SharePoint Team Services to SharePoint Server 2007, Windows SharePoint Services to SharePoint Server 2007, or SharePoint Portal Server 2001 to SharePoint Server 2007.

> **More Info** For information on how to migrate from Windows SharePoint Services to SharePoint Server 2007, please consult the *Microsoft SharePoint Products and Technologies Administrator's Pocket Consultant* (Microsoft Press, 2007).

# Overview of the Four Migration Methods

There are four approaches to upgrading a SharePoint Portal Server 2003 implementation to SharePoint Server 2007. The same four approaches can be used to upgrade Windows SharePoint Services v2 to Windows SharePoint Services v3. The four upgrade approaches follow:

1. In-place upgrade
2. Gradual upgrade
3. Content database migration
4. User copy

An *in-place upgrade* is used now for testing environments; Microsoft no longer recommends using the in-place upgrade in production environments. A *gradual upgrade* allows finer control of the upgrade process by allowing one or more site collections to be upgraded at a time. Both in-place and gradual upgrades take place on the same hardware used by your SharePoint Portal Server 2003 installation. A *content database migration* allows you to move content to a new farm or new hardware. It also upgrades one content database at a time. The *user copy* method allows you to stand up a new SharePoint Server 2007 farm on new hardware and have the end users copy over their SharePoint Portal Server 2003 content to SharePoint Server 2007.

## In-Place Upgrade

During the in-place upgrade process, the SharePoint Portal Server 2003 implementation is upgraded in real time on the same hardware to SharePoint Server 2007. The SQL content databases are upgraded to a SharePoint Server 2007 platform and, as such, the in-place upgrade is irreversible. This is why it is a best practice to back up your SharePoint Portal Server 2003 farm in case the upgrade goes poorly and you need to restore SharePoint Portal Server 2003.

During the in-place upgrade, original sites are overwritten, so you cannot view the previous versions of the sites after upgrade. You have no way to check the differences between your previous SharePoint Portal Server 2003 Web sites and the new SharePoint Server 2007 Web sites. You have only your memory, documentation, and screenshots for reference.

Originally seen as the best approach for small or single-server environments, the in-place upgrade approach is now recommended only for development, testing, and staging environments in which you need a quick and dirty upgrade. Microsoft does not recommend performing in-place upgrades in production environments because the process may fail for various reasons outside its control; with no easy recovery procedure, it has caused problems for customers.

### Advantages

The in-place upgrade method requires the least amount of administrative effort. Once the pre-upgrade tasks have been completed, all you do is start setup.exe and then order some pizza and soda so you have something to do while the upgrade process runs. In addition, if you want or need to keep your SharePoint Server 2007 farm on the existing hardware on which your SharePoint Portal Server 2003 farm is running, this method will allow you to do this.

Another advantage of the in-place upgrade is that you don't change the URLs for your content. After the upgrade is completed, the SharePoint Server 2007 farm will use the same URLs that your SharePoint Portal Server 2003 farm used.

### Disadvantages

There are three main disadvantages of doing the in-place upgrade. First, because the entire farm is upgraded at the same time, it is offline during the upgrade. For those environments where uptime is required, you may need to consider another alternative. If you have a large farm, the upgrade could take hours. We suggest that administrators plan on an upgrade of 10 GB/hour. So if you have 200 GB of data in your SharePoint Portal Server 2003 farm, it will likely require 20+ hours to conduct an in-place upgrade. This is the second disadvantage of an in-place upgrade: It can take hours to complete.

But what if the upgrade fails for some reason? Well, that leads us to our third disadvantage: There is no roll-back or revert-back process for the in-place upgrade method, so your *only* choice is to cleanse the SharePoint Portal Server 2003 servers of their farm and restore the entire farm before doing another in-place upgrade.

## Gradual Upgrade

During the gradual upgrade approach, the SharePoint Server 2007 and SharePoint Portal Server 2003 platforms are both installed side by side on all servers in the SharePoint Portal Server 2003 farm. Once installed, upgrades occur on a site-collection-by-site-collection basis at the initiation of the administrator.

The gradual upgrade process copies the data from the original content database to a new content database. The data in the new content database is then upgraded. The original data is maintained in the original database until the server administrator explicitly deletes it. As a result, you can easily roll upgraded site collections back to the previous version if necessary.

Only those site collections currently being upgraded are offline. When the upgrade process is complete, the original URLs of the SharePoint Portal Server 2003 sites point to the upgraded version of the SharePoint Server 2007 sites. This way, users can continue using the same URLs they used before the upgrade.

The gradual upgrade method allows administrators to control how many site collections are upgraded at one time. This is a clean, methodical way for large deployments to be upgraded gradually over several weeks or months while continuing to host the sites that have not yet been upgraded.

## Advantages

Probably the biggest advantage of the gradual upgrade process is the granular level of control that you'll enjoy because you'll decide which site collections are upgraded at which time. This allows for a tighter project management plan that defines a training schedule and site customization schedule to coincide with the upgrade schedule. You can determine which groups to upgrade at which time and that they are genuinely ready for the upgrade and ensure that their unique customizations are ready for the upgrade as well.

Because you can upgrade disparate, smaller groups of users at different times, the total number of users affected by any single upgrade action can be controlled and predicted. In addition, the gradual upgrade process does not delete the SharePoint Portal Server 2003 sites, so you can revert the upgrade to the SharePoint Portal Server 2003 platform if needed. Finally, this upgrade method uses existing hardware, so you can achieve economies of scale with your server hardware.

## Disadvantages

Like all things in life, the gradual upgrade process has some disadvantages. First, your hardware needs to be able to run both the SharePoint Portal Server 2003 and the SharePoint Server 2007 platforms at the same time because the gradual upgrade process requires that the SharePoint Server 2007 bits be installed side by side with the SharePoint Portal Server 2003 bits on the same servers.

Second, you'll need to create a set of URLs for the SharePoint Portal Server 2003 content that has not been upgraded to SharePoint Server 2007. The way the upgrade works is that current information sitting in SharePoint Portal Server 2003 that has not been upgraded to SharePoint Server 2007 will need a new, unique URL because the SharePoint Portal Server 2003 URLs will have been assigned to the new Web applications in the SharePoint Server 2007 farm. So, additional DNS work will be required; if you have a large farm with many Web applications, additional URL planning will be needed as well. Figure 22-1 illustrates the upgrade screen in which a new URL is entered for the old SharePoint Portal Server 2003 content.

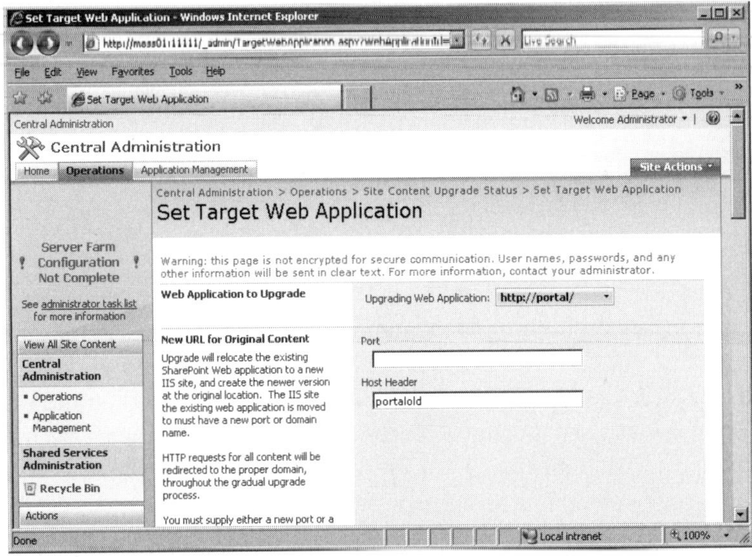


Figure 22-1 Entering a new URL for old, existing content in SharePoint Portal Server 2003

Third, this method is hardware intensive. For pockets of time, you'll have three different database sets in SQL for the same content. Factor in transaction logs, and you can see how SQL will require a lot of extra disk space and memory.

## Content Database Migration

Content database migration is an in-place upgrade performed on a copy of the content databases for an individual Web application. In the content database migration method, all databases for a SharePoint Portal Server 2003 virtual server are copied to the new SQL server (if needed) and added to an existing Web application in SharePoint Server 2007 using Central Administration to attach each one in serial. When you attach the databases to the SharePoint Server 2007 Web application, the upgrade process runs and upgrades the data and the database to the SharePoint Server 2007 platform.

### Advantages

First, this is the only method that allows the SharePoint Server 2007 farm to exist on new hardware while the SharePoint Portal Server 2003 farm continues to exist on the old hardware. Second, content is moved at the Web application level, allowing you to select which databases are moved in which order within a given database set. Third, the SharePoint Portal Server 2003 farm is not affected by content database migration because it uses copies of the SharePoint Portal Server 2003 content databases.

### Disadvantages

First, much more administrative effort is required to use this migration method because you need to build out an entire SharePoint Server 2007 farm from scratch and then ensure that all of the configurations are committed before you can start moving content to the SharePoint Server 2007 farm. In essence, you're building a new farm to which the SharePoint Portal Server 2003 databases will be migrated. Second, you'll lack the granular control that the gradual upgrade method will give you. The level of granularity will be at the database level, not the site collection level.

## User Copy

The user copy method is a manual process in which a new SharePoint Server 2007 farm is created on new hardware and then users are given a window of time to copy their SharePoint Portal Server 2003 information to the SharePoint Server 2007 platform. Usually, this window of time is three to six months.

### Advantages

The largest advantage is that a full migration project is avoided by simply having the users copy data from one location to another. In addition, there is no downtime with this method because no databases or site collections are upgraded. Instead, content is copied from one location to another by the users when they are ready to do so. Finally, you can build a new farm on new hardware and then gradually move the SharePoint Portal Server 2003 content to the SharePoint Server 2007 farm without additional consulting or migration support.

### Disadvantages

The most glaring problem with this migration method is that you're working with and trusting your end-users to move content from one location to another. Because people tend to put off until tomorrow that which isn't causing extreme pain today, there is a high probability that users will wait until the last day or two to move their content. For example, if you give your users 90 days to move their content from SharePoint Portal Server 2003 to SharePoint Server 2007, the chances are good that many will wait until day 89 to start moving their content. So, you'll need a plan to move content from one location to another and a project manager to keep everyone on track. Other than the effort of supporting two platforms for a period of time and assuming that you can work out the people factor of this migration method, we see no other disadvantages to this method.

Table 22-1 outlines the pros and cons of each method.

**Table 22-1 Pros and Cons of Different Migration Methods**

| Upgrade option | Pros | Cons |
|---|---|---|
| In-place | ■ Starts upgrade process automatically after SharePoint Product and Technologies Configuration Wizard begins.<br>■ Uses existing hardware.<br>■ Uses same URLs for upgrade process.<br>■ Easier from administrative perspective. | ■ Entire farm offline during upgrade.<br>■ No ability to easily revert.<br>■ Depending on database size, may take many hours to upgrade farm databases. |
| Gradual | ■ Allows granular control of upgrade process through site collection.<br>■ Reduces time users are affected.<br>■ Can revert to original SharePoint Portal Server 2003 Web sites.<br>■ Uses existing hardware. | ■ Requires SharePoint Server 2007 installation on SharePoint Portal Server 2003 farm.<br>■ Requires redirects for SharePoint Portal Server 2003 URLs during upgrade, which means additional administration effort.<br>■ Because upgrade is performed on same hardware that supports live SharePoint Portal Server 2003 Web sites, performance is affected for users who request pages from the SharePoint Portal Server 2003 Web sites.<br>■ Hardware intensive; requires memory and extra SQL Server storage.<br>■ Takes more time to upgrade SharePoint Portal Server 2003 Web site than when content database migration upgrade option is used. |
| Content database migration | ■ Allows moving to new farm or new hardware.<br>■ Allows Web application by Web application migration to new farm. Although you can upgrade content databases one at a time, you must first migrate the root site for Web application. Thereafter, you can migrate other content databases for Web application in any order. | ■ More complex.<br>■ Granularity in content database.<br>■ Many administrative tasks, manual steps, and high risk of error. |

**Table 22-1 Pros and Cons of Different Migration Methods**

| Upgrade option | Pros | Cons |
|---|---|---|
| Content database migration (*continued*) | ■ SharePoint Portal Server 2003 farm is not affected by upgrade process.<br>■ Better performance than gradual upgrade process. | ■ Requires new farm and double SQL Server storage.<br>■ Some features not upgraded, such as search and customization. |
| User copy | ■ SharePoint Portal Server 2003 farm experiences no downtime.<br>■ Users move content on their schedule.<br>■ Most migration project headaches are avoided. | ■ Users may procrastinate on moving content, which could cause support issues near the end of the migration window. |

Now that we have outlined the basics of the four migration methods, it's time to take a look at the pre-upgrade tasks. Once we have discussed the tasks and best practices that are part of preparing for your migration, we can then discuss the best practices and, frankly, some worst practices that need to be avoided when performing an upgrade from SharePoint Portal Server 2003 to SharePoint Server 2007.

# Pre-upgrade Tasks

A number of pre-upgrade tasks need to be performed before you will be ready to upgrade your SharePoint Portal Server 2003 farm to SharePoint Server 2007. Many of these tasks focus primarily on educating you, the administrator, about the exact state of the farm. You can regard this education as a necessary phase that is similar to seeing your doctor for a physical examination.

Because upgrades never occur in a vacuum, we'll also need to discuss the upgrade of dependent platforms and other software upgrade projects that might need to occur in your organization if you're going to take full advantage of SharePoint Server 2007. Given this, we'll first discuss the upgrade of companion and/or dependent platforms then discuss the pre-upgrade tasks that await you as you migrate from SharePoint Portal Server 2003 to SharePoint Server 2007.

## Upgrading SQL and Office Platforms

SharePoint Server 2007 depends on SQL Server. You can't use Oracle or SAP or any other database vendor for your database solution when implementing SharePoint Server 2007. You must use SQL Server. But in this vein, there are two basic questions that need to be answered.

First, what if you're running Microsoft SQL Server 2005 Express Edition as the database for your SharePoint Server 2007 farm? Well, our considered opinion is that, if you're planning on using any of the three Microsoft upgrade methods, that you first convert your SQL Server

2005 Express database to a full SQL database. The upgrade processes will not work with the Express database, so this database will need to be upgraded.

Second, what if you're running Microsoft SQL Server 2000 and you need to upgrade to SQL Server 2005 or SQL Server 2008? We strongly recommend that you not perform your SQL upgrades at the same time or as part of the same project as your SharePoint Products and Technologies upgrade. Instead, we recommend that the SQL upgrade project be started and finished either before or after the SharePoint Products and Technologies upgrade. If you need the reporting services from SQL 2005 for business intelligence in SharePoint Server 2007, then best practice would be to upgrade your SQL Server first and then upgrade your SharePoint Portal Server 2003 farm.

A second upgrade platform is at the desktop: Many companies are still running Microsoft Office 2003, and many administrators wonder about upgrading to Microsoft Office 2007. The short answer is that you'll want to upgrade to Office 2007 in order to obtain the best return on investment on your SharePoint Server 2007 investment dollars. However, because Office 2007 introduces such radical user interface changes, you'll not want to do the Office 2003 upgrade at the same time as your SharePoint Portal Server 2003 upgrade. In our opinion, that's too many changes at the desktop in too short a period of time. Because SharePoint Server 2007 will work fine with Office 2003 (minus the loss of a few minor features), you can choose the Office 2003 upgrade either before or after the SharePoint Portal Server 2003 upgrade to SharePoint Server 2007.

## SharePoint Tasks

The pre-upgrade tasks are a set of actions that represent best practices that should be performed before you begin your upgrade. Let's discuss each of these tasks now.

First, many reading this chapter will be working with multiple-server farms that need to be upgraded to SharePoint Server 2007. The order in which you upgrade the servers is important. The first server to be upgraded will be a Web front-end (WFE) server in your SharePoint Portal Server 2003 farm. After that, the next server must be the job/index server. Thereafter, any of the servers can be upgraded in any order. Best practice is to ensure that you have specified the order in which all of your SharePoint Portal Server 2003 servers will be upgraded. Of course, this doesn't apply to the content database or user copy methods because both of these methods require a new SharePoint Server 2007 farm on new hardware.

### How to Work Around the Default Web Site

If your medium- or large-server SharePoint Portal Server 2003 farm contains one or more servers that are *not* WFE servers, and you have used the Default Web Site in Internet Information Services (IIS) to host a SharePoint site, the upgrade may fail with a message that the Default Web Site cannot be upgraded. To work around this issue, before running the upgrade on all non-WFE servers, such as the Index server, do the following:

1. Rename the default Web site in IIS to something else.
2. Run the upgrade.
3. Restore the name to Default Web Site.

You do not need to rename the Web site on any WFE servers in the server farm. If you do not rename the Default Web Site in IIS before running upgrade, the upgrade will fail. You can use the following command-line operation to resume the upgrade:

```
psconfig -cmd upgrade -inplace previous versionv -wait -force
```

Second, many of the features in SharePoint Portal Server 2003 were either deprecated or transformed into new features within the SharePoint Server 2007 platform. Understanding how these feature changes occur is important. But for our purposes here, we'll focus on the best practices associated with those feature changes and deprecations.

## Deprecated Features

Features that existed in SharePoint Portal Server 2003 that are no longer in SharePoint Server 2007 include the following:

- The Topic Assistant has been removed, so you can no longer automatically categorize content.
- SPSBackup.exe has been replaced with stsadm.exe, which is the common command-line tool for both Windows SharePoint Services and SharePoint Server 2007.
- Incremental (Inclusive) and Adaptive Update index builds have been deprecated in SharePoint Server 2007.

Features that have been updated or replaced with new features are illustrated in Table 22-2.

Table 22-2 Feature Updates and Changes

| SharePoint Portal Server 2003 feature | SharePoint Server 2007 feature | Comments |
|---|---|---|
| Events list | Calendar view | Has been upgraded with a Year view in the left navigation pane that allows easier navigation between months. |
| Client-side datasheet view engine was Microsoft Office Excel 2003. | Client-side datasheet view engine is Microsoft Office Access 2007. | |
| Dataview Web part (DVWP) | Data Form Web part | The DVWP was created in Microsoft Office FrontPage 2003. The DFWP is created in Microsoft Office SharePoint Designer. |
| N/A | Microsoft Office Outlook 2007 allows for SharePoint lists to be synchronized and taken offline. | Synchronization is now a two-way process. |
| Surveys were single branched. | Surveys include multiple branches. | |
| Areas are used to implement navigation in a SharePoint Portal Server 2003 portal. | Areas are depreciated in Share-Point Server 2007 and upgrade as publishing sites. | Navigation is de-emphasized in SharePoint Server 2007, and no method is given to build a comprehensive navigation scheme. |
| Bucket webbing was implemented in a SharePoint Portal Server 2003 portal for every 20 areas in the portal. | Bucket webbing has been removed. | |
| Portal listings, which are links with metadata in SharePoint Portal Server 2003 | Pages in a publishing site in SharePoint Server 2007, which are pages with metadata that is displayed as content. | |
| Grouped Listing Web Part, used in a SharePoint Portal Server 2003 area to group portal listings | Content Query Web part | |
| Shared Services, optional feature, single provider | Shared Services, required feature, multiple providers | This is one of the most difficult parts to upgrade. Please see the, "Upgrading Shared Services" section later in this chapter for a discussion on upgrading Shared Services. |
| Alerts managed through My Site, Office Outlook and Alerts Summary Web part | Alerts managed through Outlook at the site level | The Alerts Summary Web part has been deprecated. |

Elements that are not upgraded are the following:

- Keywords and Best Bets
- Index files
- Scopes
- Search alerts
- IFilters
- Word breakers
- Thesaurus and noise word files

Based on these changes and deprecations, what are the pre-upgrade tasks that you should perform so that you know your upgrade will be successful? What follows is an expanded answer to this question.

## Perform a Full Exam of Your SharePoint Portal Server 2003 Environment

First, you'll need to thoroughly understand your SharePoint Portal Server 2003 implementation. Most SharePoint Portal Server 2003 administrators are not fully dedicated to administrating their SharePoint Portal Server 2003 environment. Most have 10-15 other platforms that they are responsible to administrate, and SharePoint Portal Server 2003 is just one of the platforms on their radar screen. Document URL topologies, permissions, and other configurations as part of your pre-upgrade effort.

## Decide Which Hardware You Will Use for Your SharePoint Server 2007 Implementation

This is no small matter because the upgrade method you choose will be predicated, in part, on the final hardware platform on which you want SharePoint Server 2007 to run. Table 22-3 outlines your choices relative to the upgrade methods and the effects those choices will have.

**Table 22-3 Upgrade Methods and Hardware Platform Choices**

| Upgrade method | Hardware platform | Effect of choice |
|---|---|---|
| In-place | Stay on same hardware | Will run your SharePoint Server 2007 implementation on the same hardware as your SharePoint Portal Server 2003 implementation. |
| Gradual | Stay on same hardware | Will run your SharePoint Server 2007 implementation on the same hardware as your SharePoint Portal Server 2003 implementation. |

Table 22-3 Upgrade Methods and Hardware Platform Choices

| Upgrade method | Hardware platform | Effect of choice |
|---|---|---|
| Content database | New hardware | Will run your SharePoint Server 2007 implementation on new hardware. |
| User copy | New hardware | Will run your SharePoint Server 2007 implementation on new hardware. |

For the vast majority of upgrade scenarios, we have found that administrators want to run their SharePoint Server 2007 implementation on new hardware. So, for those migration efforts that will use either the gradual or the in-place upgrade method, the SharePoint Portal Server 2003 farm will need to have been moved to the new hardware before the migration to SharePoint Server 2007 is commenced. In our estimation, it is easier to move SharePoint Portal Server 2003 to new hardware than it is to move SharePoint Server 2007 to new hardware. Best practice would be to run either the in-place upgrade or the gradual upgrade on the best hardware possible. To do this will mean moving your SharePoint Portal Server 2003 farm to new hardware first.

## Upgrading from 32-Bit SharePoint Portal Server 2003 to 64-Bit SharePoint Server 2007

If you'll be using either the in-place or gradual upgrade process, then you'll be forced to upgrade to a 32-bit SharePoint Server 2007 platform. You can't install a 64-bit SharePoint Portal Server 2003 version because it doesn't exist. Without a 64-bit version of SharePoint Portal Server 2003, you will be forced to move to a 32-bit version of SharePoint Server 2007, and then upgrade from there to a 64-bit version.

> **Note** If you use either the content database migration or the user copy methods, you'll simply build out your SharePoint Server 2007 64-bit farm and then either copy the databases over to the SharePoint Server 2007 environment or have users copy over their information to the 64-bit platform. These latter two methods are much easier to implement from an administrative-effort perspective.

If your migration plan calls for upgrading to a 64-bit version of SharePoint Server 2007 while using the in-place or gradual upgrade methods, then you'll have to build into your plan an intervening 32-bit SharePoint Server 2007 platform that can be upgraded to 64-bit.

So, how do you do this? Use the following steps.

1. Ensure that your SharePoint Portal Server 2003 servers are fully patched with the latest service packs and hotfixes.

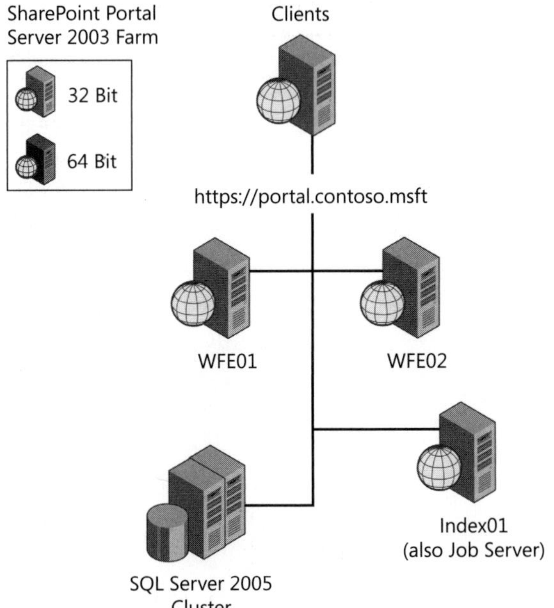


2. Upgrade your SharePoint Portal Server 2003 servers in the correct order. Ensure that your SharePoint Portal Server 2003 farm has been fully upgraded to SharePoint Server 2007 before moving on to step 3.

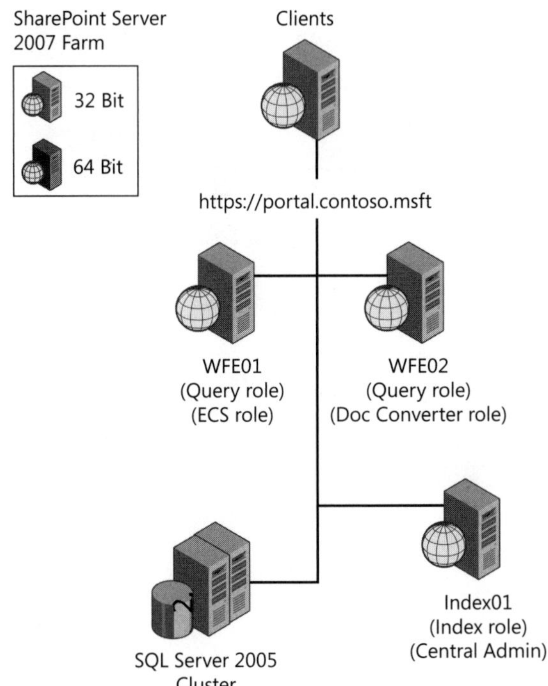

3. Assess and stabilize your SharePoint Server 2007 farm on the 32-bit hardware.
4. Add 64-bit SharePoint Server 2007 servers to your farm. Include those servers in the appropriate roles. Best practice is to move one role as one project. For example, if you have three WFE 32-bit servers, then add three 64-bit servers to your SharePoint Server 2007 farm, temporarily creating six WFE servers. Then deprecate the three 32-bit servers out of your farm, leaving only the three 64-bit servers. Best practice is to ensure that each role in the SharePoint Server 2007 farm has the same hardware platform (32-bit versus 64-bit). You can have different platforms *between* roles, but you should not have different platforms *within* roles.

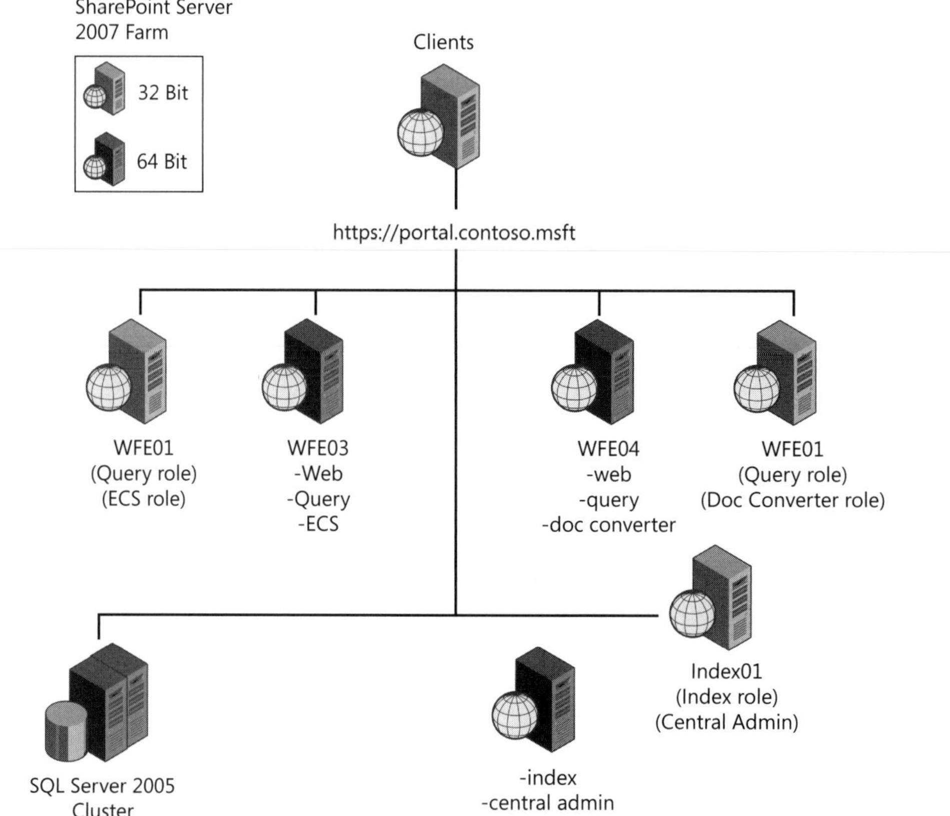


5. After adding the 64-bit servers to each farm role, be sure all of the 32-bit servers have been decommissioned from the farm. Stabilize your farm, and troubleshoot any remaining issues.

When considering the gradual upgrade process, remember that you'll be forced to run on 32-bit hardware during the entire gradual upgrade until the entire set of site collections has been moved over to the SharePoint Server 2007 implementation. Only thereafter will you be able to introduce 64-bit servers into your SharePoint Server 2007 environment.

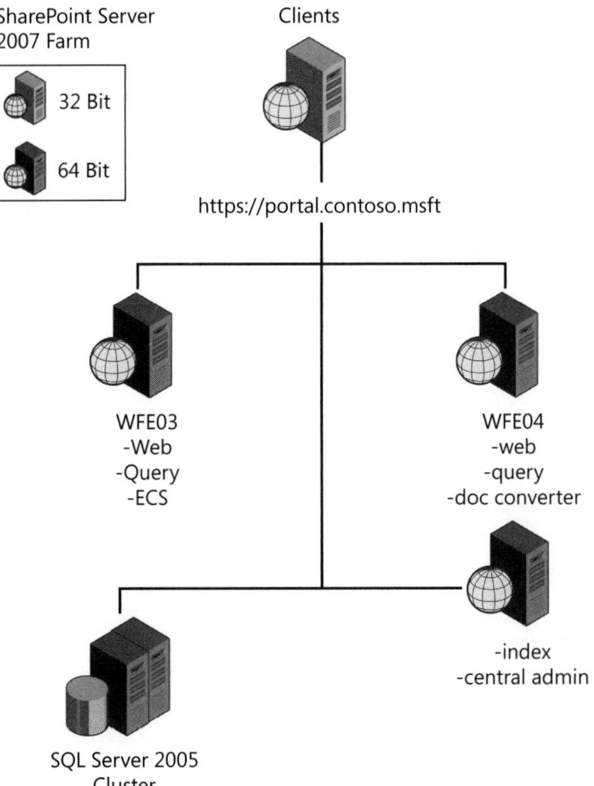


## Do You Need to Redo Your URL Topology in SharePoint Server 2007?

What we're referring to is the answer to the question, "Where does information reside in the farm?" In our experience, the vast majority of our customers did not like their URL topology and found that their first attempt at deciding where information would reside was largely a negative experience. Many were led astray by consultants who seriously didn't know what they were doing. We've run into implementations that placed all of the site collections under the sites managed path in a single portal. Others had not turned on Shared Services (SS) across multiple portals and were now facing the prospect of moving multiple indexes and sets of My Sites to a single Shared Services Provider (SSP). And others had turned users loose with Self-Service Site Creation only to find that site collections were created under the wrong wildcard-managed paths. One customer was even advised to use a single site collection for all of his collaboration activities enterprise-wide.

These and other mistakes about the information architecture occurred because governance rules were not in place and a well-thought-out information architecture was not created. Thus precious little structure existed that could inform users about where information was supposed to reside.

So, what many administrators and business stakeholders want is to leave behind the unstructured misery while moving information to the new SharePoint Server 2007 platform in such a way that everyone in the organization understands where information is supposed to reside and how it is supposed to be managed. Understanding who the content owners are and who makes overriding information architecture decisions is also foundational to not recreating the same taxonomy misery in SharePoint Server 2007.

When considering a migration to SharePoint Server 2007 from SharePoint Portal Server 2003 that requires the movement of data between site collections and, perhaps, Web applications, it is important to note that *all three* of the Microsoft migration methods will migrate your information architecture misery intact. The only migration method that will allow the movement of content from an existing URL topology to a new URL topology will be the user copy method.

Now, it can rightly be argued that after the information is migrated to SharePoint Server 2007, that you can use stsadm –export/-import commands to move sites and site collections around the farm. This is true and is the advertised way to move information. However, we see little reason to place this burden on the administrators and specially trained end-users. It is more efficient, in the long run, to have the users copy the information over to the correct locations and eliminate the movement of information between URLs.

Also, the user copy method provides the highest degree of URL flexibility in the SharePoint Server 2007 farm. All of the other three methods require the use of the old URLs from the SharePoint Portal Server 2003 farm, either at the farm level (in-place and gradual) or at the database level (content database). The user copy method allows you to create an entirely new set of URLs that isn't dependent in any way on the SharePoint Portal Server 2003 implementation. The tedious part might be mapping the old URLs to the new URLs, but this is a small cost compared to redoing your information architecture after the upgrade has been completed.

## Develop a Communication Plan to Inform Users and Management About Migration Activities

No matter which migration method you choose, there will be a need to communicate outages, downtime, training opportunities, and other unforeseen changes in the migration plan. Communication will be necessary to ensure that users and management are not unprepared by both anticipated and unforeseen events.

It might sound silly, but even anticipated, planned-for events can catch key stakeholders off guard because they either didn't record it in their calendars or they "just forgot." Communication can go a long way toward mitigating the negative effects of surprises and help keep everyone moving in the same direction for the migration.

> **More Info** For a fuller discussion about communication plans, please see Chapter 6, "Project Plans for a SharePoint Server 2007 Deployment."

> **Note** There is a sample communications plan poster job aid for you to print out on your large-scale printer. For a free hard copy of this poster, please visit the Premium Content site at *www.mindsharp.com*.

## Understand When and How to Use Prescan.exe

Prescan.exe (Figure 22-2) needs to be run on your databases immediately before each upgrade action to ensure that any problems with your databases are found and fixed before the migration starts. Prescan is a command-line utility that you'll be prompted to run by the upgrade software if you've not already run it on your databases. Especially in the gradual and content database upgrade methods, you'll want to run prescan.exe before each site collection or database is upgraded. If you don't do this, chances are nearly 100 percent that your upgrade will fail.

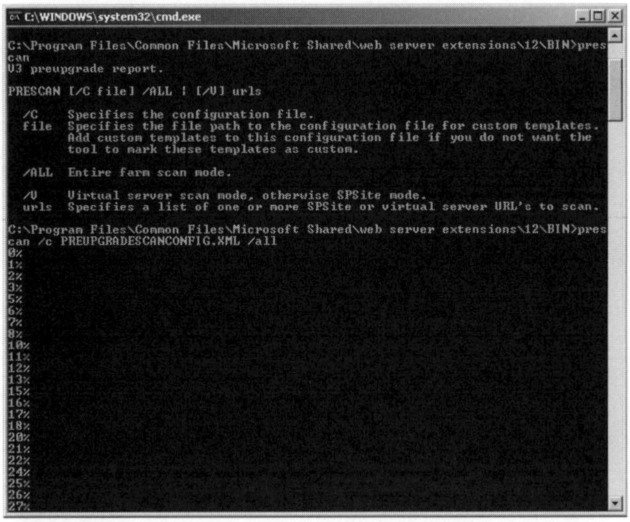

```
C:\WINDOWS\system32\cmd.exe

C:\Program Files\Common Files\Microsoft Shared\web server extensions\12\BIN>pres
can
V3 preupgrade report.

PRESCAN [/C file] /ALL | [/V] urls

  /C    Specifies the configuration file.
  file  Specifies the file path to the configuration file for custom templates.
        Add custom templates to this configuration file if you do not want the
        tool to mark these templates as custom.

  /ALL  Entire farm scan mode.

  /V    Virtual server scan mode, otherwise SPSite mode.
  urls  Specifies a list of one or more SPSite or virtual server URL's to scan.

C:\Program Files\Common Files\Microsoft Shared\web server extensions\12\BIN>pres
can /c PREUPGRADESCANCONFIG.XML /all
0%
1%
2%
3%
5%
6%
7%
8%
10%
11%
12%
13%
15%
16%
17%
18%
20%
21%
22%
24%
25%
26%
27%
```

**Figure 22-2** Prescan command-line tool being run on a SharePoint Portal Server 2003 implementation

> ### Lessons Learned **Run Prescan at the Proper Time**
>
> One customer we worked with had decided to perform a gradual upgrade for his upgrade project. What he didn't realize was that prescan had to be run between the time the SharePoint Server 2007 binaries were installed on the first WFE server and the time the SharePoint Products and Technologies Configuration Wizard was run for the first time. The customer kept receiving configuration error messages from the SharePoint

Products and Technologies Configuration Wizard. Because the error messages were inconsistent across his attempts to upgrade, the customer was sent on wild, unproductive troubleshooting research projects and Internet searches.

This customer thought that prescan could be run at a later date, right before upgrading the first site collection. Running prescan immediately after the binaries were installed on the WFE server resolved the problem, and this customer was able to move forward.

## Ensure Your SharePoint Portal Server 2003 and SQL Backups Are Working

How many times has it been suggested that an administrator first obtain and then test her backups before proceeding with an upgrade of content to a new platform? The answer is more than any of us can count. But we're not kidding. Before you embark on your upgrade plans, you first need to test your SharePoint Portal Server 2003 farm backup and restore procedures as well as your SQL backup and restore procedures. Be sure that you understand how to restore the entire SharePoint Portal Server 2003 farm from scratch so that you can revert back to your SharePoint Portal Server 2003 farm if needed. Because of the way the databases are altered during the in-place and gradual upgrade process, the chances are good that if the process fails at some point, you'll need to restore your SharePoint Portal Server 2003 farm to its original state.

## If You Choose to Perform a Gradual Upgrade, Ensure You Have Enough SQL Disk Space

When you perform a gradual upgrade, the information that is being upgraded during the upgrade process is copied from the SharePoint Portal Server 2003 database into a temporary database and then upgraded within that database. Thereafter, it is copied from the temporary database to the SharePoint Server 2007 database. This means that you'll have three database sets involved in the upgrade of information along with three transaction log sets. Be sure that you have enough SQL disk space to hold the same information in those databases and transaction log sets during the upgrade process.

Figure 22-3 shows the SQL Server database list during a gradual upgrade of a portal and its personal sites. As the portal is upgraded, the following three databases are involved:

- Portal1_site is the SharePoint Portal Server 2003 site content database.
- Portal1_site_pair is the SharePoint Server 2007 content database.
- WSSUP-Temp_<guid> is the temporary database in which the content is being upgraded. This database appears only during the upgrade of content from SharePoint Portal Server 2003 to SharePoint Server 2007. It is deleted automatically by the system when it is not needed and created again by the system when it is needed.

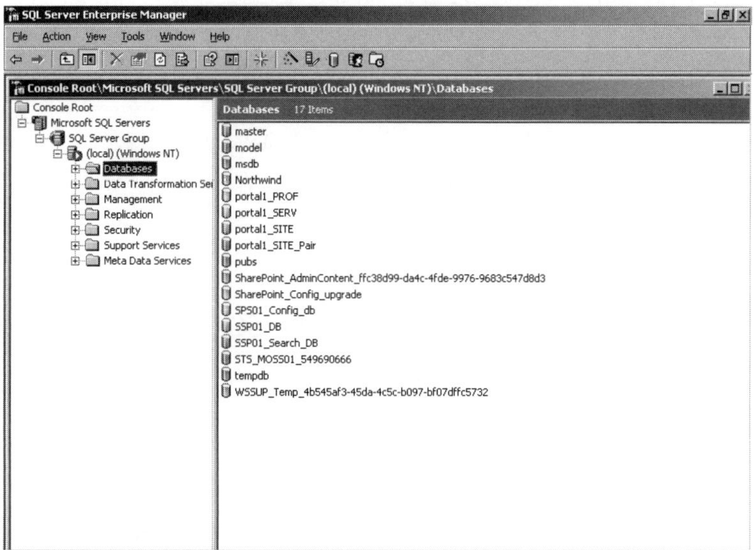


**Figure 22-3** Illustration of the three databases needed during a gradual upgrade of content

## Be Sure that You Have Removed All Orphaned Objects from the SQL Database

An *orphaned object* is an entry in one SQL database table that points to a nonexistent entry in another SQL database table. The most common orphan occurs when there is an entry for a site in the configuration database sites table but no corresponding site entry in the content database sites table. Windows SharePoint Services v2 SP2 contained two fixes to prevent orphans and contains an update to stsadm.exe, which you can use to clean orphans from the database. You may notice that you have orphans if stsadm -o restore fails to restore the site, even with the -overwrite option when you know the URL exists or stsadm -o deletesite fails to delete the site.

> **More Info** To learn more about orphaned objects and how to clean them up, please visit this series of blog articles by Keith Richie, SharePoint MVP; Joel Oleson, SharePoint Product Manager; and our friends at TechNet:
>
> - *http://blogs.msdn.com/krichie/archive/2005/10/25/484889.aspx*
> - *http://blogs.msdn.com/krichie/archive/2005/10/31/487365.aspx*
> - *http://blogs.msdn.com/krichie/archive/2006/06/30/652453.aspx*
> - *http://blogs.msdn.com/joelo/archive/2006/06/23/644954.aspx*
> - *http://blogs.msdn.com/joelo/archive/2006/07/12/663629.aspx*
> - *http://support.microsoft.com/kb/918744/*

## Increase the Web Site and ASP.NET Timeout Settings

The upgrade process will heavily tax your processor, memory, and hard disk subsystems. Some long-running processes could fail if the default Web site and ASP.NET timeouts are left unchanged. In order to avoid this, we suggest that you increase the Web sites' connection time-out on the Web Site tab to 65,000 seconds. In addition, you should increase the ASP.NET runtime timeout. This can be specified at the machine, site, application, and subdirectory levels, which is found after the <httpRuntime> element in your machine.config or web.config files.

> **More Info** For more information about timeouts, refer to *http://msdn.microsoft.com/library/en-us/cpgenref/html/gngrfHttpRuntimeSection.asp*.

## Plan for Broken Links

When we talk about broken links, we're referring to links that are embedded within a document that link to another URL location with your current SharePoint Portal Server 2003 farm. Most, if not all, of these links will be broken when you upgrade SharePoint Portal Server 2003 to SharePoint Server 2007. They will definitely be broken if you use the user copy method. In our experience of working with customers who are upgrading, nearly all report that their users must manually edit each document and redo the link(s) within each document.

For those who have a high number of links embedded within their documents, this could represent a significant effort on the part of the users. Best practice is to plan for it and train your users on how to perform this action. You might have to put up with some complaining and push back. But coding a script to find all of the links and redoing them within the documents after they have been moved to SharePoint Server 2007 would be difficult and time consuming. Consider this one of the pain points of a SharePoint Portal Server 2003 to SharePoint Server 2007 migration. There isn't much else you can do.

## Increase the SQL Transaction Log File Size

The default setting for increasing a transaction log file size in SQL is 10 percent. It is best practice that you change this setting during the upgrade process. Specifically, it is best practice to minimize the growth of the transaction log by setting the database(s) to use the simple recovery method and then to increase the growth of the transaction log by 100–500 MB, not by a percentage. What we have seen in the field is that those who leave this setting at a percentage find that, as the transaction log file size grows, the time required to increase the log file size lengthens. Some have experienced timeout errors because the increase of the transaction log took longer than the timeout limits in IIS. Increasing the IIS timeout settings will help, but changing the increase method to a set number of megabytes will ensure that the transaction log increase will not take longer than your timeout settings. Using the simple recovery method will write the data to the databases immediately after they have been committed to the transaction log. Sections of the transaction log will be re-used once the committed transactions are written to the database. Remember that the simple recovery method limits your restore of the database to the last backup of the database. After the upgrade process is completed, be sure to reset the values to the defaults or to other values that you have determined are best for your SQL and SharePoint environment.

# Upgrading Customizations

In theory, this section actually discusses a pre-upgrade task that needs to be performed, but because of the importance of this topic coupled with the various decision points, we decided to address this topic in its own major section of the chapter.

During the SharePoint Portal Server 2003 time frame, different voices in the marketplace questioned whether customize SharePoint Portal Server 2003 and, if so, how to do it. Some were vocal about never customizing anything in SharePoint Portal Server 2003 or its sites; if any customizations were to be done, they should be accomplished through the modification of site definitions and never through the use of Office FrontPage 2003. At the other end of the spectrum were those who argued that FrontPage 2003 was there for a reason and that we should not be afraid to use it. So, go ahead and customize your pages, customize your sites, and build all of the functionality you wish to have built into the site. Worry later about how that site will upgrade, and enjoy your customizations today. Well, later is now. And for those of you who have customized your sites, you now need to face some facts about customization upgrades. Unfortunately, for those who executed extensive customizations that will need to persist to the SharePoint Server 2007 platform, you have extra work ahead of you.

First, the underlying site definitions have dramatically changed in architecture and form between SharePoint Portal Server 2003 and SharePoint Server 2007. This means that whether customizations were done at the page level or at the site definition level, they will need to be redone in the SharePoint Server 2007 platform. Second, customizations performed in FrontPage 2003 (or any HTML editor) will have unghosted the page. No matter how you try, those customizations will need to be redone in SharePoint Server 2007.

> **Note** For customizations that need to be applied farm-wide, you'll use Microsoft Visual Studio.NET to create features and then wrap them up into solution deployments so the customization can be applied farm-wide. For one-off customizations at the site collection level, you can use either Visual Studio .NET or SharePoint Designer 2007.

Third, customizations committed in SharePoint Portal Server 2003 will migrate and will operate in SharePoint Server 2007, but they will be SharePoint Portal Server 2003 customizations operating in a SharePoint Server 2007 world. This means that the pages will lack the SharePoint Server 2007 features, such as a Recycle Bin, security trimming, and other SharePoint Server 2007 site and page features. In short, you'll have a 2003 page operating in a 2007 world.

Finally, any pages and sites that have not been customized will upgrade just fine to SharePoint Server 2007 and will gain the 2007 feature sets as well, such as security trimming, the global navigation bar, and the Recycle Bin. Pages that are reghosted will also migrate to the 2007 platform without any problem.

What you need to understand is that whatever customizations you did in SharePoint Portal Server 2003 will need to be redone in SharePoint Server 2007. The question is not *if* you'll re-code the customizations, but *how* and *when*. Essentially, your choices are as follows:

- Reset (reghost) your SharePoint Portal Server 2003 pages to default, then upgrade and re-customize as needed.
- Leave your SharePoint Portal Server 2003 pages customized, write new features and site definitions in the SharePoint Server 2007 platform, map those site definitions and features to the customized pages and lists in SharePoint Portal Server 2003, then upgrade and troubleshoot as needed.
- Upgrade your SharePoint Portal Server 2003 pages to SharePoint Server 2007, understanding that they will be "v2 pages in a v3 world," then re-customize the pages as needed.

What we *don't* have that everyone wishes we *did* have is a method to take all the customizations and upgrade them from SharePoint Portal Server 2003 to SharePoint Server 2007 without having to do any customization work. That scenario is not in the code. Customizations are just that: pages that have been customized to fit your individual needs.

In order to reduce your SharePoint Server 2007 customization workload, we believe that it is a best practice to take your custom Web parts and test them in the ASP.NET 2.0 environment. Most Web parts developed in Windows SharePoint Services v2 will work in SharePoint Server 2007 environments, with the following exceptions:

- If your developers used the ASP.NET 1.1 obfuscation tools on the assemblies for the Web parts, they'll need to be re-coded for ASP.NET 2.0 or 3.0.
- If the Web parts used API calls that are removed from Windows SharePoint Services v3, they will need to be recoded.
- If the Web parts used features that Microsoft has deprecated, they will need to be re-coded. This is more likely to be true if your Web part called the SharePoint Server 2003 Object Model.

Your developers will need to learn and understand how functionality is implemented in SharePoint Server 2007 using features. SharePoint Portal Server 2003 customizations will need to be mapped to SharePoint Server 2007 features if you plan to upgrade those features. What we have found is that, for most organizations, most customizations were not needed or were frivolous, leading them to reset their pages to default in SharePoint Portal Server 2003 before performing their upgrade.

Some organizations that wrote extensive applications on top of SharePoint Portal Server 2003 are not attempting to migrate or upgrade. They are simply re-coding the application in SharePoint Server 2007 and then connecting back to their data sources to complete their application customization efforts.

## Post-upgrade Tasks

After your upgrade has been completed, you will want to perform several post-upgrade tasks. These tasks are best practices.

First, if you've upgraded to 32-bit hardware and now need to move to 64-bit hardware, then refer to the earlier section, "Decide Which Hardware You Will Use for Your SharePoint Server 2007 Implementation," and visit the Lessons Learned sidebar on moving your farm from 32-bit to 64-bit hardware.

Second, you'll need to plan for your decommissioning of the SharePoint Portal Server 2003 servers. It is best practice, if possible, to leave your SharePoint Portal Server 2003 farm running in a read-only mode for a defined period of time–usually three to six months–before pulling it down entirely. You can leave this farm up and running if you're using the content database or user copy methods. The other two methods will not expose your SharePoint Portal Server 2003 farm after the upgrade has been completed.

For the gradual upgrade method, be sure to uninstall SharePoint Portal Server 2003 only after you have finalized the upgrade in the SharePoint Server 2007 Central Administration interface. Finalizing the upgrade should be a planned event and not one to be executed lightly because it is a *one-way, one-time, no-revert* action. Once you have elected to finalize the upgrade, the door is permanently shut on reverting any site collections to the SharePoint Portal Server 2003 platform, and keeping SharePoint Portal Server 2003 running on your servers is a waste of resources. Be sure your project plan specifies who will execute the finalize upgrade action and the milestones that must be met before this action is committed.

## Upgrading Shared Services

This is perhaps the most thorny and difficult part of any upgrade because of how the upgrade code is written to perform regarding SS. So we'll be straightforward and tell you that, in most circumstances, we believe it is a best practice to create a new SSP in SharePoint Server 2007 and then reassociate your portals in 2003 with the new SSP. In order to understand our best practice recommendation, it's important to first understand the differences and similarities in how SS is implemented between the two platforms and then understand how the product team was forced to write the upgrade code.

## Shared Services in SharePoint Portal Server 2003

In SharePoint Portal Server 2003, SS was an optional configuration that could be implemented if the need was perceived to exist by the farm administrator. Multiple portals were not needed to implement SS, but multiple portals were often the case for making this choice so that users would experience the same index, My Sites, audiences, and user profiles across all the portals.

What made this choice optional in SharePoint Portal Server 2003 was that each portal had its own index, My Site location, audiences, and user profiles at the time the portal was created. So, in a single portal implementation, there was little motivation to implement SS, even if the existing portal was selected as the SS portal. Doing this was like deciding to eat at a local restaurant after you had already finished your meal there. It was a redundant decision that was often perceived as unnecessary.

As a result, many SharePoint Portal Server 2003 implementations created multiple portals without configured SS. In these environments, the portals each had their own index, My Sites, audiences, and user profiles. In most cases, this redundancy was designed into obscurity because users were instructed to consume these services from a single, designated portal. Other portals were implemented for different purposes, and the My Site link was removed and/or users were instructed only to perform certain actions within that portal. In many cases, it worked just fine.

Among several drawbacks to the SharePoint Portal Server 2003 SS topology was that you couldn't have more than one SSP. Once you designated an SS portal, the other portals in the farm consumed those services from the SS portal. Any virtual servers that were not configured as portals did not participate in the SS either, leading to an inconsistent user experience. If you did need (what we would call today) multiple, disparate SS, you left SS turned off and then used different designated portals as your different SSP. Unfortunately, this randomization of SS across multiple portals was neither flexible nor scalable if you had a number of virtual servers that were configured with team sites. None of them had access to any of the portal SS, even if they were connected to one of the portals.

When SharePoint Server 2007 was developed, it was decided that, in order to obtain SS, the farm administrator would need to create a designated SSP. This SSP would then serve out the SS that the farm needed. But they also went one step further and allowed the farm to host multiple SSPs. When portals are created in SharePoint Server 2007, they have no capacity to act as their own SSP, unlike the portals in SharePoint Portal Server 2003. In other words, portals in SharePoint Server 2007 do not have a built-in index, My Site provider, audiences, or user profiles. These and other SharePoint Server 2007 SS must be provided by and consumed from a designated SSP. Consumption is by association at the Web application layer, leading the farm administrator to decide which Web applications will consume which SSP's services.

By default, when a SharePoint Portal Server 2003 portal in a non-SS environment is upgraded to SharePoint Server 2007, the upgrade code realizes that this is not only a portal, but also, in a pragmatic sense, its own SSP. So the code creates an SSP for this portal in SharePoint Server 2007 and then embeds the SSP inside the portal in the http://<portal_name>/ssp/admin location (Figure 22-4). If you look at the upgraded portal's association, you'll find that the same Web application was created for both the portal and the SSP and the portal is associated with itself (Figure 22-5). Obviously, you can change the portal's association to another SSP, but then you'll need to move the My Sites as well to the SharePoint Server 2007 My Site location.

Unfortunately, you will end up reconfiguring several Shared Service elements after an upgrade. For example, the scopes in SharePoint Portal Server 2003 are tied to the content sources; in SharePoint Server 2007, they are not. So even though the scopes will upgrade from SharePoint Portal Server 2003 to SharePoint Server 2007, the chances are good that you'll end up deleting the upgraded SharePoint Portal Server 2003 scopes and creating a new set of SharePoint Server 2007 scopes.

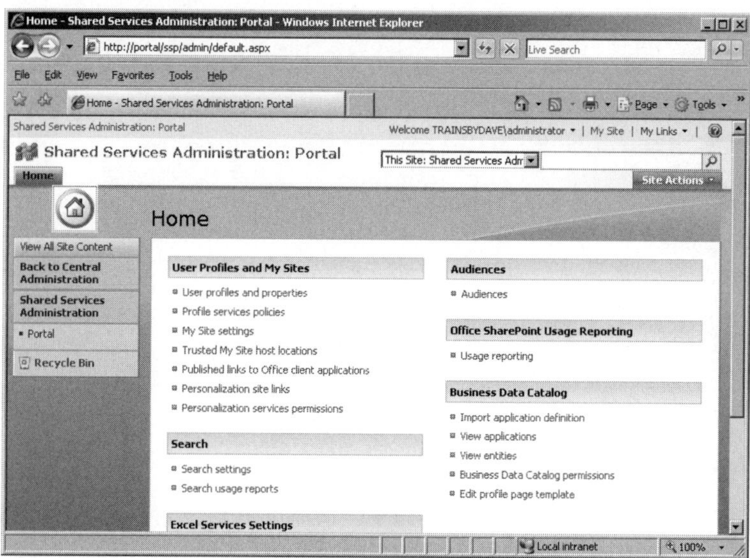


**Figure 22-4** SSP embedded inside the upgraded portal

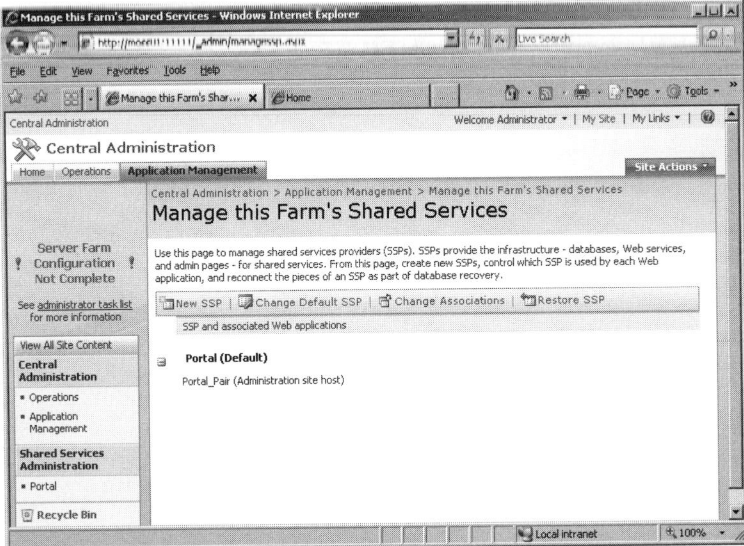


**Figure 22-5** Shared Services Administration page showing that the portal is associated with itself for SS

Another example is the index. The index doesn't upgrade and neither do the content sources. So after the upgrade of your SS portal, you'll still be in the position of having to re-create and re-crawl your content sources.

Hence, in light of what *doesn't* upgrade for an SS portal coupled with the extra work that you'll have to perform on an upgraded SS portal, perhaps you can now understand why our best practice recommendation is to create a new SSP and associate your upgraded Web applications with that new SSP.

> **Notes from the Field Upgrading an SS Portal when Using the Content Database Migration Method**
>
> If you need to upgrade an SS portal using the content database migration method, one customer we worked with was able to successfully perform this migration using the following steps.
>
> First, the customer restored a database backup of the three databases that made up the SS portal onto a SQL Server 2005 box. The customer was running SQL 2000 in production at the time of this restore and experienced no issues.
>
> Second, the customer restored the SharePoint Portal Server 2003 portal into an SP03 test environment. This resulted in repeated messages that the database was too old to join this sharepoint cluster, which was confusing because both the production environment and the test environment were both running SP2 for SharePoint Portal Server 2003. What the customer had failed to remember was that an additional patch had been

applied to the production SharePoint Portal Server 2003 environment for the changes to Daylight Savings Time early in 2007. The customer learned that, unless the SharePoint Portal Server 2003 platform versions match *exactly*, it is not possible to restore a SharePoint Portal Server 2003 portal across farms.

Third, the customer ran prescan.exe on the portal in the test environment. Prescan found nothing unusual even though there were 48 unghosted pages, but all of those were in the same site.

Fourth, in the SharePoint Server 2007 environment, the customer ran the stsadm –addcontentdb with the SITE database to an existing Web application. This action was successful and essentially imported the portal into SharePoint Server 2007.

Fifth, in the SharePoint Server 2007 environment, the customer ran the stsadm –addtossp command with the PROF database following the syntax that was referenced in the article at *http://technet2.microsoft.com/Office/en-us/library/5beaaf55-b77c-442d-88f5-eb9672f82e661033.mspx?mfr=true*. The –mysiteurl parameter was dropped because MySites were not hosted in a separate environment but were instead in the personal managed path at the parent portal. Running this command was successful.

Finally, the customer went into the SS configuration in SharePoint Server 2007 to the SSP that had been created by upgrading the SS portal from SharePoint Portal Server 2003. It had retained the customer's custom Active Directory profile import information, audiences, and user profiles. The customer completed the path to tell the SSP how to get to the upgraded My Sites, and that was how it worked. As expected, the search environment needed to be configured.

*Bill English, Microsoft MVP, Mindsharp*

If you have a large number of audiences and/or user profiles, you can use the database migration approach to bring those profiles over to your new SSP in SharePoint Server 2007. After that, you'll have to redo most of your SS customizations anyway, so performing them in a new SSP is our recommended best practice.

# Combining Migration Methods

We've seen several customers who needed their IT staff to take charge of a portion of the overall migration while allowing users to copy information over for their own sites, too. This most often happens when there is a well-established portal (or set of portals) that needs to be brought over to the SharePoint Server 2007 environment in a single effort—usually over a weekend.

The expectation isn't that IT will migrate everything from SharePoint Portal Server 2003 to SharePoint Server 2007, but that it will take charge of the migration of certain datasets, usually widely consumed portals or team sites. The rest of the content is left to the user to copy over within a prescribed time period.

Other than the in-place upgrade, you can actually combine the gradual, content database, and user copy methods to create a more customized migration approach. For example, those site collections with unique customizations can be routed through the gradual approach to ensure that the pages look, feel, and function as expected after the migration. Other site collections in other databases could be moved over and attached to new Web applications in SharePoint Server 2007 without doing harm to your gradual migration approach. You'll simply have to keep note of which information has been moved by which method because a database move will not be noticed by the gradual upgrade software. Finally, the content in some site collections or even entire database sets for a Web application can be moved by users if the scenario details will allow it.

Which approach you use will depend on a plethora of factors that need to be placed into a matrix, weighted, and then used as raw data for a final decision.

## Upgrading Between Active Directory Forests

We decided to include a section on this topic because it is frequently addressed in our contact with customers. Right now, we know of at least three implementations that need to move content from a SharePoint Portal Server 2003 farm that resides in one Active Directory forest to a SharePoint Server 2007 farm that will reside in a different Active Directory forest.

To be honest, SharePoint Products and Technologies doesn't upgrade well at all when it is moved between forests. While recent patches from Microsoft have given SharePoint Server 2007 the ability to recognize the SID History attribute in a migrated user account, the reality is that there isn't a clean way to do this.

At the time of this writing, we know that Microsoft is working on a solution with four different customers but has not released any tools or recommended best practices on this topic.

There is an stsadm –o migrateuser command that you can work with to migrate user accounts from one farm in one Active Directory to another farm in another Active Directory, but for many whose farms are heavily populated with users and content, such a manual process doesn't seem realistic. Look for third-party products to help fill this gap in the coming months.

In the absence of any tools from Microsoft or third-party providers, the user copy method might make the most sense for many who need to perform this type of migration. If that isn't a possibility for you, the only remaining option is to set up a trust relationship between the two forests and then use one of the migration methods to move over the content. Thereafter, the site administrators will need to manually add the correct accounts into their sites and site collections using the new forest's accounts. After a window of time, the trust relationship can be broken and the old accounts removed. Before breaking the trust relationship, be sure the old accounts are removed.

# When to Use the Different Upgrade Methods

As we've learned, each upgrade method has its own advantages and disadvantages. In theory, most would love to simply run a script and find that their entire SharePoint Portal Server 2003 farm was suddenly sitting on a 64-bit SharePoint Server 2007 platform, with all of the customizations upgraded and all of the content in the right locations. But alas, no such script exists. So, in Table 22-4, you will find a way to understand and think about the tradeoffs that are inherent with each upgrade method. Decision points are detailed for you, too.

> **Note** If needed, you can obtain a poster of this table at the Premium Content site of Mindsharp, at *www.mindsharp.com*.

**Table 22-4 Decision Tradeoffs Between the Four Migration Methods**

| Requirement | In-place upgrade | Gradual upgrade | Content database migration | User copy method |
|---|---|---|---|---|
| Need to run SharePoint Server 2007 on 64-bit hardware. | Must upgrade to 32-bit hardware, then leapfrog to 64-bit hardware. | Must upgrade to 32-bit hardware, then leapfrog to 64-bit hardware. | Build out 64-bit environment on new hardware and then attach databases. | Build out new 64-bit farm and have users move information as needed. |
| Need to create a new URL topology in the SharePoint Server 2007 farm. | Will retain the old URL topology. Use stsadm –export /-import to move content around the SharePoint Server 2007 farm. | Will retain the old URL topology. Use stsadm –export /-import to move content around the SharePoint Server 2007 farm. | Will retain the old URL topology. Use stsadm –export /-import to move content around the SharePoint Server 2007 farm. | Will allow users to move content to new locations in the SharePoint Server 2007 farm. Dependence on old URLs is eliminated. |
| Cannot experience farm downtime. | Do not select this upgrade method if you cannot bring your farm entirely down. | Site collections being upgraded will be down for the duration of the upgrade. Outages can be planned and communicated. | Databases will be offline during the migration. Depending on the size of the database, users may experience longer-than-wanted downtimes. | Neither farm will experience any downtime using the user copy method. |

**Table 22-4 Decision Tradeoffs Between the Four Migration Methods**

| Requirement | In-place upgrade | Gradual upgrade | Content database migration | User copy method |
|---|---|---|---|---|
| Must experience the least amount of downtime as possible. | Will bring your entire farm down for the duration of the upgrade. | Will take upgrading site collections offline. All other farm services remain up during the upgrade process. | Will take all site collections offline while the database set is upgraded. | There is no downtime with the user copy method. |
| IT needs to upgrade some content while allowing users to copy over other content. | Will not work in a combined-method solution. | Will work with the combined user copy method, but you'll need to document which content will be moved by which method. | Works well with the combined user copy method because the content to be moved by IT using this method can be clearly defined at the database level. | The user copy methods works with the gradual upgrade method but is better with the content database method. |
| We need our customizations to work in the new site collections at the time they are upgraded. | Will work only if *all* of the customizations in SharePoint Portal Server 2003 are mapped to features and site definitions in SharePoint Server 2007. | Is best suited to accomplish this purpose because the site collections can be upgraded on a scheduled basis. | Will work only if the features and site definitions are in place in the SharePoint Server 2007 platform to accept the customizations in the databases as they are upgraded. | Will require significant workflow and coordination to ensure that customizations are present when users copy their information into the SharePoint Server 2007 platform. |
| We need users trained at the time they start to work with the new technology in SharePoint Server 2007 | Will require that everyone be trained (or have access to training) when the farm is migrated. The larger the number of users, the less training that can be accomplished on a per-user basis before the migration is executed. | Is ideal for mapping the timing of content upgrades and user education classes. | Can be mapped to the timing of user education classes, but the number of users will usually be rather large for a given database set. | Will require significant workflow and project management to map the timing of the user education with their efforts to copy information into the SharePoint Server 2007 environment. |

Table 22-4 Decision Tradeoffs Between the Four Migration Methods

| Requirement | In-place upgrade | Gradual upgrade | Content database migration | User copy method |
|---|---|---|---|---|
| We need to migrate several farms (Windows SharePoint Services and SharePoint Portal Server 2003) into a single SharePoint Server 2007 farm. | Will retain the current farm topology and will do nothing to help coalesce multiple farms into a single farm environment. | Will retain the current farm topology and will do nothing to help coalesce multiple farms into a single farm topology. | Will allow you to coalesce multiple farms into a single farm by simply attaching the databases from multiple farms to a single farm's set of Web applications. | Is ideally suited for bringing multiple farms into a single farm topology. |
| We need to migrate our farm from SharePoint Portal Server 2003 to SharePoint Server 2007 while also migrating user accounts from one domain to another. | Will not achieve this goal. | Will not achieve this goal. | Will move content between farms and, assuming the Web applications are secured correctly, will move the content into the new farm and Active Directory. | Is ideally suited to achieve this goal, when worked in conjunction with other upgrade efforts, such as customization and training schedules. |

# Summary

In this chapter, we have outlined the existing best practices concerning upgrades from SharePoint Portal Server 2003 to SharePoint Server 2007 and have presented our views in various areas. What we have not tried to do is outline how to perform the upgrades because considerable information on these procedures already exists in the marketplace. Instead, we have suggested the best practices in order to achieve a successful upgrade while outlining the pros and cons of each upgrade method.

# Additional Resources

- Migration and Upgrade Resource Center: *http://msdn.microsoft.com/en-us/office/aa905505.aspx*
- Migration and Upgrade Information for SharePoint Server 2007: *http://technet.microsoft.com/en-us/office/sharepointserver/bb421259.aspx*

Chapter 23

# Capacity Planning and Performance Monitoring

**In this chapter:**



The topics of capacity planning and performance monitoring are presented together because much of the foundation is the same. Performance counters that are used for testing a farm's capacity are also used to monitor the performance of the farm. In fact, some of the capacity planning metrics will help define the baseline used for performance monitoring. For example, we will show you how to test the capacity of your farm for Web requests using performance counters. We will then use those performance tests results to define the baseline for monitoring those servers for adequate performance. When possible, the correlation between counters used for capacity planning and performance monitoring will be detailed. In this chapter, you will be presented with best practices for the following:

- Hardware and software boundaries
- Planning using System Center Capacity Planner 2007
- Testing using Visual Studio 2008
- Monitoring using System Center Operations Manager 2007

Covering the technical details of each area is not possible in a *Best Practices* book, nor do we want to repeat what is already publicly available on the Web or in other Microsoft Press books. When necessary, you will be directed to the appropriate documentation for more information. Because every environment is different, this chapter will outline the high-level best practices for planning and monitoring. There will be some farm topology examples, but these are primarily used for examples on how to use available tools and not necessarily best practices on farm topologies.

## Capacity Planning

We are often asked, "For *n* number of users, how many servers do I need?" The question really isn't that simple and cannot be reduced to a one-sentence answer. Many factors affect a given server farm configuration's ability to serve content and applications, and planning for a large deployment can be a very complex undertaking. There are five primary factors that affect a Microsoft Office SharePoint Server 2007 server farm's performance, and it is important to understand the relationship between them.

- Software configuration
- Customization
- Server and network hardware
- User load
- Traffic profiles

For a properly tuned Office SharePoint Server 2007 server farm, you *must* take all five areas of performance into account. Your software configuration greatly affects the load on your server and network hardware. The more customization of the native software, the greater your hardware needs will be. And the less substantial your hardware is, the better configured and less customized your solution must be. Finally, you need to understand how much traffic your solution will generate and what the traffic mix will be, such as reads, writes, and publishing actions. It is almost impossible to know what that mix will be in the beginning, so a best practice is monitoring your usage and refining your infrastructure as needed.

## Software Configuration

Installing a well-running SharePoint Server 2007 server farm isn't as simple as just installing the software. SharePoint Server 2007 depends upon and requires a properly installed Windows Server 2003 or 2008 operating system. If you do not follow the best practices when installing the operating system, your attempts to fine-tune your SharePoint Server 2007 installation could be negated. For example, incorrectly configuring networking, Internet Information Services (IIS), or disk management could drastically reduce the performance of SharePoint Server 2007. Likewise, most of SharePoint Server 2007 content is contained in SQL Server databases. A poorly configured and maintained SQL Server instance reduces the effectiveness of your SharePoint Server 2007 installation. Be sure to address all of the foundational software requirements for SharePoint Server 2007 before attempting to plan for capacity and performance.

Additionally, you must correctly configure SharePoint Server 2007 and all of its components. Reference the online TechNet and MSDN content for correctly planning and configuring a SharePoint Server 2007 server farm. Incorrectly configuring many options, such as diagnostic logging, can greatly reduce the ability of your server farm to render content to users. Many times, poorly running server farms are the result of incorrect application configuration and not inadequate hardware. The best way to prevent a poorly designed farm is through adequate administrator, developer, power user, and end-user training in each of their respective areas. To concretize why training is a best practice, consider the following four examples:

- **Administrator** If a SharePoint Server 2007 farm administrator did not understand the implications of logging all events to the trace logs as Verbose, while also logging all event logs as Information, your server farm would perform poorly. Configuration changes such as this are hard to find and troubleshoot because they are not technically incorrect, but affect server farm performance.
- **Developer** If a SharePoint Server 2007 developer wrote a custom Web part that queried a data source real-time and displayed the results for every user, this would adversely affect page rendering. It is equally important that the developer profile her solution to fully understand the impact to the farm as a whole, i.e., SQL Server, WFE servers, third-party content source.
- **Site Collection Administrator** A site collection administrator creates 3,000 subsites to support a project. Because SharePoint Server 2007 performs very poorly with more than 2,000 subsites, the performance of these sites would drop substantially.
- **End User** A list and library best practice is having no more than 2,000 items in a view or folder. If a user were to upload more than 2,000 items in a single view, the list performance could be reduced by as much as 100 times!

Proper training, in conjunction with creating, maintaining, and monitoring your baseline configuration, is critical to the long-term success of your SharePoint Server 2007 implementation.

> **Note** The 2,000-item limitation, at a given level, applies universally to SharePoint Products and Technologies. You can download an in-depth white paper at *http://technet2.microsoft.com/Office/en-us/library/6f03049f-5bfe-4807-b609-0e2d4a9ec3b51033.mspx* for more information. There are exceptions, such as targeted programmatic access, and these are detailed in the white paper.

## Customization

The level of application customization is usually proportional to the level of hardware required for your server farm. If you are not intimately familiar with the nuances of SharePoint Server 2007 customization, you should probably not customize in the beginning. Instead, investigate and use the native features to meet your requirements. We have seen many heavily customized SharePoint Server 2007 installations where much of the custom coding could have been accomplished through native functionality.

Customization isn't just about writing custom Web parts, it may also be adding native Web parts such as the Content Query Web Part (CQWP) or Content Editor Web Part (CEWP). While the Web parts themselves will not affect server performance, the connections they make could substantially change server load and page rendering. For example, if you are querying a third-party data source using the CQWP and the connection is very slow, the resulting page rendering time might be quite long. No amount of additional SharePoint Server 2007 server hardware will fix this issue; only addressing the query content source bottleneck will improve page performance. Likewise, poorly developed and poorly conceptualized Web parts will adversely affect server performance. Always check custom Web parts in a test environment using Visual Studio 2008 Team Suite before production deployment.

## Server and Network Hardware

Because SharePoint Server 2007 is a network-dependent application, your network infrastructure is critical to performance. Adequate wire speed for Intra-farm servers, switching, and hardware load-balancing are examples of components critical to most SharePoint Server 2007 installations.

> **More Info** Refer to TechNet for the latest in recommended and minimum server configurations: *http://technet2.microsoft.com/Office/en-us/library/4d88c402-24f2-449b-86a6-6e7afcfec0cd1033.mspx*

Be sure you have used at least the recommended hardware configurations for farm servers. Be aware that if you merely meet the minimum requirements, you may not be able to implement all of the features included with SharePoint Server 2007. The less substantial your hardware devices, whether server or network, the more carefully you must design, configure, and monitor your SharePoint Server 2007 server farm. Essentially, the less you plan, the more you buy. This might be perfectly acceptable in some instances. A real-world example is a custom Web part that doesn't perform well, but it would take 200 hours for a developer to re-code. If that developer cost $150 an hour, then the cost to mend the Web part would be $30,000! Now, if adding two WFE servers addressed the problem without an impact to the SQL Server hardware, then that would most likely represent a cost savings. Obviously, you want your code to perform well, but sometimes additional hardware can provide a quick fix.

When planning for hardware, it is important to plan for high availability first and capacity second. Many times, the planning exercise for high availability negates the need for in-depth capacity planning. For example, many small- to medium-sized SharePoint Server 2007 installations will need at least two WFE servers to support high availability. Those two WFE servers, a clustered SQL Server instance, and a single application server are usually sufficient for several thousand users in an out-of-the-box configuration with limited customizations, and provide both high availability at the Web and database tiers and substantial client capacity. A best practice is testing your high availability server farm design against your desired capacity requirements using the SharePoint Capacity Modeling tool and Visual Studio 2008 Team Suite. You will often find your capacity requirements are already met. Lastly, don't forget to plan for future growth. The user adoption rate is usually high when implementing SharePoint Server 2007, so a best practice is planning for a substantial increase in overall capacity.

## Boundaries

When designing your SharePoint Server 2007 implementation, you should consider the limits of both the software and the hardware it is installed on. This section points out many areas where there are either software limitations or hardware limitations. You will find that many of the software limitations are really "boundaries." An example is the software boundary of 2,000 items in any list view. While you can most certainly have 2,001 items in a list view, 1,999 items would yield marginally better performance, and 500 items would be substantially better. In other words, don't take the software or hardware boundaries discussed in this section as absolute values; instead, take them as recommendations.

> **More Info** See the article "Plan for software boundaries (Office SharePoint Server)" at *http://technet2.microsoft.com/Office/en-us/library/6a13cd9f-4b44-40d6-85aa-c70a8e5c34fe1033.mspx* for a full list of SharePoint Server 2007 software boundaries.

## Software Boundaries

Software boundaries are either suggested limitations by Microsoft or are hard-coded limitations imposed by the product developers. Because some of these limitations are hard-coded into the product, adding additional servers to a SharePoint Server 2007 server farm will not always address the limitation. Likewise, database schema limitations, such as 2,000 items in a list view, are also not addressed by adding additional servers into the farm. Software boundaries should be considered the upper limits when designing and not an absolute limit. Figure 23-1 illustrates an example of this by showing the performance decrease using a flat library view as the total number of items increases. This is contrasted with Figure 23-2, which demonstrates the performance improvement using Indexed Views and Folders.

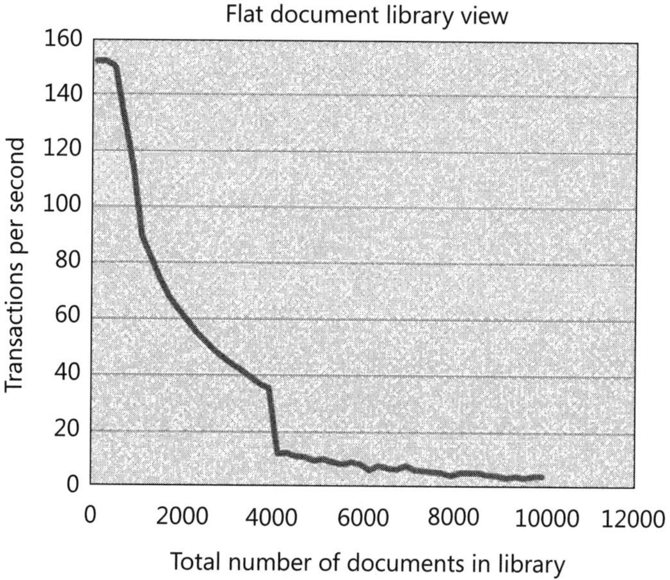


**Figure 23-1** Performance decreases as the number of documents increases.

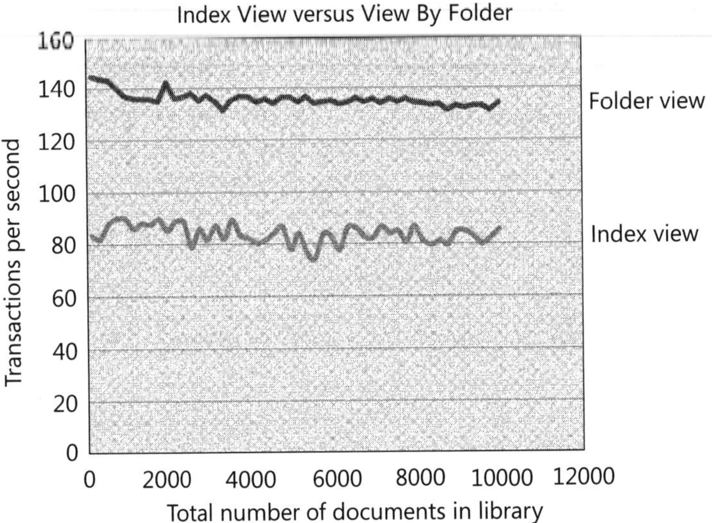


**Figure 23-2** Using either Indexed Views or Folders increases rendering performance for large lists.

Plan to stay well beneath both hard-coded and recommended limits and monitor for exceeding these software boundary thresholds. Table 23-1 shows the most common guidelines for acceptable performance. While most of this information is accessible at *http://technet.microsoft.com/SharepointServer*, it is included here for your convenience.

**Table 23-1 Guidelines for Acceptable Performance**

| Site object | Guideline | Notes | Impact scope |
|---|---|---|---|
| Site collection | 50,000 per content database | Total farm throughput degrades as site collections increase. | Farm |
| Web site | 250,000 per site collection | No more than 2,000 subsites under any single Web site. No more than 250,000 total sites in a single site collection. | Site collection |
| List items | 5 million per list | The hard-coded limit is 5 million, but only if accessed programmatically. | List |
| List view | 2,000 | You should have no more than 2,000 items in any list view. This can be accomplished via Folders or Views. See *http://office.microsoft.com/en-us/sharepointtechnology/HA101736671033.aspx?pid=CH101215281033* for more information. | List view |
| Document file size | 50 MB (2 GB max) | While you can have up to a 2-GB file upload size, server performance is directly relational to the file size. | Client file save |
| Field type | 256 per list | This is a suggested software boundary. | List view |

Table 23-1 **Guidelines for Acceptable Performance**

| | | | |
|---|---|---|---|
| Library columns | 2,000 | Suggested software boundary. | Library view |
| List columns | 4,096 | Suggested software boundary. | List view |
| Web parts | 50 per page | Suggested software boundary. Maybe less when using complex logic. | Page view |
| **People object** | **Guideline** | **Notes** | **Impact scope** |
| Users in groups | 2 million per Web site | Use Active Directory Universal Groups for sites with large user populations. | Site |
| User profiles | 5 million per farm | Imported from Active Directory or other third-party source. | Farm |
| Security principals | 2,000 per Web site | Use Active Directory Universal Groups if close to guidelines. | Site |
| **Search Object** | **Guideline** | **Notes** | **Impact scope** |
| Search index | One per SSP | Hard-coded limitation. | Farm |
| SSPs | 20 per farm | Because an SSP can be associated with only one index, the maximum number of index servers is also 20. | Farm |
| Indexed documents | 50 million per content index | While you can go past 50 million documents, it has not been tested. | Index / SSP |
| Content sources | 500 per SSP | Hard-coded. | SSP |
| Start addresses in a single content source | 500 per content source | Hard-coded. | Content source |
| Alerts | 1 million | Tested limit. | SSP |
| Scopes | 200 | Recommended. | Site |
| Scope display groups | 25 | Recommended. | Site |
| Crawl rules | 10,000 | Recommended. | SSP |
| Keyword | 15,000 | Recommended. | Site |
| Crawled properties | 500,000 | Discovered during crawl. Hard-coded. | SSP |
| Managed properties | 100,000 | Hard-coded. No more than 100 crawled properties mapped to a single managed property. | SSP |
| Authoritative pages | 200 per level | Hard-coded. | SSP |
| Results removal | 100 | Maximum number of URLs that can be removed per operation. | SSP |
| Crawl logs | 50 million items | Hard-coded. | SSP |

Table 23-1 Guidelines for Acceptable Performance

| Logical architecture object | Guideline | Notes | Impact scope |
|---|---|---|---|
| SSPs | 3 recommended, 20 maximum | After 3 SSPs in a farm, there is degradation in performance. The hard-coded maximum is 20 SSPs. | Farm |
| Zones | 5 per farm | There are 5 hard-coded zones: Default, Internet, Intranet, Extranet, and Custom. | Farm |
| Web application | 99 | Includes consuming child farms. | SSP |
| Site collection | 50,000 per Web application | Hard-coded. | Web app |
| Content database | 100 per Web app | Hard-coded. | Web app |
| Site collection | 50,000 per content database | Hard-coded limit. Realistically, the number is much lower. | Content database |
| **Physical object** | **Guideline** | **Notes** | **Impact scope** |
| Index server | 1 per SSP | Usually one per farm. | SSP |
| Excel Calculation Services | No limit | Monitor network traffic between servers. | Farm |
| Query servers | No limit | Monitor network traffic between WFE servers, index server, and SQL Server for acceptable performance. | Farm |
| Web servers per SQL Server instance | 8 WFE servers per SQL instance | Actual performance usually declines at 5 WFE servers per SQL Server instance. Dependent on server usage profile mix. | SQL Server instance |

As you can see in Table 23-1, there is much to consider when planning for a large or specialized SharePoint Server 2007 implementation. But most implementations will not approach the limitations, whether they are hard-coded limits or recommended limits.

### Notes from the Field **Reality Check**

Did you look closely at the published recommended thresholds in Table 23-1? Many are extreme limits that your implementation should never approach. Let's take a look at a few so you can see how to plan your own, real-world SharePoint Server 2007 limits. First, look at the maximum number of site collections per content database–50,000. If you think back to Chapter 3, "SharePoint Server 2007 Design Life Cycle," we discussed that a content database can only be as large as can be restored to meet your service level agreements. The average Service Level Agreement (SLA) is 4 hours, which usually equates to a 100-GB to 200-GB content database size due to restore time constraints. If your site collection quotas were 1 GB, then according to the published recommended limits you would have a 50-terabyte content database! Using a 100-GB content database size limit, you could only have 100 site collections in a content database. Most likely, your site collections will be much larger than 1 GB, and that will reduce the number of site collections in a content database even further.

Second, the recommended limit was 2,000 items in a list view. While that is true, nothing magically happens between 1,999 and 2,001 items in a view. The performance is a smooth curve, and staying well within the limits is a best practice. Realistically, you don't want more than 300 to 500 items in a single view. In fact, you should keep most document libraries under 500 items total. Why? Because users could always create a view that showed all items and kill the database performance hosting that list.

Third, you will notice that 2 GB is the maximum file upload size. Even if you increase your Web timeouts in IIS to accommodate this limit, most WAN connections will not support a 2-GB upload via HTTP. You will get tons of errors and have unhappy users. A real-world maximum file upload size is up to 300 MB. Beyond that, you will always be fighting performance and client issues.

Fourth, you notice 50 Web parts per page as a maximum. It is important to understand that all Web parts render in the browser, even if they are not presented to the client. Having 50 Web parts on a single page will most likely make the page load time unbearable to most users.

Fifth, the hard-coded maximum limit for the number of SSPs in a farm is 20. Twenty SSPs would mean 20 SSP databases, most likely 20 search databases, and 20 site collections from which to manage those SSPs. Unless you are an ISP or similar, four SSPs should be considered the maximum number. Beyond four SSPs in a farm, your implementation becomes very difficult to manage and will require significantly more hardware. Don't forget; don't create more than one SSP unless absolutely necessary.

Last, the hard-coded maximum number of crawl rules is 10,000. There are simply very, very few reasons to have more than a handful of crawl rules. If you need to crawl authenticated content sources, the best practice is adding the default content access account to the source. This simplifies your search configuration and allows you to block crawling of content by securing the source. The latter will reduce the need to create crawl rules to exclude content. Simply remove permissions from the default content access on the excluded content. Managing search in this way is more effective and results in better crawler performance than creating lots of crawl rules.

Be very thoughtful about how you design and implement SharePoint Server 2007. Don't simply assume the published limitations are "safe" in your environment because many are hard-coded limits that most SharePoint Server 2007 implementations simply cannot support. Thresholds like items in a list and sites in a site collection can be governed only via end-user training. There is no tool within SharePoint Server 2007 to monitor and report on these metrics.

*Ben Curry, Microsoft MVP, Mindsharp*

> **More Info** For a detailed guide to content database sizing and more, please see the white paper "Performance recommendations for storage planning and monitoring" at *http://technet2.microsoft.com/Office/en-us/library/ca472046-7d4a-4f17-92b1-c88a743a5e3c1033.mspx?mfr=true.*

## Hardware Boundaries

Hardware boundaries are the performance and capacity constraints imposed by the physical hardware itself. As an example, let's look at the 50 million objects per index software boundary from table 23-1. While the software allows for 50 million items, you must have the hardware to support the crawling, indexing, propagation, ranking, archiving, and other search functions related to that index. Additionally, you must have the network bandwidth between the index and query servers to propagate the index, bandwidth between the index server and content sources, and I/O available on the content sources themselves. The minimum server hardware for SharePoint Server 2007 will not support a 50 million item index; therefore, the server would be the boundary and not the software. But, just because the software boundary is well above your current or planned numbers, don't assume you will have the hardware capacity for processing. A good example is supporting large lists (lists with over 2,000 items), seen in Figure 23-1 and Figure 23-2. Those statistics were gathered using a Web server with two dual-core Xeon 2.8 GHz, 64-bit processors and 4 GB RAM. Only a 32-bit system is required to install SharePoint Server 2007. So if you installed on the minimum recommended hardware, you could expect to see the performance of large lists decrease before the 2,000 item limit, and it would be even more important to index views or create folders. Basically, the closer you get to the software boundaries, the more robust your hardware solution must be. Otherwise, you will see performance degrading long before you reach the software boundaries.

> **More Info** For detailed information on large lists, see "Working with large lists in Office SharePoint Server 2007" at *http://go.microsoft.com/fwlink/?LinkId=95450&clcid=0x409.*

There are many places in your farm that could introduce a hardware boundary. First, your SQL Server hardware can often be the performance bottleneck in your farm, specifically the I/O subsystem. You should follow SQL Server implementation best practices, including a dedicated SQL Server instance when you begin to approach any of the software boundaries mentioned previously in this chapter. In fact, you may very well need multiple SQL Server instances to support hardware requirements on disk, CPU, or network between SharePoint Server 2007 server farm members and associated databases. Be aware that when SQL Server begins to bottleneck your SharePoint Server 2007 farm, it can also impact farm member servers such as WFE servers. Two examples are immediately relevant to this discussion. First, when performance decreases and a page doesn't immediately render to a user, the users will often continually attempt to open the page, furthering the negative impact to your server farm. Second, when SQL Server bottlenecks, your WFE and application servers must queue user traffic while waiting for SQL Server to respond. Many times, these two events happen simultaneously, rendering your farm essentially inoperable. Basically, poor performance at any tier can cause a snowball effect and your farm performance could spiral downward at a rapid rate.

**More Info** There is a SQL Server Performance Recommendations guide for SharePoint Server 2007 at *http://office.microsoft.com/download/afile.aspx?AssetID=AM102509151033.*

Using 64-bit hardware for your SharePoint Server 2007 implementations is the single best way to expand hardware boundaries. First, a 64-bit server allows for more data to flow through the bus and therefore reduces the possibility of I/O bottlenecking on your SharePoint Server 2007 servers. More importantly, a 64-bit server is capable of addressing up to 1 terabyte of RAM. Contrasted with the ability of a 32-bit Windows Server to directly address only 4 GB of memory, it makes the use of 64-bit hardware very compelling.

**Note** Windows SharePoint Services 2.0 SP2 and Windows SharePoint Services 3.0 do not support the /3GB switch, as can be seen here *http://support.microsoft.com/default.aspx?scid=kb;en-us;933560&sd=rss&spid=11373*. Therefore, SharePoint Server 2007 does not support this either.

If you have a small or test scenario, you could use 32-bit hardware. But be careful testing custom code on hardware different than your production environment. If at all possible, MSF (Microsoft Solutions Framework) best practices dictate that your test environment should be identical to your production environment.

**Note** You may have to use 32-bit hardware you already own to begin with. If so, be sure to put a 64-bit upgrade plan in place and in your budget. Also note that the next versions of SharePoint Products and Technologies will not support 32-bit hardware.

## Capacity Planning Solution Tool

Capacity planning is a best practice, but performing this task has been very difficult until now. Microsoft has released a new version of their capacity planning tool named System Center Capacity Planner 2007. It was originally developed for designing medium to large Exchange Server 2007 deployments and is freely available via the Microsoft Download center. Recently, the Solution Accelerator team has released SharePoint Server 2007 and Windows SharePoint Services 3.0 models for creating and testing SharePoint Server 2007 farm architectures, including authenticated and anonymous user profiles, altering those users' traffic mix, and adding users on up to ten WAN connections. There are many benefits to using this tool. Here are some examples:

- Easy-to-use modeling wizard
- Pre-configured client profiles including light read, heavy read, light publishing, average publishing, heavy publishing, light collaboration, average collaboration, and heavy collaboration
- Pre-configured static server loads adjustable from 5 percent to 10 percent user concurrency
- Pre-configured WAN links ranging from dial-up 56 k to OC3 (Optical Carrier 156 Mbps)
- Commonly used server hardware combinations
- Ability to add custom server hardware combinations
- Ability to plan and model high availability on WFE servers and SQL Server
- Simulate one to thousands of users on LAN and WAN connections
- Create Storage Area Network (SAN) switches and storage frames
- Export drawings to Office Visio 2007 and bill of materials to Office Excel 2007 formats

As this section will show, it is a very nice planning and pre-sales tool, but should not be considered sufficient design and preparation for most SharePoint Server 2007 implementations. Although it makes a nice tool to justify hardware costs to management and customers, there are few things it will not do:

- Storage limitation of 2 terabytes
- Indexing and backup/restore loads are static and meant for small to medium deployments
- You cannot define SAN information during model creation; it must be done after creation
- You cannot create custom WAN links
- You cannot add multiple server farms for regional connectivity

The limitations will only apply to the largest deployments. If the limitations apply to your design, you should "get it close" with the capacity planning tool and use Visual Studio 2008 Team Suite for testing your actual implementation. To begin, you must have first loaded System Center Capacity Planner 2007 and added the SharePoint models to the tool. Figure 23-3 shows the farm creation screen.

While you are creating the server farm model, you can specify either an Internet or intranet deployment. Selecting an Internet deployment allows you to include anonymous users in your design. When you select Customize Usage Profiles, you can specify the exact traffic mix for each type of user. Figure 23-4 shows the editing of what average collaboration means in your environment.

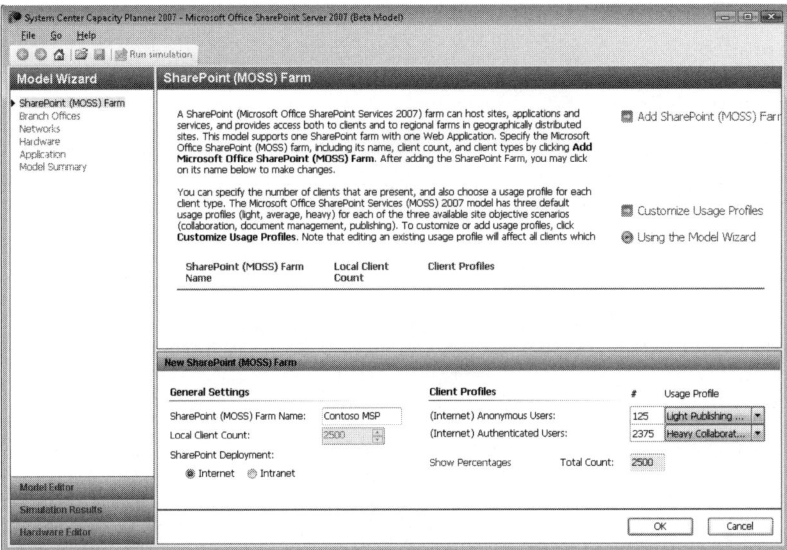


**Figure 23-3** You create a server farm and define the usage profiles for your installation.

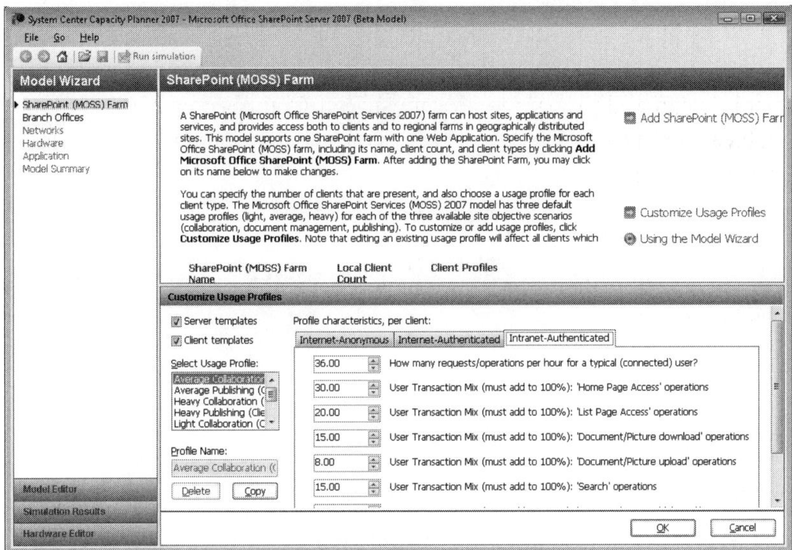


**Figure 23-4** Only change profile characteristics if you have done an analysis for your environment.

Unless you have performed detailed analysis of your current traffic, many of these settings will be guesses in the beginning. Once you have a test system in place and have captured enough traffic to have usable metrics, you can come back and redefine these for more accurate modeling.

After you have the initial farm created in the modeling wizard, you can continue to add branch office profiles. You can create all branch offices as the same profile, or create each one individually. You can create up to ten branch office profiles and define Site to Site or Shared WAN network topologies. Figure 23-5 shows an example of changing the network speeds and available bandwidth between two Shared WAN sites. Figure 23-6 shows changing the latency on a Site to Site connection.

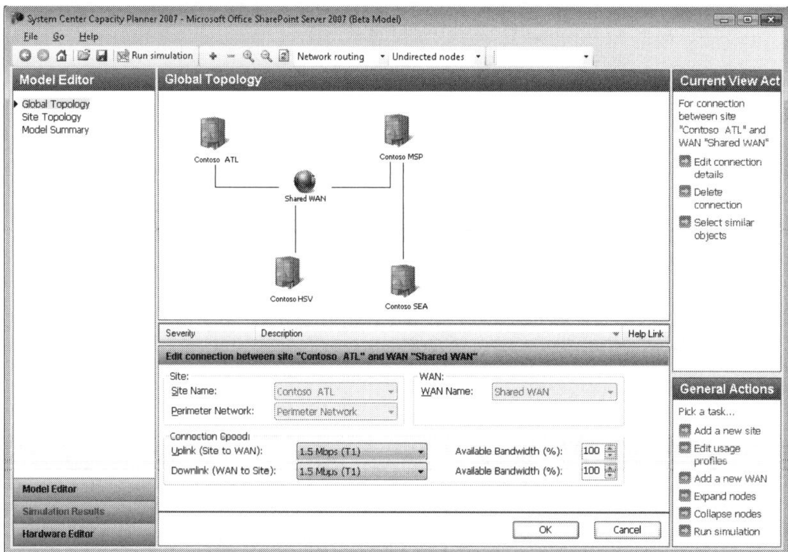


**Figure 23-5** You can set the uplink speeds and downlink speeds on WAN connections.

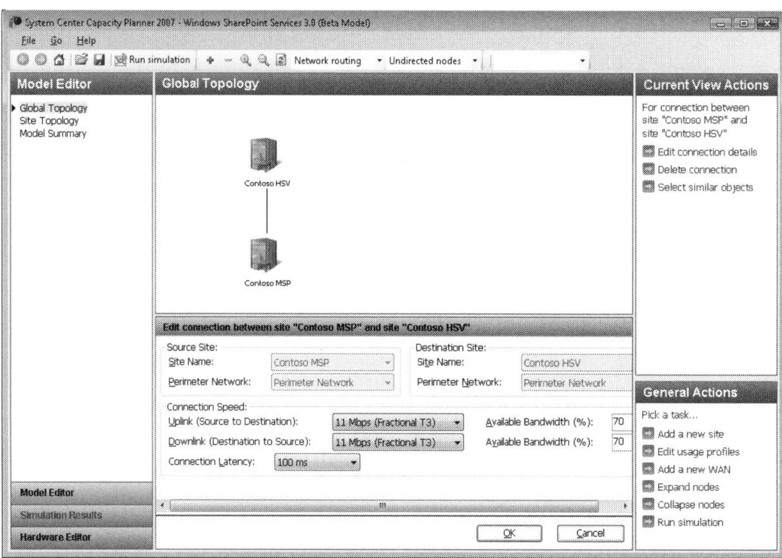


**Figure 23-6** You can change the latency on Site to Site connections.

After you have finished your model, the tool will suggest hardware configurations for your deployment. You can export this hardware list to Microsoft Office Excel 2007 to give you a basic bill of materials for hardware purchasing. You can also hover over a server in the Site Topology screen to see the suggested hardware, as seen in Figure 23-7.

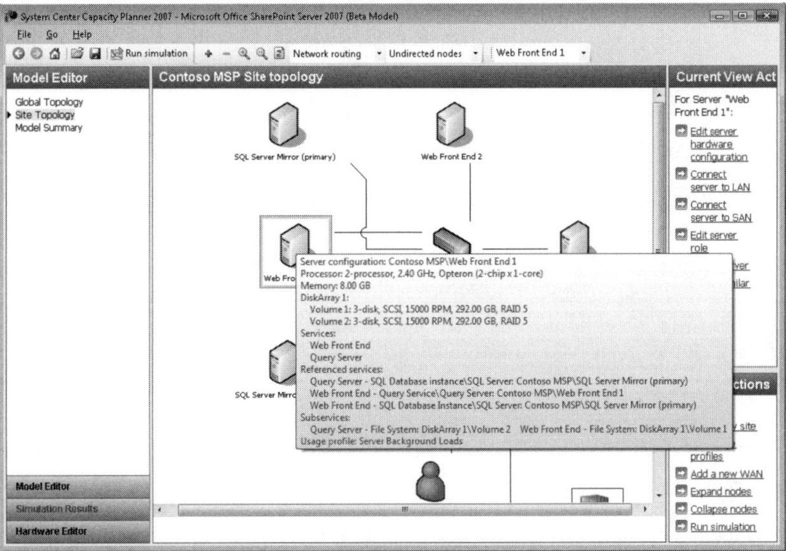


**Figure 23-7** Hover over an item to see device details.

The last benefit of the tool is the ability to run a simulation based on your input. It can show you where hardware is insufficient, WAN links are overloaded, and much more. In fact, you can perform what-if analysis after you run the initial simulation by changing the configuration in the Hardware Editor and Model Editor windows. A common example is trying slower CPUs and changing the disk configuration, then re-running the simulator to see if those bottleneck. Figure 23-8 shows an example of the simulator output when one of the WAN links is overloaded.

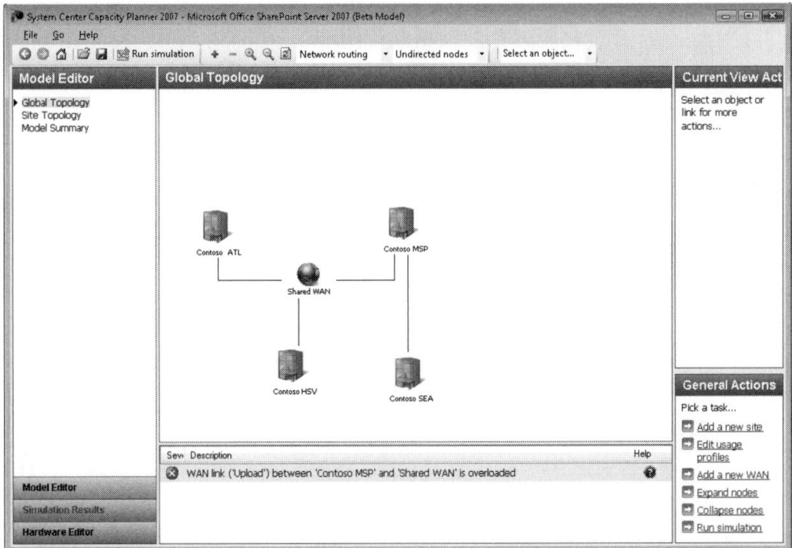


**Figure 23-8** Errors and associated Help will appear for problems encountered during simulation.

Remember, the tool can only model what you have inputted. It cannot guess at your user count, WAN connections, WAN latency, and server hardware. If your hardware devices, including storage, CPU, SAN, and WAN are incorrectly configured in the tool, you will get unreliable simulation results. Once you have completed a thorough analysis with the Capacity Planning Tool, it is time to build an actual server farm and perform testing on your production hardware to see if it performs as expected.

**On the Companion Media** On the CD, you will find SharePoint Capacity Planning Tool v1.0.msi, which will install the Windows SharePoint Services 3.0 and SharePoint Server 2007 capacity planning models. The installation instructions can be found in the accompanying SharePoint Capacity Planning ReadMe.txt file.

### IIS Compression

If you will have many remote users and users who are constrained by high-latency network connections, you could consider enabling IIS compression on one or all of your SharePoint Server 2007 farm servers. You can enable compression on both 6.0 and 7.0 versions of IIS, but only the compression of static files is enabled by default. IIS compression gives us the ability to compress files before they are sent to the client's browser. This allows large files, such as bitmaps, to be compressed before sending. The client's browser then decompresses the file to view the contents. You can compress both static files such as .htm and .bmp files, and you can compress dynamic files such as .aspx, .dll, .exe, and .asp. So why isn't IIS compression enabled and set to the maximum setting by default? After all, the higher the compression, the faster traffic will flow to WAN clients.

The reason is that, as you increase compression, you negatively affect server CPU performance due to the compression process. So even though IIS compression can really help page-load time for remote clients and should be used when needed, you may have to increase your server hardware capacity to maintain acceptable LAN service levels. If you have robust routers and firewalls, it is always possible to have some compression-enabled servers for remote users and another set of compression-disabled servers for LAN users. See *http://support.microsoft.com/kb/322603* for more information on enabling compression for dynamic files. There is also an online virtual lab where you can enable both static and dynamic compression at *http://virtuallabs.iis.net/*. (Click the link to IIS6.0 – HTTP Caching.)

## Visual Studio 2008 Team Suite

While the capacity planning tool gives you a good place to start designing and a baseline from which to purchase hardware, it cannot know all of the possible variables for a given SharePoint Server 2007 installation. Therefore, you need to test your farm architecture before deployment for production use. Additionally, you need to test all custom and third-party Web parts before deploying in a production environment. For this purpose, we use Visual Studio 2008 Team Suite (VSTS 2008). Much of this functionality was included in Visual Studio 2005 Team Center Testing Editions (VSTT), and if you were familiar with the older tool, the new one will be quite easy to learn. To adequately test the capacity of your new SharePoint Server 2007 server farm (also known as *stress testing*), you must have the Visual Studio Team System 2008 Team Suite. It provides the testing capabilities, performance statistics storage, and controller capabilities required to stress test a SharePoint Server 2007 server farm. The following lists some of the reasons we use VSTS 2008:

- Baseline farm performance
- Clearly see the impact of adding native Web parts, custom Web parts, and third-party Web parts on system performance
- Test performance changes when adding and removing servers from a farm
- Test any major configuration change in the farm, such as search and indexing

> **More Info** If you have never used a Visual Studio Testing Rig, browse to *http://msdn2.microsoft.com/en-us/vsts2008/bb872413.aspx* for an excellent how-to video by Richard Hundhausen.

You need to have a complete SharePoint Server 2007 server farm built for accurate results when using VSTS 2008 testing tools. You should build your server farm according to your preliminary design architecture. You may also want to populate your server farm with test data. There are several ways to do this, the easiest being to populate the sites and lists manually. If you need to create hundreds or even thousands of sites, lists, and items, you should consider using an automated tool that will create test data and, more importantly, remove your test data when you are finished.

> **More Info** The leading data population tool at the time this book was written was the SharePoint 2007 Test Data Population Tool, at *http://www.codeplex.com/sptdatapop*. If all you need is collaboration test data, the Windows SharePoint Services 3.0 Test Data Population Tool (*http://www.codeplex.com/sptdatapop/Release/ProjectReleases.aspx?ReleaseId=1141)* is an easier and more reliable tool to use. Refer to *http://technet2.microsoft.com/Office/en-us/library/301ed832-95da-4251-b266-7be6288f7ea01033.mspx* for detailed usage information.

Because testing SharePoint Server 2007 server farms with VSTS 2008 isn't widely understood and a critical best practice for deployment, a walkthrough is included here. For the tests described in this section, all sites, lists, libraries, and content therein were created and uploaded manually. If you follow the recommendations in the software boundaries section of this chapter, you should not need to create hundreds and thousands of sites, lists, and objects to adequately test *most* SharePoint Server 2007 deployments. The following scenario has two WFE servers that are load balanced, both hosting the search query server role, and one application server hosting Central Administration and search index role. Figure 23-9 shows a graphical representation of our scenario farm.

To begin building your test rig, you must install VSTS 2008 on a workstation or server that has direct access to all members of the SharePoint Server 2007 server farm. You will create a test project, create a test list, and then collect metrics on various client actions such as page loads and querying. While testing using VSTS 2008 can be quite elegant and complex, it doesn't have to be. This scenario only covers the basics of stress testing a SharePoint Server 2007 server farm. Begin by creating a new VSTS 2008 Test Project, as seen in Figure 23-10.

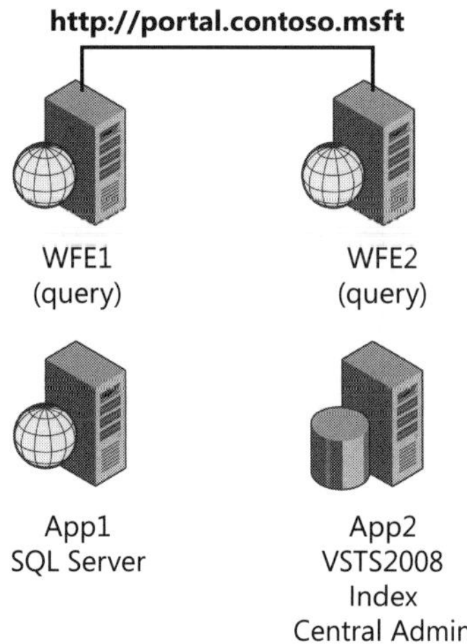


**Figure 23-9** There are four servers in the test farm, with two running as WFE servers, one indexing server, and one SQL Server instance.

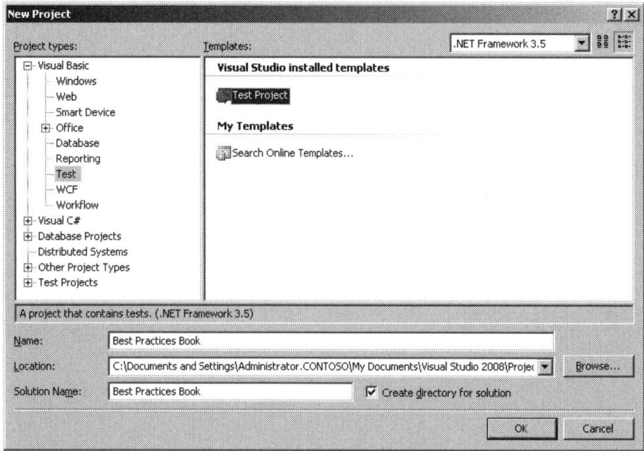


**Figure 23-10** When creating a new project for stress testing, use the Test Project template.

## Creating Web Tests

After you have created the project, you next want to begin recording Web tests. Keep in mind that the end goal of this scenario is testing the capacity of your server farm for real-world client actions such as file downloads, search queries, page rendering, list creation, and in-browser editing of a publishing site. You have two options when recording Web tests: create one large test that includes all of your users' actions, or create many individual tests. The latter is what you will do here as it allows you to change the transaction mix so that you can run multiple test scenarios from a single set of Web tests. From the Solution Explorer, add a new Web test, as seen in Figure 23-11.

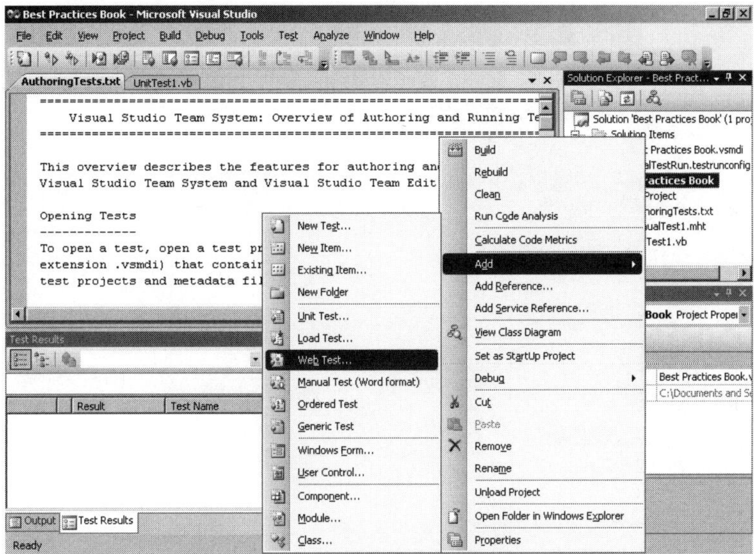


**Figure 23-11** Add a new Web test from the Solution Explorer.

After you have added a new Web test, a browser window will open allowing you to record a Web action. Browse directly to a page to begin the recording. After each record is completed, rename the Web test to match the transaction, such as Portal Home Page.webtest. You will see later why this is important. Continue to record transactions such as file uploads, querying using different terms, editing a page, and so forth. For the scenario in this section, we have recorded the following transactions, each being an individual Web test:

- Browse to the portal home page
- Edit portal home page and publish
- Manage a document library
- Upload a document
- Execute a query

You can now execute each of these Web tests individually and see results such as total time and request time. If you are only looking to see something simple, like the impact a Web part has on page rendering, then a single Web test would suffice. Simply run the test on the page before adding the Web part. Note the results. This would be considered your page performance *baseline*. Then, add the Web part to the page and re-run the test. You should easily be able to see the difference in page load times. If you require more in-depth analysis you must create a *load test*.

## Creating a Load Test

If you need to see the impact a Web test has on a server by hundreds or thousands of users, you need to create a load test. Choose Add -> Load Test from the Solution Explorer, as seen in Figure 23-12.

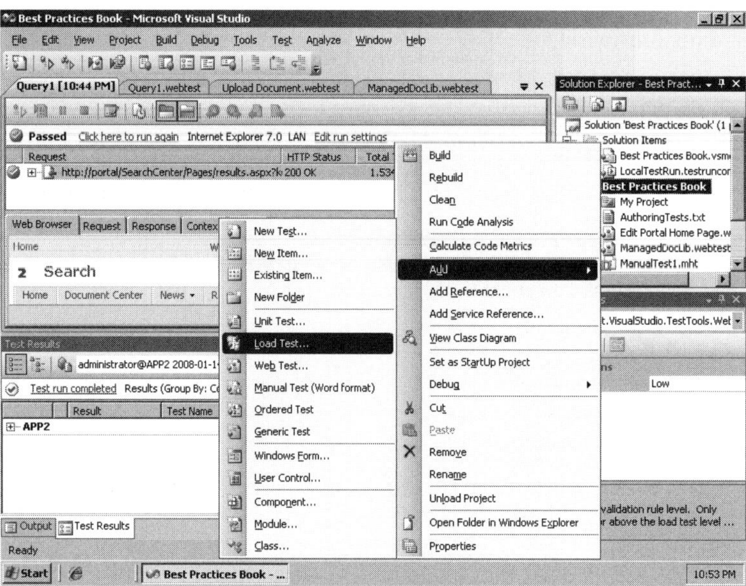


**Figure 23-12** Add a load test from Solution Explorer.

You should name the test something easy to recognize and decide whether you will include think times, use a constant or step loading pattern, and select a test mix model. Refer to your VSTS 2008 documentation for detailed information. When selecting your test mix, you can now add one or many of the individual Web tests previously recorded and select the transaction distribution, as seen in Figure 23-13. This is why you should name each individual test something easy to recognize.

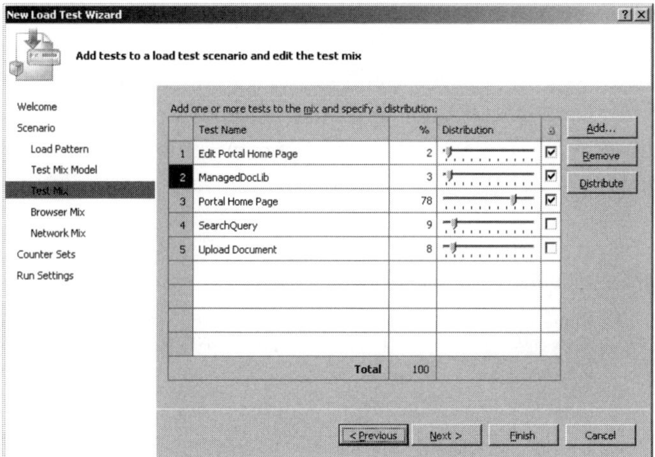


**Figure 23-13** Add the previously recorded Web test and select the distribution of those transactions.

Next, you should select the browser mix supported by SharePoint Server 2007, which includes Internet Explorer 7.0, Internet Explorer 6.0, and Firefox 2.0, as seen in Figure 23-14. Be aware other browser types can be selected, but are not supported by SharePoint Server 2007.

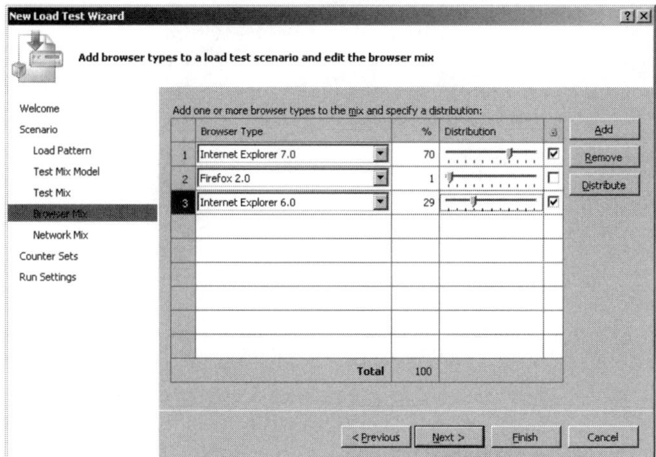


**Figure 23-14** Select the browser types and distribution.

> **Note** Using a combination of Web test, load tests, and browser types, you can test client changes such as migrating from Internet Explorer 6.0 to Internet Explorer 7.0.

The next screen will take you to the network mix. Be cautious before moving forward. If you simply want to test the impact of adding and removing features such as Web parts, you should leave the default to 100% LAN. This is the most accurate way to determine the impact of an added feature. If you want to model the impact to your server farm to ready for production deployment, then choose the network types and distribution to match your environment. We have selected a distribution of 84% LAN, 12% T3, and 4% Cable for our test scenario, as seen in Figure 23-15.

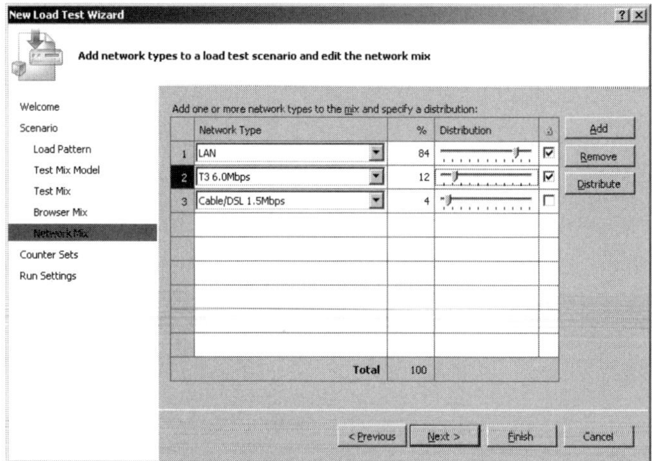


Figure 23-15 Select the network types and distribution for your environment.

To accurately monitor the load on all servers in your farm, be sure to add all servers in the farm to the Counter Sets screen. For this scenario, we have added both WFE servers in our farm with IIS and .NET counters, and APP1 server with SQL counters.

> **Note** Be sure to space the counter interval to a reasonable value such as every 15 seconds. Monitoring at a too-frequent interval will overload the testing rig and skew test results.

This should give us an overall view of our farm as we add users to the load. Last, we need to define the run settings. In Figure 23-16, you can see that we have a warm-up time of 59 seconds so we get a valid test and don't get erroneous information due to an event, such as JIT compiling. We have also defined the test duration as 2 minutes.

Once you have built your load test, you now need to run the test. While the test is in progress, you will see a graph with key indicators such as user load, request/second, and errors/second. You also see any threshold violations, as seen in Figure 23-17.

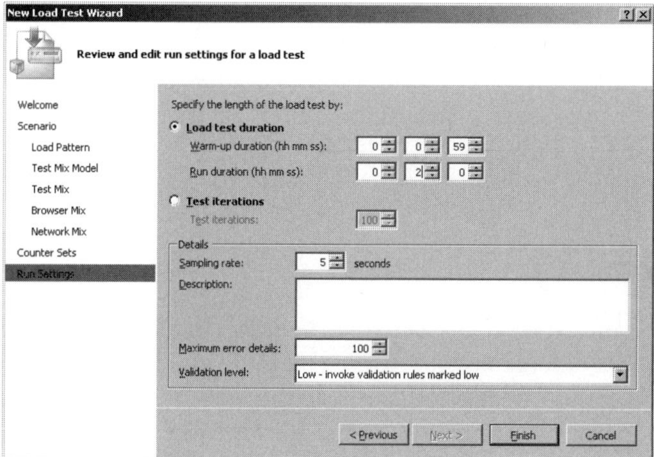

Figure 23-16 Specify the load test duration.

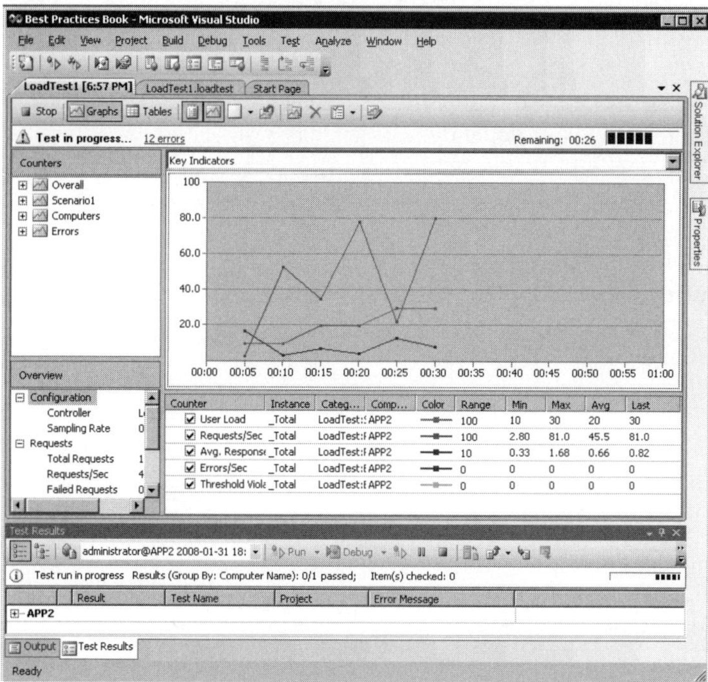

Figure 23-17 Any errors and threshold violations are displayed during load testing.

There isn't room in this chapter to discuss every possible metric that can be captured via VSTS 2008 testing. You can create custom counter sets that track any of the performance counters, including those installed with SharePoint Server 2007. You can test your farm for 100 or 100,000 users, depending on your needs. Be aware that accurate testing of more than a few hundred users requires the use of multiple VSTS 2008 Team Suite Agents to represent the actual load from these test users.

# Performance Monitoring

Performance monitoring is one of the most overlooked best practices in SharePoint Server 2007 implementations. Without monitoring, you don't know the health of your farm and will be alerted by users, instead of the system, when an application fails. With a proper monitoring solution, you many times will be notified before a hard failure actually occurs. There are many who want to monitor their solution and just don't know how. A very common question is, "What performance counters do I monitor, and what are the acceptable thresholds?" Unfortunately, there isn't a single answer for most performance counters, but there is definitely a method to define them for your implementation. Some counters, such as Processor Queue Length, are very easy to determine thresholds for—it should never be more than one. Additionally, many counters you need to monitor are not specific to SharePoint Server 2007, so you should begin with monitoring your dependencies such as SQL Server, Windows Server, and network hardware. This section will give you an overview of how to baseline your system for performance. Table 23-2 is provided as a base reference of counters you want to monitor for SharePoint Server 2007.

**Table 23-2 Base Performance Counters for SharePoint Server 2007**

| Counter | Description | Details |
|---|---|---|
| Total Processor Time | Use the % Processor Time counter to measure the percentage of elapsed time that the processor spends to execute a non-Idle thread. | Object: Processor<br>Counter: %Processor Time<br>Instance: _Total |
| Processor Privileged Time | Use the % Privileged Time counter to measure the percentage of elapsed time that the process threads spend executing code in Privileged mode. | Object: Processor<br>Counter: %Privileged Time<br>Instance: _Total |
| Processor User Time | Use the % User Time counter to measure the percentage of elapsed time the processor spends in User mode. | Object: Processor<br>Counter: % User Time<br>Instance: _Total |
| Excessive Processor Usage | It is calculated by monitoring the time that the service is inactive and subtracting that value from 100%. | Object: Processor<br>Counter: % Processor Time<br>Instance: _Total |

**Table 23-2 Base Performance Counters for SharePoint Server 2007**

| Counter | Description | Details |
|---|---|---|
| Process – W3WP Processor Time | Measures the % of elapsed time that all process threads use the processor. | Object: Processor<br>Counter: %Processor Time<br>Instance: w3wp |
| Processor Queue Length | If the threshold of this rule is exceeded, it indicates that the processor is not fast enough. | Object: System<br>Counter: Processor Queue Length |
| Page Faults per second | Use the counter Page Faults/sec to measure the average number of pages faulted per second. | Object: Memory<br>Counter: Page Faults/sec |
| Available Disk Space | Use the % Free Space counter to calculate the percentage of total usable space. | Object: LogicalDisk<br>Counter: % Free Space<br>_total |
| Disk Request Write Size | Use the Disk Write Bytes/sec counter to measure the rate at which bytes are transferred to the disk during write operations. | Object: PhysicalDisk<br>Counter: Disk Write Bytes/sec<br>Instance: _Total |
| Disk Request Write Count | Measures the rate of write operations on the disk. | Object: PhysicalDisk<br>Counter: Disk Writes/sec<br>Instance: _Total |
| Disk Usage - Disk Time | Use the % Disk Time counter to calculate the percentage of elapsed time that the selected disk drive was busy servicing read or write requests. | Object: PhysicalDisk<br>Counter: %Disk Time<br>Instance: _Total |
| Disk Block Read Size | Use the Avg. Disk Bytes/Read counter to measure the average number of bytes transferred from the disk during read operations. | Object: PhysicalDisk<br>Counter: Avg. Disk Bytes/Read<br>Instance: _Total |
| Disk Request Read Size | Measures the rate at which bytes are transferred from the disk during read operations via Disk Read Bytes/sec. | Object: PhysicalDisk<br>Counter: Disk Read Bytes/sec<br>Instance: _Total |
| Disk Request Read Count | Measures the rate of read operations from the disk. | Object: PhysicalDisk<br>Counter: Disk Reads/sec<br>Instance: _Total |
| Web Service Bytes Sent/sec | Measures the rate at which data bytes are being sent by the Web service. | Object: Web Service<br>Counter: Bytes Sent/sec<br>Instance: _Total |
| Web Service Current Connections | Monitors current IIS connections. | Object: Web Service<br>Counter: Current Connections<br>Instance: _Total (or per Web app) |

Table 23-2 **Base Performance Counters for SharePoint Server 2007**

| Counter | Description | Details |
|---|---|---|
| Web Service | Use the Total Method Requests/sec counter to measure the rate at which HTTP requests are received. | Object: Web Service<br>Counter: Total method Requests/sec<br>Instance: _Total (or specific Web apps) |
| Web Service Bytes Received/sec | Measures the rate at which data bytes are received by the Web service. | Object: Web Service<br>Counter: Bytes Received/sec<br>Instance: _Total (or per Web app) |
| Web Service Connection Attempts | Measures the rate at which connections to the Web service are being attempted. | Object: Web Service<br>Counter: Connection Attempts/sec<br>Instance: _Total |
| W3WP Private Bytes | Measures the current size, in bytes, of memory that this process has allocated and that cannot be shared with other processes. | Object: Process<br>Counter: Private Bytes<br>Instance: w3wp |
| W3WP Working Set | The Working Set is the set of memory pages recently touched by the threads in the process. | Object: Process<br>Counter: Working Set<br>Instance: w3wp |
| Committed Memory in use | Use the % Committed Bytes In Use counter to measure the ratio of the Memory\Committed Bytes counter to the Memory\Commit Limit counter. | Object: Memory<br>Counter: % Committed Bytes In Use |
| Available Memory | Use the Available MBytes counter to measure the amount of physical memory in MB immediately available for allocation to a process or for system use. | Object: Memory<br>Counter: Available MBytes |
| Memory Cache Bytes | Shows the sum of the Memory\System Cache Resident Bytes, Memory\System Driver Resident Bytes, Memory\System Code Resident Bytes, and Memory\Pool Paged Resident Bytes. | Object: Memory<br>Counter: Cache Bytes |
| .NET CLR Memory – Bytes | Use the # Bytes in all Heaps counter to sum the following four other counters: Gen 0 Heap Size, Gen 1 Heap Size, Gen 2 Heap Size, and Large Object Heap Size. | Object: .NET CLR Memory<br>Counter: # Bytes in all Heaps<br>Instance: _Global |

Table 23-2 **Base Performance Counters for SharePoint Server 2007**

| Counter | Description | Details |
|---|---|---|
| .Net CLR Data-SQL client Failed connections | Use the SqlClient: Total # failed connects counter to count the total number of connection open attempts that have failed. | Object: .NET CLR Data<br>Counter: SqlClient<br>Instance: Total # of failed attempts |
| .Net CLR Data-SQL client connections | Measures the current number of active SQL connections. | Object: .NET CLR Data<br>Counter: SqlClient<br>Instance: Current # pooled and nonpooled connections |
| .Net CLR memory – large Objects | Displays the current size of the Large Object Heap in bytes. Objects greater than 20 KB are treated as large objects by the Garbage Collector and are directly allocated in a special heap. | Object: .NET CLR Memory<br>Counter: Large Object Heap size<br>Instance: _Global |
| Succeeded Search Queries | Use the Queries Succeeded counter to count the number of queries that produce successful searches. | Object: SharePoint Search Indexer Catalogs<br>Counter: Queries Succeeded<br>Instance: Search |
| Search Query Rate | Monitors query rate. | Object: SharePoint Search Indexer Catalogs<br>Counter: Queries<br>Instance: Search |
| Search – total # of Documents | Counts the total number of documents in the index. | Object: Indexing Service<br>Counter: Total # of documents |
| Cache Faults per Second | Cache activity is a reliable indicator of most application I/O operations. | Object: Memory<br>Counter: Cache Faults/sec |
| ASP.NET Requests per Second | Counts the number of requests per second. | Object: ASP.NET Apps v2.0.50727<br>Counter: Requests/Sec<br>Instance: _Total |
| ASP.NET Cache – Hit ratio | Use the Cache Total Hit Ratio counter to sum the ASP.NET application performance counters. | Object: ASP.NET Applications<br>Counter: Cache Total Hit Ratio<br>Instance: _Total |
| ASP.NET Cache Size | Counts the total number of entries within the cache (both internal and user added). | Object: ASP.NET Applications<br>Counter: Cache Total Entries<br>Instance: _Total |
| Memory – pages per second | Measures the rate at which pages are read from or written to disk to resolve hard page faults. | Object: Memory<br>Counter: Pages/sec |

**Table 23-2 Base Performance Counters for SharePoint Server 2007**

| Counter | Description | Details |
|---|---|---|
| ASP.NET Worker Process Restart | Measures Worker Process Restarts. | Object: ASP.NET<br>Counter: Worker Process Restarts |
| Paging File | Measures the percentage of the Page File instance in use. | Object: Paging File<br>Counter: %Usage<br>Instance: _Total |
| W3WP Handle Count | This number is equal to the sum of the handles currently open by each thread in this process. | Object: Process<br>Counter: Handle Count<br>Instance: w3wp |
| Publishing Object Cache | Counts the current number of pools that are associated with the process. | Object: SharePoint Publishing Cache<br>Counter: Publishing cache hits/sec |
| Total number of ISAPI Connections | Counts the number of ISAPI connections that Windows SharePoint Services is processing simultaneously. | Object: Web Service<br>Counter: Current ISAPI Extension Requests<br>Instance: _Total |
| Total number of ISAPI Requests | Counts the number of ISAPI requests per second. | Object: Web Service<br>Counter: ISAPI Extension Request/sec<br>Instance: _Total |
| Excessive CPU Utilization | Use the % Processor Time counter to calculate the percentage of the elapsed time of all of the process threads used by the processor to execute instructions. | Object: Process<br>Counter: %Processor Time<br>Instance: _Total |

The best practice when monitoring a server farm is documenting what the counters are with no user load. Using VSTS 2008 and custom counter sets, you should obtain the exact counters in Table 23-2 before you connect users to the system. This gives you a picture of your overall server health, but also provides the counter levels when your server farm is idle. Store this baseline somewhere safe in case you should need it to troubleshoot your server farm. You can then create a monitoring solution with the tool of your choice using these numbers as a baseline, but System Center Operations Manager 2007 provides complete monitoring of all counters in Table 23-2 and has baselining functionality built in. Using System Center Operations Manager 2007 with the Windows SharePoint Services 3.0 and SharePoint Server 2007 management packs will greatly simplify your monitoring. If you do not have a monitoring product at all, you can use the built-in Windows Server tool Performance Monitor, also referred to by its executable name *perfmon.exe*.

## Perfmon.exe

Perfmon.exe provides a relatively simple way to monitor your server farm. It is very basic, is not distributed, and must keep real-time connections with farm members for performance. But it is a good starting place if you are new to monitoring. Both the *Microsoft Office SharePoint Server 2007 Administrator's Companion* (Microsoft Press, 2007) and *Microsoft SharePoint Products and Technologies Administrator's Pocket Consultant* (Microsoft Press, 2007) detail how to use perfmon.exe with SharePoint Server 2007. Because of the limitations of perfmon.exe, it should be limited to farm testing and very small implementations

**On the Companion Media** On the CD, you will find Systems Center Operations Manager management packs for SharePoint Server 2007: Office SharePoint Server (MOSS) 2007 System Center Operations Manager 2007 MP.msi and Windows SharePoint Services 3.0 System Center Operations Manager 2007 MP.msi. You'll also find the instructions for installation in the respective Office Word documents.

## System Center Operations Manager 2007

The System Center Operations Manager 2007 product suite allows for real-time monitoring of services, event logs, trace logs, WMI (Windows Management Instrumentation), and performance counters. First, the monitoring of services and WMI allow us to know the status of services, such as Office SharePoint Server Search, and automate actions like restarting the service and notifying the appropriate support staff. Second, System Center Operations Manager 2007 gives us the ability to monitor the performance counters, event logs, and applications logs. We can then create alerts, performance monitors, baselines, and tasks based on predefined thresholds for objects. In this section, we will primarily cover using System Center Operations Manager 2007 for monitoring the health of SharePoint Server 2007, including Windows SharePoint Services 3.0. Be aware that you probably need to baseline and monitor supporting applications as well, such as SQL Server, Internet Information Services, and ForeFront Security for SharePoint, if applicable.

You can install System Center Operations Manager 2007 and create custom monitors for the previously discussed performance counters and services. In fact, many advanced administrators will prefer to pick and choose what counters and services they will monitor. But for most of us, we can load System Center Operations Manager 2007 management packs. Management packs are a pre-packaged set of event rules, performance rules, and alert rules that can use many providers including the event logs, WMI, application logs, and performance counters. The management packs for specific applications, such as SharePoint Server 2007, include pertinent rules from these providers to automate responses (also called *tasks*) such as service restarting, custom scripts, SMTP notifications, SNMP traps, and command-line execution. If you have not used or tested System Center Operations Manager 2007, you will be pleasantly surprised at the ability to manage all of your applications, not just SharePoint Server 2007. Likewise, you should refer to the System Center Operations Manager 2007 product documentation for technical details and importing management packs. This section does not cover the installation, configuration, or management of System Center Operations Manager 2007 or the SharePoint Products and Technologies management packs.

> **More Info** For a full list of available management packs, browse to the System Center Pack Catalog at *http://www.microsoft.com/technet/prodtechnol/scp/catalog.aspx*. The link is also available in the System Center Operations Manager 2007 Administration Actions menu.

Because SharePoint Server 2007 is a multi- tiered, distributed application, the following management packs are relevant to SharePoint Server 2007:

- Windows SharePoint Services 3.0 Management Pack
- SharePoint Server 2007 Management Pack
- ForeFront Security for SharePoint Management Pack (if loaded)
- SQL Server Management Pack
- Web Sites and Services Management Pack

The two management packs discussed here are the Windows SharePoint Services 3.0 and SharePoint Server 2007 management packs for System Center Operations Manager 2007. At a high level, the SharePoint Products and Technologies management packs are divided into two sections: Services/Tasks and Rules/Counters. System Center Operations Manager 2007 gives you the ability to monitor relevant SharePoint Products and Technologies services, such as the SharePoint Timer service, and start or restart when the service is unavailable or stopped. Table 23-3 shows the monitored services and associated tasks included with the Windows SharePoint Services 3.0 management pack; Table 23-4 shows the monitored services and associated tasks included with the SharePoint Server 2007 management pack. If you will not use System Center Operations Manager 2007 to monitor your SharePoint Products and Technologies implementation, you should strongly consider monitoring these services manually.

**Table 23-3 Monitored Services and Tasks for Windows SharePoint Services 3.0**

| Service/Action | Description |
|---|---|
| WSS 3.0 Server Entity State | Monitors the Windows SharePoint Services 3.0 Tracing Service |
| Tracing | Monitors the Windows SharePoint Services 3.0 Tracing Service (logs events to the trace logs in the 12 Hive) |
| Timer | Monitors the Windows SharePoint Services 3.0 timing service (also called SPTimer and OWSTimer) |
| Search | Monitors the Windows SharePoint Services 3.0 Search Service |
| IIS | Monitors IIS Web Services |
| SQL Server Connections | Monitors SQL Server connections |

**Table 23-3 Monitored Services and Tasks for Windows SharePoint Services 3.0**

| Service/Action | Description |
|---|---|
| SQL Server Database Error | Monitors SQL Server Database errors |
| SQL Server Database Permissions | Monitors changes to SQL Server Database permissions |
| SQL Server Database Space | Monitors the full SQL Server Database error event log |
| **Task** | **Description** |
| Start WSS Tracing Service | Starts or Restarts the wsstracing.exe Windows service |
| Start WSS Timer Service | Starts or Restarts the owstimer.exe Windows services |
| Start WSS Search Service | Starts or Restarts Windows SharePoint Services 3.0 Search (%12 Hive%\BIN\mssearch.exe) |
| Windows SharePoint Services 3.0 IIS reset | Caution: Complete IISReset (not Windows SharePoint Services 3.0 Application specific) |

**Table 23-4 Monitored Services and Tasks for SharePoint Server 2007**

| Service/Action | Description |
|---|---|
| MOSS 2007 Server Entity State | Monitors the SharePoint Server 2007 Server Entity State |
| SSO | Monitors the Single Sign-on Service |
| Load Balance | Monitors the Office Document Conversions Load Balancer Service |
| Launcher | Monitors the Office Document Conversions Launcher Service |
| Search | Monitors the Office SharePoint Server Search Services (%program files%\Microsoft Office Servers\12.0\Bin\mssearch.exe) |
| **Task** | **Description** |
| SharePoint Server 2007 IIS reset | Caution: Complete IISReset – not only SharePoint Server 2007 Web applications |
| Start MOSS SSO service | Starts or restarts the SharePoint Server 2007 Single Sign-on Service |
| Start MOSS Load Balancer Service | Starts or restarts the SharePoint Server 2007 Load Balancer Services |
| Start MOSS Launcher Service | Starts or restarts the SharePoint Server 2007 Load Balancer Launcher Service |
| Start MOSS Search Service | Starts or restarts the SharePoint Server 2007 Search Service (Query and/or Index roles) |
| SharePoint Server 2007 Recycle Application Pool | On demand, recycles all application pools with a five-second pause in between each individual recycle |

> **Note** The best practice is to use System Center Operations Manager 2007 to monitor your SharePoint Server 2007 environment. Doing so will ensure proper services remain in the proper state, relevant events are captured, and performance counter thresholds are within range.

You could certainly use a third-party product to monitor the above services, but the real benefit to using System Center Operations Manager 2007 for monitoring SharePoint Products and Technologies is the ability to leverage the rules for countless event IDs and performance counters. System Center Operations Manager 2007 can monitor your event logs, application logs, and performance counters and execute a task you specify, such as recycling an application pool, restarting owstimer.exe, or notifying you through e-mail. Additionally, System Center Operations Manager 2007, in conjunction with the SharePoint Products and Technologies management packs, provide robust reports as follows:

- Alerts Report
- Most Common Alerts Report
- Event Analysis Report
- Most Common Events Report
- .NET CLR Data Performance Report
- .NET CLR Memory Performance Report
- ASP .NET Applications Performance Report
- Indexing Service Performance Report
- Logical Disk Performance Report
- Memory Performance Report
- MOSS Search Performance Report
- Network Interface Performance Report
- Paging File Performance Report
- Physical Disk Performance Report
- Process Performance Report
- Processor Performance Report
- System Performance Report
- Web Service Performance Report

## Summary

This chapter is not the definitive source for capacity planning and monitoring, nor was it meant to be. In fact, such a resource does not exist. There are too many variables when implementing SharePoint Server 2007 in any environment, especially large and complex ones. But you have been provided a usable resource to begin planning, testing, and monitoring your SharePoint Server 2007 implementations. At a minimum, you must do the following if you want a well-running SharePoint Server 2007 server farm:

- Educate your administrators, developers, power users, and end-users.
- Sufficiently plan your farm topology.
- Correctly configure the product.
- Test your production farm before deployment.
- Baseline your farm for monitoring.
- Monitor the performance counters in Table 23-2.

## Additional Resources

- On the CD: System Center Operations Manager 2007 management packs for both Windows SharePoint Services 3.0 and SharePoint Server 2007.
- On the CD: SharePoint Planning and Capacity models.
- White paper: *http://technet2.microsoft.com/Office/en-us/library/6f03049f-5bfe-4807-b609-0e2d4a9ec3b51033.mspx.*
- The latest information on server configurations: *http://technet2.microsoft.com/Office/en-us/library/4d88c402-24f2-449b-86a6-6e7afcfec0cd1033.mspx.*
- For a full list of SharePoint Server 2007 software boundaries, see the article "Plan for software boundaries (Office SharePoint Server):" *http://technet2.microsoft.com/Office/en-us/library/6a13cd9f-4b44-40d6-85aac70a8e5c34fe1033.mspx.*
- The most common guidelines for acceptable performance: *http://technet.microsoft.com/SharepointServer.*
- Information regarding managing lists and libraries with many items: *http://office.microsoft.com/en-us/sharepointtechnology/HA101736671033.aspx?pid=CH101215281033.*
- SQL Server Performance Recommendations guide for SharePoint Server 2007: *http://office.microsoft.com/download/afile.aspx?AssetID=AM102509151033.*

- For detailed information on large lists, see "Working with large lists in Office SharePoint Server 2007:" *http://go.microsoft.com/fwlink/?LinkId=95450&clcid=0x409*.
- Information on enabling compression for dynamic files: *http://support.microsoft.com/kb/322603*.

# Glossary

**Audiences (information)** Groups of users who are used to target content, such as Web parts. Global audiences are compiled at the SSP level based on user attributes. Active Directory distribution lists and SharePoint groups can be used as audiences at the site level.

**authenticity** Determining the validity of user activity and information.

**BLOB** Binary large object.

**BLOB caching** Storage by a Web Front-end Server of commonly used objects (normally graphics) in a local disk cache so that they do not have to be retrieved from the database each time they are needed to build a page.

**Business Data Catalog (BDC)** Used for external connections to structured content sources.

**business requirements** Clear statement of the needs of the business that can be solved through the use and application of the right technology solutions. Business requirements are expressed in a technology-agnostic format.

**CAB** Cabinet file format. Used for compressing files and archives by installers, such as Windows Installer.

**cascading style sheets (CSS)** Type of style sheet used to describe the presentation of elements in a Web site. Cascading style sheets can affect the colors, fonts, and items within a Web site, such as borders and images. With appropriate controls, they can also be used to abstract the layout of a page.

**classification (information)** Act of assigning a level of sensitivity to data.

**Code Access Security (CAS)** The .NET framework's mechanism for preventing code from performing actions beyond a specific trust level assigned to them or associated with the context within which they are executing. In the simplest possible terms, Code Access Security represents a modern approach to security that manages code with explicit permission levels similar to user access security.

**Collaboration Portal** In terms of SharePoint, one of the out-of-the-box publishing site templates that includes built-in publishing, workflow, and Web content management functionality.

**collaborative personal site** A personal site that allows the user to share thoughts, links, documents, pictures, and ideas with other users throughout the organization.

**Common Language Runtime (CLR)** An environment that executes many modern programming languages including Microsoft Visual C#, Microsoft Visual Basic, and Microsoft Visual C++.

**confidentiality (information)** Ensuring that information is accessible only to those authorized to have access.

**configuration database** SharePoint Server 2007 database that is the heart and soul of the farm. Most farm configuration data is stored in this database.

**content database** All site collections are stored in a content database. Therefore, all user content is stored in content databases.

**content database migration** Method of copying and then attaching SQL databases from the SharePoint Portal Server 2003 virtual servers to the SharePoint Server 2007 Web applications. When the database is attached, content is upgraded to the SharePoint Server 2007 platform.

**content item** Individual link in the result set to a document, list item, or object that matches the keyword query.

**ContentPlaceHolder controls** Type of ASP.NET controls that are used in master pages. ContentPlaceHolder controls define regions within a master page that can be targeted by layout pages. All controls within a layout page must target a content place holder that exists on the layout page's master page.

**content type** Defines a piece of content or information, specifically the metadata, and is a means of encapsulating a data schema and making it independent of a SharePoint list location. In SharePoint, metadata relates to the columns within a document library or list, such as the title and author of a document.

**Dashboard Designer** Component of PerformancePoint Server 2007 that plugs directly into the PerformancePoint monitoring process to generate charts, reports, and KPIs that can then be deployed directly to SharePoint sites.

**Description Document** Document that describes the metadata, content, and ownership of a document that needs to be created.

**document collaboration** Process of two or more people working together to create a document that is consumed by a larger population.

**document management** Process of applying rules and policies to a document from the time it is created to the time is it expired.

**emergent capability** New capability that is created as the result of a functioning system that was not present by simply adding together the value created by each individual component of that system.

**Enterprise Content Management** Technologies used to capture, manage, store, archive, and deliver content used in the business processes of a company.

**Enterprise FilePlan** Document that lists all of the types of information your organization creates or captures during the course of operations.

**explicit managed path** Only one site collection can be contained within it, and that site collection assumes the identity of the managed path. It establishes the named root for a single site collection.

**farm** A SharePoint Server 2007 server farm is defined by a configuration database. All servers in a farm share a common configuration database.

**feature** Modular server-side, file system level customization containing items that can be installed and activated in a SharePoint environment.

**Federated Location Definition** XML file that defines the location to which queries will be sent to obtain a result set from a remote index.

**Federated Results Web part** Web part that displays the results from a single remote index on the results.aspx page or any other results page that you customize or create.

**findability** Description of how easy or difficult it is to find an individual object or item.

**ghosted/uncustomized page** Refers to a page that resides on the file system. Until the page is customized, a pointer in the content database will reference the file system version. As soon as the page is customized, an actual copy of the page will be created in the content database for the site where the page was customized.

**Global Assembly Cache (GAC)** Stores assemblies that are designed to be shared by multiple applications. Assemblies deployed to the GAC must be signed, and they operate at full trust. The GAC is one of two possible assembly deployment locations for SharePoint Products and Technologies. Assemblies can also be deployed to the bin directory of a SharePoint Products and Technologies Web application.

**gradual upgrade** Method of upgrading a SharePoint Portal Server 2003 farm to SharePoint Server 2007 on a site-collection-by-site-collection basis. Both platforms run on the same hardware at the same time until the SharePoint Portal Server 2003 farm can be decommissioned.

**hardware boundary** When hardware is the limiting performance factor.

**hierarchy** Set of relationships between labels in a variation that determines which content is pushed from the source to the target labels.

**IDE** Integrated Design Environment.

**IIS compression** Compressing files on the Web server that are uncompressed by the client's Web browser.

**index** List of words with links to their locations in documents, objects, Web pages, and list items.

**information context** Provides a representation of the information that aligns with the way people view the work they do and the information created as a result of that work.

**information rights management** System that focuses on controlling what can be done with unstructured content once it has been downloaded from a content management system.

**in-place upgrade** Method of upgrading a SharePoint Portal Server 2003 farm to SharePoint Server 2007 that retains the same settings and hardware. This method upgrades the entire farm in one administrative action.

**integrity (information)** Ensuring that information cannot be created, changed, or deleted without authorization.

**inter-farm Shared Services** Shared Services consumed by an external server farm.

**intra-farm Shared Services** Shared Services consumed by the local server farm.

**Kerberos** Form of authentication used within SharePoint deployments that impersonates user accounts and server delegation.

**label** One of the members of a variation hierarchy. A label would include the top site of the member and any subsites.

**layout page** Used in conjunction with master pages to provide content and controls within a common framework. Layout pages flesh out the skeleton of master pages and provide unique functionality while maintaining a common layout with any other pages that share the same master page.

**long-tail** Marketing concept that describes how Web-based businesses will find that the number of seldom-requested items in their inventory will be higher than the number of often-requested items.

**master page** Define the basic structure, or skeleton, of a page. Master pages contain rectangular target areas called content place holders that are targeted by layout pages. Master pages contain a minimum number of controls, consisting largely of content place holder controls that will be targeted by layout pages. Multiple layout pages are used in conjunction with a single master page, and the layout pages provide content within the framework of the master page. Master pages are not intended for standalone use and must be used in conjunction with layout pages.

**MDX** Multidimensional Expression.

**metadata** Information that describes the content of a document or list item and is attached to that content in one or more metadata fields.

**module** Copies files from the file system to the content database. When a customizable copy is performed, a pointer is created in the content database that refers to the file system until the file is customized (for instance, by altering a page with SharePoint Designer).

**My Site** Personal, individual one-to-many collaboration site.

**native mode** Default mode in which SQL Server 2005 Reporting Services can be configured and integrated with SharePoint Server 2007 sites.

**non-collaborative personal site** Personal site that allows users to leverage important findability tools and describe themselves in their user profiles so others can find them through people search without being given collaborative tools such as shared documents or shared lists.

**NTLM** Mode of authentication.

**offline content database** Unable to accept new site collections.

**OpenSearch** Search standard developed by Amazon to allow Web sites to pass results from remote queries using RSS, Atom, HTML, and/or XHTML.

**parallel workflow** Simultaneous workflow process, such as when a document is sent for approval to all members of a project group at the same time.

**permission level** Set of SharePoint permissions that can be granted to users or SharePoint groups on an entity such as a site, library, list, folder, item, or document.

**Planning Administration Console (PAC)** Windows administration console of PerformancePoint Server 2007.

**Planning Business Modeler (PBM)** Modeler component of PerformancePoint Server 2007 that manages dimensional models and sites.

**portal** Site that presents a point of entry to the Internet or intranet that normally includes a collection of links to other sites arranged in some logical order as well as a search engine.

**precision** Measurement of how well the information retrieval system retrieves only relevant documents.

**psconfig.exe** Command-line interface for installing and provisioning SharePoint Products and Technologies.

**psconfigui.exe** Also known as the SharePoint Products and Technologies Configuration Wizard, it is used to connect a server to the farm and also to provision/unprovision Central Administration.

**recall** Measurement of how well the information retrieval system retrieves relevant documents.

**Records Management** Content management system implemented for the purpose of identifying, classifying, archiving, preserving, and destroying records, usually for legal purposes.

**recovery point objective (RPO)** Defines your data loss threshold, which is measured in time.

**recovery time objective (RTO)** Defines how long your system can be down before it is back online after a disruption.

**relevance** Measurement of how useful and helpful the content items in a result set are to an individual user.

**report** Data report generated from SQL Server 2005 Reporting Services.

**Report Builder** SQL Server 2005 Reporting Services Report Builder.

**report data source** Back-end data source that underpins reports, such as ODBC or an SQL database.

**Report Designer** Part of Visual Studio 2005 Business Intelligence, a GUI that allows developers to quickly design and deploy reports to SharePoint sites or Reporting Services.

**Report model** Model that designs the database tables, or components, from which reports can be built.

**Reporting Services** Part of SQL Server 2005 that is used to create and generate data reports.

**Reporting Services Configuration Manager** Part of the Reporting Services SharePoint Integrated mode that is used specifically to configure Reporting Services to work with SharePoint Server 2007.

**result set** Set of content items that are returned in response to a query of the index.

**scope creep** Introduction of new project requirements without those requirements being fully discussed and vetted through the normal requirements development process.

**serial workflow** Hierarchical workflow process, such as when one person must approve a document before it is sent along to the next person for approval.

**Shared Services Provider (SSP)** Hosts services that are consumed by the local farm or external farms.

**SharePoint Integrated mode** Opposite of native mode. Alternative for configuring SQL Server 2005 Reporting Services to work with SharePoint Server 2007 sites.

**site collection** One or more SharePoint webs that exist under a common URL namespace.

**site column** Re-usable column definition or template that you can assign to multiple lists across multiple SharePoint sites.

**site definition** Provides the lowest-level blueprint for creating SharePoint Product and Technologies sites. A site definition orchestrates the creation of a site only; therefore, changing a site definition will not alter sites that have already been provisioned from the site definition. Site templates are based upon site definitions.

**site template** Site Templates are based upon site definitions and are a higher-level blueprint for provisioning sites. Site templates can be created by saving an existing customized site as a site template.

**SLA** Service Level Agreement.

**software boundary** Hard-coded or suggested product limitations.

**solution** Windows SharePoint Services Solution Packages are SharePoint Product and Technologies-specific CAB files that contain instructions for the deployment of the CAB's contents in a SharePoint environment.

**structured content** Information sources that separate the storage of the content from its display, such as traditional databases or SharePoint lists.

**stsadm.exe** Command-line interface for managing and configuring SharePoint Products and Technologies.

**technical requirements** Clear statement that translates business requirements into technical requirements that are expressed in a technology-agnostic format. Technology requirements simply state what the technology needs to do without passion or prejudice for/against a particular software platform.

**unstructured content** Information sources where content is accessible only in the format in which it is stored. For example, Microsoft Office Word files contain information that can be accessed only by opening the document.

**User Copy method** Method of upgrading a SharePoint Portal Server 2003 farm by first building out a new SharePoint Server 2007 farm and then having the users copy their information from the SharePoint Portal Server 2003 farm to the SharePoint Server 2007 farm.

**variations** Set of sites (with some type of variation) established at the same level within a site collection.

**Visual Studio Team Suite (VSTS) 2008** Programming and test suite that allows granular testing of multi-server farms.

**Web application** Container for site collections rendered via Internet Information Services.

**Web Content Management** Content management system usually implemented as a Web application for creating and managing HTML content.

**Web part** Discrete, re-usable object that can be customized by users to alter its appearance, content, and behavior.

**wildcard managed path** Establishes a virtual root under which hundreds or thousands of uniquely named site collections can be created. They are appended to the managed path.

**WMI** Windows Management Instrumentations.

**workflow** Series of actions and decisions within a larger process that are committed in a particular order.

# About the Authors

This book is the result of much hard work on the part of several different authors. Each author contributed significantly to this work. What follows here is a brief introduction to each author on this book project.

## Principal Authors

**Ben Curry** (CISSP, MCP, MCTS: SharePoint Server 2007) is a SharePoint Server MVP and enterprise network architect specializing in knowledge management and collaboration technologies. As a senior instructor for Mindsharp, Ben shares his knowledge in training courses that cover the next generation of Microsoft products. In his capacity as a Mindsharp consultant, Ben draws on his years of experience to develop powerful customized solutions based on the SharePoint platform for clients. Ben has presented at TechEd, SharePoint Conference, user groups, and Dev Connections.

**Bill English** (MVP, MCT, MCTS: SharePoint Server 2007) is an author and educator specializing in Microsoft Office SharePoint Server 2007 and Microsoft Office Search Server 2008. Bill has authored or co-authored more than 10 books and regularly conducts private and public training classes for companies of all sizes. Bill is the co-owner of Mindsharp (*www.mindsharp.com*), a company that offers top-notch education on Microsoft's collaboration technologies. Bill has presented at Comdex, the Microsoft Exchange Conference, TechMentor, Networld Interop, TechEd, TechEd EMEA, and the SharePoint 2007 Conference. Bill lives in Minnesota with his wife and two children.

## Co-Author

**Kathy Hughes** (SharePoint Server MVP) is a freelance consultant based in Sydney, Australia. Her main areas of interest are architecting and customizing SharePoint and .NET deployments, specifically from a usability and design perspective. She trains the Mindsharp curriculum and consults throughout Australia.

Kathy has developed and designed Web technologies for more than 15 years and has worked with Microsoft collaborative technologies since Microsoft SharePoint Portal Server 2001. She has globally deployed and customized Microsoft Office SharePoint Portal Server 2003 since beta inception and has customized and deployed SharePoint Server 2007 since beta release. She co-authored *Microsoft Office SharePoint Server 2007 Administrator's Companion* (Microsoft Press, 2007) and developed and wrote the 5-day SharePoint Designer 2007 (design and customization) course for Mindsharp, which is now being used globally. Kathy holds a Master of Interactive Multimedia (University of Technology, Sydney, 2004-2007), having majored in Web site usability and design. Kathy blogs at *http://mindsharpblogs.com*, writes white papers on SharePoint and other collaborative technologies, and consults and delivers training on SharePoint technologies and user-centered Web design solutions.

## Contributing Authors

**James Curry** is a respected computer scientist and consultant with more than 15 years of programming experience. In his role as a Mindsharp instructor, James uses his knowledge of Microsoft products to provide students with a dynamic, hands-on classroom experience. James is a contributing author of *Microsoft SharePoint Products and Technologies Administrator's Pocket Consultant* (Microsoft Press, 2007) and has been invited to speak at user groups on topics such as customizing Microsoft Office SharePoint Server 2007. As a computer scientist with InfoPro Corporation in Huntsville, Alabama, James developed information management solutions for organizations of all sizes. James focused on developing Web applications for large governmental organizations. James resides in Madison, Alabama, with the love of his life, his wife Joy.

**Paul Schaeflein** (MCP) is a developer for Barracuda (*www.barracuda.net*), working on tools and utilities to ease the administration of SharePoint installations. Before joining Barracuda, Paul was an independent consultant specializing in development of solutions and components built in SharePoint.

**Paul Papanek Stork** (MBA, CTT+, MCT, MCSE+I, MCSA, MCSD, MCDBA, MCITP, MCPD, MS CRM Certified Master) has specialized in Microsoft products since the mid-1990s. Paul is a jack-of-all-trades who has developed expertise as an administrator, developer, and DBA. His primary area of expertise is Microsoft application servers, which defy compartmentalization and leverage multiple technologies. Paul's depth of knowledge makes him ideally suited to teach custom courses for Mindsharp that combine modules from their Administrative, Development, and SharePoint Designer courses. In addition, Paul manages updates to Mindsharp's development courseware. Paul maintains an active blog at *http://www.mindsharpblogs.com/pauls* and has contributed chapters to several books on Microsoft technologies. Paul lives outside of Cleveland, Ohio, with his wife. He has two grown children.

**Daniel Webster** is an author, educator, and speaker currently specializing in SharePoint Products and Technologies. Daniel is a senior instructor and administrator courseware lead for Mindsharp. He also assists organizations with their SharePoint architecture and design plans. Daniel held his first MCSE in NT 3.51 and continues through Windows 2003 with specialties in security and Internet. He was a co-author of *Microsoft Office SharePoint Server 2007 Administrator's Companion* (Microsoft Press, 2007). Daniel has spoken at conferences such as NetWorld InterOp, Comdex, HDI, Support Services, FrontLines, MCTCon, IT Infrastructure Management, and CeBIT America.

**Mark Ferraz** is President of SolutionsMark, a Houston-based consulting firm specializing in the design, development, and implementation of information management solutions using SharePoint Products and Technologies. Mark is the Senior Information Architect and Developer specializing in information management, collaboration tools, and knowledge management systems for medium to large enterprises. Mark has more than 10 years of experience designing, managing, and implementing complex technology projects involving application implementation, supporting infrastructure, custom development, and integration. Visit SolutionsMark online at *http://www.solutionsmark.com*.

**Mark Schneider** (PMP) provided technology leadership and planning to organizations big and small for more than 25 years. He focuses on bridging the strategic planning gap between business and technology stakeholders. His passion is developing the skills and capabilities of others, and toward that end, he teaches workshops on strategic technology planning, taxonomy planning, technology governance, and project management. He is currently serving as Vice President of Barracuda, a developer and publisher of enterprise software tools. Mark can be reached at *mark@vitalskill.com* and at his blog site *www.sharepointplan.com.*

## Content Contributors

This book is the result of many people giving input and ideas into the final product. The folks listed in this section contributed in ways that range from reviewing individual chapters to offering ideas through informal conversations. Ben and Bill wish to thank these people for the time and effort that was given to make this book better. These individuals include Doran Bar-Caspi, Sam Crewdson, Joel Oleson, Andrew Woodward, Todd Bleeker, Keith Richie, Ross Brookshire, Scott Edwards, Bob Fox, Daniel Galant, Jack Dougher, Woodrow Windischman, Steve Mong, Eric Larson, Kuda Nhiwatiwa, Oleg Glubochansky, Satish Mathew, Sean Livingston, Steve Smith, Todd Klindt, Satish Mathew, James Petrosky, John Moh, Don Scott, Mike Watson, Robert Bogue, Matthew McDermott, and Frank Zakrajsek.

# Index

## C

## D

## J



## K



## L

## O



## P

## Q



## R

## S

## T

## U



## V



## W

## X



## Z

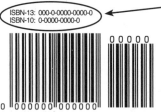